Lecture Notes in Computer Science 15348

The series Lecture Notes in Computer Science (LNCS), including its subseries Lecture Notes in Artificial Intelligence (LNAI) and Lecture Notes in Bioinformatics (LNBI), has established itself as a medium for the publication of new developments in computer science and information technology research, teaching, and education.

LNCS enjoys close cooperation with the computer science R & D community, the series counts many renowned academics among its volume editors and paper authors, and collaborates with prestigious societies. Its mission is to serve this international community by providing an invaluable service, mainly focused on the publication of conference and workshop proceedings and postproceedings. LNCS commenced publication in 1973.

Avo Schönbohm · Francesco Bellotti ·
Antonio Bucchiarone · Francesca de Rosa ·
Manuel Ninaus · Alf Wang · Vanissa Wanick ·
Pierpaolo Dondio
Editors

Games and Learning Alliance

13th International Conference, GALA 2024
Berlin, Germany, November 20–22, 2024
Proceedings

Springer

Editors
Avo Schönbohm
Hochschule für Wirtschaft und Recht Berlin
Berlin, Germany

Antonio Bucchiarone
Fondazione Bruno Kessler
Trento, Italy

Manuel Ninaus
University of Graz
Graz, Austria

Vanissa Wanick
University of Southampton
Winchester, UK

Francesco Bellotti
University of Genova
Genova, Italy

Francesca de Rosa
Center for Advanced Preparedness
and Threat Response Simulation (CAPTRS)
Austin, TX, USA

Alf Wang
Norwegian University of Science
and Technology
Trondheim, Norway

Pierpaolo Dondio
Technological University Dublin
Dublin, Ireland

ISSN 0302-9743 ISSN 1611-3349 (electronic)
Lecture Notes in Computer Science
ISBN 978-3-031-78268-8 ISBN 978-3-031-78269-5 (eBook)
https://doi.org/10.1007/978-3-031-78269-5

This Springer imprint is published by the registered company Springer Nature Switzerland AG
The registered company address is: Gewerbestrasse 11, 6330 Cham, Switzerland

Preface

This volume includes contributions from the Games and Learning Alliance (GALA) conference, which is dedicated to the advancement of research into serious games. The thirteenth edition of the GALA conference was held in Berlin, Germany, November 20th – November 22nd, 2024. This edition was organized by the Serious Games Society (SGS) and Berlin School of Economics and Law.

The fascinating three-day event provided an international discussion forum to advance the theories, technologies, and knowledge that support the design, development, and research of serious games. GALA 2024 received 103 paper submissions from academic researchers and practitioners from 35 countries. Each paper was reviewed by three Program Committee members. The accepted papers, covering various aspects of serious game theories and applications, were presented in 7 paper sessions (30 full papers) and a poster session (15 short papers).

This year's anthology presents a rich variety of research and innovation across six distinct sections. The *Advances in Game-Based Learning* section highlights cutting-edge approaches to adaptive expertise, language acquisition, and the use of artificial intelligence in educational games. The *Designing for Engagement* section delves into how cognitive and emotional responses are influenced by serious game mechanics, with a focus on feedback, gamification, and player motivation. In the *Sustainability and Environmental Literacy in Serious Games* section, the papers explore how game-based learning can address global challenges, including sustainability, environmental literacy, and civic engagement. The *Detecting Deception and Developing Leadership* section examines the role of serious games in ethical decision-making, leadership development, and deception detection, showcasing games that tackle real-world challenges. The *Futures Literacy* section focuses on games designed to foster futures thinking, with topics ranging from civic learning to business innovation, and how serious games can be tools for envisioning future scenarios. Lastly, the *Serious Games for Health and Immersive Learning* section covers innovative uses of games in healthcare and pharmacology education, from non-pharmacological therapies to immersive augmented reality for learning.

Finally, the *Poster* section addresses a wide range of topics, from gender-based analysis of gamification preferences and motion design for emotional engagement, to VR interaction modalities and learning effects. This section also features research on gamification and artificial intelligence in education, moral decision-making through social media marketing, and the integration of historical and cultural content in role-playing games. Additional studies explore 360° spaces and social VR, VR-based puzzle games, participatory approaches to forced migration, and visual inquiry tools for designing educational escape games. The section concludes with an evaluation of collaborative learning games on history, cognitive and psychosocial rehabilitation through multiplayer games, the use of LEGO® in adult playful learning, and an AI-focused board game aimed at increasing teachers' awareness of artificial intelligence.

We were delighted to have three prominent keynote speakers, Alessandro Canossa (Royal Danish Academy), Jan L. Plass (New York University), and Eric Klopfer (Massachusetts Institute of Technology). Alessandro Canossa discussed data-driven behavioral profiling and evaluation in digital games, Jan Plass delivered a talk on designing effective games for learning, and Eric Klopfer, based on his experience at the Education Arcade @ MIT, talked about the games resonating with learners and technologies.

The conference featured a Game Exhibition and a *"Games for Better Futures"* game competition with the aim of rewarding games that positively impact society, community, and well-being. The game competition received 56 submissions in the following three categories: business, academic, and student. Twelve shortlisted games were invited to demo their games at the conference.

As in previous years, the authors of the selected best papers presented at the GALA conference were invited to submit an extended version of their paper for a dedicated special issue of the International Journal of Serious Games, the scientific journal managed by the Serious Games Society, indexed by the Emerging Sources Citation Index (ESCI), in the Web of Science Core Collection since 2015, and by Scopus since 2020.

We thank the authors for submitting many interesting papers and the international Program Committee for their careful and timely review of these papers. We are also thankful to our conference sponsors for their financial support: CAPTRS, the center for Advanced Preparedness and Threat Response Simulation. Finally, we gratefully acknowledge the Serious Games Society and Berlin School of Economics and Law for organizing the conference.

November 2024

Avo Schönbohm
Francesco Bellotti
Antonio Bucchiarone
Francesca de Rosa
Manuel Ninaus
Alf Wang
Vanissa Wanick
Pierpaolo Dondio

Organization

General Chair

Avo Schönbohm	Berlin School of Economics and Law, Germany

Program Chairs

Vanissa Wanick	University of Southampton, UK
Antionio Bucchiarone	Bruno Kessler Foundation, Trento, Italy
Pierpaolo Dondio	Technological University Dublin, Ireland
Francesca de Rosa	Center for Advanced Preparedness and Threat Response Simulation, USA
Alf Inge Wang	Norwegian University of Science and Technology, Norway
Manuel Ninaus	University of Graz, Austria

Keynotes Chairs

Sander Bakkes	Utrecht University, The Netherlands
Avo Schönbohm	Berlin School of Economics and Law, Germany

Competition and Exhibition Chairs

Kristina Risley	University of Southampton, UK
Mariana Rocha	Technological University Dublin, Ireland
Jonny-Bix Bongers	Berlin School of Economics and Law, Germany
René Röpke	RWTH Aachen University, Germany

Publication Chair

Pierpaolo Dondio	Technological University Dublin, Ireland

Communication Chairs

Vanissa Wanick	University of Southampton, UK
Sander Bakkes	Utrecht University, The Netherlands

Local Chair

Jonny-Bix Bongers	Berlin School of Economics and Law, Germany

Administrative and Financial Chair

Francesco Bellotti	University of Genova, Italy

Program Committee

Alf Inge Wang	Norwegian University of Science and Technology, Norway
Angel Torres Toukoumidis	Universidad Politécnica Salesiana, Ecuador
Antionio Bucchiarone	Bruno Kessler Foundation, Italy
Antti Koskinen	Tampere University, Finland
Attracta Brennan	University of Galway, Ireland
Avo Schönbohm	Berlin School of Economics and Law, Germany
Bettina Schneider	Northwestern Switzerland University of Applied Science and Arts, Switzerland
Carlos Marín Lora	Universitat Jaume I, Spain
Carolina Islas Sedano	University of Turku, Finland
Chiara Eva Catalano	CNR IMATI, Italy
Dipti Jadhav	Don Bosco Institute of Technology, India
Elena Camossi	NATO Science and Technology Organization, Centre for Maritime Research and Experimentation, Italy
Eliana Silva	University of Porto, Portugal
Elizabeth Cloude	Tampere University, Finland
Enes Yigitbas	Paderborn University, Germany
Federica Gini	University of Trento, Italy
Federico Bonetti	Bruno Kessler Foundation, Italy
Francesca de Rosa	Center for Advanced Preparedness and Threat Response Simulation, USA
Francesco Zanichelli	University of Parma, Italy

Frutuoso Silva	University of Beira Interior, Portugal
Galih Dea Pratama	Bina Nusantara University, Indonesia
George Kritikos	EPS, Greece
George Lepouras	University of the Peloponnese, Greece
Georgios Fesakis	University of the Aegean, Greece
Giuseppe Città	CNR Palermo, Italy
Heinrich Söbke	Bauhaus University, Weimar, Germany
Herre Van Oostendorp	Utrecht University, The Netherlands
Ioana Andreea Stefan	Advanced Technology Systems, Romania
Iza Marfisi Schottman	Le Mans University, France
Jannicke Baalsrud Hauge	University of Bremen, Germany
Jonny-Bix Bongers	Berlin School of Economics and Law, Germany
Ju Ling Shih	National Central University, Taiwan
Kendra M. L. Cooper	Independent, Canada
Kevin Körner	Eberhard Karls University of Tübingen, Germany
Kristina Risley	University of Southampton, UK
Lahcen Oubahssi	Le Mans University, France
Luca Forneris	University of Genova, Italy
Luca Lazzaroni	University of Genova, Italy
Ludovic Hamon	Le Mans University, France
Mads Haahr	Trinity College Dublin, Ireland
Maira B. Carvalho	Tilburg University, The Netherlands
Manuel Ninaus	University of Graz, Austria
Manuel Gentile	National Research Council, Italy
Marco Temperini	Sapienza University of Rome, Italy
Margarida Romero	Côte d'Azur University, France
Maria Saridaki	University of Athens, Greece
Maria Rauschenberger	University of Applied Science Emden-Leer, Germany
Maria Popescu	Carol I National Defence University, Romania
Mariana Rocha	Technological University Dublin, Ireland
Marianna Cossu	University of Genova, Italy
Matheus Cezarotto	NMSU, USA
Matthias Teine	University of Paderborn, Germany
Micael Sousa	CAPTRS, USA
Michael Kickmeier Rust	Graz University of Technology, Austria
Michela Mortara	CNR Imati Genova, Italy
Mohammad Fadhli Asli	University Malaysia Sabah, Malaysia
Nour El Mawas	Université de Lille, France
Phuong Bui	University of Turku, Finland
Pierpaolo Dondio	Technological University Dublin, Ireland
Pierre Laforcade	Le Mans University, France

Rafael Bidarra	Delft University of Technology, The Netherlands
Ramesh Gorantla	Arizona State University, USA
René Röpke	RWTH Aachen University, Germany
Riikka Aurava	Tampere University, Finland
Rob Nadolski	Open University of the Netherlands, The Netherlands
Roger Azevedo	University of Central Florida, USA
Sander Bakkes	Utrecht University, The Netherlands
Simon Hoermann	University of Canterbury, New Zealand
Simone Bassanelli	Università di Trento, Italy
Sinead Impey	ADAPT Centre, Ireland
Stelios Xinogalos	University of Macedonia, Greece
Thierry Nabeth	P-Val Conseil, France
Thomas Hainey	University of the West of Scotland, UK
Thorsten Händler	Ferdinand Porsche FErnFH, Germany
Toby Best	Queen Mary University of London, UK
Valentina Rossi	EPFL, Switzerland
Vanissa Wanick	University of Southampton, UK
Varvara Garneli	Ionian University, Greece
Ville Kankainen	Tampere University, Finland
Vinicius Andrade	Universidade Estadual Paulista "Júlio de Mesquita Filho", Brazil
Vipin Verma	Arizona State University, USA
Yasser Khazaal	Lausanne University, Switzerland
Yoones Sekhavat	Tabriz Art University, Iran

Contents

Detecting Deception and Developing Leadership: Games Tackling Real-World Challenges

Futures Literacy: Games for Civic Participation and Futures Thinking

Serious Games for Health and Immersive Learning: E-Health and Pharmacology

Short Papers

Advances in Game-Based Learning: AI, Adaptive Expertise, and Language Acquisition

A Growing Community of Practice on Games and Learning: A Literature Review with Bibliometric and Thematic Analyses

Kristina Risley[1(✉)] and René Röpke[2]

[1] University of Southampton, Park Ave, SO23 8DL Southampton, UK
k.risley@soton.ac.uk
[2] TU Wien, Favoritenstr. 9-11, 1040 Vienna, Austria
rene.roepke@tuwien.ac.at

Abstract. The Games and Learning Alliance (GALA) community, established in 2013, represents a growing interdisciplinary network focused on advancing serious games research and practice through innovation and knowledge sharing. This study provides an overarching introduction to the contributions of the GALA community by employing bibliometric and thematic analyses to map the community's composition, geographic origins, academic disciplines, and prevailing topics of interest. Results highlight the community's interdisciplinary nature, integrating fields such as Education, Psychology, Computer Science and Health Education. The analysis reveals robust collaborative networks, exemplifying a Community of Practice that stimulates innovation and learning opportunities through shared practices and mentorship. Limitations of the study include the scope of analyses and AI tool constraints, necessitating further human validation of the insights gained. Future research will focus on longitudinal mapping and detailed examination of specific disciplines and frameworks.

Keywords: Community of Practice · Serious Games · Bibliometric Analysis · Thematic analysis

1 Introduction

The Serious Games Society (SGS) was established in 2013 from a consortium of European organizations joined in the EU FP7 framework program to foster collaboration on information and communication technologies. The GALA Network of Excellence funding scheme also led to the founding the Games and Learning Alliance (GALA) conference in the same year [11]. The GALA community is now an influential network of interdisciplinary researchers and practitioners, committed to fostering technological innovation and excellence in serious games through exploration and knowledge sharing. This dynamic community spans a diverse set of disciplines, e.g., Education, Psychology and Computer Science.

A. Schönbohm et al. (Eds.): GALA 2024, LNCS 15348, pp. 3–13, 2025.
https://doi.org/10.1007/978-3-031-78269-5_1

The primary aim of this systematic literature review was to map the composition of the GALA community in line with geographical representation, topics and disciplines. To achieve this, the review was guided by several research questions: who makes up the community, including their geographic origins and the academic disciplines they represent; how have research collaborations evolved over time; what are the topics of interest at the GALA conference and what interests the community in terms of topics, frameworks and theories?

Several bibliometric and thematic analyses chronicling the maturation of research disciplines such as gamification [1,13] and learning analytics [3,4], have been shown to enable research communities to map the prevailing topics and frameworks of relevance to the field [5,6]. Furthermore, this practice enhances understanding of internal relationships and how newcomers and junior researchers can move from peripheral involvement [7] to full participation as part of their development. By employing bibliometric analysis, this work charts the growth and interdisciplinary makeup of the GALA community. Furthermore, following with a high-level thematic analysis of all published papers, this work presents an overview of the community's research approaches and key topics [10]. This analysis is underpinned by the principles of the Communities of Practice theory [14,15] in that the GALA community not only shares a common domain of interest but also demonstrates mutual engagement and a shared repertoire of resources and practices. As such, this review sought to provide an overarching introduction to the community and its contributions to date, without over-analyzing individual themes, thus setting the stage for further exploration and discussion of the community's growing impact on the field of serious games.

2 Related Work: Theory of Community of Practice

The term Community of Practice (CoP) was coined by Lave and Wenger [7] and further built upon by Wenger [15] as *"groups of people who share a concern or a passion for something they do and learn how to do it better as they interact regularly"* (p. 11). CoP theory explains how professionals with common interests interact, share knowledge and develop expertise. Membership of a CoP implies a commitment to the domain and a shared "regime of competence" [14], which distinguishes CoP members from others. These concepts are particularly useful for understanding dynamic communities centered around shared interests in specific domains. For instance, through CoP mechanisms, these communities develop and maintain unique identities, practices and authority systems [4].

Legitimate peripheral participation is a key aspect of the CoP model, explaining how newcomers progress from the periphery the center of the community as their engagement and expertise and grow [7]. This process enables early career academics to transition from peripheral to full participation, gaining experience and academic standing through community activities. Applying CoP principles involves providing newcomers with an entry mechanism and a structured pathway or natural scaffolding, allowing them to learn specific skills and absorb the community's norms, culture and practices. As newcomers interact more productively, they become central participants, shaping the community's practices and creating pathways for other newcomers. Experienced members mentor newcomers as future successors, ensuring the research field's future.

Research CoPs offer several benefits including enhanced learning opportunities, innovation through collaboration, support and mentorship for newcomers and increased motivation and engagement [8] [12]. However, CoPs in research settings also present potential pitfalls including risk of conformity, barriers to entry and knowledge silos. Strong community norms can stifle innovative contributions and discourage deviation from accepted methodologies [2]. Newcomers may also struggle to break into established CoPs, where the value of social capital can at times outweigh the value of individual contributions [9].

3 Methodology

This review covers a decade of research conducted by the GALA research community, with evaluation including both bibliometric and inductive style thematic analyses [10]. It covers all accepted papers to the GALA conference between 2013 and 2023, including full papers and posters that were part of the conference proceedings. A total of 444 papers appear in the GALA conference proceedings between 2013 and 2023. However, 5 papers from the 2017 proceedings were excluded from the analysis as they were poster submissions that did not conform to the GALA paper or poster standards, also lacking abstracts and author-defined keywords. Consequently, the final review was based on 439 papers.

Data Selection and Cleaning: Data for all 444 papers were initially collected from Scopus, including metadata and PDF files of the articles. The data was then cleaned by cross-referencing with the PDFs to fill in missing information for corresponding authors, correct date issues where publication years were merged (with some listed as published in the year the conference took place and others in the following year) and add missing abstracts and author-defined keywords.

Analysis 1 Calibration: An initial analysis was conducted using 20 randomly selected papers, categorizing them based on target groups, educational contexts, topics, summaries, game modes/types, game technologies, theories/ conceptual frameworks, paper type and methodology used. Both authors independently read and reviewed the abstracts, further interrogating the full papers where necessary. The results from both authors were compared to identify consensus and deviations, in order to calibrate the evaluators' approaches. Elicit[1], an automated AI-based analysis tool, was used in parallel to perform the same analysis on these 20 papers and Elicit's results were also compared with those of the authors. This calibration showed broad consensus between the authors, although there were differences in the depth and subcategorization of the papers. Elicit provided consistent and accurate categorization, consistently matching the main points identified by the authors and it was therefore decided that all content analysis

[1] https://elicit.com/, last accessed 04.07.2024.

would be facilitated by Elicit. Through this process, subcategories and codes for each criterion were refined and consolidated into a final list for the content analysis which followed in Analysis 3.

Analysis 2 Bibliometric Review: The bibliometric analysis of 439 papers examined authorships to identify the key authors active in the community over time, as well as the countries represented to determine the geographic distribution of authors. Co-author networks were analyzed in order to map collaboration networks among authors within the broader CoP. The objective was to identify the structure of the network and any possible alignment with CoP concepts.

Analysis 3 Content Analysis: All 439 papers were uploaded into Elicit and grouped by year. Elicit was then used to scan each paper and categorize its content based on the categories defined in the calibration phase. Categories were finally clustered thematically by the research team This review focused on several key areas, identifying themes in the types of papers presented at the conference, as well as the types of game studied, relevant target user groups and educational contexts. Identification of the primary theoretical frameworks applied in each paper allowed for broad insight into the disciplines represented within the community, based on the disciplinary origins of each theory [6]

4 Results

4.1 Analysis of Authorships

Across the 439 papers, 1178 different authors were from 48 different countries. As GALA was founded by the SGS and originally a consortium of 30 European partners [11], it comes as no surprise that most authors are affiliated with European institutions, with Italy, Germany and the Netherlands occurring most often (see Fig. 1). Illustrating the worldwide growth of the GALA CoP, results show that in 2013 35 papers were presented by authors from 13 different countries, while in 2018, 46 papers were presented by authors from 35 different countries.

Next, the number of authors mapped to the number of papers published at GALA was analyzed. This revealed that the majority of authors only published once (80.5%) or twice (11.1%) and less than 8.6% of authors published three or more times. Interestingly, six authors published at least 15 papers, so on average more than one paper per year. Among these authors are Francesco Bellotti (26), Riccardo Berta (22), Kristian Kiili (20), Jannicke Baalsrud Hauge (17), Alessandro De Gloria (16), and Manuel Ninaus (15). Overall, the core of authors at GALA is rather small with about 100 authors with three or more publications and more than 940 authors with only one paper so far.

When further analyzing collaborations among GALA papers, the average number of co-authors is 3.93 and only 25 of 439 papers (0.6%) were written by single authors. Since collaborations between authors can be viewed as a graph, where nodes represent different authors and the edges whether they collaborate,

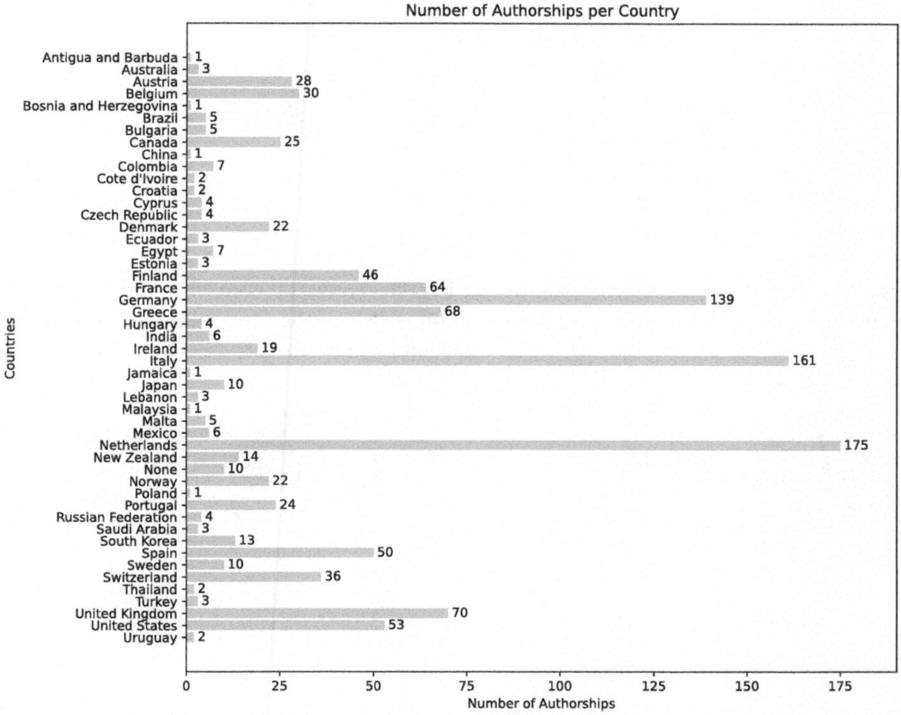

Fig. 1. Number of different authors per country from 2013 until 2023.

it can be plotted using the Fruchterman-Reingold force-directed algorithm. The collaboration graph consists of a strongly connected core of authors collaborating with each other and various loosely coupled authors in the periphery (Fig. 2). Upon zooming in (Fig. 3), the dense graph implies various collaborations in a tightly-knit community. Darker nodes are authors with a higher number of edges.

4.2 Analysis of Publications

Paper Types and Focus: Of the 439 papers reviewed, the majority presented some kind of case study analyzing real-world applications of games or game-based approaches with different target groups. The next largest paper type discussed or proposed frameworks for technology use in learning. This at times included introducing new technologies or frameworks to apply technology, as well as papers exploring technological trends and their impacts. Papers with a diagnostics/analytics focus discussed the development or application of analytical and diagnostic tools, techniques, or diagnostic instruments. As shown in Fig. 4, the remaining paper types include literature reviews, papers showcasing particular methodologies as their focus and articles that propose or expand theories, models or conceptual frameworks. The categories themselves are debatable and papers could potentially be interpreted as belonging to different categories by

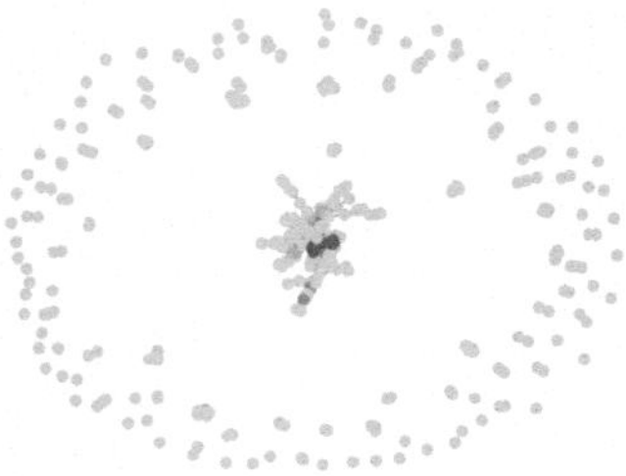

Fig. 2. Complete graph with highly connected center and sparse periphery

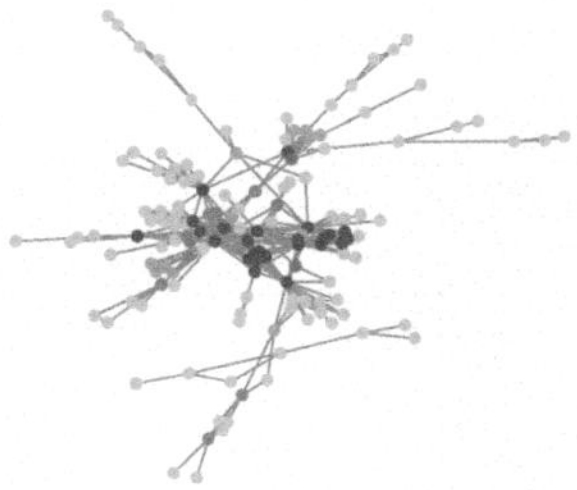

Fig. 3. Zoom of core showing highly connected authors as dark blue nodes (Color figure online)

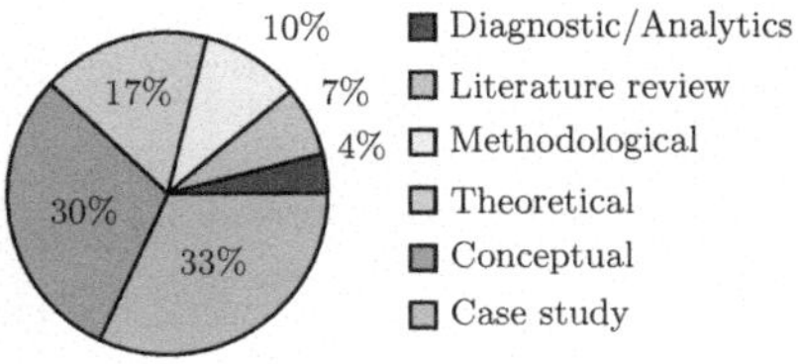

Fig. 4. Paper type

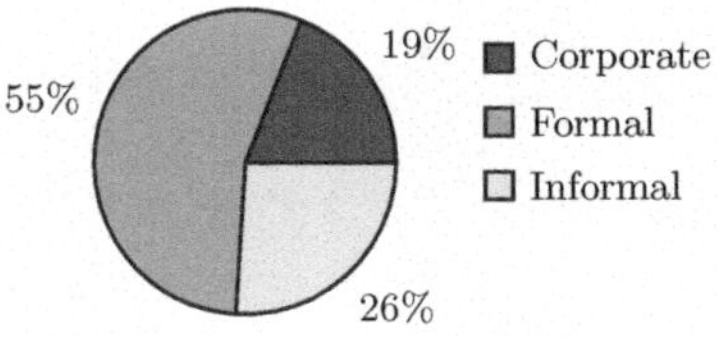

Fig. 5. Type of learning

different disciplines. However, a broad trend can be seen, with a large amount of case studies and comparatively less focus on diagnostics or analytics as the main area discussed. This supports the notion that the GALA CoP enjoys a shared 'regime of competence' [14], favouring the practical contributions of games.

Figure 5 shows the educational context discussed in the sample of papers, with formal learning accounting for the largest proportion of papers and referring to structured education (e.g., school, university). This is relatively unsurprising as the GALA community is largely made up of academics, who have ease of access to user groups in formal education. However, the community does also reach out of the academic playground to informal learning contexts, which are more self-directed, occurring outside of educational institutions or certifications. Finally, corporate learning was the least represented and covered the development of skills, knowledge and/or competencies within an organizational setting.

Game Subject Matter. Of the 439 papers reviewed, 344 (78%) discussed a specific game, which was either a newly developed game or a review of an existing game for new purposes. This further supports findings regarding case study being the most preferred paper type. Table 1 shows a breakdown of the subject matter represented in the sample of games. These groupings could potentially be aggregated further into broad categories, but due to the multidisciplinary nature of the GALA research community, an excessively reductive approach would likely oversimplify the rich diversity of game topics utilised. Furthermore, the type of game used does not necessarily determine the research focus or outputs.

Table 1. Subject matter covered in games presented

Game subject matter	#(%)	Game subject matter	#(%)
Mathematics education	38 (11%)	Language and literacy education	15 (4%)
Business and management	35 (10%)	Driving or flight training	14 (4%)
Social skills/behavioural training	29 (8%)	Cybersecurity education	12 (3%)
Science and engineering education	28 (8%)	Pedagogy/educator training	12 (3%)
Sustainability/environmental education	24 (7%)	Computer science/programming	11 (3%)
Health and well-being	23 (7%)	Music education	5 (1%)
Cultural and historical education	23 (7%)	Emergency preparedness	5 (1%)
Diagnostic and treatment/rehabilitation	23 (7%)	Research methods and statistics	4 (1%)
Cognitive training games	20 (6%)	Economics education	4 (1%)
Clinical skills education	16 (5%)	Information/media literacy	3 (1%)

Disciplines Represented. In order to gauge which disciplines were represented in the GALA research community, the dominant academic theory or framework was identified from each paper (Table 2). This use of a theoretical base was then clustered into the relevant disciplines represented, as shown in Fig. 6. The proportion of GALA community members whose focus is mainly technical would appear to be low. This is to some extent unsurprising as review of publications shows the community is primarily united by a shared interest in the domain of games for impactful learning, rather than the technical design of games. This may also however present opportunities for development interventions to raise technical competence across willing members of the community.

5 Discussion

This work's key contribution is an introductory overview to the GALA research community's makeup and academic works. Analyzing the CoP's composition, collaborative evolution and thematic interests has provided insights to inform regular internal evaluations ensuring the community maintains its quality, relevance and inclusivity. Methodically this contribution elaborates on established approaches of systematic bibliometric and thematic literature reviews [10], by including carefully calibrated and systematic use of an automated AI-based tool.

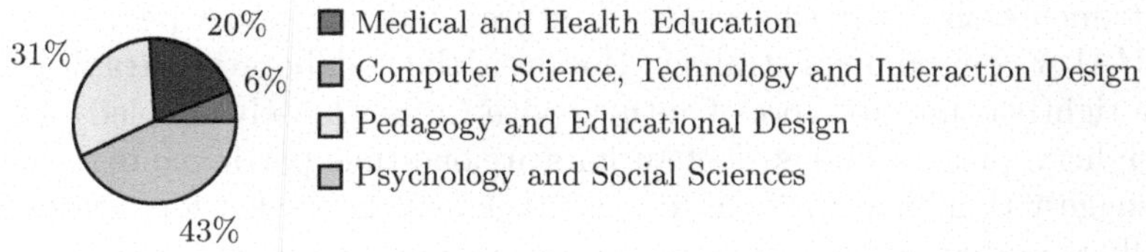

Fig. 6. Disciplines represented

Table 2. Frameworks used in papers

Theoretical Framework	#(%)	Theoretical Framework	#(%)
Constructivism	32 (7.3%)	Scaffolding Theory	8 (1.8%)
Flow Theory	29 (6.6%)	Theory of Planned Behavior	7 (1.6%)
Self-Determination Theory	27 (6.2%)	Activity Theory	7 (1.6%)
Learning Analytics	11 (2.5%)	Cognitive Load Theory	6 (1.4%)
Computational Thinking	10 (2.3%)	Social Constructivism	6 (1.4%)
Evidence-Centered Design	10 (2.3%)	Bloom's Taxonomy	6 (1.4%)
Theory of Multiple Intelligences	9 (2.0%)	Motivation Theory	5 (1.1%)
Situated Learning Theory	8 (1.8%)		

The interdisciplinary nature of the GALA community is an important finding of this study, highlighting the integration of various fields, e.g., Education, Psychology, Health Education, Computer Science. In line with CoP theory, GALA exemplifies the ways in which interdisciplinary collaboration can enhance learning opportunities and drive innovation [8]. This supports Wenger et al. [14,15] ideas that CoPs provide a fertile ground for continuous learning and collective growth; the GALA community has also grown its reach considerably from representing just 13 countries to contributors from 48 countries around the world. Furthermore, findings support previous calls for a unified theoretical approach to game-based learning [6] and examining how different theoretical perspectives within the community contribute to innovation and the growth of research CoP.

In an emerging discipline such as serious games, the development of expected quality standards and tools is crucial for continuing the field's advancement and is the responsibility of pioneering CoPs like GALA. Meanwhile, maintaining a broad and inclusive approach to research on games and learning is essential. For instance, Fig. 6 shows a low representation of technical disciplines compared to a large number of educators. While this is to be expected in an academic CoP, it presents further opportunity to capitalize on the interdisciplinary nature and further develop the skill mix. Similarly, regarding game subject matter, Table 1 shows some representation of diagnostics, clinical skills and emergency preparedness. These could represent small sub-communities or areas too be explored and expanded, along with increased applications in the corporate domain (Fig. 3).

In alignment with the CoP principle of legitimate peripheral participation [7], support, mentorship and succession of future academics must be vital aspects of the GALA community's strategy. However, the collaboration graph in Fig. 2 shows a tightly connected core of authors with various loosely coupled authors in the periphery, plus around 80% of authors are one-time participants so far. This could suggest that more deliberate encouragement is needed for newcomers to gradually move towards full engagement. It must be noted however that specialist contributors may join to collaborate with core authors only once. Alternatively, new authors' first contribution may be individual, before they partner with other new-found collaborators from the CoP for future contributions. The authorship trends and collaborative networks plus their development over time therefore warrant further investigation and ongoing interrogation. This is important to ensure the GALA community remains focused on academic quality and contribution, avoiding operation based on social capital, which can make it difficult for newcomers to break in [9]. This reflects common challenges within CoPs, where strong community norms may stifle innovation by preventing members from breaking CoP conventions [2]. Encouraging wide participation in decision-making and outreach to other areas, including geographical regions (as shown in Fig. 1) is essential. As the academic leadership of the community, the central core of practitioners must continue to focus on developing junior researchers, passing on their knowledge and succession planning to ensure the future continuation of the community. As such, regular reviews like this are crucial to understanding the community's makeup and interests, also uncovering any potential biases, barriers to entry or limited developmental pathways.

Limitations: This study's limitations include the scope of the bibliometric and content analyses and the inherent constraints of the AI tools employed. The bibliometric analysis, while comprehensive, may not capture the full complexity and nuance of the GALA community's research outputs due to the selection criteria and database limitations. Additionally, AI tools are powerful in processing large datasets and identifying patterns, cognizance of their limitations must be maintained, including potential biases in algorithmic design, accuracy issues and the inability to interpret context in the same way a human researcher would. Despite these limitations, it is anticipated that the systematic approach adopted in this study, which included consistent use of AI across all analyses, helped mitigate some of these issues. The methodology ensured a degree of uniformity and repeatability in the findings, which may have been less consistent if they stemmed from two human researchers. While this lends credibility to the initial insights generated, it is important to emphasize that this work represents the first stage of a more extensive investigation and at this stage, the intention was not to over-analyze. The AI-generated insights need to be validated through human review and expert feedback from the GALA community to ensure their accuracy and relevance. This human validation is crucial to refining the analysis, correcting any AI-induced errors and enhancing the overall robustness of the study.

6 Conclusion and Outlook

This study provides an introduction to the GALA community and its contributions, guided by the primary research questions regarding the community's composition, geographic origins, academic disciplines, the evolution of research collaborations, and topics of interest. Results indicate that there is growth in the community, along with strong collegiate ties, and highlight the community's robust and interdisciplinary collaborative networks. To maintain these strengths and succession plans for the future, the core of academic leadership in the community must continue to develop junior researchers and include other CoP members in decision-making to mitigate the risks typically facing such communities.

Future research will focus on longitudinal analysis, mapping trends, exploring specific disciplines and further developing intellectual frameworks. Regularly updating and validating these analyses will ensure that the GALA community continues to foster innovation and excellence in the field of serious games, supporting its members in driving the boundaries of research and practice forward.

References

1. Behl, A., Jayawardena, N., Pereira, V., Islam, N., Giudice, M.D., Choudrie, J.: Gamification and e-learning for young learners: a systematic literature review, bibliometric analysis, and future research agenda. Technol. Forecast. Soc. Chang. **176**, 121445 (2022)
2. Chen, C.V.H., Kearns, K., Eaton, L., Hoffmann, D.S., Leonard, D., Samuels, M.: Caring for our communities of practice in educational development. Improve Acad. J. Educ. Dev. **41** (4 2022)
3. Chen, G., Rolim, V., Mello, R.F., Gašević, D.: Let's shine together! a comparative study between learning analytics and educational data mining. In: 10th International Conference on Learning Analytics & Knowledge, pp. 544–553. ACM, New York (2020)
4. Dawson, S., Gašević, D., Siemens, G., Joksimovic, S.: Current state and future trends: a citation network analysis of the learning analytics field. In: 4th International Conference on Learning Analytics and Knowledge, pp. 231–240. ACM, New York (2014)
5. Hwang, G.J., Chen, P.Y.: Interweaving gaming and educational technologies: clustering and forecasting the trends of game-based learning research by bibliometric and visual analysis. Entertainment Comput. **40** (2022)
6. Krath, J., Schürmann, L., von Korflesch, H.F.: Revealing the theoretical basis of gamification: a systematic review and analysis of theory in research on gamification, serious games and game-based learning. Comput. Hum. Behav. **125** (2021)
7. Lave, J., Wenger, E.: Situated learning: legitimate peripheral participation. Cambridge University Press (1991)
8. Pyrko, I., Dörfler, V., Eden, C.: Thinking together: what makes communities of practice work? Hum. Relations **70**, 389–409 (2017)
9. Roberts, J.: Limits to communities of practice. J. Manage. Stud. **43**, 623–639 (2006)
10. Rojas-Sánchez, M.A., Palos-Sánchez, P.R., Folgado-Fernández, J.A.: Systematic literature review and bibliometric analysis on virtual reality and education. Educ. Inf. Technol. **28**, 155–192 (2023)
11. Serious Games Society: About the Serious Games Society. https://seriousgamessociety.org/about/ (2024). Accessed 10 Jul 2024
12. Sánchez-Cardona, I., Sánchez-Lugo, J., Vlez-González, J.: Exploring the potential of communities of practice for learning and collaboration in a higher education context. Procedia. Soc. Behav. Sci. **46**, 1820–1825 (2012)
13. Trinidad, M., Ruiz, M., Calderón, A.: A bibliometric analysis of gamification research. IEEE Access **9**, 46505–46544 (2021)

14. Wenger, E.: Communities of practice and social learning systems: the career of a concept. In: Blackmore, C. (ed.) Social Learning Systems and Communities of Practice, pp. 179–198. Springer London, London (2010). https://doi.org/10.1007/978-1-84996-133-2_11
15. Wenger-Trayner, E., Wenger-Trayner, B., Reid, P., Bruderlein, C.: Communities of practice within and across organizations. The Social Learning Lab (2023)

Gameplay Performance as a Predictor of Adaptive Expertise in Primary School Students

Mariana Rocha(✉) and Pierpaolo Dondio

School of Computer Science, Technological University Dublin, Dublin, Ireland
mariana.rocha@tudublin.ie

Abstract. The present study explores the potential of gameplay performance to predict gains in adaptive expertise among primary school students. More specifically, this research evaluates adaptive number knowledge (ANK), an ability to understand whole-number relations and apply this knowledge flexibly to solve new problems. Our study involved 130 primary school students playing the digital game "Seven Spells", which focuses on arithmetic operations and numeric tables. Students' ANK skills were assessed through a pen-and-paper timed task before and after playing the game for six weeks. Three gameplay performance metrics were collected: the highest level achieved in a multi-player mode, the highest score in single-player mode, and the leaderboard position in single-player mode. Linear regression analysis revealed that the progress against virtual opponents significantly predicted various improvements in ANK skills. Conversely, higher leaderboard positions in the single-player mode were unexpectedly correlated with some reduced ANK gains, likely due to a lack of engagement in this game mode. Student feedback indicated a preference for multiplayer mode, which may have fostered higher engagement and skill development. Our contribution suggests games can support adaptive expertise development and highlights the importance of identifying specific game design features for learning.

Keywords: Adaptive Expertise · Adaptive Number Knowledge · Maths games

1 Introduction

Extensive research has investigated the impact of games to improve learning outcomes in mathematics education. More recently, researchers have started investigating the impact of digital and non-digital games on developing higher-order maths skills, such as adaptive expertise. This paper explores the potential of gameplay performance in revealing the development of Adaptive Number Knowledge (ANK) skills.

1.1 The Impact of Games in Mathematics Learning

A recent systematic review of 28 open-access articles identified that maths games impact students' cognitive domain, supporting the development of their intellectual skills and

A. Schönbohm et al. (Eds.): GALA 2024, LNCS 15348, pp. 14–24, 2025.
https://doi.org/10.1007/978-3-031-78269-5_2

boosting engagement during learning [1]. Previously, [2] meta-analysis suggested a small but significant potential for maths games to provide higher learning gains compared to traditional learning methods. However, it is not possible to generalise that games outperform nongame teaching as the design within the game plays a crucial role in the learning outcome [3]. The design of a maths game can impact, for instance, the development of high-order thinking, which includes abilities such as problem-solving and critical thinking [4].

1.2 Adaptive Expertise in Mathematics

The seminal work by [5] defines an adaptive expert as "those who not only perform procedural skills efficiently but also understand the meaning of the skills and nature of their object" (p. 2). Understanding their own knowledge can allow learners to flexibly apply their skills to new settings. In maths, adaptive expertise can be illustrated by Adaptive Number Knowledge (ANK) – the ability to understand whole-number relations and apply this knowledge creatively and flexibly to solve unfamiliar problems [6]. ANK contrasts with routine expertise, commonly emphasised in traditional teaching methods for arithmetic problem-solving. Routine expertise focuses on limited procedures and is often efficient only when applied to familiar tasks [7]. For instance, memorising that $4 + 5 = 9$ is a familiar task while knowing the different paths to move from 12 to 146 ($12 + 134$; $12 \times 12 + 2$; $12 \times 10 + 26$, etc.) requires adaptive expertise [8].

1.3 Game-Based Learning and High-Order Skills

Games designed to promote rich tasks and multiple levels of inquiry allow children to practice their adaptive expertise, leading to the development of ANK skills [9]. Games can provide, for example, the option to solve tasks through a surface or more complex approach, motivating the player to adapt their knowledge to each task. However, games do not automatically make learning more efficient or motivating [10]. The game design must allow the integration of the educational content into the game context [9], promoting learning in an approach that might not be achievable in traditional classroom practice. To support ANK skills development, students must have opportunities for extensive practice solving tasks in which numbers and operations are connected in novel ways [9]. According to [11], efficient game-based learning should provide clear goals, allow learners to play the game in various situations, and offer feedback.

1.4 Current Research

Emerging research suggests that games can support the development of adaptive expertise. However, the relationship between gameplay performance and the development of adaptive expertise skills in maths learning remains unclear. This study aims to address part of this gap by answering the following research question:

RQ: Can performance in mathematics games predict the development of students' adaptive number knowledge skills?

We hypothesise that students who engage with and perform well in maths games designed to support higher-order thinking will demonstrate better performance in adaptive expertise tests. Our goal is to evaluate if in-game variables can be directly linked to the improvement in the ANK skills as an attempt to specifically understand what aspects of game design can support the development of these abilities.

2 Methods

The current research took place in primary schools in Ireland, evaluating the potential of gameplay performance metrics in predicting ANK skills through a digital game designed for children between 8 and 12 years old, currently played by over 2,000 students.

2.1 Participants

Participants were recruited by contacting the list of National Primary Schools in Ireland and enrolled on a first-come-first-serve basis. Data collection took place from April 2024 to June 2024. The students were required to provide a signed parent's consent form to join the study. To play the game, children received an anonymous username, also used as the participant's ID for data collection, protecting the student's identity. Game logs were collected automatically by saving game events into an online relational database managed by the researchers.

2.2 Seven Spells

This study used the game Seven Spells as an intervention for ANK skills development in primary school. Seven Spells is a digital card game that covers learning outcomes such as arithmetic operations and numeric tables. Players aim to score high by strategically using their cards to capture the opponent's cards by performing the most efficient moves. Scaffolding learning is available through the support of a character, the game master, who guides the player on what each card can do. The points are scored by capturing number cards presented on a digital board using maths knowledge. Cards with the same number can be matched and captured. The game also includes spell cards, which use numeric operations or properties to modify existing numbers by increasing or reducing them or even combining them with other numbers. Spell cards can add, subtract, multiply or divide existing numbers cards. For instance, a spell card "Divide by 3" can be used to convert a number card 18 into a number card 6, which can then capture another number card 6. Some number cards have special abilities, such as the 'total' card, allowing the player to capture multiple number cards from the opponent by combining them. Figure 1 illustrates a game move, where the blue card 15 (player's card) is used to capture the red card 15, and a 21 total card is used to capture the numbers 1, 13, and 7 as their sum results in 21. When clicking on card '21 total', the master character indicates the possible action to be taken using this card.

The game can be played in single or multi-player mode, when the student can play against up to 35 virtual opponents. In the single mode, players have a deck of 40 cards and use those to capture other cards to and score the highest they can. In this mode,

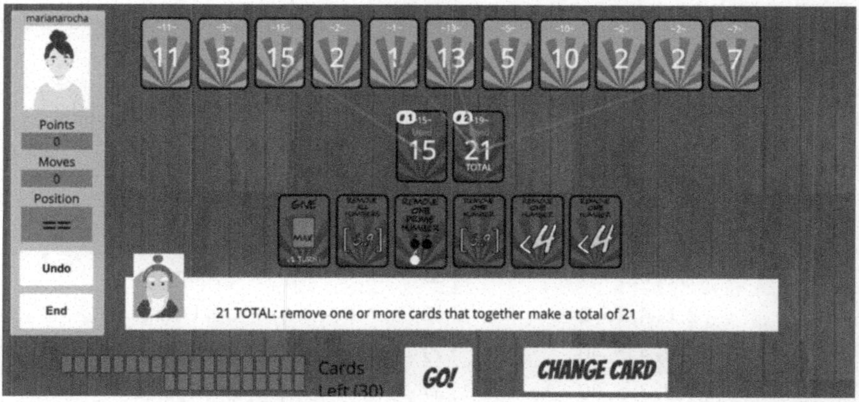

Fig. 1. The gameplay screenshot shows a move that uses a number card and a total card to score 36 points in total.

the game does not end automatically – the player needs to have the initiative to end it when they do not have more cards available. Students can access a leaderboard that compares their highest scores to their classmates' when playing single-player mode. The game is turn-based when playing against virtual opponents: the player tries to use their unlimited deck of cards to capture the virtual opponent's cards. Once one of the two players (human or virtual) scores 100 points, the interface announces the winner, and the game ends automatically. Considering that Seven Spells is designed to emphasise arithmetic operations and flexible number manipulation, this game can mirror the idea of adapting players' maths knowledge to solve new problems, which is in line with ANK principles.

2.3 Adaptive Number Knowledge Tasks

To identify participants' ANK skills before and after playing the game, students were asked to complete the Arithmetic Sentence Production Task, developed by [8]. The pen-and-paper task combined four to five numbers with the four basic operations to reach a target number. For example, one item in the task could be to provide as many combinations as possible of the numbers 2, 4, 6 and 8 to find the number 16 (for instance: $8 \times 2 = 16$; $4 \times 4 = 16$; $8 + 2 + 6 = 16$ etc.). Students had to provide as many answers as possible in 8 min and were allowed to repeat numbers or operations as long as they only used the items illustrated in the task.

Each pre- and post-test included four items, one of which was a dense item and three of which were sparse. Dense items have many arithmetical relations between given and target numbers. For example, students might find it easy to identify the combinations between the numbers 2, 4, 6, 16 and 24 that result in the target number 12. Sparse items, in contrast, have a smaller number of relations between the given and target numbers. Students might find it more challenging to make 79 by combining the numbers 1, 2, 4, 5 and 40 using the basic operations. Table 1 describes the items included in the pre- and post-tests.

Table 1. Dense and sparse items included in the pre- and post-tests used to measure students' levels of ANK skills before and after playing the game.

Time	Given numbers	Target number	Problem type
Pre-test	2, 4, 8, 12, 32	16	Dense
	1, 2, 3, 5, 30	59	Sparse
	2, 4, 8, 10	22	Sparse
	1, 3, 5, 7	35	Sparse
Post-test	2, 6, 4, 16, 24	12	Dense
	1, 2, 4, 5, 40	79	Sparse
	1, 2, 3, 5, 30	37	Sparse
	3, 4, 5, 6	63	Sparse

Following [8] research, participants' ANK abilities were calculated considering the number of correct solutions across all items, the number of correct solutions that used both additive (addition and/or subtraction) and multiplicative (multiplication and/or division) operations and the proportion of multi-operation solutions per correct solution.

2.4 Experiment Design

The research design involved six weekly one-hour visits to the classrooms. During these visits, students played both modes (single and multi-player) of the Seven Spells game. In the first (week 1) and last (week 6) visits, trained researchers carried out pre- and post-ANK tasks. In the final visit, students also answered a questionnaire providing feedback on their experience playing the game. Students could also play the game from home after week 2. Besides the results of ANK tests and gameplay experience feedback, the study collected data on each participant's gameplay performance. Table 2 provides an overview of the variables collected and included in the data analysis.

Table 2. Description of the data collected during the study.

Variable name	Definition
id	Student identification
all_correct_diff	Difference between the number of all correct answers in the pre- and post-ANK test
all_multi_op_diff	Difference between the number of correct multi-operation answers in the pre- and post-ANK test
all_propmult_diff	Difference in the proportion of multi-operation solutions per correct solution in the pre- and post-ANK test

(continued)

Table 2. *(continued)*

Variable name	Definition
dense_correct_diff	Difference between the number of correct dense items answers in the pre- and post-ANK test
dense_multi_op_diff	Difference between the number of correct multi-operation answers for dense items in the pre- and post-ANK test
dense_prop_mult_diff	Difference in the proportion of multi-operation solutions per correct solution for dense items in the pre- and post-ANK test
sparse_correct_diff	Difference between the number of correct sparse items answers in the pre- and post-ANK test
sparse_multi_op_diff	Difference between the number of correct multi-operation answers for sparse items in the pre- and post-ANK test
sparse_propmult_diff	Difference in the proportion of multi-operation solutions per correct solution for sparse items in the pre- and post-ANK test
score	Highest score achieved by a player in the solo mode
leaderboard	The position of a student in the classroom solo mode leaderboard
cpu_progress	Students' progress when playing against a computer player, measured by the number of opponents defeated during the gameplay

3 Results

Only students present for the whole 6-week cycle were included in the study, resulting in 130 participants (19 from 3rd grade – ages 8 to 9, 42 from 4th grade – ages 9 to 10, 61 from 5th grade – ages 10 to 11, and 8 from 6th grade – ages 11 to 12). To answer the research question, linear regression was used to evaluate the impact of gameplay performance (independent variables) on predicting the development of adaptive number knowledge, measured by the difference between pre-test and post-test scores (dependent variables). No multicollinearity was detected for the independent variables.

The results of the pre-test for each variable related to the ANK pre-test were included in each analysis model as an independent variable, allowing control for the student's initial ability. Students with higher pre-test scores may have less room for improvement than those with lower pre-test scores. By including the pre-test values in the model, we account for this initial ability, making it easier to isolate and see the impact of the game-related variables on the improvement. The models have R^2 values between 0.25 and 0.51, meaning that the model explained between 25% and 51% of the variance in the pre- and post-test differences. The linear regression results suggest that the three independent variables considered significantly correlate with a number of pre and post-test differences (Table 3).

According to our results, the more virtual opponents the player managed to defeat (*cpu_progress*), the higher the general improvement in their ANK skills ($p = 0.016$), as the direction of the effect is positive ($\beta = 0.116$). A good performance when playing against the opponents explains the majority of differences between pre and post-ANK

Table 3. Linear Regression results show the impact of in-game metrics in predicting ANK skills progress.

Dependent variables	Independent variables						
	cpu_progress		score		leaderboard		R^2
	β	p	β	p	β	p	
all_correct_diff	0,116	0.016*	0,001	0.389	-0,034	0.495	0.25
all_multi_op_diff	0,106	0.002**	0,002	0.050	0,058	0.110	0.27
all_propmult_diff	0,007	0.009**	0	0.115	0,007	0.022*	0.36
dense_correct_diff	0,059	0.022*	-0,001	0.254	-0,071	0.011*	0.51
dense_multi_op_diff	0,013	0.097	0,001	0.001**	0,018	0.038*	0.47
dense_prop_mult_diff	0,002	0.209	0	0.001**	0,004	0.031*	0.29
sparse_correct_diff	0,092	0.012*	0,003	0.017*	0,038	0.343	0.36
sparse_multi_op_diff	0,098	0.002**	0,002	0.155	0,042	0.210	0.28
sparse_propmult_diff	0,014	0.001**	0	0.760	0,005	0.327	0.26

tests, including the proportion of multi-operation solutions per correct solution for sparse items, as the *cpu_progress* has a significant impact ($p = 0.005$) on that variable. The direction of the effect is also positive ($\beta = 0.014$), showing that this gameplay performance could predict the development of the ability to solve sparse items using multiple operations.

The results also suggest that the highest score when playing the single-player mode can predict some improvements in the player's ANK skills, such as their performance in solving dense items using multiple operations (*dense_multi_op_diff* and *dense_prop_multi_diff*) and their general performance in solving sparse items (*sparse_correct_diff*). However, a surprising result was obtained when looking at the leaderboard position as a possible predictor of ANK skills improvement. For the *all_propmult_diff*, *dense_multi_op_diff* and *dense_prop_mult_diff*, the coefficients have positive values, indicating that the higher the leaderboard position value (bottom of the leaderboard, meaning worse single-player mode performance), the better the improvement on the ANK skills. This result was unexpected as students at the top of the leaderboard were likely to perform better in the ANK test. As the leaderboard states the scores of players in the game's single-player mode, a deeper investigation is needed.

To better understand the potential of the different gameplay modes in predicting ANK skills improvement, we evaluated which mode the players preferred. In a survey after the 6-week playing cycle, students were asked to provide a score (1: did not like it, 10: loved it) for each gameplay mode (single-player and multi-player). Table 4 shows each score's mean, standard deviation, and maximum and minimum values.

The mean indicates that the students might prefer the multi-player mode. Wilcoxon Signed-Rank Test results show that the score given to the single-player mode is significantly lower than the score for playing against virtual characters ($W = 1838.5$, $p < .05$,

Table 4. Descriptive analysis of the students' feedback about their gameplay experience.

Student feedback	Mean	SD	Min	Max
Single-player	7.3	2.1	2	10
Multi-player	7.9	2.2	1	10

Z = -6). This result suggests that because students preferred playing against virtual characters, more effort was dedicated to this game mode, resulting in higher improvements in their ANK skills.

4 Discussion

The present study aimed to identify if gameplay performance could predict gains in players' ANK skills, abilities related to adaptive expertise. The gameplay performance metrics used included the highest level achieved when playing against virtual players, the highest score in single-player mode and the leaderboard position in single-player mode. The number of opponents defeated when playing against virtual players significantly predicted an improvement in most variables related to ANK skills development. The highest single-player score also managed to predict, on a smaller scale, some of the ANK skills developed. The single-player leaderboard position, however, showed an unexpectedly significant result: students at the bottom of the leaderboard had better improvements in their ability to use multiple operations to solve maths problems. When looking into the players' preferred game mode, the multiplayer mode is significantly preferred compared to the single-player mode. This could explain why the multi-player mode better predicted the ANK skills development in our study – as students preferred to play against the virtual characters, more effort was put into this game mode.

In the Seven Spells game, the leaderboard is generated by the highest score achieved in the single-player mode, and the whole classroom can see the players' positions. Previous literature suggests that the peer pressure caused by leaderboards can demotivate students from engaging in gameplay [12, 13]. Even though leaderboards are added to games as a competitive element to motivate players to succeed [14], the social pressure it brings to the environment might not benefit a learning game. In a study involving a competition where 271 students played a nationwide maths game, [15] identified that the leaderboard could only motivate students whose teams were performing well in the competition. In contrast, those underperforming teams felt demotivated to play. A previous study on the Seven Spells game suggested that students with higher levels of mathematics anxiety can be sensitive to the presence of a leaderboard [16].

Our results suggested that players' performance when playing against virtual characters positively predicted their improvement in the ANK test. As previous studies demonstrated, multiplayer games tend to be more engaging [17], which can result in players spending more time and effort improving their performance in this game mode. Students developed their ANK skills by engaging more in playing against computer players and improving their game performance. More specifically, students significantly improved using multi-operations to solve sparse items, which are more difficult to solve than dense items. The post-gameplay results confirm the preference for a multiplayer version of the game, where students preferred playing against virtual characters instead of the single-player mode. Even though playing solo can give the child a sense of control and the possibility of getting used to the game mechanics and rules before facing an opponent [18], multiplayer allows open-ended learning, motivating the players to achieve abstract and difficult-to-measure learning objectives such as adaptive expertise [19].

5 Conclusions

Our results do not mean to compare the efficacy of multi against single-player maths games but to better understand how the performance in different game modes can help to predict students' gains in adaptive expertise skills such as ANK. Previous work demonstrates that single-player games are great for focused, self-paced learning and reinforcing basic skills, while multiplayer games promote collaboration, engagement, and the development of higher-order thinking skills [20]. Balancing both types of games in an educational setting can provide a comprehensive approach to mathematics education. This study suggests that games have the potential to support adaptive expertise development in maths since primary school age. However, more effort is needed to identify what specific game design features can be relevant to give space for game-based learning tools beyond drill and practice activities.

6 Limitations and Future Work

Our study contributed to better understand the potential of digital maths games in developing adaptive expertise at the primary school level and how in-game metrics can support the assessment of these skills. However, our research was limited to 130 primary school students and further investigation with larger samples is needed. For better generalisability, we aim to explore different age groups and educational contexts. Considering students could play both at home and at school, future work should also include an analysis of the amount of time playing and how that can be related to our current results. We also aim to evaluate qualitative data that might reveal how students feel about each Seven Spells game mode. The post-gameplay survey provided an open space for students to reveal positive and negative aspects of the game. Comments such as "the leaderboard made me feel under pressure" or "I felt bad because my classmates could see my leaderboard position" were common. However, students appreciated playing against virtual characters. They mentioned enjoying reading about each character and the fact they could try to beat them as many times as they wished.

References

1. Hui, H.B., Sofwan Mahmud, M.: Influence of game-based learning in mathematics education on the students' cognitive and affective domain: A systematic review. Front. Psychol. **14**, 01–15 (2023)
2. Tokac, U., Novak, E., Thompson, C.G.: Effects of game-based learning on students' mathematics achievement: a meta-analysis. J. Comput. Assist. Learn. **35**, 407–420 (2019). https://doi.org/10.1111/jcal.12347
3. Clark, D.B., Tanner-Smith, E.E., Killingsworth, S.S.: Digital games, design, and learning: a systematic review and meta-analysis. Rev. Educ. Res. **86**, 79–122 (2016). https://doi.org/10.3102/0034654315582065
4. Chen, P.Y., Hwang, G.J., Yeh, S.Y., Chen, Y.T., Chen, T.W., Chien, C.H.: Three decades of game-based learning in science and mathematics education: an integrated bibliometric analysis and systematic review. J. Comput. Educ. **9**, 455–476 (2022). https://doi.org/10.1007/s40692-021-00210-y
5. Hatano, G., Inagaki, K.: Two courses of expertise (1986)
6. Hickendorff, M.: Flexibility and Adaptivity in Arithmetic Strategy Use: What Children Know and What They Show. J Numer Cogn. **8**, 367–381 (2022). https://doi.org/10.5964/jnc.7277
7. Baroody, A.J., Rosu, L.: Adaptive expertise with basic addition and subtraction combinations: the number sense view (2006)
8. McMullen, J., Brezovszky, B., Rodríguez-Aflecht, G., Pongsakdi, N., Hannula-Sormunen, M.M., Lehtinen, E.: Adaptive number knowledge: Exploring the foundations of adaptivity with whole-number arithmetic. Learn. Individ. Differ. **47**, 172–181 (2016). https://doi.org/10.1016/j.lindif.2016.02.007
9. McMullen, J., et al.: A game-based approach to promoting adaptive rational number knowledge. Math. Think. Learn. (2023). https://doi.org/10.1080/10986065.2023.2177818
10. Wouters, P., Van Oostendorp, H.: A meta-analytic review of the role of instructional support in game-based learning. Comput. Educ. **60**, 412–425 (2013). https://doi.org/10.1016/j.compedu.2012.07.018
11. Husain, L.: Getting serious about math: serious game design framework & an example of a math educational game (2011)
12. Alexander, S., De La Porte, A.: Exploring the inner workings of the leaderboard for use in educational contexts (2022)
13. Huang, R., et al.: The impact of gamification in educational settings on student learning outcomes: a meta-analysis. Educ. Tech. Res. Dev. **68**, 1875–1901 (2020). https://doi.org/10.1007/s11423-020-09807-z
14. Cagiltay, N.E., Ozcelik, E., Ozcelik, N.S.: The effect of competition on learning in games. Comput. Educ. **87**, 35–41 (2015). https://doi.org/10.1016/j.compedu.2015.04.001
15. Ninaus, M., De Freitas, S., Kiili, K.: Motivational potential of leaderboards in a team-based math game competition
16. Dondio, P., Almo, A., Amaral, M., Tibebe, E., Rocha, M., Brennan, A.: Not (Only) a matter of position: player traits which influence the experience with the leaderboard in a digital maths game. In: Lecture Notes in Computer Science (including subseries Lecture Notes in Artificial Intelligence and Lecture Notes in Bioinformatics), pp. 183–193. Springer Science and Business Media Deutschland GmbH (2024). https://doi.org/10.1007/978-3-031-49065-1_18
17. Gitarana, G.R.E., Fithratu, C., Muis, A.N., Darmakusuma, R.: Analysis and evaluation of player engagement in serious education game using game refinement theory case study: arithmatopia game. In: 6th International Conference on Interactive Digital Media, ICIDM 2020. Institute of Electrical and Electronics Engineers Inc. (2020). https://doi.org/10.1109/ICIDM51048.2020.9339633

18. Sommerfelt, E.F.: The Effect of Opponent on Player Experience Solo Play vs. Human vs. Artificial Intelligence (2024)
19. Harteveld, C., Bekebrede, G.: Learning in single-versus multiplayer games: the more the merrier? Simul. Gaming **42**, 43–63 (2011). https://doi.org/10.1177/1046878110378706
20. Araya, R., Jiménez, A., Bahamondez, M., Calfucura, P., Dartnell, P., Soto-Andrade, J.: Teaching modeling skills using a massively multiplayer online mathematics game (2014). https://doi.org/10.1007/s11280-012-0173-5

Cipher in Classrooms: Evaluating Digital Game-Based Language Learning for Irish Vocabulary Acquisition

Liang Xu[1](✉), Mark Andrade[2], Elaine Uí Dhonnchadha[2], and Monica Ward[1]

[1] Dublin City University, Dublin, Ireland
{liang.xu,monica.ward}@dcu.ie
[2] Trinity College Dublin, Dublin, Ireland
{andradem,uidhonne}@tcd.ie

Abstract. This study explores the educational outcomes of Cipher, a Digital Game-Based Language Learning (DGBLL) application, focusing on vocabulary acquisition in Irish language learning. Cipher integrates engaging game mechanics with pedagogical principles, with the aim of enhancing Irish learners' language skills. Using a double-baseline model, we assess learning gains among 45 primary school students. Results show vocabulary improvements in the experimental groups compared to the control group, underscoring Cipher's educational potential. Key factors contributing to its success include a pedagogical focus, cultural responsiveness, curriculum alignment, content co-creation and innovative game design. This study highlights the potential of DGBLL applications like Cipher to support language acquisition, particularly in less commonly taught languages.

Keywords: Digital Game-Based Language Learning · L2 Learning Outcomes · Vocabulary Acquisition · Indigenous Language · Intervention Evaluation

1 Introduction

The integration of digital technologies into education has increasingly reshaped traditional learning paradigms, offering innovative methods which can enhance student engagement and learning effectiveness. DGBLL combines the immersive and interactive aspects of gaming with educational content, making learning more enjoyable and effective [1, 2]. In the context of the Irish language, DGBLL presents a unique opportunity to address several educational challenges. Irish, an official language of Ireland, is spoken very well by only approximately 4% of the population [3]. Traditional language learning methods often fail to maintain student interest, leading to a decline in engagement and retention in the Irish context [4]. Cipher, a DGBLL for Irish, integrates game elements with educational content to enhance the learning experience for Irish language students. It incorporates storytelling, culturally responsive content, and interactive challenges to make language learning more appealing and effective. To evaluate the educational effectiveness of Cipher, we used the rigorous double baseline model, which

A. Schönbohm et al. (Eds.): GALA 2024, LNCS 15348, pp. 25–35, 2025.
https://doi.org/10.1007/978-3-031-78269-5_3

involved conducting two pre-tests to establish a comprehensive baseline before implementing a 5-week intervention period and a post-test. The research was conducted in an English-medium primary school, focusing on vocabulary acquisition as a key measure of language learning. The study compared the performance of control and experimental groups, assessing Cipher's impact on vocabulary learning.

2 Related Research

Digital Game-Based Language Learning (DGBLL) merges the realms of gaming and language education, utilising digital games as a medium to enhance language acquisition [1]. This approach leverages the engaging and interactive nature of games to create learning environments that can motivate learners and improve their language skills [2]. Research has shown the positive impact of DGBLL on language acquisition, particularly vocabulary development. A meta-analysis [6] of DGBLL studies reveal medium to large effect sizes for vocabulary acquisition, underscoring its effectiveness compared to non-gaming instructional methods. However, there is a need for more comprehensive analyses of DGBLL for less commonly taught languages, such as Irish. The current body of research on DGBLL for the Irish language is very limited, with only a few available studies [7–9]. One of the challenges in measuring the effectiveness of a learning intervention is making sure that observed improvements in vocabulary knowledge are due to the intervention rather than other factors. A significant issue arises from the fact that participants can potentially learn from the tests themselves. When the same or similar tests are used for both pretests and post-tests, there is a risk that improvements in scores are partially due to test familiarity or practice effect rather than the educational intervention. Additional challenges include the diversity of contexts, participants, methodologies and curriculum alignment. Many studies focus on English and adult learners and are not integrated into a structured classroom setting, leading to results that may not generalise to the learning experiences of schoolchildren [10]. Games designed purely for entertainment have been found to be more engaging and effective for language learning compared to those specifically developed for educational purposes [6]. However, this also means that curriculum integration and assessment is challenging.

One common approach to ensure that observed improvements in vocabulary knowledge are due to the intervention rather than test familiarity is using pretests and post-tests with the same items presented in different orders [10, 11]. This method reduces the practice effect. Contextualised testing involves embedding test words in meaningful sentences or providing cues to ensure that students understand the context and meaning of the words. Including both experimental and control groups is one of the most common testing approaches. This allows researchers to distinguish the effects of the intervention from test familiarity [10], and allows for a clear comparison of vocabulary gains attributable to the intervention versus traditional learning methods. Delayed post-tests assess long-term retention, distinguishing between immediate recall and sustained learning. The double baseline model presents a novel approach to evaluating language learning effectiveness [5]. This model involves establishing two baseline measurements before implementing an intervention. Traditional pretest post-test designs often struggle with issues arising from test familiarity. By incorporating a second baseline, researchers can better distinguish between genuine learning gains due to the intervention and those resulting from repeated exposure to test materials. If improvement 1 (i.e. the difference between pretest 1 and pretest 2 scores) is none or very small and improvement 2 (i.e. the difference between pretest 2 scores and post-test scores) is significantly greater than improvement 1, it shows that repeated exposure to the test words does help slightly but the learning intervention contributed more significantly to learning. Collectively, these methodological strategies aim to ensure that observed vocabulary gains are attributable to the educational intervention rather than simply due to repeated test exposure.

3 Methodology

Cipher is a DGBLL application that fosters language acquisition through an engaging game environment, where players solve language challenges to uncover stories and defeat villains. Developed with a pedagogically informed, learner-oriented approach, the game incorporates elements such as levels, power-ups, game characters and scoring systems to maintain player interest and motivation. The game content is culturally responsive, utilising Irish folklore and mythology to enhance relevance for learners. Additionally, it features AI-generated images and text-to-speech technology to support vocabulary acquisition, reading comprehension and writing [12]. Designing and developing a DGBLL game is both exciting and challenging. With this in mind, Cipher was designed with five key principles in mind. They are a green approach (i.e. reuse and repurpose), a focus on pedagogy, cultural responsiveness, curriculum alignment and co-creation. When designing a DGBLL resource, it can be tempting to focus on the game elements, but a pedagogical focus is important. The Cipher game uses storytelling to immerse learners in tasks that involve deciphering "magic stones" (ciphered words) and "enchanted scrolls," (ciphered texts). AI-generated images are integrated for context illustration of vocabulary and to enhance understanding (see Fig. 1). A culturally responsive approach to teaching involves taking into consideration cultural differences and focusing on what students can do [13]. Cipher was designed to provide learners with an opportunity to read more Irish, in a rich and visually appealing way which complements the school curriculum. Using co-creation with teachers, Cipher texts at an appropriate level of difficulty help students to focus on spellings and reading.

Fig. 1. Vocabulary, reading and writing.

Testing took place in a suburban, English-medium, all boys school, with mixed-ability classes. As our test methodology, we use a double baseline approach [5], conducting two pre-tests for both the experimental and control groups. The primary school had three 4th class classes (age range 9 - 12). One class was randomly selected as the control group (Room 5), while Room 1 and Room 3 were the experimental groups having 24 students in each class. The control group attended regular Irish classes, similar to the experimental groups, but without Cipher's intervention. The experimental groups received the same standard instruction with the addition of Cipher as a supplementary tool. There were 45 participants in total as some students were exempt from Irish. Each teacher was given an overview of the Cipher game and understood the purpose of the experiments. The researchers led the initial session of the intervention to ensure the game was properly introduced and any technical issues were addressed. For the remaining sessions, the classroom teachers were able to facilitate the game sessions themselves without difficulty. This was important, as the game was designed to be integrated into regular Irish classes without requiring ongoing researcher involvement. Specific vocabulary tasks were developed in conjunction with teachers for the Cipher experiment. It was important to have a mix of easy and difficult words, and also a mix of target words (Cipher words) and non-target words (non-Cipher). The first task was a **vocabulary checking task** whereby students were asked to spell a word. There were 30 words in this task: 20 Cipher words (5 easy and 15 difficult) and 10 non-Cipher words (5 easy and 5 difficult). During the test, each word was spoken, then read in the context of a sentence and then the word was repeated again. The words were read out in blocks of 10 words with a short break in between each block. There were two unrelated practice words before the start of the experiment. The second task was a **vocabulary matching task**, which is generally easier for learners. Students are asked to match words in Irish (L2) to their meaning in English (L1). To reduce guessing, there were more English words than Irish words in the matcher task. The same list of vocabulary words was used for this test. The double baseline design involved a first pretest (pretest 1), a second pretest one month later (pretest 2), a 5-week game block, followed by a post-test. Additionally, a user satisfaction survey was conducted at the end of the intervention, but it was not included in the paper due to limited space. However, previous user satisfaction research for Cipher was conducted and can be found in study [14].

4 Results and Discussion

4.1 Data Analysis

The data analysis is conducted according to a double-baseline model [5]. The data was separated into two overall categories for further classification: the scores achieved in the vocabulary checker scores exercises, which checked for the student's ability to spell the Irish words, and the vocabulary matcher scores exercises, which checked their understanding of the words, i.e. their ability to match the Irish words to their English translations. In the vocabulary checker task, for each word was scored 0 or 1. A score of 0.5 was given where the word was correct except for incorrect accent marks (*síneadh fada*) or missing/unnecessary double consonant. In the vocabulary matcher exercise, a 0 or 1 score was given, depending on whether the words were matched correctly. In both exercises each student was given a percentage score. Within the two task groups, the data was split using the student's room number and the testing round. All testing and game-playing were anonymous but each student was assigned a unique user ID. Students were asked to write their user ID on their test sheets. However, some issues arose that made it difficult to track students across the three rounds. Some students did not include their user ID on their test sheets, or their ID did not match their user IDs from the game. A final problem occurred where multiple students used the same ID in the same test round, presumably as they had shared a game device and user ID or may have used the same ID as a friend. Additionally, the decision was made not to merge the two experimental groups in the analysis due to variations in teacher involvement. Specifically, in one experimental group (Room 1), the regular teacher was absent for several sessions, and substitute teachers covered the class. The lack of continuity may have been an issue, as it usually takes a substitute teacher some time to become familiar with the students and their progress in each subject. This variation may have influenced the results. Such variability reflects the challenges of conducting real-world educational experiments and was accounted for in the analysis.

To gain an initial understanding of the performance of the three classrooms, each student's scores were split between their performance on target words, those that the student encountered in-game, and non-target words. Both lists had a mixture of easier and more difficult words. Running the Shapiro-Wilk test on each of the thirty-six data sets (target and non-target words, in each of the three rooms, across three rounds, in both forms of tests) established whether they were normally distributed. Half of the vocabulary checker tests (9/18) had a normal distribution, as did three-quarters of the vocabulary matcher tests (15/18). Specifically, regarding the data for the third round (post-test), most of the data was also normally distributed. Both the vocabulary checker and vocabulary matcher target word scores are normally distributed for all students with p-values of 0.106 and 0.109 respectively. While the vocabulary matcher non-target word scores were normally distributed (p-value of 0.235), the same wasn't true for the vocabulary checker non-target word scores ($0.0003 < 0.05$). This limited the scope of statistical analysis that could be performed as discussed in greater detail below. To graph the performance of each classroom, the mean and standard deviations of each of the 36 sets of scores were calculated and then plotted using Google Sheets. The data is shown in Table 1 and the graphs are shown in Fig. 2.

The performance of Room 1 for **vocabulary checker target words** exhibits an almost uniform increase from pre-test 1 to the post-test. The pre-test 2 to the post-test incline is slightly greater than between the two pre-tests ($m_{2\text{–}3} = 0.05 > m_{1\text{–}2} = 0.04$). This learning gain is less than had been expected, and maybe somewhat explained by the fact that Room 1 had several different teachers during the Cipher testing period. Room 3's performance is closer to the expected (and hoped for) outcome, as the slope between rounds 2 and 3 for target words is greater than that between the two pre-test rounds, implying the existence of an influence from the game. Room 5, the control group, also fits the model as very little increase in performance is seen between rounds 2 and 3. However, there is a strong increase between the two pre-test rounds. This may be explained by the teacher's strong focus on Irish in the classroom, especially through the use of interactive tools such as Duolingo. However, it seems that this progress flattens out in these cases during the intervention period. The equivalent scores for the **vocabulary checker non-target words** also give differing results. In Room 1 there's slight progress from round 1 to 2, which is then lost in the post-test. This could be due to teaching disruption, where the exposure to Irish outside of the game might have been reduced.

Room 3's scores on both of the pre-tests have a marginal difference but do improve after playing the game. It's not immediately clear what causes the difference, but it can be posited that the game increased their interest in learning Irish [14]. The slope of Room 5's graph is almost identical to that in the target words, albeit starting and ending at higher points.

Table 1. The mean (μ) and standard deviation (σ) of each data set across the two exercises.

Vocab Checker		Target words			Non-Target words		
	R1 (μ σ)	R 2 (μ σ)	R3 (μ σ)		R1 (μ σ)	R 2 (μ σ)	R3 (μ σ)
Room 1	11% 7%	15% 8%	20% 12%	**Room 1**	18% 12%	23% 15%	17% 17%
Room 3	8% 6%	14% 9%	24% 12%	**Room 3**	13% 11%	13% 11%	20% 15%
Room 5	7% 7%	17% 9%	17% 10%	**Room 5**	14% 12%	22% 14%	23% 17%
Vocab Matcher		**Target words**			**Non-Target words**		
	R1 (μ σ)	R 2 (μ σ)	R3 (μ σ)		R1 (μ σ)	R 2 (μ σ)	R3 (μ σ)
Room 1	21% 10%	24% 12%	29% 12%	**Room 1**	29% 13%	25% 10%	22% 12%
Room 3	22% 6%	26% 12%	39% 15%	**Room 3**	24% 11%	26% 6%	29% 11%
Room 5	21% 15%	30% 7%	30% 14%	**Room 5**	27% 14%	25% 12%	27% 11%

Turning to the results for the **matching exercise target words** we see similarly shaped slopes in the target word scores to those in the vocabulary checker. Again, the difference for Room 1 in the increase between pre-test 1 and the post-test appears almost uniform, but there is a slightly greater incline between rounds 2 and 3. For Room 3, the increase between rounds 2 and 3 is greater than that of Room 1 for the **matching exercise target words**, as well as the increase in their score from round 2 to 3 for **the vocabulary checker target words**. Room 5 once again progressed between the two pre-tests, and then maintained the latter score in the third round. The final set of charts for the **matching exercise non-target words** is the most ambiguous and difficult to analyse. It's not immediately clear why Room 1's trajectory is worse here than in the vocabulary checker, even if it does start and finish at higher scores. Room 3's score again shows steady progress, which aligns well with the hypothesis of learning through testing. Room 5's score in rounds 1 and 3 are the same but appear to have a slight drop in round 2.

In summary, for the target words, the pattern was observed in both the vocabulary checker and matching exercise in both experimental groups, where the increase from pre-test 2 to the post-test was sharper than between the two pre-tests. This demonstrates that the game had a positive effect on vocabulary acquisition, even considering that participants learned from the tests. This pattern was not observed in the control group, nor for the non-target words. Additionally, in terms of the performance of the three classes at each data point for each task (e.g., vocabulary checker), comparative analyses were conducted across three rounds, with a total of 36 comparisons made. The majority of the differences between the classes are not statistically significant (21/36). Of the remaining differences, eleven showed a medium effect size, and four had a large effect size. The differences with a medium effect size (Cohen's d between 0.35 and 0.65) were fairly evenly distributed among the three comparisons (Room 1 vs. Room 3, Room 1 vs. Room 5, and Room 3 vs. Room 5). In Round 2, there are three comparisons with a large effect size. In the vocabulary checker for non-target words, there is a statistically significant difference between Room 1 and Room 3, and between Room 3 and Room 5. The difference between Room 1 and Room 3 can be attributed to the improvements made by Room 1 and Room 5 due to learnings from the test, with no difference between the first two rounds for Room 3. In the vocabulary matcher for the targeted words, there is a large effect size between Room 1 and Room 5. Although all rooms improved from the test, Room 5 showed a more significant improvement compared to Room 1. The final significant difference is between Room 1 and Room 3 in the final round, for target words in the matcher exercise. This is also the most significant difference (Cohen's d of 0.76). This difference is due to Room 1 not improving as much as Room 3 between the second and third rounds. This demonstrates that the rooms do not have statistically different baseline scores, which could be problematic if there are large variations, as starting from a lower baseline typically allows for greater improvement in the post-test.

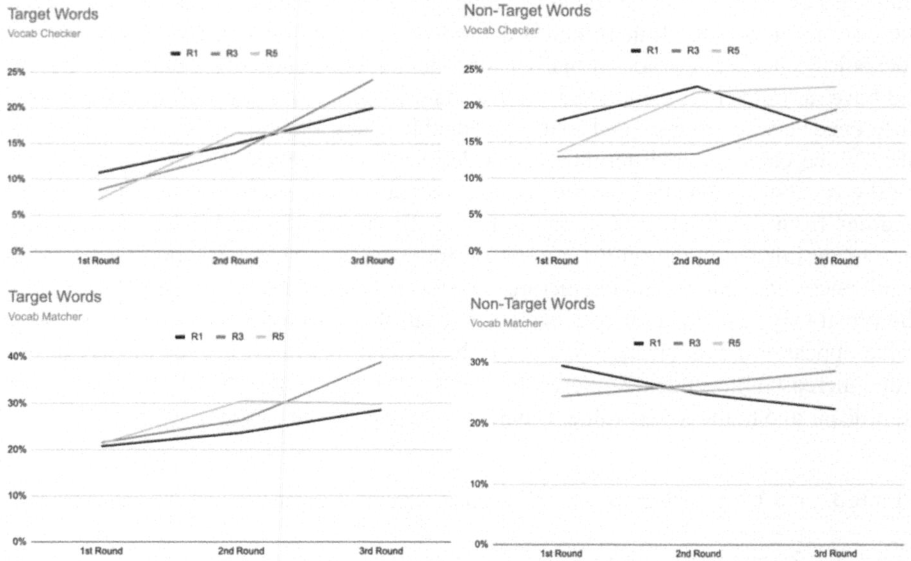

Fig. 2. Four graphs showing the trajectory of each class across the three different testing periods, for both the targeted and non-target words.

4.2 Application of Statistical Methods

As not all the data was normally distributed, non-parametric testing was used. The **Kruskal-Wallis** test is used to compare the means of three or more independent groups, in this case the three different classrooms. Due to the marking scheme there were several cases where multiple students had the same score and thus were ranked with the same value. As we see in Table 2 no p-value fell below the 0.05 significance level, with the closest score coming from the second round of the vocabulary matcher for target words, where the mean scores differences nearly reach the significance level. This can be explained by low progress made by Room 3, even less progress made by Room 1, and the relatively better performance by Room 5 at Round 2.

Table 2. Kruskal-Wallis H- and p-values from tests (3 classrooms, each round, 2 exercises).

Vocabulary Checker							
Target words				Non-Target words			
	Round 1	Round 2	Round 3		Round 1	Round 2	Round 3
H	3.85	1.25	2.22	**H**	1.62	4.97	2.10
p-value	0.146	0.535	0.330	**p-value**	0.445	0.083	0.351

Vocabulary Matcher							
Target words				Non-Target words			
	Round 1	Round 2	Round 3		Round 1	Round 2	Round 3
H	0.30	5.91	4.23	**H**	1.72	0.83	1.27
p-value	0.861	0.052	0.121	**p-value**	0.422	0.659	0.531

Parametric tests were also carried out on the data where possible. **ANCOVA** (analysis of covariance) was carried out using classroom number and testing round as factors, with the covariate '*Cipher*', a binary variable added to indicate whether that class play the game or not. Results can be found in Tables 3 and 4. It was only possible to conduct the test on three of the four Round 3 datasets, as the data for non-target words in the vocabulary checker was not normally distributed. Table 3 shows that playing the game did have an impact on the student's performance. The *Round* value shows the overall difference between rounds, and so it is reasonable to say that the improved performance of all three classes, for different reasons, led to this difference. Regarding the scores for the vocabulary matcher, the results from the target words also appear to back up the findings from the group trajectories in Fig. 2. Both variables and the covariate had a significant impact on the scores of the classrooms at each stage. The non-target words result once again paints a mixed picture. The low p-value of *Room* can be justified given the previously explained decline in Room 1, but the reason for the covariate's low p-value appears far less clear. While it can be posited that the influence of playing the game increased the student's interest for the Irish language overall [14], it appears very significant due to the low p-value. Clearly, more research in this area is needed.

Table 3. ANCOVA findings on the 3 classrooms' scores on vocabulary checker target words.

Vocabulary Checker – Target Words				
	Sum Sq	df	F	PR(>F)
Room	20.14	2	1.241	0.381
Round	205.56	2	12.671	**0.019**
Cipher	62.77	1	7.739	**0.050**
Residual	32.44	4	NaN	NaN

Two types of t-tests were conducted: independent and paired t-tests. The results from the **independent t-tests** did not return any significant information, while the **paired t-tests** did. As with ANCOVA, the tests were conducted on the Round 3 (post-test) results.

Table 4. The findings from ANCOVA, 3 classrooms' scores on all vocabulary matcher words.

Target Wds	Sum Sq.	Df	F	PR(>F)	Non target Wds.	Sum Sq.	df	F	PR(>F)
Room	299.35	2	11.563	**0.022**	Room	440.61	2	23.604	**0.006**
Round	195.89	1	7.451	**0.045**	Round	2.67	2	0.143	0.871
Cipher	149.03	1	11.513	**0.027**	Cipher	330.88	1	35.452	**0.004**
Residual	51.78	4	NaN	NaN	Residual	37.33	4	NaN	NaN

Cohen's d for each test was grouped into three ranges, low effect size (less than 0.35), high effect size (greater than 0.65), and a medium effect size. In Table 5, there is a medium effect size between Room 3 and Room 5 in the target words, both in the vocabulary checker and matcher, which is to be expected by comparing the experimental and control groups. The most significant difference from the data appears to be in the vocabulary matcher scores between Room 1 and Room 3, in the target words but also to some extent in the non-target words. It was only possible to conduct the paired t-tests on Room 3, for target and non-target words, as the rest of the data was not normally distributed for both word lists. For the vocabulary matcher, the **paired t-tests** compared the values that the three classes had achieved in the third round, again in the target and non-target words. The calculation returned both Cohen's d and p-values, with the former categorised in the three categories and p-values being compared against a 0.05 significance level. As the other two room's datasets were not normally distributed, Room 3's results from the paired t-tests do not give a lot of information (Table 6). The interpretation for the vocabulary matcher appears clearer, and again supports the argument that playing Cipher did improve the student's ability to match the Irish words to their English translations. (Table 7) The low p-values of 0.01 and 0.02 are quite significant, as are the Cohen's d of 0.76 and 0.73. This shows a significant difference in the student's scores in the target word list compared to the non-target words. While it is not as clear in Room 1, for Room 3 it does show the positive difference that playing the game had on the student's ability in Irish.

Table 5. Cohen's d of comparisons between classrooms for target words in the vocabulary checker (left) and vocabulary matcher (right).

Vocabulary Checker	
Target Words	
	Cohen's d
Room 3 / Room 1	0.32
Room 1 / Room 5	0.29
Room 3 / Room 5	0.63

Vocabulary Matcher			
Target Words		Non-Target Words	
	Cohen's d		Cohen's d
Room 3 / Room 1	0.73	Room 3 / Room 1	0.50
Room 1 / Room 5	0.09	Room 1 / Room 5	0.34
Room 3 / Room 5	0.60	Room 3 / Room 5	0.18

In summary, at first glance, the data does not present straightforward evidence for the hypothesis that playing Cipher did improve the student's Irish, and most of these

Table 6. Paired t-test between target and non-target words (Room 3 vocab. Checker).

Vocabulary Checker					
	Cohen's d	Mean of diff	Std. Dev. Diffs	t-statistic	p-value
Room 3	0.39	4.615	11.948	1.393	0.19

Table 7. Paired t-test between target and non-target words (all rooms, vocab. Matcher).

Vocabulary Matcher					
	Cohen's d	Mean of diffs	Std dev. Diffs	t-statistic	p-value
Room 1	0.76	6.143	8.056	2.853	**0.01**
Room 3	0.73	10.286	14.030	2.743	**0.02**
Room 5	0.29	3.333	11.566	1.223	0.24

discrepancies (e.g., the vocabulary matcher scores between Room 1 and Room 3) arose from real-world factors (e.g., the absence of the regular teacher in Room 1) outside the control of this study. However, there are many positive indicators to be found. It appears clear that Cipher can work well when paired within a regular classroom context without additional assistance from researchers, as shown by the performance of Room 3 across the three rounds of testing. In the case of Room 1, where there had been some disruption to regular teaching the results were more mixed. The distribution of the data restricted the testing that could be performed. Independent t-tests showed the positive effect size between Room 3 and Room 5, the control group. Carrying out paired t-tests on the vocabulary matcher showed the large effect size between target and non-target words in the classes that used Cipher, and the smaller effect size in the control group.

5 Conclusion

Our findings indicate weak but observable evidence that Cipher positively influences language learning, particularly in vocabulary acquisition. The double-baseline model represents an advancement in the context of DGBLL, which provides a robust method for assessing the learning gains associated with the use of educational games. It highlighted that students in the experimental groups showed improvements in vocabulary checker and matcher tasks compared to the control group, demonstrating Cipher's educational potential. The integration of pedagogical principles, cultural responsiveness, and curriculum alignment contributed to its success. Future research should address the limitations of this study, such as the small sample size and lack of diversity in participant demographics. Conducting similar experiments in different educational settings and with larger, more diverse cohorts could provide a more comprehensive understanding of Cipher's effects. This study focuses on vocabulary acquisition as a starting point for assessing the effectiveness of Cipher. Further research could explore the impact of Cipher on other language skills, such as reading comprehension and writing proficiency.

Addressing these areas will help refine DGBLL applications and their implementation in educational contexts, ultimately enhancing their pedagogical value.

Acknowledgments. This research was supported by the Science Foundation Ireland Centre for Research Training in Digitally-Enhanced Reality (d-real) under Grant No. 18/CRT/6224. For the purpose of Open Access, the author has applied a CC BY public copyright licence to any Author Accepted Manuscript version arising from this submission.

References

1. Chowdhury, M., et al.: Digital game-based language learning for vocabulary development. Computers and Education Open **6**, 100160 (2024)
2. Janebi Enayat, M., Haghighatpasand, M.: Exploiting adventure video games for second language vocabulary recall: A mixed-methods study. Innov. Lang. Learn. Teach. **13**(1), 61–75 (2019)
3. Census of Population 2022 - Summary Results, https://www.cso.ie/en/releasesandpublications/ep/p-cpsr/censusofpopulation2022-summaryresults/educationandirishlanguage/, last accessed 2024/07/25
4. O'Sullivan, K., Bird, N., Burns, G.: Students' experiences of the teaching and learning of Irish in designated disadvantaged schools. International Journal of Education, Culture and Society **4**(5), 87–97 (2019)
5. Üstün-Yavuz, M.S. Supporting struggling readers in later primary years: current practice in schools and a multicomponent reading comprehension intervention for year 3 children, Doctoral Thesis, University of Sheffield (2024)
6. Dixon, D.H., Dixon, T., Jordan, E.: Second language (L2) gains through digital game-based language learning (DGBLL): A meta-analysis. Lang. Learn. Technol. **26**(1), 1–25 (2022)
7. Collins, N., Vaughan, B., Cullen, C.: GaeltechVR: measuring the impact of an immersive virtual environment to promote situated identity in irish language learning. Journal of Virtual Worlds Research **12**(3). (2019)
8. Dalton, G., Devitt, A.: Irish in a 3D world: engaging primary school children. Lang. Learn. Technol. **20**(1), 21–33 (2016)
9. Chiaráin, N. N., Chasaide, A. N.: The Digichaint interactive game as a virtual learning environment for Irish. In CALL communities and culture–short papers from EUROCALL 2016, pp. 330–336. (2016)
10. Noroozloo, N., Ahmadi, S.D., Mehrdad, A.G.: The effect of using a digital computer game (sims) on children's incidental english vocabulary learning. Cumhuriyet Üniversitesi Fen Edebiyat Fakültesi Fen Bilimleri Dergisi **36**(3), 1991–2000 (2015)
11. Alfadil, M.: Effectiveness of virtual reality game in foreign language vocabulary acquisition. Comput. Educ. **153**, 103893 (2020)
12. Xu, L., Uí Dhonnchadha, E., Ward, M.: Harnessing the power of images in CALL: AI image generation for context specific visual aids in less commonly taught languages. In EUROCALL 2023 Short Papers, 92–96 (2023)
13. Samuels, A.J.: Exploring culturally responsive pedagogy: teachers' perspectives on fostering equitable and inclusive classrooms. Srate Journal **27**(1), 22–30 (2018)
14. Xu, L., Dhonnchadha, E. Uí., Ward, M.: User experience study of" Cipher: Faoi Gheasa", a digital educational game for language learning and student engagement. In Proceedings of the 2nd Workshop on Games Systems, pp. 5–8 (2022)

Involving Teachers in Gamified Learning Activities Using Generative Artificial Intelligence Tools

Cecilia Fissore, Francesco Floris, Valeria Fradiante(✉), Marina Marchisio Conte, and Matteo Sacchet

Dipartimento di Biotecnologie Molecolari e Scienze per la Salute, Università di Torino, Via Nizza, 52, 10126 Torino, Italy
{cecilia.fissore,francesco.floris,valeria.fradiante, marina.marchisio,matteo.sacchet}@unito.it

Abstract. Incorporating Generative Artificial Intelligence (GenAI) and gamification into the educational curriculum can make learning more engaging and effective for students. Based on previous research on these topics, we present the results of training teachers to design educational activities using gamification and GenAI. This paper analyses the 32 activities designed by 47 lower secondary school teachers from all disciplines during the training course. The research questions of this study concern teachers' ability to make significant use of both gamification and GenAI in the design of the activity and their added value in education. The activities designed by teachers and their responses to the initial and final questionnaires were analyzed. The results show a paradigm shift in the implementation of gamification with the use of GenAI tools, a large variety of strategies such as involvement, rewards, progression, and challenge, and the need for further training to offer students innovative teaching methods.

Keywords: Design of Game Mechanics · Gamified Educational Activities · Generative Artificial Intelligence for Gamification · Teacher Training

1 Introduction

Introducing Generative Artificial Intelligence (GenAI) and gamification into the educational curriculum can create more engaging and effective student learning experiences. Our experience on the topics started with two workshops where teachers were asked to design didactic activities using AI in 2022 [1] and a gamification approach in 2023 [2]. During the first half of 2023, we asked ourselves how GenAI could support the development of gamification strategies in the classroom. To this end, we conducted a national survey of Italian teachers at all levels of education [3, 4], in order to understand the background of Italian teachers on these topics. The results showed that in Italy, there currently needs to be more knowledge about AI and gamification in education, while teachers are interested in using them in their didactics. Between December 2023 and

A. Schönbohm et al. (Eds.): GALA 2024, LNCS 15348, pp. 36–46, 2025.
https://doi.org/10.1007/978-3-031-78269-5_4

April 2024, we organized a training course for 73 lower secondary school teachers participating in the Compiti@casa project designed to fight educational fragility [5]. The course aims to explain basic concepts of AI and gamification to teachers and have them design activities using game mechanics and GenAI. This research explores whether teachers can significantly use both gamification and GenAI in the design of didactic activities, explicitly investigating the most used gamification elements and GenAI tools and the added value in their use. To this end, the activities designed by the teachers and their responses to an initial and final questionnaire were analysed.

2 Related Works

2.1 Gamification in Education

Gamification in education involves incorporating elements and principles of game design into the learning environment, such as points, leaderboards, badges, challenges, and storytelling, to improve student engagement, motivation, and overall learning outcomes [6]. By integrating gamification into educational environments, educators can create a more dynamic and effective learning experience that makes learning fun and improves critical thinking and teamwork. Implementing gamification in education requires careful planning and specific strategies to ensure that it effectively enhances learning [7]. The literature highlights several strategies that can be used to effectively implement gamification in education, such as involvement through a challenge, a sense of control and adaptability, the ability to make choices, encouraging players to keep playing through prizes and points accumulation, the use of levels to encourage the user to progress through the challenge, or personalization, for example through the choice of an avatar to develop a unique identity [3, 7–9]. Teacher training plays a crucial role. It is important to provide them with the necessary resources to implement gamification effectively, such as selecting appropriate gamification strategies to develop learning outcomes and integrating them well into their didactic practices [7]. Our previous research on designing didactic activities using gamification [3, 10] found that teachers are willing to actively involve and motivate their students in the learning process, but they need to learn how to implement it in their daily teaching practice. This research has helped to raise awareness of the difficulties teachers face when planning gamified activities; for example, it has emerged that teachers find it difficult to achieve learning adaptability [3, 10]. Another main challenge in designing gamified activities is rethinking the activity using gamification strategies, making them a fundamental part of the activity itself, and putting them into practice correctly [10]. As Tomczyk and Teckchandani [11] pointed out, a potential danger of using gamification strategies is that educators may focus too much on designing a game or making the experience enjoyable, resulting in the educational element being overshadowed or lost in the fun. Alternatively, an educator may lean too heavily on the conventional approach, resulting in a lesson that closely mirrors a traditional classroom setting. In order to guide teachers in the design phase, the authors in [11] identify some steps to gamify a lesson: determine the necessary concepts to be covered in the experience (1), identify learning outcomes, decide how much time one has to create (2), prepare, explain, run, and debrief the experience (3), select and use gamification strategies to build the experience (4). Some advice is given on the last steps:

encouraging students' curiosity, allowing them to make meaningful choices so that they are not just passive players, and using game-based learning activities to provide a shared experience and encourage collaboration between students. As pointed out in [12], there is a general lack of knowledge about the process of gamification systems, which leads to the introduction of gamification elements without a specific criterion. Therefore, there is a need to introduce gamified practices in teacher training, providing experiential learning that allows them to apply this methodology to their professional life in a relevant way [4].

2.2 Integrating Artificial Intelligence into Gamified Learning

According to the UNICEF definition: "AI refers to machine-based systems that can, given a set of human-defined objectives, make predictions, recommendations, or decisions that influence real or virtual environments" [13], AI systems interact with us and act on our environment, either directly or indirectly; often, they appear to operate autonomously and can adapt their behaviour when provided with additional context. This is just one of the many definitions of AI, but it seems relevant to us due to its future-proof, human-oriented, and data-dependent nature [14]. The integration of AI in education should be thoughtful and with a human-centered approach to support pedagogy or learning activities [15]. According to the DigComp 2.2 framework, educators should develop age-appropriate tools and materials to ensure that students at all levels can access basic AI concepts and identify, evaluate, and navigate the complex information landscape in the AI age. Achieving these goals is essential to understand the importance of AI from both a theoretical and technical perspective. The use of AI in education is characterized by a large gap between the ease of use of AI-based tools (for educational purposes and other aspects of daily life) and the difficulty for teachers to explain the mechanisms and technologies behind them, given their complexity. It is essential to train teachers not only in the theoretical content related to these topics but also in planning didactic activities based on innovative pedagogical approaches. The relationship between AI and education involves three areas [4]: learning with AI, which encompasses the use of AI-powered tools in classrooms; learning about AI, which involves the study of its technologies and techniques; preparing for AI, which entails empowering all citizens to gain a better understanding of the potential impact of AI on human lives. In [1] some examples regarding the use of AI in education are shown, such as the one that aim to develop an AI algorithm to recognize from images of microscopic sections of plastics if they are recyclable. In our previous research on designing educational activities using AI, teachers emphasized the importance of adaptability, interactivity, and the use and integration of different techniques and tools when planning educational activities. One of the difficulties that emerged in the workshop was how to design educational activities on AI topics or how to use AI tools in a way that would be attractive to students [1, 3]. This paper focuses on GenAI tools: AI capable of generating text, images, video, or other data using generative models, often in response to prompts. As recent research has shown, gamification can benefit from new AI tools. In terms of designing gamified activities, GenAI enables the rapid creation of dynamic and interactive educational and narrative content that keeps students engaged and motivated. It will significantly benefit teachers who want to incorporate gamification experiences into their teaching practice but feel discouraged by the challenges associated with the time required to produce student materials [16]. GenAI creates a compelling narrative, for example in the form of badges that can be awarded to students when they achieve specific goals. Additional elements can be added to customize the learning experience and make it more immersive (e.g. speech synthesizers, content translation, or text to video converter).

3 Research Context and Methodology

3.1 Research Context

The context of this research is an 8-h training course (divided into four 2-h sessions) for 73 secondary school teachers from all over Italy. The course was held between December 2023 and April 2024. The first 4 h were dedicated to an introduction to gamification and GenAI topics and to the presentation of examples of gamified activities design using AI tools. They were asked to rethink their teaching and to create an activity to develop disciplinary and transversal skills, using game mechanics and GenAI tools. Group work between teachers from different disciplines was encouraged. The aim of the course was not the development of advanced AI skills but helping teachers understand how to integrate GenAI into their teaching using open online tools (i.e. https://www.futuretools.io/), also using a gamification approach. At the beginning, teachers were asked to fill in an initial questionnaire to understand if they knew and used AI and gamification in their didactic practices. At the end, they were asked to fill in a final questionnaire to express their appreciation of the course and their intentions to use the tools and methodologies learned in the course. On completion of all the activities, a certificate was issued by the University of Turin.

3.2 Designing Didactic Activities Using Gamification and AI

We created a design form with 14 items to guide teachers in planning gamified didactic activities enhanced by GenAI tools (Table 1). Based on the steps for gamifying a lesson outlined by Tomczyk and Teckchandani [11], the first 6 items resume steps (1) and (2), and items from 9 to 12 are based on steps (3) and (4). Since we asked teachers to include GenAI tools, we invited them to explain which tools they chose and how they used them [4], and to highlight the potential of using gamification and GenAI. The design form represents a cost-free tool for teachers, and it does not require advanced technological skills, thus making gamification accessible.

Table 1. Example of a gamified activity using AI tools developed with the design form.

Title	Numberia
Discipline	Mathematics
School grade	Grade 6/7/8 students
Topic	Numbers, using numbers in everyday life
Type of activity	In groups of 2 or 3 students
Goals	Classify numbers according to one or more properties Make comparisons between known numbers Interpret numbers in concrete contexts Communicate, discuss, and argue correctly
AI Area	Learning with AI
GenAI tools	ToolBaz, Edrawmind, Adobe Firefly
Gaming factors	Involvement, rewards, progress, accumulation
Gaming element	Challenge, points, prizes, storytelling
Brief description of the activity (detailing the previous answers)	In the kingdom of Numberia, ruled by the mathematician King Alaric, all the numbers have disappeared due to a spell cast by the evil sorcerer Malakar. Desperate, King Alaric decides to challenge the students of the Universe to bring the numbers back to his kingdom. Students are divided into groups of 3/4 and must think about numbers that give information to re-establish using numbers in Numeria. Each valid piece of information gives the team a maximum of 5 points. The team with the highest score will receive a certificate as an honorary citizen of Numeria. Finally, a leaderboard is created based on the points scored
For what purpose(s) did you use gamification?	The story was used to make the activity more engaging Accumulation of points as an incentive to think and bring out as many concepts as possible related to the numbers Final recognition to reward the students' efforts

(*continued*)

Table 1. (*continued*)

Title	Numberia
For what purpose(s) did you use GenAI?	To create a story (ToolBaz), the diagrams with students (Edrawmind), and the final badge (Adobe Firefly)
What was the added value of using AI and gamification in the design of the activity?	AI tools have made it possible to produce materials within seconds, significantly speeding up the process of planning didactic activities. The gamification strategies make the activity more engaging and invite students to participate actively

3.3 Research Questions and Methodology

The research questions are:

- (RQ1) Were teachers able to make significant use of both gamification and AI in the design of the activity?
- (RQ2) What are the most used gamification elements and AI tools?
- (RQ3) What was the added value of using AI and gamification?

To answer the research questions, we considered the 45 didactic activities designed by the 73 teachers participating in the training course. Out of those 45, we selected the 36 activities created by the teachers who had completed the initial and final questionnaires. Reviewers A and B examined the 36 submissions individually. First, the activities were individually classified into three categories by the two reviewers A and B: GenAI gamified activity (the activity consistently uses both gamification strategies and GenAI tools), gamified activity (GenAI is not used), GenAI activity (the activity uses GenAI tools but has no gaming elements or they are not well integrated into the design). To understand which of the three categories to place the activities in, they had to be comprehensible: each field of the form had to be filled in and any gamification strategies or GenAI tools had to be consistently integrated and justified in the activity. For the most critical activities, a discussion was held between the two reviewers and the other authors, to avoid the possibility that a submission deemed incomprehensible was the result of a misinterpretation by one reviewer. Therefore, the forms that did not clearly indicate how the gamification strategies were developed and how the AI was used were discarded. The result of the selection process of the design forms was a list of 32 didactic activities designed by 47 teachers, since 26 of them collaborated in the creation of the multidisciplinary activities. The second classification concerns the division in the 3 areas [4]: "learning about AI", "preparing for AI", "learning with AI". In most cases, there was no disagreement between the two reviewers. The only point of conflict concerned the classification of activities in the 'Learning with AI' category chosen by the teachers. According to reviewer A, only the activities in which the students use AI tools belong to this category, because if only teachers use AI in their didactic practice, it is a gamification activity without AI. Reviewer B felt that it was important to highlight the use of AI by teachers. It was agreed to divide the category "learning with AI" into two subcategories: "learning with AI used by teachers" and "learning with AI used by students" depending on whether it is the teacher using AI to design the activity or the student using AI to perform it. In the first case, it is the teacher who benefits, for example it speeds up the lesson planning; in the second case, it is the student who can, for example, use GenAI and critically evaluate the output. So, the four categories became: "learning about AI", "preparing for AI", "learning with AI used by teachers" and "learning with AI used by students". Descriptive analysis was used to examine the answers to the other fields of the form and for the initial and final questionnaires. The responses to the initial and final questionnaire were used to understand the initial background of the teachers' satisfaction with the proposed activity, and the impact of the training course.

4 Results

The sample of 47 teachers who designed the 32 activities is 78% female and evenly distributed across the age groups: 26–35, 36–45 and over 46. Although the teachers involved come from the north, centre and south of Italy, the majority (48%) come from Piedmont, due to the local influence of the University of Turin in this region. A mere six respondents indicated that they had attended workshops or training courses on AI, while 17 stated that they had done so for gamification. Teachers showed more confidence in their knowledge of gamification strategies than artificial intelligence, although the self-confidence level for gamification knowledge averaged 2.02 on a scale of 1 to 5. Regarding the GenAI tools, the most frequently cited was ChatGPT (the specific applications were not inquired about). The initial questionnaire indicates that teachers are cognizant of the potential of AI to augment gamification methodologies, even if many of them lack the knowledge to leverage this technology effectively. The analysis of the design forms showed that 11 of the 32 activities were multidisciplinary (Fig. 1), involving two or more disciplines, and were aimed at students in grade 6 (43.75%), grade 7 (21.88%), and grade 8 (40,63%).

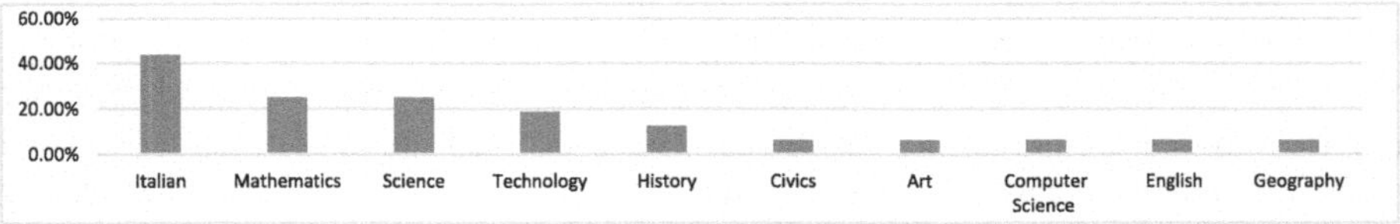

Fig. 1. Disciplines involved in the activities

Regarding the use of both gamification and AI in the design of the activity, 66% were classified by the two reviewers as GenAI gamified activities, 25% as GenAI activities, and 9% as gamified activities. Therefore, we can observe that teachers found it easier to rethink their teaching using GenAI, with 91% of activities using GenAI tools, compared to 75% of activities with significantly implemented gamification strategies, although the responses to the initial questionnaire showed that teachers were more confident in using gamification than AI. Another relevant aspect is how GenAI is integrated into education and, as mentioned above, an important finding is the identification of a fourth area in addition to the three identified in the theoretical framework [4]. As shown in Fig. 2, the most common use of GenAI in designing gamified activities is "learning with AI used by students" (75%), suggesting that most teachers designed activities that directly involved students in using AI. Teachers could indicate more than one of the four AI areas and 14 out of 32 were classified as having more than one use.

Fig. 2. How teachers used Gen AI in didactic activities

We expected the area of learning with AI to be the most common, as it is probably more suited to the development of gamification strategies and there are now several tools that allow the development of different game elements (e.g. creating stories, badges, images). In terms of game elements in the design of activities, involvement, rewards, progression, storytelling, and challenge are the most common game elements used in over 70% of activities. The possibility for students to make choices is also very common in the activities (65%); this may be due to the use of GenAI by students, which requires the ability to think critically and make choices. Instead, the adaptability of the didactic activities is quite low (around 22%), so the introduction of GenAI into the design of gamified activities did not make them particularly adaptable. Regarding the most recurring GenAI tools, teachers used more than one GenAI tool; chatbots were widely used (93.75%), followed by the frequent use of image creators (62.50%). Just over a third of activities also experimented with interactive diagramming and concept mapping tools (34.38%) or used ad hoc storytelling tools (37.50%). Only a small number of teachers (6.25%) used GenAI for other purposes (e.g. translation and language, music creation). The main empowerment of GenAI, as indicated by the teachers and found in the designed activities, concerns the possibility of creating didactic material quickly and easily (Table 2). The use of GenAI also encourages students to be critical and active users of AI tools. Another strength is the ability to create innovative and original materials, especially for those who struggle to create imaginative materials. Some teachers mentioned the benefit of using GenAI to personalise learning, but did not fully apply it. Regarding the potential of gamification strategies, the greatest benefits were seen in making learning more engaging and fun (23 of the 32 activities that effectively implemented gamification strategies were considered). Table 3 shows the results from the final questionnaire, on a Likert scale from 1(Strongly disagree) to 5(Strongly agree).

Table 2. Added value of using GenAI and gamification according to teachers.

To what extent do you think that GenAI	Freq. (%)
Quickly produces great materials for teachers	100
Creates innovative and original material	59.38
Makes learning more engaging and fun	58.33
Encourages students to be aware, critical, and active users of AI tools	42.57
Creates a challenging environment	33.33
Stimulates creative thinking	25
Encourages sharing and collaboration	21.88
Makes the evaluation phase more pleasant	16.67

Table 3. Level of engagement and appreciation of the methodologies and activities.

Teachers' answers	Mean
The methodologies and activities proposed were interesting	4.07
The methodologies and activities proposed were clear	3.9
These methodologies and activities significantly facilitate students' learning	4.01
They allow students to develop transversal and disciplinary competences	3.93
I would like to deepen my understanding of these methodologies	3.96
I would like to integrate these methodologies into my teaching practice	3.91

5 Conclusion and Future Development and Research

The paper analysed 32 selected didactic activities using gamification and AI tools developed by 47 lower secondary school teachers and their answers to the initial and final questionnaires. To answer RQ1, the results showed that 66% of teachers were confident in using GenAI tools to create gamified didactic activities for developing disciplinary and transversal skills. Regarding RQ2, as noted in previous research [2], involvement, rewards, progression, and challenge are the most common game elements used in over 70% of activities. Storytelling has increased significantly compared to our past research: more than 70% added a mission or a story to the activity. Moreover, there has been a clear improvement in the possibility for students to make choices within the activity; we note that it is much more frequent (65%) compared to what was found in the past (44%), which could be due to the use of GenAI by students, which requires the ability to think critically and make choices. Instead, like what was found previously, the adaptability of the didactic activities remains low (around 22%). Therefore, the introduction of GenAI in the design of gamified activities has not made them more adaptable. It will be necessary to rethink how to implement this aspect in learning; in the future we would like to study and implement targeted gamification strategies based, for example, on students' characteristics (such as initial motivation or different gamification user types) [17]. Regarding the GenAI tools employed, chatbots have been used extensively, probably because they are one of the most widely used and well-known tools, although most teachers have tried using tools to create pictures, concept maps, and stories. To answer RQ3, all the teachers found GenAI an excellent advantage for quickly creating didactic material and stimulate critical thinking and an active use of AI tools. Most of them highlighted the advantage of creating innovative and original resources and making learning more engaging and fun. The teachers tested these activities with their students. They gave us feedback on their validity and any modifications they would like to make. Future research will be based on this analysis. The research is limited to the Italian context; even if the teachers involved come from different Italian regions, the majority (48%) come from Piedmont, due to the local influence of the University of Turin in its region. The study involved lower secondary school teachers, but it would be interesting to extend it to other categories of teachers and countries for comparison. It would be also interesting to include students' feedback or to support teachers in the experiment to make other observations. The design form can be shared and adapted from teacher to teacher, fostering a community of practice where innovative ideas can be exchanged and continuously improved. To encourage collaboration and sharing of best practices among teachers, we plan to share the 32 activities in an open database in a digital learning environment. There is a need to continue to train teachers so that they can offer innovative teaching methods to their students. We intend to train and provide them with ready-made activities they can use in a project like Compiti@casa to fight educational fragility and help disengaged students who could benefit from this material.

Acknowledgements. The research was carried out within the Indam—Istituto Nazionale di Alta. Matematica "Francesco Severi" and Compiti@casa project, which was made possible with the collaboration and the support of Fondazione De Agostini, and the support of IGT, Fondazione Alberto e Franca Riva and Fondazione Comunità Novarese.

References

1. Fissore, C., Floris, F., Marchisio, M., Sacchet, M.: Didactic activities on artificial intelligence: the perspective of STEM teachers. In: Proceedings of the 19th international conference on Cognition and Exploratory Learning in the Digital Age, pp.11–18. IADIS press, Lisbon (2022)
2. Fissore, C., Fradiante, V., Marchisio, M., Pardini, C.: Design didactic activities using gamification: the perspective of teachers. In: Proceedings of E-Learning and Digital Learning, pp. 11–18. IADIS Press, Porto (2023)
3. Fissore, C., Floris, F., Fradiante, V., Marchisio Conte, M., Sacchet, M.: From theory to training: exploring teachers' attitudes towards artificial intelligence in education. In: Proceedings of the 16th International Conference on Computer Supported Education, vol.2, pp. 118–127. SciTePress, Angers (2024)
4. Fissore, C., Floris, F., Fradiante, V., Marchisio Conte, M., Sacchet, M.: Applications of Artificial Intelligence and gamification for teaching and learning purposes. In PRESS
5. Balbo, A., Barana, A., Boetti, G., Marchisio Conte, M., Omegna, S.: Digital technologies and their impact on metacognitive aspects in learning recovery in scientific and humanistic

subjects. In: Proceedings of the 18th International Conference on E-Learning and Digital Learning, pp. 105–112. IADIS Press, Budapest (2024)
6. Deterding, S., Dixon, D., Khaled, R., Nacke, L.E.: Gamification: toward a definition. In: CHI 2011 Gamification Workshop Proceedings, pp. 12–15. Vancouver (2011)
7. Qasim, S.H.: Beyond the Classroom: Emerging Technologies to Enhance Learning. Book Bazooka Publication (2024)
8. Bunchball, I.: Gamification 101: an introduction to the use of game dynamics to influence behavior. White paper (2010)
9. Floris, F., Fradiante, V., Marchisio Conte M., Rabellino, S.: Design Gamification Strategies in a Digital Learning Environment: The Impact on Students. In: Games and Learning Alliance, 12th International Conference, pp. 464–469. Springer, Dublin (2023)
10. Fissore, C., Fradiante, V., Marchisio, M., Pardini, C.: Teachers' strategies and difficulties in designing gamification activities. In: IADIS Int. J. WWW/Internet, **21**(2), 86–100 (2023)
11. Tomczyk, D., Teckchandani, A.: Using gamification strategies to create effective experiential exercises. Manage. Teach. Rev. **0**(0), (2023)
12. González-Fernández, A., Revuelta-Domínguez, F., Fernández Sánchez, M.: Models of instructional design in gamification: a systematic review of the literature. Educ. Sci. **12**(44) (2022)
13. Dignum, V., Penagos, M., Pigmans, K., VoslooPolicy, S.: UNICEF policy guidance on AI for children: version 2.0. In: Recommendations for Building AI Policies and Systems that Uphold Child Rights. United Nations Children's Fund (UNICEF) (2021)
14. Holmes, W., Persson, J., Chounta, I. A., Wasson, B., Dimitrova, V.: Artificial intelligence and education: a critical view through the lens of human rights, democracy and the rule of law. Council of Europe (2022)
15. Romero, M., Frosig, T., Taylor-Beswick, A.M.L, Laru, J., Bernasco, B.: Manifesto in defence of human-centred education in the age of artificial intelligence. In: Creative Applications of Artificial Intelligence in Education. Palgrave Studies in Creativity and Culture. Springer Nature, Switzerland (2024)
16. Zolezzi, D., Iacono, S., Vercelli, G.: Star words re-generated: gamification and GenAI for effective training. Int. J. Emerging Technol. Learn. (iJET) **19**(4), 97–104 (2024)
17. Dumas Reyssier, S., Serna, A., Hallifax, S., Marty, J. C., Simonian, S., Lavoué, E.: How does adaptive gamification impact different types of student motivation over time? Interact. Learn. Environ., 1–20 (2023)

Game-Based Learning Can Enhance Students' Understanding of AI Ethics

Antti Koskinen(✉), Antero Lindstedt, and Kristian Kiili

Faculty of Education and Culture, Tampere University, Tampere, Finland
antti.koskinen@tuni.fi

Abstract. As AI technologies advance and become more integrated into society, it is crucial for students to develop a strong understanding of AI ethics. However, interventions specifically targeting AI ethics are scarce, as are those using game-based learning in AI literacy education, presenting an opportunity to explore the potential of game-based learning for teaching AI ethics. In this paper, we report the results of a pilot study in which we investigated the usefulness of a game-based learning environment titled MediaWatch - AI Ethics. The game was designed to foster an understanding of AI ethics. The study was conducted with 40 Finnish 9th-grade students who played MediaWatch - AI Ethics for about ten minutes during the regular school day. Pre-and post-test measurements were used to assess changes in students' understanding of AI ethics and epistemic curiosity, while in-game measurements were used to examine self-efficacy and epistemic curiosity during gameplay. The findings revealed that even a short duration of gameplay can positively influence students' understanding of AI ethics, suggesting that game-based learning is a promising approach to AI ethics education. However, the game did not significantly impact students' epistemic curiosity or self-efficacy. The results contribute to the discussion of approaches to foster AI literacy and encourage further exploration of game-based learning in AI ethics instruction.

Keywords: AI ethics · game-based learning · AI literacy · secondary education · learning outcomes

1 Introduction

Artificial Intelligence (AI) is a rapidly growing field that will profoundly impact society. Consequently, understanding AI's capabilities and limitations is becoming increasingly crucial [1]. However, despite the increasing exposure to AI-based systems in daily life, students rarely possess a deep understanding of these systems and may hold misconceptions about them [2]. For example, students may underestimate AI systems' limitations [3] or overestimate their capabilities, such as believing that AI systems have no weaknesses [3]. Such naive assumptions can have serious consequences, as they may severely hinder students' future career options involving AI-based technologies [4]. Consequently, education should emphasize enhancing students' understanding of the societal implications, ethical principles, guidelines, and standards governing the development and deployment of AI-based technologies, referred to as AI ethics [5–8].

A. Schönbohm et al. (Eds.): GALA 2024, LNCS 15348, pp. 47–56, 2025.
https://doi.org/10.1007/978-3-031-78269-5_5

AI ethics is a crucial sub-concept of AI literacy, that often also encompasses affective, behavioral, and cognitive dimensions [6, 8]. AI ethics explores the benefits, risks, and implications of AI development and deployment, considering issues such as human-AI interaction, potential biases, transparency, and accountability [5–8]. Research has shown that understanding AI ethics is positively related to AI self-efficacy, attitude toward using AI solutions, and behavioral intention to use AI-based technologies [9]. These findings suggest that a strong grasp of AI ethics can foster confidence, positive attitudes, and a willingness to engage with AI tools, which all are essential factors contributing to active and meaningful participation in the future society [10].

Given the importance of AI ethics in shaping individual engagement with AI-based systems and societal participation, scholars have called for the implementation of AI ethics instruction in educational curricula [11]. Recent studies have shown that curriculum design can positively influence students' AI literacy through various pedagogical approaches [5, 12], such as using games to teach machine learning principles [13]. However, interventions using game-based learning and specifically targeting AI ethics are extremely rare [5, 14].

Further, previous AI literacy studies that included AI ethics component have primarily focused on investigating cognitive impacts [5, 12]. However, it is imperative to recognize that learning outcomes are not solely determined by cognitive factors [14]. According to the cognitive-affective model of learning with media [15], motivational factors (e.g., self-efficacy) and perceived emotions (e.g., curiosity) also play a significant role in influencing cognitive processing and, thus learning outcomes [16, 17]. Consequently, exploring also motivational and emotional outcomes can substantially extend our understanding of the factors contributing to the effectiveness of AI ethics education. Furthermore, there has been a growing recognition of the importance of exploring motivational and emotional outcomes during instruction [18]. Recently, it has been shown that this can be achieved by implementing measurements in the gameplay [19–21].

Given the shortcomings of previous research, this presents a unique opportunity to explore the potential of game-based learning as a tool for teaching AI ethics. Game-based learning refers to modifying basic instructional tasks (beyond the mere implementation of reward systems) to create learning experiences that are more meaningful, interesting, and effective [22]. Extensive research has demonstrated that game-based learning is a prominent instructional method across various educational disciplines and age groups [23, 24]. However, its potential for AI ethics instruction remains unexplored. To address this gap, we have developed a learning game, MediaWatch - AI Ethics, designed to support students' understanding of AI ethics. By focusing on cognitive, emotional, and motivational factors, such a study could provide valuable insights into the effectiveness of game-based learning in promoting AI ethics understanding.

In particular, examining how the game affects students' epistemic curiosity and self-efficacy about AI ethics can increase our understanding of the potential of game-based learning in AI ethics instruction. Epistemic curiosity has been considered to positively influence, without extrinsic rewards, what a student voluntarily chooses to pay attention to, study, attempt to solve, retrieve, or explore [25]. Consequently, provoking epistemic curiosity can have a substantial effect on the learning process [26]. Self-efficacy refers to an individual's belief in their ability to succeed in specific tasks and is most strongly influenced by successful task completion, referred to as mastery experience [27]. Studies indicate that self-efficacy is positively related to learning outcomes [28] and can be affected by game design [20].

For these reasons, we address the following research questions: 1) How does the use of a game-based learning environment (MediaWatch - AI Ethics) affect students' understanding of AI ethics? 2) Does the use of a game-based learning environment affect students' epistemic curiosity and self-efficacy in AI ethics?

In this paper, we report the results of a pilot study in which we examined the usefulness of the first version of the MediaWatch - AI Ethics game. We piloted the game with secondary school students, as they may be better able to understand the sometimes complex AI ethics issues and have more experience with AI than primary school students [5]. The findings of this study will contribute to our understanding of AI ethics instruction, the understanding of how motivational and emotional factors are related to the learning outcomes, and the iterative, evidence-based development of the MediaWatch - AI Ethics game. Consequently, we believe that this study may serve as a foundation for future research and educational initiatives, helping to inform the development of more comprehensive and effective AI literacy and ethics curricula.

2 Methods

2.1 Participants

The sample consisted of 40 Finnish 9th-grade students (Age: M = 15.53 SD = .51; Gender: boy/girl/do not want to report: 17/23/0). The participants' guardians were informed about the study in advance, and they had the right to refuse their children to participate. Students were asked to give informed consent to use their data. The school principal gave permission for the study. The study protocol complies with national legal and ethical requirements, including the ethical guidelines of the Finnish National Board on Research Integrity, legislation for the protection of privacy, and the EU General Data Protection Regulation (GDPR).

2.2 Game-Based Learning Environment: MediaWatch – AI Ethics

MediaWatch - AI Ethics is a web-based game-based learning environment designed to foster a deeper understanding of AI ethics in particular the benefits and weaknesses of AI applications. The game design encourages active learning and critical thinking, as students must grapple with diverse ethical dilemmas and receive targeted feedback on their choices. Previously, the MediaWatch game platform has been used in critical reading skills instruction [29]. The key game elements of MediaWatch - AI Ethics are *competition*, *character identification* and *feedback*, which theoretically should be beneficial for enhancing cognitive [24] and motivational outcomes [30].

In MediaWatch - AI Ethics, the player selects one of four characters to compete against three fictional rivals for the position of AI ethics expert (Fig. 1, left). The game presents the player with 7 tasks (Fig. 1, right), each of which is evaluated by a fictional grand AI ethics committee. These tasks are designed to challenge students' understanding of AI ethics by presenting them with ethical dilemmas related to the use of AI. For instance, one task asks whether difficult decisions should be left to AI, while another explores how society should adapt to changes in the nature of work brought about by AI.

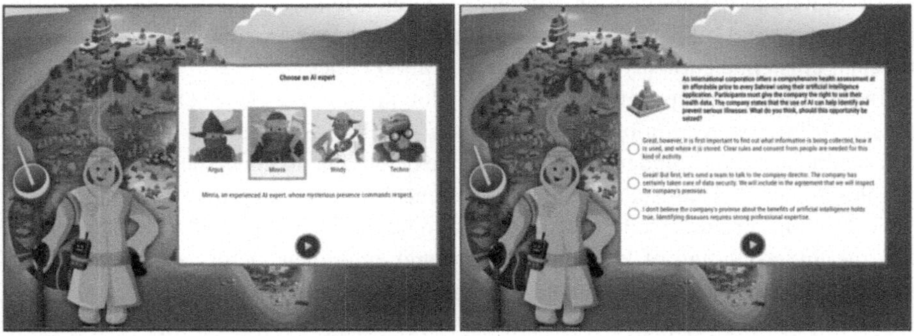

Fig. 1. On the left is the character selection. On the right is an example of a task.

Each task offers the player three options to choose from, with four tasks including correct, partly correct, and incorrect options, and three tasks presenting only one correct and two incorrect options. After the player submits the answer, the grand AI ethics committee provides argumentation for their evaluation of the given answer along with corrective feedback (Fig. 2, left). The player can also access additional arguments related to the evaluation by clicking on a designated button. However, in-game metrics revealed that less than ten students used this feature. Players only had one attempt on each task.

Following each task, a scoreboard displays the player's position relative to their fictional competitors (Fig. 2, right). The scoreboard is designed to create a dynamic and engaging competitive environment. The game randomly selects one of the virtual competitors as the main challenger, who provides a constant challenge to the player. To become the AI ethics expert, the player must answer approximately two-thirds of the questions correctly. The other two competitors demonstrate lower levels of performance. Upon completing the final task, the player is presented with the final scoreboard, showing the player's overall performance in the game.

2.3 Measurements

All the measurements were conducted in the game-based learning environment. The study featured pre-and post-test measurements as well as in-game measurements.

Understanding of AI-Ethics Measurements. Students' understanding of AI ethics was measured at the pre-and post-test. The AI-ethics questionnaire was based on the existing AI-ethics scales [8, 31]. The existing scales were not directly used as the game contents did not cover all the aspects featured in these scales. The AI ethics measurements consisted of 8 items (e.g., AI must benefit everyone; Users should be aware of the potential limitations of AI) on a Likert scale from one (totally disagree) to five (totally agree). The measurements demonstrated good reliability, with Cronbach's $\alpha = .82$ and

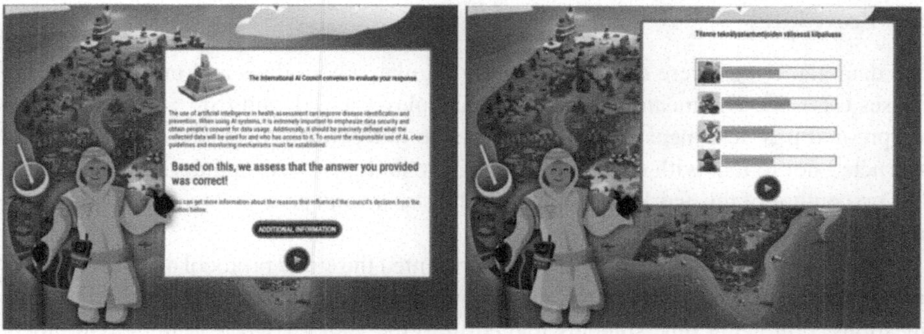

Fig. 2. On the left is an example of feedback for a correctly answered question. On the right is the scoreboard. The player (top character) is currently in second place.

.84 for the pre-test and post-test, respectively [31]. The *pre-and post-test score* variables were calculated as an average of the responses.

Epistemic Curiosity Measurement. Students' epistemic curiosity was measured at the pre-and post-test using a scale derived from [33]. The Scale consisted of 6 items (e.g., I would like to explore this topic in depth) measured on a Likert scale from one (totally disagree) to five (totally agree). The measurements demonstrated good reliability, with Cronbach's $\alpha = .84$ and .79 for the pre-test and post-test, respectively [32]. The *pre-and post-test curiosity* variables were calculated as an average of the responses.

Game Like Measurement. Students' game liking was measured at the posttest using four items (e.g., I liked the game), measured on a Likert scale from one (totally disagree) to five (totally agree). The measurement demonstrated excellent reliability with Cronbach's $\alpha = .96$ [32]. The *Game-like* variable was calculated as an average of the responses.

In-Game Measurements. Students' in-game self-efficacy and curiosity were measured using repeated single-item in-game measurements. The main argument for using single-item measures is that they minimally disrupt the learning process and have satisfactory predictive validity [21].

Both in-game self-efficacy and curiosity were measured on a continuous scale from one (totally disagree) to five (totally agree) three times during the learning activity: at the beginning, in the middle, and at the end. Self-efficacy was measured with an item stating, "I will certainly perform well on the following tasks" [20]. Curiosity was measured with an item stating, "I am really curious to know more about this topic" [33].

In-Game Metrics. In-game metrics were used to calculate students' *playing time* and mean *game score*. In tasks, students could earn 2 points for a correct answer, 1 point for a partly correct answer, and 0 points for an incorrect answer.

2.4 Procedures

The data gatherings were conducted during regular school days and in regular school classes (N = 3). The mean length of the gameplay was 7.1 min (SD = 1.53) (excluding pre-and post-test measurements). To ensure independent responses, students were instructed not to talk with each other during pre-and post-tests and during the playing. The first author of this work participated in the classes and provided technical assistance to the students as needed.

Before the intervention, the researcher presented the study protocol and gave general instructions, such as encouraging students to do their best and be honest in answering the questions. Following this, students logged in to the game-based learning environment using their anonymized individual codes. They then completed a background questionnaire and a consent form. Next, students completed a pre-test including AI ethics and epistemic curiosity measures. Upon completing the pre-test, students proceeded directly to the gameplay. After concluding the final task in the game, students immediately proceeded to the post-test. The post-test was arranged similarly to the pre-test but also included a game-like measurement.

3 Results

3.1 Descriptive Statistics

Table 1 shows descriptive statistics and zero-order correlations. These indicate that the students had a good prior understanding of AI ethics, and their mean game score was high. These suggests that the game and the pretest may have been relatively easy.

3.2 RQ1: Learning Outcomes

A paired-sample t-test was conducted to determine the effect of MediaWatch - AI Ethics on students' understanding of AI ethics by comparing their pre-test and post-test scores. The analysis revealed a significant difference between the pre-test (M = 4.24, SD = 0.58) and post-test (M = 4.35, SD = 0.61) scores, $t(39) = 2.652$, $p < .05$. The effect size, calculated using Cohen's d, was 0.27, which indicated a small positive effect [34]. This finding indicates that the game did significantly enhanced students' understanding of AI ethics.

3.3 RQ2: Epistemic Curiosity and Self-efficacy

Another paired-sample t-test was conducted to determine the effect of MediaWatch - AI Ethics on students' epistemic curiosity about AI by comparing their pre-test and post-test evaluations. The analysis revealed a nonsignificant difference between the pre-test (M = 3.25, SD = 0.72) and post-test (M = 3.21, SD = 0.75) curiosity scores, $t(39) = 0.327$, $p > .05$. Two one-way repeated measures ANOVA's were conducted to examine the changes in in-game measurements of self-efficacy and epistemic curiosity across three-time points during the instruction. The results showed no significant main effect of time on self-efficacy, $F(2, 78) = 0.527$, $p > .05$, partial $\eta 2 = 0.01$, or epistemic curiosity

Table 1. Descriptive statistics and zero-order correlations

	1	2	3	4	5	6	7	8
1. Pre-Score	1							
2. Post-Score	$.90^{**}$	1						
3. Pre-CU	$.44^{**}$	$.52^{**}$	1					
4. Post-CU	$.34^{*}$	$.45^{**}$	$.71^{**}$	1				
5. Game-like	$.32^{*}$	$.47^{**}$	$.62^{**}$	$.60^{**}$	1			
6. Game Score	.11	.22	$.36^{*}$	$.40^{*}$	.30	1		
7. In-game SE	.11	.24	$.40^{*}$	$.74^{**}$	$.42^{**}$	$.40^{**}$	1	
8. In-game CU	−.09	0.07	$.44^{**}$	$.72^{**}$	$.52^{**}$	$.41^{**}$	$.71^{**}$	1
Range	1–5	1–5	1–5	1–5	1–5	0–2	1–5	1–5
M	4.24	4.35	3.25	3.22	3.49	1.55	3.49	3.12
SD	0.58	0.62	0.72	0.75	1.09	0.31	0.74	0.83

Note, Correlation (**) is significant at the 0.01 level (2-tailed); Correlation (*) is significant at the 0.05 level (2-tailed); Pre = Pre-test; Post = Post-test; CU = Curiosity; In-game SE = Average of in-game self-efficacy measurements; In-game CU = Average of in-game curiosity measurements.

$F(2, 78) = 0.252$, $p > .05$, partial $\eta^2 = .006$. These findings suggest that the MediaWatch - AI Ethics, in its current form, may not be effective in promoting students' curiosity and self-efficacy on AI ethics.

4 Discussion

This study examined whether game-based learning can be used to foster students' understanding of AI ethics. The results revealed that even a short duration of gameplay can positively influence students' understanding of AI ethics, even though students had a relatively good understanding of AI ethics before the gameplay. Consequently, scholars should continue exploring the potential of game-based learning in AI ethics instruction to gain a more nuanced understanding of its potentials and shortcomings.

The findings of this study are consistent with previous research highlighting the effectiveness of game-based learning in various educational contexts [23, 24], but also add a new context. Our findings suggest that even brief exposure with simple game-based learning environment can have a positive impact on students' understanding of AI ethics. This finding is particularly encouraging, as it suggests that educators can incorporate game-based learning into their curricula without a significant time commitment. In general, game-based learning environments have the potential to provide opportunities to explore complex ethical dilemmas, make decisions, and observe the consequences of their choices in a safe, virtual environment. To create a more engaging and realistic environment for exploring AI ethics, game designers could focus on increasing the impact of players' choices on the game's progression and outcomes, more than was the case in our game.

However, it is important to note that the results of this study are based on a pilot study in which a small sample of students from one school used one game. Furthermore, the study did not include a comparison group, hence it cannot be ruled out that students may have learned from taking the pre-test. Additionally, the high correlation between the pre-test and post-test scores suggests that students' performance on the post-test was strongly related to their performance on the pre-test. This finding, together with the relatively high mean scores on both the pre-test and post-test, may indicate a ceiling effect. For these reasons, the results should be interpreted and generalized with caution.

Several factors could have contributed to the lack of significant changes in students' epistemic curiosity and self-efficacy. Regarding self-efficacy, the combination of relatively high game scores, high pre-test scores, and relatively high self-efficacy values may indicate that the game failed to offer meaningful situations for students to experience mastery experiences. In other words, tasks may have been too easy for the students, and they did not need to devote substantial cognitive resources to complete the tasks successfully, resulting in a lack of a sense of accomplishment upon completing tasks [26]. Given the students' high prior knowledge and relatively high self-efficacy, the game did not naturally trigger curiosity. For example, the findings of [25] have indicated that curiosity is maximal when people believe they almost know the answer to a task but are not totally sure. In contrast, curiosity is minimal when people are entirely sure that they know the answer. That is students might have been too confident to feel curious. Furthermore, as the game was relatively easy, it can be assumed that students did not perceive the knowledge gap in AI ethics, and thus, they did not yearn for more knowledge on the topic [33]. However, the short gameplay duration should be taken into account when considering these potential reasons for the nonsignificant findings.

The findings of this study encourage exploring the possibilities of game-based learning in AI ethics education also with younger participants. The possible ceiling effect suggests that the game and the pre-and post-test may be more appropriate for bit younger students, who may find the content more challenging and have more room for improvement in their understanding of AI ethics. For students with a level of understanding similar to that of the 9th-grade participants, more challenging instructional tasks may be necessary to promote further learning in their AI ethics knowledge and skills. Furthermore, to maximize the effectiveness of game-based learning in AI ethics education, future studies should investigate the impact of different game design elements and instructional strategies using a variety of different measures and research methods. For example, studies could use value-added study designs [35] to compare the impact of different feedback, different consequences of choices, and game mechanics. In addition, researchers should explore the optimal duration and frequency of gameplay sessions, as well as the role of teacher support and debriefing. Moreover, future studies should examine the long-term effects of game-based learning on students' understanding of AI ethics and their ability to apply this knowledge in real-world contexts. Lastly, studies should compare game-based AI ethics instruction to more conventional AI ethics instruction approaches.

In conclusion, this study provides promising evidence for the use of game-based learning in AI ethics education. The results suggest that even short gaming sessions have the potential to positively influence students' understanding of AI ethics, highlighting the potential of games as effective educational tools. As AI technologies continue to advance and transform various aspects of society, it is crucial that students have the knowledge and skills necessary to understand the ethical implications of these technologies. By further exploring the potential of game-based learning, educators may be able to create engaging experiences that foster AI ethics and prepare students for the challenges and opportunities of the AI-driven future.

Acknowledgments. This study was supported by the Strategic Research Council (grant: 358250).

References

1. Vinuesa, R., et al.: The role of artificial intelligence in achieving the sustainable development goals. Nat. Commun. **11**(1), 1–10 (2020)
2. Bewersdorff, A., Zhai, X., Roberts, J., Nerdel, C.: Myths, mis-and preconceptions of artificial intelligence: a review of the literature. Comput. Educ. Artif. Intell., 100143 (2023)
3. Kim, K., Kwon, K., Ottenbreit-Leftwich, A., Bae, H., Glazewski, K.: Exploring middle school students' common naive conceptions of artificial intelligence concepts, and the evolution of these ideas. Educ. Inf. Technol. **28**(8), 9827–9854 (2023)
4. Yang, S.J., Ogata, H., Matsui, T., Chen, N.S.: Human-centered artificial intelligence in education: Seeing the invisible through the visible. Comput. Educ. Artif. Intell. **2**, 100008 (2021)
5. Ng, D.T.K., Su, J., Leung, J.K.L., Chu, S.K.W.: Artificial intelligence (AI) literacy education in secondary schools: a review. Interact. Learn. Environ., 1–21 (2023)
6. Huang, C., Zhang, Z., Mao, B., Yao, X.: An overview of artificial intelligence ethics. IEEE Trans. Artif. Intell. **4**(4), 799–819 (2022)
7. Ng, D.T.K., Leung, J.K.L., Chu, S.K.W., Qiao, M.S.: Conceptualizing AI literacy: an exploratory review. Comput. Educ.: Artif. Intell. **2**, 100041 (2021)
8. Ng, D.T.K., Wu, W., Leung, J.K.L., Chiu, T.K.F., Chu, S.K.W.: Design and validation of the AI literacy questionnaire: the affective, behavioural, cognitive and ethical approach. Br. J. Edu. Technol. **55**(3), 1082–1104 (2024)
9. Kwak, Y., Ahn, J.W., Seo, Y.H.: Influence of AI ethics awareness, attitude, anxiety, and self-efficacy on nursing students' behavioral intentions. BMC Nurs. **21**(1), 267 (2022)
10. Dai, Y., Chai, C.S., Lin, P.Y., Jong, M.S.Y., Guo, Y., Qin, J.: Promoting students' well-being by developing their readiness for the artificial intelligence age. Sustainability **12**(16), 6597 (2020)
11. Borenstein, J., Howard, A.: Emerging challenges in AI and the need for AI ethics education. AI and Ethics **1**, 61–65 (2021)
12. Su, J., Yang, W.: Artificial intelligence in early childhood education: a scoping review. Comput. Educ. Artif. Intell. **3**, 100049 (2022)
13. Voulgari, I., Zammit, M., Stouraitis, E., Liapis, A., Yannakakis, G.: Learn to machine learn: designing a game based approach for teaching machine learning to primary and secondary education students. In: Proceedings of the Interaction Design and Children, pp. 593–598 (2021)
14. Plass, J.L., Kaplan, U.: Emotional design in digital media for learning. In: Emotions, Technology, Design, and Learning, pp. 131–161. Academic Press (2016)
15. Moreno, R., Mayer, R.: Interactive multimodal learning environments: special issue on interactive learning environments: contemporary issues and trends. Educ. Psychol. Rev. **19**, 309–326 (2007)

16. Tyng, C.M., Amin, H.U., Saad, M.N., Malik, A.S.: The influences of emotion on learning and memory. Front. Psychol. **8**, 235933 (2017)
17. Howard, J.L., Bureau, J.S., Guay, F., Chong, J.X., Ryan, R.M.: Student motivation and associated outcomes: a meta-analysis from self-determination theory. Perspect. Psychol. Sci. **16**(6), 1300–1323 (2021)
18. Pekrun, R., Marsh, H.W.: Research on situated motivation and emotion: progress and open problems. Learn. Instr. **81**, 101664 (2022)
19. Koskinen, A., McMullen, J., Hannula-Sormunen, M., Ninaus, M., Kiili, K.: The strength and direction of the difficulty adaptation affect situational interest in game-based learning. Comput. Educ. **194**, 104694 (2023)
20. Koskinen, A., McMullen, J., Ninaus, M., Kiili, K.: Does the emotional design of scaffolds enhance learning and motivational outcomes in game-based learning? J. Comput. Assist. Learn. **39**(1), 77–93 (2023)
21. Koskinen, A.: Enhancing the Effectiveness of Digital Game-Based Learning with Adaptive Instructional Support. Ph.D. thesis. Tampere University, Tampere (2023)
22. Plass, J., Homer, B., Mayer, R.E., Kinzer, C.K.: Theoretical foundations of game-based and playful learning. In: Plass, J., Mayer, R.E., Homer, B. (eds.) Handbook of Game-based Training, pp. 3–24. MIT Press, Cambridge, MA (2020)
23. Clark, D.B., Tanner-Smith, E.E., Killingsworth, S.S.: Digital games, design, and learning: a systematic review and meta-analysis. Rev. Educ. Res. **86**(1), 79–122 (2016)
24. Wouters, P., Van Oostendorp, H.: A meta-analytic review of the role of instructional support in game-based learning. Comput. Educ. **60**(1), 412–425 (2013)
25. Metcalfe, J., Vuorre, M., Towner, E., Eich, T.S.: Curiosity: The effects of feedback and confidence on the desire to know. J. Exp. Psychol. Gen. **152**(2), 464–482 (2023)
26. Von Stumm, S., Hell, B., Chamorro-Premuzic, T.: The hungry mind: intellectual curiosity is the third pillar of academic performance. Perspect. Psychol. Sci. **6**(6), 574–588 (2011)
27. Usher, E.L., Pajares, F.: Sources of self-efficacy in school: critical review of the literature and future directions. Rev. Educ. Res. **78**(4), 751–796 (2008)
28. Hattie, J.A., Donoghue, G.M.: Learning strategies: a synthesis and conceptual model. NPJ Sci. Learn. **1**(1), 1–13 (2016)
29. Kiili, K., Juho, S., Cloude, E., Dindar, M.: Demystifying the relations of motivation and emotions in game-based learning: insights from co-occurrence network analysis. Int. J. Serious Games **10**(4), 93–112 (2023)
30. Plass, J.L., Homer, B.D., Kinzer, C.K.: Foundations of game-based learning. Educ. Psychol. **50**(4), 258–283 (2015)
31. Ng, D.T.K., Wu, W., Leung, J.K.L., Chu, S.K.W.: Artificial intelligence (AI) literacy questionnaire with confirmatory factor analysis. In: 2023 IEEE International Conference on Advanced Learning Technologies (ICALT), pp. 233–235. IEEE (2023)
32. Taber, K.S.: The use of Cronbach's alpha when developing and reporting research instruments in science education. Res. Sci. Educ. **48**, 1273–1296 (2018)
33. Schmidt, H.G., Rotgans, J.I.: Epistemic curiosity and situational interest: distant cousins or identical twins? Educ. Psychol. Rev. **33**, 325–352 (2021)
34. Kraft, M.A.: Interpreting effect sizes of education interventions. Educ. Res. **49**(4), 241–253 (2020)
35. Mayer, R.E.: Computer games in education. Annu. Rev. Psychol. **70**, 531–549 (2019)

Design and Pilot Evaluation of an RPG Game for Self-assessment of Informatics and Economics Knowledge in Secondary Education

Theoklitos Tataris(✉) and Stelios Xinogalos

University of Macedonia, Egnatia 156, 54636 Thessaloniki, Greece
teoklitostat@gmail.com, stelios@uom.edu.gr

Abstract. In this paper the educational game Mythical Empires is proposed. Mythical Empires is a role-playing game (RPG) that aims at supporting Upper Secondary Education students getting prepared for the nationwide exams for admission in Tertiary Education in the fields of Economics and Informatics, in self-assessing their knowledge on the aforementioned fields. The design of the game is presented in the context of the CMX framework, along with the results of its evaluation by 88 prospective Informatics teachers through a survey based on the MEEGA+ model and the key criteria for game design proposed by Sanchez. Positive results on the perceived didactic utility and the anticipated player experience of the target group users were recorded, while improvements were highlighted. This pilot evaluation was deemed necessary for confirming and improving the design of the game prior its evaluation by the actual target group in order to draw solid conclusions on its didactical effectiveness and entertaining dynamics.

Keywords: Educational Game · Serious Game · Self-assessment · Economics · Informatics

1 Introduction

Nowadays, technology plays a crucial role in education. Educational games are recognized as significant tools in improving the educational process and can also be used to enhance perception, raise awareness of serious issues, and inform [1]. However, there is a notable lack of educational games parametrised to the needs of High School seniors, especially in subjects like Economics and Informatics, taught in High Schools in Greece. This gap has significant consequences, as educational games can boost students' understanding and interest, thereby enhancing their performance [2]. A game with enhanced graphics and unique gameplay focused on these subjects could encourage students to explore the topics further, and improve the effectiveness of the educational process.

The lack of educational games focusing on the Economics and Informatics subjects taught in Greek High schools and examined in nationwide scale for their entrance in tertiary education is a serious gap. While some games address economics or programming

A. Schönbohm et al. (Eds.): GALA 2024, LNCS 15348, pp. 57–67, 2025.
https://doi.org/10.1007/978-3-031-78269-5_6

and serve as useful educational tools, they often lack quality graphics and gameplay. Existing games fail to provide the desired experience that would encourage students to explore and understand these subjects. The need for games combining educational value with engaging graphics and exciting gameplay is imperative and should be considered [3]. Only then can they capture students' interest and encourage them to discover the secrets of these subjects in a fun and engaging way [1, 4]. Therefore, it is crucial to invest in creating high quality educational games that meet students' needs and enhance learning in these important academic fields.

The purpose of this study is to present the design of an educational game which combines enjoyment with education in the subjects of Economics and Informatics taught in High Schools in Greece. The primary objective is to create a game with high quality graphics and engaging gameplay that offers students an enjoyable educational experience. The game includes questions and exercises related to the respective subjects, providing an educational dimension that aims to assist players in testing their knowledge and enhancing their understanding of the topics covered. The questions and exercises included in the game reflect the difficulty level and type of questions that students may encounter in the national exams for entrance in relevant tertiary education schools, as well as simpler ones adapted to the current level of the player. In this way, the proposed educational game not only provides enjoyment, but also serves as an effective tool for enhancing learning and preparing student players for their exams.

Eventually, a pilot evaluation of the game is conducted with 88 participants, which are undergraduate Applied Informatics students attending a program on "Pedagogical and Didactical Efficiency" as part of their Bachelor studies. The pilot evaluation aimed at investigating the participants' perceptions on the didactical utility of the proposed game, as well as the anticipated player experience of the target group users. Qualitative data are also collected, offering valuable insights for the improvement of the game, but also for the development of future games on the specific subjects.

The rest of the paper is organised as follows. In Sect. 2, we briefly present related work, while in Sect. 3 the design of the educational game "Mythical Empires" is presented. In Sect. 4, the methodology of the pilot evaluation is briefly presented, followed by the results in Sect. 5. Finally, in Sect. 6 the main conclusions and the limitations of the study are presented.

2 Related Work

Several educational games for economics [5] and programming [6] have been proposed in the literature and some of them are freely available. However, these games are not tailored to the needs of the Economics and Informatics subjects taught in Upper High Schools in Greece for the following reasons: the games are in English and this is rather problematic when scientific terminology is used in their educational content and tasks; the educational content is not in accordance with the school curriculum. Some of these games are characterized by visually appealing graphics and although they could not be used they provided the motivation to develop an equally aesthetically pleasing game capable of capturing the player's attention.

It is true that some games tailored to the needs of the Informatics and Economics subjects taught in Greek schools are available. Specifically, there are a few quizzes for mobile devices, such as a quiz game for the Informatics subject [7], or webpages, such as [8] with typical mini-games (hangman, crosswords etc.) for the Economics subject. The problem with these games lies in the lack of interaction, while they become monotonous and tiresome as the game progresses. Despite this fact, the aforementioned games include a plethora of carefully selected questions and the way that they are presented to the player and their tone served as a source of inspiration for our game.

3 The Educational Game "Mythical Empires"

During the design and development phases, the priority was to create an engaging, fun, and attractive game that offers students a memorable educational journey. The game aims to provide students with a break from the stress of studying and school obligations. Thus, a game environment was created to relax the student and allow them to enjoy the educational experience in an entertaining way. Simultaneously, the game serves as an educational tool that enables students to test their knowledge throughout the gameplay. The incorporated questions and exercises allow students to apply their knowledge and assess their progress.

The design of a serious game, or more specifically an educational game, is a challenging task that can be supported by using dedicated conceptual design frameworks that have been proposed in the literature. The design of "Mythical Empires" was based on the framework proposed in the context of the MMO-RPG game CMX that aimed at teaching computer programming [9]. The CMX framework was designed taking into account several existing frameworks, including [10]: the Four dimensional Framework by de Freitas and Jarvis; the Conceptual framework for educational games by Yusoff et al.; the Design, Play, and Experience Framework by Salen and Zimmerman; the Experiential Gaming Model by Kiili; the EFM Model for educational game design by Song and Zhang; and the Educational Games Design Model Framework by Ibrahim and Jaafar. The CMX framework includes various features organized in the following axes: User, Scenario, Activities, Pedagogy, Learning Objectives, and Learning Outcomes. The design of "Mythical Empires" is briefly presented in the following paragraphs in the context of the CMX framework.

User. The target group for this game is Upper High School students, aged 17–18 years old that are preparing for the national exams in Greece for their admission in Tertiary Education studies in the fields of Informatics and Economics. The students are taught Informatics and Economics subjects at school and consequently have relevant knowledge. The game is considered to fall into the types of games that students prefer to play, such as Massively-Multiplayer Online Games (MMO-RPG), Multiplayer Online Battle Arena (MOBA), Battle Royale, and Role Playing Games (RPG).

Scenario. At the beginning of the game, the player chooses from six different characters. After selection, they are transported to the game world where interaction starts immediately with an NPC who directs them to their first missions. Throughout the game, there are NPCs that assist the player by giving advice and directions. The player faces enemies that have spawned over the world, collects useful materials that can either be sold to the wizard or used to craft spells, and interacts with "Wise" NPCs who help the player by giving money, directions, and rare items for answering their questions correctly. "Wise NPCs" and NPCs are visually distinguishable since they are dressed differently.

The game comprises of four distinct regions, each possessing its own unique attributes. For example, the desert region is distinguished by its light colour palette and suitable assets. Each region maintains a self-contained economy, ensuring that transactions made by the player do not influence the markets in other regions. Furthermore, players receive information on the specific goods produced in each area, leading to reduced prices for those items. Additionally, the game features a laboratory dedicated to technical questions, specifically those related to information technology. Successfully answering technical questions results in a reduction of the prices of military equipment available at the Weaponsmith. Transitioning between levels within the game does not inherently increase the difficulty of the questions posed to the player. The complexity of the questions is determined by the player's previous responses, both correct and incorrect. Consequently, a player may progress to the final region without necessarily encountering the most challenging questions, which are reserved for the upper quartile. Based on the design of the game, the player gets one attempt per question, while the correct answer is always presented after submitting a response in order to assist the players in learning from their mistakes. The final mission requires the player to face the main villain, "The Spider," located in a dungeon. Upon defeating the boss, the player can choose either to continue playing or exit the game.

Activities. The player can interact with NPCs, such as the "Wise" NPCs and NPCs giving directions. Additionally, when dealing with the wise NPCs, the user faces theoretical questions and small exercises in the form of multiple choice and true/false questions (see Fig. 1). Within the game, the player can customize their gameplay by choosing weapons, spells, and abilities to encounter the enemies. The player's weapons and other items, spells and abilities are accessible through an inventory.

Pedagogy. Tailored to the curriculum of Economics and Informatics for last-year High School students, the game includes fundamental economic principles, such as: market structures, the role of different economic agents, the law of demand and supply, the production possibilities curve, price determination based on production costs, as well as key concepts and theories of macroeconomics. Additionally, the game focuses on programming skills in the context of Informatics: algorithmic structures (sequence, selection, and repetition), data structures (arrays), algorithm design using pseudocode in a specialized programming language with statements in Greek, as well as the principles of object-oriented design. The questions refer mainly to theoretical issues or short exercises (such as completing excerpts of code) for the Economics and Informatics subjects, combining questions included in previous years of the exams. The learning content is designed to be relevant to the educational level and prior knowledge of the students, providing an engaging way to reinforce their understanding of these subjects through interactive gameplay. The game aims at assisting players in dealing with the stress and pressure of the preparation for the national exams, while simultaneously self-assessing their knowledge. Simple questions are asked at the beginning, and depending on the number of correct answers, the questions become more difficult. The player knows that within the game, they must answer at least 16 mandatory questions presented as quests, and thereafter, they can decide whether to continue interacting with the Wise NPCs to answer more questions and earn rewards. In any case, incorrect answers do not negatively impact the player's progress, ensuring that their overall experience in the game is not hindered.

Fig. 1. Interaction with a "Wise NPC" posing the question "In microeconomic analysis the reference point is:". The player must choose between: the total consumption of an economy; the total income of an economy; the determination of the price of a good; the total volume of output of an economy.

Learning Objectives. In the first two levels/areas, the player is required to confront 16 "Wise" NPCs in total by answering correctly in the questions they pose. Correct answers prize the player with certain coins and rare items that can only be obtained this way. Throughout the game, the player has access to a bar visible at the bottom of the screen (see Fig. 1) that indicates their current level of knowledge based on the correct answers provided so far. For example, each incorrect answer shifts the indicator to the left, showing a decrease in the player's level, while correct answers increase the level by shifting the indicator to the right. The player can decide whether to continue playing without answering the questions posed by the NPCs, but this will create problems in terms of items and difficulty, as they will be unable to purchase better equipment due to a lack of coins, making it harder to face enemies.

Learning Outcomes. The game helps high school seniors self-assess their existing knowledge, identify potential knowledge gaps they did not know they had, face questions similar to those on national exams, and interact with a game environment where every action creates a reaction in the game world, such as the purchase (increase in demand) of items increasing their price in order to help students comprehend in practice economics concepts.

The game was developed using the C# programming language and the Unity game engine, with assets sourced from the Unity Asset Store. Additionally, some 2D UI graphics were utilized from the Udemy course "Create an RPG Game in Unity" by the instructor Pete Jepson [11]. Furthermore, GitHub was employed to facilitate better control of the game development process, as well as to manage and track the changes effectively (https://github.com/TeoSaloufardos/My_RPG).

4 Study Methodology

Research Questions. The aim of the study was to investigate the degree of acceptance of the game by prospective Informatics teachers, as well as their perceptions on the attractiveness and the effectiveness of the game for its target group. Two research questions were investigated:

- RQ1: How do prospective Informatics teachers evaluate the didactic utility of the game "Mythical Empires" as a tool for self-assessment of Informatics and Economics knowledge in High School?
- RQ2: What are the perceptions of prospective Informatics teachers regarding the attractiveness of the game and the player experience for the target group users?

Participants. The game was play tested and evaluated by 88 last year students of an Informatics Department attending an elective "Didactics of Informatics" course, in the context of acquiring a certificate of "Pedagogical and Didactical Competency". In the context of the aforementioned course, alternative teaching approaches are presented to students, including serious/educational games, as well as relevant frameworks for designing and evaluating such games. Due to their knowledge on the subject and their interest in education, this group of participants was considered to be ideal for an initial pilot evaluation of the game prior its usage by the actual target group in a follow-up study. The average age of the participants was 22.63 years (st.dev: 4.76), while the majority (88%) of them were in their fourth year of their studies (of a four year Bachelor program). Moreover, 77% of the participants had studied and given nationwide exams on Informatics and Economics for entering their Bachelor studies.

Data Collection Instruments and Analysis. Data was collected through a questionnaire (using Google Forms). The questions were based on the MEEGA+ educational game evaluation framework [12] and Sanchez's key criteria for game design [13]. The MEEGA+ evaluation model is one of the most reliable and widely used frameworks for an initial evaluation of perceived player experience and short-term learning. The questionnaire included mainly closed-type questions on a 5-point Likert scale (1 = Strongly Disagree, 5 = Strongly Agree).

5 Results

The results on the game's perceived didactic utility and the anticipated target group player experience are presented in Table 1 and Table 2 respectively.

The vast majority of the participants evaluated positively the didactic utility of the game giving a median value of 4 for all the ten items for this part of the survey. The

Table 1. Results on the perceived didactic utility of the game.

Statement	Mean	Std.dev.	Median
[T1.1] The content fits the characteristics of the students (age, prior knowledge etc.) that will play it	3.79	0.87	4
[T1.2] The content fits the curriculum	4.13	0.79	4
[T1.3] The game provides appropriate guidance to students	3.71	0.9	4
[T1.4] The game provides clear and relevant feedback to students regarding their choices in the game	3.77	0.93	4
[T1.5] The game can be used as a supplement to the educational process	4.12	0.85	4
[T1.6] The game is suited to the pedagogical objectives of the teacher	3.76	0.85	4
[T1.7] The tasks of the students within the game are relevant to their educational background	3.92	0.8	4
[T1.8] There is a balance between the elements of the game and the achievement of the educational goal	3.8	0.89	4
[T1.9] By playing, students improve their knowledge	3.95	0.8	4
[T1.10] The content is relevant (no errors)	3.78	0.87	4

participants agree that the learning content of the game fits the curriculum (T1.2) and is free of errors (T1.10), while the tasks are relevant to students' educational background (T1.7). The game is considered to provide appropriate guidance (T1.3) and feedback to the students (T1.4). The game achieves a balance between fun and learning (T1.8) and students learn through playing (T1.9), and consequently the game can be used as a supplement to the educational process (T1.5).

The participants also evaluated positively the anticipated player experience of the target group of users. Specifically, the participants agree (median = 4) with most of the statements that exhibit a game of good quality in terms of usability, players' confidence, level of challenge, feeling of satisfaction, fun, focused attention or else immersion, and relevance of the game in terms of its contents and intended learning goals. The participants' were divided as to whether the game becomes monotonous as it progresses (median = 3), although they agree (median = 4) that this is appropriately challenging for students and provides new challenges at an appropriate pace. Improvements are necessary in order to achieve focused attention and further immerse students, since the participants were indifferent (median = 3) as to whether students will become so involved while playing as to lose track of time and forget their immediate surroundings. Moreover, the participants identified the following problems: ambiguities in the path that the player should follow; unclear questions; having the same questions being posed by the Wise NPCs. These problems that could only be identified by having the game play tested by a significant number of players with experience both on the educational content and entertainment games, might also have affected the perceived focused attention and immersion.

Table 2. Results on anticipated player experience.

Dimension	Statement	Mean	Std.dev.	Median
Usability ~ Aesthetics	The game design is attractive (interface, graphics, etc.)	3.73	0.8	4
	The text font and colors are well blended and consistent	3.93	0.9	4
Usability ~ Learnability	Students will need to learn a few things before they could play the game	3.72	1.03	4
	Learning to play this game will be easy for students	3.89	0.94	4
	I think that students would learn to play this game very quickly	3.89	0.98	4
Usability ~ Operability	I think that the game is easy to play for students	3.87	1	4
	The game rules are clear and easy to understand	3.79	1.05	4
Usability ~ Accessibility	The fonts (size and style) used in the game are easy to read	3.95	1.01	4
	The colors used in the game are meaningful	3.93	0.79	4
Usability ~ Error Prevention & Recovery	The game prevents the student from making mistakes	3.36	0.97	3
	When the student makes a mistake it is easy to recover from it quickly	3.6	0.95	4
Confidence	When the students first look at the game, I think they will have the impression that it will be easy for them	3.79	0.84	4
	The contents and structure will help students to become confident that they will learn with this game	3.82	0.81	4
Challenge	This game is appropriately challenging for students	3.68	0.92	4
	The game provides new challenges (offers new obstacles, situations or variations) at an appropriate pace	3.72	0.81	4

(continued)

Table 2. (*continued*)

Dimension	Statement	Mean	Std.dev.	Median
	The game does not become monotonous as it progresses (repetitive or boring tasks)	3.19	0.93	3
Satisfaction	Completing the game tasks will give students a satisfying feeling of accomplishment	4.14	0.63	4
	It is due to the student's personal effort that they will manage to advance in the game	4.22	0.62	4
	A student will feel satisfied with the things that they learned from the game	3.64	0.89	4
	I would recommend this game to students	3.95	0.95	4
Fun	I had fun with the game	3.63	1.05	4
	The game will be fun for students	3.77	0.9	4
	During the game I think that there are features (game elements, competition, etc.) which would make a student smile	3.65	0.93	4
Focused Attention	There is something interesting at the beginning of the game that I think it will capture students' attention	3.68	0.79	4
	A student could be so involved in the gaming task that will lose track of time	2.92	1.2	3
	A student could forget about their immediate surroundings while playing this game	2.64	1.16	3
Relevance	The game contents are relevant to the interests of upper Secondary education students	3.85	0.82	4

(*continued*)

Table 2. (*continued*)

Dimension	Statement	Mean	Std.dev.	Median
	It is clear to me how the contents of the game are related to the Informatics & Economics courses	4.43	0.67	5
	This game is an adequate assessment method of students' knowledge on the underlying subjects	3.57	1	4

6 Conclusions

Economics and Informatics are two subjects taught at the last year of Upper High Schools in Greece and examined in nationwide scale for their entrance in related fields of study in tertiary education. In this paper, the design of an RPG game that aims to assist students in their self-assessment of the aforementioned subjects is presented in the context of the CMX framework [9]. The pilot evaluation of the game by 88 participants that are prospective Informatics teachers in terms of the didactic utility of the game and the anticipated player experience of High School students, as recorded in a questionnaire based on the MEEGA+ model [12] and the key criteria for game design proposed by Sanchez [13], showed promising results and at the same time highlighted several improvements. However, it is clear that although this pilot study provided some preliminary results for the quality of the game, it is necessary to investigate its actual didactic utility and player experience through a follow-up study with High School students.

Besides the conclusions drawn in the context of its research questions, this work can be viewed as a constructive case study of designing and evaluating an educational game with limited human and financial resources. Utilizing a design framework, ideally a specialized one according to the domain of the game, can assist educational game designers in taking into account important educational and entertaining factors and achieving a better balance between learning and fun. Moreover, having the game play-tested and evaluated through specialized questionnaires that have been validated in the literature can provide valuable conclusions both for the perceived player experience and didactic utility of a game, as well as problems that have to be dealt with prior its formal evaluation in the classroom by the intended target group.

Disclosure of Interests.. The authors have no competing interests to declare that are relevant to the content of this article.

References

1. Yu, Z., Gao, M., Wang, L.: The effect of educational games on learning outcomes, student motivation, engagement and satisfaction. J. Educ. Comput. Res. **59**(3), 522–546 (2021)

2. Cheung, S.Y., Ng, K.Y.: Application of the educational game to enhance student learning. Front. Educ. **6**, 623793. Frontiers Media SA (2021)
3. Mitgutsch, K., Alvarado, N.: Purposeful by design? A serious game design assessment framework. In: Proceedings of the International Conference on the foundations of digital games, pp. 121–128. (2012)
4. Caserman, P., et al.: Quality criteria for serious games: serious part, game part, and balance. JMIR Serious Games **8**(3), e19037 (2020)
5. Platz, L.: Learning with serious games in economics education a systematic review of the effectiveness of game-based learning in upper secondary and higher education. Int. J. Educ. Res. **115**, 102031 (2022)
6. Miljanovic, M.A., Bradbury, J.S.: A review of serious games for programming. In: Serious Games: 4th Joint International Conference, JCSG 2018, Darmstadt, Germany, November 7–8, 2018, Proceedings 4, 204–216. Springer International Publishing (2028). https://doi.org/10.1007/978-3-030-02762-9_21
7. </informatics>{the game}. https://play.google.com/store/apps/details?id=gr.digart.plirofori kithegame&hl=el&pli=1. Accessed 21 Sept 2024
8. Apla.oikonomika. https://aplaoikonomika.gr/. Accessed 21 Sept 2024
9. Malliarakis, C., Satratzemi, M., Xinogalos, S.: CMX: the effects of an educational MMORPG on learning and teaching computer programming. IEEE Trans. Learn. Technol. **10**(2), 219–235 (2017)
10. Malliarakis, C., Satratzemi, M., Xinogalos, S.: Designing educational games for computer programming: a holistic framework. Electron. J. e-Learn. **12**(3), 281–297 (2014)
11. Udemy course "Create an RPG Game in Unity" by Pete Jepson. https://www.udemy.com/course/create-an-rpg-game-in-unity/. Accessed 24 Sept 2024
12. Petri, G., Wangenheim, G. C., & Borgatto, F.A.: MEEGA+: an evolution of a Model for the Evaluation of Educational Games, p. 8, INCoD, Brazilian Institute for Digital Convergence. Federal University of Santa Catarina, Brazil (2016)
13. Sanchez, E.: Key Criteria for Game Design: A Framework. IFE/Ecole Normale Supérieure, de-Lyon, France (2011)

Using LLMs to Adapt Serious Games with Educators in the Loop

Federico Bonetti[1], Antonio Bucchiarone[1,3](✉), and Vanissa Wanick[2]

[1] Motivational Digital Systems (MoDiS) - Fondazione Bruno Kessler, Trento, Italy
fbonetti@fbk.eu

[2] Winchester School of Art, University of Southampton, Southampton, UK
vwv1n12@soton.ac.uk

[3] SWEN, Universitá degli Studi dell'Aquila, 67100 L'Aquila, Italy
antonio.bucchiarone@univaq.it

Abstract. Recently, the advancement of generative AI has brought about the opportunity to adapt and personalize learning material to individual students with little effort. This paper explores the application of large language models, such as ChatGPT, to help educators adapt educational serious games at runtime. To incorporate adaptation into serious games in a systematic way, we employ the MAPE-K loop framework. A key focus is the inclusion of educators in the adaptation process, who ensure that AI-driven changes align with educational goals. We thus propose an architecture that integrates player/learner data, game logic, and AI-generated adaptations, monitored and approved by educators via a dedicated browser-based dashboard, in a human-in-the-loop fashion. We show how we integrated this architecture into *Untitled Bee Game*, an existing educational serious game for eco-sustainability.

Keywords: serious games · adaptation · mape-k loop · education · sustainability

1 Introduction

Generative Artificial Intelligence (GAI) refers to the capability of machines to autonomously generate content, such as text, images, and audio [11]. Recent generation models, such as Large Language Models (LLMs) like ChatGPT and Gemini represent a viable direction to explore new possibilities to generate game content and address previously identified challenges in educational serious games (SGs) [14,19]. ChatGPT, for instance, is a fine-tuned dialogue-oriented version of the GPT model (the latest version being 4.0o at the time of writing) which took advantage of billions of parameters during training. Through *textification* of data (e.g., player/learner profile data, game session data, etc.) and prompt engineering techniques that produce standardized, reusable templates [9,32], challenges in content generation and adaptation for SGs can be faced in new ways. In the field of game-based learning, for example, [12] have applied ChatGPT to the

A. Schönbohm et al. (Eds.): GALA 2024, LNCS 15348, pp. 68–77, 2025.
https://doi.org/10.1007/978-3-031-78269-5_7

design of educational escape rooms, by using ad-hoc prompts. Although this direction may sound promising, little has been discussed regarding the applicability of these strategies to *adapt educational SGs at runtime using LLMs.* This is particularly crucial in educational settings where maintaining attention and motivation facilitates effective learning experiences. By integrating AI-driven generation and adaptation processes within SGs, we aim to enable educators to dynamically tailor the gameplay experience to their learners. Large language models (LLMs) can make educational SGs easily adaptable to different users and scenarios. Their one- and zero-shot learning capabilities, which allow them to learn new tasks with little or no examples [32], are useful for creating systems with multiple components, like chatbot assistants and text summarizers. Yet one of the main challenges is how to include humans (educators in particular) in the loop to monitor and assess the adaptations carried out by the system [4,10,14]. Adaptation and personalization help to maintain player motivation over time, since people play for widely different reasons [20] Although adaptative and personalized learning material has been shown to have positive effects on student learning [25], adaptation is all but a straightforward process and different adaptation criteria may yield very different results [16]. Having a human expert make decisions, especially in the educational domain, is crucial. Technical limitations of the AI, such as the phenomenon of hallucination [22,30], further highlight the need to include educators in the adaptation stack. We propose a vision for an AI-driven architecture for SG adaptation with educators involved. This entails collecting and analyzing player data, planning adaptations with the educator, and dynamically integrating them into the system. Storing data enables faster future adaptations and material improvements. We identified the MAPE-K loop [1,15] as the most appropriate framework for such an approach as it involves a *Monitoring*, an *Analysing*, a *Planning*, and an *Execution* phase, as well as a data repository represented by the *Knowledge* component. In addition, it has already been applied to adaptive serious games [29] and has significant overlap with some concepts derived in serious game frameworks [14] as explained in Sect. 3. The research questions guiding this exploratory work are: *How can generative AI aid SG adaptation? And how can educators be involved in the process?* The remainder of this paper is organized as follows: In Sect. 2 we describe the related work on SG adaptation, player modelling, and the MAPE-K loop. In Sect. 3 we outline the proposed architecture. In Sect. 4 we show how our architecture is applied to an existing educational SG, namely Untitled Bee Game. We discuss limitations and future work in Sect. 5.

2 Related Work

2.1 Player Modelling and Adaptation in SGs

SGs can be defined as games whose primary purpose goes beyond amusement alone as they integrate educational design and content and do not have entertainment as their primary purpose [2,23]. SGs may be designed for education, well-being, military training, advertisement, and healthcare, among other purposes [13,18]. SGs pose a significant challenge in terms of design and development, as they need to engage players while pursuing a concurrent objective (e.g., learning or exercising) and provide personalized experiences. Thus, AI strategies might help software engineers and designers exploit the potential of personalization in SGs. Areas in which AI is commonly used in SGs include assessment of scores, game design, difficulty balancing, player profiling, and content adaptation [28,31]. Content adaptation, in particular, is key to overcoming the one-size-fits-all approach [8,27] and tailoring the experience to individual user needs, and is one of the key success factors of SGs identified by [18]. Many attempts exist that try to establish frameworks to categorize and cluster players [3,21] and to address the improvement of educational SGs with player profiles and types [7]. In their review, Hare and Tang [14] compare different player modelling and adaptation strategies. Two key modules are essential for adaptive serious games: a player model and an adaptation module [14]. These two modules are included in our architecture in Sect. 3, which is largely based on the framework extracted by [14]. The framework by Berger and Müller [4] is also relevant, as they extract a flowchart for explainable adaptive AI where manipulated variables (similar to the MAPE-K effectors) influence players while they interact with other variables (similar to the MAPE-K sensors); adaptation is supervised by a human. Speaking of humans in the loop, in a similar vein Dobrovsky et al. [10] introduce an educator-in-the-loop approach to correct serious game adaptations.

2.2 MAPE-K Loop

The MAPE-K loop is a fundamental concept in autonomic computing, providing a systematic approach to optimising complex systems [1,15]. The loop consists of four interconnected phases over a *Knowledge base*: *Monitor*, *Analyse*, *Plan*, and *Execute*. The *Monitoring* phase involves the continuous observation and collection of data regarding the system's behaviour and performance metrics. It helps to assess the current state of the system and detect any deviations from expectations. In the *Analysis* phase, the collected data is processed and analysed to identify patterns, anomalies, and potential issues within the system. Based on the this phase, decisions are made in the *Planning* phase on how to adapt the system to meet its objectives. This may involve formulating strategies and action plans to improve system performance. In the *Execution* phase, the planned actions or changes are implemented. Finally, the *Knowledge base* is employed for capturing and storing the lessons learned throughout the process. Various uses of MAPE-K loops can be found across different application domains (i.e., cloud, cyber-physical systems, Internet of Things) [26]. In the field of adaptive SGs, The MAPE-K loop has been adopted for dynamic difficulty adjustment in an exergame where physiotherapists can monitor their patients' cycling performance [29]. These examples underscore the versatility of MAPE-K loops in diverse contexts, highlighting their significance ragarding adaptive systems.

3 Proposed Architecture

Hare and Tang [14] propose a framework that involves 5 entities or components and that constitutes the basis of our architecture: a *Player*, a *Virtual Environment*, an *Adaptation Module*, a *Player Model*, and *External Sensors* (as depicted in Fig. 1). We keep the *Player* (and name it Player/Learner) and the *Adaptation Module* and introduce small changes for the other components: we split the *Virtual Environment* into *Game Front-end* and the *Game Back-end*. The rationale behind this choice is that it should be possible for researchers and practitioners to decide where the actual game mechanic computations are carried out (i.e., on the player's computer versus the server). The Game Front-end module contains the *Effectors* and *Sensors* (overlapping with External Sensors) provided by the MAPE-K loop. These consist mainly of dynamic *Game Parameters* and *Interaction Logs* respectively. *Game Parameters* in our case study reflect the style and difficulty of educational exercises such as reading and quizzes. The *Game Back-end* contains the logic and data needed to run the game. The *Player Model* by [14] is contained in the Knowledge component in the form of *User Data*. The User Data should include anything that reflects how the Player/Learner interacts with the SG. For example, scores, preferences, and interaction logs such as reading speed. Our architecture also largely conforms to the model extracted by the authors in [4], where their *Game* component (the Game Front-end/Back-end) is divided into *Player-influenced Variables* (the Sensors) and *Manipulated Variables* (the Effectors); their *Adaptation Function* is mirrored by the Adaptation Module, except we treat the user data (the Knowledge) separately. Our proposed architecture thus conforms to the previous literature while being integrated with LLMs (through ad hoc APIs). In their architecture, [14] conceptualize the loop as a sequence in which the Player interacts with the Virtual

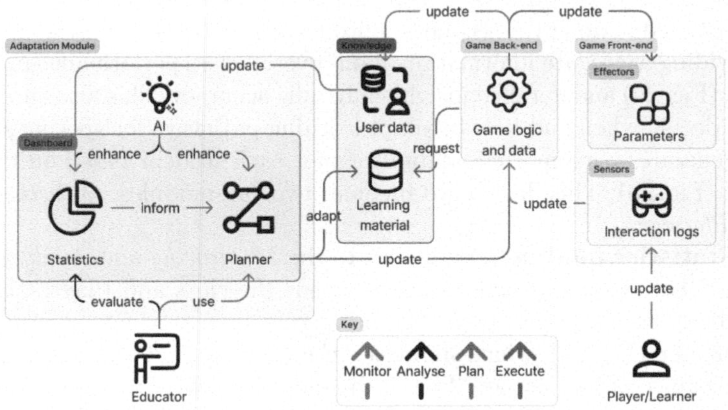

Fig. 1. Architecture design for LLMs in Adaptive SGs. Modules and flows are represented according to the MAPE-K loop (in particular, the Knowledge, Effector, and Sensor components, and the four phases).

Environment, their data are saved and analysed, together with those collected by the External Sensors, and then the Adaptation Module adapts the Virtual Environment. Our approach is similar, except we add the Educator entity and a Dashboard to control AI's adaptations. Here we propose the step-by-step of the architecture flow (see Fig. 1). In the ***Monitoring*** phase, the Player/Learner interactions are saved, and the Game Logic and Data are updated along with the User Data stored in the Knowledge component. In the ***Analysis*** phase, the AI produces human-readable statistics that the Educator evaluates. Then, in the ***Planning*** phase, the AI produces potential plans that the Educator may greenlight or customize. Finally, in the ***Execution*** phase, the Planner component of the Adaptation Module outputs the adaptations to the Learning Material (if the Educator made any changes), and the Game Logic and Data, which in turn updates the Effectors to produce an impact on learning. Crucially, in our architecture, adaptations can be approved and customized for one student only or for an entire class. To sum up, the AI is adopted in this architecture to i) suggest adaptations automatically, and ii) refine adaptations through specific textual prompts inserted by the Educator.

3.1 Educators in the Loop: Dashboard Design

The Dashboard is the Conversational User Interface (CUI) between the AI and the Educator. It suits the vision proposed by [25] and is conceptualized as a Toolkit (see Fig. 2) that supports the Educator in creating learning material and summarizing how the learning progresses within the game. It is built using `React` and `JavaScript` for the front-end, and `Node.js`, `Express`, and `MongoDB` for the back-end and data management. Generative AI is used to create educational materials, while `Chart.js` provides data visualization for monitoring student performance. It is made up of two main components: the first is a user interface to generate educational materials using generative AI[1], simplifying the creation of content for educators; the second monitors the progress of the student's learning[2], providing aggregate information about overall class performance in learning activities (Fig. 2a) and detailed insights into quiz accuracy. This also enables educators to decide when and how to adapt learning pathways for specific students. The AI generates personalized adaptations for each student based on their performance (Fig. 2b). This dashboard includes two sub-modules, *Statistics module* and the *Planner*.

The **Statistics module** corresponds to the *Monitoring* and *Analysis* phases of the MAPE-K loop and offers insights about the class and Players/Learners. One is about the direction of the learning rate in a tab named ***Aggregated Performance*** (Fig. 2a), which showcases the aggregated data from quizzes and the performance of the learner. This is the more heuristic part of the data visualization and it should help Educators grasp at first sight how the adaptation is faring. In the second tab, named ***Correct/Incorrect Performance*** or just

[1] https://gala24demo-genmaterial-production.up.railway.app/.
[2] https://gala24demo-ui-production.up.railway.app/.

Performance, it is possible to see the raw scores. The **Planner** corresponds to the Planning and Execution phases of the MAPE-K loop and is responsible for co-generating correct adaptations with the Educator. It is always up to the Educator to approve a specific adaptation strategy or to generate a new one. To carry out the necessary adaptations, the architecture is connected to a specific learning content generation API, based on GPT-3.5Turbo, which we detail in Sect. 3.2. Suggested adaptations are proposed to Educators in the form of buttons that, once clicked, send the necessary updates to the Game Back-end and then to the Front-end effectors. Additional adaptation suggestions can be generated by requesting new ones. The Dashboard planner makes ideal adaptation suggestions (red point in the chart of Fig. 2a and the Educator can choose which students to apply the adaptation to (Fig. 2b).

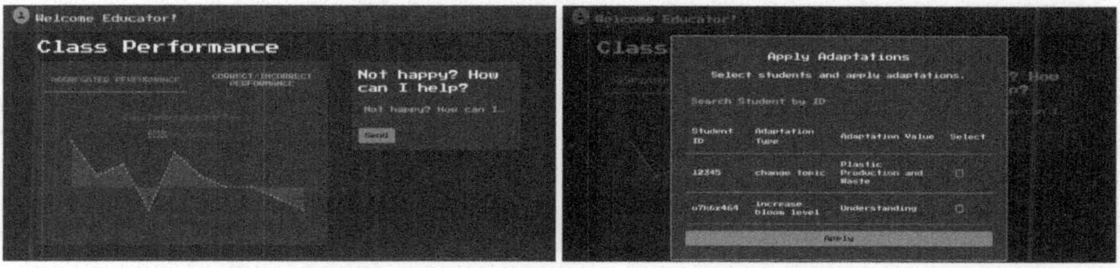

(a) Aggregated Performance View.

(b) Adaptation View.

Fig. 2. The Educator Dashboard.

3.2 Learning Content Generation APIs

Our approach uses a set of Application Programming Interfaces (APIs)[3] to enhance the teaching experience. These APIs, developed to leverage LLM capabilities, offer a comprehensive range of features that support Educators in any of their tasks. While they can be used individually, they are designed to work sequentially to streamline the educator's workflow within our architecture. This module can be used to generate the material beforehand. However, it also has the purpose of generating adapted material dynamically. For each learning material used in our system (i.e., PDF documents), we utilize the **Text Analyser API**, which extracts parameters like language, macro subject, title, educational level, and covered topics. It also suggests possible assessment categories based on the identified topics. The final step involves populating the learning activities. The **Activity Generator API** requires additional specifications such as activity type, assignment type, and parameters such as the number of correct answers and distractors. The generated activity includes the assignment, solutions, and necessary details, making it ready for our application. The generative AI APIs

[3] https://skapi.polyglot-edu.com/swagger/index.html.

support a variety of educational activities and exercises. In particular, for the sake of simplicity, in our architecture, we focus on multiple-choice questions. This category allows for both single and multiple correct answers. To adapt learning content and define learning objectives and levels, the current version of our architecture employs Bloom's taxonomy [17], a widely recognized framework for classifying educational objectives into levels of complexity and specificity.

4 Applying Our Architecture: Untitled Bee Game

Untitled Bee Game (UBG) [6] is a serious game about eco-sustainability developed in Unity[4] that lets players control a bee in a small town (see Fig. 3). It was inspired by Untitled Goose Game[5], where players control a goose and disrupt human activities. The objective is to dissuade the NPCs from pursuing certain behaviours. The game implements two non-player characters (NPCs): the first one wastes plastic bottles, while the second one uses polluting substances to wash her car. If the behaviour is harmful, players are asked to sting the NPCs. If this is performed correctly, new flowers and new fish appear. Once a flower has appeared, players can interact with it and read facts. The game then quizzes players with multiple-choice questions about the materials.

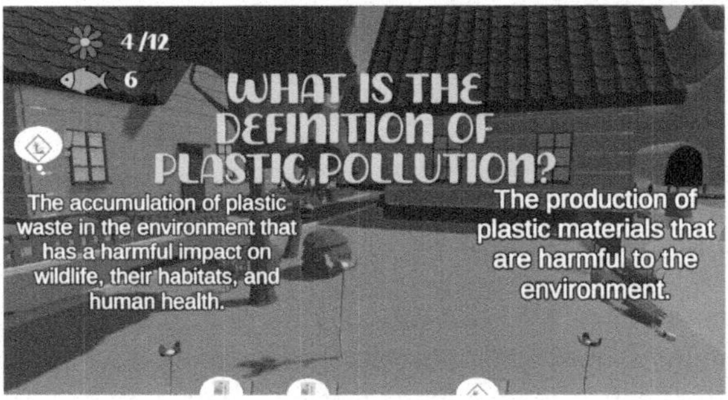

Fig. 3. A multiple choice quiz in Untitled Bee Game.

4.1 Learning Path and Game Loop: Adapting UBG

Learning paths are defined as "*a sequence of activities with designated goals to help students build up their knowledge or skills in a subject area*" [33]. This sequence is composed of 'nodes' also known as *knowledge elements* (KEs) [33] or *learning objects* (LOs) [24]. To explore the feasibility of our approach, we start from a repository of learning materials, which we call *learning map*. We include

[4] http://www.unity.com.
[5] https://goose.game/.

a very simple learning path in Untitled Bee Game that can be adapted. We focus on micro-level adaptivity (providing adaptation to the learner's needs in real-time) as opposed to macro-level adaptivity [25] (suggesting new materials or courses). The path is made of *learning nodes*, each of which contains several *activities* consisting of a reading node and an assessment node. We mapped the learning path onto the *game loop*, that is, the sequence of actions performed by the player in a typical play session. The game loop integrating the learning path unfolds as follows. Players have to complete a learning node, i.e., they read a fact (e.g., how plastic garbage is polluting the environment) by a flower and answer a quiz in a specific game location (e.g., asking how much plastic is not recycled globally). Performance information is stored as a binary correct/incorrect variable from a multiple-choice question. Then, they perform game actions (mainly stinging humans), and finally they get back to the learning location for the next learning node[6]. When all learning nodes have been done, the learning path is complete. When the first learning node has been completed Educators can apply adaptations. There are two possible outcomes: i) if performance (the number of correct answers) is below a threshold set by the Educator, the AI planner suggests making variations on the activity **topic** to pass the learning node; ii) if performance is above the threshold, the planner suggests a higher **Bloom level** and moves on to the next learning node in the path, which may be adapted or not. In the current implementation, adaptations are suggested according to thresholds. The Educator's intervention is crucial to aid the system in maintaining learner motivation high by integrating specific user needs that could be voiced in classrooms. This is a straightforward way to adapt the learning content, suiting our current design needs and constraints, and will be replaced in the next version by LLM predictions from prompts including the student's performance history. In terms of MAPE-K components, the learning material and the user performance history are the *knowledge*; the content of learning nodes is the *effectors*; the quiz history is the *sensors*.

5 Conclusion and Future Work

We have presented an architecture for GAI-Educator collaboration in educational SGs where adaptation is driven by LLMs. It is based on the MAPE-K loop, a well-known framework for self-adaptive systems. The adaptation is based on the Bloom taxonomy [5]. We show how the LLM-based approach and the MAPE-K loop can function in synergy to provide dynamic and robust adaptation, in compliance with Bloom taxonomy components, curated by a human in the loop. In addition, we have shown how the generated content is integrated into an existing educational serious game. The main limitation is that we have not yet evaluated the architecture in an experimental setting, which corresponds to the next step in our work. In the future, we aim to adjust the granularity of the adaptation to smaller bits of the learning path, i.e. the individual activities that make up the learning nodes. We will employ open-source LLMs that can be

[6] A video is available at https://youtu.be/wNMfLPgJhDU.

run locally (e.g., Gemma[7] instead of ChatGPT 3.5). Running models locally also allows to mitigate ethics-related issues, like feeding the learner demographics and preferences to public models, by limiting the processing of the learner-generated data to proprietary or institutional machines. Research in this area is still in its infancy. We expect this paper to be a starting point for researchers and practitioners willing to include LLMs in Education and SG design and execution.

Acknowledgments. We acknowledge the support of the PNRR project FAIR - Future AI Research (PE00000013), under the NRRP MUR program funded by the NextGenerationEU.

References

1. An architectural blueprint for autonomic computing. Tech. rep., IBM (2005)
2. Abt, C.: Serious Games. Viking Press, Viking compass book (1970)
3. Bartle, R.: Hearts, clubs, diamonds, spades: Players who suit MUDs
4. Berger, F., Müller, W.: Back to basics: explainable AI for adaptive serious games. In: Fletcher, B., Ma, M., Göbel, S., Baalsrud Hauge, J., Marsh, T. (eds.) Serious Games, pp. 67–81. Springer International Publishing (2021)
5. Bloom, B., Krathwohl, D.: Taxonomy of Educational Objectives: The Classification of Educational Goals. No. v. 1 in Taxonomy of Educational Objectives: The Classification of Educational Goals, Longmans, Green (1956)
6. Bonetti, F., Bassanelli, S., Bucchiarone, A., Gini, F., Marconi, A.: Untitled bee game: be(e)ing mean to learn more about eco-sustainability. In: Proceedings of the 8th Annual International GamiFIN Conference 2024. Ruka, Finland (2024)
7. Brandl, L., Schrader, A.: Student player types in higher educationtrial and clustering analyses. Edu. Sci. **14**, 352 (2024)
8. Böckle, M., Micheel, I., Bick, M., Novak, J.: A design framework for adaptive gamification applications. In: Proceedings of the 51st Hawaii International Conference on System Sciences (2018)
9. Clarisó, R., Cabot, J.: Model-driven prompt engineering. In: 2023 ACM/IEEE 26th International Conference on Model Driven Engineering Languages and Systems (MODELS), pp. 47–54. IEEE (2023)
10. Dobrovsky, A., Borghoff, U., Hofmann, M.: An approach to interactive deep reinforcement learning for serious games.
11. Feuerriegel, S., Hartmann, J., Janiesch, C., Zschech, P.: Generative AI **66**(1), 111–126 (2024)
12. Fotaris, P., Mastoras, T., Lameras, P.: Designing educational escape rooms with generative AI: a framework and ChatGPT prompt engineering guide. In: European Conference on Games Based Learning **17**(1), 180–189 (2023)
13. Frutos-Pascual, M., Zapirain, B.G.: Review of the use of AI techniques in serious games: decision making and machine learning. IEEE Trans. Comput. Intell. AI Game **9**(2), 133–152 (2017)
14. Hare, R., Tang, Y.: Player modeling and adaptation methods within adaptive serious games. IEEE Trans. Comput. Soc. Syst. **10**(4), 1939–1950 (2023)
15. Kephart, J.O., Chess, D.M.: The vision of autonomic computing. Computer **36**(1), 41–50 (2003)

[7] https://huggingface.co/blog/gemma.

16. Koskinen, A., McMullen, J., Hannula-Sormunen, M., Ninaus, M., Kiili, K.: The strength and direction of the difficulty adaptation affect situational interest in game-based learning **194**, 104694 (2023). https://doi.org/10.1016/j.compedu.2022.104694
17. Krathwohl, D.R.: A revision of bloom's taxonomy: an overview. Theory Pract. **41**(4), 212–218 (2002)
18. Laamarti, F., Eid, M., El Saddik, A.: An overview of serious games **2014**, 1–15 (2014)
19. Lavoue, E., Monterrat, B., Desmarais, M., George, S.: Adaptive gamification for learning environments **12**(1), 16–28 (2018)
20. Lopes, R., Bidarra, R.: Adaptivity challenges in games and simulations: a survey. IEEE Trans. Comput. Intell. AI Game. **3**(2), 85–99 (2011). https://doi.org/10.1109/TCIAIG.2011.2152841
21. Marczewski, A.: User types HEXAD, pp. 65–80
22. McIntosh, T.R., Liu, T., Susnjak, T., Watters, P., Ng, A., Halgamuge, M.N.: A culturally sensitive test to evaluate nuanced GPT hallucination. IEEE Trans. Artif. Intell. 1–13 (2023)
23. Michael, D., Chen, S.: Serious Games: Games that Educate, Train and Inform. Thomson Course Technology
24. Nabizadeh, A.H., Leal, J.P., Rafsanjani, H.N., Shah, R.R.: Learning path personalization and recommendation methods: a survey of the state-of-the-art. Expert Syst. Appl. **159**, 113596 (2020)
25. Ninaus, M., Sailer, M.: Closing the loop The human role in artificial intelligence for education. Front. Psychol. **13**, 956798 (2022). https://doi.org/10.3389/fpsyg.2022.956798
26. Oh, J., Raibulet, C., Leest, J.: Analysis of MAPE-K loop in self-adaptive systems for cloud, IoT and CPS. In: Service-Oriented Computing - ICSOC 2022 Workshops - ASOCA, AI-PA, FMCIoT, WESOACS 2022, Sevilla, Spain, November 29 - December 2, 2022 Proceedings. Lecture Notes in Computer Science, vol. 13821, pp. 130–141. Springer (2022)
27. Orji, R., Tondello, G.F., Nacke, L.E.: Personalizing persuasive strategies in gameful systems to gamification user types. In: Proceedings of the 2018 CHI Conference on Human Factors in Computing Systems, pp. 1–14. ACM (2018)
28. Pérez, J., Castro, M., López, G.: Serious games and AI: challenges and opportunities for computational social science. IEEE Access **11**, 62051–62061 (2023)
29. Souza, C.H.R., De Oliveira, S.S., Berretta, L.O., De Carvalho, S.T.: DDA-MAPEKit: a framework for dynamic difficulty adjustment based on MAPE-k loop. In: Proceedings of the 22nd Brazilian Symposium on Games and Digital Entertainment, pp. 1–10. ACM (2023)
30. Wang, T.: Navigating generative AI (ChatGPT) in higher education: opportunities and challenges. In: Anutariya, C., Liu, D., Kinshuk, Tlili, A., Yang, J., Chang, M. (eds.) Smart Learning for A Sustainable Society, pp. 215–225. Springer Nature Singapore (2023)
31. Westera, W., et al.: Artificial intelligence moving serious gaming: presenting reusable game AI components. Educ. Inf. Technol. **25**(1), 351–380 (2020)
32. White, J., et al.: A Prompt Pattern Catalog to Enhance Prompt Engineering with ChatGPT (2023)
33. Yang, F., Li, F.W., Lau, R.W.: An open model for learning path construction. In: Advances in Web-Based Learning–ICWL 2010: 9th International Conference, Shanghai, China, December 8-10, 2010. Proceedings 9, pp. 318–328. Springer (2010)

Designing for Engagement: Cognitive and Emotional Responses in Serious Games

Establishing a New Computational Method to Predict Effects of Gaming: A Feasibility Study on Growth Mindset

Manuel Ninaus[1,2(✉)], Moritz Edlinger[1], Nathalie Scheucher[1], and Stefan E. Huber[1]

[1] Department of Psychology, University of Graz, Graz, Austria
manuel.ninaus@uni-graz.at
[2] LEAD Graduate School and Research Network, University of Tübingen, Tübingen, Germany

Abstract. We present a novel method for approximating potential psychological effects of video games on players utilizing computational text analysis and artificial intelligence. Focusing specifically on growth mindset – a psychological construct associated with learning and resilience – we analyze player-generated reviews on the Steam gaming platform. In particular, reviews were examined using a specifically developed growth mindset dictionary derived from key psychological texts and validated questionnaires. Utilizing over 1 million user-generated reviews across eight distinct game genres, we identified that puzzle, roguelike, and platformer games showed a higher prevalence of growth mindset-related terms when compared to genres that we considered unrelated to growth mindset (e.g., zen, cozy, walking simulator). This aligns well with a growth mindset meaning system, as these genres inherently involve setting objectives, exerting effort, learning from setbacks, and refining strategies through gameplay. In addition, exploratory BERTopic modeling identified four topics with a clear relation to the concept of a growth mindset. These topics emerged differentially across genres with a pattern like the one found with the dictionary, further corroborating our findings. These results confirm theoretical assumptions in the field with a new methodological approach, opening avenues for precisely targeted research on video game effects and informed selection of video game-based interventions.

Keywords: natural language processing · text mining · artificial intelligence · video games · growth mindset

1 Introduction

Video game effect research is usually concerned with investigating the associations with or consequences of gaming. These are usually studied using cross-sectional and intervention studies, for instance, by investigating the effects of a particular video game or genre by studying a video game exemplary for that genre. In fact, video games have been suggested to improve cognitive, emotional, motivational, and social skills [1–3].

Video games are frequently built on mechanics like coping with challenges and failure, or learning via trial and error, and developing corresponding skills [4]. For this

A. Schönbohm et al. (Eds.): GALA 2024, LNCS 15348, pp. 81–91, 2025.
https://doi.org/10.1007/978-3-031-78269-5_8

reason, it was suggested that video gaming can promote the development of a growth mindset [1, 5–7] by cultivating an incremental belief of intelligence and ability in players. The concept of a growth mindset thus simply reflects the belief that individuals can develop and enhance their personal abilities and talents through effort and learning [8]. Whereas perceiving intelligence or ability as unchangeable (= fixed mindset) can cause feelings of inadequacy, seeing them as a result of dedicated effort (= growth mindset) makes failure a cue for increased persistence and effort. The advantages of a growth mindset over a fixed mindset were extensively studied and supported by many research studies in the field of education [9, 10] as well as mental well-being [11].

Mindsets are assumed to be part of a broader "meaning system", comprising a person's goals, effort beliefs, attributions, and strategies, significantly shaping how individuals respond to setbacks and adversities [12]. In the context of gaming, such a "meaning system" might be more or less explicit. Certain games require the players to (i) set objectives to overcome obstacles (i.e., goals; e.g., setting goals aimed at improving a skill), (ii) evaluate the relationship between effort and outcome (i.e., effort beliefs; e.g., effort can lead to improvement), (iii) make sense of successes and failures (i.e., attributions; e.g., failure can be corrected by effort), and (iv) adopt various approaches to overcome obstacles (i.e., strategies; e.g., trying harder after failure). Hence, one might assume, that games more explicit with regard to the aspects of a "meaning system" are either more likely to be played by persons with a growth mindset or that some games may even provide an excellent environment to develop a growth mindset [1, 5, 7]. However, so far, strong empirical evidence supporting these notions is lacking.

One crucial problem for empirical research in this respect is the selection of potential games that might promote the construct or skills in question. This is exacerbated by the fact that games are becoming continuously more complex and can hardly be categorized into a single genre [13, 14]. Further, much of video game research is quickly outdated due to the fast pace of technological innovation and game development. In 2023, 30 new games were (on average) released daily just on Steam, amounting overall to 12.000 games released over the year (https://steamdb.info). Therefore, a so far missing, scalable method is required for identifying games that are potentially linked to or even affect the psychological construct in question. Systematic research on the effects of video games requires further a detailed understanding of their distinct characteristics, which is also potentially missed by relying on the current genre classification system [13].

To address these issues, we developed a new and scalable method using openly available user-generated reviews of video games. In digital gaming ecosystems like Steam, player-written game reviews can serve as a rich source of data on user experiences, game mechanics, and even mental health [15, 16]. That is, reviews not only reflect individual players' preferences but also reveal underlying connections between games beyond their genres or tags. Drawing on the lexical hypothesis (e.g. [17]), which suggests that language reflects key personal traits, the analysis of natural language in reviews might reveal information about a game's potential psychological impact.

Here, we apply modern computational text analysis methods to game reviews to isolate the most significant elements of gaming experiences. This approach could help narrow down the large annual output of video games to a smaller sample for in-depth study of certain (psychological) effects. In the current study, we set out to examine the feasibility of our method to identify games that are likely related to a growth mindset.

2 Methods

2.1 Data Collection

The reviews were collected in the first week of March 2024. The Steam Review Explorer (https://project.joshhills.dev/steam-review-explorer/) was used to download reviews of games on Steam using the Steam API, resulting in a total of 1,125,185 reviews.

Table 1. Matching game genres to mindset meaning system. + indicates high relevance; ~ indicates some relevance; - indicates low relevance. Yellow/grey color represents game genres more/less likely to be related to a growth mindset.

	Mindset meaning system			
	Goal behavior	Effort beliefs	Attributions	Strategies
Game genres				
Roguelike	+	+	+	+
Puzzle	+	+	+	+
Platformer	+	+	+	+
Life simulations	~	~	~	~
Cozy	-	-	-	-
Zen	-	-	-	-
Walking simulation	-	-	-	-
Design & illustration	-	-	-	-

2.2 Selection Criteria and Data Preprocessing

The examined genres in this study were selected by categorizing the genres into the mechanisms of the mindset's meaning system (Table 1). This procedure involved assessing which mechanisms of *goal behavior*, *effort beliefs*, *attributions,* and *strategies* [12] seem more/less relevant for certain game genres and could accordingly represent a growth mindset environment. The selection of genres was guided by the idea of identifying those that are strongly related to a growth mindset environment or preferred by players with a growth mindset. Growth mindset-related genres that were identified in this way were *roguelike*, *puzzle*, and *platformer,* as they all revolve around overcoming (difficult) obstacles and progress. Additionally, we considered *life simulation games* in the growth mindset category because of a preliminary finding in an unpublished survey study by the authors. Note that the mechanisms of the mindset's meaning system do not appear to be overly relevant for this genre (see Table 1). Using the same procedure, a control group consisting of four genres supposedly unrelated to a growth mindset was conceptualized. The genres included in the control group (neutral category) were *cozy*, *zen*, *walking simulation*, and *design & illustration*, as they do not heavily revolve around overcoming (difficult) obstacles and progress.

For each of the investigated genres, three, prototypical games were selected for analysis: *Roguelike*: The Binding of Isaac: Rebirth; Dead Cells; Enter the Gungeon; *Puzzle*: The Witness, BaBa is you; Talos Principle. *Platformer*: Ori and the Will of the Wisp, Getting Over It, Portal 2. *Life simulation*: Sims 4; Dinkum; Stardew Valley. *Zen*: Abzu; Journey; Gris. *Cozy*: Spiritfarer; KindWords; Unpacking. *Walking simulator*: Gone Home; Firewatch; What Remains of Edith Finch. *Design & Illustration*: Passpartout: The Starving Artist; House Flipper; House Flipper 2. These selected games should be rather consistent with the typical mechanics of their genre. To ensure sufficient data for analyses only games with at least 1500 reviews in English and a primarily positive overall rating were selected. This guarantees a minimum level of quality of the game.

During the reviews' preprocessing, the contractions within them were split, the reviews were converted to lowercase, emojis were converted to ASCII symbols, and special characters and digits were removed. All reviews with less than ten words were excluded to ensure that they could be meaningfully analyzed. After preprocessing, 563,047 reviews remained for subsequent analyses. *Stemming*, a natural language processing method in which words are reduced to their stem, was not done, to avoid a potential loss of information. This allows us to differentiate between different words of a common root word, such as "try" and "tried", which may be used in different contexts in the reviews, such as in the phrases "try something new" or "tried stardew valley".

2.3 Creation of the Growth Mindset Dictionary

Three different sets of texts served as the basis for the creation of a dictionary specifically tailored to the concept of a growth mindset. These three sets were: 1) the book "Mindset - The New Psychology of Success" by Carol Dweck [8]; 2) the transcripts of talks by Carol Dweck [23–25]; and 3) three (growth) mindset questionnaires [8, 26, 27]. These sets were analyzed using a frequency count of their respective unigrams to create a growth mindset-related dictionary. An n-gram is a sequence of n consecutive words, meaning that unigrams are a special case of n-grams with only one word. A researcher subsequently manually evaluated all relevant terms. Common proper names such as "Carol" and toponyms such as "Bronx" were excluded. In another round of inspection, the contextual usage of the remaining terms was evaluated by inspecting the frequencies of their bigrams in the reviews, to determine whether the terms (e.g., *"challenge"*) were predominantly used in a manner related to growth mindset (e.g., *"overcome challenge"*) or not (e.g., *"no challenge")*. Network graphs were created to visualize and inspect the most common co-occurrences of the terms of interest. This allowed for a more refined and precise construction of a growth mindset-related dictionary. Only terms showing a relation to the growth mindset concept through the analysis of their respective bigrams and network graphs were retained.

The final version of the context-adjusted growth mindset dictionary consisted of 31 unique terms derived from the book, transcripts, and questionnaires: abilities, ability, become, challenge, challenges, challenging, constantly, develop, difficulty, fail, failure, feedback, goal, harder, improves, learn, learned, learning, mindsets, motivation, practice, problems, process, setbacks, skills, strategies, succeed, success, taught, try, trying.

2.4 Topic Modelling Using BERTopic

Topic Modelling using BERTopic [28] was performed on the reviews to determine whether growth mindset-related topics emerged from the data. This approach provided additional information on the extent to which growth mindset-related topics or themes were discussed in the reviews. Furthermore, it allowed a comparison of the frequency of the respective topics between the specified genres. BERTopic leverages state-of-the-art embedding models such as BERT (Bidirectional Encoder Representations from Transformers) to capture semantic information effectively and yield coherent and interpretable results. To ensure an equal influence of each genre on the topic modelling, 26 376 reviews were chosen randomly per genre resulting in 211 008 reviews (26 376 * 8) being analyzed during the topic modelling. The number 26 376 was chosen as it represents the number of reviews in the genre with the smallest number of reviews (i.e., *puzzle*), which is described in more detail in Sect. 3.1.

3 Results

The terms defined in the growth mindset dictionary were used to calculate the frequency of their occurrences, relative to the number of reviews in the respective genre. Hence, for each genre an average frequency of the growth mindset-related terms in the dictionary was calculated, which controls for differences in the number of reviews per genre. The results of parametric significance tests in this section were further checked with non-parametric equivalents, yielding qualitatively equivalent results.

3.1 Descriptive Results

Reviews of games in genres part of the growth mindset category (i.e., *platformer, life simulation, roguelike*; *puzzle*) were shorter (*mean* = 52 words, *SD* = 88) than reviews of games in the neutral category (i.e., *zen, cozy, walking simulation, design & illustration;* mean = 72 words, *SD* = 103). The average playtime (*mean* = 195.99 h, *SD* = 433.47) was higher in the growth mindset category than in the neutral category (*mean* = 34.68 h, (*SD* = 16.42). Each genre yielded a different number of reviews: *puzzle* (26 376), *design & illustration* (27 833), *zen* (30 944), *cozy* (33 094), *walking simulation* (53 954), *roguelike* (89 191), *platformer* (107 592) and *life simulation* (194 063).

3.2 Differences between the Groups

A t-test was used to assess the differences in the occurrences of the terms in the growth mindset dictionary between the growth mindset-related genres and the neutral category, revealing a significant difference between the two categories $t(327123) = 31.865$, $p < .001$, $d = .086$. Reviews in the growth mindset category were associated with a higher average frequency of the terms defined in the growth mindset dictionary ($M = .265$, $SD = .791$) than reviews in the neutral category ($M = .201$, $SD = .611$).

3.3 Differences between the Genres

Statistical differences regarding the relative frequencies of the growth mindset-related terms between the genres were analyzed using an analysis of variance including the factor *genre* with the eight factor levels roguelike, platformer, puzzle, life simulation, zen, cozy, walking simulation, design & illustration. The analysis revealed significant differences between genres regarding the average frequency of growth mindset expressions $F(7{,}563039) = 1885, p < .001, \eta^2 = 0.023$.

Pair-wise differences between the genres were assessed using Tukey's HSD method to compute p-values adjusted for multiple comparisons. All pairwise differences between the genres were significant except for two comparisons among genres of the neutral category (see Table 2). Notably, all growth mindset-related genres showed significantly higher values than genres in the neutral category in the pairwise comparisons, except for the life simulation genre which showed the lowest values (Fig. 1).

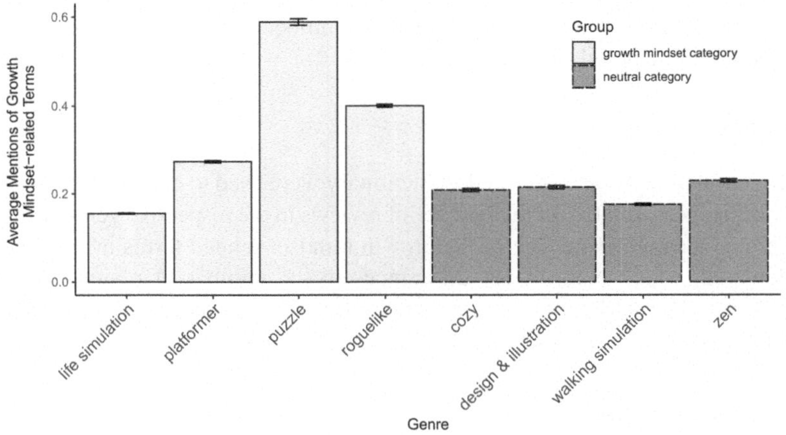

Fig. 1. Average Mentions of growth mindset-related expressions, depicted by genre. The absolute frequencies of growth mindset expressions per genre are relativized by the total number of reviews per genre. The standard errors are depicted by error bars.

3.4 Results of the Topic Modelling Using BERTopic

The topic modelling yielded 910 topics. Four out of the 910 identified topics via BERTopic showed a clear relation to the concept of growth mindset in an exploratory observation of these topics (Fig. 2). The number of reviews being classified as belonging to one of the four identified topics varied by genre: *platformer*: 303, *life simulation*: 39, *roguelike*: 491, *puzzle*: 274, *zen*: 17, *cozy*: 15, *walking simulation*: 8 and *design & illustration*: 23. Growth mindset-related topics are mentioned in 0.6% of reviews overall (1% in the growth mindset category and 0.06% of neutral category). These results serve as another indicator of the stability and validity of the findings of this paper. Moreover, the prevalence of the topics indicates that a discussion of growth mindset-related topics

Table 2. Effect sizes (Cohen's d), highlighted by color, from highest (red) to lowest (blue), of the pairwise comparisons between the genres (upper triangle) and the corresponding p-values using Tukey HSD test (lower triangle). Three asterisks (***) signify p-values < .001. Platf. = platformer, Life S. = life simulation, D&I = design and illustration, W. Sim = walking simulation.

VS		Growth Mindset Category				Neutral Category			
		Puzzle	Rogue-like	Platf	Life S	Cozy	Zen	D&I	W. Sim
Growth Mindset Category	Puzzle		.179	.350	.680	.416	.384	.397	.512
	Roguelike	***		.138	.342	.207	.182	.197	.259
	Platf	***	***		.182	.084	.056	.075	.132
	Life S	***	***	***		-.097	-.134	-.109	-.037
Neutral Category	Cozy	***	***	***	***		-.032	-.010	.057
	Zen	***	***	***	***	.009		.022	.091
	D&I	***	***	***	***	.971	.238		.067
	W.Sim	***	***	***	***	***	***	***	

is not the focus of most reviews and underscores the value of employing computational text analysis for our approach rather than relying on manual qualitative analyses [16].

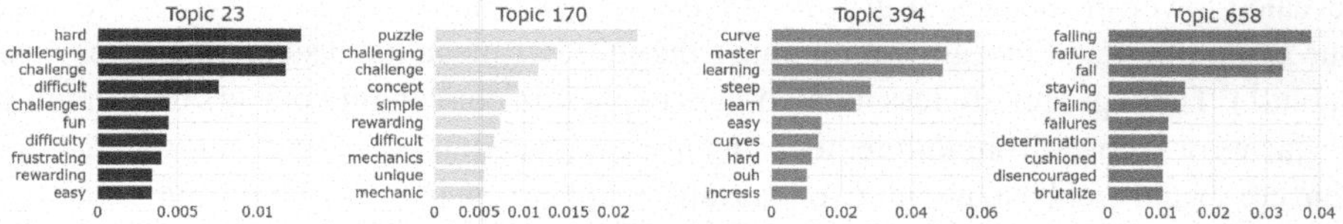

Fig. 2. Four identified growth mindset-related topics identified via exploratory BERTopic modelling. The x-axis of the topics depicts the representativeness of the term for the specific topic, calculated by a class-based TF-IDF (term frequency-inverse document frequency) procedure.

4 Discussion

The current study examined the feasibility of a new method to identify potential psychological effects of video gaming by analyzing user-generated reviews of video games on Steam using text mining and natural language processing. With the lexical hypothesis as our theoretical foundation, suggesting that language is a proxy for personal traits, we hypothesized that player reviews would reveal insights into how certain game genres might relate to or even foster a growth mindset.

Using the developed growth mindset dictionary, our results indicated that puzzle games had the highest frequency of growth mindset-related terms in player reviews, which supports the notion that this genre seems to be either particularly interesting for players with a growth mindset or even constitutes an environment to foster such a mindset. Specifically, overcoming challenges in puzzle games often necessitates setting clear objectives and learning goals, the belief that (cognitive) effort can help overcome challenges, the attribution of failures to lack of effort than fixed abilities, and the flexibility to adopt new approaches/strategies (e.g., players would otherwise stop playing if a puzzle was not solved on first try). Furthermore, games of the genres roguelike and platformer exhibited a high presence of growth mindset terminology, second only to puzzle games. Roguelike games, for example, require learning goal-oriented gameplay and trial-and-error strategies where players are expected to learn and adapt from repeated failures, effectively requiring learning from setbacks. Similarly, platformers require players to refine their strategies and exert effort to navigate progressively challenging levels, fostering an environment potentially conducive to cultivating a growth mindset.

Despite not seeing a strong relevance of the mindset meaning system categories for life simulation games (see Table 1), we initially considered life simulation games as part of the growth mindset category because of preliminary correlational results of a survey study by the authors. However, life simulation games showed the lowest mentions of growth mindset-related terms. Yet, a potential link between life simulation games and a growth mindset cannot be ruled out due to their structure around task accomplishment and progress. However, such tasks are sometimes – at least partly – simulated (e.g., sending your Sims to work in Sims 4), and thus, motives for playing such games [29] might also differ considerably from puzzle or roguelike games.

The control game genres cozy, zen, walking simulation, and design & illustration revealed lower incidences of growth mindset language in reviews. This is in line with our assumption and categorization along the mindset meaning system categories (see Table 1). These genres are less likely or less explicit in challenging players to overcome obstacles or recover from failure, focusing more on creating a soothing atmosphere (i.e., zen, cozy) and emphasizing more on narrative exploration (i.e., walking simulations) or personal expression (i.e., design and illustration).

Overall, these results, which were qualitatively supported by the BERTopic model, seem to be in line with theoretical assumptions made in the field regarding the relationship between video gaming and a growth mindset [1, 5–7], demonstrating the usefulness of the current approach. However, it's important to note that by analyzing a large number of reviews, already very small effects result in significant differences between genres. In fact, almost every comparison of genres was significant. Thus, the reported effect sizes are necessary to contextualize the practical significance of these findings (Table 2). For instance, while our comparison between the grouped genres is significant – the effect size is negligible (Cohen's $d < 0.2$). This, however, is driven by our categorization of life simulation games as a growth mindset-related genre. In fact, we find the largest difference between puzzles and life simulation games. Importantly, considering the obtained small to medium effect sizes (Cohen's $d \sim 0.2–0.5$), it seems that puzzle and roguelike games seem to be more relevant for growth mindset as compared to games in our neutral control genres.

As this feasibility study set out to develop novel methods for supporting video game effect research, it is also confronted with some limitations. First and foremost, it is imperative to note that the mere mention of growth mindset-related terms in player reviews does not necessarily indicate that the players themselves possess a growth mindset, or that the games with frequent mentions of such terms effectively promote the development of this mindset. This represents a significant challenge and needs to be carefully studied in future validation studies. Second, the dictionary constructed in this paper required substantial manual coding efforts and is not definitive. While the current outcomes suggest its utility, future studies should focus on its refinement and validation, such as examining additional genres and in-depth analysis of individual games. Further, expanding the dictionary to include bi- and trigrams, such as "overcoming this challenge," could potentially enhance both accuracy and specificity. Additionally, with further advancement in automatic text processing and natural language processing, such word-specific dictionaries might no longer be necessary – increasing the approach's scalability. However, a thorough understanding of the constructs/skills being investigated will remain crucial for guiding AI models, such as generative pre-trained transformers, which might still require manual coding (e.g., fine-tuning models).

Taken together, using this new approach, we found that games traditionally associated with overcoming challenges and performance improvements, such as puzzle and roguelike games, yielded the highest mentions of growth mindset-related terms. Thus, applying computational text analysis to user-generated reviews might be feasible in determining how gaming preferences are related to latent psychological constructs. Importantly, this approach might also support video game effect research by filtering the large number of video games published each year to a more manageable subset of games for in-depth psychological examinations or identifying games potentially effective in cultivating specific skills, such as those associated with a growth mindset.

References

1. Granic, I., Lobel, A., Engels, R.C.M.E.: The benefits of playing video games. Am. Psychol. **69**, 66–78 (2014). https://doi.org/10.1037/a0034857
2. Bediou, B., Rodgers, M.A., Tipton, E., Mayer, R.E., Green, C.S., Bavelier, D.: Effects of action video game play on cognitive skills: a meta-analysis. Technol. Mind Behav. **4** (2023). https://doi.org/10.1037/tmb0000102
3. Greitemeyer, T.: The dark and bright side of video game consumption: effects of violent and prosocial video games. Curr. Opin. Psychol. **46**, 101326 (2022). https://doi.org/10.1016/j.copsyc.2022.101326
4. Gee, J.P.: Learning by design: good video games as learning machines. E-Learn. Digit. Media. **2**, 5–16 (2005). https://doi.org/10.2304/elea.2005.2.1.5
5. Pusey, M., Wong, K.W., Rappa, N.A.: Resilience interventions using interactive technology: a scoping review. Interact. Learn. Environ. **30**, 1940–1955 (2022). https://doi.org/10.1080/10494820.2020.1772837
6. O'Rourke, E., Haimovitz, K., Ballweber, C., Dweck, C., Popović, Z.: Brain points: a growth mindset incentive structure boosts persistence in an educational game. In: Proceedings of the SIGCHI Conference on Human Factors in Computing Systems, pp. 3339–3348. ACM, To-ronto Ontario Canada (2014). https://doi.org/10.1145/2556288.2557157
7. Anderson, C.G., Campbell, K., Steinkuehler, C.: Building persistence through failure: the role of challenge in video games. In: Proceedings of the 14th International Conference on the Foundations of Digital Games, pp. 1–6. ACM, San Luis Obispo California USA (2019). https://doi.org/10.1145/3337722.3337741

8. Dweck, C.S.: Mindset: The new psychology of success. Random House (2006)
9. Burnette, J.L., et al.: A systematic review and meta-analysis of growth mindset interventions: For whom, how, and why might such interventions work? Psychol. Bull. **149**, 174–205 (2023). https://doi.org/10.1037/bul0000368
10. Yeager, D.S., Dweck, C.S.: Mindsets that promote resilience: when students believe that personal characteristics can be developed. Edu. Psychol. **47**, 302–314 (2012). https://doi.org/10.1080/00461520.2012.722805
11. Burnette, J.L., Knouse, L.E., Vavra, D.T., O'Boyle, E., Brooks, M.A.: Growth mindsets and psychological distress: A meta-analysis. Clin. Psychol. Rev. **77**, 101816 (2020). https://doi.org/10.1016/j.cpr.2020.101816
12. Bernecker, K., Job, V.: Mindset theory. In: Sassenberg, K. and Vliek, M.L.W. (eds.) Social Psychology in Action, pp. 179–191. Springer International Publishing, Cham (2019). https://doi.org/10.1007/978-3-030-13788-5_12
13. Dale, G., Joessel, A., Bavelier, D., Green, C.S.: A new look at the cognitive neuroscience of video game play. Ann. N. Y. Acad. Sci. **1464**, 192–203 (2020). https://doi.org/10.1111/nyas.14295
14. Vargas-Iglesias, J.J.: Making sense of genre: the logic of video game genre organiza-tion. Game. Culture. **15**, 158–178 (2020). https://doi.org/10.1177/1555412017751803
15. Zhu, M., Fang, X.: A lexical approach to study computer games and game play experience via online reviews. Int. J. Human-Comput. Int. **31**, 413–426 (2015). https://doi.org/10.1080/10447318.2015.1036228
16. Phillips, C., Klarkowski, M., Frommel, J., Gutwin, C., Mandryk, R.L.: Identifying commercial games with therapeutic potential through a content analysis of steam reviews. Proc. ACM Hum. Comput. Interact. **5**, 1–21 (2021). https://doi.org/10.1145/3474682
17. Pennebaker, J.W., Mehl, M.R., Niederhoffer, K.G.: Psychological aspects of natural language use: our words. Our Selves. Annu. Rev. Psychol. **54**, 547–577 (2003). https://doi.org/10.1146/annurev.psych.54.101601.145041
18. Hemenover, S.H., Bowman, N.D.: Video games, emotion, and emotion regulation: expanding the scope. Ann. Int. Commun. Assoc. **42**, 125–143 (2018). https://doi.org/10.1080/23808985.2018.1442239
19. Macnamara, B.N., Burgoyne, A.P.: Do growth mindset interventions impact students' academic achievement? a systematic review and meta-analysis with recommendations for best practices. Psychol. Bull. **149**, 133–173 (2023). https://doi.org/10.1037/bul0000352
20. Carras, M.C., Kowert, R., Quandt, T.: Psychosocial effects of gaming. In: Attrill-Smith, A., Fullwood, C., Keep, M., and Kuss, D.J. (eds.) the Oxford Handbook of Cyberpsychology, pp. 556–587. Oxford University Press (2019). https://doi.org/10.1093/oxfordhb/9780198812746.013.30
21. Clarke, R.I., Lee, J.H., Clark, N.: Why video game genres fail: a classificatory analysis. Game. Culture. **12**, 445–465 (2017). https://doi.org/10.1177/1555412015591900
22. Wang, X., Goh, D.H.-L.: Components of game experience: an automatic text analysis of online reviews. Entertainment Comput. **33**, 100338 (2020). https://doi.org/10.1016/j.entcom.2019.100338
23. Developing a Growth Mindset with Carol Dweck. https://www.youtube.com/watch?v=hiiEeMN7vbQ
24. The power of yet. https://www.youtube.com/watch?v=J-swZaKN2Ic
25. The Growth Mindset. https://www.youtube.com/watch?v=-71zdXCMU6A
26. Levy, S.R., Stroessner, S.J., Dweck, C.S.: Stereotype formation and endorsement: the role of implicit theories. J. Pers. Soc. Psychol. **74**, 1421–1436 (1998). https://doi.org/10.1037/0022-3514.74.6.1421

27. Abd-El-Fattah, S.M., Yates, G.: Implicit Theory of intelligence scale: testing for factorial invariance and mean structure. In: Presented at the Paper presented at the Australian Association for Research in Education Conference, Adelaide, Australia (2006)
28. Grootendorst, M.: KeyBERT: minimal keyword extraction with BERT (2020)
29. Demetrovics, Z., et al.: Why do you play? The development of the motives for online gaming questionnaire (MOGQ). Behav. Res. Methods **43**, 814–825 (2011). https://doi.org/10.3758/s13428-011-0091-y

Is There Cognitive Engagement When They Comment 'Haha': A Dynamic Analysis of Cognitive and Emotional Engagement in Game Video Comments

Jiayi Cen(✉), Nora McIntyre, and Christian Bokhove

Southampton Education School, University of Southampton, Southampton, UK
J.Cen@southampton.ac.uk

Abstract. Enhancing students' emotional involvement and enjoyment is key to improving their concentration and educational outcomes in game-based learning (GBL), which is widely recognised as a benefit of this approach. However, concerns remain about students becoming overly immersed, which could lead them to stray from the learning goals of GBL. This study utilises Cross-recurrence quantification analysis (CRQA) to investigate the dynamic relationship between cognitive and emotional engagement in GBL settings. Fifty participants watched two Minecraft gameplay videos and engaged in cognitive tasks that involved identifying creative gameplay behaviours. The timesync comments technology was used to record students' timed responses. After categorising these comments into cognitive or emotional engagements using Content Analysis, CRQA was used to explore these engagements. Findings revealed a high synchronicity in cognitive and emotional engagement across both videos. The second video, notable for its exaggerated narration and imaginative gameplay, triggered more frequent recurring emotional and cognitive states, indicating a pattern of more consistent engagement. The study discusses how to balance cognitive and emotional stimulation when designing serious games.

Keywords: video games · CRQA · emotion · cognition

1 Introduction

Video games are becoming more prominent in education, with nearly half of the teachers in the UK and the US incorporating gamification into their teaching to better engage students [1]. Enhancing student engagement in games to help them gain knowledge is seen as a key benefit of game-based learning (GBL) [2]. In educational gaming, engagement encompasses three components: affective, behavioural, and cognitive engagement [3]. This study primarily focuses on the affective and cognitive engagement. The emotional engagement relates to how the game make students feel, which can range from interest to boredom, from happiness to anxiety, and other ranges of affective states. The cognitive dimension of engagement is typically defined as the cognitive effort expended by students within educational games, along with the resultant thought processes or attention they entail.

A. Schönbohm et al. (Eds.): GALA 2024, LNCS 15348, pp. 92–100, 2025.
https://doi.org/10.1007/978-3-031-78269-5_9

Some research indicates that the emotions experienced by learners while playing games can enhance their cognition, thereby influencing learning outcomes. For example, Franceschini et al. [4] suggested that the positive emotions and biochemical activation generated by playing video games can enhance visual perception, sensorimotor functions, and reading skills in the short term. Cheng et al.'s study [5] found that seventh graders improved their learning outcomes through game-based learning, with long-term effects being consistent regardless of whether they felt mostly positive emotions or a combination of positive and negative emotions during the game. Furthermore, neuroscience experiments [6] have also demonstrated that GBL leads to an invigoration of learning processes through emotional engagement. Conversely, some researchers [7] are concerned that although video games do provide enjoyment, they also tread a fine line between promoting motivation and fostering distraction. If students' gameplay activities are too intense, they might become overly involved in the action and score achievement in the game itself and instead wander away from the learning goals.

Most research on cognitive and emotional engagement in GBL still uses static methods. Typically, this involves students using emotion scales to report their feelings after GBL activities and evaluating learning outcomes with pre-tests and post-tests through academic exams. However, these studies do not reveal how cognitive and emotional engagement dynamically interact throughout the game-based learning environment.

The current study aims to more precisely investigate the cognitive and emotional dynamics exhibited by students while engaging in cognitive tasks to identify creative gameplay behaviours in video games. The research question is: As students identify creativity within video games, do their emotional and cognitive engagements synchronize and mutually affect each other over time?

2 Methods

2.1 Research Design

This study adopts a dynamic perspective to understand the creative process (i.e., The Creative Process Model [8]) and the interaction between emotion and cognition (i.e., The Integrated Model of Cognitive-Affective Learning with Media [9]).

Therefore, for the research materials, this study chose two Minecraft construction videos to illustrate how the creative process is manifested through gameplay behaviours. To capture the dynamics of emotional and cognitive engagements when students watch Minecraft videos, this study utilises the timesync comment feature of the Bilibili video platform to collect data. Timesync comments can simultaneously record both the time when participants post their comments and the content of those comments. This means the timesync comments capture the exact moments (timestamps) when students react emotionally or cognitively to Minecraft videos, and also identify the nature of these reactions (by analysing the content of the comments). Figure 1 shows an example of a timesync comment on the Bilibili platform.

In this study, students logged into their personal accounts on the Bilibili video platform, watched the selected videos, and posted timesync comments at moments they perceived as creative gameplay behaviours. Content Analysis was used to categorise comments as either cognitive or emotional engagement, then Cross-Recurrence Quantification Analysis (CRQA) was used to analyse the dynamic structure of emotional and cognitive engagement.

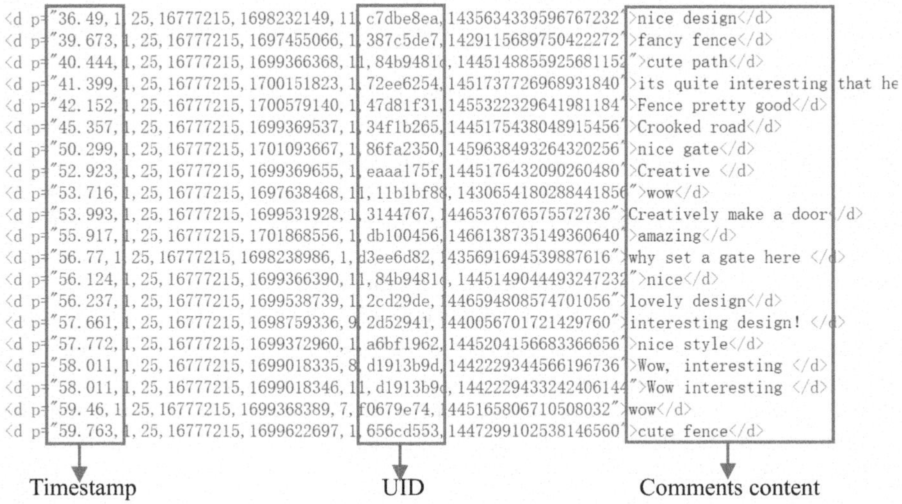

Fig. 1. The sample of timesync comments on the Bilibili platform

2.2 Participants

A total of 50 participants (23 females, 26 males and 1 participant "prefer not to say" the gender) were recruited at the university through poster advertisements and the snowball sampling method. To ensure participants are representative and reflect the diversity of the population being studied, this research tried to include undergraduate students (42%), postgraduate taught students (52%), and postgraduate research students (6%) from different faculties. All participants have had gaming experience in Minecraft for a period exceeding more than three months.

2.3 Materials

Two videos about how seasoned players create top Minecraft buildings that reflect creative insights were used as materials. First, used the different combinations of the terms 'Minecraft buildings' 'top' 'idea' and 'creative' to search videos through YouTube platforms. And using YouTube's *Filter* option, videos were sorted by their 'Rating'.

Then the selection process for the videos was divided into two stages. In the initial selection stage, researchers applied three criteria to filter the videos: (1) The video must document the entire building process of the player, not just display or a tour guide of the final result. (2) The building structure should feature a variety of parts or designs, which could demonstrate different creative behaviours as much as possible. (3) The video should be between 5–15 min long. The top 50 videos from the search results were reviewed, and 8 met these criteria. These 8 videos were then evaluated using The Patient Education Materials Assessment Tool for Audio-visual [10] a tool typically employed in the medical field to measure the quality of educational materials based on their understandability and action ability. The highest-scoring video, which featured the construction of a roller coaster theme park, was chosen as the first material for the study (Video 1). Video 1 features no spoken commentary, just short subtitles during crucial building sections.

After video 1 was confirmed, a second video also featuring roller coaster construction was added to help students make cognitive decisions more easily. Using 'Minecraft' and 'roller coaster' as search terms on YouTube, a video was selected as the second material (Video 2). This video was chosen because it has distinctly different characteristics from Video 1: it features no subtitles, but includes constant, exaggerated narrated commentary. The duration of the first video is 885 s, while the second video spans 845 s.

2.4 Data Collection Procedure

Participants were invited separately to a quiet room where the researcher first introduced the purpose and process of this study. Then used their own digital device to register or log in to their personal account on the Bilibili platform. Next, participants were given an hour to watch the two videos and send timesync comments on where they felt the construction processes or behaviours exemplify creativity. During this process, students were required not to pause or rewatch the video—a feature characteristic of the timesync comments system, which allows viewers to post their thoughts instantly using brief texts and symbols. The timesync comments recorded user IDs, the timestamps of comments, and the comments' content.

2.5 Data Analysis

Content Analysis. Students often become emotionally or cognitively engaged while viewing video game scenes or clips. These comments expressed students' emotional or cognitive engagement towards the video (or a part of it, or the video's creator) [11].

Content analysis is often utilised to identify the emotions or cognitions [12] expressed in texts. This study used content analysis to categorise the timesync comments students make while watching gaming videos. The coding process is inductive. Comments that reflect cognitive engagement often clearly express their perceptions of gameplay behaviours or structures in response to tasks aimed at identifying creativity. These kinds of comments reveal complex thoughts through linguistic features, demonstrating the students' deep understanding and reflection on the video content. For instance, a comment like 'Very interesting sign design' suggests that the participant found an architectural feature in the game—specifically, a roller coaster sign—to be creative. Comments that consist of emotional words or only one or two exclamations or symbols are coded as emotional engagement, which carries information about the most direct personal response. For example, surprise (e.g. 'wow', '!!!'), praise (e.g. 'good'), enjoy (e.g. 'haha'), and affection (e.g. 'love this').

Some cognitive comments inherently involve affective elements. Affective processing—linked to authentic reactions, is generally automatic and rapid. In contrast, cognitive processing requires more extensive cognitive resources as it is associated with analytical thinking and understanding [13]. This study suggests that if comments display cognitive engagement (even alongside emotional content) it indicates that students have moved from immediate reactions to a complex stage of thought, involving more time and cognitive resources. Consequently, a binary coding approach is utilised for analysing the comments.

Cross-Recurrence Quantification Analysis (CRQA). CRQA is a nonlinear correlational analysis technique used to explore dynamic interactions and synchronizations between two or more time series [14]. The core concept of CRQA is recurrence – repetition of elements or patterns in a sequence. The core tool of this analysis is the recurrence plot and recurrence matrix. The recurrence plots are constructed by marking the times at which the states of one time series are similar to the states of another within a predefined threshold. The versatility of CRQA lies in its ability to detect and quantify the degree of similarity and coupling between time series, without the need for the data to be stationary or linear. This makes CRQA particularly suitable for analysing the relationship between emotional and cognitive engagement, where the underlying dynamics are non-linear [15].

In this study, CRQA was conducted on the raw data without embedding the data. Therefore, when setting the parameters for CRQA [16], the Delay parameter is set to 1 ($d = 1$), the Embedding parameter to 1 ($m = 1$), and the Radius parameter to 0.1 ($r = 0.1$). Furthermore, previous work has indicated that, for categorical time series, this parameter setting is adequate to extract empirically useful CRQA measures [17].

3 Results

3.1 Higher Cognitive Engagement Highlighted in Video 1 Comments

After cleaning the data, 5 duplicate comments were removed. There were 962 timesync comments in total, with 508 from Video 1 and 454 from Video 2. These were duplicates where the same UID sent the same content at the same time, likely due to the participant hitting the 'enter' key twice in quick succession. After coding timesync comments through Content Analysis, Video 1 showed a higher proportion of cognitive engagement, with 335 comments making up 65.94% of the total. Emotional engagement comments numbered 173, representing 34.06%. Video 2 had a slightly higher count of cognitive comments at 239, accounting for 52.64%, while emotional comments were 215, making up 47.36%.

3.2 Emotional and Cognitive Engagement in Video 2 Demonstrates Higher Recurrence

The Cross-Recurrence Quantification Analysis (CRQA) delineated marked differences in emotional and cognitive engagement across two educational videos, revealing nuanced variations in how students interacted with the content. Video 2 demonstrated a higher Recurrence Rate (RR) of 49.86% compared to 44.92% in Video 1, indicative of more frequent recurring emotional and cognitive states, thus suggesting a pattern of greater periodic engagement. This consistent recurrence was reinforced by a higher Determinism (DET) rate in Video 2 (75.18%) as opposed to Video 1 (72.04%), reflecting more predictable and structured cognitive and emotional engagement patterns within Video 2. The average diagonal line length (L) in Video 2 was slightly longer at 3.01 compared to 2.94 in Video 1, which might suggest marginally more extended episodes of synchronized cognitive and emotional states in Video 2.

Table 1. The recurrence measure parameters

	RR	DEF	L	LAM	TT	ENTR
Video 1	44.92%	72.04%	2.94	78.44%	3.80	1.34
Video 2	49.86%	75.18%	3.01	78.77%	3.25	1.39
V1_shuffled	44.92%	68.96%	2.83	68.27%	3.27	1.27
V2_shuffled	49.86%	74.66%	2.98	76.66%	3.12	1.36

Further differentiation between the videos is evident in their entropy metrics; Video 2 recorded a slightly higher entropy (ENTR) (1.39) compared to Video 1 (1.34). This increased entropy suggests more complex patterns of engagement in Video 2, reflecting a richer interplay between cognitive inputs and emotional responses. Video 2 displayed marginally higher Laminarity (LAM) (78.77% versus 78.44% for Video 1). This suggests more stable phases of engagement, likely due to more consistently aligned cognitive and emotional states.

Notably, the average Trapping Time (TT) was shorter in Video 2 (3.25 s) compared to Video 1 (3.80 s), indicative of quicker transitions between different states of cognitive and emotional engagement. This dynamic suggests that while Video 2 may foster quicker shifts in engagement states, it maintains a higher order and predictability in how these transitions occur, potentially enhancing the learning experience by keeping students cognitively and emotionally engaged with evolving content.

The recurrence plots from Video 1 (Fig. 2A) and Video 2 (Fig. 2B) illustrate significant structured behaviour in viewer engagement, with Video 2 displaying denser and more prolonged engagements. To corroborate these patterns as genuine, this study randomised the response order using a distributed shuffling technique to ensure that each sequence had an equal probability of selection, thereby eliminating any video content dependencies for CRQA analysis. The recurrence measure results of shuffled data are shown in Table 1. The recurrence plots for the shuffled data from Video 1 are shown in Fig. 2C, and those for Video 2 shuffled data are illustrated in Fig. 2D. These results suggested that although the recurrence measure parameters have changed compared with the original response sequences, the overall recurrence regularity in time didn't disappear.

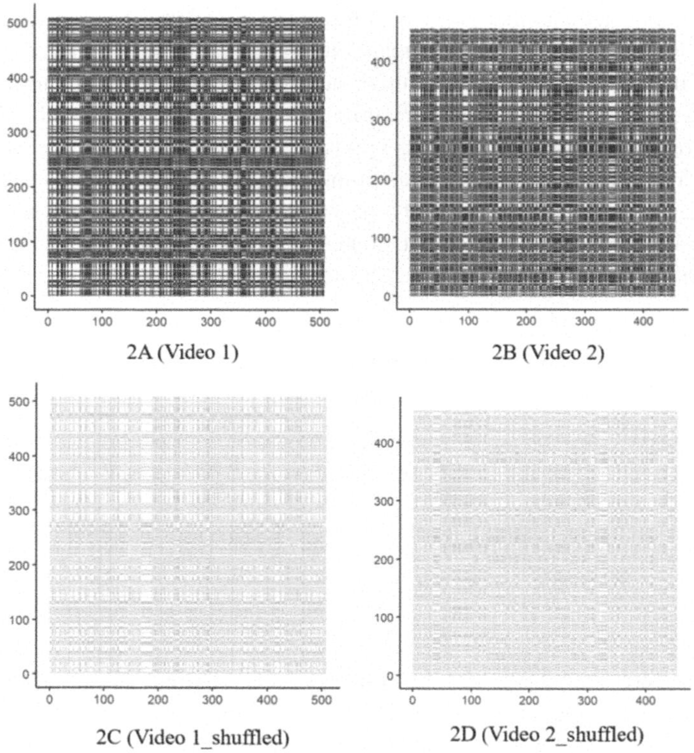

Fig.2. The recurrence plots of emotional and cognitive engagement

4 Discussion

4.1 Interplay of Cognitive and Emotional Engagement

The results suggested that moments of high emotional engagement are often accompanied by intense cognitive activity. This is particularly evident in Video 2, where increased determinism (75.18%) and higher recurrence rates (49.86%) suggest that emotional responses are not random but are aligned with specific cognitive tasks. This finding, to some extent, alleviates concerns among educational researchers that students might become overly absorbed in the emotional aspects of video games—such as animations and sound effects, potentially detracting from their cognitive involvement [18]. In addition to the findings presented in this study, where Video 2's more pronounced artistic style and sound effects were found to enhance students' emotional engagement, serious game design might also consider incorporating emotionally resonant episodes within the storyline, such as problem-solving events and moral dilemmas. These elements can simultaneously evoke cognitive processing, thereby requiring students to employ both emotional judgment and cognitive strategies [19]. This dual activation not only deepens the learning experience by engaging students on multiple levels but also highlights the intricate relationship between emotional and cognitive faculties in GBL contexts.

4.2 Balancing Cognitive and Emotional Dynamics in Educational Games

The complexity and transition dynamics highlighted by the trapping time metrics further illustrate how emotional and cognitive engagements are dynamically linked. Specifically, the faster transitions between states observed in Video 2, as indicated by shorter trapping times of 3.25 s, suggest a highly dynamic environment. Such environments are likely designed to keep students continuously engaged by presenting them with rapid shifts in cognitive and emotional challenges. This aspect of game design, which prompts students to adapt quickly to changing conditions, is crucial for educational settings as it helps avert cognitive stagnation and sustains emotional interest, both of which are essential for continuous learning [20].

However, while the dynamic nature of such environments can enhance learning by preventing boredom and disengagement, it may also pose risks of cognitive overload. While moderate levels of challenge and emotional engagement can enhance learning by fostering attention and motivation, excessively challenging or emotionally intense scenarios could detract from learning by causing anxiety or confusion. Thus, an optimal balance needs to be struck in the design of educational games to maximize learning outcomes without overwhelming the students.

5 Conclusion

This study used timesync technology to collect students' emotional and cognitive engagement while they watched Minecraft gameplay videos. Cross Recurrence Quantification Analysis results (CRQA) showed that in the video game environment, there is a high synchrony between emotional and cognitive engagement. The study suggests that blending cognitive challenges and emotional triggers effectively within the design can enhance engagement, fostering a video game setting that stimulates both the intellectual and emotional capacities of students.

The limitation of this study is that analyses textual data from students watching game videos, with a specific focus on how to enhance the attractiveness of video clips in educational games and improving their effectiveness in demonstrated concepts [21]. However, this approach overlooks the emotional and cognitive engagement that occurs during direct interactions with the game elements of Minecraft, such as its mechanics and storyline. To address this gap, future research will explore the use of physiological measurement devices to capture more precise signals of cognitive and emotional engagement during video game interactions, providing a deeper understanding of the dynamic processes involved.

References

1. G2A: Educators Turn to Gaming to Enable Pandemic Learning, https://www.g2a.co/educators-turn-to-gaming-to-enable-pandemic-learning-study-commissioned-by-g2a-com-finds/. Accessed 16 July 2024
2. Kiili, K., Ketamo, H.: Evaluating cognitive and affective outcomes of a digital game-based math test. IEEE Trans. Learn. Technol. **11**(2), 255–263 (2017)

3. Ge, X., Ifenthaler, D.: Designing engaging educational games and assessing engagement in game-based learning. In: Gamification in Education: Breakthroughs in Research and Practice, pp. 1–19. IGI Global (2018)
4. Franceschini, S., Bertoni, S., Lulli, M., Pievani, T., Facoetti, A.: Short-term effects of video-games on cognitive enhancement: the role of positive emotions. J. Cogn. Enhancement, 1–18 (2022)
5. Cheng, M.T., Huang, W.Y., Hsu, M.E.: Does emotion matter? An investigation into the relationship between emotions and science learning outcomes in a game-based learning environment. Br. J. Edu. Technol. **51**(6), 2233–2251 (2020)
6. Greipl, S., et al.: When the brain comes into play: neurofunctional correlates of emotions and reward in game-based learning. Comput. Hum. Behav. **125**, 106946 (2021)
7. Rieber, L.P., Noah, D.: Games, simulations, and visual metaphors in education: antagonism between enjoyment and learning. Educ. Media Int. **45**(2), 77–92 (2008)
8. Sawyer, R.K., Henriksen, D.: Explaining Creativity: The Science of Human Innovation. Oxford University Press (2012)
9. Plass, J.L., Kaplan, U.: Emotional design in digital media for learning. In: Emotions, Technology, Design, and Learning, pp. 131–161. Academic Press (2016)
10. Shoemaker, S.J., Wolf, M.S., Brach, C.: The patient education materials assessment tool (PEMAT) and user's guide. https://www.ahrq.gov/health-literacy/patient-education/pemat.html. Accessed 16 July 2024
11. Du Bois, J.W.: The stance triangle. Stancetaking Discourse Subjectivity Eval. Interact. **164**(3), 139–182 (2007)
12. Sundararajan, L., Ting, R.S.-K., Hsieh, S.-K., Kim, S.-H.: Religion, cognition, and emotion: what can automated text analysis tell us about culture? Hum. Psychol. **50**(2), 213–233 (2022)
13. Lutz, B., Adam, M., Feuerriegel, S., Pröllochs, N., Neumann, D.: Which linguistic cues make people fall for fake news? A comparison of cognitive and affective processing. Proc. ACM Hum. Comput. Interact. **8**(CSCW1), 1–22 (2024)
14. Wallot, S.: Multidimensional cross-recurrence quantification analysis (MdCRQA)–a method for quantifying correlation between multivariate time-series. Multivar. Behav. Res.. Behav. Res. **54**(2), 173–191 (2019)
15. Gao, N., Shao, W., Rahaman, M.S., Salim, F.D.: N-gage: predicting in-class emotional, behavioural and cognitive engagement in the wild. Proc. ACM Interact. Mobile Wearable Ubiquitous Technol. **4**(3), 1–26 (2020)
16. Wallot, S., Leonardi, G.: Analyzing multivariate dynamics using cross-recurrence quantification analysis (CRQA), diagonal-cross-recurrence profiles (DCRP), and multidimensional recurrence quantification analysis (MDRQA)–a tutorial in R. Front. Psychol. **9**, 2232 (2018)
17. Main, A., Paxton, A., Dale, R.: An exploratory analysis of emotion dynamics between mothers and adolescents during conflict discussions. Emotion **16**(6), 913 (2016)
18. Lei, H., Wang, C., Chiu, M.M., Chen, S.: Do educational games affect students' achievement emotions? Evidence from a meta-analysis. J. Comput. Assist. Learn.Comput. Assist. Learn. **38**(4), 946–959 (2022)
19. Luo, J., Yu, R.: Follow the heart or the head? The interactive influence model of emotion and cognition. Front. Psychol. **6**, 573 (2015)
20. Park, B., Brünken, R.: The rhythm method: a new method for measuring cognitive load—an experimental dual-task study. Appl. Cogn. Psychol.Cogn. Psychol. **29**(2), 232–243 (2015)
21. Abdul Jabbar, A.I., Felicia, P.: Gameplay engagement and learning in game-based learning: a systematic review. Rev. Educ. Res. **85**(4), 740–779 (2015)

The Role of Feedback Type and Task Performance on Concurrent Emotions and Interest During Game-Based Learning

Elizabeth B. Cloude[1(✉)], Eva Kormann[2], Marco Steiner[2], Antero Lindstedt[1], Kristian Kiili[1], and Manuel Ninaus[2]

[1] Faculty of Education and Culture, Tampere University, 33100 Tampere, Finland
{elizabeth.cloude,antero.lindstedt,kristian.kiili}@tuni.fi
[2] Department of Psychology, University of Graz, Graz, Austria
{e.kormann,marc.steiner,manuel.ninaus}@edu.uni-graz.at

Abstract. Building adaptive game-based learning (GBL) interventions (e.g., immediate feedback) has been a recent effort to maximize learning effectiveness. State-of-the-art algorithms often overlook the concurrent emotions and motivation of individuals and its impact on GBL interventions. This pilot study utilized a 3 (feedback type: results, elaborative, attribution) x 2 (graph type: misleading, non-misleading) within-subjects design with MediaWatch, a GBL environment built to improve critical graph literacy. At an Austrian university, 41 students' concurrent emotions and motivation were measured using validated surveys immediately after different types of feedback on tasks during GBL. Results showed a significant improvement in graph literacy after GBL. Different types of feedback and task performance influenced concurrent emotions and interest, but individual differences accounted for the largest variability explained in emotions and interest. The findings suggest that within-subject variability is crucial for understanding concurrent emotions and motivation to feedback types and task performance during GBL.

Keywords: Emotions · Motivation · Game-based Learning · Feedback

1 Introduction

Game-based learning (GBL) interventions offer promising solutions for improving critical-literacy skills (e.g., graph literacy) [4]. Using inoculation theory [15], GBL environments (GBLEs) expose individuals to weakened doses of misinformation, while simultaneously scaffolding emotional engagement, motivation, and cognitive skills [5]. GBLEs can be further exploited via adaptive scaffolding, where game features, e.g., feedback, can be customized to meet individual learning needs, thereby enhancing learning effectiveness [21]. However, state-of-the-art algorithms driving adaptive scaffolding primarily target the cognitive aspects of learning [8,26], overlooking the influence of emotions and motivation on learning [8,9,16].

F. Bellotti et al. (Eds.): GALA 2024, LNCS 15348, pp. 101–111, 2025.
https://doi.org/10.1007/978-3-031-78269-5_10

Negative emotions can hinder learning and motivation to persist [11,27], while positive emotions can enhance learning and encourage continued engagement [10,11]. A GBL study [17] found that more positive emotions co-occurred with more interest, suggesting emotions and motivation have interdependent relations [9]. Thus, building adaptive GBL interventions that consider emotions and motivational on learning is essential.

1.1 Feedback, Emotions, and Motivation

Feedback on tasks can evoke different emotions and motivation that influence persistence and engagement [12,18]. According to control-value theory (CVT), the attributions an individual makes affects their motivation, emotions, and learning [7]. In response, feedback strategies have been developed to scaffold specific learning processes [6]. In its simplest form, feedback provides task evaluation results: correct vs. incorrect. Studies find that feedback on failed (FOF) tasks is often associated with negative emotions, while feedback on success (FOS) is associated with positive emotions [13]. Whether different emotional responses to FOS or FOF influenced motivation and learning is understudied.

A common feedback strategy is elaborative, providing detailed information about the task evaluation. First, the outcome expectation (standard) and the answer selected is highlighted. Next, hints, examples, and next steps for future improvement are provided [6]. Studies find that when individuals receive elaborative feedback, they demonstrated more learning compared to only feedback of task results [20]. Attribution-based (AB) feedback is another strategy grounded in CVT [7] that strategically directs an individual's attention to the cause of the evaluation. AB highlights internal vs. external attributions that support positive emotions and motivation [14,19]. E.g., if an individual received FOS, the evaluation is attributed to an internal cause, while FOF to an external cause.

[14] found that subjects who received AB feedback outperformed and reported more positive emotions than those receiving results feedback. Another study [19] found that elaborative feedback with AB elements was associated with more learning strategies than only received elaborative feedback. However, both groups used more learning strategies than those who received no feedback. More questions remain about the role of emotions and motivation in response to different types of feedback and its influence on GBL outcomes. In some cases, negative emotions that arise from FOF can motivate individuals to overcome challenges, depending on how they attribute the causes of their performance and whether it is within their control [7,22,23]. Other limitations exist as few studies account for individual variability in emotions and motivation and its influence on GBL outcomes. Prior studies and CVT [7] emphasize that individual characteristics shape the attributions about a task result, which in turn influence the nature, timing, and intensity of emotions and motivation.

1.2 Current Study and Novel Contributions

Emotions and motivation to feedback and its influence on critical-literacy skill development is understudied. The challenges stem from methods for measuring emotions and motivation. Objective, continuous data are common approaches for measuring emotions (e.g., electrodermal [18], neuro-imaging [27]), and while these data provide useful insights, inferences are made about emotions and motivation without input from the individual's subjective experience. This study provides novel insights into concurrent emotions and motivation to feedback during GBL in two ways. First, emotions and motivation were collected using validated surveys to capture the subjective experience following different feedback: AB, elaborative, and results. Second, we studied the role of individual differences on concurrent emotions and motivation after feedback during GBL [9].

2 Methods

2.1 Sample and Materials

Forty-one students ($n = 41$; $M^{\text{Age}} = 23.73$ ($SD = 3.23$); 62% female) enrolled at a University in Austria completed an online study with a GBLE called MediaWatch. Subjects were removed if they did not complete the surveys before and after GBL. One subject was removed for starting the game twice and 2 subjects were removed as they completed the GBL tasks in English, but were instructed to complete them in German. The study lasted roughly 60 - 90 min. After completing the study, subjects could voluntarily enroll in a raffle prize. Pre-/post-surveys were administered before and after GBL to assess graph-literacy skills. Graph-literacy skills were measured using a validated, 13-item instrument [2]. After each GBL task, emotions and motivation were measured using the Emotions & Values (EV) survey [1], a 5-pt Likert scale (*1=Strongly Disagree, 5=Strongly Agree*) capturing anger, boredom, surprise, neutral, confusion, interest, and eureka (e.g., "Right now I feel bored"). Prior work has found a high agreement between facial expressed emotions and EV data (75.6%) [1].

2.2 MediaWatch

MediaWatch is a web-based, GBLE grounded in inoculation theory [15][1]. Subjects are exposed to misleading graphs to build critical graph-literacy skills [5]. On an island called Sahramao, subjects act as a fact-checker to identify misleading graphs marketed by corporations. Subjects must complete 12 graph-reading tasks; each graph-reading task includes a question, a 4-option, multiple-choice answer, and a graph representation. Six of the 12 graphs are misleading, while the rest are non-misleading. Misleading graphs had one of many manipulations, including x- or y-axis scale-/text-spatial conflicts [2,3] (Fig. 1).

[1] https://webpages.tuni.fi/gamelab/2022/mediawatch/.

2.3 Experimental Design

A 2 (graph type: misleading, non-misleading) x 3 (feedback: results, elaborative, AB) block-based, within-subject design was used. Three blocks were used and each block consisted of 4 graphs (2 misleading, 2 non-misleading). Graph type was randomized for each block and subjects received immediate feedback regardless of correctness. The feedback varied for each block: 1) evaluation results, 2) elaborative, and 3) AB feedback (Fig. 1). The results feedback only stated whether their answer was correct or incorrect. For block two, the elaborative message was designed using to the Feedback Strategies Framework [6]. The feedback highlighted (a) the gap between their performance and the standard [6], (b) the answer selected, and (c) a recommendation for how to improve in the future. For all misleading graphs, hints were provided where the misleading graph and its corrected version were presented along with the feedback message (see Fig. 1). In block 3, AB feedback was designed similarly to elaborative but was grounded in CVT [7]. In this case, at least one attribution of the result was highlighted to elicit a positive emotional-motivational response [14]. For FOF, subjects competence was highlighted and the failure was attributed to an external cause, while FOS was attributed to an internal cause. After feedback was provided, EV measures were immediately administered.

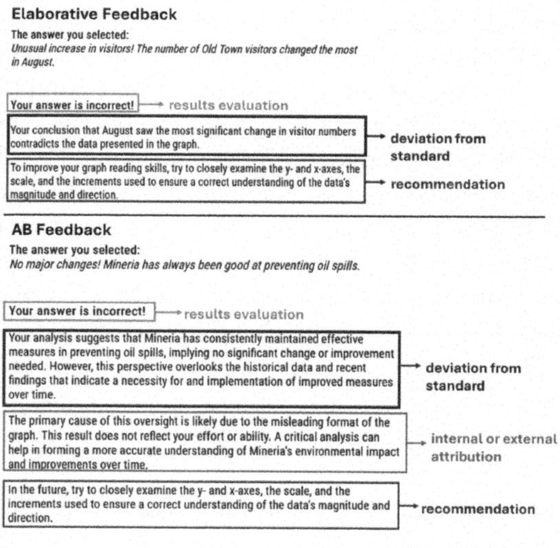

Fig. 1. Elaborative and AB feedback (left); misleading graph hint example for y-axis scale-spatial conflict (right).

2.4 Procedure

Subjects were recruited via email with university listservs. A survey link was shared, which could be accessed using a laptop, where individuals could enroll in the study. Once the link was selected, subjects were directed to the study information. If they decided to participate, they received a random key code. Next, they completed a pre-test survey and were then directed to the game. During GBL, they were presented with brief instructions and then they were asked to complete multiple graph tasks. Once subjects completed the tasks, a post-test survey was immediately administered. After the post-test survey, subjects were thanked and offered enrollment in a raffle.

3 Results

3.1 Are There Differences in Graph-Literacy Skills Before and After GBL with MediaWatch?

A paired Wilcoxon signed rank test was conducted with a one-sided test (we expected improvement in graph-literacy skills after GBL with MediaWatch [5]). Results showed that there was significant improvement in graph-literacy scores from before GBL ($Med = 81.25$, $SD = 7.86$) to after GBL ($Med = 87.5$, $SD = 9.35$), $V = 36.5$, $p = .0006698$, Cohen's $d = .591$. The findings confirmed our hypothesis, where we expected graph-literacy skill improvement after GBL [5].

3.2 Are There Differences in Task Performance During GBL Between Feedback Types (Results, Elaborative, AB) and Graph Types (Misleading, Non-Misleading)?

A standard logistic regression was fitted to assess the relationships between feedback and graph types on task performance during GBL (correct vs. incorrect). The results showed that there were significant, negative relations between task performance and graph type (non-misleading) ($\beta = 1.15$, $p < .01$), $\chi^2(3) = 20.07$, $p < .01$, McFadden $R^2 = .05$. This finding suggests that the odds of an correct answer was approximately .32 times (or 68%) higher when the graph was non-misleading compared to when the graph was misleading. There were no relations with feedback and task performance ($ps < .05$). It is important to note that the model explained 5% of variability in task performance, leaving 95% unexplained by other factors. The findings partially supported our hypothesis, where we expected graph types and feedback to influence task performance [4,5].

3.3 Are There Relations Between Emotions and Motivation, Task Performance (Correct, Incorrect), Feedback Types (Results, Elaborative, AB), and Graph Types (misleading, Non-misleading)?

Cumulative link mixed models (CLMM) make it possible to analyze ordinal responses while allowing the use of random effects [24]. To examine whether feedback, graph type, and task performance were associated with concurrent emotions and motivation, a CLMM with a LaPlace approximation was calculated with a random effects term to partition within-subject variability in dependent variables over time. A separate model was calculated for each dependent variable: anger, boredom, surprise, neutral, confusion, interest, and eureka, using the 'clmm' function with the ordinal package [25] in RStudio [Version 4.3.2] [28]. Results are presented in Table 1 due to page restrictions. Follow-up pairwise Tukey tests were calculated for all significant predictors with a false discovery rate post hoc correction. The post hoc pairwise Tukey results are in Table 2.

Overall, the findings suggest that concurrent emotions and interest were significantly related to feedback, except for anger. Bored responses were highest after AB (compared to elaborative and results), while surprise, confusion, and interest were lowest after AB feedback (compared to results and elaborative feedback). Eureka responses were highest after elaborative compared to AB feedback. This result did not support our hypothesis where we expected more positive emotions and interest after AB. In contrast, surprise was the only emotion related to graph type. More surprised responses were higher after misleading than non-misleading graphs, which is to be expected since misleading graphs had manipulations. In general, there were positive and significant relationships with anger, surprise, and confused responses with incorrect answers, but neutral responses were higher after correct than incorrect answers. Across the models, the fixed effects (feedback, graph type, and task performance) explained at least 5 - 10% variability in emotional and motivational states. In contrast, the random effects explained 40 - 70% of variability in emotional and motivational states, suggesting within-subject variability played a large role in concurrent emotions and motivation during GBL.

4 Discussion

This study examined concurrent emotions and motivation to different feedback types (AB, elaborative, results) for misleading and non-misleading graphs with MediaWatch and whether graph-literacy skills improved after GBL. Research question one (RQ1) suggested there was significant graph literacy skill improvement after GBL, supporting our hypothesis and prior findings [5]. RQ2 investigated the effect of graph type and feedback on task performance during game-based learning (GBL). The results suggested that non-misleading graphs were associated with a higher likelihood of correct answers compared to misleading graphs. Yet, we did not observe any relations between feedback and task performance, which contradicts prior work [19,20]. A possible explanation for this result could be due to the block-based design of the study. Subjects were exposed to all feedback messages across the GBL tasks, which may have diminished the impact of feedback on task performance over time, unlike a controlled experimental condition. Future studies should leverage experimental designs to investigate the role of different types of feedback on task performance during GBL.

In RQ3, we examined whether task performance, feedback, and graph types were associated with concurrent emotions and motivation during GBL. Results

Table 1. CLMM results.

	Anger			Boredom			Surprise		
Fixed Effects	OR	95% CI	p	OR	95% CI	p	OR	95% CI	p
Feedback (E)	0.67	0.45-0.98	.039	0.52	0.39-0.68	<.001	1.41	1.04-1.91	.028
Feedback (R)	0.62	0.42-0.91	.015	0.34	0.25-0.45	<.001	1.72	1.27-2.32	<.001
Graph type (NM)	0.89	0.64-1.23	.472	1.20	0.96-1.50	.102	0.76	0.59-0.98	.033
TP (INC)	4.02	2.67-6.05	<.001	1.17	0.83-1.65	.358	2.84	2.05-3.94	<.001
Random Effects	σ^2	τ_{00}	ICC	σ^2	τ_{00}	ICC	σ^2	τ_{00}	ICC
Individual	1.00	1.09	.52	1.00	3.17	.76	1.00	0.95	.49
Model Diagnostics									
n	41			41			41		
Observations	492			492			492		
Fixed R^2	0.121			0.047			0.105		
Total R^2	0.580			0.772			0.540		
	Neutral			Confusion			Interest		
Fixed Effects	OR	95% CI	p	OR	95% CI	p	OR	95% CI	p
Feedback (E)	2.08	1.62-2.69	<.001	1.26	0.91-1.75	.162	2.24	1.71-2.95	<.001
Feedback (R)	2.42	1.87-3.13	<.001	1.50	1.09-2.07	.014	3.74	2.82-4.96	<.001
Graph type (NM)	1.22	0.99-1.50	.065	0.81	0.62-1.05	.116	1.06	0.85-1.31	.625
TP (INC)	0.47	0.34-0.64	<.001	5.13	3.63-7.25	<.001	0.80	0.57-1.11	.183
Random Effects	σ^2	τ_{00}	ICC	σ^2	τ_{00}	ICC	σ^2	τ_{00}	ICC
Individual	1.00	2.04	.67	1.00	0.81	.45	1.00	3.14	.76
Model Diagnostics									
n	41			41			41		
Observations	492			492			492		
Fixed R^2	0.071			0.180			0.067		
Total R^2	0.694			0.548			0.775		
	Eureka								
Fixed Effects	OR	95% CI	p						
Feedback (E)	1.45	1.07-1.95	.015						
Feedback (R)	1.35	1.00-1.82	.050						
Graph type (NM)	0.89	0.69-1.13	.331						
TP (INC)	1.08	0.75-1.54	.682						
Random Effects	σ^2	τ_{00}	ICC						
Individual	1.00	2.32	.70						
Model Diagnostics									
n	41								
Observations	492								
Fixed R^2	0.009								
Total R^2	0.701								

Note. Feedback(E)/(R) = Elaborative/Results; Graph type (NM) = Non-misleading; TP(INC) = Task Performance Incorrect

Table 2. Significant findings from pairwise Tukey tests for various models.

Model	Predictor	Comparison	M	p
Anger	Task Performance	Incorrect - Correct	1.83 - 1.18	< .0001
Boredom	Feedback	AB - Elaborative	2.89 - 2.43	< .0001
		AB - Results	2.89 - 2.09	< .001
		Elaborative - Results	2.43 - 2.09	.0061
Surprise	Feedback	Results - AB	1.83 - 1.48	.0011
	Graph Type	Misleading - Non-misleading	1.78 - 1.52	.033
	Task Performance	Incorrect - Correct	2.57 - 1.5	< .0001
Neutral	Task Performance	Correct - Incorrect	3.32 - 2.64	< .0001
	Feedback	Results - AB	3.46 - 2.83	< .0001
Confusion	Feedback	Results - AB	1.67 - 1.41	.0373
	Task Performance	Incorrect - Correct	2.64 - 1.35	< .0001
Interest	Feedback	Results - AB	2.96 - 2.09	< .0001
		Elaborative - AB	2.59 - 2.09	< .0001
		Results - Elaborative	2.96 - 2.59	.0003
Eureka	Feedback	Elaborative - AB	1.87 - 1.66	.0406

showed that the effect of feedback was significantly related to concurrent emotions and interest, with the exception of anger. Boredom was the highest and interest was the lowest after AB compared to elaborative and results feedback, which is contradictory to prior work [7,14,19]. Surprise, neutral, and confused responses were significantly higher after results compared to AB feedback. Eureka was significantly higher after elaborative compared to AB feedback. Our findings partially support prior studies, where there were less positive emotions and motivation after results feedback (possibly explaining the higher confusion). In general, there were less positive emotions and interest after AB compared to results and elaborative feedback. A possible explanation could again be due to an ordering effect caused by the study design. In block 3, individuals reported the most boredom compared to block 2 and 1. This suggests that there was an increase in boredom and decrease in interest across the order of the blocks. In terms of task performance, there were significantly more negative emotions after incorrect compared to correct answers, where there was more anger and confusion after incorrect, but more surprise and neutral responses after correct answers compared to incorrect answers. The findings support our hypothesis, where we expected more confusion and anger after incorrect than correct answers [7,13].

Our study has limitations. First, relying solely on self-report data to measure concurrent emotions and motivation is problematic as individuals may not always be aware of their emotions or motivation. Future studies should utilizing mixed-mulitmodal methods, where both subjective (e.g., think-/emote-alouds, surveys) and objective measures (e.g., facial recognition, electrodermal activity, field observations) are used. Second, the block order design of the study may have influenced emotions and motivational responses. Future studies should consider emotional and motivational changes as well as an control group to account for the possible ordering effect of the feedback blocks on emotions and motivation.

Acknowledgements. This study was funded by the European Union ([EU] ID No. 101105874). Views and opinions expressed are however those of the author(s) only and do not necessarily reflect those of the EU.

References

1. Harley, J., Bouchet, F., Hussain, M., Azevedo, R., Calvo, R.: A multi-componential analysis of emotions during complex learning with an intelligent multi-agent system. Comp. Hum. Behav. **48**, 615–625 (2015)
2. Galesic, M., Garcia-Retamero, R.: Graph literacy: a cross-cultural comparison. Med. Decis. Making **31**(3), 444–457 (2011)
3. Okan, Y., Garcia-Retamero, R., Galesic, M., Cokely, E.: When higher bars are not larger quantities: on individual differences in the use of spatial information in graph comprehension. Spat. Cogn. Comput. **12**(2–3), 195–218 (2012)
4. Kiili, K. Siuko, J. Ninaus, M.: Tackling misinformation with games: a systematic literature review. Interact. Learn. Environ. 1–16 (2024)
5. Siuko, J. Cloude, E. Kiili, K.: Improving critical graph reading skills: the potential might lie in game-based learning. In: DSouza, P., Bujić, M. Xi, N., Hamari, J. (eds.) Proceedings of 8th International GamiFIN Conference, vol. 3669, pp. 79–87 (2024)
6. Narciss, S., et al.: Exploring feedback and student characteristics relevant for personalizing feedback strategies. Comput. Educ. **71**, 56–76 (2014)
7. Pekrun, R.: The control-value theory of achievement emotions: assumptions, corollaries, and implications for educational research and practice. Edu. Psych. Rev. **18**, 315–341 (2006)
8. Aleven, V., McLaughlin, E., Glenn, R.A., Koedinger, K.: Instruction based on adaptive learning technologies. Handb. Res. Learn. Instr. **2**, 522–560 (2016)
9. Pekrun, R., Marsh, H.: Research on situated motivation and emotion: progress and open problems. Learn. Instr. **81**, 101664 (2022)
10. Goetz, T. Hall, N.: Emotion and achievement in the classroom. In: Hattie, J., Anderman, E.M. (eds.) International Guide to Student Achievement, pp. 192–195. Routledge (2013)
11. Loderer, K., Pekrun, R., Lester, J.: Beyond cold technology: a systematic review and meta-analysis on emotions in technology-based learning environments. Learn. Instr. **70**, 101162 (2020)
12. Peterson, E., Brown, G., Jun, M.: Achievement emotions in higher education: exploring emotions across an assessment event. Cont. Edu. Psych. **42**, 82–96 (2015)
13. Lipnevich, A., Murano, D., Krannich, M., Goetz, T.: Should I grade or should I comment: links among feedback, emotions, and performance. Learn. Individ. Differ. **89**, 102020 (2021)
14. Schrader, C. Grassinger, R.: Tell me that I can do it better: the effect of attributional feedback from a learning technology on achievement emotions and performance and the moderating role of individual adaptive reactions to errors. Comp. Edu. **161**, 104028 (2021)

15. Ecker, U.K.H., et al.: The psychological drivers of misinformation belief and its resistance to correction. Nat. Rev. Psychol. **1**(1), 13–29 (2022)
16. Cloude, E.B., Taub, M., Lester, J., Azevedo, R.: The role of achievement goal orientation on metacognitive process use in game-based learning. In: Isotani, S., Millán, E., Ogan, A., Hastings, P., McLaren, B., Luckin, R. (eds.) AIED 2019. LNCS (LNAI), vol. 11626, pp. 36–40. Springer, Cham (2019). https://doi.org/10.1007/978-3-030-23207-8_7
17. Kiili, K., Juho, S., Cloude, E., Dindar, M.: Demystifying the relations of motivation and emotions in game-based learning: insights from co-occurrence network analysis. Int. J. Serious Games **10**(4), 93–112 (2023)
18. Horvers, A., Molenaar, I.V., Der West, H., Bosse, T., Lazonder, A.: Multimodal measurements enhance insights into emotional responses to immediate feedback. Front. Psych. **14**, 1294386 (2024)
19. De Sixte, R. Mañá, A. Ávila, V. Sánchez, E.: Warm elaborated feedback: exploring its benefits on post-feedback behaviour. Edu. Psychol. **40**(9), 1094–1112 (2020)
20. Van der Kleij, F., Feskens, R., Eggen, T.: Effects of feedback in a computer-based learning environment on students' learning outcomes: a meta-analysis. Rev. Educ. Res. **85**(4), 475–511 (2015)
21. Koskinen, A., McMullen, J., Hannula-Sormunen, M., Ninaus, M., Kiili, K.: The strength and direction of the difficulty adaptation affect situational interest in game-based learning. Comp. Edu. **194**, 104694 (2023)
22. Vogl, E. Pekrun, R.: Emotions that matter to achievement: student feelings about assessment. In: Handbook of Human and Social Conditions in Assessment, pp. 111–128. Routledge (2016)
23. Lim, L.-A., et al.: Students' perceptions of, and emotional responses to, personalised learning analytics-based feedback: an exploratory study of four courses. Assess Eval. High Edu. **46**(3), 339–359 (2021)
24. Agresti, A.: Categorical Data Analysis, vol. 792. Wiley (2012)
25. Christensen, R.: Ordinal-regression models for ordinal data. R Package Vers. **10**(2019), 54 (2019)
26. Chen, C., Law, V., Huang, K.: Adaptive scaffolding and engagement in digital game-based learning. Educ. Tech. Res. Dev. **71**(4), 1785–1798 (2023)
27. Lei, H., Wang, C., Chiu, M., Chen, S.: Do educational games affect students' achievement emotions? Evidence from a meta-analysis. J. Comp. Assist. Learn. **38**(4), 946–959 (2022)
28. R Core Team: R: a language and environment for statistical computing. R Foundation for Statistical Computing (2023)

On the Design of Gamified Learning Analytics for Immersive Virtual Reality Games

Zacharoula Papamitsiou[1(✉)], Sobah Abbas Petersen[1], Chrysoula Psyllaki[2], Gunnar Lamvik[1], and Hans Torvatn[1]

[1] SINTEF Digital, 7031 Trondheim, Norway
{zacharoula.papamitsiou,sobah.petersen,gunnar.lamvik, hans.torvatn}@sintef.no
[2] SQLearn, 18536 Pireaus, Greece

Abstract. Immersive Virtual Reality (IVR) games are gaining popularity for acquiring practical skills and tacit knowledge in formal education and professional contexts. Enhancing such games with learning analytics (LA) can add value to the learning process. However, research on the design of LA for IVR games is limited. This paper launches *gamified LA as game elements 'by design'*. It presents a process to design LA that (a) provide the most insightful information about learners' behavior and performance to support self-monitoring and trigger reflection, and (b) inherit game properties from the IVR game to improve interactivity and promote learners' engagement. We adopted basic principles of human-centric design and explored a space of game elements ideas to inspire desired outcomes. We involved 55 participants (pupils, teachers, domain experts, UX-designers, LA experts) in multiple rounds of workshops to co-design gamified LA that are educationally meaningful and relevant and at the same time intuitive and fit the playful nature of the IVR game. This paper explicates the design process and presents the results from the evaluation of the design outcomes.

Keywords: human-centered design · gamified learning analytics · immersive virtual reality · practical skills · seamanship · vocational education

1 Introduction

The integration of Immersive Virtual Reality (IVR) into educational settings can foster truly student-centered learning experiences [32] via autonomous, exploration-based, active learning paradigms, that promote learning by doing, experiential learning, and the flow of learning [26, 30, 32]. In Vocational Education and Training and professional contexts, IVR affords realistic simulations of real-world scenarios in a highly intuitive, cost-effective, and memorable environment [27, 31], without real-life risks.

This safe and controlled environment helps trainees acquire hands-on experience, build their competences, and apply their knowledge [31]. IVR allows trainees to explore complex concepts and processes, rehearse specific sequences with high resemblance to their real-world counterparts [17, 31], and receive immediate feedback [5, 17]. Trainees

A. Schönbohm et al. (Eds.): GALA 2024, LNCS 15348, pp. 112–122, 2025.
https://doi.org/10.1007/978-3-031-78269-5_11

can engage in situations that are difficult to observe in the physical world due to inaccessibility, cost and real-life dangers, or ethical issues, among others, making learning possible to anyone, anywhere, anytime. Such situated learning experiences can enhance trainees' engagement and creativity [10] and improve attention [24].

To achieve the desirable learning outcomes, user interactivity with the IVR environment is crucial. IVR as a learning platform has two primary affordances: *sense of presence* and *agency* [20, 25]. Sense of presence is determined by *immersion* and *interaction* and is key for the enjoyment of the learning activities [5, 18]; agency is the *degree of freedom and control* that learners have in order to perform meaningful actions in the learning space [21, 23]. Interactivity facilitates both sense of presence and agency.

Games and gamification are natural ways to achieve high levels of interactivity [7], as they are designed to provide players with a sense of identity and autonomy that can prolong engagement and motivation [27]. Integrating game-like elements (e.g., rewards, achievements) in the IVR learning environment [7, 13, 28], and exploiting affordances stemming from interactivity (i.e., engagement, enjoyment) can support the development of physical and mental capabilities and boost knowledge [7, 22, 28].

However, adding gaming interactivity and educational content in an IVR intervention cannot guarantee its effectiveness. It is necessary to line-up the technological, gaming, and pedagogical characteristics of the intervention with the desired learning outcomes and the learning design [3, 32, 34]. IVR and games bring their affordances in the educational context, yet, achieving the alignment that will yield improved learning outcomes, depends on considering the learning design and enhancing the educational process [30, 34]. Learning Analytics (LA) can offer insights by visualizing learning traces and support decision-making in digitally enhanced game-based and IVR learning environments due to their predictive capabilities and by creating feedback opportunities [8, 14, 15]. Although LA have been acknowledged for supporting the learning design [29], yet, research in the direction of enhancing the IVR games is, at the moment, sparse.

Despite their potential, our knowledge on the design and integration of LA in IVR educational games is limited. Thus, this study was motivated by the following research question (RQ): *How can we design and seamlessly integrate LA in IVR games to support learning and promote interactivity for enhancing sense of presence and agency?*

The overall objective of this study is to address this RQ and provide a generalizable and scalable method to design LA that are fitting for and seamlessly enhance environments with special characteristics and additional affordances, by *considering those as design requirements.* On that basis, we aimed at a design process that is easy to adapt and apply to other educational contexts that have similarities with either IVR or games.

2 Related Work

Research in LA primarily focused on exploiting learner data to study learning performance, behavioral/emotional/cognitive aspects, engagement patterns, and self-regulation among others, and drive interventions accordingly [9, 29]. Another trend concerns approaches for designing LA. The early designs usually followed top-down processes. Researchers and developers were making decisions in advance, without considering theories in human-computer interaction, learning science, and information visualization [1, 11, 19], and the outcomes did not always meet user needs and expectations.

Emphasis is now shifted on co-creation practices that involve the end-users in all phases of the LA design, integrating experiences and values of the end-users, thus, aiming to improve usability and usefulness [4, 11], and indirectly, acceptance and adoption. Common design practices employ cards (e.g., [1, 6, 35]) or involve users in participatory workshops (e.g., [11, 12]). Those human-centric paradigms aim to guide the design by mapping which indicators are good for which data types and for which task, to get better insights, enabling a shift from a data-first to a people-first approach [1, 4, 6, 12].

Although human-centricity and pedagogical aspects are evident in those attempts, the particularities of the learning environment *per se* are not considered. This is rather important when designing LA for environments such as games and IVR, as additional requirements emerge from the affordances of these environments (e.g., playfulness, sense of presence, agency). Such requirements must be embedded in the design of LA [2] to avoid noise or disruption of the learning process. The challenge is to design LA that are educationally meaningful and useful, and fit the playful nature of the IVR game.

As a response to this challenge, the novelty of our approach is to *think of LA as game elements*. LA are not game elements '*by design*'. Gamifying the LA, i.e., adding affordances that invoke the same psychological experiences as games do [36] can have a powerful impact on learning achievements, and cognitive, motivational, and behavioral engagement [33]. Gamified LA (*referred to as 'GLA' from this point on*) have two dimensions: (a) a learning dimension that is inherent, carried out by *gamifying the content* to ensure that LA are still about learning, and (b) an interactivity dimension that is inherited from the IVR game, added by *gamifying the structure* to ensure that LA carry properties of the game for the seamless integration in it. GLA are fundamentally different from gamification LA. Gamification LA are *analytics about the use of gamification elements* in a non-gaming learning environment, focusing on measuring the effectiveness of gamification elements (e.g., badges, leaderboards) within the learning environment and assessing their impact on student engagement and performance. GLA are *gaming elements per se*, i.e., organic components of a *gaming* learning environment to support the player to perform tasks (e.g., a virtual 'smartwatch' placed on the wrist of the player to inform the player about attempts/time-spent to solve the task correctly).

GLA are more than gamification elements; they are active elements of the game itself, and thus, their design is a delicate process. Game attributes (in serious games) have the intention to directly affect learning, and, thus, each indicator needs to be seen through game design principles in terms of mechanics, dynamics, and aesthetics [2].

This paper presents a step-by-step, coherent approach for co-designing GLA. For each step, we outline the objectives, questions, methods and participants, as well as outcomes, to highlight the roles of diverse contributors to consistent design outcomes.

3 Methods

3.1 Overall Research Design and Participants

This study explicates a step-by-step process for designing a set of GLA, i.e., the gaming visual elements and interaction modes, for an IVR game, and presents the results from their empirical evaluation. In line with principles for designing playful and immersive systems [2, 7, 13, 36] and with current trends to design LA [4, 11, 12], we adopted human-centered design, and involved 55 participants (pupils, teachers, LA experts, VR experts, UX designers, game experts, instructional designers, domain experts) in workshops, focus groups, testing, and critique, from April 2023 to March 2024. The approach (Fig. 1) builds on participants' interdisciplinarity to foster engagement.

Three overarching questions guided the research design: **(a)** *What do the users expect?* **(b)** *What is technically feasible?* **(c)** *What value is delivered?* To address those question, we followed an iterative approach of four phases that aimed to: (1) understand the problem-space and set the foundations; (2) explore the solutions-space and co-design alternatives; (3) test the solutions and refine the designs; (4) evaluate the final solution and provide feedback. The first question governed phases 1 and 2; the second was explored across phases 1 to 3; the third was probed in phases 3 and 4.

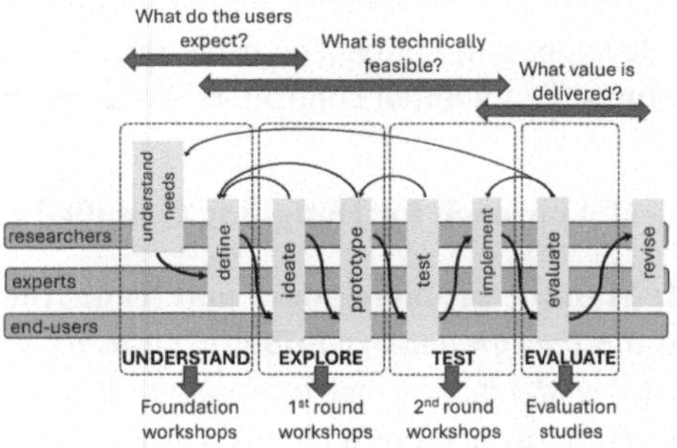

Fig. 1. The overall methodological approach.

Each phase had its own objectives, questions, methods, and participants who were recruited on the basis of their expertise and expected contribution to the activities. For activities that involved pupils and teachers, permission was granted by authorized personnel (i.e., the schools' headmasters), and *no personal data was collected at any stage.* The pupils that were involved were 16–17 years old (upper secondary maritime education) with some experience in games/gaming, and that was a criterion for recruitment. Participation was totally voluntary and free of special rewards or external motivation.

3.2 The IVR Game

An IVR game (available here) provided the learning space in which the pupils would acquire, develop, and retain practical skills and tacit knowledge (i.e., seamanship). The game consists of four scenarios that simulate real-life maritime situations related to on-board safety. Each scenario incorporates realistic images, sound, and motion. The pupils have to complete a set of tasks and activities, following instructions and highlighted interactions, followed by practice ('exams') to test the acquired skills and knowledge (Fig. 2). The pupils can monitor the status and achievements, as well as their progress.

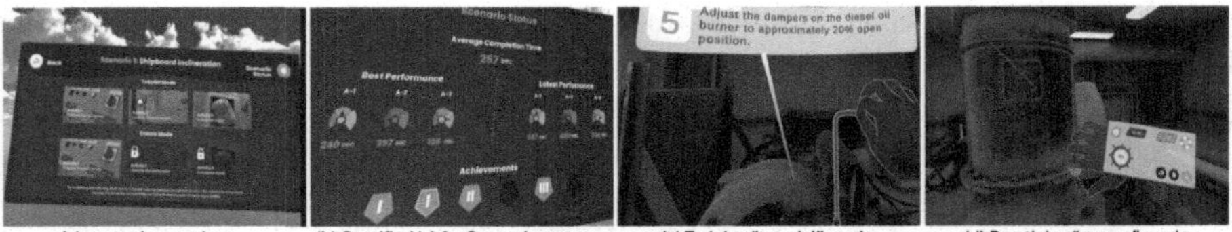

(a) scenario overview (b) Gamified LA for Scenario status (c) Training "tutorial" mode (d) Practicing "exams" mode

Fig. 2. IVR Game Scenario 1: (a) overview (b) status (c) tutorial mode (d) exams mode.

The learning objectives are in line with the official maritime education curriculum. The primary learning materials and game content were developed in the learning design phase, in collaboration with instructional designers, maritime experts, and pedagogical experts, and were deployed in the IVR game. Here, we focus on the design of secondary elements, i.e., the GLA, to complement the primary learning environment.

The IVR game had been developed in Unity prior to this study and was available as material for this study. The GLA were administered on Oculus Quest 2 Head Mounted Displays (HDMs) and developed in Unity. The users interact with the artifacts in the IVR game via hand gestures, i.e., without controllers, for a natural experience.

3.3 The Methodological Approach for Designing Gamified LA

Phase 1 - Understand: Map the problem-space and frame the problem.

Objective: Prepare *the background regarding what users would expect and what is technically feasible*: (a) *understand* what information has the educational value to support pupils in their efforts to acquire and retain practical skills in the IVR game (learning goal) and how to deliver this information to suit the IVR game (interactivity goal); (b) *define* properties and game mechanics of the LA (reduce the problem-space).

Questions: Q1.1 What are the goals of gamified LA? What will learners gain? (*understand*) Q1.2 What are the mechanics, and characteristics of gamified LA? (*define*).

Methods & Participants: A divergent style of thinking was promoted in a 2-h physical workshop. A group of three researchers on LA, VR, and instructional design assumed a beginner's mindset and followed a think-aloud protocol to identify pupils' needs and expectations from gamified LA that could address learning and interactivity in the IVR game, exploring Q1.1. A convergent style of thinking was followed in a second 2-h online workshop. A group of six experts (LA/VR/game experts, UX/UI designers, maritime domain experts) joined a brainstorming session for mapping the characteristics and affordances of IVR, games, and LA for practical skills, and extracted a set of game mechanics stemming from them, as candidates for gamified LA in Q1.2.

Outcomes: (a) a typology of LA for supporting learning and interactivity goals; (b) loosely designed digital sketches of gamified LA for IVR games in PowerPoint.

Phase 2 - Explore: Investigate the solutions-space.

Objective: *Collect design ideas that meet what users expect and are technically feasible*: (a) *ideate* possible GLA and visualize solutions that make sense to pupils; (b) *prototype* solutions to experiment with GLA and interaction modes, rethink about their complexity, mechanics, aesthetics, and feasibility, revise sketches, and spark new ideas.

Questions: Q2.1 How might we gamify LA to support learning and interactivity? How could the GLA look like? What game mechanics can support the pedagogical goals of LA? (*ideate*) Q2.2 How complex are the suggested solutions and which of them are realistically feasible? (*prototype*).

Methods & Participants: A divergent-convergent style of thinking was followed in two co-design workshops that adopted an assertion-based gestalt view with a semi-structured design. The workshops took place physically at two maritime schools. Each workshop's duration was 2,5 h and they were facilitated by 5 experts from Phase 1. In total, 14 teachers (8 males and 6 females) and 4 pupils (males) participated. The participants were introduced to main concepts of LA and games, the logic in the digital sketches from Phase 1, and the scenarios in the IVR game, to familiarize with the context and learning objectives. Next, they were invited to reflect on the perceived understandability of the GLA sketches and challenge the assumptions regarding their appropriateness to support learning and interactivity. Participants engaged in brainstorming to loosely visualize their ideas (divergence) and revise the sketches, providing input to Q2.1. They were prompted to explore the visualizations they created and the interaction modes and elaborate on how complex they were (convergence), answering Q2.2.

Outcomes: (a) feedback on the sketches and challenges posed by VR. Authentic designs on paper, including the positions of the LA; (b) low-fidelity prototypes in Miro.

Phase 3 - Test: Try-out the solutions.

Objective: *Demonstrate ideas that are technically feasible and deliver value, and collect early feedback:* (a) *test* the prototypes to discover strengths and weaknesses and seek feedback on the pedagogical soundness of the designs, their relevance for enhancing practical skills and appropriateness for the maritime context, visual consistency, and intuitiveness of functionalities; (b) *implement* the solutions and integrate feedback.

Questions: Q3.1 Do the designed gamified LA successfully support their dual goal? How well do those prototypes reflect and meet the specifications from previous workshops? (*test*) Q3.2 What are the final characteristics of the gamified LA? (*implement*).

Methods & Participants: A '*show, don't tell*' approach utilized think-aloud testing in a semi-structured workshop at a school for 2, 5 h. Three teachers (2 male and 1 female) and 4 pupils (3 male and 1 female) – different from Phase 2 – participated and contributed. The same experts as before synopsized the objectives, scenarios, gamified LA designs, and feedback from previous workshops to provide background. Next, participants were given printed copies of the gamified LA and tasks in a scenario and were prompted to interact with and try the solutions, reflecting on the dual prospects (*value*) facilitated by them. This aimed to understand user experiences, identify ambiguities, uncertainties, and pain points, and design technically feasible solutions to enhance usability, intuitiveness, and satisfaction, addressing Q3.1. The feedback pointed at truly needed improvements of the elements and was integrated in the final solution, in Q3.2.

Outcomes: (a) materials with feedback; (b) final designs implemented in the game.

Phase 4 - Evaluate: Assess the single solution.

Objective: Reflect on the value delivered by the designed GLA by evaluating them.

Questions: Q4.1 What are pupils' attitudes towards using GLA in IVR games for acquiring practical skills/tacit knowledge (learning goal)? Q4.2 What are pupils' perceptions on the usability, clarity, and engagement level of the GLA (interactivity goal)?

Methods & Participants: A mixed-methods evaluation with 29 pupils (7 females and 22 males) – different from Phases 2 & 3 – was conducted in two 3-h physical sessions. Pupils received practical information about the HMDs and a brief demonstration of basic interactions in the game (e.g., how to use their hands to navigate and grab objects, 'tele-transferring' in the VR space, etc.). After logging in the IVR game (using anonymous-IDs), approx. 5 min. Were given to pupils to familiarize with the VR space, locate the interaction functionalities and explore the navigation panels. Then, a '*learning by doing*' training started, and pupils were free to decide the order of the scenarios and repeat them as many times as they wanted to (*agency*). Their interactions were tracked to generate the GLA (progress bars, time-spent, errors, statistics) (*sense of presence*). After completing the training, pupils filled-in a survey about the GLA: (a) learning goals; and (b) interactivity (engagement, enjoyment). Finally, pupils joined a focus group discussion on the efficiency of GLA to achieve the dual goals (Q4.1 and Q4.2).

Outcomes: Evaluation results and comprehensive feedback for revising the designs.

3.4 Data Collection

Qualitative and quantitative data was collected throughout the four phases. The primary data was produced by the participants, i.e., the authentic designs, the reflections and feedback, the survey responses, and focus group discussion. The survey consisted of 8 items to rate using a 5-point Likert-like scale, configuring GAMEFULQUEST [16], to assess pupils' perceived learning and interactivity support provided by the GLA. Additional secondary data was produced by the researchers who were keeping notes.

4 Results

Phases 1 – 3: Fig. 3 demonstrate the evolution of the design from conceptualization to implementation, integrating users' ideas. These results included the selection of visualized information, the reasoning of game mechanics, the placement of the LA elements in the game, and the interaction modes. *Pedagogically*, the GLA are designed to enhance pupils' self-awareness about their errors, time-spent, and progress via monitoring those indicators during an activity and every time they repeat it. From an *interactivity (*i.e., *sense of presence and agency)* perspective, the LA are organic elements of the game, located on the main panel and on the wrist of the player, inspired from the common functionalities of 'smart watches'.

Phase 4: Regarding the evaluation of the GLA, Fig. 4 synopsizes the results. Pupils express their confidence that '*gamified LA elements supported my learning and added value to the training content (Q1)*' (93,10%, N = 27), helping them '*be more effective on reaching learning goals (Q3)*' (89,66%, N = 26), since they '*comprehensively supported*

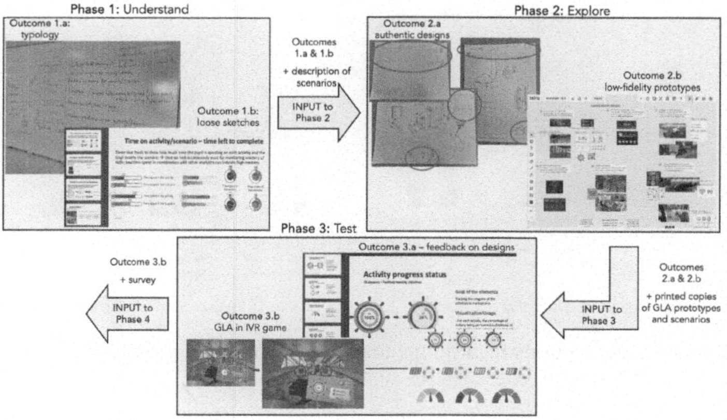

Fig. 3. The evolution and progress of the gamified LA elements' design through Phases 1 – 3.

the educational materials and content (Q2)' (82,76%, N = 24). They agree that '*the gamified LA make the course enjoyable (Q5)*' (93,10%, N = 27) associating success with accomplishment (*Q6*) (89,66%, N = 26). Pupils understand that these elements intent to help them in their learning and acknowledge that they keep them on track (*Q7*) (93, 10%, N = 27), yet the entertainment part is useful (*Q8*) (41, 38%, N = 12).

These results were elaborated and strengthened during the focus group where all pupils agreed that GLA is useful for learning practical skills (*Q4*) for seamanship and claimed that it is a fun way to self-monitor their learning (one of the students made the following comment: '*it was about time serious learning to be fun too!*'). Pupils also explained that '*the gamified LA felt really intuitive*' and the realistic graphics in the scenarios helped them understand the operations they had to do, incentivizing them to try the scenarios more than once, and revealing the authenticity of IVR interactions. Yet, pupils were concerned regarding the understanding of errors and the scaffolding with feedback when errors occurred. Pupils asked for improvements in the feedback mechanisms that would help them realize and acknowledge their errors and deepen their knowledge and skills retention. They also explicitly expressed the wish to contribute to future design initiatives by participating in similar co-design and validation processes, as they believe that they create learning opportunities for them.

5 Discussion and Conclusions

Designing and integrating LA in IVR games to support learning and promote interactivity is pivotal for promoting educational experiences that are instructive, yet engaging and playful [3, 32]. The LA should provide insightful information in line with learning science, comply with principles from information visualization, be intuitive and human-centric [4, 11], and also be playful for their seamless integration in the IVR game. Those challenges inspired us to think of *LA as game elements by design*, and gamify them by following a participatory design process, with multiple stakeholders and experts.

All phases of the design contributed to improving the knowledge on what users expect, what is technically feasible, and what value is delivered (Fig. 1). From Phase 1,

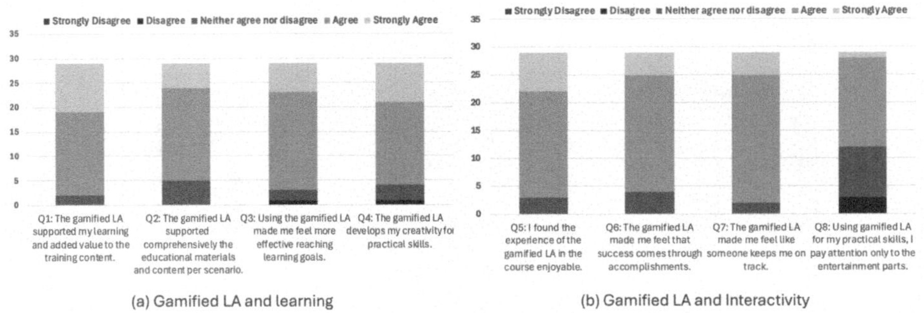

Fig. 4. Pupils' perceptions regarding gamified LA and (a) learning, (b) interactivity.

our priority was to understand pupils' expectations, mindset, and needs, both in learning terms and playful interactions-wise. In Phase 2, the participants featured gameful designs that are intuitive, aligned with pedagogical goals, and relevant for maritime, narrowing the solution-space and resulting in authentic prototypes that targeted pupils' *sense of presence,* in line with [5]. Similarly, in Phase 3, discussion through follow-up questions revealed important factors related to inclusion and semantics relevant for the maritime sector and highlighted the value of following the order of steps to complete a task (*flow*) and having a minimum of distractions or 'noisy' features in the IVR game, improving pupils' *agency* [23]. Throughout Phases 1 to 3, pupils and teachers exhibited high levels of cognitive stimulation and expressed a strong disposition to actively contribute to the design of educational artifacts that create value via gameful experiences. This was reflected in the results from the evaluation in Phase 4, which showed that the GLA can achieve the dual goal to support learning and enhance interactivity.

This study contributes to literature by launching a step-by-step design process for bringing together the worlds of IVR games and LA. The GLA approach that incorporates secondary interactive game elements attributes to the development of soft skills, particularly among younger learners. The GLA promoted pupils' freedom to make meaningful choices (agency) that impact the learning outcome and enhanced their sense of presence through visualizations of meaningful personal learning information. Furthermore, the step-by-step presentation of the approach in this paper makes it totally generalizable, scalable, and reproducible in any given IVR game, yet the final design outcomes (i.e., the GLA), should be expected to be different every time.

Our future work plans involve the deeper and systematic exploration of the effects of GLA on the learning value they create, as well as on enjoyment and continuance intention to use. Additional studies are needed to also explore differences between groups of users with different profiles (e.g., gaming/IVR backgrounds, experience with LA in other learning settings). Those are withing our future research scope.

Acknowledgments. This study was funded by the EEA and Norway Grants (Grant Number: 2022/348154).

Disclosure of Interests. The authors have no competing interests to declare.

References

1. Alvarez, C.P., Martinez-Maldonado, R., Buckingham Shum, S.: LA-DECK: a card-based learning analytics co-design tool. In: Proceedings of the 10th International Conference on Learning Analytics & Knowledge, pp. 63–72. ACM, New York, NY, USA (2020)
2. Arnab, S., et al.: Mapping learning and game mechanics for serious games analysis. Br. J. Edu. Technol. **46**(2), 391–411 (2015)
3. Boel, C., et al.: Applying educational design research to develop a low-cost, mobile immersive virtual reality serious game teaching safety in secondary vocational education. Educ. Inf. Technol. **29**, 8609–8646 (2024)
4. Buckingham Shum, S., Ferguson, R., Martinez-Maldonado, R.: Human-centred learning analytics. J. Learn. Anal. **6**(2), 1–9 (2019)
5. Buttussi, F., Chittaro, L.: Effects of different types of virtual reality display on presence and learning in a safety training scenario. IEEE Trans. Visual Comput. Graphics **24**(2), 1063–1076 (2017)
6. Chatti, M.A., et al..: How to design effective learning analytics indicators? A human-centered design approach. In: 15th European Conference on Technology Enhanced Learning, pp. 303–317. Springer (2020)
7. Checa, D., Bustillo, A.: A review of immersive virtual reality serious games to enhance learning and training. Multi. Tools Appl. **79**(9), 5501–5527 (2020)
8. Christopoulos, A., Pellas, N., Laakso, M.J.: A learning analytics theoretical framework for stem education virtual reality applications. Edu. Sci. **10**(11), 317 (2020)
9. De Freitas, S., et al.: Foundations of dynamic learning analytics: using university student data to increase retention. Br. J. Edu. Technol. **46**(6), 1175–1188 (2015)
10. De Freitas, S., Veletsianos, G.: Crossing boundaries: Learning and teaching in virtual worlds. British J. Edu. Technol. **41**(1) (2010)
11. Dimitriadis, Y., Martínez-Maldonado, R., Wiley, K.: Human-centered design principles for actionable learning analytics. In: Research on E-learning and ICT in education: Technological, pedagogical and instructional perspectives, pp. 277–296 (2021)
12. Dollinger, M., Liu, D., Arthars, N., Lodge, J.M.: Working together in learning analytics towards the co-creation of value. J. Learn. Anal. **6**(2), 10–26 (2019)
13. Ferguson, C., Van den Broek, L., Van Oostendorp, H.: On the role of interaction mode and story structure in virtual reality serious games. Comput. Educ. **143**, 103671 (2020)
14. Freire, M., et al..: Game learning analytics: learning analytics for serious games. In: Learning, design, and technology: An international compendium of theory, research, practice, and policy, pp. 3475–3502. Springer (2023)
15. Heinemann, B., et al.: A learning analytics dashboard to investigate the influence of interaction in a VR learning application. In: LAK Workshops, pp. 251–259 (2024)
16. Högberg, J., Hamari, J., Wästlund, E.: Gameful experience questionnaire (GAMEFULQUEST): an instrument for measuring the perceived gamefulness of system use. User Model. User-Adap. Inter. **29**(3), 619–660 (2019)
17. Huang, H., Hwang, G.J., Jong, M.S.Y.: Technological solutions for promoting employees' knowledge levels and practical skills: an SVVR-based blended learning approach for professional training. Comput. Educ. **189**, 104593 (2022)
18. Iachini, T., et al.: The experience of virtual reality: are individual differences in mental imagery associated with sense of presence? Cogn. Process. **20**(3), 291–298 (2019)
19. Jivet, I., Scheffel, M., Specht, M., Drachsler, H.: License to evaluate: preparing learning analytics dashboards for educational practice. In: Proceedings of the 8th International Conference on Learning Analytics and Knowledge, pp. 31–40 (2018)

20. Johnson-Glenberg, M.C.: The necessary nine: design principles for embodied VR and active stem education. Learning in a Digital World: Perspective on Interactive Technologies for Formal and Informal Education, pp. 83–112 (2019)
21. Kilteni, K., Groten, R., Slater, M.: The sense of embodiment in virtual reality. Presence Teleoperators Virtual Environ. **21**(4), 373–387 (2012)
22. Lampropoulos, G.: Kinshuk: virtual reality and gamification in education: a systematic review. Edu. Technol. Res. Dev. 1–95 (2024)
23. Lehikko, A., Nykänen, M., Lukander, K., Uusitalo, J., Ruokamo, H.: Exploring interactivity effects on learners' sense of agency, cognitive load, and learning outcomes in immersive virtual reality: a mixed methods study. Comput. Edu. X Reality **4**, 100066 (2024)
24. Lu, F., et al.: Evaluating engagement level and analytical support of interactive visualizations in virtual reality environments. In: 2018 IEEE International Symposium on Mixed and Augmented Reality (ISMAR), pp. 143–152. IEEE (2018)
25. Makransky, G., Andreasen, N., Baceviciute, S., Mayer, R.: Immersive virtual reality increases liking but not learning with a science simulation and generative learning strategies promote learning in immersive virtual reality. J. Educ. Psychol. **113**(4), 719 (2021)
26. Marougkas, A., Troussas, C., Krouska, A., Sgouropoulou, C.: Virtual reality in education: a review of learning theories, approaches and methodologies for the last decade. Electronics **12**(13), 2832 (2023)
27. Merchant, Z., Goetz, E.T., Cifuentes, L., Keeney-Kennicutt, W., Davis, T.J.: Effectiveness of virtual reality-based instruction on students' learning outcomes in k-12 and higher education: a meta-analysis. Comput. Educ. **70**, 29–40 (2014)
28. Mondragón Bernal, I.F., et al.: An immersive virtual reality training game for power substations evaluated in terms of usability and engagement. Appl. Sci. **12**(2), 711 (2022)
29. Papamitsiou, Z., Giannakos, M.N., Ochoa, X.: From childhood to maturity: Are we there yet? Mapping the intellectual progress in learning analytics during the past decade. In: Proceedings of the 10th International Conference on Learning Analytics & Knowledge, pp. 559–568 (2020)
30. Pellas, N., Mystakidis, S., Kazanidis, I.: Immersive virtual reality in k-12 and higher education: a systematic review of the last decade scientific literature. Virtual Reality **25**(3), 835–861 (2021)
31. Radhakrishnan, U., Koumaditis, K., Chinello, F.: A systematic review of immersive virtual reality for industrial skills training. Behav. Inf. Technol. **40**(12), 1310–1339 (2021)
32. Radianti, J., Majchrzak, T.A., Fromm, J., Wohlgenannt, I.: A systematic review of immersive virtual reality applications for higher education: design elements, lessons learned, and research agenda. Comput. Educ. **147**, 103778 (2020)
33. Sailer, M., Homner, L.: The gamification of learning: a meta-analysis. Educ. Psychol. Rev. **32**(1), 77–112 (2020)
34. Sun, W., Chen, Q.: The design, implementation and evaluation of gamified immersive virtual reality (IVR) for learning: a review of empirical studies. In: European Conference on Games Based Learning. vol. 17, pp. 789–797 (2023)
35. Vezzoli, Y., Mavrikis, M., Vasalou, A.: Inspiration cards workshops with primary teachers in the early co-design stages of learning analytics. In: Proceedings of the 10th International Conference on Learning Analytics & Knowledge, pp. 73–82 (2020)
36. Zichermann, G., Cunningham, C.: Gamification by design: Implementing game mechanics in web and mobile apps. Inc, O'Reilly Media (2011)

Adding Chance to a Serious Game's Mechanics to Encourage Action in Uncertain Situations

Jessica L. Bitter, Rieke Deborah Koßmann, Michael Lurz, Lorena Müller, and Ulrike Spierling(✉)

Hochschule RheinMain, Wiesbaden, Germany
{jessicalaura.bitter,deborah.kossmann,michael.lurz, lorena.mueller,ulrike.spierling}@hs-rm.de

Abstract. For a serious game to support the primary prevention of intimate partner violence (IPV), we have developed game mechanics that resemble actions in situations with risky or uncertain outcomes. While the game conveys its learning objectives about the complex structural problem largely through narration, the underlying game mechanics, with a combination of choice and chance, allow players to experience the uncertainties of difficult decision making. We compare three variants of the representation of random probabilities by means of quantitative anonymous evaluation (n=44) and measure their effect on the attribution of internal or external control.

Keywords: Serious game · Game mechanics · Intimate partner violence

1 Introduction

In an ongoing interdisciplinary project with experts from game design and applied social science, we develop a serious game to support the primary prevention of intimate partner violence (IPV) [6]. Addressing the complex societal problem, the game's learning goal is to sensitize players in the role of the social environment for often hidden signs and symptoms and to show possibilities to act. It is crucial to highlight the difficulties in finding simple solutions and thus to raise empathy for victims of ongoing violence. Players need to learn that single heroic rescue attempts may fail, and that it is important to build a social environment that supports the victims and stands up against violence. However, in reality, the road to success is usually paved with failures and setbacks, so that the success of one's own help attempts in the role of the environment depends on other people and thus on uncertainties.

The game is intended to illustrate these contingencies while still encouraging the players to act. To avoid having to program a complex social simulation, we abstract the uncertain factors and dependencies by mapping them to

A. Schönbohm et al. (Eds.): GALA 2024, LNCS 15348, pp. 123–132, 2025.
https://doi.org/10.1007/978-3-031-78269-5_12

chance. While the game conveys its learning objectives about the complex structural problem largely through narration, the underlying game mechanics, with a combination of choice and chance, allow players to experience the ambiguity of difficult decision making. In this study, we compare three designed variants of random outcome determination with differences in visual representation and interaction. Using a quantitative, anonymous evaluation, we measure their impact on the respondents' attribution of internal or external control.

While introducing uncertainty into games through random elements is a well-used strategy to keep players engaged [2], our motivation lies in the learning objective of the theme. IPV is a serious and emotionally distressing topic that few people want to deal with and is fraught with taboos. The experience of failing with offers of help is particularly frustrating and an important learning process is to understand these circumstances in order to gain knowledge and resilience.

2 Game Description

Before designing, we have analyzed IPV together with experts in the field as a structural problem [7]. There are often networked structures that maintain taboos and create dependencies in the relationships of a social network, which enable perpetrators to evade responsibility, hinder victims from getting support and make it difficult for other members of the network to notice the violence and provide help. This is taken up in our narrative game.

The player's task is to create a supportive network for a victim of IPV, taking on the role of different people from the couple's social environment. Each scene presents a character with the opportunity to intervene upon observing signs of violence (see Fig. 1, left). Players must select from three possible courses of action, each leading to either a positive outcome (strengthening the network, e.g. raising awareness) or a negative one (maintaining the status quo, e.g. facing opposition, trivialization, ridicule or evasion). The game determines the result at random, whereby each option is assigned a specified probability of a positive result by design. This chance mechanic is visualized as a spinning wheel (see Fig. 1, right), with the probability for the positive and negative outcomes represented as green and red slices. Over the course of several scenes, the probability of a positive outcome can increase depending on the strength of the support network that has been built up, which is also visualized.

By combining the choice mechanic with elements of chance, we aim to convey the message that individuals can indeed make a difference and have a responsibility. At the same time, we seek to highlight the complexity of the issue, emphasizing that there are no easy solutions and that no one has complete control. The mechanics ought to abstractly model the real challenges, and while we recognize that they may frustrate players, we hope to encourage acceptance of uncertainty while fostering a sense of agency.

We assumed that this intended mixed feeling of agency can be influenced by the way the uncertain outcome is presented. In our study, we therefore investigated how three different visualizations influence this desired effect in order to inform further development. The three variations are (V1, V2, V3):

Fig. 1. Left: Choice interface; Option of a colleague of the victim to suggest that they look for information on an IPV counseling center together. Right: Visualization of a spinning wheel that shows unequal probabilities for outcomes.

V1: The spinning wheel is started by the players and gradually decelerates until stopping at a random position.
V2: The spinning wheel is started by the players and spins until the players click a button causing an immediate stop. However, the wheel spins too fast for the players to consciously control the outcome by stopping at the right time.
V3: Instead of a wheel there is only a button for players to click to determine the outcome. The rest of the interface is the same as in the other variations.

Both wheels (V1 and V2) display the probabilities for the respective option, as well as the increase in probability due to a strong network.

3 Related Work

Zhang et al. [9] investigate the role of randomness with regard to when it occurs in a game by comparing four different variations of the same game. Their findings indicate that input randomness, defined as a "random information or element brought into the game before players make a decision", results in lower gameplay satisfaction than the other variations. These insights are derived from a study involving 18 participants and were assessed using the GUESS scale.

Howard-Jones et al. [4] observed higher engagement with learning games containing elements of randomness. The games used in three studies with children, adolescents and adults "focused on learning in simple terms (i.e. basic maths and factual recall)" and included randomness elements such as coin flips or dice rolls which influenced the player's score.

In a study with 110 college students, Zysberg et al. [10] explored the relationship between results in a betting game and participants' perceptions of randomness. Those who experienced a win or loss viewed these events as more predetermined compared to participants who encountered a neutral outcome.

4 Evaluation

4.1 Method

To evaluate how the three designed alternatives influence the player's learning concerning 'agency under uncertainty', we conducted a pre/post study in which we surveyed participants both before and after they played our game. Participants completed the "Positive And Negative Affect Schedule" (PANAS) questionnaire [5] before and after playing the game to indicate their emotional state, as well as a modified version of the attributional style questionnaire (ASQ)[8], which we customized to a specific situation of the topic IPV. We chose ASQ because it measures the weighting of attributed influence (internal or external) on the outcome of a situated action, which fits with our learning objective of 'agency under uncertainty'. We prompted our participants to imagine a situation in which they try to help someone close to them who is affected by intimate partner violence, and then asked them to rate explanations for the assumed outcome in three bipolar items using a 100 point scale as follows:

The reasons whether my attempts at help are successful...

- ... are related to other people or circumstances. <-> ... are related to me. (Internality)
- ... only affect this situation. <-> ... affect many other situations, too. (Globality)
- ... will change over time. <-> ... will remain stable over time. (Stability)

Following gameplay, we also asked participants how they perceived the influence of chance on their game result, specifically to what extent they believed the game outcome was determined by their own actions, by chance, or was predefined by the game. This was measured using connected sliders, ensuring that the total for all three items equaled 100%.

Participants were divided into three groups, with each group playing one of our designed chance representations (V1, V2, V3) described in Sect. 2. The assignment of participants to each game variant was randomized. Our hypotheses, based on the learning goals presented in Sect. 2, are as follows:

H1: The perceived control (attributional style "Internality") changes after playing the game.
H2: The more extreme (internal or external) the attributional style is pre playing, the more it shifts towards the center post playing.
H3: The players assess the extent of the influence of 'chance' on their game result differently in each group.
H4: The greater the perceived influence of chance, the more external the attributional style after playing the game.
H5: The affect (PANAS) post playing differs per group.

4.2 Participants

We recruited participants from our student body, acquaintances, and an online survey portal. They confirmed their voluntary participation after reading a content warning indicating the serious topic. After excluding 6 datasets for not meeting our criteria (at least 90% completion and over three minutes spent in the game) we received 44 valid datasets. Among these, 17 participants were male, 25 female, and 2 identify as diverse. Ages range from 18 to 85, with clusters reported in decades, except for 18–25. The majority of participants was below the age of 35, with 12 participants aged 18–25 and 15 participants aged 26–35.

4.3 Results

H1. For each group, we conducted a Wilcoxon test since we could not assume a Gaussian distribution in our sample. For the test we focused on the 'Internality' item from our adapted ASQ questionnaire, as detailed in Sect. 4.1.

We compared the attributional style before and after playing the game. As illustrated in Table 1, only the group that engaged with the third game variant without a wheel depiction exhibited a significant change (p=0.003). Furthermore, Table 2 indicates that the difference between the means is greatest for this group. In each group, there is a slight shift towards a more internal attributional style.

Table 1. H1 Wilcoxon test.

Attributional style pre game - post game	W	z	p	Hodges-Lehmann Estimate
V1: Auto stopping wheel	32.500	−0.909	0.382	−9.000
V2: Manually stopped wheel	35.000	−1.706	0.093	−17.000
V3: Without wheel	11.000	−2.783	0.003	−26.000

Table 2. H1 Descriptives.

Attributional Style Internality	N	Mean	SD	SE	Coefficient of variation
V1: Auto stopping wheel, pre game	13	51.154	29.117	8.076	0.569
V1: Auto stopping wheel, post game	13	60.077	29.042	8.055	0.483
V2: Manually stopped wheel, pre game	16	42.313	30.819	7.705	0.728
V2: Manually stopped wheel, post game	16	60.625	29.193	7.298	0.482
V3: Without wheel, pre game	15	50.600	21.980	5.675	0.434
V3: Without wheel, post game	15	76.667	16.646	4.298	0.217

H2. Aligning with our learning goal that IPV, while a structural problem, can still be influenced by individual members of the social environment, we aimed to determine whether individuals with distinct external or internal attributional styles regarding IPV would shift towards a moderate attributional style after engaging with our game. From our total sample, we formed two groups (based on their pre-game either external or internal attribution style) without differentiating between the game variants. We conducted a Wilcoxon test to examine if the external group shifted towards internal attribution post-game and vice versa. We defined group membership based on the mean of the pre-game attributional style question's item 'Internality' (μ=47.00, σ=27.25). We compared our mean with existing literature, such as Deichstetter [3], who reported a mean of 78.72, and Peterson et al. [8] who used a 7-point scale resulting in a range from 3.80 to 5.39. In contrast to those our mean value is more external (3.82, after mapping it to the 1–7 scale Peterson et al. used) which met our expectations, as our scenario referred to a more structural problem than the events Peterson et al. and Deichstetter used. As Table 3 shows, the shift from external to internal is significant (p<.001), while the shift from internal to external is not (p=0.458).

Table 3. H2 Wilcoxon test. AS = Attributional Style.

Group	Measure	W	z	p
Below mean	AS Internality pre game - post game	8.500	−3.939	< .001
Above mean	AS Internality pre game - post game	119.000	0.122	0.458

Table 4. H2 Descriptives. AS = Attributional Style.

Group	N	Mean	SD	SE
Below mean (external) AS 'Internality' pre game	23	25.478	13.564	2.828
Below mean (external) AS 'Internality' post game	23	60.348	27.400	5.713
Above mean (internal) AS 'Internality' pre game	21	72.143	14.104	3.078
Above mean (internal) AS 'Internality' post game	21	72.048	23.863	5.207

H3. We used the non-parametric Kruskal-Wallis test due to our small sample size. The test shows that we can continue to support our hypothesis that the assessment of the influence of 'chance' on the game result differs between the groups, as p=0.044 (Factor variable is 'Grouping', statistic=6.236, df=2). To estimate implications for game design, we examined the mean values for the other items ('own influence' and 'predefined by game') as well (see Table 5). The mean values suggest that group V3 (without wheel) assessed their own influence higher and chance lower than the other groups. Group V2 (manually stopped wheel) rated the influence of chance higher than the other groups.

Table 5. H3 Descriptives: Assessment of 'chance' aspect.

Item	Group	N	Mean	SD	SE
Perceived own influence	V1: Auto stopping wheel	13	57.692	29.021	8.049
	V2: Manually stopped wheel	16	49.000	29.326	7.331
	V3: Without wheel	15	54.933	34.454	8.896
Perceived influence of chance	V1: Auto stopping wheel	13	22.154	21.729	6.026
	V2: Manually stopped wheel	16	32.750	25.072	6.268
	V3: Without wheel	15	15.667	25.626	6.616
Perceived predetermination by the game	V1: Auto stopping wheel	13	23.154	28.062	7.783
	V2: Manually stopped wheel	16	21.250	23.837	5.959
	V3: Without wheel	15	32.400	27.079	6.992

H4. We computed a linear regression using the item of the perceived influence of 'chance' and the attributional style item 'Internality' of our post game ASQ adaptation, using the total number of participants not divided into groups. As shown in Table 6, we cannot keep our hypothesis (p=0.277).

Table 6. H4 Linear Regression.

Model		Sum of Squares	df	Mean Square	F	p
H_1	Regression	824.406	1	824.406	1.211	0.277
	Residual	28584.389	42	680.581		
	Total	29408.795	43			

Table 7. H4 Model Summary and Coefficients.

Model		Unstandardized	Standard Error	Standardized	t	p	R	R^2	Adjusted R^2	RMSE
H_0	(Intercept)	65.932	3.943		16.723	< .001	0.000	0.000	0.000	26.152
H_1	(Intercept)	70.121	5.473		12.812	< .001	0.167	0.028	0.005	26.088
	Perceived influence of chance	−0.176	0.160	−0.167	−1.101	0.277				

H5. Due to our non-normally distributed data, we performed a Kruskal-Wallis test instead of an ANOVA to test whether there is a difference in the positive affects of the PANAS per group after the game. The test was not significant (Factor variable is 'Grouping', statistic=0.445, df=2, p=0.801). To nevertheless obtain hints for our game design, we exploratively employed a directional Wilcoxon test to find out whether there was a downward shift in positive affect or an increase in negative affect within each group. For both cases, the results for all groups are significant (see Table 8).

Table 8. H5 explorative directional Wilcoxon test using the PANAS pre game score vs. post game score. PA: Positive Affect (PANAS), NA: Negative Affect (PANAS).

Group	Affect	W	z	p	Affect	W	z	p
V1: Auto stopping wheel	PA	69.500	1.677	0.050	NA	5.000	−2.667	0.004
V2: Manually stopped wheel	PA	104.000	2.499	0.007	NA	12.000	−2.341	0.011
V3: Without wheel	PA	83.000	1.915	0.030	NA	20.000	−2.272	0.012

Table 9. H5 Descriptives. PA: Positive Affect, NA: Negative Affect. Group V1: Auto stopping wheel, group V2: Manually stopped wheel, group V3: Without wheel.

Group	N	Measure	Mean	SD	SE	Measure	Mean	SD	SE
V1	13	PA pre	3.038	0.790	0.219	NA pre	1.685	0.365	0.101
V1	13	PA post	2.569	0.749	0.208	NA post	1.954	0.564	0.156
V2	16	PA pre	2.825	0.467	0.117	NA pre	1.837	0.466	0.117
V2	16	PA post	2.382	0.496	0.124	NA post	2.144	0.581	0.145
V3	15	PA pre	2.653	0.658	0.170	NA pre	1.760	0.659	0.170
V3	15	PA post	2.327	0.726	0.187	NA post	2.080	0.624	0.161

5 Discussion

In the following, we relate the results to our learning objective outlined in Sect. 2. We observed differences between the groups in their attributional style "Internality" with regard to an IPV situation. Our educational goal to encourage agency under accepted uncertainty means that we hoped for our participants to exhibit a balanced attributional style after playing the game. This corresponds with a value around 47 (standard deviation = 27.25), which is the pre-game midpoint between external and internal attribution in our sample. Groups V1 and V2 matched this goal (mean post value around 60), while in group V3, there was a stronger and significant shift towards an internal attributional style.

H2 about the game's balancing effect on attributional styles was partially supported. Independent of the game variants, subjects that started with a more external attributional style showed a significant shift towards a more internal attributional style after playing (Tables 3 and 4). The other respondents with a previous internal attributional style showed no significant shift towards external. Since we made the grouping for this test based on the attributional style mean values of the entire sample, we did not take into account the game variations and thus did not consider a possible variance that could influence the results.

The perception of the influence of chance varied between the tested design variants and was reported least by the participants in group V3 (without wheel), who instead felt most strongly that their own actions determined the game's outcome. This supports our assumption that participants may be less inclined to recognize IPV as a structural issue when the chance mechanics are not visualized. This is consistent with the findings from H1.

The data does not support the hypothesis that the greater the perceived influence of chance, the more external the attributional style after playing the game (H4, Table 6).

Further, we have to reject the hypothesis H5 that the post-playing affect differs among the groups. Due to our small sample size we could not test this hypothesis as planned. However, an exploratory comparison between the positive affect pre and post for each group indicated that the positive affect is lower after playing in all three groups as can be deduced from Tables 8 and 9. The shift is strongest in group V1. Group V3 has the lowest average positive affect but only exhibits weak tendencies. This suggests that, as expected, we can assume a certain level of frustration from the game.

6 Limitations

One limitation of this study is the small sample size of 44 participants in total, distributed unevenly across the three groups. The results are to be considered first indications, and there were five hypotheses resulting in many tests being conducted. Further limitations are that the results have not been tested for alpha errors, and people's prior understanding of concepts of 'chance' has not been assessed.

7 Conclusion and Future Work

In this work, we presented a design study on a prosocial serious game about IPV with complex learning objectives. Our goal was to evaluate the effects of three design alternatives, introducing game elements of chance as an abstraction of complex possible outcomes of player decisions. Despite the small sample size, we see tendencies that we will consider in further design steps. In particular, we see the results as supporting our approach of achieving one of our diverse game goals of encouraging acceptance of uncertainty while fostering a sense of agency.

Overall, our findings indicate that the game may influence the situational attributional style of the players in this topical context. Variant V3 of our chance visualizations (without the wheel indicator) shows the greatest shift from external to internal attribution, which runs counter to our goal of achieving an ambivalent attribution of "internal" control with our game. We conclude that it is worthwhile to continue the development with an explicit chance visualization, whereby its variants could be examined further, also using qualitative means. Experiencing randomness should not take precedence over the realization that success is not only in one's own hands, while at the same time, it should be encouraged to take a stand against violence. Specifically, this should promote the acceptance of uncertainties with regard to (difficult) direct solutions in the problem area and thus contribute to resilience in an overall frustrating context.

Further research includes exploring the relationship between the players' attributional styles and their attitude towards IPV in order to estimate the game's intended educational effect.

On a broader level, this could also provide general indications for the development of other serious games about intimate partner violence and may perhaps even be applicable to games about similar topics (i.e. other forms of structural discrimination).

Acknowledgments. This work was funded [in part] by the German Federal Ministry of Education and Research (BMBF), funding program "Forschung an Fachhochschulen", contract number 13FH035SX8, in the interdisciplinary project "AusWege" involving two research teams [1] (https://www.auswege-online.de/). The game prototype has been designed and developed in the Faculty of Design, Computer Science, Media of Hochschule RheinMain, Wiesbaden, Germany. Members of the Faculty of Applied Social Sciences initiated this project and contributed social science expertise and research findings on IPV, as well as scenarios for the game scenes.

Disclosure of Interests. The authors have no competing interests to declare that are relevant to the content of this article.

References

1. AusWege: Project website (2024). https://www.auswege-online.de/
2. Costikyan, G.: Uncertainty in Games. MIT Press, Cambridge Massachusetts, Playful thinking series (2013)
3. Deichstetter, D.: Untersuchung möglicher Einflussfaktoren auf die Ausprägung erlernter Hilflosigkeit durch die Vorgabe lösbarer und unlösbarer Zahlenreihen. Diploma thesis, Universität Wien, Wien (2012)
4. Howard-Jones, P.A., Demetriou, S.: Uncertainty and engagement with learning games. Instr. Sci. **37**(6), 519–536 (2009). https://doi.org/10.1007/s11251-008-9073-6
5. Janke, S., Glöckner-Rist, A.: Deutsche version der positive and negative affect schedule (panas). Zusammenstellung sozialwissenschaftlicher Items und Skalen (ZIS) (2012). https://doi.org/10.6102/zis146
6. Müller, L., Spierling, U., Bitter, J.L., Schwarz, S.: Challenges in designing a game for the prevention of intimate partner violence. In: Proceedings of the ECGBL 2023, pp. 852–855 (2023). https://doi.org/10.34190/ecgbl.17.1.1838
7. Müller, L., Spierling, U., Merkle, A., Dackweiler, R.M.: Systems mapping to support interdisciplinary understanding in serious game design. In: Proceedings of the ECGBL 2022, pp. 403–4011 (2022). https://doi.org/10.34190/ecgbl.16.1.772
8. Peterson, C., Semmel, A., von Baeyer, C., Abramson, L.Y., Metalsky, G.I., Seligman, M.E.P.: The attributional style questionnaire. Cogn. Ther. Res. **6**(3), 287–299 (1982). https://doi.org/10.1007/BF01173577
9. Zhang, Y., Monteiro, D., Liang, H.N., Ma, J., Baghaei, N.: Effect of input-output randomness on gameplay satisfaction in collectable card games. In: 2021 IEEE Conference on Games (CoG), pp. 1–5 (2021).https://doi.org/10.1109/CoG52621.2021.9619020
10. Zysberg, L., Kimhi, S.: Winning or losing a bet and the perception of randomness. J. Gambl. Stud. **29**(1), 109–118 (2013). https://doi.org/10.1007/s10899-011-9289-2

Evaluating Phillips' Game Rewards Taxonomy: Implications for the Gamification Design

Brunella Botte[1,4](✉), Giada Marinensi[2], Henk Aarts[3], Sander Bakkes[4], and Remco Veltkamp[4]

[1] Department of Life Sciences, Health and Medical Professions, Link Campus University, Rome, Italy
b.botte@unilink.it, b.botte@uu.nl

[2] Department of Human Sciences, Link Campus University, Rome, Italy
g.marinensi@unilink.it

[3] Department of Psychology, Utrecht University, Utrecht, The Netherlands
h.aarts@uu.nl

[4] Department of Information and Computer Science, Utrecht University, Utrecht, The Netherlands
{s.c.j.bakkes,r.c.veltkamp}@uu.nl

Abstract. This study evaluates the relevance of Phillips' reward taxonomy in the context of contemporary video game design, with implications for modern gamification strategies. Phillips' taxonomy categorizes game rewards into six types based on their functions within game systems. Given the rapid evolution of video games, this research investigates whether this taxonomy remains applicable to current gaming landscapes. The study consisted of two main steps: firstly, a detailed analysis of rewards in seven video games from various genres was performed and secondly, a card sorting activity with expert players was conducted. Results shown that while Phillips' taxonomy resulted to be still applicable, the need for two additional categories, rewards of currency and rewards of self-expression, emerged, reflecting the evolving dynamics in game design and player preferences. Future research will explore the relationship between these reward categories and the fulfilment of basic psychological needs as outlined by Self-Determination Theory, to enhance the motivational impact of gamification.

Keywords: gamification · reward taxonomy · video games · motivation · Game design · Self-Determination Theory

1 Introduction

The maturation of gamification has led to its widespread adoption across diverse domains [1–6] fostering the need for a deeper comprehension of its mechanisms and its effect on users' motivation. As conventionally understood, gamification entails the integration of game elements into non-game contexts [7], thereby imbuing such activities with game-like qualities, with the final aim of fostering user engagement and motivation [8]. Central to this approach are rewards, namely game elements such as points, badges and leader

A. Schönbohm et al. (Eds.): GALA 2024, LNCS 15348, pp. 133–141, 2025.
https://doi.org/10.1007/978-3-031-78269-5_13

boards, employed to promote user engagement, mirroring the challenges and progression inherent in gaming experiences. Consequently, an in-depth exploration of rewards, their bestowal mechanisms, and their intricate interplay with motivational dynamics emerges as pivotal for refining the efficacy of gamification design and counteract the potential negative effect of gamification on intrinsic motivation (e.g. overjustification effect) [9–11]. Indeed, in terms of rewards variety and complexity, video games represent an excellence, and systematically studying them can deeply contribute to the improvement of gamification design.

A number of studies have highlighted the pivotal role of rewards in gamified systems [12, 13], with a specific emphasis on the influence of reward scheduling and contingency factors on the efficacy of gamification. Over time, several studies, regarding video game reward systems, have also proposed game rewards taxonomies focusing on reward typologies rather than conferral modalities [14–18]. Among those studies, the ones carried out by [14, 15] resulted to be particularly interesting for their innovative approach to categorising rewards according to their role within the game system. However, given that Phillips' taxonomy was published a decade ago and that game design is evolving rapidly, the objective of this research is to ascertain whether it remains an appropriate means of evaluating the reward systems of contemporary video games.

2 Motivation and Rewards

As previously mentioned, one of the objectives of gamification would be to motivate users [19], preferably not only in the short period of time. In fact, game-elements are adopted in gamified system to satisfy users basic psychological needs, enhance their overall experiences, and then motivate them to consistently engage with the specific content and activities proposed by the system [7, 20–22]. Although the core concept of gamification is rooted in accomplishing activities through selectively applied incentives (rewards), adhering to a fundamental behaviouristic idea [23], the contemporary approach to gamification design strives to evoke intrinsic motivation processes that extend beyond the transient behavioural changes resulting from a reward system [24]. This shift has broadened the meaning of the term gamification which, as already suggested by Deterding et al. (2011), should be considered as "an informal umbrella term for incorporating video game elements into non-gaming systems to enhance user experience (UX) and user engagement". In fact, building on the foundation laid by Self-determination Theory (SDT), which explored how motivation is developed in video games [25] we can conclude that gameplay itself can be part of an inherently rewarding experience. It would be safe, then, to suppose that the basic psychological demands that are required to create intrinsically engaging video game experiences could be also required to create intrinsically motivating gamified experiences. However, in contrast with this assumption, it must be noticed that gamification usually intends to reach its objective by leveraging game elements like badges, points or leader boards used as extrinsic reinforcement for users' actions in the gamified system, more from the point of view of behaviourists [23, 26] than from the SDT's one [25, 27].

To improve the approach to the use of rewards in gamification, one necessary step would then be to better understand the rewards' nature. In general, the majority of the studies investigating rewards motivational power is focused mostly on their ability to foster motivation according to the circumstances under which they are awarded [28–31].

To contribute to improving the gamification design would be interesting to adopt a different approach and investigate the impact of rewards on motivation according to their function in the system (i.e., how the reward affects the player's experience and the players' abilities within the system), instead of the circumstances under which they are awarded. To achieve this final objective, this study first intends to verify whether any of the existing taxonomies categorising game rewards based on their function in the game system [14–18] would be suitable for contemporary games' rewards.

3 Why Phillips' Taxonomy

A preliminary search in the main scientific databases, namely Scopus, IEEE-Xplore, ACM Libraries and Science Direct, was performed to identify the main existing rewards taxonomies. A total of 54 papers were found, but only 6 were considered being consistent with the aim of this study, as they provided a systematic analysis of the types of rewards included in video games.

Among all the examined taxonomies, the one from [14, 15], seemed to be the most suitable for describing a video game reward system: in fact, in comparison to alternative taxonomies [16–18, 32], the one advanced by [14, 15] exhibits a more inclusive and abstract nature, emphasising the function of rewards within the system rather than their discrete attributes. Moreover, it draws from a broader spectrum of videogame analyses in contrast to [16, 17].

Finally, among the array of taxonomies analysed, the one posited by [14, 15], emerges as particularly aligned with the primary objective of this investigation. This taxonomy prompts contemplation regarding the potentiality that rewards themselves may not inherently serve as motivators. Rather, it is the function they assume within the system that elicits motivational responses. According to [14, 15] rewards can be categorised as follows:

Rewards of access: locations or resources that, at some point in the game, become accessible (e.g. A new level, a new area on a map, etc.);

Rewards of facility: give players the ability to do things they were not capable of or improve abilities that they already have (e.g. power ups);

Rewards of sustenance: help players to stay longer in the game (e.g. extra lives or medi kits);

Rewards of glory: they have no direct impact on the gameplay itself, but they are an integral part of the gaming experience (e.g. points, achievements, etc.);

Rewards of praise: like rewards of glory they don't have a direct impact on the gameplay but work as encouragement to the players, and highlight their success (e.g. phrases of congratulations).

Rewards of sensory feedback: are audio/video/aptic feedback given to the player when things happen in the game (e.g. vibration of the controller, special sounds, animations, etc.).

Furthermore, [14] identified what they defined as "emerging categories", which described the duration rewards had in the games they examined.

4 Research Questions

To derive the aforementioned categories, Phillips et al. examined popular games from different genres in 2013. Given the evolving nature of the video game market, it is reasonable to assume that in this last decade gameplays have evolved, and, consequently, the types of rewards they include as well. To identify a reward taxonomy able to classify rewards according to their role could be the starting point of a broader research aiming at further understanding the link between rewards and motivation. Given that, the research questions this paper aim at answering to are:

RQ1: Can the Phillips et al. taxonomy still be considered as representative of contemporary video games reward systems?

RQ2: Are there new emerging reward categories in the current game video industry?

5 Method

Initially, to address the research questions, 21 games were selected from among the most prominent titles within the gaming milieu, 3 for each of the genres listed in Table 1. The subsequent step was to identify the experts that would have to examine the game rewards in the light of the selected taxonomy. For convenience reasons, the selection of expert players was predicated on their voluntary participation among students enrolled in the Applied Games course, part of the bachelor's degree in Innovative Technologies for Digital Communication at Link Campus University, thus ensuring their familiarity with Phillips' taxonomy and the overarching aims of this investigation. Students were asked to fill in a questionnaire to self-assess their expertise in the 21 games previously identified. Specifically, they were asked for an estimation of how many hours per week they spent playing each game and their level of appreciation of them. According to questionnaire results, a short list of 7 games was drafted, as synthetised in Table 1.

Also, a pool of seven evaluators was selected for the first step of the analysis: they were initially requested to compile an inventory of the principal rewards embedded within the game they played the most, based on their memory of the entire game. Subsequently, through a closed card sorting session [33], the evaluators categorised the identified rewards according to the taxonomy established by [14, 15]. In case of rewards not fitting any of the Phillips categories, a session of discussion through an open card sorting session was organized [33]. Finally, to assess the consistency of the categorisation performed by the evaluators the Inter-rater Agreement [34] was conducted: fourteen more raters were chosen among the respondents to the questionnaire, to individually rate their agreement (1) or disagreement (0) with the categorisations of the evaluators. Two raters were assigned to each game: they received the list of the rewards with a brief description and the categories of the taxonomy they were in. Given the small number of items to be rated, to calculate such agreement, the Percent Agreement Method was adopted [35–37].

Table 1 Games selected for the study

Title	Genre	Single player/Multiplayer	Monetisation model
Clash royale	Pay-to-win real-time strategy	Multiplayer	Freemium/in-app purchase
Cyberpunk2077	Action role-playing in an open world	Single player	Premium + DLC
Dark Souls	Action role-playing game	Both	Premium + DLC
Dead by daylight	Survival horror asymmetric multiplayer online game	Multiplayer	Premium/in-app purchase
HayDay	Mobile simulation game	Multiplayer	Freemium/in-app purchase
League of legends	Multiplayer online battle arena (MOBA)	Multiplayer	Freemium/in-app purchase
Valorant	Tactical first-person hero shooter	Multiplayer	Freemium/in-app purchase

6 Results

A total of N = 190 rewards were identified over the seven selected games. After the closed card sorting session the distribution under the Phillips categories resulted to be uneven, fact that can be mostly ascribed to the games' different genres. Furthermore, the 20% of the total of the rewards (n = 38) resulted as not classifiable under any of the available categories. In this phase, an open card sorting activity was carried out, resulting in two more categories added to the Phillips' taxonomy:

Rewards of currency: including all the rewards that could be used in the game to buy (or in exchange for) other rewards (e.g. coins, gold, special currency, etc.);

Rewards of self-expression: become popular in recent years, have the only purpose of allowing players to customize their gaming equipment, with no impact on the gameplay or on the game performances (e.g. avatar skins, weapons skins, etc.).

The last step was to calculate the level of agreement among raters regarding the belonging of a reward to a specific category. In Table 2 all the percentage agreements are summarised.

Percentage agreement is acceptable in a range between 70 and 90% (Hartmann, 1977; Stemler, 2019). Considering all the agreements being higher than 80% it was reasonable to consider the single rewards of each game as representative of the category they were associated with.

Table 2 Each game percentage agreement between raters

Title	Percentage agreement	Title	Percentage agreement
Clash royale	100%	HayDay	93.75%
Cyberpunk2077	96%	League of legends	82.93%
Dark Souls	84.62%	Valorant	81.48%
Dead by daylight	80%		

7 Discussion and Conclusion

The objective of this paper was to verify if the reward taxonomy, theorized by [14] was still valid if applied to contemporary video games and to determine if any new reward category emerged after the analysis of contemporary videogames.

Results shown that the taxonomy is still applicable, and that two more categories can be added to the existing ones: rewards of currency and rewards of self-expression. It can be noticed that concept of currency already existed in Phillips taxonomy, but it was presented under one of the "emerging categories" referred to the duration of the rewards, "Consumable Rewards". This shift into a proper category could be ascribed to the prominent role that currency, in its broader sense, has in contemporary games, both as items that can be spent in the game and as in-game currency to be bought through real money. As for the rewards of self-expression, this is a completely new category, representing the rewards that don't affect the gameplay in any way, but that have the sole role of allowing players to express themselves within the game environment, which has been identified as a growing need in new generations of players [40]. Lastly, it can be highlighted that these two new rewards categories have one element in common, namely micro-transactions, that is payments made for buying mobile applications or purchasing extra content within video games [41]. In recent years, this business model (freemium and/or with in-app purchase, as shown in Table 1) has become predominant in the games industry [42], and it has largely been studied in relation to its implication in gambling and ludopathic behaviour [43, 44] but, in the light of the results of this study, it can be hypothesised that such business model has also had an impact on game design itself.

This research also highlights how the variety of rewards included in video games is wide, and how they are used to generate different experiences within the game system. This is also the case in Serious Games, which retain the structure and constituent elements of the video games developed just for entertainment pourposes. In this sense, the design of Gamification can take its cue, trying to diversify the rewards bestowed, having as a framework of reference precisely the role that these rewards play within the system, and moving forward from the superficial kind of gamification approaches relying mainly on points, badges and leaderboards (PBL), which have been largely criticised for being of limited efficacy [45].

8 Limitations and Future Work

As a first attempt of analysing video games rewards in the light of their role in the game system, this study suffers from some limitations. The plethora of games chosen for the study, even though representative of the main game genres, is limited and could be extended both, to specific genre niches and in terms of numerosity. It must be also noticed that in this specific study the gamer point of view was adopted, while it could be explored if, changing the perspective, for instance involving other professionals, the results of the study would be different.

This research represents the first step of a broader study about the role of rewards in gamified application as elements supporting motivation. The next step of this study would be to verify if, and to what extent, categories of rewards, as defined in this paper, are correlated to the satisfaction of the three Basic Psychologic Needs theorized by the Self-determination Theory [27].

References

1. Huang, W.D., Loid, V., Sung, J.S.: Reflecting on gamified learning in medical education: a systematic literature review grounded in the structure of observed learning outcomes (SOLO) taxonomy 2012–2022. BMC Med. Educ. **24**(1), 1–10 (2024). https://doi.org/10.1186/s12909-023-04955-1
2. Pradhan, D., Malik, G., Vishwakarma, P.: Gamification in tourism research: a systematic review, current insights, and future research avenues. J. Vacat. Mark. (2023). https://doi.org/10.1177/13567667231188879
3. Jarnac de Freitas, M., Mira da Silva, M.: Systematic literature review about gamification in MOOCs. Open Learn. **38**(1), 73–95 (2023). https://doi.org/10.1080/02680513.2020.1798221
4. Irwanto, I., Wahyudiati, D., Saputro, A.D., Laksana, S.D.: Research trends and applications of gamification in higher education: a bibliometric analysis spanning 2013–2022. Int. J. Emerg. Technol. Learn. **18**(5), 19–41 (2023). https://doi.org/10.3991/ijet.v18i05.37021
5. Khodabandelou, R., Roghanian, P., Gheysari, H., Amoozegar, A.: A systematic review of gamification in organizational learning. Learn. Organ. **30**(2), 251–272 (2023). https://doi.org/10.1108/TLO-05-2022-0057
6. S. Lehtoranta, Xi, N., Hamari, J.: Gamification and employee well-being: a systematic literature review. In: International Conference on System Sciences, vol. 1, pp. 5277–5286 (2024). [Online]. Available: https://researchportal.tuni.fi/files/112198818/0518.pdf
7. S. Deterding, Dixon, D., Khaled, R., Nacke, L.: From game design elements to gamefulness: Defining gamification. In: Proceedings of the 15th International Academic MindTrek Conference: Envisioning Future Media Environments, MindTrek 2011, pp. 9–15 (2011). https://doi.org/10.1145/2181037.2181040
8. Krath, J., Schürmann, L., von Korflesch, H.F.O.: Revealing the theoretical basis of gamification: a systematic review and analysis of theory in research on gamification, serious games and game-based learning. Comput. Human Behav. vol. 125, no. August, p. 106963 (2021). https://doi.org/10.1016/j.chb.2021.106963
9. Deci, E.L., Koestner, R., Ryan, R.M.: Extrinsic rewards and intrinsic motivation in education: reconsidered once again. Rev. Educ. Res. **71**(1), 1–27 (2001). https://doi.org/10.3102/00346543071001001
10. Lepper, M.R., Greene, D., Nisbett, R.E.: Undermining children's intrinsic interest with extrinsic reward: a test of the overjustification hypothesis. J. Pers. Soc. Psychol. **28**(1), 129–137 (1973). https://doi.org/10.1037/h0035519

11. Dah, J., et al.: Gamification is not working: why?. Games Cult. 1–24 (2024). https://doi.org/10.1177/15554120241228125
12. Vranešic, P., Aleksic-Maslac, K., Sinkovic, B.: Influence of gamification reward system on student motivation. In: 2019 42nd International Convention on Information and Communication Technology, Electronics and Microelectronics, MIPRO 2019 - Proceedings, pp. 766–772 (2019). https://doi.org/10.23919/MIPRO.2019.8756848
13. Zhao, F., Guo, D.: Rewards in gamification. In: Lecture Notes in Computer Science (including subseries Lecture Notes in Artificial Intelligence and Lecture Notes in Bioinformatics), vol. 11595, LNCS, pp. 453–462 (2019). https://doi.org/10.1007/978-3-030-22602-2_34
14. Phillips, C., Johnson, D., Wyeth, P.: Videogame reward types. In: ACM International Conference Proceeding Series, pp. 103–106 (2013). https://doi.org/10.1145/2583008.2583025
15. Phillips, C., Johnson, D., Wyeth, P., Hides, L., Klarkowski, M.: Redefining videogame reward types. In: OzCHI 2015: Being Human - Conference Proceedings, pp. 83–91 (2015). https://doi.org/10.1145/2838739.2838782
16. Rapp, A.: The value of rewards: exploring world of warcraft for gamification design. In: Proceedings of the 2016 Annual Symposium on Computer-Human Interaction in Play Companion Extended Abstracts, in CHI PLAY Companion 2016. New York, NY, USA: Association for Computing Machinery, pp. 253–259 (2016). https://doi.org/10.1145/2968120.2987721.
17. Rapp, A.: From games to gamification: a classification of rewards in world of warcraft for the design of gamified systems. Simul. Gaming **48**(3), 381–401 (2017). https://doi.org/10.1177/1046878117697147
18. Wang, H., Sun, C.T.: Game reward systems: gaming experiences and social meanings. In: DiGRA conference (2011)
19. Schöbel, S., et al.: A research agenda for the why, what, and how of gamification designs: outcomes of an ecis 2019 panel. Commun. Assoc. Inf. Syst. **46**, 706–721 (2020). https://doi.org/10.17705/1CAIS.04630
20. Bunchball, I.: Gamification 101: an introduction to the use of game dynamics to influence behavior. White paper **9**, 1–18 (2010)
21. Kapp, K.M.: The Gamification of Learning and Instruction: Game-Based Methods and Strategies for Training and Education. John Wiley & Sons (2012)
22. Zichermann, G., Cunningham, C.: Gamification by design: implementing game mechanics in web and mobile apps. O Reilly Media, Inc., (2011)
23. Skinner, B.F.: Operant conditioning. Encycl. Educ. **7**, 29–33 (1971)
24. Deci, E.L., Koestner, R., Ryan, R.M.: A meta-analytic review of experiments examining the effects of extrinsic rewards on intrinsic motivation. Psychol. Bull. **125**(6), 627–668 (1999). https://doi.org/10.1037/0033-2909.125.6.627
25. Ryan, R.M., Rigby, C.S., Przybylski, A.: The motivational pull of video games: a self-determination theory approach. Motiv. Emot. **30**(4), 347–363 (2006). https://doi.org/10.1007/s11031-006-9051-8
26. Thorndike, E.L.: Educational Psychology. Vol. I: The Original Nature of Man. Columbia Univ.: New York (1913)
27. Ryan, R.M., Deci, E.L.: Self-Determination Theory: Basic Psychological Needs in Motivation, Development, and Wellness, 9th edn. Guilford publications, New York, NY, USA (2017)
28. Ryan, R.M., Mims, V., Koestner, R.: Relation of reward contingency and interpersonal context to intrinsic motivation: a review and test using cognitive evaluation theory. J. Pers. Soc. Psychol. vol. 45, no. 4, p. 736 (1983)
29. Houlfort, N., Koestner, R., Joussemet, M., Nantel-Vivier, A., Lekes, N.: The impact of performance-contingent rewards on perceived autonomy and competence. Motiv. Emot. **26**(4), 279–295 (2002). https://doi.org/10.1023/A:1022819120237

30. Harackiewicz, M., Manderlink, G.: A process analysis of the effects of performance-contingent rewards on intrinsic motivation. J. Exp. Soc. Psychol. **20**(6), 531–551 (1984). https://doi.org/10.1016/0022-1031(84)90042-8
31. Yamaguchi, M., Nishimura, A.: Modulating proactive cognitive control by reward: differential anticipatory effects of performance-contingent and non-contingent rewards. Psychol. Res. **83**(2), 258–274 (2019). https://doi.org/10.1007/s00426-018-1027-2
32. Lewis, Z.H., Swartz, M.C., Lyons, E.J.: What's the point?: a review of reward systems implemented in gamification interventions. Games Health J **5**(2), 93–99 (2016)
33. Soranzo, A., Cooksey, D.: Testing taxonomies : beyond card sorting the need for user testing of taxonomies. Bull. Assoc. Inf. Sci. Technol. **41**, 34–39 (2015)
34. Gisev, N., Bell, J.S., Chen, T.F.: Interrater agreement and interrater reliability: Key concepts, approaches, and applications. Res. Social Adm. Pharm. **9**(3), 330–338 (2013). https://doi.org/10.1016/j.sapharm.2012.04.004
35. Hayes, J.R., Hatch, J.A.: Issues in measuring reliability: correlation versus percentage of agreement. Writ. Commun. **16**(3), 354–367 (1999). https://doi.org/10.1177/0741088399016003004
36. Graham, M., Milanowski, A., Miller, J.: Measuring and promoting inter-rater agreement of teacher and principal performance ratings (2012)
37. Park, C.U., Kim, H.J.: Measurement of inter-rater reliability in systematic review. Hanyang Med. Rev. **35**(1), 44 (2015). https://doi.org/10.7599/hmr.2015.35.1.44
38. Hartmann, D.P.: Considerations in the choice of interobserver reliability estimates. J. Appl. Behav. Anal. **10**(1), 103–116 (1977). https://doi.org/10.1901/jaba.1977.10-103
39. Stemler, S.E.: A comparison of consensus, consistency, and measurement approaches to estimating interrater reliability. Pract. Assess. Res. Eval. **9**(4) (2004)
40. van Berlo, K., Liblik, K.C.: The business of micro transactions. pp. 1–106, 2016.
41. Tomic, N.: Effects of micro transactions on video games industry. Megatrend Rev. **14**(3), 239–257 (2017). https://doi.org/10.5937/megrev1703239t
42. Gibson, E., Griffiths, M.D., Calado, F., Harris, A.: Videogame player experiences with micro-transactions: an interpretative phenomenological analysis. Comput. Human Behav. **145**, 107766 (2023). https://doi.org/10.1016/j.chb.2023.107766.
43. Nielsen, D.: The moral economy of micro-transactions in digital games. Baltic Screen Media Rev. **8**(1), 92–110 (2020). https://doi.org/10.2478/bsmr-2020-0009
44. McCaffrey, M.: The macro problem of microtransactions: the self-regulatory challenges of video game loot boxes. Bus. Horiz. **62**(4), 483–495 (2019). https://doi.org/10.1016/j.bushor.2019.03.001
45. Manzano-León, A., et al.: Between level up and game over: a systematic literature review of gamification in education. Sustainability (Switzerland) **13**(4), 1–14 (2021). https://doi.org/10.3390/su13042247

Sustainability and Environmental Literacy in Serious Games

Design and Evaluation of a Serious Game on Household Sustainability

Jan Sau[1](✉), Imma Boada[2], Aleix Dorca Josa[1], and Laura Sánchez-Pascuala Gómez[2]

[1] Universitat d'Andorra, AD600 Sant Julià de Lòria, Andorra
JSAU@UDA.AD
[2] Graphics and Imaging Laboratory, Universitat de Girona, 17003 Girona, Catalonia

Abstract. Sustainability education has evolved from a necessity to a responsibility, or even an obligation. Numerous awareness initiatives have been implemented to meet this, including advertising campaigns and educational materials. Serious games combine entertainment with education and offer a powerful communication strategy to engage society and promote sustainability awareness. This paper presents Pick Energy Cards, a prototype of a serious game designed to educate players on energy consumption, water waste, and environmental pollution. The study's primary focus is the evaluation process, which aims to validate the game concept and assess both its usability and playability before testing its educational impact. To achieve this, the EGameFlow usability survey has been employed. A diverse group of 24 participants, aged 18 to 60, with varying levels of video game experience, participated in the study. After playing the game, participants completed the survey. The results demonstrate that Pick Energy Cards has the potential to serve as an effective learning tool for players across all age groups.

Keywords: Serious games · Evaluation · Gamification · Sustainability · Energy · Household ecology

1 Introduction

Sustainability is defined by United Nations Brundtland Commission as *"meeting the needs of the present without compromising the ability of future generations to meet their own needs"* [19]. This definition offers a broad perspective on sustainability, revealing the complexity of conveying its pedagogical content to educate the population. This complexity arises from interconnected systems, long-term considerations, the balance between human needs and environmental limits, and the call for active engagement. In this context, serious games can be a good strategy to engage the population, as they both entertain and educate, making complex sustainability concepts more accessible and compelling to the audience.

Serious games are an effective strategy for transmitting important concepts across various domains. They are used in fields such as climate change adaptation, corporate settings, research, rehabilitation, and team building to engage

A. SchÃűnbohm et al. (Eds.): GALA 2024, LNCS 15348, pp. 145–155, 2025.
https://doi.org/10.1007/978-3-031-78269-5_14

audiences, improve efficiency, gather data, aid recovery, and build trust. These games offer an accessible and cost-effective approach that traditional methods cannot match [4,6].

Focusing on sustainability, a variety of serious games can be found in the literature. Among these, there are: *Cansuyu Elektrik*, a game proposed by Abdusselam to educate on energy consumption that requires players to manage energy sources to keep lights on and enemies away [2]. Tests with the game demonstrated a significant increase in students' awareness of energy sources after playing, indicating a positive effect on behavior change; Gustafsson et al. proposed *Power Agent*, a serious game designed to engage teenagers and families in reducing home energy consumption by tracking the energy consumption in the participants' homes and competing with rival households [14]; Liu et al. proposed *Smarter households*, a serious game aimed to influence energy use in social housing. Households received dashboards displaying real-time data, collected via utility meters and indoor sensors, on energy consumption, costs, and indoor environmental conditions, comparing weekly consumption [17]. There are also *Climate Challenge* and, *EnerCities*, designed for societal and environmental studies at various educational levels, and *Shortfall*, for industrial management and targeted to engineering students. These three games, evaluated by Katsaliaki and Mustafee [16], effectively incorporate environmental, economic, and societal sustainability, providing players with a comprehensive understanding of sustainable decision-making. Casals et al. proposed *EnerGAware* where players complete missions to learn energy efficiency, using real energy data for the decisions [7]. Initial findings showed promising short-term energy savings, with tenants voluntarily participating in the engaging and visually appealing game. More recently, Gawel et al. presented *BizArena* that seeks to integrate sustainability into virtual business simulators for higher education to boost students' environmental awareness [13]. Their findings emphasize the complexity of incorporating all aspects of sustainability into a single game, as it complicates the interactions between various business elements, making the objective of business diversification more challenging. For a review of how serious games can enhance understanding of sustainability issues, see Stanitsas et al. [22].

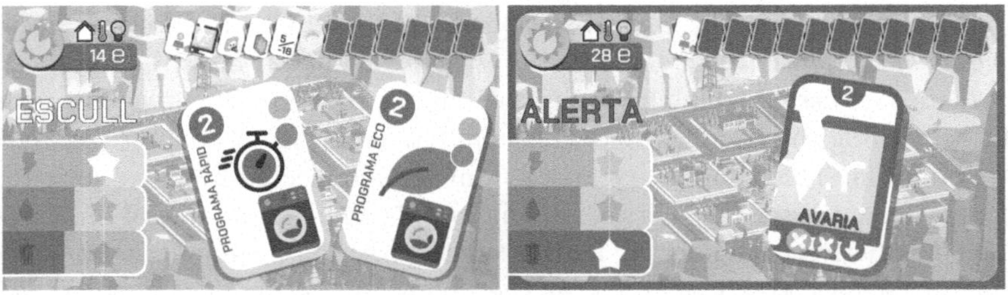

(a) (b)

Fig. 1. The two types of situations that may appear in the game: (a) *Pick Situation*, (b) *Event Situation*.

This paper presents Pick Energy Cards, the prototype and validation of a serious game to educate on sustainability and focused on energy consumption, water usage, and environmental impact to all ages. The game design allows for content customization, making it adaptable to evolving sustainability topics and various learning situations. Following this introduction, the paper is structured as follows: Sect. 2, Materials and Methods, presents the serious game, the testing scenario, and the evaluation methodology. Section 3 presents Results and Discussion. Finally, Conclusions and Future Work are given in Sect. 4.

2 Material and Methods

2.1 Pick Energy Cards Serious Game

Pick Energy Cards aims to promote sustainable lifestyles by integrating insights from various disciplines. The goal is to reduce the ecological footprint of domestic activities through engaging gameplay focused on waste management, energy consumption, and water usage. To design the game the Learning Mechanics-Game Mechanics design model [5] has been applied. This ensures coherence between learning objectives, game mechanics, learning mechanics, and assessment strategies [3,15]. The key concepts of the game are presented below.

Learning Objectives. In the game, Andorra's government official guides on household ecology were analyzed and used as a reference [1]. The referenced guide introduces daily household actions, such as managing different types of waste, using electricity-consuming appliances, regulating energy for heating or cooling rooms, and using water resources for various purposes. It also informs about the implications of each situation in terms of consumption, pollution, and cost, and it offers useful advice to be more sustainable in the short and long run.

Game Mechanics and Learning Mechanics. The game integrates Andorra's guide actions using the *dilemma choice mechanic*, presenting binary choices that impact sustainability, based on source material [1]. The gameplay of Pick Energy Cards revolves around players engaging in decision-making processes concerning energy consumption, water waste, and environmental pollution using a card-based mechanism, while keeping track to stay on budget. Players are tasked with selecting pairs of actions, named situations, that are presented as cards to manage resources at both the household and neighborhood levels effectively. These cards (as shown in Fig. 1) feature a relevant image, a pick cost that affects the budget on the corresponding level, the resources they affect (represented as colored circles), and an icon if the card may impact future situations. There are two types of possible situations (see Fig. 1), i.e., Pick Situations, where the player must select between two different options (such as taking a shower or having a bath), and Event Situations, which are unpredictable misfortunes that may affect your scores if you have not provisioned it (such as a heat wave, where having an isolated home can palliate the energy consumption effects of it). Strategic decision-making is crucial as players navigate sustainability challenges, strive to optimize their resource usage, and not spend all the level coins before obtaining all three stars.

Assessment. The game pathway initiates with an interactive tutorial designed to familiarize players with the core mechanics of the game. Subsequently, players progress to the main gameplay, where they are presented with a level selection interface featuring nine levels and three difficulty settings. Following each level attempt, players receive a color grading score reflective of their performance, mirroring the European Energy Label system [8], achieved through their progression and solving of situations presented and their budget management. Score follows the three-star system, that many games have and that has shown a potential to encourage players to follow the desired behaviour [12]. High scores unlock bonus playtime, serving as an incentive for players to excel and engage further.

The game employs a feedback mechanism to motivate players and maintain engagement. Upon completing a level or when the allotted time runs out, players receive a final score reflecting their performance across levels. The final score is obtained by aggregating the three-star scores achieved in each level, resulting in a score ranging from 0 to 27. The score is then graded using the color coding and the lettering system of the European Energy Label.

Global Game Overview. In Fig. 2 the structure followed by the main game and each level to complete them is illustrated. This structured game progression reinforces learning outcomes and enhances decision-making skills. Based on learning and game mechanics principles, Pick Energy Cards guides players through distinct stages: *Situation events*: These present players with realistic scenarios to solve; *Resource management challenges*: Players must make strategic decisions about allocating limited resources; *Level recaps*: These provide a recap of key learning points from each level; and *Feedback loops*: Players receive immediate feedback on their actions, allowing them to learn and improve.

2.2 Evaluation Based on EGameFlow

To validate the game concept, test the prototype's usability and playability, and green-light the game for evaluation in a future learning effectiveness study, the EGameFlow questionnaire was selected. This questionnaire [11] follows a seven-point Likert scale and gauges how much a player enjoys themselves while playing a serious game. Therefore, it serves as a reliable predictor of the game's capacity for learning, according to previous research [9], as well as the validity of its results [11,21]. To assess Pick Energy Cards eight EGameFlow criteria have been considered. These are *focus*, *challenge*, *objective clarity*, *feedback*, *autonomy*, *immersion*, *social interaction*, and *knowledge enhancement*. The *social interaction* element of the survey was excluded since the game does not partake in social engagement in-game. The seven selected EGameFlow scales have a list of sub-scales, that measure in detail each of the seven main items. For each scale,

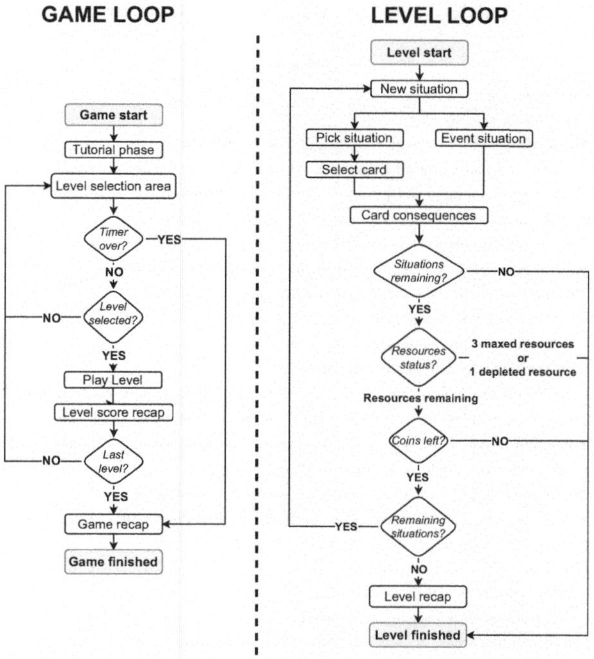

Fig. 2. A game flux diagram for both the full game and for each level.

four questions were selected forming the 7 sub-scales and 28 items included in the overall assessment as shown in Table 1.

Additionally, questions regarding demographics were incorporated (see Table 2), which can also be found in previous related research [18]. These questions provide further insight into the study participants, allowing the possibility to determine whether the designed prototype can be utilized by all user types or if it only caters to specific target audiences. Questions in this demographic poll focused on participants' age and occupation status, as well as topics related to the participants' familiarity with games.

2.3 Participants

To obtain information from a diverse sample, the prototype concept was tested on a demographically varied group of 24 people, spanning ages 18 to 60, who were contacted via email to participate. This range of participants was considered appropriate for the assessment because the base document, used to design the game, is targeted at all types of audiences, and adults and young adults are familiar with the everyday decisions the game portrays.

Participants received a fixed set of instructions to conduct the experiment. In these, the participants needed to download the game, play it to completion, without any more guides or clues than the ones already included in the serious game,

Table 1. EGameFlow survey questions

EGameFlow survey		
Scale	Code	Sub-scale
Concentration	C1	The game grabs my attention.
	C2	The game provides content that stimulates my attention.
	C3	I can remain concentrated throughout the game.
	C4	Most of the gaming activities are related to the learning task.
Goal Clarity	GC1	Overall game goals were presented in the beginning of the game.
	GC2	Overall game goals were presented clearly.
	GC3	Intermediate goals were presented in the beginning of each scene.
	GC4	Intermediate goals were presented clearly.
Feedback	F1	I receive feedback on my progress in the game.
	F2	I receive immediate feedback on my actions.
	F3	I am notified of new tasks immediately.
	F4	I receive information on my success (or failure) of intermediate goals immediately.
Challenge	CH1	The game provides "hints" in text that help me overcome the challenges.
	CH2	The game provides video or audio auxiliaries that help me overcome the challenges.
	CH3	I enjoy the game without feeling bored or anxious.
	CH4	The game provides new challenges with an appropriate pacing.
Autonomy	A1	The game does not allow players to make errors to a degree that they cannot progress in the game.
	A2	I feel a sense of control and impact over the game.
	A3	I know next step in the game.
	A4	I feel a sense of control over the game.
Immersion	I1	I forget about time passing while playing the game.
	I2	I become unaware of my surroundings while playing the game.
	I3	I can be involved in the game.
	I4	I feel emotionally involved in the game.
Knowledge Improvement	K1	The game increases my knowledge.
	K2	I catch the basic ideas of the knowledge taught.
	K3	The game motivates the player to integrate the knowledge taught.
	K4	I want to know more about the knowledge taught

and once completed respond to the designed questionnaire. After responding the questionnaire participants' game data was retrieved, to verify the game was played to completion, as well as the overall game time. This procedure aimed to avoid any variance in experience for the participants and ensure their experience was homogeneous. Participants were also encouraged to send written feedback on their experience, which will be taken into account in further iterations.

2.4 Evaluation Metrics

The answers from the demographic survey and the EGameFlow survey have been analyzed to evaluate the outcome of the testing. Demographic questions served two purposes. First, they were used as sub-setting items to identify relevant discrepancies between groups. Second, they provided a profile of the participants, helping to validate that a diverse sample had been selected. For the EGameFlow survey seven-point Likert answers, have been analyzed numerically to get a mean score for each scale and subs-scale, as well as an overall score.

The Mann-Whitney U test was selected to evaluate differences between groups. This non-parametric test was deemed most appropriate because the data comprised ordinal satisfaction ratings on a 1 to 7 scale, which do not meet the normality assumptions required for parametric tests like the t-test. By comparing the distributions of these ranked satisfaction scores between groups, the Mann-Whitney U test allows for the identification of statistically significant differences in perceived satisfaction levels without assuming normality in the data.

3 Results and Discussion

Table 2 displays demographic questions and results gathered through the survey. Results show that the survey received responses from a varied group, ranging between 18 and 60 years old, with almost half of them ranging between 27 and 35 years old (50%), followed by 18 to 26 years old (25%). In terms of occupation, the survey received no answers from unemployed people, and the majority of the responses came from employed people (75%).

In terms of their relationship with video games, around 29,17% of participants do not play video games regularly, which correlates with the novice (8.33%) and less experienced gamer (20.83%) in the experience with video game questions. In terms of participants who regularly play video games, most view themselves as experienced players (45.83%) and all of them play games for their entertainment, but only a set of them play to learn something (29.41%). These varied results will allow the possibility of having a more global view of the perception of the game by many player profiles, through the EGameFlow survey.

Results for the overall EGameFlow test are positive, as seen in Table 3. For each of the seven scales, and each question the mean was calculated to show the overall perception for each dimension of the test, also a mean for all categories was calculated to give an overall perception of the game. Having a seven-point Likert test sets 4 as the average score, so all scores surpassing 4 show a positive perception. In terms of scoring the overall score for the game, for all categories, is 5,32, with *Feedback*, *Goal Clarity*, and *Knowledge Improvement* graded as the highest ones, and *Immersion* graded as the worst one, being the only scale under 5. Concentration is also close to third best score. These results show that the game gives clear instructions, guides the players and communicates their performance through feedback, and makes the players perceive a gain of knowledge, as well as incites their curiosity to expand it.

Figure 3 shows the results for each question and each of the 7 Likert score answers (from Strongly Disagree to Strongly Agree) by percentage. This visual representation further displays that the majority of results are positive. Also, data was analyzed by grouping answers to analyze if there were any significant differences. Separations aimed to ensure that the lack of games literacy of the participants and the particular ways a game uses to communicate were not affecting the overall game experience, since they can hinder the transmission of knowledge [20]. Grouping participants between people who do not play often (n=7) and people who play weekly (n=17) showed no statistical difference in any of the survey questions. Conversely, when separating the age groups into two (35 and younger and 36 and older), out of the 28 questions analyzed using

Table 2. Demographic survey answers

Characteristics	Item	Amount	Percentage
Age	18–26	6	25,00%
	27–35	12	50,00%
	36–44	3	12,50%
	45 and older	3	12,50%
Current occupation	Student	6	25,00%
	Employed	18	75,00%
	Unemployed	0	0,00%
How many hours do you spend playing video games per week?	I don't play video games	7	29,17%
	0–2 hours per week	5	20,83%
	3 h per week	2	8,33%
	4 - 6 h per week	3	12,50%
	7 - 9 h per week	1	4,17%
	10 h or more	6	25,00%
I play computer games: (Multiple choice) *(Only answers from people who play weekly)*	To learn something	5	29,41%
	For a challenge	8	47,06%
	For fun	17	100,00%
	To fulfill my leisure time	12	70,59%
I feel that I am a/an	Experienced gamer	11	45,83%
	Moderate experience gamer	6	25,00%
	Less experienced gamer	5	20,83%
	Novice gamer	2	8,33%

the Mann-Whitney U test, four questions-GC1, GC4, F3, and A1-showed statistically significant differences between the groups (p-values below 0.05). Specifically, for GC1, the test statistic was $W = 81$ ($p = 0.041$), for GC4, $W = 85$ ($p = 0.034$), for F3, $W = 81$ ($p = 0.041$), and for A1, $W = 82.5$ ($p = 0.045$). These results indicate that, while the majority of the questions did not show significant differences, responses to these four questions revealed a meaningful distinction between the groups. Even though the overall responses are positive in both groups, results may imply that the detailing of goals can be improved and rewritten to be clearer. These results highlight the potential of the developed prototype to educate users of all profiles on the importance of household ecology. Data from the written commentaries for the participants, as well as the survey results, provides crucial information to iterate on the developed prototype and release the game.

Table 3. EGameFlow survey average answers

Scale	Code	Mean	Scale	Code	Mean	Scale	Code	Mean	Scale	Code	Mean
Concentration	C1	5,63	**Feedback**	F1	6,00	**Autonomy**	A1	5,38	**K. Improvement**	K1	5,75
	C2	5,29		F2	6,46		A2	5,58		K2	6,33
	C3	6,08		F3	6,54		A3	6,00		K3	5,71
	C4	6,21		F4	6,33		A4	5,54		K4	5,71
	All	**5,80**		All	**6,33**		All	**5,63**		All	**5,88**
Goal Clarity	GC1	6,33	**Challenge**	CH1	5,42	**Immersion**	I1	4,63	**EGameFlow**	Global	**5,66**
	GC2	5,92		CH2	4,88		I2	4,46			
	GC3	5,83		CH3	5,29		I3	5,58			
	GC4	5,58		CH4	5,50		I4	4,54			
	All	**5,92**		All	**5,27**		All	**4,80**			

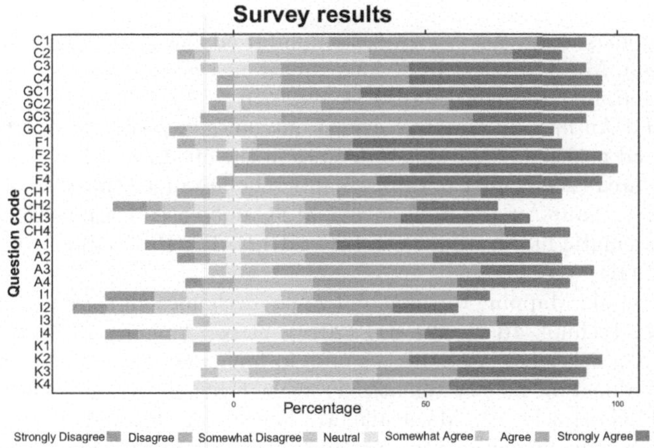

Fig. 3. EGameFlow survey results in percentage

4 Conclusions and Future Work

This paper introduced Pick Energy Cards, a game designed to educate players about sustainability. The game employs a card-based system where players must select the best options to efficiently preserve their resources, addressing a broad range of sustainability issues. This design allows for easy expansion and scalability. The study reports the results of the EGameFlow survey, which was conducted with a diverse group of participants varying in age and video game experience. Survey results suggest that the game has strong potential as an effective educational tool. From the results obtained and discussed, the game provides an enjoyable way to learn about sustainable practices in households, benefiting people of all ages by increasing their interest and desire for knowledge on home sustainability.

Future work will focus on testing the game in real-world environments (e.g. Fijnheer et al. [10], a game that engages players in real-world energy-saving missions, where they complete tasks while receiving feedback on their energy consumption). A key area of interest is evaluating the amount of knowledge players acquire about sustainability. To achieve this, in-game statistics will be collected and analyzed quantitatively. Additionally, the game will be expanded to include more cards and scenarios, covering a broader range of sustainability themes. Improvements will be made to enhance game immersion and challenge scaling based on survey results. The goal is to ensure the final game is accessible and beneficial for all types of players, regardless of their video game experience.

Conflict of interest. The authors declare that they have no conflict of interest.

References

1. Ecologia domèstica, https://www.sostenibilitat.ad/docs/ecologia_domestica.pdf
2. Abdüsselam, M.: The effect of serious games on the awareness of energy sources consumption. Int. Technol. Educ. J. **4**, 7 (2020)
3. Adam, S.F.: An introduction to learning outcomes a consideration of the nature , function and position of learning outcomes in the creation of the European higher education area (2006). https://api.semanticscholar.org/CorpusID:8549631
4. Aragonez, T., Saur-Amaral, I., Gouveia, M.: Game-based learning in higher education: a systematic literature review. In: EDULEARN Proceedings, pp. 1849–1856. IATED (2021)
5. Arnab, S., et al.: Mapping learning and game mechanics for serious games analysis. Br. J. Edu. Technol. **46**(2), 391–411 (2014). https://doi.org/10.1111/bjet.12113
6. Brandl, L.C., Schrader, A.: Serious games in higher education in the transforming process to education 4.0—systematized review. Educ. Sci. (Basel) **14**(3), 281 (2024)
7. Casals, M., Gangolells, M., Macarulla, M., Fuertes, A., Vimont, V., Pinho, L.M.: A serious game enhancing social tenants' behavioral change towards energy efficiency. In: 2017 Global Internet of Things Summit (GIoTS), pp. 1–6 (2017)
8. Comission, E.: Understanding the energy label. https://energy-efficient-products.ec.europa.eu/ecodesign-and-energy-label/understanding-energy-label_en
9. Espinosa-Curiel, I.E., Pozas-Bogarin, E.E., Martínez-Miranda, J., Pérez-Espinosa, H.: Relationship between children's enjoyment, user experience satisfaction, and learning in a serious video game for nutrition education: empirical pilot study. JMIR Serious Game. **8**(3), e21813 (2020)
10. Fijnheer, J.D., van Oostendorp, H., Giezeman, G.J., Veltkamp, R.C.: Competition in a household energy conservation game. Sustainability **13**(21) (2021). https://doi.org/10.3390/su132111991, https://www.mdpi.com/2071-1050/13/21/11991
11. Fu, F.L., Su, R.C., Yu, S.C.: EGameFlow: a scale to measure learners' enjoyment of e-learning games. Comput. Educ. **52**, 101–112 (2009)
12. Gaston, J., Cooper, S.: To three or not to three (2017)
13. Gawel, A., Strykowski, S., Madias, K.: Implementing sustainability into virtual simulation games in business higher education. Educ. Sci. (Basel) (2022)
14. Gustafsson, A., Katzeff, C., Bang, M.: Evaluation of a pervasive game for domestic energy engagement among teenagers. Comput. Entertain. **7**(4), 1–19 (2009)
15. Kalmpourtzis, G., Romero, M.: Constructive alignment of learning mechanics and game mechanics in serious game design in higher education. Int. J. Serious Game. **7**(4), 75–88 (2020)
16. Katsaliaki, K., Mustafee, N.: Serious games for sustainable development. J. Manag. Educ. **37**(6), 889–894 (2013)

17. Liu, S., et al.: Impact of emerging interaction techniques on energy use in the UK social housing. Futur. Cities Environ. **4**(1) (2018)
18. Johari, N.F.M., L, Ishak, N., Zaini, H.: Adopting the eGameFlow model in an educational game to increase knowledge about vaccination. JOIV : Int. J. Inf. Vis. **7**, 338–344 (2023) https://doi.org/10.30630/joiv.7.2.1809
19. Nations, U.: Sustainability defintion. https://www.un.org/en/academic-impact/sustainability (2024), [Online; Accessed 3 June 2024]
20. Sherrick, B.: Video games and communication (Mar 2018), title of the publication associated with this dataset: Oxford Bibliographies Online Datasets
21. Shu-Hui, C., Wann-Yih, W., Dennison, J.: Validation of eGameFlow: a self-report scale for measuring user experience in video game play. Comput. Entertain. **16**(3) (2018). https://doi.org/10.1145/3238249,https://doi.org/10.1145/3238249
22. Stanitsas, M., Kirytopoulos, K., Vareilles, E.: Facilitating sustainability transition through serious games: a systematic literature review. J. Clean. Prod. **208**, 924–936 (2019)

Graveler - Global Awareness Education Through Virtual Voyages

Kevin Körner[1(✉)], Esther Fink[2], Ann-Kathrin Steiner[3], Jennifer Chupakhin[3], and Glaucia Peres da Silva[3]

[1] MA Specialization Digital Humanities, University of Tübingen, Keplerstr. 2, 72074 Tübingen, Germany
kevin.korner@uni-tuebingen.de
[2] Center for Teaching and Learning, University of Tübingen, Sigwartstr. 20, 72076 Tübingen, Germany
esther.fink@uni-tuebingen.de
[3] Global Awareness Education, University of Tübingen, Rümelinstraße 19, 23, 72070 Tübingen, Germany
{ann-Kathrin.steiner,jennifer.chupakhin, glauciaperes.dasilva}@uni-tuebingen.de

Abstract. This paper examines the course "*What is Globalization?*" offered through the Global Awareness Education program at the University of Tübingen, which seeks to transcend the typical media focus on the economic dimensions of globalization. Instead, this fully online course aims to deepen students' understanding of the complex effects of globalization on politics, cultures, the environment, and interpersonal interactions across diverse global communities. Utilizing the 2D, web-based, role-play serious game Graveler - Globe Traveler - as both a learning and communication platform, the course employs a "virtual trip around the world" didactic concept. Presented here are the findings from four classes conducted since 2023 using this innovative educational approach. We detail the capabilities of Graveler that enhance student learning experiences and discuss the methodology and outcomes of our study, including a quantitative survey on the game's acceptance and a qualitative analysis of students' final assignments to assess learning outcomes. Additionally, we explore the Graveler backend, which allows users to create their own virtual journeys on topics beyond globalization, and discuss potential applications of this tool.

Keywords: Serious Games · Global Awareness Education · e-learning platform

1 Introduction

Over the past few decades, the term globalization has become increasingly prevalent in academia and the media. Often associated primarily with economic processes, as Smith [1] explains, globalization encompasses much more. The course

A. Schönbohm et al. (Eds.): GALA 2024, LNCS 15348, pp. 156–166, 2025.
https://doi.org/10.1007/978-3-031-78269-5_15

"*What is Globalization*", offered by the Global Awareness Education program at the University of Tübingen, explores the multifaceted effects of globalization on politics, cultures, the environment, and interpersonal interactions.

Through the web-based, 2-dimensional, multiplayer role-playing game "*Globe Traveler*" (Graveler), students engage with standard literature on globalization topics. Additionally, they virtually visit cities directly connected to scientific globalization research, gaining deeper insights into the conditions under which scientific work was produced, such as the economic or political contexts and cultural changes influencing researchers. Graveler was designed and developed by an interdisciplinary team from the Global Awareness Education, the MA Specialization Digital Humanities and University Didactics. The game incorporates interactive elements for knowledge presentation and referencing web resources, along with a quest-like gameplay to motivate long-term engagement. Furthermore, a spatial chat feature, which enables players to initiate video calls directly within their browser when multiple characters converge in the virtual world, is included to facilitate interaction among students and promote the exchange of their experiences.

The course provides students with a common foundation for understanding globalization, and through Graveler, it offers the opportunity to comprehend the cultural background of research findings, thereby fostering a nuanced understanding of the topic. In this paper, we present the evaluation results from four classes conducted since summer 2023. Initially, we conducted a quantitative survey to assess whether the system was intuitive to use, if it motivated the players, and which elements were perceived positively versus those needing improvement. Additionally, we qualitatively analyzed learning outcome patterns based on the assignments students submitted for course assessments.

Section 2 provides an overview of related work. Section 3 details the didactic concept and how Graveler was integrated into the course. Section 4 presents the results of a quantitative survey on the acceptance of Graveler and qualitative findings based on student term papers. Section 5 discusses the benefits of the underlying class creation functionality, which facilitates the implementation of Graveler games in various settings, and provides an outlook on ongoing work. Finally, Sect. 6 concludes our work.

2 Related Work

The use of role-playing in digital games can be traced back to the worldwide success of the tabletop game Dungeons & Dragons in the early 1970 s. As Brad King and John Borland state, "*Scratch almost any game developer who worked between the late 1970 s and the early 2000 s, and you're likely to find a vein of role-playing experience*" [2]. Since then, a wide range of role-playing games (RPGs) have been developed, including those used in educational settings. Lehto [3], for example, provides an overview of serious RPGs developed for well-being, categorizing them into subcategories such as cultural, therapeutic, and even erotic role-playing games that actively promote well-being. She notes that "*the common feature is that the player plays a role: he performs actions, thinks and speaks for the character, and sometimes even feels the emotions of his character.*" Hammer et al. offer an overview of RPGs as an educational method in [4], stating that "*role-playing games can, under the right circumstances, help players learn new skills, motivate them to engage with academic or non-academic content, support collaboration, and much more*". They identify the "*right circumstances for effective learning*" as including "*portraying a character; manipulating a fictional world; experiencing an altered sense of reality, which can either heighten the stakes of fictional decisions or lower the stakes of realistic ones; supporting collaboration through shared imaginative spaces; and learning through making role-playing games.*" MacCallum-Stewart et al. additionally provide a research overview on the impact of RPGs on Western culture in [5].

Through such opportunities to "experience" learning coupled with reflection activities during or post gameplay allows learners to gain valuable insights as Mekler [6] explains. Building on the rules and success factors of non-digital RPGs used in teaching, digital serious RPGs have been developed. For example, the work of Herrero et al. [7] motivated us to develop 2D educational multiplayer escape rooms in Graveler. Another influence on Graveler's multiplayer strategy was the serious game Masters of Air (SAIR), a digital multiplayer chemistry RPG developed by Varvara Garneli [8]. Both examples illustrate how to create the right learning circumstances as proposed by Hammer. However, both lack the capability for geographically distributed players to participate.

A significant inspiration for Graveler was Gather[1], a web-based meeting platform that offers basic 2D role-playing gameplay with features like character customization, movement within regions, multiplayer elements, and spatial chat functionality. Additionally, it allows users to create individual sceneries and integrate references and interactive elements. However, it lacks core RPG elements such as a quest system and tools for manipulating the fictional world.

In her research, Oygardslia presents seven serious games developed to teach topics related to promoting global awareness [9] which we took in consideration during our planning phase. However, the games analyzed include strategy, adventure, and point-and-click games, but none belong to the RPG genre.

3 Didactic Concept

3.1 A Virtual Trip Around the World

The *What is Globalization?* course is designed to be delivered entirely online and aims to introduce students to the fundamentals of globalization and its impacts on societies worldwide. The didactic concept is illustrated in Fig. 1 and described below. During the course, participants embark on a virtual journey to four replicas of cities around the globe, where they discuss well-regarded scientific publications on the topic. After a short stop in virtual Tübingen, the

[1] https://www.gather.town/, last accessed 17.07.24.

journey begins in Milton Keynes, starting with "*Introduction in Global Transformations*" by David Held et al. [10]. Next, in Mexico City, students explore "*Globalization and the Ethics of Liberation*" by Enrique Dussel [11]. The third city is Jerusalem, where "*Multiple Modernities in an Age of Globalization*" by Shmuel N. Eisenstadt [12] is discussed. Finally, the course concludes with visiting Johannesburg with "*Walking on Water: Globalization and History*" by Dilip M. Menon [13].

Week	**1**	**2 + 3**	**4 + 5**	**6 + 7**	**8 + 9**	**10-12**
City	TÜ	MK	MC	JE	JO	-
Task	Onboarding	Held [10]	Dussel [11]	Eisenstadt [12]	Menon [13]	Essay

Fig. 1. Didactic Schedule of *What is Globalization?*: Each city (Tübingen, Milton Keynes, Mexico City, Jerusalem, Johannesburg) is explored over a two-week period, with one week dedicated to individual exploration and literature review, followed by the task to write a term paper (essay) in the subsequent weeks.

To provide students with a more immersive experience during the course, the serious game *Graveler* was developed. It is a web-based, multiplayer role-playing game featuring spatial chat and elements from learning platforms such as Moodle[2]. Graveler draws significant inspiration from RPG Maker[3] and Gather. To maximize the game's success, we incorporated Caserman et al.'s [14] recommendations during development, ensuring the inclusion of clear feedback, well-defined targets, and graphics appropriate for the target audience.

The course utilized Graveler as follows: In the initial session in virtual Tübingen, students underwent a digital onboarding to familiarize themselves with Graveler's technical and organizational aspects. This session also addressed any technical issues, such as incorrect login data or browser setting errors. Over the following weeks, asynchronous and group sessions alternated biweekly. During the asynchronous sessions, students explored virtual cities within Graveler independently and completed related exercise tasks. The lecturer was only available for technical questions during that time. The subsequent group sessions utilized the course's spatial chat functionality for discussions, enriching these exchanges by occasionally including external scientists as guest discussion partners. This approach aimed to immerse students in the cities and cultures they studied, ensuring a shared knowledge base. The course culminated in a group discussion, after which each student was required to write an essay detailing their understanding of the class topic and their experiences with Graveler.

[2] https://moodle.org/, last accessed 16.07.24.
[3] https://www.rpgmakerweb.com/, last accessed 16.07.24.

3.2 Graveler

Within Graveler, students gain brief insights into the local cultural and academic environments during their virtual trips to various cities, as depicted in Fig. 2. Players navigate through scenic environments and engage with a variety of interactive elements. Non-Player Characters (NPCs) guide the players and contribute to storytelling. Furthermore, interaction spots offer textual information and link to external resources on the World Wide Web, such as videos, 360-degree pictures, browser games, or collaborative workspaces like an Etherpad[4] instance.

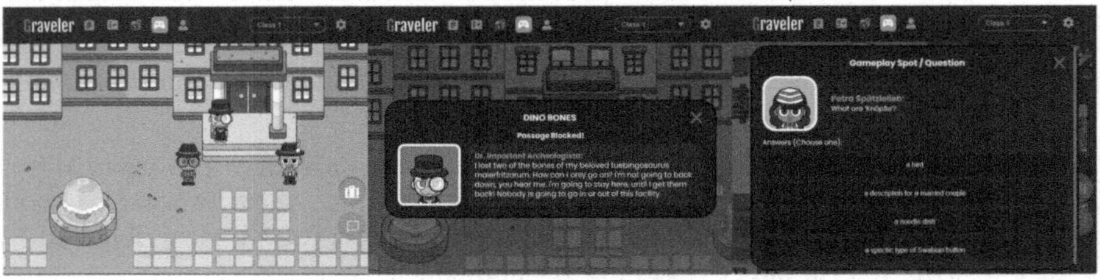

Fig. 2. Left: In-game scenery featuring an avatar and NPCs. Center: Blocked passage. Right: Question spot.

Throughout their journey, students are accompanied by their travel diary, the so-called Traveldex, inspired by Japanese Eki Stamp books. This diary graphically records key events of their virtual journey, such as the arrival and departure dates for the cities and achievements unlocked. Interactions at designated sightseeing spots within the virtual cities - highlighting unique objects, places, or persons - result in stamps added to the Traveldex and provide structured information. Additionally, can collect their notes, thoughts and ideas in a notebook.

Players encounter four types of gameplay spots during their experience: multiple-choice questions, object collection, object delivery, and minigames. These spots primarily serve to advance the storyline by blocking passage through certain areas of the map until resolved. Players must gather information and objects in the virtual city and utilize associated resources to progress. Additionally, some delivery-based gameplay spots may add entries to the Traveldex, especially if the main quest of a city is completed.

In addition to traditional role-playing elements, Graveler features spatial chat functionality. This integration facilitates student interaction during exploration phases, allowing them to share and discuss their findings. It also serves as the primary communication channel during the group discussions of the course.

Graveler also incorporates elements from learning platforms for course and document management. It stores additional documents in a structured manner, making them accessible to players at predefined times. These include literature for further research and exercises that must be completed within a specified

[4] https://etherpad.org/, last access 16.07.24.

period. Students upload their solutions directly to Graveler, where tutors can download and evaluate the submissions before providing feedback.

4 Evaluation

4.1 Research Questions

To evaluate student acceptance of Graveler, we conducted a voluntary survey in the final session for research purposes. The survey aimed to test several research questions: (1) *Was the system intuitive to use*, (2) *Did the system motivate the players*, (3) *Identify positively perceived elements*, and (4) *Identify elements in need of improvement.*

Additionally, to assess the effectiveness of the didactic concept in terms of content-related knowledge transfer, we analyzed the essays submitted by the students. The primary focus was on (5) *Identify learning outcome patterns based on the students' independent engagement with the content provided in Graveler.* Since there was no control group, we refrained from concluding whether the knowledge transfer was better or worse compared to other methods; this aspect is reserved for future research.

4.2 Methodology

Since the summer term of 2023, the educational concept described has been implemented in several classes at the University of Tübingen. In this paper, we investigate the first four of these classes, which were conducted entirely online, were part of CIVIS, Europe's Civic Universities Alliance network[5], and attracted 51 students from universities across Europe. The participants came from a variety of academic backgrounds, including sociology, computer science, and political science. Due to this diversity, all course materials and the language of instruction were in English. The execution of the classes followed the procedures outlined in Sect. 3.1.

4.3 Survey Results

Of the 51 students who participated, 43 completed a survey evaluating their experience. The questionnaire consisted of 39 questions covering details about the students, the course overall, and their specific experiences with Graveler. Due to space constraints in this document, we will focus exclusively on the questions related to Graveler. The survey included a range of question types: 5-point Likert scale questions (ranging from 1 for "*strongly agree*" to 5 for "*strongly disagree*"), single and multiple choice questions, and free text answers.

58% of the students identified themselves as somewhat regular computer game players, with an additional 25% playing rarely, indicating that the majority had some gaming experience. However, only two students had previously

[5] https://civis.eu.

taken a class that utilized serious games as a didactic method. The technical environment was reported to function mostly flawlessly, with mean (M) scores of 1.9, a standard deviation (SD) of 0.7, and a skewness of 0.6. The onboarding process was generally perceived as intuitive (M: 2.0, SD: 1.0, skew: 0.9). The user interface (M: 1.6, SD: 0.6, skew: 0.5) and gameplay (M: 1.8, SD: 0.8, skew: 1.7) were rated as mostly easy to understand, though students with little to no gaming experience found the gameplay and interface more challenging.

Of those who participated, 35 students customized their avatars, and 28 of these reported that customization enhanced their sense of identity and engagement in the virtual learning environment. Regarding the use of spatial chat functionality, only 14 students utilized it beyond scheduled meetings with the lecturer to communicate and collaborate with peers, and merely 5 found it an effective communication channel.

Of the students participating, 39 used Graveler to explore all four cities, while 4 explored only three. Those who visited all four cities also reported successfully completing the voluntary gameplay objectives in each location. The duration of gameplay was perceived by students as appropriate, though slightly lengthy (M: 2.7, SD: 0.6, skew: -0.8). The learning objectives were viewed as mostly clear (M: 1.7, SD: 0.65, skew: 0.9), and the content was recognized as relevant to the study of globalization (M: 1.7, SD: 0.7, skew: 0.4). Additionally, students reported that the game facilitated reflection on their intercultural competence (M: 1.7, SD: 0.9, skew: 1.5) and enhanced their understanding of the history of different regions around the world (M: 1.4, SD: 0.6, skew: 1.7).

Overall, the game experience received a positive rating, with an average grade of 1.7 on a 1 (great) to 5 (poor) scale (SD: 0.7, skew: 0.4).

In their free-text comments, students highlighted the appealing graphics and user-friendliness of Graveler. They appreciated the game's ability to familiarize them with the history, culture, and society of each city, noting the advantage of "*getting to know these aspects without needing to travel there*". Additionally, many remarked on the educational value of the game, stating that it was "*a lot of fun and increased my interest and knowledge in the topic. Time flew by and it didn't seem like that much work*". Some students also enjoyed the humorous elements of the game, such as playful interactions with silly NPCs and jokes integrated into the gameplay.

However, certain elements of Graveler received criticism from the students. Some expressed concerns about information overload, stating, "*At some point, there were so many open links and tabs that I felt like there was an information overflow*". They suggested integrating external web pages into Graveler's user interface rather than opening new browser tabs. Additionally, some students were dissatisfied with the browser compatibility limitations, as Graveler functioned properly only on Google Chrome and Mozilla Firefox.

Some students mentioned that the content within Graveler was overwhelming and found it "*time-consuming to complete 100% of a region*". However, many students also expressed satisfaction with the learning experience, noting that it was gratifying "*to learn so much about a city while playing a game*".

Many students provided suggestions to improve the user experience with Graveler. They recommended reducing the sometimes long loading times, increasing the movement speed of characters, and enhancing the visibility of interactive areas to make them easier to locate. Additionally, some students reported feeling "*lost in the regions*" during the asynchronous sessions, noting that they "*couldn't ask anyone for help because no one used Graveler at the same time*". To address this, they suggested offering additional, voluntary group sessions where interested students could concurrently explore the regions and interact using the spatial chat.

4.4 Essay Results

Of the 51 students who participated in the class, 41 submitted an essay as term paper, which were analyzed following the methodology suggested by Mayring and Fenzl [15]. The analysis was conducted step by step in a methodically controlled manner, aimed at developing a theory-guided category system. This process involved summarizing, explicating, and structuring the material. Specifically, the reduction procedure of summarizing qualitative content analysis was applied to the essays to retain essential content and create a representative corpus. The inductive approach was deemed particularly suitable for evaluating the essays, as it strives for the most naturalistic and object-oriented representation of the material without distortions from the researcher's preconceptions.

All term papers confirmed that the primary motivation for attending the course was the topic of globalization. Analysis of the essays revealed a common understanding among students regarding the influences of globalization; we identified clusters on the fields of impact on politics, culture and nature. There was considerable variation in how students weighted these effects. The analysis also showed that students recognized how framework conditions directly influenced the literature discussed.

Furthermore, clusters within the term papers indicated that the exploratory and discussion components of the course were generally received positively. Students appreciated the engaging nature of learning, which facilitated reflection on the history of various global regions. Many students expressed increased motivation to learn more about specific regions and globalization, noting that the interactive format helped them retain more information than traditional reading. Additionally, they valued the satisfaction derived from completing assignments and the flexibility to progress at their own pace.

4.5 Discussion

The results pertinent to our research question (1) indicate that the application is intuitive to use. This supports our plans to develop additional classes and adjust the scale of technical support accordingly. Concerning (2), the application's capacity to motivate the audience is confirmed by the survey results. The main takeaways for research question (3) are presented in Sect. 4.3.

However, the primary criticisms identified in response to research question (4) relate to technical issues and the time needed to navigate through external sources. A significant drawback was the under-utilization of the spatial chat functionality beyond the group meetings. One of our considerations was that the students used other channels as Discord[6] for communication. However, this finding indicates a need to revisit and better integrate this feature into the didactic plan's workflow.

Regarding (5), it was found that a majority of the students developed a common understanding of globalization and its multifaceted impact on countries, extending beyond mere economic aspects.

5 Graveler as Tool and Outlook

Graveler was designed as a learning management system that facilitates the creation of virtual worlds and classes centered around them. It provides an interface for entering class-specific parameters, such as customized travel maps and a pool of literature and exercises with publication and due dates. Virtual worlds are constructed using a grid aspect of world creation drew significant inspiration from tools like RPG Maker and Gather. Based on various tiles and objects lifelike and engaging environments can be created. The grid also delineates areas for interactive elements, sightseeing spots, and gameplay. The input dialogs for these areas also offer options for a speaker's name and illustrations, enhancing the storytelling aspect.

To explore the adaptability of the Graveler backend across various academic disciplines, initial courses beyond *What is Globalization?* have already been developed and implemented. These include topics such as *History of Ancient and Chinese Numismatics* and *Climate Change.*

We are grateful for receiving a grant from the German *Stiftung Innovation in der Hochschullehre*[7] to extend and further develop Graveler in response to feedback from students and stakeholders groups. The current development phase includes the integration of new gameplay elements such as a workflow system to control interactive elements. Additionally, we are enhancing organizational tools for lecturers, including a statistics survey feature that tracks student activities, such as play durations and interactions with gameplay elements.

6 Outlook and Conclusion

In this paper, we introduced the didactic concept behind the class *What is Global Awareness* and the serious game *Graveler.* We explored its technical capabilities as a versatile tool for developing various class concepts, analyzed its acceptance within the target audience, and assessed the effectiveness of content knowledge transfer through a qualitative examination of student essays.

[6] https://discord.com/, last access 23.07.24.
[7] https://stiftung-hochschullehre.de/, last accessed 17.07.2024.

Based on our findings, we are updating the didactic concept for future classes, focusing on enhancing collaborative interactions between students. Moreover, thanks to funding, we are further developing *Graveler* and organizing a community of practice to shape and utilize it as a platform for creating customized educational experiences. We invite interested lecturers to collaborate with us in developing a support network and shared resources.

References

1. Smith, K.E.I. (Ed.).: Sociology of Globalization: Cultures, Economies, and Politics (1st ed.), Routledge (2013). https://doi.org/10.4324/9780429493089
2. King, B., Borland, J., Stewart, Roger.: Dungeons and Dreamers: The Rise of Computer Game Culture from Geek to Chic (1st. ed.), Osborne (2003). ISBN-13: 978-0072228885
3. Lehto, K.: Role-playing games and well-being. Int. J. Role-Playing 72–93 (2021). 10.33063/ijrp.vi11.284
4. Hammer, J., To, A., Schrier, K., Bowman, S., Kaufman, G.: Learning and Role-Playing Games (2018). 10.4324/9781315637532-15
5. MacCallum-Stewart, E., Stenros, J., Björk, S.: The Impact of Role-Playing Games on Culture (2018). 10.4324/9781315637532-9
6. Mekler, E.D., Iacovides, I., Bopp, J.A.: A game that makes you question...: exploring the role of reflection for the player experience. In: Proceedings of the 2018 Annual Symposium on Computer-Human Interaction in Play (CHI PLAY 2018). Association for Computing Machinery, New York, NY, USA, 315-327 (2018). https://doi.org/10.1145/3242671.3242691
7. Herrero, A., et al.: Game-based learning with role-playing elements using RPG maker MZ. Model. Sci. Educ. Learn. **16**, 55–65 (2023). https://doi.org/10.4995/msel.2023.18975
8. Garneli, V., Patiniotis, K., Chorianopoulos, K.: Game mechanics of a character progression multiplayer role-playing game with science content. In: Marfisi-Schottman, I., Bellotti, F., Hamon, L., Klemke, R. (eds.) GALA 2020. LNCS, vol. 12517, pp. 415-420. Springer, Cham(2020). https://doi.org/10.1007/978-3-030-63464-3_40
9. Oygardslia, K.: Computer games for promoting global awareness: Methods and modes. Reading: Academic Conferences International Limited (2015). Retrieved from https://www.proquest.com/conference-papers-proceedings/computer-games-promoting-global-awareness-methods/docview/1728409586/se-2
10. Held, D., McGrew, A., David, G., Perraton, J.: Introduction in Global Transformations. Politics, Economics and Culture. Stanford. Stanford University Press, pp. 1-28 (1999)
11. Dussel, E.: Globalization, organization and the ethics of liberation. Organization **13**(4), 489 – 508 (2006)
12. Eisenstadt, S.N.: Multiple modernities in an age of globalization. Can. J. Sociol. **24**(2), 283–295 (1999)
13. Menon, D.M.: Walking on water: globalization and history. Global Perspect. **1**(1), 1–6 (2020)

14. Caserman, P., et al: Quality criteria for serious games: serious part, game part, and balance. JMIR Serious Games **8**(3), e19037 (2020). URL: https://games.jmir.org/2020/3/e19037https://doi.org/10.2196/19037
15. Mayring, P., Fenzl, T.: Qualitative Inhaltsanalyse. In: Baur, N., Blasius, J. (eds) Handbuch Methoden der empirischen Sozialforschung. Springer VS, Wiesbaden (2019). https://doi.org/10.1007/978-3-658-21308-4_42

Wicked Problems as a Frame to Teach Environmental Literacy in a Digitally-Mediated Seminar Game

Mikhail Fiadotau[1,3(✉)], Peadar Callaghan[1], Michela Tramonti[2], and Alden Dochshanov[2]

[1] School of Digital Technologies, Tallinn University, Tallinn, Estonia
fiadotau@tlu.ee
[2] EU-Track, Terracina, Italy
[3] College of Science and Technology, Nihon University, Tokyo, Japan

Abstract. The paper presents a design case study of *BIG GAME*, a digitally-mediated seminar game aimed at developing environmental literacy and STEM skills among middle-school students. The game employs a series of open-ended missions based on real-life environmental issues, framing the missions as wicked problems, i.e., complex problems that resist straightforward solutions due to their evolving and often contradictory requirements. This approach was chosen since real-life environmental issues fall under the domain of wicked problems, yet traditional education largely focuses on unambiguous problems with clear-cut solutions. The paper introduces the choices taken during the design process and reflects on the results of implementing the game as a competition involving 27 schools in four European countries.

Keywords: Wicked problems · Environmental education · Seminar game

1 Introduction

Contemporary environmental issues can be described as wicked problems: complex problems that have "a resistance to resolution because of incomplete, contradictory, or changing requirements," attempts at solving which may lead to unintended complications [14]. Traditional education, with its emphasis on clearly defined problems with unambiguous solutions, has struggled to address the uncertainty and open-endedness of wicked problems such as climate change [7]. At the same time, many educators agree that 21st century classrooms *should* aim to help students develop both tolerance for uncertainty and practical problem-solving skills that can help them tackle wicked problems in real life [3,7].

Games, both serious and otherwise, are known to facilitate learning about and reflection on wicked problems [1]. Many examples can be found in the wargaming tradition [11], including so-called seminar games: experiences in which players

F. Bellotti et al. (Eds.): GALA 2024, LNCS 15348, pp. 167–176, 2025.
https://doi.org/10.1007/978-3-031-78269-5_16

"are presented with a scenario consisting of a set of ... events that must be resolved through deliberation, with the process being facilitated by an umpire" [2]. Seminar games provide a way to predict and prepare for possible futures [9], as well as promote a deeper understanding of wicked problems [11], as player decisions "are not based on clear and complete understanding of all the facts, but on how players view those facts through a cloudy and possibly incomplete frame of reference" [10]. This results in "clumsy solutions"—solutions that are tentative, ad-hoc, and partial [16]—confronting players with uncertainty and complexity.

Although traditional seminar games operate similarly to a pen-and-paper role-playing game like *Dungeons & Dragons*, with players and the facilitator sat around a table, recent years have seen an increasing number of digital adaptations and computer-mediated versions. While sacrificing traditional seminar games' physical immediacy and social dynamics, this approach allows for asynchronous and larger-scale play, as well as building data-driven scenarios and tracking player performance [5,13].

This paper is a design case study focusing on *BIG GAME*: a digitally-mediated seminar game for middle-school students, aimed at raising their environmental literacy and capacity to navigate wicked problems. Structurally, the paper follows the three main stages of design-based research as outlined by McKenney and Reeves: analysis and exploration (understanding the problem and stakeholder needs); design and construction (creating and implementing an intervention to address the problem); and evaluation and reflection (assessing the results of implementing the intervention and their significance) [8].

2 Analysis and Exploration

2.1 Context

The game was designed as part of an Erasmus+ project titled "BIG GAME: Immersive and Multidisciplinary STEM Learning through A Cooperative Story-Driven Digital Game." The project targeted European school students aged 11–16 and aimed to facilitate STEM learning and digital skills, as well as to promote environmental literacy and awareness of climate issues. A key output of the project was an online game environment, and the design goal for the team in charge of the game was to support the above objectives by facilitating collaborative, problem-based, and playful learning. We decided to adopt the prism of wicked problems, believing it would allow us to additionally facilitate domain-general skills like creative thinking and analytical skills. The project consortium included representatives of several schools in multiple European countries, who actively provided input throughout the design process. More information about the project can be found on the website: https://big-game.eu-track.eu/.

2.2 Design Requirements and Constraints

The first step in the design process was to outline the requirements and constraints for the game. This was done during several brainstorming sessions with teachers and other project consortium members, using the initial project proposal as a point of reference, and resulted in the following key points:

- **Groupwork and team play**: the game must support teamwork and collaboration rather than individual play.
- **Suitable for classroom use**: the game must be playable in class or as homework at middle-school level (a challenge since many seminar games are "too complex and lengthy to be used by students in a class context" [13]).
- **Curriculum alignment**: the game must be usable within different national school curricula, as well as IB and Montessori schools.
- **Open-ended, local problems**: every problem in the game must be specific and localized (to be more immediate and relatable to players), but reflective of a broader, global issue, as well as support multiple ("clumsy") solutions.
- **Ease of play**: the game must not require experience with videogames or advanced technical skills.
- **Feedback and scale**: the game must be playable by 100–200 teams in parallel and offer a way of providing timely feedback.
- **Asynchronicity**: the game must be playable asynchronously and not depend on time zone and class schedule.
- **Accessible language**: game content must be understandable to middle-schoolers for whom English is a second language.
- **Player privacy**: given the players are minors, the game must not collect any personal data, while at the same time being able to track teams' performance.
- **User experience**: game content must be viewable in the classroom (on a projector) as well as students' personal devices; players must be able to clearly see their progress.

3 Design and Implementation

3.1 Gameplay

We designed the game as a series of scenarios ("missions")—made available one at a time—depicting fictional emergencies rooted in real-life environmental issues. The missions would be presented to the participating teams of around 4–5 students by their teacher. The teams would then develop and submit solutions via the game environment, after which the solutions would be reviewed and scored. Given the focus on wicked problems, we would design complex, open-ended missions with no single optimal solution.

This complexity also meant that solutions could not be evaluated by a computer. Like other researchers on seminar games and wargaming [9,13], we felt that programming the game to automatically review submissions based on predetermined parameters would compromise complexity and nuance. Despite advances in large language models, their inability to consistently fact-check and critically evaluate their own output [12] made them unsuitable for the task. Instead, we would need human evaluators to review submissions and provide feedback.

Each mission would be announced on Monday and be open for 10 days to accommodate different teaching schedules. Then, we would spend 4 days on evaluating solutions and preparing the debriefing session. The following Monday, a new mission would be introduced, prefaced by the debriefing session.

3.2 Narrative

A meaningful narrative was crucial to ensure the game was engaging and supported situated learning: i.e., provided a meaningful context for players to apply their knowledge [6]. We opted for a near-future setting, which allowed some creative license while enabling missions based on current environmental issues:

> The year is 2030. The Earth is facing a massive climate crisis, and the situation is getting worse. The United Nations establishes the UN Anti-Apocalypse Force (UNAAF) to help save the planet. In *BIG GAME*, student teams play as task forces within UNAAF. Their task is to formulate solutions to local environmental issues presented as missions in the game.

This allowed us to design the game as a series of missions following environmental crises around the globe, providing a degree of continuity between the missions. It also justified the team-based competition aspect of the game, since UNAAF was depicted as having many teams working in parallel.

To reinforce the fictional premise, we designed three non-player characters (NPCs) for mission (de)briefings. We gave them different backgrounds, roles within UNAAF, and personalities: Chief Operations Officer Dr. Anita Silva was calm and authoritative; Senior Logistics Officer Maj. Petru Marin was a straight talker with a dryly humorous manner; Senior Analyst Dr. Ken Hashimoto displayed more urgency and had a more empathetic personality. As such, the social aspect of the game included collaborative (intra-team), competitive (between the teams), and parasocial (non-player characters) dimensions.

3.3 Mission Design and Presentation

Given the limited classroom time available for the game, we kept the main campaign to three missions, with seven more to be made freely available after the competition's conclusion. Each mission was framed as a request for help sent to UNAAF by a local authority. For example, Mission 1 involved an imminent glacial dam burst in the Peruvian Andes threatening the nearby city of Huaraz but also highlighted the broader issue of climate change and glacier melting.

The missions were designed to afford a variety of solutions. For example, Mission 2 dealt with an invasive fish species in river Rhône in France, able to reproduce due to thermal pollution from a nearby power plant. Measures suggested by the players ranged from adding more water cooling stations to the power plant, to creating an underwater fence to stop the fish from spreading further, to using electrofishing to stun the fish and remove the invasive specimens.

Mission content was presented as a briefing (see Fig. 1) with the non-player characters introducing the issue to the player similar to a visual novel [4]. Character images were displayed in front of a background (UNAAF meeting room), with a textbox next to them containing their dialogue. Clicking the textbox advanced the dialogue. Some dialogue lines were accompanied by an illustration (e.g., a photo of a bush fire, or a map of the area where the issue is happening). In the initial design, players could choose between several dialogue options, eliciting different responses from the characters; this was ultimately scrapped to make sure that players did not miss any relevant information. To make briefings easier to follow, we recorded audio dialogue to accompany the text and made the text appear one letter at a time in sync with the audio.

Fig. 1. Briefing screen: non-player character (Anita Silva) introducing a mission.

Each mission also included a mission report: a text document with more detailed information. These documents could also be accessed as PDFs outside of the game and were intended as a starting point for teams when conducting their research. In practical terms, this helped avoid forcing players to rewatch the briefing every time they needed a specific bit of information.

3.4 Team Creation

We initially planned to let teams pick their own names to encourage player expression and a stronger sense of group identity. However, this would have required a self-registration system and pose challenges such as monitoring the team names for duplicates and inappropriate language. Instead, we assigned each team a randomly generated name. In keeping with the game's environmental theme, the team names consisted of an animal name and a color adjective, e.g., Black Capybaras, Purple Eagles, etc. A login and a password were created for each team and sent to their teachers to maintain students' privacy.

3.5 Submission

To simplify the submission process, we used a standardized submission format. Upon discussion with teachers, we decided on a slide deck with five slides:

- **Your Solution:** "Replace this text with a description of how to deal with the problem. You are welcome to add an image to illustrate your solution."
- **Expected Outcome:** "If UNAAF follows the steps you proposed, how do you expect the situation to change?"
- **Requirements:** "For your solution to work, what equipment and resources does it need?"
- **Risks and Limitations:** "What can the solution help with—and what are things it cannot help with? What might go wrong when the solution is put into practice?"
- **Sources:** "Please paste links to the information sources you used when working on your solution."

The slide deck was structured so that players had to justify their solution and reflect on its pros and cons. "Expected Outcome" was intended to encourage players to consider the consequences of their solution, rather than simply outlining a series of steps. Asking the teams to list the solution's requirements was a way to get them to reflect on practical limitations (resources, logistics, technology, human effort, etc.), which is a major challenge when tackling wicked problems in real-life settings. The "Risks and Limitations" section highlighted that attempts at solving wicked problems often must focus on specific aspects and may have unintended consequences. The "Sources" slide was intended as evidence of the teams' research process and as a way to encourage them to do research in the first place, rather than speculate without knowledge of the subject.

Upon consulting the teachers, we realized that having teams create and share their own slide decks could lead to complications with file sharing and submissions. Instead, for each mission, we pre-created a separate empty slide deck (a copy of the template) for each team and made it accessible as a shared online document. Teams could collaboratively edit their copy of the slide deck via a web-based interface by logging in using their team login credentials. We eliminated the need for manual submission by automatically changing access to read-only after 10 days, marking the start of the evaluation phase.

3.6 Submission Review and Feedback

Submission evaluation posed both practical and conceptual challenges. The tentative, imperfect nature of "clumsy" solutions to wicked problems made quantified grading difficult, while purely qualitative feedback was not feasible given the game's competitive nature and the need to rapidly assess many teams. Ultimately, we developed a consistent rubric in collaboration with teachers, applicable across all three missions and aligned with the slide deck structure:

- **Efficacy:** would the proposed solution help solve the problem? (Bearing in mind solutions would inevitably be "clumsy.")
- **Pragmatism:** how practical, efficient, and doable is the solution?
- **Scholarship:** does the solution cite multiple relevant and reliable sources?
- **Persuasion:** is the solution clearly explained and presented well?

While the first two criteria were used to evaluate the content of the solution, Scholarship was based on the final slide (Sources) and reflected the quality of the underlying research. Persuasion was introduced to encourage clear, structured presentation of ideas (which we hoped would aid players in structuring their own thought process). Other criteria were considered at different points but ultimately discarded: e.g., Innovation was scrapped for fear of incentivizing novelty over realism and pragmatism, which were deemed a higher priority (even though tackling wicked problems does certainly involve creative thinking and exploring novel solutions). To reduce bias, each solution was reviewed by three evaluators from different countries, who graded each criterion on a 1 to 5 scale, after which the average scores were calculated.

The next question was how to present the evaluation results to the students. Releasing the results as is could demotivate lower-scoring teams, as well as feel like being graded for a school assignment (a mentality we wanted to avoid). Instead, we wanted to offer encouragement even to teams with weaker submissions, as well as create a sense of progression to incentivize continued play.

We framed the four evaluation criteria like character attributes in role-playing games. Each team would start with a single star in each of the four attributes, out of a maximum of four stars. These attributes would be displayed on the team information screen, the first screen teams would see after logging into (see Fig. 2)). For each completed mission, teams could earn an additional star in one or more categories. The best, most well-rounded submissions would earn a star in all four categories. The lowest-scoring submissions would earn a star in the single category where they got the highest average score. Most submissions would fall between these two extremes and earn a star in two or three categories per mission. This system ensured every submission was rewarded proportionately, while also providing simplified feedback and helping teams identify where their strengths were and what areas needed improvement.

4 Evaluation and Reflection

4.1 Results and General Observations

The game was played over 6 weeks (two weeks for each of the three missions) in November-December 2023. Overall, 121 teams representing 27 schools in 4 countries took part. (While the school competition has concluded, the mission content remains available at https://dlg.tlu.ee/big-game/.)

A survey of the teachers who used the game in their classes yielded 61 responses. (The survey design and a separate survey of the players are discussed more fully in a separate article [15]). The questionnaire contained a number

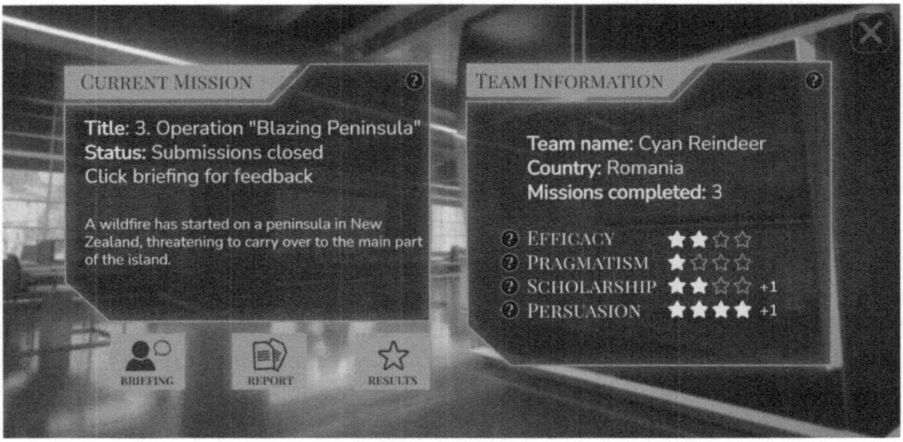

Fig. 2. Team information screen with RPG-style attributes

of Likert-type items (1 = strongly disagree; 5 = strongly agree) and indicated that teachers found the game materials to be useful in their teaching (median = 4, mean = 4.2, SD = 0.9). Teachers were also asked to what extent the game helped facilitate specific skills, and agreed that the game can help develop problem-solving, analytical skills, creative thinking, research skills, as well as collaboration and communication skills (median = 4 for all of the above).

Based on free-form feedback, teachers agreed that the overall premise of the game was useful, the game materials were a helpful starting point for classroom discussion, and that playing was motivating for students: "The idea behind a role-play type of game [involving] finding solutions for real life problems is very good"; "The enthusiasm of my students surprised me. They had good ideas, ... worked together and really had fun solving the scenario."

Many teachers specifically praised the missions and submission templates as being well-structured and easy to use, and pointed out that the mission content was varied and interesting and allowed players to develop interdisciplinary skills. Another aspect that some teachers appreciated was the game's visual presentation and design. Several responses also pointed out that the mission content was presented appropriately for young non-native English speakers: "It worked well in developing the students' interdisciplinary skills in multiple ways and was well-suited to their proficiency level in English as a foreign language."

In sum, teachers' feedback suggests that the game design and implementation was successful in terms of promoting critical thinking, problem-solving, and teamwork, and helping students apply those skills to wicked problems focused on the environment.

4.2 Challenges

Despite the overall positive response, several challenges were identified by the design team and/or reported by teachers. The wide age range of the players made it difficult to evaluate submissions fairly, even though several teams of 11–12 year olds outperformed our expectations and submitted the best solutions. While in traditional seminar games, the immediacy of the social interaction tends to ensure player engagement, our asynchronous implementation resulted in differing levels of engagement and motivation. Notably, the total number of teams who submitted a solution dropped by around 30% from Mission 1 to Mission 3, indicating some teams lost motivation to play.

A key challenge for solution evaluation was that we could only review the final product (i.e., slide deck), but not the process behind it. Some teams may have received more teacher support than others; other teams may have had only one or two actively contributing members. In fact, a couple of the solutions for Missions 2 and 3 were protest submissions, whose authors, rather than focus on the solution, mostly lamented the lack of teamwork and support. The biggest limitation, however, is that this format did not allow us access to what, in traditional seminar games, is a pivotal part of the process: player deliberation.

The focus on specific, local issues and "clumsy" solutions also meant the game emphasized damage reduction and stop-gap solutions, while not addressing how the broader underlying issue (e.g., glacial melting or loss of biodiversity) should be tackled on a global, long-term scale.

4.3 Takeaways and Future Directions

This case study demonstrates that wicked problems offer a productive frame for environmental education, and that seminar games, thanks to their compatibility with open-ended problems and "clumsy" solutions, can support this approach. While a majority of research on wargames and seminar games focuses on adult players, our example shows that it is possible to adapt the format for younger audiences, including for larger-scale, asynchronous play—as long as the needs and features of this demographic are taken into account. The game design outlined in this paper suggests that storytelling can help make the play experience more meaningful and cohesive, and integrating different social aspects (teamwork, inter-team competition, relationships with non-player characters) can further engagement. Using local scenarios makes global issues more relatable and helps students see their impact on real-life communities. Attribute systems can provide a way to efficiently deliver feedback in larger-scale contexts where detailed qualitative feedback is not feasible.

At the same time, larger-scale, asynchronous seminar games pose their own challenges in terms of player engagement and focus on product (solution) over process (deliberation). How to navigate these challenges is a direction for future research. For example, training teachers in how to facilitate play sessions and asking them to take and submit observation notes could provide the umpires with more insight into the process. Future studies could also adopt a more player-centered approach to design, which could help understand how to improve player retention and motivation for play.

Acknowledgments. This study was supported by the European Commission through the Erasmus+ KA2 program (Cooperation Partnerships in School Education), grant agreement no. 2021-1-FI01-KA220-SCH-000024098. The authors have no competing interests to declare relating to the content of this article.

References

1. Bosman, F.G.: There Is No Solution!: "Wicked Problems" in digital games. Games Cult. **14**(5), 543–559 (2019). https://doi.org/10.1177/1555412017716603
2. Callaghan, P., Fiadotau, M.: Using meaningful choices and uncertainty to increase player agency in a cybersecurity seminar game. In: Dondio, P., et al. (eds.) Games and Learning Alliance, vol. 14475, pp. 23–32. Springer, Cham (2024). https://doi.org/10.1007/978-3-031-49065-1_3
3. Earle, A.G., Leyva-de la Hiz, D.I.: The wicked problem of teaching about wicked problems: design thinking and emerging technologies in sustainability education. Manage. Learn. **52**(5), 581–603 (2021). https://doi.org/10.1177/1350507620974857
4. Fiadotau, M.: Visual novel. In: Lee, N. (ed.) Encyclopedia of Computer Graphics and Games, pp. 2085–2088. Springer, Cham (2024). https://doi.org/10.1007/978-3-031-23161-2_193
5. Haggman, A.: Cyber wargaming: finding, designing, and playing wargames for cyber security education. Doctoral thesis, Royal Holloway, University of London (2019)
6. Kirk, D., MacPhail, A.: Teaching games for understanding and situated learning: rethinking the Bunker-Thorpe model. J. Teach. Phys. Educ. **21**(2), 177–192 (2002)
7. McDiarmid, G.W., Zhao, Y.: Learning for Uncertainty: Teaching Students How to Thrive in a Rapidly Evolving World. Routledge, New York (2022)
8. McKenney, S.E., Reeves, T.C.: Conducting Educational Design Research, 2nd edn. Routledge, London and New York (2019)
9. Pace, D.K.: Seminar gaming: an approach to problems too complex for algorithmic solution. J. Hopkins APL Tech. Dig. **12**(3), 290–296 (1991)
10. Perla, P.P.: What wargaming is and is not. Naval War Coll. Rev. **38**(5), 70–78 (1985)
11. Pournelle, P.E.: The use of M&S and wargaming to address wicked problems. In: Turnitsa, C., Blais, C., Tolk, A. (eds.) Simulation and Wargaming, pp. 203–221. Wiley, Hoboken (2021). https://doi.org/10.1002/9781119604815.ch8
12. Quelle, D., Bovet, A.: The perils and promises of fact-checking with large language models. Front. Artif. Intell. **7** (2024)
13. Sabin, P.: The benefits and limits of computerization in conflict simulation. Literary Linguist. Comput. **26**(3), 323–328 (2011). https://doi.org/10.1093/llc/fqr024
14. Thollander, P., Palm, J., Hedbrant, J.: Energy efficiency as a wicked problem. Sustainability **11**(6), 1569 (2019). https://doi.org/10.3390/su11061569
15. Tramonti, M., et al.: Game on for climate action: Big Game delivers engaging STEM learning. Educ. Sci. **14**(8), 893 (2024). https://doi.org/10.3390/educsci14080893
16. Verweij, M., et al.: Clumsy solutions for a complex world: the case of climate change. Public Adm. **84**(4), 817–843 (2006)

Detecting Experts Using a MiniRocket: Gaze Direction Time Series Classification of Real-Life Experts Playing the Sustainable Port

Gianluca Guglielmo(✉), Michal Klincewicz, Elisabeth Huis in 't Veld, and Pieter Spronck

Tilburg University, Tilburg, Netherlands
G.Guglielmo@tilburguniversity.edu

Abstract. This study aimed to identify real-life experts working for a port authority and lay people (students) who played The Sustainable Port, a serious game aiming to simulate the dynamics occurring in a port area. To achieve this goal, we analyzed eye gaze data collected non-invasively using low-grade webcams from 28 participants working for the port authority of the Port of Rotterdam and 66 students. Such data were used for a classification task implemented using a MiniRocket classifier, an algorithm used for time-series classification. The classifier reached an F1 score of 0.75 (SD = 0.07), a PR AUC of 0.73 (SD = 0.14), and an ROC AUC of 0.75 (SD = 0.15) providing evidence that it is possible to identify real-life experts about maritime port management using data that can be obtained from a webcam. We speculate that the gaze direction used to train the MiniRocket may contain relevant information about the cognitive processes and decisions occurring throughout the gameplay. We suggest that the methods here presented not only can be used to detect experts playing simulations, such as serious games, but also to identify experts tackling screen-presented tasks.

Keywords: Gaze · Expertise · Machine Learning · Maritime Port · Serious Games · Sustainability · Time Series Classification

1 Introduction

Serious games are valuable tools that have already been used for training, educational purposes, and hiring new employees [6]. This last point seems to suggest that relevant skills that a candidate may have can emerge during the game play of a serious game; such skills may be those that experts in a specific field already have. Therefore, it may be not surprising that experts in real-life play and experience a serious game differently than lay people. One such example is The Sustainable Port [2], a serious game that simulates the real-world environment of the Port of Rotterdam (PoR). Players put themselves into the role of

A. Schönbohm et al. (Eds.): GALA 2024, LNCS 15348, pp. 177–187, 2025.
https://doi.org/10.1007/978-3-031-78269-5_17

executive decision-makers at PoR with the goal of balancing the port's profits and emissions. Seventy percent of PoR employees who played The Sustainable Port reported that they used their previous experience acquired at the Port of Rotterdam during their gameplay and indeed, they achieved better scores than university students [14]. The main goal of the current study is to evaluate whether it is possible to discriminate experts from lay people based on their eye movements during the gameplay using non-invasive methods such as the eye gaze information extracted from OpenFace [3] combined with a fast algorithm for timeseries classification such as the MiniRocket [9]. The secondary goal was to further test the assumption that real-life expertise is applied in a simulation and that this transfer is detectable not only by overt, conscious actions and decisions during the gameplay, but also by covert, automatic physiological changes tracked by non-invasive methods. The results of this study explore additional avenues in which serious games, combined with accessible technology, can detect interesting decision-making profiles for hiring or training purposes.

2 Expertise, Physiology, and Gaze

Prior experience and knowledge of experts affects their behavior and physiological responses. Experts show different eye-related patterns during a task compared to their less experienced counterparts. For example, expert radiologists have different eye gaze patterns of fixation and saccades while looking at X-rays [25]. One way to interpret this pattern of results is that eye gaze [12] reflects more effective working memory use, with experts being more effective in encoding and retrieving task-related information [10]. Another possible explanation is that experts are more effective in the selective allocation of their attentive resources focusing on relevant stimuli and neglecting the non-relevant ones [12, 15]. What may also play a role, at least for some of these differences, is familiarity with the task [2], which is reflected in more efficient use of working memory or more effective allocation of attentive resources [5].

3 Methods

3.1 The Sustainable Port Game

The Sustainable Port is a game simulating port dynamics introduced by a previous study by Guglielmo, Klincewicz, Huis in 't Veld, and Spronck [14]. Such a game unfolds across ten rounds, and the player has to adjust their strategy across the game to balance CO2 emission and the Added Value (the revenues). The final score obtained in the game is calculated by subtracting the CO2 emissions from the Added Value. Furthermore, all players know that they need to have a CO2 $<=$ 10 in order not to lose the game outright and that their score at the end of round 10 is the final measure of performance. During the game, the participants can build, destroy, upgrade, and close facilities.

3.2 Sample

In this experiment, a total of N = 109 people were recruited to play The Sustainable Port, of which n = 75 students (Nmales = 27, Nfemales = 47 females, Nnd = 1; Mage = 21.20, SD = 3.4) from Tilburg University and n = 34 (Nmales = 23, Nfemales = 11; Mage = 40.67, SD = 10.82) from the Port of Authority of the Port of Rotterdam. Two PoR employees were excluded from the analysis due to a corrupted video recording. Additionally, 4 PoR employees and 9 students were excluded due to their inability to understand the game mechanics. More specifically, the participants were asked the following question: "During which round did you develop confidence in the game mechanics? (for example: which button or option is associated to specific actions)". The final sample used for analysis consisted of N = 94 participants (28 PoR employees and 66 students).

3.3 Data Collection Procedure

The students were recruited through the recruitment system at Tilburg University in exchange for a formative credit. PoR employees were recruited from the HRM department, Strategy department, Finance department, Environmental management, Port Development department, Commercial Department & Policy Department of the Port Harbour Master. All of these departments were relevant for our study since they are involved in strategic decisions concerning the green transition and the future development of the Port of Rotterdam. Participants were recruited anonymously with the help of a spreadsheet shared through the internal Port of Rotterdam newsletter. Interested employees were asked to create an alphanumeric code making sure they do not use any information about their identity (like their date of birth or name). Once they signed up, all participants were informed that the study was approved by the ethics committee of Tilburg University (REDC 2021.35f + study number 1) and that it would involve expertise and decision-making.

Both the participants' faces and the gameplay were recorded using the Open Broadcaster Software [18]. After the final 10th round, participants were presented with their score and whether they reached the necessary CO2 threshold to not lose the game. They were also asked, through a questionnaire, to indicate during which round they understood the game mechanics (or to declare that they did not understand them at all) if they paid attention to the game dynamics, and if they were motivated to play the game on a Likert scale between 1 (strongly disagree) to 7 (strongly agree), Each experimental session lasted approximately 60 min.

3.4 Preprocessing

To extract gaze direction, the video recordings were cropped to just contain the faces of participants. Gaze direction was extracted, using OpenFace [3], from eye gaze angle as two series of values: `gaze_angle_x` and `gaze_angle_y`, which respectively refer to the horizontal axis and the vertical axis of the area that participants are looking at during the gameplay.

Participants took 19.90 min (SD = 6.63) on average to finish all 10 rounds of the game. All the recordings had a variable length with PoR employees spending significantly more time playing the game (M = 23.88, SD = 6.48) than students (M = 18.21, SD = 5.94; Welch t-test results: $t(46.82) = 3.92$, $p < .001$). Therefore, the data extracted from the video recordings were padded using the single individual mean of each participant for the `gaze_angle_x` (horizontal movements) and the `gaze_angle_y` (vertical movements), so that they had the same lengths [4]. In this specific case, we used the single individual mean of each participant for the `gaze_angle_x` (horizontal movements) and the `gaze_angle_y` (vertical movements). This approach has several advantages over other methods. First, it is better than truncation given evidence of its non-robustness [4] and the distortion it generates to the original time series. Second, zero padding, a commonly used technique, was also excluded because it may introduce a bias. This 0-based bias would likely arise due to students and PoR employees having significantly different lengths of average recordings. A significantly higher number of zeros at the end of the recordings for a specific group (as it would occur for the students' group), due to padding, may result in potentially extracting misleading features from such zeros. Given these reasons, we chose the single mean padding [23], which is based on the mean of the distribution of gaze direction for each participant and should not introduce class-specific bias. The padded-time series used as inputs were as long as the longest time series in our data (69361 data points which corresponds to 38.53 min at 30 fps). At the end of the classification task, we still compared the padded length of the misclassified instances with the padded length of the correctly classified instances. This approach was used to evaluate if the padded length played a role in correctly classifying or misclassifying our participants even after using the individual means of each participant. If the padded length played a role in correctly identifying the two groups we would expect the correctly classified instances and the incorrectly classified ones to have a significant difference in their padded length. Such analyses were run after controlling for the normality of the residuals with a KS test [27] and the homogeneity of variance with the Bartlett test [32]. Besides evaluating the effect of padding, we also trained the same classifier (MiniRocket), using the truncated version of the time series. Therefore, all the time series were truncated at 15902 datapoints (8.83 min) corresponding to the shortest recording in our data. Such a process was adopted to evaluate if even in case of reduced and limited information our classifier still performs above baseline suggesting emerging differences between the two groups before the end of the recordings.

3.5 Evaluation of Confounding Variables

Even though previous studies found a significant correlation between the ranges of gaze angles and age due to younger individuals having presumably wider eye movements [21] no significant correlation (Pearson's r coefficient) was found between age and vertical gaze ($r = -0.07$, $p = .51$) or horizontal gaze ($r = -0.09$, p = .38) in our sample. Furthermore, given that previous studies showed that attention [28] and motivation [17] influence eye gaze, we evaluated if there was a significant difference between the two groups we analyzed. Our results show no significant difference in self-assessed motivation (PoR employees M = 5.64, SD = 0.97; Students M = 5.55, students SD = 1.16; t(59.60) = 0.41, p = .68) and self-assessed attention (t(42.48) = 0.14, p = .89; PoR employees M = 5.54, PoR employees SD = 1.18; Students M = 5.50, Students SD = 0.96) between the two groups.

3.6 MiniRocket Time Series Classifier

MiniRocket (MINImally RandOm Convolutional KErnel Transform) is an algorithm for time series classification. Compared to other time series classification algorithms, it offers an optimal balance between accuracy, computational power, and computational complexity [7,9]. MiniRocket has two uniquely engineered phases: a feature extraction phase and a classification phase. Features are extracted using randomly generated convolutional kernels with a fixed length of 9 [7]. The kernel operation in the MiniRocket maps a problem that is not linearly separable, as in most time series problems, into a multi-dimensional space that makes them linearly separable [20]. Like convolutional neural networks, zero padding is applied at the beginning and at the end of the input, so that convolution operations are centered on values composing it. The weights are drawn between −1 and 2 while the bias is directly obtained from the convolution output [9]. After that, the generated kernels are convoluted with the input data (the time series used as input for the MiniRocket) to generate the final set of features that should make the problem linearly separable.

A single feature per kernel is extracted: the proportion of positive values pooling (PPV), which is the output of each convolution operation. The PPV is the proportion of positive values in the convoluted region [9]. This process retains the most essential information reducing computational complexity [19]. However, unlike the convolutional neural network, in the MiniRocket there are no hidden layers and no linear combinations of features [9]. MiniRocket does not have many hyperparameters and they are not supposed to be tuned, such hyperparameters are the max dilations per kernel (equal to 32) and the number of kernels, which is 9996. From each kernel, the PPV is extracted thereby always generating 9996 features (the number of kernels multiplied by the PPV extracted). After the features are extracted, during the second phase (the classification phase), these features are used to train a linear classifier, such as a Support Vector Machine, a Logistic Regression, or in the case of small datasets a Ridge Classifier [9].

MiniRocket proved to have satisfactory performance on several datasets compared to competitors' algorithms [9] while maintaining a relatively small computation time [1]. Furthermore, this algorithm has already been successfully used for different purposes: from virtual price currency prediction [7] to identifying subjects with atrial fibrillation [1]. However, despite its success, one of the problems of the MiniRocket is potential multicollinearity among extracted features (the PPVs) which can contain noise generating significant correlation among the features [20]. This can be mitigated by using a Ridge Classifier, with an optimized alpha shrinkage parameter, known to be resistant to multicollinearity [8].

3.7 Pipeline for Classification Task and Model Evaluation

The MiniRocket was combined with a ridge classifier using sktime given our small sample. We also used the default options for in MiniRocket in sktime, and we did not scale the time series inputs since MiniRocket does not require this process [9]. This approach was demonstrated effective for small datasets [1] and on multivariate time series data [29]. A 5-fold stratified cross-validation respecting the original class imbalance present in the dataset (approximately composed of 70% students and 30% PoR employees) was used. During each of the 5 folds, the data were partitioned so that 80% of the data was used as a train set and 20% as a test set. During each fold, the train set is split again using another 5-fold stratified cross-validation to detect the best alpha parameter for the ROC AUC, given its alleged robustness towards class imbalances [30]. The range of values for alpha used for the optimization was between 10 and 100 opting for a stronger regularization to better cope with potential multicollinearity and overfitting considering the small size of our dataset. The input for the MiniRocket consists of a dataset of 94 participants (instances) with 2 dimensions (`gaze_angle_x` and `gaze_angle_y`) where each time series had a length of 69361 data points. This 2-dimensional input data (the mean padded time series of the `gaze_angle_x` and `gaze_angle_y`) was fed to the MiniRocket algorithm that extracted the PPV value for each of the 9996 kernels. After having extracted the features (the PPV extracted per kernel), the RidgeClassifierCV function available in sklearn was used for the classification task, balancing the class weights during training.

The ROC, AUC, weighted F1 score, and PR AUC metrics were used to evaluate the performance of the classifier (considering the PoR employees as the positive class) [16,22,30]. The extracted sample weights for the train splits (during each fold) were applied when computing the PR AUC; this process was adopted since sklearn does not have a weighted option for the PR AUC (examples of how to calculate the PR AUC with sklearn can be found at the following link: https://sinyi-chou.github.io/python-sklearn-precision-recall/). The evaluation of the model was done after the optimal value of alpha for the ROC AUC was detected on each of the 5 train splits generated by the 5-fold stratified cross-validations. The final metrics (ROC AUC, PR AUC, and F1) were first calculated on the test set for each original split and after that, at the end of the process, averaged across all the 5-folds defined. The same process, with the same data split, was used to train another MiniRocket classifier with the truncated version of the time series (94 participants with 2 dimensions, `gaze_angle_x` and `gaze_angle_y`, where each time series had a length of 15902 data points in this case).

Finally, we compared MiniRocket's performance with a Dummy Classifier that uses a "constant" as strategy to find the baseline F1 and "stratified" as strategy to find the baseline ROC AUC and PR AUC. The Dummy Classifier, used to define classification baselines, ignores the features provided and just looks at the distributions of the instances according to the class labels (More information about the Dummy Classifier and its classification strategies can be found at: https://scikit-learn.org/stable/modules/model_evaluation.html).

4 Results

MiniRocket managed to correctly identify around 70% of the PoR employees and 74% of the students. After having extracted a confusion matrix, we found that, across the entire dataset on the test splits of the 5-fold stratified cross-validation, MiniRocket correctly detected 19 PoR employees (9 misclassified as students) and 51 students (15 misclassified as PoR employees). Overall, MiniRocket correctly detected 70 participants out of the 94 collected. Furthermore, the classifier always outperformed the Dummy Classifier (baseline) as displayed in Table 1.

Table 1. The scores of the chosen metrics and the comparison with the Dummy Classifier (baseline).

	F1	ROC AUC	PR AUC
MiniRocket	0.75 (SD = 0.07)	0.75 (SD = 0.14)	0.73 (SD = 0.15)
Dummy Classifier	0.46 (SD = 0.03)	0.70 (SD = 0.00)	0.45 (SD = 0.13)

The padded lengths of the correctly and incorrectly classified instances did not differ for either the PoR employees (Correct: M = 23.95 min, SD = 2.90. Incorrect M = 19.90 min, SD = 2.90; $t(35) = 1.77$, $p = .09$), or the students (Correct: M = 18.32 min, SD = 4.60. Incorrect M = 21.37 min, SD = 5.77; $t(24.48) = 1.93$, $p = .08$). Furthermore, when evaluating the results obtained by the MiniRocket using the truncated data we found out that even in this case the classifier performed above baseline (Dummy Classifier). The MiniRocket with the truncated data obtained a mean F1 score of 0.66 (SD = 0.12), a mean ROC AUC of 0.59 (SD = 0.14), and a mean PR AUC = 0.56 (SD = 0.21). In this case, using truncated data, 10 PoR employees (18 misclassified) and 51 students (15 misclassified) were successfully detected across the 5-fold stratified cross-validation.

5 Discussions

The results here presented suggest that PoR employees can be discriminated from lay people (students) using information contained in gaze direction. MiniRocket, combined with OpenFace gaze information [3] could therefore offer a fast, effective, and accessible solution to detect real-life experts playing serious games. Our results show the classifier likely does not rely on group differences in age [21], self-assessed motivation [28], or attention during gameplay [17]. Furthermore, we saw that padding seems to have a limited role or no role at all in our classification task; this is further confirmed when looking at the results obtained using truncated data. Such results, despite not reaching an acceptable ROC AUC of 0.70 [26], still obtained a performance above baseline in all the metrics further suggesting the limited effect of padding and the emergence of differences even before the classifier was provided with complete information about the recordings. Altogether, these results suggest that the classifier was actually able to successfully detect participants in the two groups and the effect of the considered confounders was lacking or negligible.

Unfortunately, the features used for the classification task by the MiniRocket have no intuitive interpretation being based on kernels [33]. However, it is likely that the PoR employees used what they already know about port environments to play the game better than students [14] as the game introduces very niche innovative technologies such as hydrogen-oriented technology [31], which is very related to the expertise of the PoR employees involved in this study, who all work for departments that actively participate in the modern debate about green transition. Furthermore, the gaze direction observed in these two groups may reflect different ways of dealing with the presented information, which may be connected to experiences obtained in similar informational environments [10] or different styles of suppressing irrelevant information [2]. If that is right, then our study provides some evidence that expertise learned in real life is reflected in behavior and physiological responses occurring during serious games. Another possibility is that differences in gaze patterns reflect different decisions made during gameplay. PoR employees performed better than students [14], so what we may be seeing in gaze could be connected to the specific in-game mechanics, and actions that experts happen to do during play. We can assume that similar behaviors may emerge in other serious games and screen-presented tasks. Therefore, future studies may focus on using these methods with other serious games and screen-presented tasks to evaluate their degree of generalizability. Obtaining similar results may pave the way for using the method here proposed for business applications to train or hire new employees [6].

Despite the promising results, our study has several limitations. First, our dataset was small and strongly imbalanced (notably, this reflects the distribution of experts in the general population) and we just presented results from one game: The Sustainable Port. Furthermore, besides the results obtained by the MiniRocket, there are still problems that need to be addressed when it comes to using this classifier. MiniRocket features are based on kernels that are not humanly interpretable [33] even though methods such as SHAP could help detect the relevant kernels used for classification [24]. However, a more transparent algorithm would yield better explanations of performance. Future studies should apply other, more computationally expensive and time-consuming, classifiers such as learning shapelets [31] or pattern-based embedding for time series classification [13] to have more accessible interpretations of the results. Third, using other sources of behavioral and physiological signals, such as the ones extractable from eye trackers [11] may provide better and more information to discriminate experts from lay people or novices [34] compared to the gaze angle extracted in OpenFace; however, such data may require more expensive tools to be collected. If the results we report here can be replicated in other serious games and if a more interpretable classifier combined with eye-tracking data is used with them, we may obtain deeper insights into the physiological patterns and behaviors making specific people better decision-makers in complex environments.

Acknowledgments. This research is founded by the MasterMinds project, part of the RegionDeal Mid- and West-Brabant, and it is co-founded by the Ministry of Economic Affairs and Municipality of Tilburg.

References

1. Alagoz, C.: Robust and efficient atrial fibrillation detection from intracardiac electrograms using MiniRocket. Int. J. Eng. Res. Dev. **16**(1), 432–447 (2024)
2. Alonso, A., van der Meij, J., Tse, D., Genzel, L.: Naïve to expert: considering the role of previous knowledge in memory. Brain Neurosci. Adv. **4**, 2398212820948686 (2020)
3. Baltrusaitis, T., Zadeh, A., Lim, Y., Morency, L.: OpenFace 2.0: facial behavior analysis toolkit. In: 2018 13th IEEE International Conference on Automatic Face & Gesture Recognition (FG 2018) (2018)
4. Bier, A., Jastrzębska, A., Olszewski, P.: Variable-length multivariate time series classification using rocket: a case study of incident detection. IEEE Access **10**, 95701–95715 (2022)
5. Brams, S., et al.: The relationship between gaze behavior, expertise, and performance: a systematic review. Psychol. Bull. **145**(10), 980–1027 (2019)
6. Bylieva, D., Lobatyuk, V., Rubtsova, A.: Serious games as a recruitment tool in educational projects. In: European Proceedings of Social and Behavioural Sciences, vol. 51 (2018)
7. Byrd, J., Lin, B., Loesch, F., Neubarth, M., Peng, Z., Tian, F.: The application of minirocket in virtual currency price prediction (2024)
8. Cule, E., Iorio, M.D.: Ridge regression in prediction problems: automatic choice of the ridge parameter. Genet. Epidemiol. **37**(7), 704–714 (2013)
9. Dempster, A., Schmidt, D., Webb, G.: MiniRocket: a very fast (almost) deterministic transform for time series classification. In: Proceedings of the 27th ACM SIGKDD Conference on Knowledge Discovery & Data Mining, pp. 248–257 (2021)
10. Ericsson, K., Kintsch, W.: Long-term working memory. Psychol. Rev. **102**, 211–245 (1995)
11. Feremans, L., Cule, B., Goethals, B.: PETSC: pattern-based embedding for time series classification. Data Min. Knowl. Disc. **36**(3), 1015–1061 (2022)
12. Gegenfurtner, A., Lehtinen, E., Säljö, R.: Expertise differences in the comprehension of visualizations: a meta-analysis of eye-tracking research in professional domains. Educ. Psychol. Rev. **23**, 523–552 (2011)

13. Grabocka, J., Schilling, N., Wistuba, M., Schmidt-Thieme, L.: Learning time-series shapelets. In: Proceedings of the 20th ACM SIGKDD International Conference on Knowledge Discovery and Data Mining, pp. 392–401 (2014)
14. Guglielmo, G., Klincewicz, M., Huis in 'T. Veld, E., Spronck, P.: Introducing sustainable port. In: Proceedings of the International Conference of Games, Entertainment, and Media (GEM). IEEE (2024)
15. Haider, A., Frensch, P.: Eye movement during skill acquisition: more evidence for the information-reduction hypothesis. J. Exp. Psychol. Learn. Mem. Cogn. **25**, 172 (1999)
16. Jeni, L., Cohn, J., Torre, F.D.L.: Facing imbalanced data–recommendations for the use of performance metrics. In: 2013 Humaine Association Conference on Affective Computing and Intelligent Interaction, pp. 245–251 (2013)
17. Khan, A., Blohm, G., McPeek, R., Lefevre, P.: Differential influence of attention on gaze and head movements. J. Neurophysiol. **101**(1), 198–206 (2009)
18. Kristandl, G.: "All the world's a stage"–the open broadcaster software (OBS) as enabling technology to overcome restrictions in online teaching. Compass: J. Learn. Teach. Univ. Greenwich **14**(2), 1–16 (2021)
19. Krizhevsky, A., Sutskever, I., Hinton, G.E.: ImageNet classification with deep convolutional neural networks. In: Advances in Neural Information Processing Systems, vol. 25 (2012)
20. Kung, S.: Kernel Methods and Machine Learning. Cambridge University Press, Cambridge (2014)
21. Lee, W., Kim, J., Shin, Y., Hwang, S., Lim, H.: Differences in eye movement range based on age and gaze direction. Eye **33**(7), 1145–1151 (2019)
22. Lu, H., Ehwerhemuepha, L., Rakovski, C.: A comparative study on deep learning models for text classification of unstructured medical notes with various levels of class imbalance. BMC Med. Res. Methodol. **22**(1), 181 (2022)
23. Mann, M.: Smoothing of climate time series revisited. Geophys. Res. Lett. **35**(16) (2008)
24. Marcílio, W.E., Eler, D.M.: From explanations to feature selection: assessing SHAP values as feature selection mechanism. In: 2020 33rd SIBGRAPI Conference on Graphics, Patterns and Images (SIBGRAPI), pp. 340–347. IEEE (2020)
25. McLaughlin, L., Bond, R., Hughes, R., McConnell, J., McFadden, S.: Computing eye gaze metrics for the automatic assessment of radiographer performance during X-ray image interpretation. Int. J. Med. Informatics **105**, 11–21 (2017)
26. Metz, C.: Basic principles of ROC analysis. Semin. Nucl. Med. **8**(4), 283–298 (1978)
27. Mishra, P., Pandey, C.M., Singh, U., Gupta, A., Sahu, C., Keshri, A.: Descriptive statistics and normality tests for statistical data. Ann. Card. Anaesth. **22**(1), 67 (2019). https://doi.org/10.4103/aca.ACA_157_18
28. Nikitin, J., Freund, A.: Age and motivation predict gaze behavior for facial expressions. Psychol. Aging **26**(3), 695 (2011)
29. Pantiskas, L., Verstoep, K., Hoogendoorn, M., Bal, H.: Taking rocket on an efficiency mission: a distributed solution for fast and accurate multivariate time series classification. In: Proceedings of the XYZ Conference, pp. 123–130 (2021)
30. Richardson, E., Smith, M., Doe, J., Johnson, A., Williams, L.: The ROC-AUC accurately assesses imbalanced datasets. Available at SSRN 4655233 (2024)
31. Sazali, N.: Emerging technologies by hydrogen: a review. Int. J. Hydrogen Energy **45**(38), 18753–18771 (2020)
32. Viwatwongkasem, C.: A comparison of type I error and power of Bartlett's test, Levene's test and Cochran's test under violation of assumptions. Ph.D. thesis (2004)

33. Wu, C., Miller, J., Chang, Y., Sznaier, M., Dy, J.: Solving interpretable kernel dimension reduction. arXiv preprint arXiv:1909.03093 (2019)
34. Zhu, M., Bao, D., Yu, Y., Shen, D., Yi, M.: Differences in thinking flexibility between novices and experts based on eye tracking. PLoS ONE **17**(6), e0269363 (2022)

Detecting Deception and Developing Leadership: Games Tackling Real-World Challenges

"Deception Detected!"—A Serious Game About Detecting Dark Patterns

Kevin Fiedler[1(✉)], René Schäfer[1], Jan Borchers[1], and René Röpke[2]

[1] RWTH Aachen University, Templergraben 55, 52062 Aachen, Germany
{kfiedler,rschaefer,borchers}@cs.rwth-aachen.de
[2] TU Wien, Favoritenstr. 9-11, 1040 Vienna, Austria
rene.roepke@tuwien.ac.at

Abstract. Dark patterns are malicious user interface design strategies that nudge users toward decisions that may be against their best interests. As countermeasures, related work has explored legislation, detecting and modifying web content with such patterns, and educating users about dark patterns. Serious games that teach detecting and classifying dark patterns, however, have received little attention so far. We present a web-based prototype of such a game targeting adults and the results of a comprehensive user study investigating its effectiveness and knowledge retention among participants. Our findings demonstrate that participants became better at detecting dark patterns, indicating that they became more aware of such design manipulations. While our analysis of participants' classification abilities yields mixed results, our game log data confirms that their detection skills increased.

Keywords: Dark Patterns · Deceptive Design · Serious Game

1 Introduction

Dark patterns are malicious user interface design strategies widely used in apps and online services [5,13,18] that aim to manipulate users into specific actions and decisions that may go against their best interests, such as expensive purchases or hidden subscriptions [7,18]. To mitigate the manipulative effects of these patterns, researchers have called for effective countermeasures [1,8]. Examples of such countermeasures include legislation [7] and techniques to detect and counteract dark patterns in the user interface [1,4,23]. Educating users, however, presents a complementary approach to fighting dark patterns [1,2,17]. As related work in IT security education has demonstrated, serious games can enable learning about such topics in a risk-free and engaging learning environment [21].

Therefore, we introduce a web-based serious game about detecting and classifying dark patterns in online content (see Sects. 3 and 4). It lets users familiarize themselves with different manipulation techniques widely applied online and in apps. Our game adopts the preliminary ontology by Gray et al. [9]. After describing the design of our game, we present the results of a comprehensive user study

A. Schönbohm et al. (Eds.): GALA 2024, LNCS 15348, pp. 191–200, 2025.
https://doi.org/10.1007/978-3-031-78269-5_18

that evaluates the game's effectiveness and knowledge retention (see Sect. 5). We use a pre-/post-/re-test experimental study design. Lastly, we discuss our findings and possible limitations (see Sect. 6) before concluding the paper and outlining future work (see Sect. 7).

2 Related Work

2.1 Dark Patterns

The term *dark pattern*[1] was introduced by UX researcher Harry Brignull in 2010 on his website[2]. Nowadays, Brignull [3] refers to them as *deceptive patterns* and defines them as "tricks used in websites and apps that make you do things that you didn't mean to, like buying or signing up for something" on his website.

Such manipulative design strategies can be found in mobile games [6], social media [19], shopping websites [18], and many other domains. Because of this, researchers have collected existing types of dark patterns [10,18] and call for effective countermeasures to mitigate the manipulative effects of these patterns [8]. Bongard-Blanchy et al. [1] propose an intervention space for such countermeasures. This space contains the fields *Regulatory* (e.g., [7]), *Technical* (e.g., [2,18]), *Design* (e.g., [11,20]), and *Educational* (e.g., [1]). While current research does not agree on the impact of user awareness on resilience [1,12], sensitizing people to dark patterns could help them detect patterns themselves and, thus, reduce the influence of prevalent manipulations. One approach to sensitizing people is to provide real-world examples combined with an explanation, as Brignull does on his website[3]. Another approach involves serious games, as they allow people to expose themselves to manipulative designs without the risk of harm [22].

2.2 Serious Games on Dark Patterns

Work on game-based learning regarding dark patterns is still sparse. "The Dark Pattern Game" is a board game focusing on dark patterns and privacy [24]. It targets adolescent players and can be played in groups of three to five people. Its objective is to set up a mobile phone with a selection of apps while trying to minimize data sharing for privacy reasons. Although playing the game had only limited impact on participants' knowledge about dark patterns, there was a significant influence on behavioral intention, i.e., students with higher prior dark pattern knowledge reported higher intentions to protect their personal data and privacy. Our own work intends to further this research through a web-based game prototype on the topic.

[1] While the ACM Diversity, Equity and Inclusion Council already considers the term to be problematic, the research community has not agreed on a different name yet. Therefore, we use the term to better connect with the existing literature.

[2] https://www.deceptive.design, last accessed July 17, 2024.

[3] https://www.deceptive.design/hall-of-shame, last accessed July 17, 2024.

In a workshop at CHI'24 [8], two papers presented games in the context of dark patterns[4]: The first game [15] tackles dark patterns in a virtual 3D setting in which a narrator tries to keep players in a location as long as possible. To do this, the narrator uses 3D analogies of dark patterns, like manipulating the light sources in a room to create a prolonged path for the players.

The second game [16] is a decision-making game in which players always choose between two options and try to maximize their score. However, as they play, they are also confronted with several manipulative techniques. For example, players may choose to quickly walk to a low-scoring item or take a longer path to reach a higher-scoring item, which resembles the "Obstruction" dark pattern. With their game, the authors propose a new paradigm to better estimate the deceptive potential of dark patterns. Additionally, aspects like decision time or cognitive load can also be adjusted in this game by altering, e.g., task complexity, level of distraction, or time pressure.

In contrast to both games, our approach focuses on dark patterns as a learning object by actively requiring players to find and classify them.

3 Concept and Design

Our game design takes inspiration from serious games on anti-phishing education due to the similarity of subject matter: In both areas, users need to detect and understand manipulation and deception. However, research in anti-phishing games has also shown that detection alone is not sufficient to prepare users [22] since it does not offer much insight into players' decision-making processes and allows for guesswork. Therefore, using classification in addition to detection allows for deeper insights into players' understanding of the manipulation and helps to identify possible misconceptions. For this game, we use the high-level patterns from Gray et al.'s ontology [9] for classification[5].

As a first step, we evaluated three game mechanics on three different levels of Bloom's Revised Taxonomy [14] with paper prototypes in a preliminary user study: (a) classifying (i.e., determining the correct category of) a potential dark pattern, (b) finding and classifying a single dark pattern hidden on a full website, and (c) finding and classifying an unknown number of dark patterns on a website. Our results show that players prefer the latter game mechanic as it closely mimics the real-world situation and was perceived as the most fun and most satisfying game mechanic. Considering [14], we argue that the step of identifying or finding a dark pattern matches to "Analyze", while classifying it would be "Evaluate".

Consequently, our game prototype uses this as its core game mechanic. We use a level-based design with each level themed around a specific type of website (e.g., a hotel booking website, or a smartphone shop). In each level, the player is presented with a partially interactive website that they can search for dark

---

[4] All accepted papers to the workshop are available at https://ceur-ws.org/Vol-3720/, last accessed July 17, 2024.

[5] When conducting the study, the updated version of the ontology presented at CHI'24 [10] was not available yet. Hence, our game still uses *Nagging* as a high-level pattern.

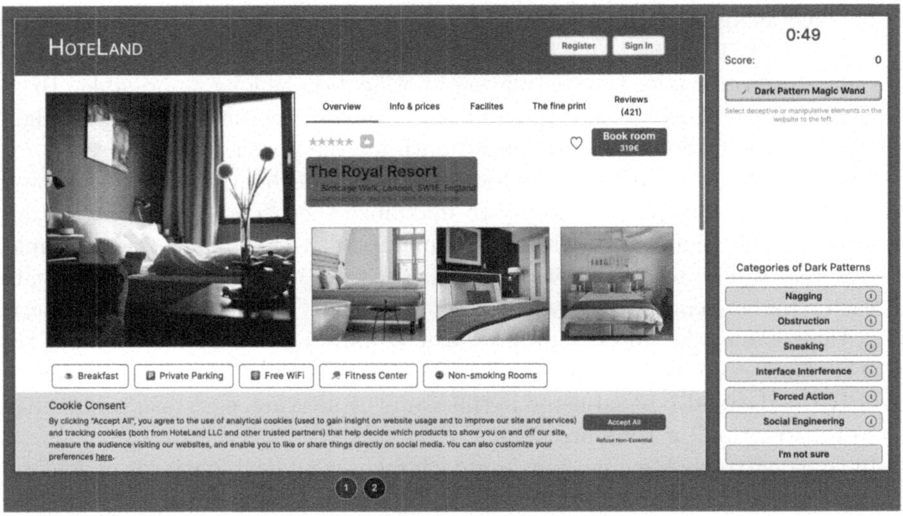

Fig. 1. In our game, players select elements from a website that they believe to be dark patterns. The active selection is highlighted in red. They then classify the element based on the high-level patterns by Gray et al. [9] shown on the right. (Color figure online)

patterns. To select a potential dark pattern, they activate a "magic wand" and click the element (see Fig. 1). This displays the list of high-level dark pattern categories from the ontology for classification. After the classification, players receive instant feedback with a short explanation and are scored for the detection and classification aspect. False positives deduct points, and choosing the *"unsure"* classification only rewards half points.

Additionally, we use storytelling elements to increase player engagement: Players assume the role of the newest recruit in the fictional "Dark Pattern Defense Force" and can climb a metaphorical career ladder to higher positions by completing levels and earning more points. The look of the game and its tutorial are themed to match this storytelling.

4 Implementation

The game is implemented as a web application to make it easily accessible and widely available. It is built with React[6] and Next.js[7]. The React framework allows for a very modular design with reusable components and offers a modern state-based implementation, making it easy to maintain and extend. We provide exemplary gameplay in an OSF repository[8].

Currently, the game offers a tutorial to teach the categories for classification and six levels in three different themes: a hotel booking website, a smartphone

[6] https://react.dev/, last accessed July 21, 2024.
[7] https://nextjs.org/, last accessed July 21, 2024.
[8] https://doi.org/10.17605/OSF.IO/UQ9ZF, last accessed September 20, 2024.

shop, and a concert ticket shop. All except one level contains multiple dark patterns from different categories. One level does not contain any dark patterns. The levels themselves are built in a modular fashion with parameters to generate different versions. Currently, this is only used for design variations (e.g., with cookie banners), but in the future this can be extended to vary the dark patterns and thus increase replayability.

Since the game itself and the game content (i.e., the levels) are written in the same language, exchanging data between them is straightforward, which enables the core game mechanic: selecting dark pattern elements on the website. Every HTML tag can be augmented with the class "darkPatternContainer" to make it selectable as a possible dark pattern. Additionally, the correct category of dark patterns and links to other elements (e.g., siblings) are modeled using HTML classes. Custom attributes let us specify explanations for each tag (with a list of pre-defined explanations for common dark patterns) and custom scoring information. That way, the level contents remain compatible with basic HTML.

Lastly, we implemented extensive gameplay logging to capture events like users selecting an element, choosing a category, or hovering a tooltip. The resulting log data can be used to analyze gameplay using game learning analytics or to discover user behaviors to improve countermeasures against dark patterns.

5 Evaluation

5.1 Study Design and Procedure

Our user study was designed as a two-part within-subjects experiment with pre-post-test (part 1) and re-test (part 2). Each player completed the tutorial (~ 5 min) and the actual game (2.5 to 5 min per level) between the pre- and post-test. The order of levels was randomized. As part of the pre-, post-, and re-test, participants were presented with images of potentially manipulative websites and had to decide if they were manipulative and why. We used the same ten sample websites from Bongard-Blanchy et al. [1] for the pre-test, plus twice an additional five websites in a similar style each for the post- and re-test to check for learning biases. For the re-test, four months later, players first classified the $10 + 5$ potentially manipulative images before playing four levels: one new level and three levels from the previous session. No additional tutorial was offered, but explanation tooltips were available throughout the game if players needed to refresh their knowledge on the different types of dark patterns [9].

5.2 Participants

We conducted the study with 22 university students (12 female, 9 male, 1 diverse), all between 20 and 35 years old ($M = 25.0$, $SD = 3.86$). 15 participants had a technical background (computer science, engineering), seven a non-technical background (economics, musicology). Eleven participants were undergraduate students and held a high school diploma as their highest academic degree, four completed their Bachelor's, and four a Master's degree. Participants reported spending an average of 4.86 hours/day online ($SD = 2.17$). For the re-test, 19 of these students participated again and as such, only the $n = 19$ participants who completed all steps of the study were considered for analysis.

5.3 Results

For performance improvements between pre- and post-test, we checked for learning bias first. We calculated the mean of correct answers (in %) for the pre-test items ($M_{\text{pre}} = .73$, $SD = .16$), the combined post-test items ($M_{\text{post}} = .87$, $SD = .06$), the post-test items that were part of the pre-test ($M_{\text{post-pre}} = .88$, $SD = .1$), and the new post-test items ($M_{\text{post-new}} = .86$, $SD = .11$). The descriptive results show that the improvements in the post-test are similarly higher for the pre-test images and the new images. Furthermore, both are substantially higher than in the pre-test. As such, potential learning bias should be negligible. Similarly, the results for the re-test suggest that the learning bias is negligible too ($M_{\text{re}} = .8$, $SD = .12$; $M_{\text{re-pre}} = .79$, $SD = .13$; $M_{\text{re-new}} = .82$, $SD = .17$).

To determine the influence on the participants' performance as learning effects, we performed paired t-tests with a Bonferroni correction for the correctly identified percentages between the pre-test and post-test and the pre-test and re-test, all on the data of $n = 19$ participants who completed all three tests. For assumption checking, we confirmed a normal distribution for the differences with a Shapiro-Wilk test ($p_{\text{pre-post}} > .48$, $p_{\text{pre-re}} > .54$). The results of the paired t-tests show significant differences both between the pre- and post-test results ($t(19) = -4.89$, $p = .0002$, $df = 18$, Cohen's $d = 1.12$) and between the pre- and re-test results ($t(19) = -4.02$, $p = .0016$, $df = 18$, Cohen's $d = .92$).

On average, participants' performance improved between the pre-test and the post-test by 13.64% ($SD = 12.6$, $CI = [8.03, 19.24]$). The gain in performance was less pronounced the better participants already were in the pre-test. In the re-test, participants' performance improved by 7.19% on average compared to the pre-test ($SD = 7.8$, $CI = [3.43, 10.95]$).

When analyzing gameplay log data, results show that player performance within the game also improved during the second play session (as part of the re-test) compared to the first play session. The average detection rate for a level during the first playthrough was 68.08% ($SD = 7.62$). In the re-test, players detected 13.83% ($SD = 6.48$) more dark patterns for levels that they had encountered four months prior. However, while the detection rate of dark patterns improved during the second playthrough, the correct classification score decreased by 3.44% ($SD = 13.15$). While the improvement in detection was quite uniform (all except one participant detected more dark patterns than in the first study), the successful classification varied greatly between participants, with the majority doing slightly worse and four participants each doing considerably worse and considerably better, respectively.

6 Discussion and Limitations

Based on the data collected in our user study, we are able to discuss and reflect on the results, their interpretation and limitations applicable to our work.

6.1 Performance Between Pre-, Post and Re-test

The improvement between the pre- and post-test shows that the game fulfilled one of its core purposes: imparting domain knowledge. It does so in two steps: first by teaching dark patterns terminology, and then by testing that knowledge in an interactive and playful way. The improvements were more pronounced for participants who detected less than half the manipulations during the pre-test, thus indicating its benefits for novices.

Even though participants' performance in the re-test was lower than in the post-test, it was still significantly higher than in the pre-test. This indicates that at least some knowledge was retained over the four months between the tests. However, we would still recommend that players continue to play the game from time to time to refresh their knowledge, similar to practices with regular compliance and safety trainings.

6.2 Performance During Gameplay

The improvements between re- and pre-test are also reflected during gameplay. Players were better at detecting dark patterns not just in the replayed level but also in the new level. However, performance improvements in the replayed level were more pronounced. While this is true for the re-test in general, it also extends to recurring instances of dark patterns. Our log data also indicates that players appear more likely to detect further instances or variations of the same type of dark pattern after encountering it once. For instance, the initial instance of a *disguised ad* dark pattern was only detected by 27% of participants. Its second instance was detected and correctly classified by 41%. Additionally, participants were more decisive in their selection and classification of recurring dark patterns. These findings support our goal to teach detection and classification of different dark patterns so that users can remember their characteristics and make informed decisions.

Players were able to detect (and correctly classify) certain dark patterns better than others: Generally, they were best at detecting and classifying dark patterns from the *social engineering* category of the ontology [9], such as *low stock messages* (e.g., "only one room left") and *countdown timer*. Similarly, *false hierarchy* dark patterns were detected in 90% of all occurrences. Dark patterns from the *sneaking* category, which hide information, were detected least often. Our findings match the results of [1] on people's ability to detect certain dark patterns better than others.

Participants often mistook either *sneaking* or *forced action* for obstruction (less often vice versa) because the hidden information or required action was considered an unnecessary step and thus made the task unnecessarily harder.

Participants also frequently classified *nagging* as *forced action*. Interestingly, in the recent update of the ontology [10], *nagging* was re-classified as a sub-category of *forced action*. This seems to match our participants' mental model.

For a more comprehensive performance evaluation, we need to consider socio-demographical participant data. All participants were students in higher education or with a university degree. In the first part of our study, there were 15 participants with a technical and 7 with a non-technical background. Their respective detection and classification rates were very similar, suggesting that affinity to technology does not influence one's ability to resist dark patterns.

Furthermore, we analyzed performance in correlation to time spent online. Participants who spend less time online (1–3 h per day) detected slightly more dark patterns, whereas participants who spend much time online (6 or more hours per day) were slightly better in classifying them. However, these differences were minimal, and the rather small sample size does not allow us to draw general conclusions from this.

6.3 Limitations

One limitation derives from our implementation of how the game handles multiple dark patterns. While it is possible for one element to contain multiple dark patterns (in this case selecting any one would be considered correct), a problem arises with nested dark patterns (i.e., an outer container being one dark pattern and an inner container being another one). During the study, it became apparent that participants often *meant* the right thing, but their selection was either too broad or too narrow.

Another limitation is that our participant sample is small and only consisted of university students. The perception of dark patterns might vary by age [1]. As such, generalizability of our results to other demographics is limited and requires further validation, e.g., in a larger study with a more diverse user group.

7 Conclusion and Future Work

In this paper, we presented the design, implementation, and first evaluation of a serious game about detecting and classifying dark patterns in sample websites. Through an empirical user study with pre-, post-, and re-test and two game-play sessions, we evaluated possible learning effects by focusing on participants' performance improvements. Our results show that participants' performance in detecting dark patterns improved significantly after playing the game, both in the immediate post-test as well as in a re-test four months later. Furthermore, participants showed differences in classifying different types of dark patterns; e.g., *social engineering* was correctly classified more often than *sneaking*. This may allow further reasoning on participants' misconceptions and difficulties.

For future work, we plan to make our game publicly available to validate our study results with a larger and more diverse participant sample. Using detailed game log data, we want to extract participants' mental models and possible misconceptions for specific instances of dark patterns, and use this data to improve countermeasures against dark patterns.

References

1. Bongard-Blanchy, K., Rossi, A., Rivas, S., Doublet, S., Koenig, V., Lenzini, G.: "I am Definitely Manipulated, Even When I am Aware of it. It's Ridiculous!" - dark patterns from the end-user perspective. In: Designing Interactive Systems Conference 2021, pp. 763–776. ACM, Virtual Event, USA (2021). https://doi.org/10.1145/3461778.3462086
2. Bösch, C., Erb, B., Kargl, F., Kopp, H., Pfattheicher, S.: Tales from the dark side: privacy dark strategies and privacy dark patterns. Privacy Enhancing Technol. **2016**(4), 237–254 (2016). https://doi.org/10.1515/popets-2016-0038
3. Brignull, H.: Deceptive Patterns: Exposing the Tricks Tech Companies Use to Control You. Testimonium Limited (2023)
4. Conti, G., Sobiesk, E.: Malicious interface design: exploiting the user. In: 19th International Conference on World Wide Web, WWW 2010, pp. 271–280. ACM, New York (2010). https://doi.org/10.1145/1772690.1772719
5. Di Geronimo, L., Braz, L., Fregnan, E., Palomba, F., Bacchelli, A.: UI dark patterns and where to find them: a study on mobile applications and user perception. In: Proceedings of the 2020 CHI Conference on Human Factors in Computing Systems, CHI 2020, pp. 1–14. Association for Computing Machinery, New York, NY, USA (2020). https://doi.org/10.1145/3313831.3376600
6. Di Geronimo, L., Braz, L., Fregnan, E., Palomba, F., Bacchelli, A.: UI dark patterns and where to find them: a study on mobile applications and user perception. In: CHI Conference on Human Factors in Computing Systems, CHI 2020, pp. 1–14. ACM, New York (2020). https://doi.org/10.1145/3313831.3376600
7. European Commission and Directorate-General for Justice and Consumers, Lupiáñez-Villanueva, F., Boluda, A., Bogliacino, F., Liva, G., Lechardoy, L., Rodríguez de las Heras Ballell, T.: Behavioural study on unfair commercial practices in the digital environment: dark patterns and manipulative personalisation (final report). Publications Office of the European Union, Brussels (2022). https://doi.org/10.2838/859030
8. Gray, C.M., et al.: Mobilizing research and regulatory action on dark patterns and deceptive design practices. In: Extended Abstracts of the 2024 CHI Conference on Human Factors in Computing Systems, CHI EA 2024. ACM, New York (2024). https://doi.org/10.1145/3613905.3636310
9. Gray, C.M., Santos, C., Bielova, N.: Towards a preliminary ontology of dark patterns knowledge. In: Extended Abstracts of the 2023 CHI Conference on Human Factors in Computing Systems, CHI EA 2023. ACM, New York (2023). https://doi.org/10.1145/3544549.3585676
10. Gray, C.M., Santos, C.T., Bielova, N., Mildner, T.: An ontology of dark patterns knowledge: foundations, definitions, and a pathway for shared knowledge-building. In: CHI Conference on Human Factors in Computing Systems, CHI 2024. ACM, New York (2024). https://doi.org/10.1145/3613904.3642436
11. Graßl, P., Schraffenberger, H., Zuiderveen Borgesius, F., Buijzen, M.: Dark and bright patterns in cookie consent requests. J. Digit. Soc. Res. **3**(1), 1–38 (2021). https://doi.org/10.33621/jdsr.v3i1.54

12. Grossklags, J., Acquisti, A.: When 25 cents is too much: an experiment on willingness-to-sell and willingness-to-protect personal information. In: WEIS. Citeseer (2007)
13. Gunawan, J., Pradeep, A., Choffnes, D., Hartzog, W., Wilson, C.: A comparative study of dark patterns across web and mobile modalities. Proc. ACM Hum.-Comput. Interact. **5**(CSCW2), 1–29 (2021). https://doi.org/10.1145/3479521
14. Krathwohl, D.R.: A revision of bloom's taxonomy: an overview. Theory Pract. **41**(4), 212–218 (2002)
15. Kronhardt, K., Gerken, J.: Start playing around-serious & persuasive games as a viable counter-measure against deceptive patterns? In: Mobilizing Research and Regulatory Action on Dark Patterns and Deceptive Design Practices Workshop at CHI 2024, Honolulu (2024). https://ceur-ws.org/Vol-3720/paper7.pdf
16. Löschner, D.M., Pannasch, S.: Measuring the deceptive potential of design patterns: a decision-making game. In: Mobilizing Research and Regulatory Action on Dark Patterns and Deceptive Design Practices Workshop at CHI 2024, Honolulu (2024). https://ceur-ws.org/Vol-3720/paper9.pdf
17. Lu, Y., Zhang, C., Yang, Y., Yao, Y., Li, T.J.J.: From awareness to action: exploring end-user empowerment interventions for dark patterns in UX. Proc. ACM Hum.-Comput. Interact. **8**(CSCW), 1–41 (2024). https://doi.org/10.1145/3637336
18. Mathur, A., et al.: Dark patterns at scale: findings from a crawl of 11K shopping websites. Proc. ACM Hum.-Comput. Interact. **3**(CSCW), 1–32 (2019). https://doi.org/10.1145/3359183
19. Mildner, T., Freye, M., Savino, G.L., Doyle, P.R., Cowan, B.R., Malaka, R.: Defending against the dark arts: recognising dark patterns in social media. In: 2023 ACM Designing Interactive Systems Conference, DIS 2023, pp. 2362–2374. ACM, New York (2023). https://doi.org/10.1145/3563657.3595964
20. Potel-Saville, M., Da Rocha, M.: From dark patterns to fair patterns? Usable taxonomy to contribute solving the issue with countermeasures. In: Privacy Technologies and Policy, pp. 145–165. Springer, Cham (2024). https://doi.org/10.1007/978-3-031-61089-9_7
21. Roepke, R., Schroeder, U.: The problem with teaching defence against the dark arts: a review of game-based learning applications and serious games for cyber security education. In: Lane, H., Zvacek, S., Uhomoibhi, J. (eds.) 11th International Conference on Computer Supported Education, CSEDU 2019, pp. 58–66. SciTePress, Heraklion, Greece (2019). https://doi.org/10.5220/0007706100580066
22. Röpke, R.: Extending game-based anti-phishing education using personalization: design and implementation of a framework for personalized learning game content in anti-phishing learning games. Doctoral thesis, RWTH Aachen University, Aachen (2023). https://doi.org/10.18154/RWTH-2023-04991
23. Schäfer, R., Preuschoff, P.M., Röpke, R., Sahabi, S., Borchers, J.: Fighting malicious designs: towards visual countermeasures against dark patterns. In: CHI Conference on Human Factors in Computing Systems, CHI 2024. ACM, New York (2024). https://doi.org/10.1145/3613904.3642661
24. Tjostheim, I., Ayres-Pereira, V., Wales, C., Manna, A., Egenfeldt-Nielsen, S.: Dark pattern: a serious game for learning about the dangers of sharing data. ECGBL **16**(1), 774–783 (2022). https://doi.org/10.34190/ecgbl.16.1.872

HeartGuard VR: Immersive Romance Scam Education

Octavia Lea, Lynsay A. Shepherd(✉), and Andrea Szymkowiak

School of Design and Informatics, Abertay University, Dundee, UK
octavial@gmx.com, {lynsay.shepherd,a.szymkowiak}@abertay.ac.uk

Abstract. Romance scams are a form of social engineering whereby a scammer leads a victim to believe they are in a romantic relationship. The scammer typically lures the victim to an alternative communication method before requesting money under the guise of an urgent situation, such as medical or travel expenses. Victims are left emotionally and financially devastated. Although dating platforms and law enforcement provide information on spotting scammers, it is often text-based and not interactive. We present HeartGuard VR, an immersive, virtual reality (VR) serious game environment which aims to educate the public about romance scams in an engaging manner. This paper describes the game's design and development, alongside the results of a user evaluation. In the future, it is anticipated the experience will become a publicly available intervention to reduce romance scam victimisation.

Keywords: Romance scams · Virtual reality · Serious games

1 Introduction and Background

Romance scams are a specific type of cybercrime where victims are drawn in, often via online dating platforms, and conned out of money as a product of a fake romantic relationship. Scammers use a number of tactics to achieve their goal [12]; the resulting financial and emotional costs can devastate victims. Furthermore, the crime is often under-reported because victims may be too embarrassed to admit they have been scammed. It is not a new crime, however, the COVID-19 pandemic led to an increase in cybercrime [13], while the associated lockdowns meant many people felt isolated, turning to online dating for companionship.

Dating platform providers and law enforcement often run information campaigns to help raise awareness of romance scams to prevent further victimisation. However, such initiatives are often text-based and may be limited in terms of engagement, with users preferring more interactive approaches [11]. Additionally, it can be challenging for users to find relevant safety information produced by dating platforms. Existing work by Dickerson et al. [8] highlights that interaction rates with static safety information pages are likely to be low without providing users with contextualised romance scam warnings on a dating platform. There

A. Schönbohm et al. (Eds.): GALA 2024, LNCS 15348, pp. 201–211, 2025.
https://doi.org/10.1007/978-3-031-78269-5_19

is a recognised need to raise awareness of romance scams and encourage users to adopt protective mechanisms when using online dating platforms [6,16].

Serious games have previously been used to educate people about various cybersecurity topics, including phishing [5], password security [10], and attack/defence scenarios [24]. This suggests that a serious game can serve as an appropriate mechanism to address the challenges associated with romance scam education. Due to the immersive experience of VR environments, the technology may enhance learning and training in serious games [4], e.g., there are cybersecurity specific VR education environments available such as Cyberinfrastructure Security Education for Professionals and Students (CiSE-ProS) [20]. Thus, we present HeartGuard VR, a VR-based serious game designed to educate the public about romance scams. Through immersive gameplay, we seek to demonstrate the nature of this crime and reduce future victimisation.

2 Game Design and Implementation

2.1 Narrative

In HeartGuard VR, the player takes the role of an AI security assistant, marking messages on a given device as genuine or a scam. This style of gameplay is similar to *"Papers, Please"* [15], where the player takes the role of an immigration inspector at a border checkpoint for the fictional country of Arstotzka. In comparison, HeartGuard VR's gameplay revolves around the player reading messages sent to the main character's (Claire's) device, immersing themselves into the story and determining if the messages received are genuine or a scam.

One core narrative takes place in the game: a romance scam targeting Claire, perpetrated by an individual named Freddie. Alongside this narrative are smaller conversation threads between Claire, her best friend, and her mother, to maintain a sense of social realism, whilst Claire is sucked deeper into the romance scam.

If the romance scam messages are incorrectly categorised by the player, slight changes occur in the dialog, such as Claire apologising for a late reply. Incorrectly classifying the miscellaneous scam messages (e.g., typical phishing messages) will result in consequences like Claire's bank reporting unauthorised activity. To maintain story flow, consequences do not result in a game over.

As the narrative progresses, different types of messages appear. Firstly, the messages arrive from a dating application - this is where Claire first encounters Freddie, then emails are unlocked and finally text messages are shown to the player. This follows the natural progression of romance scams, as the scammer moves a victim away from a dating platform and isolates them [7,23]. Additional scammer tactics are represented in the serious game, for example, Freddie uses time limits and emotive language to pressure Claire into sending money [3]. At the end of the VR experience, Claire receives an email from her mum, with a link to a news article. It reveals that a romance scammer has been arrested, and one of his identities was Freddie.

2.2 Technology

HeartGuard VR was developed in Unity, a game engine supporting a wide variety of platforms [21], and has been used for developing other cybersecurity VR-based serious games [20]. Whilst Unity has native support for VR, SteamVR [22] allows Unity and other game engines to interface to a connected VR headset. SteamVR supports a plethora of VR headsets, expanding the target audience. Additionally, SteamVR's Unity package [22] comes pre-bundled with a demonstration world showcasing the different mechanics supported. Of note were the default VR controls, physics-based interactive items and buttons that can be pressed. These mechanics were integrated in HeartGuard VR.

2.3 World

To foster a sense of escapism and to prevent the environment feeling like a traditional office, the theme of old technology was used, also known as retro computing, where TVs were chunky, and data came on floppy disks, potentially invoking a sense of nostalgia. Messages in HeartGuard VR appear as floppy disks and are inserted into either a floppy drive or a grinder to dispose of them, if they are classified as a scam attempt. These actions are accompanied by matching sound effects. The main play space is an old metal desk (Fig. 1), with a clock on the right displaying the current date/time and, on the left, a radio playing relaxing music, and a small decoration to add colour. Above the desk is a corkboard displaying security focused public domain posters from America's National Security Agency [17], a motivational poster and two posters to inform the player that the floppy drive on the left is for approving messages, and the grinder on the right is for marking messages as spam.

Fig. 1. The main desk play area on the left, the AI assistant control room environment on the right.

The play area sits inside a lifeless, control room (Fig. 1). This prevents the environment from distracting the player, instead focusing them on the desk in front. To the right of the player is a message on the wall. This message welcomes the player, reminds them to go through a questionnaire (see Sect. 3, methodology) and tells them how to reset their position in the game for a more comfortable experience. To the left of the player is a wall of CRT TVs, which add to the aesthetic of a security room. Behind the player is an exit doorway and a list of assets used in the project with their respective Creative Commons licences.

3 Methodology

The development and evaluation of HeartGuard VR was approved by Abertay University's Ethics Committee (submission no. EMS7314). Before playing the game, participants provided informed consent and were asked to complete a survey relating to their past experience of VR and knowledge of romance scams. The VR experience began by asking if the participant had used a VR device before. If they had, more questions appeared in relation to the participant's past experience (*What do you find comfortable in VR?* and *What is the maximum length of time comfortable for you in VR?*). Regardless of previous VR experience, all participants were asked if they had experienced motion sickness or had epilepsy. If the participant was comfortable to continue, they were asked if they had heard about romance scams. If they answered *yes*, they were asked to provide a definition, and where they had heard the term (e.g., on social media, or on the news). All participants were asked if they were comfortable playing a game that shows the effects of romance scams on an individual (e.g., tactics used by scammers, and victim responses). The player was then instructed to play through the HeartGuard VR experience (either on-campus at Abertay University, or at home with the game files downloaded from itch.io if they owned a VR headset).

After game play, a post-questionnaire was then used to explore the participant's experience with HeartGuard VR, and to capture demographics. A modified version of the System Usability Scale [2] was used for gaining usability insights, where 1 equalled Strongly Disagree and 5 equalled Strongly Agree. Questions included: *I want to play more of the game, The game was unnecessarily complex, The game was easy to play, I needed previous VR experience to play the game, The different parts of the game were well integrated, There was inconsistency between the different parts of the game, Learning how to play the game was quick, Performing actions in the game felt cumbersome, Playing the game felt natural, It took a long time to figure out how to play the game.*

A modified version of the Experience Economy Model [19] used for VR experiences in museums [14] was adapted to suit HeartGuard VR (Table 1). The score for each section was produced by taking the average of each question, with the answer ranging from 1 (Strongly Disagree) to 7 (Strongly Agree). Questions marked with a * in Table 1 were negatively framed, and were thus reverse coded for analysis (i.e., response values were subtracted from 8).

Additional questions were designed to garner players' personal feelings on the game including features they liked and disliked (e.g., gameplay, the story, graphics, controls, sounds), and if they had learned about romance scams. There was a space for the participant to provide any additional comments about the game. Finally, demographics were captured, after this, including country of residence, age, gender, education, employment, industry, and VR usage. To conclude the HeartGuard VR study, participants were given a debrief, including resources on romance scam victim support.

Table 1. Modified Experience Economy Model questions.

Section	Questions
Education	I learnt something new from the game
	The game made me more knowledgeable
	The game provided a good experience for learning
	The game stimulated my curiosity to learn new things
Entertainment	Playing the game was amusing
	Playing the game was captivating
	Playing the game was entertaining
	Playing the game was fun
Aesthetics	I felt a sense of harmony in the game's environment
	Just being in the game's environment was very pleasant
	The game's environment was pretty bland*
	The game's environment was very attractive
Escapism	I felt like I was in a different time or place
	The game let me imagine being someone (or something) else
	I completely escaped from reality
	I felt I played a different character in the game
Overall VR Experience	Using VR contributed positively to learning about romance scams
	Using VR helped me enjoy learning about romance fraud
	Using VR gave me a meaningful experience about romance fraud
	I would like to use VR to learn about other things in the future
Romance Scam Education	I will look into romance scams after playing this game
	I will forget about romance scams soon after playing this game*
	I see romance scams in a different light after playing this game
	I will think about this game when thinking about romance scams

4 Results and Discussion

The study was advertised on campus at Abertay University, and on social media platforms. The study was conducted in August 2023 and recruited ($n = 10$) participants. The VR experience took approximately 1 h to complete.

4.1 Demographics

The majority of the participants were in the 18–24 age category ($n = 6$) and most participants resided in the United Kingdom or the USA ($n = 9$). Half of the participants ($n = 5$) were in full-time employment. Gender, education level, and industry were mixed (Table 2).

Table 2. Participant demographic information.

Category	Answers	n	Category	Answers	n
Gender	Male	5	Age	18–24	6
	Female	3		25–34	1
	Non-Binary	1		35–44	2
	Prefer not to say	1		45–54	1
Residing country	United Kingdom	5	Highest education level	High School/College	4
	USA	4		Undergraduate	3
	France	1		Postgraduate	2
				Doctoral	1
Employment	Student	2	Industry	Public	1
	Unemployed	1		Private	1
	Part-time	2		Accommodation & food	1
	Full-time	5		Professional, scientific & technical	2
				Education	3
				Other services	1

4.2 Experience with VR and Romance Scams

Just over half of the participants owned a VR headset ($n = 6$) and most had used VR before ($n = 9$). Responses to frequency of VR usage were varied, and most participants were comfortable with static standing experiences ($n = 8$). Half said they had not experienced VR sickness ($n = 5$). Just over half of the participants had heard of romance scams ($n = 6$), and most had heard the term from the news or online. Table 3 shows the full breakdown of responses.

4.3 SUS Scores

SUS scores varied between 90 and 72.5 (mean = 79.75, SD = 9.46, $n = 10$), which suggests the usability of the VR experience was considered to be above average (68). To assess the internal consistency of the survey, Cronbach's alpha was calculated, $\alpha = 0.4$, indicating limited consistency with the small user group.

Table 3. Experience with VR and romance fraud.

Question	Answers	n	Question	Answers	n
Own a VR headset	Yes	6	Used VR before	Yes	9
	No	4		No	1
Last time in VR	Last 7 days	4	VR usage	Every day	1
	Last month	1		Once a week	1
	Last year	2		2–3 times a week	2
	Last 3 years	1		<once a month	4
	Over 3 years	1		2–3 times a month	1
	Never	1			
Comfortable with VR experiences	Seated	6	Comfortable time in VR	10–30 min	2
	Static standing	8		31–60 min	3
	Roomscale	4		Over 2 h	4
	Moving using teleportation	4		No answer	1
	Moving using a thumbstick	5			
Experience of motion sickness	Not at all	4	Experience of VR sickness	Not at all	5
	Minor	4		Minor	2
	Moderate	1		Moderate	1
	Severe	1		Not sure	2
Epilepsy	Not at all	9	Heard about romance scams	Yes	6
	Minor	1		No	2
				Maybe	2
Heard about them from:	Awareness campaign	1			
	News	6			
	Online	8			
	Friends or family	4			
	Other (Scambaiting)	1			

Table 4. Mean, standard deviation, median and Cronbach's alpha for each section.

Descriptives	Education	Entert-ainment	Aesthetics	Escapism	Overall VR Experience	Romance Scam Education
mean	5.55	5.45	4.98	5.00	6.23	5.68
SD	1.14	1.46	1.21	1.51	0.59	0.85
median	6.00	6.00	5.00	5.00	6.00	6.00
α	0.797	0.864	0.909	0.920	0.802	0.584

4.4 Experience Economy Model Questions

For each of the sections of the Experience Economy Model, the mean was calculated, along with standard deviation, median and Cronbach's alpha (Table 4).

Participants were generally positive towards aspects of their experience involving education, entertainment, aesthetics, escapism, overall VR experience, and romance scam education questions, with the standard deviation reflecting some variation. The Cronbach's alpha value ranged between 0.797 and 0.909 for education, entertainment, aesthetics, escapism, and overall VR experience, suggesting reliable internal consistency. The romance scam education Cronbach's alpha of 0.584 suggests low reliability for this section.

4.5 Qualitative Results

Narrative. One of the key reasons cited as to why participants enjoyed the game was the immersive storyline. These results are consistent with previous research which highlights the importance of narrative in serious games [18]. Additionally, the strength of the narrative, alongside positive participant responses to the game aesthetics (Sect. 4.4) may have positively influenced how much participants perceived they learned from HeartGuard VR [1].

- P04 - *"The story was well written and felt realistic, having to physically choose a side made it more immersive"*
- P09 - *"the storyline was really helpful in understanding how real-life romance scams may play out"*

Gameplay and VR Experience: Participants enjoyed aspects of HeartGuard VR, in particular the interaction and immersiveness of the experience, which links in with findings by Seo et al. [20].

- P05 - *"Different experience, less passive than usual IT teaching. Interactive compared to just reading"*
- P08 - *"the simple feedback of sorting and grinding things ... Seeing the messages from Mom did hit me, and the VR in-person experience I think amplified the effect ..."*
- P09 - *"the graphics were awesome and really well-designed, and the sound design really helped with immersion. The setup was really innovative..."*

Conversely, some of the participants felt HeartGuard VR needed to be more engaging, with a branching narrative and consequences for actions. Player characteristics may influence how people respond to a game based environment [9], which needs to be investigated further.

- P01 - *"I would have liked a more clear ending, rather than the game closing itself (I thought it had crashed!)"*
- P03 - *"Needs to be more engaging."*
- P04 - *"I feel like the choices i made didn't have any influence on the story"*

Romance Scam Education: When participants were asked if HeartGuard VR has changed their view on romance scams, although some had previous knowledge, they still found the experience useful. A longitudinal study is required to investigate whether participants retain information they have learned [25].

- P07 - *"it made me feel the effects of them more strongly, as it made me feel personally involved in the situation"*
- P08 - *"I think it's made it more clear what could happen when vulnerable people are preyed on, but it kind of doesn't sell to me how people who do not perceive themselves as vulnerable can fall prey to these kind of things"*
- P09 - *"This was a really good refresher on what romance scams can look like and I would definitely encourage people to play it"*

Overall View of HeartGuard VR: Generally, comments received from participants were positive, suggesting the experience may help raise awareness of romance scams and the tactics used.

- P01 - *"Overall I think this was very well made and informative. It also made me realize that (other than the motion sickness) learning in VR is very very effective. Being able to interact with my environment and play a game while learning is so so helpful to me. A lot of times I struggle with textbook-style learning, and so something interactive like this is HUGELY helpful."*
- P08 - *"... This is not an inaccurate portrayal of a romance scam. It's actually quite realistic. That being said I do think that the player agency is in this game is rather low... it does feel a little not fun to play."*

Limitations. The sample size in the user evaluation was small ($n = 10$), however, a further study with a larger participant pool would help generalise our findings.

5 Conclusion and Future Work

Romance scams continue to pose a challenge for law enforcement, online dating platforms, and those using online dating for companionship. The generally positive results from the user evaluation of HeartGuard VR demonstrate that serious games in a VR environment have the potential to contribute towards educating users about romance scams. Future work seeks to develop the HeartGuard VR experience further, and it can serve as an intervention to reduce romance scam victimisation which can be deployed by law enforcement, dating platforms, and academia.

Acknowledgments. The authors would like to thank Abertay University's Emergent Technology Centre for supporting this work.

Disclosure of Interests. The authors have no competing interests to declare that are relevant to the content of this article.

References

1. Alexiou, A., Schippers, M.C., Oshri, I., Angelopoulos, S.: Narrative and aesthetics as antecedents of perceived learning in serious games. Inf. Technol. People **35**(8), 142–161 (2022)
2. Brooke, J., et al.: SUS-a quick and dirty usability scale. Usability Eval. Ind. **189**(194), 4–7 (1996)
3. Carter, E.: Distort, extort, deceive and exploit: exploring the inner workings of a romance fraud. Br. J. Criminol. **61**(2), 283–302 (2021)
4. Checa, D., Bustillo, A.: A review of immersive virtual reality serious games to enhance learning and training. Multimedia Tools Appl. **79**(9), 5501–5527 (2020)
5. Gokul, C.J., Pandit, S., Vaddepalli, S., Tupsamudre, H., Banahatti, V., Lodha, S.: PHISHY-a serious game to train enterprise users on phishing awareness. In: Proceedings of the 2018 Annual Symposium on Computer-Human Interaction in Play Companion Extended Abstracts, pp. 169–181 (2018)
6. Cross, C.: Using artificial intelligence (AI) and deepfakes to deceive victims: the need to rethink current romance fraud prevention messaging. Crime Prev. Community Saf. **24**(1), 30–41 (2022)
7. Cross, C., Dragiewicz, M., Richards, K.: Understanding romance fraud: insights from domestic violence research. Br. J. Criminol. **58**(6), 1303–1322 (2018)
8. Dickerson, S., Apeh, E., Ollis, G.: Contextualised cyber security awareness approach for online romance fraud. In: 2020 7th International Conference on Behavioural and Social Computing (BESC), pp. 1–6. IEEE (2020)
9. Hookham, G., Nesbitt, K.: A systematic review of the definition and measurement of engagement in serious games. In: Proceedings of the Australasian Computer Science Week Multiconference, pp. 1–10 (2019)
10. Jayakrishnan, G.C., Sirigireddy, G.R., Vaddepalli, S., Banahatti, V., Lodha, S.P., Pandit, S.S.: Passworld: a serious game to promote password awareness and diversity in an enterprise. In: Proceedings of the Sixteenth USENIX Conference on Usable Privacy and Security, pp. 1–18 (2020)
11. Karagiannis, S., Papaioannou, T., Magkos, E., Tsohou, A.: Game-based information security/privacy education and awareness: theory and practice. In: Themistocleous, M., Papadaki, M., Kamal, M.M. (eds.) EMCIS 2020. LNBIP, vol. 402, pp. 509–525. Springer, Cham (2020). https://doi.org/10.1007/978-3-030-63396-7_34
12. Kydd, M., Shepherd, L.A., Szymkowiak, A., Johnson, G.I.: Love at first sleight: a review of scammer techniques in online romance fraud. In: Onwubiko, C., et al. (eds) The International Conference on Cybersecurity, Situational Awareness and Social Media, pp. 327–341. Springer, Cham (2023). https://doi.org/10.1007/978-981-99-6974-6_18
13. Lallie, H.S., et al.: Cyber security in the age of Covid-19: a timeline and analysis of cyber-crime and cyber-attacks during the pandemic. Comput. Secur. **105**, 102248 (2021)
14. Lee, H., Jung, T.H., Tom Dieck, M.C., Chung, N.: Experiencing immersive virtual reality in museums. Inf. Manage. **57**(5), 103229 (2020)
15. Pope, L.: Papers, Please (2013). https://papersplea.se/. Accessed 15 July 2024
16. Luu, V., Land, L.P.W., Chin, W.W.: Safeguarding against romance scams - using protection motivation theory. In: European Conference on Information Systems (2017). https://api.semanticscholar.org/CorpusID:4426698
17. National Security Agency: National Security Agency (NSA) security/motivational posters from the 1950s and 1960s (2017). https://www.governmentattic.org/28docs/NSAsecurityPosters_1950s-60s.pdf. Accessed 15 July 2024

18. Naul, E., Liu, M.: Why story matters: a review of narrative in serious games. J. Comput. Res. **58**(3), 687–707 (2020)
19. Pine, B.J., Gilmore, J.H., et al.: Welcome to the Experience Economy, vol. 76. Harvard Business Review Press Cambridge, MA, USA (1998)
20. Seo, J.H., Bruner, M., Payne, A., Gober, N., McMullen, D., Chakravorty, D.K.: Using virtual reality to enforce principles of cybersecurity. J. Comput. Sci. Educ. **10**(1), 81–87 (2019)
21. Unity Technologies: Unity (2024). https://unity.com/. Accessed 15 July 2024
22. Valve Corporation: SteamVR Plugin (2024). https://assetstore.unity.com/packages/tools/integration/steamvr-plugin-32647. Accessed 15 July 2024
23. Whitty, M.T.: Anatomy of the online dating romance scam. Secur. J. **28**, 443–455 (2015)
24. Yamin, M.M., Katt, B., Nowostawski, M.: Serious games as a tool to model attack and defense scenarios for cyber-security exercises. Comput. Secur. **110**, 102450 (2021)
25. Yasin, A., Fatima, R., Wen, L., JiangBin, Z., Niazi, M.: What goes wrong during phishing education? A probe into a game-based assessment with unfavorable results. Entertain. Comput. **52**, 100815 (2025)

Virtual Battlefields: The Rise of Video Games "Inspired" by War in Ukraine

Elena Shliakhovchuk[1(✉)] and Miguel Chover[2]

[1] The Polytechnic University of Valencia, camino de Vera s/n, 46022 Valencia, Spain
olsh@upvnet.upv.es
[2] Jaume I University of Castellón, Vicent Sos Baynat, s/n, 12071 Castellón de la Plana, Spain

Abstract. The intersection of video games and real-world global issues represents a growing field of interest within the academic community. This study contributes to the discourse by examining video games that incorporate narratives related to the war in Ukraine. From storyless simple arcades to richly detailed immersive RPGs, a diverse range of fifty-six games were examined from multiple perspectives to reflect on the unique lens through which players are invited to engage with the complexities of the Russian-Ukrainian War. The study analyses content, themes, and distinctive common features, considering the broader implications of using interactive media to engage with contemporary global conflicts. The findings reveal that these games transcend mere entertainment, serving as powerful mediums for conveying complex themes and educating players about significant world events.

Keywords: Video Games · Game Development · War in Ukraine

1 Introduction

Russia's invasion of Ukraine on the 24th of February in 2022 initiated the largest military conflict in Europe since World War II, demonstrating far-reaching consequences that have affected global security, economies, and various industries [1]. The video game industry is no exception; in response to international sanctions against Russia, many gaming companies exited the Russian market to comply with these sanctions and show solidarity with Ukraine, effectively blocking Russian businesses and players. The major console platforms (PlayStation, Nintendo, Xbox) and publishers (Activision Blizzard, CD Projekt Red, EA, Ubisoft) withdrew their products and services [2]. In addition, numerous game developers and video game companies launched fundraising campaigns to support humanitarian efforts in Ukraine, conducted awareness campaigns, and organised in-game events such as virtual charity races to support Ukraine and educate players about the situation [3, 4]. Numerous video game companies have issued public statements condemning the invasion and expressing solidarity with Ukraine, while the global game development community rallied support for Ukrainian developers [5, 6].

A. Schönbohm et al. (Eds.): GALA 2024, LNCS 15348, pp. 212–221, 2025.
https://doi.org/10.1007/978-3-031-78269-5_20

At the same time, after February 24, 2022, many Ukrainian and some international developers began to see themselves as representatives of unique perspectives on the intersection between video games and social impact [7]. As an integral part of public discourse and a significant media market, video games have become arenas of political and social expression. Consequently, the video game industry has responded to Russia's war against Ukraine by developing impactful games that have emerged as a result of this war [8, 9].

This study analyses video games developed in response to the war in Ukraine from multiple perspectives, seeking to document and analyze video games' content, themes, and common features. It aims to understand how these games can contribute to public discourse and how they can serve as tools for education and advocacy in the context of an ongoing global conflict.

2 Literature Review

Video games that draw inspiration from real-world events have emerged as a significant genre within the gaming industry. This trend of grounding game narratives provides players with unique perspectives on history and current affairs in the hope of enhancing their understanding of complex events [10].

One notable example is "This War of Mine", inspired by the Siege of Sarajevo during the Bosnian War, which starkly depicts the harsh realities faced by civilians in wartime. The game uses gameplay and storytelling to explore themes of bureaucracy, conflict, and human suffering, fostering player empathy [11]. Similarly, "Liyla and the Shadows of War" employs interactive storytelling to convey the experiences of Palestinian families during a siege. "Valiant Hearts: The Great War" chronicles the hardships of World War I through diverse lives, intertwining historical accuracy with emotional storytelling to prompt reflection on personal sacrifices and the conflict's global impact. By blending unconventional narratives with established gaming mechanics, it exemplifies video games' potential in public history practice [12]. "1979 Revolution: Black Friday" provides an immersive experience of the Iranian Revolution, accentuates the intricacies of political unrest and personal sacrifice, and illustrates video games' efficacy in addressing societal, political, and cultural biases and prejudices [13]. "Czechoslovakia 38–89: Assassination" allows players to interactively partake in key moments of Czechoslovakia's modern history, offering a multi-perspective "experience" of these events. This game underscores the influential role of video games in promoting historical consciousness and understanding historical and social dynamics [14].

Parallelly, research highlights the unique ability of video games to convey political and social messages effectively and influence players' attitudes and understanding. For example, engagement with "PeaceMaker," which simulates the Palestinian-Israeli conflict, led to a marked reduction in metrics associated with religious convictions and extremist political leanings [15]. "Papers, Please" influences players' opinions on political issues and helps to explore the themes of immigration, border control, and bureaucratic ethics [16]. Titles such as "Finding Home", "Bury Me, My Love", "Path Out", and "North", based on real-life experiences of displaced people, have the potential to spark discussions on critical political issues surrounding refugees, raise awareness, and encourage engagement in political discourse at various levels [17]. Moreover, video games based on real events have demonstrated their effectiveness as instruments for advocacy and activism, raising awareness, and mobilising support for various causes. For instance, players' exposure to "Darfur is Dying," a game spotlighting the Darfur crisis, led to an increased readiness to help the people of Darfur [18]. Similarly, "Against All Odds" and "Survival" developed to depict the realities faced by refugees, resulted in players reporting a heightened interest in the topic, increased empathy, and greater motivation to support individuals in need [19, 20]. These examples illustrate the growing prevalence of video games based on real-world events as a significant form of cultural expression capable of addressing complex social, historical, and political issues [21].

The ongoing war has brought military action to the forefront of public consciousness, yet popular culture, particularly video games, continues to focus on past and future conflicts, highlighting a societal reluctance to engage with the harsh realities of current conflicts and a preference for the clear-cut victories of past and future wars [22]. As games increasingly shape our understanding of the world [23], this study aims to examine how digital media interacts with real-world events by exploring the intersection of video game development and the war in Ukraine.

3 Video Games Developed Post-2022 Full-Scale Invasion

3.1 Video Games Selection

To analyse video games developed after February 24, 2022, when the Russian full-scale invasion occurred, the following selection criteria were established: (1) games must have been developed after February 24, 2022; (2) games must have themes connected to the war in Ukraine; (3) games must be developed by developers with a clear stance on the war (pro-Ukrainian position); (4) games should have received a minimum threshold of critical reviews or feedback to ensure recognition within the gaming community. In this context, the term "videogames" is used broadly to include smaller-scale projects such as mods or limited levels that are significant for their thematic relevance and player engagement.

The search for these games was conducted with thoroughness and diligence, using various platforms and sources. Popular digital game distribution services such as Steam, Gamejolt, Itch.io, and Google Play were scoured, as were social media platforms, gaming forums, and articles from various search engines on the video game industry's response to the war in Ukraine [7, 9]. This comprehensive approach yielded a total of fifty-six video games[1] that met the established criteria. The reasons behind including "Power & Revolution (2022 Edition)" and "Microsoft Flight Simulator (An-225 'Mriya' edition)" which have additional content to the main game connected to the war, is that they broaden the scope of engagement and awareness of the war in Ukraine, offering diverse gameplay experiences and perspectives from international developers. Seven games, including "Broken Life" and "Back to Hearth," are on the list despite not yet being released. They are expected to be released soon or available for preorder, with demos available on platforms such as Reddit, TikTok, and YouTube, along with press releases

[1] Each of the fifty-six games listed is mentioned in the text at least once.

and developer interviews. Although these games do not meet criterion (4), the anticipation generated by their pre-release materials, coupled with the developers' reputable track records (e.g., "Zero Losses") and strategic partnerships (e.g., "Project Palianytsia" received a large grant from Epic Games), suggests a promising reception upon release. Furthermore, robust community support, evidenced by crowdfunding success (e.g., "One More Day") and awards-winning ("Critics Choice," in the case of "Hollow Home") or award-nominating ("Most Anticipated Game" nomination in the case of "Glory to Heroes") underscores their potential impact. Collectively, these factors advocate for their early recognition and study, highlighting the multifaceted value they add to the industry beyond conventional review metrics.

Eleven video games, among them "DDOS-game.playforukraine", "путлера на пляшку/put putler on the bottle," "Fight For Ukraine", "Все буде Україна/Everything will be Ukraine" have been rendered inaccessible for gameplay due to the reasons discussed further. However, an abundance of walkthroughs, critiques, reviews, and visual documentation remain readily available on digital platforms, as well as mentions in various gaming forums and resources aimed at a broader audience, making them eligible to be included in the list.

3.2 Developers

Of the 56 games identified, at least 50 were developed by Ukrainian developers, making up approximately 90% of the total. Notable exceptions include "Power & Revolution (2022 Edition)," created by French developers, "Welcome to Chornobayivka VR," produced by German developers, and the project "It's Ukraine, not a Game" that unites seven mini-games is a collaborative development between Ukrainian and German teams. Additionally, "Death from Above" is a product of Finnish and Ukrainian cooperative efforts, "Ukraine Defense Force Tactics" is developed by a Polish team, and "Microsoft Flight Simulator (An-225 'Mriya' edition)" by American developers. It merits acknowledgment that the attribution of several games to specific individuals or collectives posed a challenge, leading to the provisional assumption that they were the endeavours of Ukrainian independent developers.

Of 56 games, at least 50 are developed by indie developers, representing approximately 90% of the total. Exceptions include "Power & Revolution (2022 Edition)" by EverSim, "Microsoft Flight Simulator (An-225 'Mriya' Edition)" by Microsoft, "Project Palianytsia" by Ukrainian studio Frogwares with a grant from Epic Games, "yeBayraktar" and "Drone Operator" created in cooperation with the Ukrainian Ministry of Digital Transformation and published on the Ukrainian state portal Diia, and "Whose Tank is This?" by the Ukrainian independent media channel Texty.org.ua. Notably, the youngest developer is 14 years old, who, along with a 17-year-old friend, created the secret level "Russian Warship, Go Fu*k Yourself" in the game "Trash is Fun".

3.3 Themes and Genres

The video games analysed exhibit a diverse range of genres with a strong focus on Simulator, Shooter, Action, Shoot 'Em All, Adventure, Strategy, and Role-Playing Games (RPG) (see Word Cloud 1). Additionally, genres such as Visual Novels, Casual, Arcade,

Horror, and Satire are present, showcasing the wide range of creative expressions used to address serious topics and evoke emotional responses from players. Some games have very unusual concepts, like players having to use a condom to catch sperm with Putin's face on it, like in "Stop Huilo", or the player needs to steal Russian tanks with the help of a tractor, like in "Steal Russian Tank".

The common roles in these video games also encompass a wide range of perspectives, from Ukrainian civilians striving for survival in besieged cities like Bucha and Mariupol to military personnel operating drones and leading tactical units. Players may also assume combat and tactical roles, embodying elite soldiers or anti-tank operators, or take on non-combat roles, such as tractor drivers capturing Russian tanks and volunteers contributing to reconstruction efforts. Other roles offer a diverse array of characters, including a history teacher, a 14-year-old teenager, an ordinary student, a detective, a combat duck or someone wielding a sunflower to torture a bloody dictator (see Word Cloud 2).

Word Cloud 1. Genres of the video games

Word Cloud 2. The roles in video games

3.4 Platforms

An analysis of the distribution reveals that 39 are browser-based, indicating a trend towards more accessible and immediate platforms for game deployment. These browser games are available on a variety of platforms, including Steam, Itch.io, and through their own dedicated links. The remaining titles are designed for mobile devices, showcasing the versatility and reach of gaming in contemporary times.

3.5 Common Distinctive Features

Free-to-Play Model. Of the games analysed, 38 explicitly incorporate the Free-to-Play model, enhancing accessibility and allowing players to engage without upfront costs. Most paid games are priced between 1.99 euros and 9.75 euros, with a few exceptions. For the unreleased games, promotional materials clearly indicate a paid model, often accompanied by various charity and donation initiatives.

Fundraising Initiatives. Many games, at least 33 out of 56 with explicit messages on their pages, integrated various donation mechanisms to support the Ukrainian military and humanitarian. Methods of contribution include direct donations, redirecting profits from advertisements or in-game purchases, offering paid access to games with proceeds directed to military support, and providing options for in-game purchases where funds are allocated to charity initiatives (e.g., "For the Victory with Ukraine", "Rebuild Ukraine"). For instance, players are encouraged to donate to well-known military funds such as "Return Alive" through direct links to in-game menus (e.g., "Putin Caput"). Additionally, some developers have committed to transferring a portion of their profits to different NGOs or to support the Armed Forces of Ukraine (e.g., "Putler Stress Relieve Game", "Tile Cities").

Boom in 2022. Most games were designed and published in 2022, after full-scale invasion, accounting for 41 out of 56 games. In 2023, six additional games were released, followed by three in 2024. One game is planned for release in 2025; five others are coming soon, currently available for preorder.

Pixel World: Orcs Attack. An analysis of explicit reviews available for at least 30 games reveals a predominantly positive reception. Many of these games receive positive or mostly positive feedback (e.g., on Steam), with numerical ratings often ranging from 4 to 5 points (e.g., on Google Play). In particular, mobile games such as "Stugna" and "Pixel World" have achieved high ratings of 4.6 and 4.5, respectively, based on over 5,000 reviews.

Political Discussions in Review Sections. The review sections of these videos on platforms like Steam and YouTube often transcend beyond mere game evaluations. It is common to encounter heated political discussions, especially contributions from Russian users and their suspected bots. The discourse often delves into contentious debates, reflecting polarised views on the war.

Meme Putin Character. A notable feature in at least 11 games is the incorporation of satire and meme-based dictator, his army, and the elite, which are hyperbolised into grotesque personas. For example, players can punish the dictator with a sunflower ("Sunflowerslap"), throw different items at him, beat and torture him in a variety of ways ("Fuck Putin", "Catch Crazy Dictator", "Putler is Dead").

Purposely Not Available in Russian. A notable trend among these games is the deliberate choice to limit language availability, particularly excluding Russian. This decision underscores a form of digital protest or solidarity with Ukraine. For instance, titles like "The Death from Above" have been made accessible in 18 languages, and "The Twenty-Second: Stories of Underground Kharkiv" is available in 6 languages, which still excludes Russian. Some games are exclusively in English (e.g., "Slava Ukraini!", "Ukraine Defense Force Tactics") or Ukrainian (e.g., "Sniffer Dog Quest," "Битва за Україну/Battle for Ukraine"), underscoring the targeted audiences and the developers' intent to support and reach specific linguistic communities.

Real-Life Events, People, and Sources Incorporation. These games often feature real photos and locations, such as Hostomel, Bucha, Mariupol, and Kharkiv underground station (e.g., "What's up in a Kharkiv bomb shelter," "The Nightmare Winter"), accurately recreated using real-world heightmap data and photogrammetry. Some games specifically highlight well-known events, like those in Chornobaivka or Zmiiny Island (e.g., "Chornobaivka. The Day of the Groundhog", "Chornobaivka") or iconic locations like Independence Square in Kyiv. Real people are frequently depicted in these games, including notable figures like Putin, Kadyrov, Zelensky, and Elon Musk (e.g., "Musk vs. Putin," "Putinist Slayer"). Additionally, these games incorporate real-life stories, offering players a chance to engage with narratives that reflect the experiences and struggles of actual individuals (e.g., "Ukraine War Stories"). Incorporating educational elements, numerous video games serve as interactive platforms to enlighten the general public about, for example, Ukrainian geography ("Learn Ukraine"), types of tanks ("Whose tank is this?"), and dangerous explosive objects such as mines ("Sniffer Dog Quest").

Focus on the Unique Features of the Russian-Ukrainian War. Reflecting the modern nature of the war and its brand-new technologies, such as unmanned aerial and naval vehicles, copters, and anti-tank guided missiles, games like "Ukrainian Bayraktar vs. Orcs" and "Bavovna.Drone Attack" allow players to operate all types of drones to combat enemy forces. These games also portray Ukrainian guerrilla strategies, notably the "tractor army" phenomenon, where tractors are used to tow tanks from the battlefield (e.g., "Ukrainian army", "Tractor vs. Tank", "Farmers stealing tanks"). With Ukrainian national symbols, music, motifs, and phrases gaining international recognition, they incorporated in games (e.g., "Slava Ukraini!/Glory to Ukraine", "Smert' Vorogam/Death to the Enemies", "Glory to the Heroes"). Furthermore, they lampoon the reported looting behaviours of Russian soldiers stealing washing machines and toilets and the alleged recruitment from socioeconomically disadvantaged classes, using caricatures and irony to depict the enemy as fantastical creatures such as orcs and marauders (e.g., "Ukraine Defender", "Fella Game", "Putin Orcs Defender", "Birds Attack 2022").

4 Discussion

The emergence of video games centred on the war in Ukraine represents a significant shift in the medium's role as the tool for capturing the moment, documenting, and broadcasting it [7, 8]. The analysis of these games reveals a rich tapestry of genres, roles, and perspectives, each offering a unique and varied entry point into the complexities of the war, ultimately suggesting an intention to provide a holistic view of the conflict. They invite players to participate in simulated real events and support the Ukrainian side. The concentrated development of games following the full-scale invasion in 2022 indicates a responsive and engaged Ukrainian gaming community that prolongs unprecedented solidarity among Ukrainians in the face of a common disaster.

The genre and roles diversity is not merely a testament to the creative versatility of game developers but also an indication of the medium's potential to engage with serious topics in a manner that is both accessible and profound [19]. The predominance of indie developers in creating these games underscores the indie gaming community's ethos of prioritising creative freedom and innovation. The anonymity of some developers can serve as a protective measure against potential backlash or harassment, given the politically sensitive nature of war-related content. The unavailability of some titles at the moment of writing this article, shows, on the one hand, the fluidity of the medium, and, on the other hand, it points to the challenges faced by indie games, such as the lack of financial and technical support, which lead to their discontinuation. On the bright side, the generally positive reception of these games underscores their quality and the resonance of their themes, with players affirming their success in captivating and satisfying their audience.

The varying degrees of impact and outreach of these games are evident in several ways. Firstly, the prevalence of the Free-to-Play model allows developers to make a strategic move to democratize access, making it possible for individuals from different economic backgrounds to participate, thereby increasing the potential impact. Additionally, in many cases, fundraising efforts to support the Armed Forces of Ukraine through these games underscore the medium's role in activism and volunteerism [18] as it challenges "apolitical" Western players who believe that donations should only be for humanitarian, not military, needs. Secondly, the use of satire and humour in some titles, which ridicules and undermines Russian leadership and army, offers a provocative way to critique the war, using levity to process the gravity of real-world events [8]. Thirdly, the inclusion of actual events, locations, and figures serves to ground the virtual experiences, where the games inform and enlighten. Lastly, the political statements made through language choices and narrative elements are a demonstration of the medium's capacity to participate in geopolitical discourse and to reach beyond typical gaming communities to include activists, educators, and policymakers [23]. This idea is further reinforced by the fact that virtual spaces become extensions of the ideological battles associated with war with players engaging in discussions that mirror real-world polarized views. This highlights the intersection of gaming, politics, and social issues, adding complexity to the reception of these games as arenas for geopolitical arguments and propaganda efforts [22, 23].

Limitation of the Study. The study examines games developed after the full-scale invasion in 2022, meaning the conclusions drawn are significantly shaped by the immediate response to recent events, potentially overlooking longer-term trends in the development of such games. Moreover, this research offers somewhat reductionist analyses of specific features, potentially neglecting broader contextual factors and the intricate interplay between various game elements. Another limitation is the potential bias in the selection of games analysed, which might not represent the full spectrum of Ukraine war-themed games, such as games with neutral or pro-russian perspectives.

Future Research. Several observations from this analysis merit further investigation. These include concerns about trivializing serious issues, the morality of creating such games during an ongoing war, the appropriateness of softening war's harsh realities, and the potential reputational risks of developers and publishers. Additionally, there's the question of whether these games should resonate with the Ukrainian people or appeal to Western audiences. Future research also calls for examining the long-term trends of war-themed games, as well as their influence on public perception, audience reception, and societal attitudes toward contemporary conflicts.

To sum up, the analysis of video games "inspired" by the war in Ukraine highlights the medium's evolving role as a multifaceted platform for engagement and means of persuasion. While many of the games may not always capture a global mainstream audience, their developers aspire to foster empathy, create a deeper understanding of the ongoing war, raise awareness, stir up pro-Ukrainian sentiment, shape perceptions, help disseminate information, facilitate counter-propaganda, and do fundraising among the interested audience. As the war, unfortunately, continues to unfold, video games on the "topic of the day" stand as for sure a testament to the power of interactive media to serve as a digital archive of events and act as a virtual battlefield.

5 Conclusions

Meaningful and engaging video games are often those that most effectively immerse players in the narrative, allowing them to empathize with and connect to the experiences of others. In the face of the Russian-Ukrainian war, video games discussed in the article are no longer neutral spaces devoid of politics; instead, they are dynamic, contested, and highly lucrative environments where game developers pretend to shape the perspectives of their audiences. They may not achieve immediate mass impact, but their long-term influence on the discussions surrounding the war and contributions to digital activism should not be underestimated.

Acknowledgments. The research is supported by the Margarita Salas Grant (MS/62) from UPV and the Ministry of Universities-the Recovery, Transformation, and Resilience Plan financed by Next Generation EU and the CIAICO/2021/037 project funded by the Generalitat Valenciana.

References

1. Götz, E., Ekman, P.: Russia's war against Ukraine: context, causes, and consequences. Probl. Post-Communism **71**, 193–205 (2024)
2. Osborn, G.: Vladimir Putin's Video Games Console: Taking the console wars up a notch or two. https://www.videogamesindustrymemo.com/p/vladimir-putins-video-games-console
3. LeBlanc, W.: Game Studios Show Support For Ukraine. https://www.gameinformer.com/2022/04/04/game-studios-show-support-for-ukraine
4. Ukraine war: Fortnite maker Epic Games raises $144m (£110m) to help victims. https://www.bbc.com/news/technology-60983344
5. Wald, H.: How the video game industry is rallying around Ukraine. https://www.gamesradar.com/how-the-video-game-industry-is-rallying-around-ukraine/
6. The European Games Developer Federation (EGDF): National Initiatives Supporting Ukrainian Gamedev Community. https://www.egdf.eu/national-initiatives-supporting-ukrainian-gamedev-community/
7. Shchotkina, K.: This is no playing: Who and how creates games about the tragic pages of our history. https://zn.ua/eng/this-is-no-plaything.html
8. Zinovieva, T.: War in Ukraine through the lens of interactive media: a typological study of video games. Rocz. Inst. Eur. Środkowo-Wschodniej. **21**, 213–229 (2023)
9. Brovinska, M.: Games about war: 25 games about the war in Ukraine. https://dev.ua/ru/news/15-igor-pro-viynu
10. Boltz, L.O.: Like hearing from them in the past. Int. J. Gaming Comput. Simul. **9**, 1–18 (2017). https://doi.org/10.4018/IJGCMS.2017100101

11. Pergerson, C.: How this war of mine creates empathy for virtual characters. In: ART 108: Introduction to Games Studies (2021)
12. Hartman, A., Tulloch, R., Young, H.: Video games as public history: archives, empathy and affinity. Game Stud. **21**(4) (2021)
13. Rad, S.R.: Politics of language in video games: identity and representations of Iran. Int. J. Persian Lit. **6**, 103–119 (2021). https://doi.org/10.5325/intejperslite.6.0103
14. Kolek, L., Šisler, V., Martinkovа́, P., Brom, C.: Can video games change attitudes towards history? Results from a laboratory experiment measuring short- and long-term effects. J. Comput. Assist. Learn. **37**, 1348–1369 (2021). https://doi.org/10.1111/jcal.12575
15. Marengo, L.G., Imhoff, D., Godoy, J.C., Cena, M., Ferreira, P.D.: Videojuegos y socialización política: evaluación del potencial de los videojuegos para promover aprendizajes sociopolíticos. Cuad. del Cent. Estud. en Diseño y Comun. Ensayos, ISSN-e 1853-3523, ISSN 1668-0227, N^{O}. 130, 2021 (Ejemplar Dedic. a Deriv. Conc. y aperturas los game Stud.), pp. 151–168 (2021)
16. Peña, J., Hernández Pérez, J.F., Khan, S., Cano Gómez, Á.P.: Game perspective-taking effects on players' behavioral intention, attitudes, subjective norms, and self-efficacy to help immigrants: the case of "Papers, Please." Cyberpsychol. Behav. Soc. Netw. **21**, 687–693 (2018). https://doi.org/10.1089/CYBER.2018.0030
17. Navarro-Remesal, V., Zapata, B.P.: First-person refugee games: ludonarrative strategies for playing the stories of refugees and asylum seekers. In: Zagalo, N., Veloso, A., Costa, L., Mealha, Ó. (eds.) Videogame Sciences and Arts, VJ 2019. CCIS, vol. 1164, pp. 3–17. Springer, Cham (2019). https://doi.org/10.1007/978-3-030-37983-4_1
18. Peng, W., Lee, M., Heeter, C.: The effects of a serious game on role-taking and willingness to help. J. Commun. **60**, 723–742 (2010). https://doi.org/10.1111/j.1460-2466.2010.01511.x
19. Shliakhovchuk, E.: Video games as awareness raisers, attitude changers, and agents of social change. Int. J. Comput. Games Technol. (2024). https://doi.org/10.1155/2024/3274715
20. Shliakhovchuk, E.: Learning about refugee life with educational video games. Inf. Technol. Learn. Tools **98**, 94–106 (2023). https://doi.org/10.33407/itlt.v98i6.5168
21. Cerezo-Pizarro, M., Revuelta-Domínguez, F.I., Guerra-Antequera, J., Melo-Sánchez, J.: The cultural impact of video games: a systematic review of the literature. Educ. Sci. **13**, 1116 (2023). https://doi.org/10.3390/EDUCSCI13111116/S1
22. Robinson, N.: Military videogames: more than a game. RUSI J. **164**, 10–21 (2019). https://doi.org/10.1080/03071847.2019.1659607
23. Schulzke, M.: Video Games and the Simulation of International Conflict. https://www.e-ir.info/2014/08/01/video-games-and-the-simulation-of-international-conflict/

Use of Game Design and Game Elements in Serious Project Management Games

Alf Inge Wang(✉)

Norwegian University of Science and Technology, N7491 Trondheim, Norway
alfw@idi.ntnu.no

Abstract. Using serious games to teach project management is a logical choice, as it al-lows students to practice skills without facing real-world economic or human consequences. These games offer a realistic learning environment where players can experiment with different ideas and retry projects after failure. Additionally, game-based learning enhances learning outcomes, motivation, and engagement. However, to fully realize these benefits, serious games must incorporate established game design principles and elements. This paper presents a literature review examining how well existing project management games apply such principles. The study analyzes 64 games using Malone's Taxonomy for Intrinsic Motivation, the GameFlow framework, eight reward systems, and other recognized game design elements.

Keywords: Game-based Learning · Serious Games · Project Management

1 Introduction

Project management (PM) is challenging to teach because it requires practical experience in managing unpredictable events, people, tools, and processes. Poor PM can be costly, leading to resource overruns, delays, and, in extreme cases, project failure. The growing complexity and uncertainty in project environments highlight the need for more focus on PM education [1]. However, increased knowledge alone will not resolve these challenges; it also requires training in applying that knowledge effectively in real-world scenarios [2]. Since project managers make daily decisions on schedule, quality, risks, and resources, soft skills are essential for success [3]. A viable solution is to train decision-making skills through experimentation [4], without the associated real-world costs or risks [5]. Given that project performance is strongly linked to accumulated experience, practical PM training through games is crucial [6].

One promising solution for effective PM training is video games, as well-designed games are efficient learning tools [7]. Game-based learning enhances learning outcomes, motivation, and engagement [8]. Video games are particularly suited to PM, as they provide a safe environment for experimentation, allowing players to learn from mistakes without financial repercussions [9]. Serious games, such as simulators, can create realistic learning experiences using real project data, closely mimicking the role of a project manager [10]. However, for serious games to be effective learning tools, they must be

A. Schönbohm et al. (Eds.): GALA 2024, LNCS 15348, pp. 222–232, 2025.
https://doi.org/10.1007/978-3-031-78269-5_21

designed with the same care and attention as successful commercial games. This literature study explores the extent to which serious PM games incorporate established game design principles and elements.

2 Material and Methods

This section describes the research focus, method, and background theory for the study.

2.1 Research Goal, Question, and Approach

The research method in this literature review follows the Goal-Question-Metric (GQM) approach [11], which involves defining the research goal at the conceptual level, formulating research questions at the operational level, and establishing metrics to answer these questions at the quantitative level. In this study, the metrics consist of data extracted from the literature review. Using the GQM template, the research goal of this study was defined as follows:

> The purpose of this study was to *investigate how game design and game features are used in serious project management games* from the point of view of a *researcher* in the context of the *serious games research community.*

The research goal was broken down into the following research questions:

- RQ1: What elements from Malone's Taxonomy are used in serious PM games?
- RQ2: What elements from the GameFlow framework are used in serious PM games?
- RQ3: What reward systems are implemented in serious PM games?
- RQ4: Are serious PM games scripted (linear) or emergent experiences?
- RQ5: What other game design elements are used in serious PM games?

2.2 Research Methodology for the Literature Review

The data to address these research questions was gathered through a systematic review of articles describing serious PM games. This review followed the systematic method outlined in [12], which includes five stages:

1) <u>Development of review protocol:</u> Ensure broad literature coverage, include relevant studies on serious PM games, and synthesize data related to the research questions.
2) <u>Identification of inclusion and exclusion criteria:</u> Include articles published in peer-reviewed international conferences or journals, written in English, and featuring "project management," "serious game," or "gamification" in the title, abstract, or keywords. Exclude non-English, inaccessible, or out-of-scope articles.
3) <u>Search for relevant studies:</u> Four databases were searched (see Table 1). Search string used was: +"project management" AND (+"serious game" OR "gamification").
4) <u>Critical appraisal:</u> The articles were reviewed, with relevant studies added and those outside the scope or duplicates removed. Articles were rejected if they did not focus on teaching project management or if they described the gamification of PM rather than a serious PM game. Sixty-four studies were accepted.

5) Data extraction: All accepted papers were reviewed to extract data relevant to the research questions, which was entered into a spreadsheet. The extraction focused on identifying game design elements by examining each article for terms and descriptions matching the elements outlined in the following section. The analysis was based solely on the text within the articles, without playing the games or viewing game footage.
6) Synthesis: Analyze the spreadsheet data in relation to the defined research questions. For more details and references to papers, see online: https://t.ly/GFWZ5.

Table 1. Search for Articles

Research Database	Articles found	Articles added to the review
Scopus	221	87
Web of Science	80	12
IEEE Xplore	68	13
ACM Digital Library	11	1
Total	**380**	**113**

2.3 Motivational and Game Design Theory

Well-designed video games can be highly effective learning machines, as they are so engaging and motivating that the player learns without been aware of it [7]. The challenge for serious games is to balance the pedagogical with the engaging elements. This section will present some theories, frameworks, and game design elements that have proven to increase engagement and enjoyment of games used in our study analysis.

Malone's taxonomy of intrinsic motivation focuses on what makes an activity enjoyable or rewarding for its own sake, rather than through external rewards [13]. This taxonomy, grounded in experiments and theories of intrinsic motivation, highlights three key characteristics. First, learning games must provide a *challenge*, with uncertain outcomes (randomness), so that reaching goals enhances the player's self-esteem. *Fantasy* can increase enjoyment and motivation, while *curiosity* drives the desire to learn, independent of specific goals or fantasies [13]. Malone distinguishes between two types of curiosity: sensory curiosity, which uses changes in stimuli like light and sound, and cognitive curiosity, which motivates players by presenting incomplete or inconsistent information—similar to how crime novels gradually reveal plots. In our literature review analysis, we assessed whether the games incorporated these elements: challenge, uncertainty, fantasy, sensory curiosity, and cognitive curiosity.

The **GameFlow framework** is a model designed to evaluate player enjoyment in games [14], drawing from Csikszentmihalyi's flow theory [15]. GameFlow identifies eight elements that contribute to game enjoyment: *Concentration* – the game must require and support focus; *Challenge* – games should offer challenges that match player skill levels; *Player Skills* – games should foster skill development and mastery; *Control* – players need to feel a sense of control over their actions; *Clear Goals* – games must provide clear, timely goals; *Feedback* – players should receive relevant feedback at appropriate times; *Immersion* – games should create deep, effortless involvement; and *Social Interaction* – games should enable and encourage social interactions. Our study analyzed how serious PM games incorporated these eight elements.

Reward systems are crucial for making games enjoyable and motivating. Wang and Chuen-Tsai identified eight reward types from their research on motivation and games [16]: *Score* – use of points that do not affect gameplay directly; *Experience Point (XP)* – earned during gameplay, allowing players to level up when goals are achieved; *Item Granting* – providing graded items that players can use; *Resources* – valuables that players can collect and use to affect gameplay (e.g., virtual wood, extra life); *Achievements* – titles or badges earned by fulfilling specific conditions; *Feedback Messages* – instant positive feedback for successful actions; *Plot animations and pictures* – advancing the game's story during key events or achievements; and *Unlocking mechanisms* – giving players access to new content when requirements are met. We classified the reward systems in serious PM games based on these categories.

Our analysis also included well-known game design elements found in existing games [17–19]. These elements, used in the literature review, include: *Time pressure* – creating urgency to increase engagement [20, 21]; *Levels* – representing game sessions that progress in difficulty; *Inventory* – allowing players to store and use items; *Non-playable characters* (NPCs) – characters controlled by the computer; *Avatars* – playable characters representing players; *Role Play* – where players assume roles of interacting characters; *Quest* – rewarded tasks players can complete; *Appointment* – tasks to be completed later in the game; *Narrative* – the story or story elements within the game; and *Gambling* – where players risk something of value in hopes of winning more. Additionally, our literature review classified the games as either *scripted* (linear) or *emergent* [22]. *Scripted* gameplay guides players through pre-defined actions, while *emergent* gameplay is driven by global rules that lead to unpredictable gameplay experiences.

3 Results

Our literature review identified 64 serious games that met the study's criteria, all focusing on project management (PM). However, they varied in specific areas, as shown in Table 2. Approximately half of the games centered on software PM, one-third on general PM, and one-fifth on construction PM.

Table 3 offers an overview of the mediums and user interfaces used in the reviewed games. The majority (56%) were digital games for PCs, 31% were web-based, and 5% ran on mobile devices. Physical games mainly consisted of board games, with some in-real-life (IRL) exercises and card games.

3.1 Support for Malone's Taxonomy for Intrinsic Motivation

Table 4 highlights how these games support elements of Malone's taxonomy. More than half incorporate *uncertainty* (randomness), which aims to enhance realism rather than

Table 2. Focus on Specific Domains in Serious PM Games.

Specific Domain	Count	Percentage	Citations	Citation %
Construction Project Management	11	17%	336	14%
Entrepreneurship Project Management	1	2%	0	0%
General Project Management	18	28%	520	22%
Information Technology Project Management	1	2%	4	0%
Insurance Project Management	1	2%	3	0%
Software Project Management	31	48%	1439	62%
Sustainability Project Management	1	2%	32	1%

Table 3. Medium and User Interfaces Provided by the Games.

Medium	User Interface	Count	Percentage
Digital	38% No game UI, 18% Some game UI, 44% Game UI	39	61%
Hybrid	43% Board, 57% IRL exercise + sim, tools, Lego	7	11%
Physical	78% Board, 11% Card, 17% IRL exercise	18	28%

motivation. Over one-third offer *sensory curiosity* through graphics, animation, and audio. Several games also include *fantasy* elements or adaptive difficulty (*challenge*) settings to optimize the player experience.

Table 4. Support for Malone's Elements for Intrinsic Motivation.

Characteristics	Count	Percentage
Malone's taxonomy for intrinsic motivation is mentioned	3	5%
Challenge (difficulty settings, adapted challenge level)	12	19%
Uncertainty (random)	35	55%
Fantasy	16	25%
Sensory Curiosity	22	34%
Cognitive Curiosity	6	9%

3.2 Support for GameFlow

Table 5 outlines how the games reviewed support elements of the GameFlow framework. Social interaction is the most supported feature, present in 61% of the games. Nearly half (49%) offer collaborative, team-based experiences. Other social interaction features include scoreboards (18%), team vs. team (15%), player vs. player (15%), and collaboration among teams (3%).

Table 5. Support for GameFlow.

Characteristics	Count	Percentage
GameFlow theory is mentioned	0	0%
Challenge (difficulty settings, adapted challenge level)	12	19%
Concentration	8	13%
Player Skills	7	11%
Control	10	16%
Clear Goals	15	23%
Feedback	25	39%
Immersion	3	5%
Social Interaction	39	61%

3.3 Support for Reward Systems

Table 6 highlights the use of reward systems in the reviewed games. *Scoring* systems are the most common, featured in 69% of the games, with various metrics such as points, time, money, cost, quality, letter grade, correct moves/decisions, total earnings, revenue, stars, ranking, and XP. Additionally, 20% of games use *leaderboards* for score comparison. *Feedback messages*, provided in 11% of the games, rank as the third most common reward system.

Table 6. Support for Reward Systems.

Reward System	Count	Percentage
Leaderboard	13	20%
Score	44	69%
Experience Points (XP)	5	8%
Item Granting	0	0%
Resources	0	0%
Achievements	5	8%
Feedback Message	7	11%
Plot Animations/Pictures	2	3%
Unlocking	1	2%

3.4 Scripted or Emergent Gameplay

Table 7 compares the ratio of scripted to emergent gameplay in the games. While most games are characterized as *scripted* or linear, many incorporate both scripted and emergent elements. The prevalence of *emergent* gameplay is largely due to the use of simulators, where models dictate the interaction of elements. Random elements are often introduced to make the games less predictable and less scripted.

Table 7. Scripted or Emergent Gameplay.

Characteristics	Count	Percentage
Scripted (linear)	39	61%
Emergent	25	39%

3.5 Support for Other Game Design Elements

Table 8 highlights additional game design elements used in the surveyed games. The most common features were *levels* and *role-playing*, both present in 25% of the games. These were followed by *narrative* elements, *NPCs*, and *time pressure*.

Table 8. Support for Other Game Design Elements.

Game Design Element	Count	Percentage
Time Pressure	9	14%
Levels	16	25%
Inventory	1	2%
Non-Playable Character (NPC)	11	17%
Avatar	7	11%
Role Play (Role-playing elements)	16	25%
Quest	1	2%
Appointment	1	2%
Narrative	15	23%
Gambling	1	2%

4 Discussion

Adding more game design elements to serious games does not automatically improve them, but it can increase the chances of making the game more enjoyable, immersive, and motivating, which can, in turn, enhance learning. This section examines how much emphasis serious PM games place on game design and its elements.

Regarding game UIs, our analysis shows that most serious PM games lack a proper game UI, instead focusing on simulation or business-style interfaces. This holds true for both digital and physical/hybrid games. Notable exceptions that offer more sophisticated game UIs include PMG-2D [23] and SimSE [24]. An evaluation of PMG-2D with 35 professionals yielded highly positive feedback: 88% found the game design attractive, 92% felt motivated to learn more about project management, 76% lost track of time while playing, 80% expressed a desire to play again, and 84% reported increased knowledge of project management. Similarly, SimSE showed significant learning outcomes in PM and was generally considered enjoyable, though it was critiqued for being repetitive and requiring instruction to play effectively.

Only three papers explicitly mentioned using Malone's taxonomy in their game design. The most common elements were *randomness* (55%), *sensory curiosity* (34%), *fantasy* (25%), and *challenge* (19%). In many cases, randomness was added to simulate a realistic project environment rather than to increase engagement. Since Malone's characteristics can make games more engaging and fun, there is significant untapped potential here. For example, Sharkworld is a pervasive PM game that effectively applies Malone's taxonomy [25]. Although its evaluation was limited, results showed that 83% of players felt the game enhanced their knowledge, 100% reported it captured their attention, and 83% were satisfied with the experience. However, only 14% believed the game improved retention.

Most games in our study also lack support for various GameFlow elements. *Social interaction* (61%), *feedback* (39%), and *clear goals* (23%) were the most commonly used features, but none of the reviewed papers explicitly mention the GameFlow framework. Only 5% of the papers highlighted immersion as a design goal. Since GameFlow is focused on creating immersion and player enjoyment, it is clear that there is significant potential to improve player experience in these games.

Similarly, the focus on reward systems in these games is limited. While 69% of games include a *scoring* system, most are designed to provide educational feedback rather than to motivate or engage players. Common scoring methods include points, and combinations of time and cost, but only 20% of games featured leaderboards. Other reward systems, such as *feedback messages*, *experience points (XP)*, *achievements*, *plot animations*, *unlocking*, *item granting*, and *resources*, were rarely used. ATIC, for instance, uses a diverse array of rewards, including leaderboards, points, XP, achievements, and feedback messages [26].

As for other game design elements, many remain underutilized. Features like *levels*, *role-play*, *narrative*, and *time pressure* were only used by 25% or fewer games. Elements such as *inventory*, *quests*, *appointments*, and *gambling* appeared in just a few games. Surprisingly, only 11% of the games offered avatars for player representation, despite their potential to enhance immersion. A notable exception is "My Life as a Software Engineer", which included levels, NPCs, avatars, role-play, and a narrative [27]. This game showed significant educational benefits, with a 43% increase in knowledge and a high player rating (Mean = 4.22 on a 5-point Likert scale). However, despite featuring many design elements, the gameplay remained relatively simple, focusing heavily on answering multiple-choice questions.

Our review of 64 serious PM games revealed a limited emphasis on game design elements that could enhance player enjoyment and immersion, which in turn could improve learning motivation and outcomes. Notably, we did not identify a single serious game that matched the quality of well-designed, popular entertainment games. Additionally, the limited evaluation of these games makes it difficult to assess the impact of game design on the overall learning experience. More research and development are needed to explore how game design can better support educational effectiveness in serious PM games.

One limitation of this study is that the analysis is based on textual descriptions of the games rather than direct gameplay. Some games may contain more design elements than were identified in the study.

5 Conclusion

The goal of this study was to explore how game design and features are applied in serious PM games. The findings revealed that only three papers explicitly referenced Malone's taxonomy, with most games neglecting key elements apart from *uncertainty* (randomness) (RQ1). Even in games incorporating *challenge*, *fantasy*, and *curiosity*, these elements were often inadequately designed and implemented. Similarly, most games supported only *social interaction* and *feedback* from the GameFlow framework, with minimal attention to other elements (RQ2). This suggests that serious PM games tend to prioritize simulation and learning over player enjoyment and engagement.

In terms of reward systems, most games featured a basic *scoring* system, with around 20% offering a *leaderboard* (RQ3). Few games incorporated other reward mechanisms like *feedback messages*, *XP*, *achievements*, or *unlocking features*. The study also found that 61% of the games followed *scripted* or linear gameplay, while 39% offered *emergent* gameplay (RQ4), largely due to their simulation-based features.

Finally, support for additional game design elements was limited. The most frequently used elements were *levels*, *role-playing*, *narrative*, *non-playable characters* (NPCs), and *time pressure* (RQ5). This highlights an untapped potential to enhance player enjoyment, engagement, and motivation in serious PM games. Future research should explore the broader application of game design principles in serious games and investigate how these elements can be leveraged to maximize educational outcomes.

Acknowledgments. This research was conducted during my tenure as a visiting professor at the Department of Informatics, University of California, Irvine, 2023/2024.

References

1. Thomas, J., Mengel, T.: Preparing project managers to deal with complexity–advanced project management education. Int. J. Project Manag. **26**, 304–315 (2008)
2. Rumeser, D., Emsley, M.: A systematic review of project management serious games: identifying gaps, trends, and directions for future research. J. Mod. Project Manag. **6** (2018)
3. Belzer, K.: Project management: still more art than science - a paper, pp. 1–6 (2001). https://www.coursehero.com/file/49303444/More-art-than-sciencepdf/

4. Navarro, E.O., Van Der Hoek, A.: Design and evaluation of an educational software process simulation environment and associated model. In: 18th Conference on Software Engineering Education and Training (CSEET'05), pp. 25–32. IEEE (2005)
5. Iansiti, M.: How the incumbent can win: managing technological transitions in the semiconductor industry. Manag. Sci. **46**, 169–185 (2000)
6. Caird-Daley, A., Harris, D., Bessell, K., Lowe, M.: Training decision making using serious games. Human Factors Integration Defence Technology Centre. Report No: HFIDTC/2/WP4 6, pp. 1–66 (2007)
7. Gee, J.P.: What video games have to teach us about learning and literacy. Comput. Entertain. **1**, 20 (2003)
8. Wang, A.I., Tahir, R.: The effect of using Kahoot! for learning–a literature review. Comput. Educ. **149**, 103818 (2020)
9. Saenz, M.J., Cano, J.L.: Experiential learning through simulation games: an empirical study. Int. J. Eng. Educ. **25**, 296 (2009)
10. Calderón, A., Ruiz, M., O'Connor, R.V.: A serious game to support the ISO 21500 standard education in the context of software project management. Comput. Stand. Interfaces **60**, 80–92 (2018)
11. Basili, V.R.: Software modeling and measurement: the Goal/Question/Metric paradigm. University of Maryland for Advanced Computer Studies (1992)
12. Dybå, T., Dingsøyr, T.: Empirical studies of agile software development: a systematic review. Inf. Softw. Technol. **50**, 833–859 (2008)
13. Malone, T.W.: What makes things fun to learn? Heuristics for designing instructional computer games. In: The 3rd ACM SIGSMALL Symposium and the First SIGPC Symposium on Small Systems. ACM Press, Palo Alto, California, United States (1980)
14. Sweetser, P., Wyeth, P.: GameFlow: a model for evaluating player enjoyment in games. ACM Comput. Entertain. **3** (2005)
15. Csikszentmihalyi, M.: Flow. In: Csikszentmihalyi, M. (ed.) Graph Theory. Graduate Texts in Mathematics, vol. 173, pp. 149–172. Springer, Heidelberg (2014). https://doi.org/10.1007/978-3-662-53622-3_6
16. Wang, H., Sun, C.-T.: Game reward systems: gaming experiences and social meanings. In: DiGRA Conference. Citeseer (2011)
17. Deterding, S., Dixon, D., Khaled, R., Nacke, L.: From game design elements to gamefulness: defining gamification. In: Proceedings of the 15th International Academic MindTrek Conference: Envisioning Future Media Environments, pp. 9–15. ACM (2011)
18. Hamari, J., Koivisto, J., Sarsa, H.: Does gamification work?–A literature review of empirical studies on gamification. In: 2014 47th Hawaii International Conference on System Sciences (HICSS), pp. 3025–3034. IEEE (2014)
19. Chou, Y.-k.: The octalysis framework for gamification & behavioral design (2015). https://yukaichou.com/gamification-examples/octalysis-complete-gamification-framework/. Accessed 03 Nov 2019
20. Yildirim, I.G.: Time pressure as video game design element and basic need satisfaction. In: Proceedings of the 2016 CHI Conference Extended Abstracts on Human Factors in Computing Systems, pp. 2005–2011 (2016)
21. Wang, A.I.: The wear out effect of a game-based student response system. Comput. Educ. **82**, 217–227 (2015)
22. Sweetser, P., Wiles, J.: Scripting versus emergence: issues for game developers and players in game environment design. Int. J. Intell. Games Simul. **4**, 1–9 (2005)
23. Lino, J.E.N., Paludo, M.A., Binder, F.V., Reinehr, S., Malucelli, A.: Project management game 2D (PMG-2D): a serious game to assist software project managers training. In: 2015 IEEE Frontiers in Education Conference (FIE), pp. 1–8. IEEE (2015)

24. Navarro, E.O., Van Der Hoek, A.: Comprehensive evaluation of an educational software engineering simulation environment. In: 20th Conference on Software Engineering Education and Training (CSEET'07), pp. 195–202. IEEE (2007)
25. Jerman Blažič, A., Džonova Jerman Blažič, B.: Exploring and upgrading the educational business-game taxonomy. J. Educ. Comput. Res. **52**, 303–340 (2015)
26. Crespo-Martinez, E., Bueno, S., Gallego, M.D.: A Video game for entrepreneurship learning in Ecuador: development study. JMIR Form. Res. **7**, e49263 (2023)
27. Evangelou, S.M., Stamoulakatou, G., Xenos, M.: A serious game for mobile phones used in a software engineering course: usability evaluation and educational effectiveness. In: 2021 IEEE Global Engineering Education Conference (EDUCON), pp. 219–225. IEEE (2021)

Asking the Experts: A Delphi Method Investigation into Serious Games for Leadership Development

Kristina Risley(✉) and Vanissa Wanick

University of Southampton, Park Avenue, Southampton SO23 8DL, UK
{k.risley,v.w.vieira}@soton.ac.uk

Abstract. In an increasingly digital business environment, the development of critical leadership skills such as emotional intelligence and critical thinking is paramount for individual and organisational success. As organisations evolve, innovative and experiential development methods such as serious games become indispensable but these remain underutilised due to reservations around credibility and return on investment. This study employed the Delphi method to consult a panel of experts in leadership development and serious games design, exploring how serious games can foster the development and application of leadership skills. Three master themes emerged, outlining elements of successful serious games for leadership development: simulated interpersonal dynamics, reinforcement for behavioural adjustment and authenticity of learning experience. Sub-themes included motivation and reward, feedback provision, adaptive learning and personalisation, experience of consequences, competitive versus co-operative environments and simulation of complex decisions. Findings are discussed in relation to Flow theory, Social Constructionism and Identity Theory in order to advance the understanding and implementation of serious leadership games for modern contexts.

Keywords: Serious games · Leadership development · Flow · Identity · Social Constructionism

1 Introduction

In today's digital business landscape, the need for critical leadership skills or 'soft skills' like emotional intelligence and critical thinking cannot be overstated. Furthermore, as business practices and organisations evolve, adopting innovative development methods is essential to keep the development of both current and future leaders on pace. Experiential development opportunities are considered crucial for nurturing these complex skills [6], with serious games (SGs) extending the possibilities of replicating and even co-creating replicated workplace scenarios [19]. This can include rare or extreme scenarios such as severe workplace conflicts, pandemics or financial crises, which leaders may seldom encounter over

A. Schönbohm et al. (Eds.): GALA 2024, LNCS 15348, pp. 233–242, 2025.
https://doi.org/10.1007/978-3-031-78269-5_22

the span of a career [23]. These scenarios are however contained within psychologically safe environments [13] where learners can explore strategies without the real-life risks of career-ending consequences [20]. Enhanced feedback mechanisms also support learners' capacity for self-analysis and awareness, allowing autonomous behavioural adjustment [14]. Despite their potential however, SGs face challenges like time constraints, costs and resource limitations, which hinder their widespread adoption in leadership training, often due to doubts about their effectiveness, credibility and return on investment [21].

This work therefore sought to address the following research question: *How can SGs foster the development and application of leadership skills as methods of experiential learning?* By exploring and converging the opinions of experts themselves, utilisation of the Delphi method allowed for interrogation of intelligence from a range of practitioners in the fields of leadership development and SGs design [8,9]. This process explored the space where experiential learning meets the immersive state of Flow [12], where in-game and real-life emotions influence each other [4] and this is integrated into their learners' self-concepts and the socially constructed realities [15] in which critical leadership skills development can develop. Ultimately this research aims to enhance pedagogical understanding and practices in leadership development, broadening theoretical frameworks and enriching literature on the roles of Flow [11], identity bleeding or stretching [4,25], and immersive 'other realities' [7,15] in cultivating leadership skills.

2 Background Literature Overview

Review of academic literature around SGs for leadership development uncovers parallels between three distinct yet complementary schools of thought: Flow, Identity Theory, and Social Constructionism. These are all commonly associated with SGs and experiential leadership development, but the potential interactions between these constructs are not yet fully explored. This work is directed towards exploring the applications of SGs for leadership development, synthesising existing academic thought and identifying future research directions to fill these noted literature gaps.

Identity Theory [25] partly explains how individuals shape their self-concepts and leadership identities through SGs. These simulated environments allow players to adopt and practice various leadership roles, influencing their self-perception through individual actions and group dynamics [22]. As players engage with challenges and receive feedback, they internalise their experiences, shaping their identity as leaders. The concept of "bleed," where in-game experiences influence real life and vice versa [4], extends Identity Theory, suggesting that skills and emotions from the game can affect real-world behaviour. It is anticipated that this phenomenon enhances leadership development by integrating learned skills and behaviours into the player's professional identity [18]. SGs therefore not only teach soft skills but also promote personal growth, transforming players' self-perceptions and leadership capabilities. Social interactions within the game further cement these new identity aspects, promoting collective identity development [24] and reinforcing these identities through feedback.

Flow as defined by Csikszentmihalyi [11,12] is a state of deep immersion which enhances concentration and learning in game-based environments. This psychological state is said to stem from a balance between challenges and the individual's skill level, transcending typical learning barriers such as fear of failure and self-consciousness. Although Flow is noted as beneficial for engagement and motivation in learning, its effectiveness in nurturing complex leadership skills requires further exploration. Furthermore, the related concept of team Flow, which involves a group collectively experiencing Flow [16] is particularly relevant for interpersonal dynamics and leadership as it facilitates collaboration, reinforcing shared mental models [15] and collective identities [24].

Social Constructionism emphasises the role of social interactions in the creation and perception of reality [7], suggesting that simulated environments in SGs provide alternative realities for practicing leadership skills in a risk-free setting [15]. These simulated realities allow learners to experiment with and internalise various leadership identities, behaviours and outcomes, with feedback illustrating the implications of their choices, reinforcing behaviours and identifying areas for improvement [14]. Furthermore, the interactive nature of SGs supports social learning [3], as players observe, emulate and receive feedback on behaviours within the game. This facilitates not only individual learning but also enhances group dynamics and the co-construction of knowledge [15], making these environments ideal for exploring and developing leadership skills and identities collaboratively [24].

Although there are clear parallels between these schools of thought, each faces significant criticisms, such as being deemed too general and vague for effective measurement and application in SGs, where specific behavioural outcomes are necessary. Moreover, these theories predominantly reflect Western cultural norms, potentially limiting their relevance in diverse global contexts where leadership styles vary. Further exploration of how these constructs present and interact is therefore required for a useful framework relating to leadership SGs.

3 Research Design

3.1 Delphi Method

This study employed the Delphi method [5], a structured communication technique which has been used in previous works to explore emerging fields in SGs and capture insights from a panel of expert practitioners [8,9]. The method was used to allow experts to contribute asynchronously and consider their views independently, focusing solely on the merit of presented ideas rather than interpersonal dynamics or status. A panel of 20 experts participated, contributing through 3 iterative rounds of qualitative questionnaires, 3 weeks apart. Each round began with a set of 5 open-ended questions, with responses forming the basis of the questions for the following round. Feedback from each round was summarised and shared with the panel. Reviewing the anonymised responses from other panellists as well as their reasoning allowed participants to evaluate the evidence whilst crafting their next answer. The rounds procedure continued for 3 rounds, until the answers from all of the experts converged into a series of consensus views, with no significant areas of disagreement in the responses provided and no new lines of discussion to pursue.

3.2 Expert Panel

The expert panel for the study was selected through purposive sampling, targeting individuals with substantial experience in Flow, SGs or leadership development. In total 20 participants began the study and 90%(18) continued to the end, surpassing the British Psychological Society's 70% standard [5]. Expertise distribution among participants included 15% in Flow, 15% in SGs, 30% in leadership development, 15% in pedagogy and 25% as game developers. Most worked in education (50%), leadership development outside higher education (30%) and games industry (20%). Geographically, 60% were from the UK, 25% from the rest of Europe and 15% from the USA. The panel was diverse in years of experience, with 56% having 20+ years in their respective fields, though skewed towards male participants, with only three women remaining by the study's end.

3.3 Data Analysis

Responses were analysed thematically using close coding in order to identify prevailing themes and divergent opinions at the end of each round. Following the completion of all rounds, this thematic analysis was repeated taking into account the progression of the rounds and highlighting themes which presented over multiple questions and rounds. These sub-themes were clustered into master themes following an inductive approach to drawing conclusions.

4 Results

4.1 Summary of Rounds

Round 1 addressed five key questions, covering: advancements in people development, ideal conditions for developing soft skills, immersive learning experience examples, assessing soft skills with SGs and the role of social learning in skills development. General consensus was reached on the importance of psychological safety, immersive learning experiences and the role of social learning in developing soft skills. However, a number of new lines of investigation presented as part of participants' responses, which informed the questions for round 2.

Round 2 explored unresolved issues and discrepancies from the initial discussions, including: important elements of feedback and reinforcement of behaviour, how transfer of learning works best and the merits and challenges associated with SGs in the business world. Consensus was reached when emphasising the alignment of learning interventions with real-world scenarios and the effectiveness of cooperative environments. Incorporating rewards/reinforcement that capitalise on intrinsic motivation was also agreed.

Several areas for further investigation presented from Round 2, which informed the questions for the final round. These included the ideal delivery mechanisms of feedback, how learning SGs can be made most authentic to real life and how SGs can be adapted to account for individual differences and situational factors. By the end of the round, opinions had noticeably converged, showing stability in the group's responses with no significant disagreements or new discussion topics and therefore the panel was disbanded.

4.2 Summary of Themes

Three overarching themes appeared through thematic analysis of the responses over the Delphi rounds: *simulated interpersonal dynamics*, *reinforcement for behavioural adjustment* and *authenticity of learning experience.*

Simulated Interpersonal Dynamics: across all rounds, the panel consistently highlighted the importance of simulated interpersonal dynamics in leadership development, along with the ability for learners to engage in complex social interactions which reflect real-world leadership challenges. The foundational principles of Social Learning Theory [3] - role-modeling, observation, imitation and reinforcement - were identified as crucial for effective learning in themes weaving throughout all responses and rounds. Additionally, narrative and storytelling within games were noted for their capacity to create emotional resonance, enhancing engagement and the internalisation of leadership skills.

> *"The games teach the player what the skills are, shows examples of their use, and then lets players experiment with them in different scenarios to see the consequences ... In the context of a game, these consequences are ephemeral – no one is actually going to be hurt, no project is going to be derailed, you're not going to lose your job – but if the game has managed to foster an emotional connection to these characters, the emotional response to these consequences can be real and effective."* (Participant 1).

As illustrated by Participant 16, experts also consistently discussed the safe exploration of leadership styles and decision-making consequences, particularly emphasising the value of psychological safety [13] and the opportunity to experience risk and failure without real-world repercussions. In line with this, panellists suggested that co-operative gameplay is more conducive to a sense of psychological safety than competitive environments, which introduce more psychological risk and are not appropriate for the depth of behavioural change required for leadership development. This is also supported by previous research where competitive approaches were associated with lower performance [19,20].

> *"Soft skills and learning per se, require a climate of trust, as people are out of their normal comfort zone. As such, a cooperative learning environment is likely to create this. Even if the learning event is about how to manage in a competitive environment, the activity can backfire."* (Participant 16).

Overall however, many participants heralded the benefits of both environments and recommended mixed approaches, with players operating as part of a co-operative team, engaged against a shared 'enemy' such as a competing team, the computer itself or a teacher.

Reinforcement for Behavioural Adjustment: the second master theme revolved around the reinforcement strategies integral to modifying leadership behaviour effectively. Various guises of learning cycles and loops were discussed as facilitated by SGs with blended approaches, involving self-assessments, learning analytics and reflective practice - importantly, scaffolded by teachers and mentors [10]. When considering learner motivation and how reward or reinforcement can be incorporated into SGs for leadership development, the primary debate revolved around intrinsic versus extrinsic motivation and rewards [1]. Panellists were in agreement that rewards associated with intrinsic motivations are most effective and therefore desirable, with some cautioning deliberately regarding the risks and dangers associated with extrinsic rewards.

> *"Extrinsic rewards need to be used cautiously/critically as they can have a negative impact, or act as a 'perverse incentive' ... stop being about the learning itself and instead be about the reward ..."* (Participant 15).

Experts also advocated for the integration of both diegetic (within the narrative) and non-diegetic (outside the narrative) feedback. This was as diegetic feedback maintains player immersion [17], but non-diegetic can be more tailored to improve learning transfer [2], which is an existing theme in the academic literature. Immediate and frequent feedback was emphasised as crucial for real-time correction and reinforcement of leadership skills, as was a variety of feedback types to suit different learning preferences and enhance training impact.

> *"Appreciation via a real other person, makes you glow your heart more. It makes feel 'really' appreciated. This also counts for personal feedback Task-related feedback (about someone's progress) is most optimal via systems as avatar, chatbot, dashboards, etc. It is not personal, so better when a valid system give the feedback. Feels better"* (Participant 9).

As discussed by Participant 9, a consensus view was achieved regarding the value of feedback from both human and non-human sources, where human feedback offers depth and empathy and non-human systems such as in-game analytics and AI-generated feedback can ensure consistency and objectivity.

Authenticity of Learning Experience: a common theme of discussion was the degree of realism in SGs how this may impact the effectiveness of leadership development and learning transfer. The panel highlighted that experiential learning elements need to be able to reflect the unpredictability and decision-making complexity of real-life, along with failure in social context, as these are essential for deep engagement and long-term retention of skills [2].

> *"Simplest way would be to use real-life situations, including sanctions that would be applied. ... would also be important (or at least useful) to ensure that some 'successes' cannot ever be achieved, just as in real life"* (Participant 17).

Furthermore, responses consistently emphasised the need to tailor digital learning experiences to the specific context of the industry or sector to increase relevance and authenticity. The need to represent diversity in terms of team composition and adherence to industry-specific regulations within the simulations was widely acknowledged and the importance of decision-making in leadership highlighted, potentially incorporating different leadership styles. Moreover, the adaptability of games to include personalised learning paths appropriate to player preferences [26], learner ability work experience and seniority and culturally relevant content was noted as crucial for ensuring that SGs meet the diverse needs of learners across various contexts.

Alternatives to highly tailored, industry-specific simulations were presented however, as several participants believed that leadership skills can be generic and that digital learning should focus on broader, transferable skills.

> *"The other method would be to abstract the context into a more general format. This would involve identifying the core skills, behaviors, actions, etc., that one wishes to target and creating a new context to teach those targets in that doesn't necessarily resemble the specific real-world context at all. This abstract representation could apply to a wider variety of real world contexts, provided generalization of learning objectives is achieved"* (Participant 1).

Some panellists suggested that abstracting the context into more general formats might be more effective in teaching core leadership skills applicable across various real-world scenarios. These uncertain and sometimes self-contradictory views are reflected in wider academic discussions around situated learning, authenticity and generalisability, with scaffolding suggested to bridge cognitive gaps [10].

5 Discussion

The central research question of this investigation was: *"How can SGs foster the development and application of leadership skills as methods of experiential learning?"* Analysis of participants' responses support the premise that a Delphi investigation was required to explore gaps in existing literature regarding SGs for leadership development. Furthermore, the insights gained shed further light on the linkages between Flow, Identity Theory and Social Constructionism.

Participants' views confirm existing thinking that for SGs to induce Flow, they must present challenges which are finely tuned to match the player's ability level (avoiding boredom and anxiety) [11]. This is echoed in participants' calls for learner-centred design, personalised learning paths, adaptable difficulty settings and feedback mechanisms which respond to individual performance. Furthermore, the concept of psychological safety [13] as cited by participants has long been regarded as a prerequisite for Flow [11] and team Flow [16] experience, as well as the experiential exploration needed to develop critical leadership skills. The expert panel's responses support the idea that immersive and engaging narratives and diegetic feedback within SGs facilitate Flow [17], enabling learners to lose themselves in scenarios that mimic real-life leadership challenges. This deep engagement has been cited by the panel as crucial for the effective internalisation of skills and emotional resonance, which enhances learning retention and transfer. Furthermore, the immediate and varied feedback mechanisms within games, as part of the reinforcement for behavioural adjustment, also contribute to maintaining Flow by providing continuous engagement cues and satisfaction from overcoming challenges [11,12].

Principles of Social Constructionism [7] are distinctly reflected in the master theme of *simulated interpersonal dynamics.* Here Social Learning Theory's mechanisms [3] were cited as game elements for learners to construct understanding and develop leadership skills through social processes of observing and interacting with other characters or players. This illustrates how players can incorporate in-game experiences and behaviours into their real-life leadership identities [18], a phenomenon akin to 'bleed' [4] where the boundary between player and character blurs. The narrative context of the games embeds learners in socially constructed realities [15] where they experiment with and reshape their leadership identities within a community. As players navigate roles and challenges, their real-world self-concepts evolve, reflecting the integration of their in-game experiences. Furthermore, participants' recognition of diverse leadership styles and the importance of context within the game narratives suggests an alignment with Social Constructionism. As outlined by participants, leadership is not a fixed trait but a set of skills and behaviours shaped by social norms, cultural values and situational demands. SGs that allow for this diversity enable players to construct their understanding of effective leadership in a meaningful and applicable way to their unique social and cultural context. However, current limitations of SGs make this challenging; participants therefore suggested that scaffolding should be provided around the usage of SGs for learners to be assisted by another individual to apply their learning in context [10].

The theme of *authenticity in learning experiences* relates strongly to Identity Theory, which explains the roles individuals adopt and the personal meaning they derive from them. The panel agreed SGs provide realistic and contextually rich scenarios, safe exploration of different leadership identities and integration into learners' self-concepts [25]. Reinforcement mechanisms through feedback, reflection and behavioural adjustments in the game also support identity development by allowing learners to see the consequences of their actions and refine their leadership approach. Additionally, how processes akin to bleed [4] may impact when players are immersed or how learners' identities may instead *stretch* to incorporate new identity elements warrant further exploration.

6 Conclusion and Outlook

In response to the research question: *"How can SGs foster the development and application of leadership skills as methods of experiential learning?"*, this Delphi study identified three key themes: *simulated interpersonal dynamics*, *reinforcement for behavioural adjustment* and *authenticity of learning experience.* Consensus among experts supports the use of theories like Flow, Identity Theory and Social Constructionism in game design to enhance leadership learning. This indicates substantial potential to design these interventions taking into account sub-themes such as motivation and reward, feedback provision and scaffolding, adaptive learning and personalisation, experience of consequences, competitive versus co-operative environments and simulating complex decisions.

However, the study faced limitations due to its small sample size and the diverse backgrounds of participants, which sometimes obscured common theoretical understandings and could affect the generalisability of the findings. A 10% dropout rate further impacted data continuity, although this did surpass guideline retention rates. To address potential biases and ensure understanding of complex theories, future research studies should incorporate semi-structured interviewing where participants' understanding can be checked and addressed. Future works to validate this study's findings and develop a practical framework for serious leadership games will involve observing learners before, after and during game play. The next stage will further explore the constructs which emerged from this study such as socially constructed realities and team play, psychological safety and scaffolding, player identity stretching and Flow experience, alongside the effectiveness of 'soft skills' development in players.

Acknowledgements. Great appreciation is extended to the panel of expert participants, as well as Dr Christopher Buckingham and Professor Seth Giddings for their invaluable insights, guidance and contributions to this research.

References

1. Abuhamdeh, S., Csikszentmihalyi, M.: Intrinsic and extrinsic motivational orientations in the competitive context: an examination of person-situation interactions. J. Pers. **77**, 1615–1635 (2009)
2. Allal-Chérif, O., Lombardo, E., Jaotombo, F.: Serious games for managers: creating cognitive, financial, technological, social, and emotional value in in-service training. J. Bus. Res. **146**, 166–175 (2022)
3. Bandura, A., Cervone, D.: Social Cognitive Theory: An Agentic Perspective on Human Nature. Wiley, New York (2023)
4. Bowman, S.L.: Immersion and Shared Imagination in RolePlaying Games, pp. 379–394. Routledge, London (2018)
5. British Psychological Society: The Delphi method (2009). https://www.bps.org.uk/psychologist/delphi-method
6. Buchanan, J.L.: Leadership development and experiential methodology: the impact on learning leadership. Int. J. Arts Sci. **10**, 601–608 (2017)
7. Burr, V.: Social Constructionism. Routledge, London (2015)

8. Calabor, M.S., Mora, A., Moya, S.: The future of 'serious games' in accounting education: a Delphi study. J. Account. Educ. **46**, 43–52 (2019)
9. Chalki, P., Mikropoulos, T.A., Tsiara, A.: A Delphi study on the design of digital educational games. In: Antona, M., Stephanidis, C. (eds.) HCII 2019. LNCS, vol. 11572, pp. 433–444. Springer, Cham (2019). https://doi.org/10.1007/978-3-030-23560-4_32
10. Chen, D.T., Hung, D.: Two kinds of scaffolding: the dialectical process within the authenticity-generalizibility (a-g) continuum. Educ. Technol. Soc. **5** (2002)
11. Csikszentmihalyi, M.: Flow: The Psychology of Optimal Experience, 2nd print. edn. Harper I& Row, New York (1990)
12. Csikszentmihalyi, M.: Applications of Flow in Human Development and Education: The Collected Works of Mihaly Csikszentmihalyi. Springer, Dordrecht (2014). https://doi.org/10.1007/978-94-017-9094-9
13. Edmondson, A.C., Lei, Z.: Psychological safety: the history, renaissance, and future of an interpersonal construct. Annu. Rev. Organ. Psych. Organ. Behav. **1**, 23–43 (2014)
14. Freitas, S.D., Routledge, H.: Designing leadership and soft skills in educational games: the e-leadership and soft skills educational games design model (ELESS). Br. J. Edu. Technol. **44**, 951–968 (2013)
15. Hoffman, S.G.: The practical use of other realities: taking Berger and Luckmann into the wild. Cult. Sociol. **10**, 109–124 (2016)
16. van den Hout, J.J., Davis, O.C., Weggeman, M.C.: The conceptualization of team flow. J. Psychol. **152**, 388–423 (2018)
17. Iacovides, I., Cox, A., Kennedy, R., Cairns, P., Jennett, C.: Removing the hud: the impact of non-diegetic game elements and expertise on player involvement. In: CHI PLAY 2015 - Proceedings of the 2015 Annual Symposium on Computer-Human Interaction in Play, pp. 13–22. Association for Computing Machinery, Inc (2015)
18. Komives, S.R., Mainella, F.C., Longerbeam, S.D., Osteen, L., Owen, J.E.: A leadership identity development model: applications from a grounded theory. J. Coll. Stud. Dev. **47**, 401–418 (2006)
19. Lebrón, M.J., Lasley, J.: Game design: re-imagining learning and teaching leadership through active gameplay. New Dir. Stud. Leadersh. 111–120 (2022)
20. Lovelace, K.J., Eggers, F., Dyck, L.R.: I do and I understand: assessing the utility of web-based management simulations to develop critical thinking skills. Acad. Manag. Learn. Educ. **15**, 100–121 (2016)
21. López, F.R., Arias-Oliva, M., Pelegrín-Borondo, J., Marín-Vinuesa, L.M.: Serious games in management education: an acceptance analysis. Int. J. Manag. Educ. **19** (2021)
22. Salas, E., Wildman, J.L., Piccolo, R.F.: Using simulation-based training to enhance management education. Acad. Manag. Learn. Educ. **8**, 559–573 (2009)
23. Schrier, K., Zahradnik, A., Shaenfield, D.: Playful approaches to leadership development: three innovative uses of games in the classroom. J. Manag. Educ. (2023)
24. Snow, D.A., Corrigall-Brown, C.: Collective Identity. Elsevier Inc., Amsterdam (2015)
25. Stryker, S., Burke, P.J.: The past, present, and future of an identity theory. Soc. Psychol. Q. **63**, 284–297 (2000)
26. Van Gaalen, A.E.J., Schönrock-Adema, J., Renken, R.J., Jaarsma, A.D.C., Georgiadis, J.R.: Identifying player types to tailor game-based learning design to learners: cross-sectional survey using q methodology. JMIR Serious Games **10**(2) (2022)

Development of a Simulation to Aid Navigation in First Year CS Students

Chloe Woods, Aaron Tasker-Lynch, Joseph Le Seelleur, Stephen McBride, Ryan Gilbride, Daniel Brice, and Darragh Lydon(✉)

School of Arts, English & Languages Queen's University Belfast, Belfast, UK
d.lydon@qub.ac.uk

Abstract. Transferring to university for the first time can be an exciting and potentially overwhelming experience for students, particularly those from less privileged backgrounds or those prone to anxiety. These students can sometimes face difficulties integrating into campus life leading to increased access to disability services. This case study details the development and testing of simulation of the Computer Science building at Queen's University Belfast with the aim of aiding students in their transition to university.

Keywords: Simulation · Case Study · VR

1 Introduction

Acclimatising to university life, particularly for those students who are the first from their family to attend higher education, can be a stressful and confusing time. The increased autonomy compared to secondary level educational institutions, where students jave clear guidance on class times and school navigation stands in contrast to the onboarding process offered to first year students. This anxiety could be increased by large class sizes (Mulryan-Kyne, 2010), something that is quite common in computer science courses. Students can feel isolated in these large environments as it is hard to ask questions in front of a large group of their peers. A further complication involves students with ASD/anxiety, who can struggle with this lack of routine and guidance (Elias and White, 2018). The Disability Services team in Queen's University Belfast (QUB) have noted this in their surveys of current and past computer science students, and approached the authors to help students with ASD/Anxiety understand in advance which areas of the Computer Science Building (CSB) have potentially uncomfortable levels of noise, lighting, and crowds, and where certain facilities and rooms are, reducing the stress of navigating the building in real time.

Virtual reality experiences have been proven to be a useful tool for campus navigation in work by (Salleh et al., 2021). An issue with this work was that the level of detail present in the simulation was not high enough to give a fully accurate representation of the environment, resulting in less-than-optimal user experience. Additional work by (Patil, 2022) presented a high-fidelity model of the electronics building in VTU Belgaum. The structure of this work, where immersive sounds, navigation to points and

A. Schönbohm et al. (Eds.): GALA 2024, LNCS 15348, pp. 243–252, 2025.
https://doi.org/10.1007/978-3-031-78269-5_23

a free roam mode provided inspiration for the design presented in this work. The model presented by Patil did not have additional information for locations in the building, and their navigation system was steered by the system instead of allowing the user to follow a guided path. Guidance was provided using Augmented Reality (AR) in the prototype developed by (Paetow et al., 2021), this type of navigation was used as a starting point for the "Guided Tour" option discussed below. AR was also used in the work by (Rehman and Cao, 2016), where the authors compared the use of head mounted device to paper/smartphone navigation. They determined that digital navigation aids were superior to paper maps with regards to navigation time and cognitive workload. Further investigation on the applicability of digital navigation by (Tahir and Krogstie, 2023) indicated that the use of AR devices does not aid with route retention, and that 3D models or immersive experiences would be of greater benefit to users in this area.

There have been numerous studies to ascertain whether virtual reality applications can be used to alleviate anxiety (Anderson et al., 2017; Pallavicini et al., 2016). This has also been extended to university students in work by (Camara and Hicks, 2019; Rajabalee and Ravi, 2019). The latter work also faced the same issue as Salleh, as the resolution and level of detail present in the experience resulted in a less immersive experience than is possible using newer technologies.

Our research question is: 'Can a simulated Computer Science Building 1) Increase the user's navigation and knowledge of the building?' 2) Reduce anxiety for users visiting the building.

2 QUB Specific Investigation

To address the specific case of simulation at QUB, we looked at the virtual tour options already offered by the university: the QUB Virtual Tour app and Virtualexperiencce.qub.ac.uk. Both products include the interiors of various buildings, using high resolution 360° images with fixed point player perspective navigated by clicking and dragging. This approach is taken by many 'virtual tours' online and does not feel very immersive (Fig. 1).

One insightful simulation was the replica of the CSB on Minecraft built by students. This is a simplified abstraction of the building due to the style and limitations of the game but is still recognisable as the CSB due to the accurate layout and colouring. Nevertheless, it can be hard to tell what certain objects are, and there is no signage indicating the names of the rooms (Fig. 2).

Based on this research, there appears to be no immersive high fidelity game experience of the CSB like the one that we proposed to create. We believe that there is a need for such an experience, and so we sought to understand what current Computer Science students think of the CSB, and how a virtual tour may benefit them.

We already had anecdotal evidence about the kinds of problems the Disability Services team heard from students regarding over-stimulating lighting, décor, and sounds that could potentially cause discomfort or distress. They also pointed out that many students can be confused about the layout.

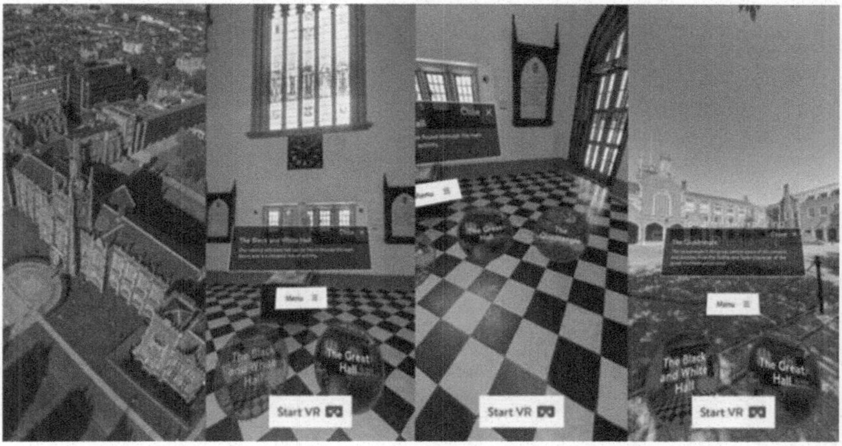

Fig. 1. Previous QUB Tour Options

Fig. 2. Minecraft CSB

We wanted to corroborate this with a user survey to CS students. The survey received 12 responses from students from 1st to 4th year with the following highlights:

- 83% stated they would be interested in a virtual tour and would be likely to use it, showing that there is a desire for such a product.
- Many respondents did not know about the quiet rooms or lounge or how to find them. This allowed us to focus on the rooms that would be most helpful to show (Fig. 3).
- One student claimed that they would avoid going to the CSB as it was too crowded, and another mentioned the excessive light from the LEDs.

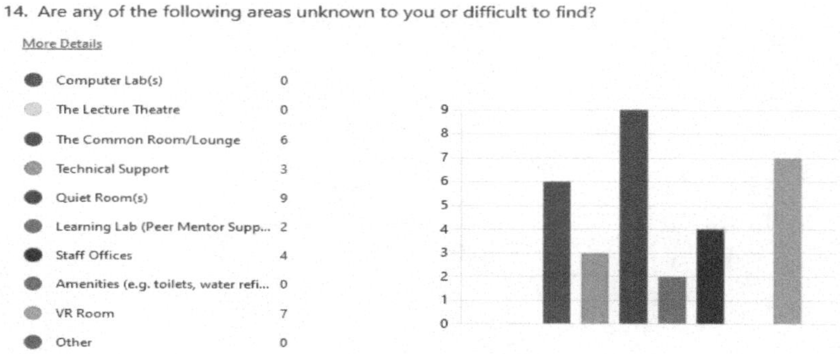

Fig. 3. Survey question related to navigation of the CSB

3 Technical Development

Our project is a desktop and VR simulation and tour of the Computer Science Building (CSB) in Queen's University Belfast. The goal of this project is to provide a tool for newcomers to the building that they can use to understand the layout of the building, obtain knowledge about the facilities offered and operation of the building, and experience typical light and sound levels.

The project accomplishes these goals through the three 'Game Modes' offered that the user can switch between.

1) A fully automated tour guiding the user around different locations of the building and providing detailed information (Fig. 4) at each waypoint via narration by Dr. Neil Anderson and subtitles. The information at these waypoints ranges from the name and function of important rooms to useful knowledge for EEECS students to know such as the opening times of the building or what to do if they lose their student card.

Fig. 4. Waypoint Information

2) A free roam option with the tour waypoints active so that the user can choose which areas they want to learn more about. This is also the best mode to make use of the 'Location Finder'(Fig. 5), a dropdown menu of rooms the user can select and is then shown how to get to that room.

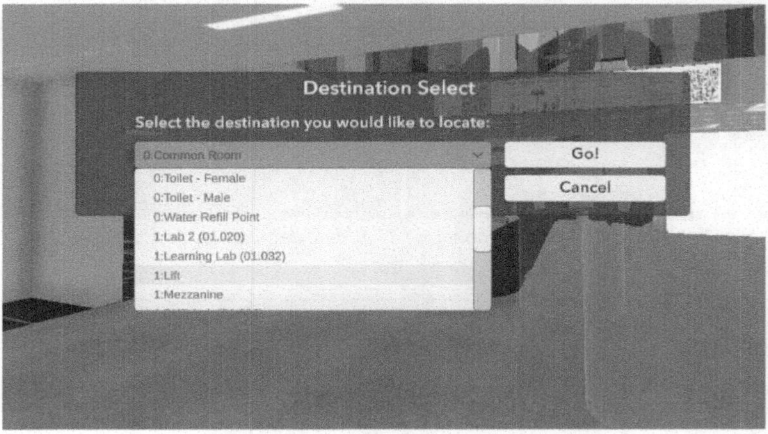

Fig. 5. Location Finder Menu

3) An immersive free roam option with no tour elements. This mode is focused on experiencing the audiovisual environment of the building.

Many design choices have been made to increase the immersivity of the simulation:

- Every room contains ambient noise, simulating sounds heard at different times of the day. The simulation includes 24 environmental sounds, the vast majority of which were made using samples of audio recordings taken during visits to the CSB. The volume of sounds associated with specific objects (e.g. server rooms) will change depending on the user's proximity to the object.
- Realistic style of modelling and texturing. The building itself was made to scale using the floorplans and by taking measurements. Colour schemes, textures, and room items (desks, stools, PC's etc.) were also made as true to their real life CSB equivalents as possible within the project timeframe.
- The menu was designed to replicate the style of QUB signage.

All these design choices and features were informed by user needs defined by anecdotes from Disability Services and surveys we sent to students from the school of Electronics, Electrical Engineering and Computer Science. This feedback was indispensable for prioritising work, refining the simulation, and maximising accessibility. For example, we designed the simulation for both desktop and VR, and we added extra accessibility options for audio, game controls, and interface settings so the user can cater the experience to their individual needs and preferences.

3.1 Environment Modelling and Design

To facilitate creating an accurate model, we used the floorplan, accurate measurement information and reference photos captured from visits to the CSB. We used Blender to model the building. Modelling of the CSB went through the following phases:

1 - Modelled building that followed general floor plan

2 - Added detail such as windows/doors/trim etc

3 - Added item models (desks, chairs, computers etc.)

4 – More objects added, model textured.

3.2 Texturing and Optimisation

To ensure adequate performance for a WebGL application that could be run on weaker machines, and to fall within data limits, it was necessary to optimise textures prior to importing them into Unity. This required two approaches:

The first, trim sheet texturing, involved the creation of 2D textures (or capturing, in the case of photographic textures), and arranging them into a single image file; object UVs could be arranged on this to project different parts of the texture onto the model. This process was repeated for each element of that material (diffuse, normals, etc.).

The second approach was to create texture atlases, which entailed a reversed approach, whereby object UVs were packed into a single texture space and their textures (procedurally created in Blender) were baked to a single file. With these techniques, it was possible to compress a large number of textures (30+) into less file space and only 7 Unity materials. In addition to this, we used dynamic occlusion on all our objects so that the simulation was only rendering models that were visible to the user.

3.3 Navigation

Unity's AI Navigation package enabled us to create a NavMesh based on our CSB model. A NavMesh is a navigation system that allows characters to move around a game world by using a mesh that defines navigable areas and obstacles. We then optimised the mesh using NavMeshModifier, which is a tool that allows developers to add fine detail to an automatically generated mesh, in this case we added in detail for desk and chairs in the computer laboratories. The NavMeshAgent functionality was used to facilitate automatic navigation, which meant the player character would travel around the experience without any input from the user, and we also implemented a custom waypoint solution that enabled us to place waypoints around the building. These waypoints were used in the Guided Tour and Destination Selection features.

3.4 VR

Our research into effective VR GUI and Control methods helped us tailor the VR experience to provide the user with a good VR experience. For example, Richie's Plank Experience is a VR game that has good staples of intuitive VR menuing, e.g. making buttons change colour and play a sound when you hover over (Fig. 6).

Fig. 6. UI Concepts used for Design inspiration

In addition, VR controls were researched to ensure that we implemented intuitive VR controls. Resident Evil 4 and Darth Immortal are a couple of example VR games we reviewed to learn from how they implemented their control systems.

Unity XR packages have inbuilt features such as the XR Rig, Teleport Provider and Continuous Movement Provider which enabled us to implement a VR solution that was flexible to the user's needs. We also had to consider factors that can make VR experiences uncomfortable and so implemented a Tunnel Vision System and tuned movement speed to alleviate motion sickness issues.

We implemented two VR control methods to suit the preferences of users. One was based on teleport movement which is effective for new VR users and those susceptible to motion sickness. The other was based on continuous movement which gives users more detailed control of their movement via the controller joysticks.

4 Results

When we had a working prototype, we sought feedback to understand how well the application helps people navigate the building and to improve the user experience. Highlights from this feedback:

- 61% mentioned the simulation helped them discover the existence of the rooms, in particular the quiet rooms and lounge that were highlighted in the first survey.
- Out of the respondents who did not already know where everything was, 75% said the simulation increased their knowledge of the building and 85% said the simulation increased their ability to navigate
- 84% said the simulation would be a useful resource for newcomers
- Many respondents stated that they would be more likely to use the tour on desktop, verifying our choice to make a desktop version (Fig. 7).

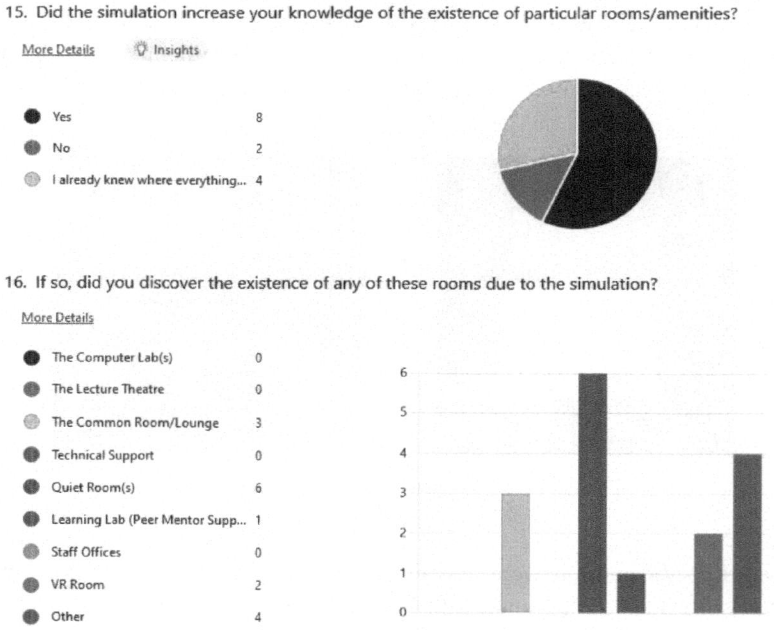

Fig. 7. Post experience evaluation survey results

Based on this, we can conclude that users are happy with the product and would use it, and it helps with navigating the building, which had been our primary research question. Because the focus of the project shifted away from anxiety reduction, we did not survey students on this element of the experience.

5 Next Steps

While the application currently fulfils the necessary functions for a virtual tour, we do have features in our backlog and our user feedback survey has provided insight into additional ways to improve user experience. While the survey was useful for initial feedback during development, it is quite limited in terms of scope as it mainly focuses on navigation experience. We intend to repeat the testing process implementing more survey elements to measure the behavioural effects of the navigation, as outlined in the work by (van Oostendorp and Karanam, 2013).

In terms of development, first would be minor fixes to usability and quality of life such as adjusting mouse sensitivity, softening the UI sounds, and a faster movement option. To help with navigation, a map of the building to go along with the Destination Select tool will also be available in future. On the visual side, we are yet to finish the lighting. This means currently the environment looks quite bland and the night version is too dark. Creation of a lighting setup in Unity will improve this, below is an example render from Blender (Fig. 8).

Fig. 8. Example render with improved lighting

We are also evaluating the purpose of our Game Modes, how to distinguish them, and how to onboard users to the different experiences. Currently, you can swap Game Mode at any time, and all options are available regardless of what mode you are in. It may make more sense to only make Mode selection available in the main menu and reduce the number of decisions a player must make, such as control settings.

Related to this, we need to refine our onboarding/tutorial process for each mode so users know how to get the most out of the application. For example, the Location Selector was the second most popular feature, but it was not explicitly shown, so many testers did not know it existed. One potential fix for this is making the feature exclusive to Informational and having the dropdown menu constantly on screen in this mode.

Finally, one potential feature that would help those with ASD/Anxiety is the implementation of crowds.

Acknowledgments. This research was carried out with the assistance of Disability Services at Queen's University Belfast.

Disclosure of Interests. The authors have no competing interests to declare that are relevant to the content of this article.

References

Anderson, A.P., Mayer, M.D., Fellows, A.M., Cowan, D.R., Hegel, M.T., Buckey, J.C.: Relaxation with immersive natural scenes presented using virtual reality. Aerosp. Med. Hum. Perform. **88**(6), 520–526 (2017). https://doi.org/10.3357/AMHP.4747.2017

Camara, D., Hicks, R.: Using Virtual Reality to Reduce State Anxiety and Stress in University Students: An Experiment, vol. 4, p. 15 (2019)

Elias, R., White, S.W.: Autism goes to college: understanding the needs of a student population on the rise. J. Autism Dev. Disord. **48**(3), 732–746 (2018). https://doi.org/10.1007/s10803-017-3075-7

Mulryan-Kyne, C.: Teaching large classes at college and university level: challenges and opportunities. Teach. High. Educ. **15**(2), 175–185 (2010). https://doi.org/10.1080/13562511003620001

Paetow, T., Wichmann, J., Wißotzki, M.: Campus-Navigation-System Design for Universities – A Method Approach for Wismar Business School, pp. 3–12 (2021). https://doi.org/10.1007/978-981-16-3264-8_1

Pallavicini, F., Argenton, L., Toniazzi, N., Aceti, L., Mantovani, F.: Virtual reality applications for stress management training in the military. Aerosp. Med. Hum. Perform. **87**(12), 1021–1030 (2016). https://doi.org/10.3357/AMHP.4596.2016

Patil, A.: in Rted – interactive navigation by virtual reality tour of electronics department. Int. J. Res. Appl. Sci. Eng. Technol. **10**(6), 295–300 (2022). https://doi.org/10.22214/ijraset.2022.43633

Rajabalee, Y., Ravi, R.: Virtual reality and 3D tours as pedagogical support to improve students experiences at the university (2019)

Rehman, U., Cao, S.: Augmented-reality-based indoor navigation: a comparative analysis of hand-held devices versus google glass. IEEE Trans. Hum.-Mach. Syst. **47**, 1–12 (2016). https://doi.org/10.1109/THMS.2016.2620106

Salleh, S., Ujang, U., Azri, S.: Virtual 3D campus for Universiti Teknologi Malaysia (UTM). ISPRS Int. J. Geo Inf. **10**(6), 356 (2021). https://doi.org/10.3390/ijgi10060356

Tahir, R., Krogstie, J.: Impact of navigation aid and spatial ability skills on wayfinding performance and workload in indoor-outdoor campus navigation: challenges and design. Appl. Sci. **13**(17), 9508 (2023). https://doi.org/10.3390/app13179508

van Oostendorp, H., Karanam, S.: Navigating in a virtual environment with model-generated support. In: Proceedings of the 31st European Conference on Cognitive Ergonomics, pp. 1–8 (2013). https://doi.org/10.1145/2501907.2501948

Futures Literacy: Games for Civic Participation and Futures Thinking

Making Games to Make Futures

Playfully Co-designing Games for Civic Learning and Thinking About Futures

Anna O. Meshcheryakova(✉) and Fabian Hemmert

University of Wuppertal, Gaußstr. 20, 42119 Wuppertal, Germany
anna.meshcheryakova@uni-wuppertal.de

Abstract. This paper reports on a co-design workshop conducted to examine how co-designing board games could be conceptualised as an activity for supporting people in critical engagement with potential futures and civic learning. We follow a*research-through-design* approach to investigate how such formats may be designed and used to facilitate creative and collaborative engagement with futures. Thereby, we attempt to position the design activity itself as playful and explore how the idea of how playing and engaging in experiments with prototypes could be seen as making. We reflect on both the workshop blueprint and overall workshop outcomes, exploring to what extent the approaches of criticality, making and play can be balanced, and how they may contribute to supporting workshop participants in engaging with futures in a context of civic learning.

Keywords: co-design · making games · designing as play · civic learning · critical making · critical play

1 Introduction

Games can be seen as effective tools for imagining futures [7] and civic learning [25]. In civic learning, people can exchange knowledge, explore ideas, pursue community interests and connect with each other [1]. While serious games and game-based learning have produced many proposals for games that can support such processes, Kafai and Burke [14] argue that having people make their own games may have a greater effect on learning in regards to systems thinking and collaboration. We believe these aspects to be crucial for imagining, learning about and building collective futures. Hence, we followed a *research-through-design* approach [9] to design, conduct and evaluate a game-making workshop in which participants designed board games for engaging with futures. Our understanding of "futures" is rooted in the futures literacy concept used by UNESCO, which focuses on how people not only "use" future to shape their lives through anticipation, but also how they deal with emerging complexity [17]. We were specifically interested in examining how designing games could be conceptualised as an activity for supporting people in mutual learning about and critical engagement with emergent and complex anticipatory ideas.

A. Schönbohm et al. (Eds.): GALA 2024, LNCS 15348, pp. 255–264, 2025.
https://doi.org/10.1007/978-3-031-78269-5_24

Building on the concepts of *critical play* [10], *critical making* [20] and *designing as play* [4], the workshop blueprint that we developed attempts to fuse making and playing as two ways of learning. Both modes have been underrepresented in traditional learning environments, yet their experiential nature holds great potential for learning and dealing with complexity [6]. Thus, these approaches may be very fruitful for the context of civic learning, participation and futures literacy. Our workshop aims to enable people to experiment with and experience playful tools and interactions as a way of collaboratively imagining futures. Thereby, we attempt to position the design activity itself as playful [4] and examine the idea of how playing with prototyping materials could be seen as designing and making.

This paper presents both the workshop outline and outcomes. We examine to what extent criticality, making and play can be balanced and reflect on how they may contribute to supporting workshop participants in engaging with futures. The workshop blueprint is made available online with a CC BY-NC-SA 4.0 license linked here.

2 Background

2.1 Civic Learning, Game-Based Learning and Futures

Research interest in educational approaches like futures literacy that aim to enable people to actively shape their futures and (creatively) navigate the complexity of our world have surged in recent years [17]. We see civic learning with its focus on supporting citizens in becoming empowered actors in democratic societies [13] as a relevant related approach. Ampatzidou [1] describes civic learning as complex social process that is not only about acquiring domain knowledge, e.g. about political institutions, but also exchanging opinions and negotiating of collective decisions. Hoggan et al. argue that civic learning is about ways of living in a democratic society, hence it can be understood as education that helps people build the social relations needed for active citizen participation [13].

Whilst game-based learning and serious games have been used in civic learning, e.g. to promote efficacy or teach concepts relevant to society [25], it seems that less attention has been paid to learning to engage with novel ideas and other citizens in constructive ways. The latter is particularly relevant for imagining, constructing and negotiating futures - processes that occur not in isolation but always in relation to other people [12]. Games in particular can have strong social components, promote collaboration and interaction amongst players [1], therefore we believe game-based learning to hold great potential for our purpose.

2.2 Making Futures and Co-creation

One area with a rich tradition of collaboratively engaging with the future is the realm of co-creation and participatory design (PD). Here, the mode of *making* - oftentimes brought to life through collaboratively constructing and prototyping representations of desired futures - is used to facilitate learning about people's needs and desires [8,21]. Brandt et al. refer to these types of activities as a "new game of possible futures" [3, p. 171].

Typically, this takes the shape of a co-creative process in which researchers or practitioners interact with non-designers and facilitate their engagement with one another and provided prototyping materials. Even though PD practitioners have used games widely in the past [2] and arguments for incorporating co-creation of games in education have been made [23], there seems to be little engagement between the two disciplines. We believe that drawing from co-creation's strengths - deep involvement, addressing player/learner needs and collaboration - may be particularly effective in supporting meaningful learning related to imagining and debating collective futures.

We suggest drawing from the triad of *telling, making* and *enacting* that Brandt et al. have proposed as ways of engaging with the future in PD [3]. Specifically, this could mean looking at ways in which people can tell stories, build things or physically act out imagined scenes as ways of illustrating and experimenting with ideas. These modes make use of sensory and embodied experience - similar to what has been done with games in education - to support learning [24], and therefore could be useful pathways for fostering civic learning though combining games with co-creation. Notably, all three modes may be particularly well supported by analogue games and prototyping materials that allow direct and intuitive interaction. Whilst modding has already been discussed as a (playful) approach to game-making in the digital realm [27], it seems that analogue games such as board games hold particular promise for (civic) learning due to their rich materiality that allows for embodied experimentation, and may serve to support meaningful social interactions.

2.3 Critical Play and Critical Making in Relation to Learning

We draw additional inspiration from the concepts of *critical play* and *critical making*. Brown and Douglas have noted that both playing and making are effective, albeit undeserved, modes of learning [6]. They argue that making and playing enable learning on a deep level, because they allow people to participate in imagining the world - not merely receiving information about it, but *being* in and shaping it [6]. Whilst Brown and Douglas hint at the potential that lies in fusing these modes, Kafai and Burke point out that although games are increasingly used in education, the idea of *making games* as a way of learning has received less attention [14]. They refer to this as constructionist gaming, a concept that shows many parallels to Ratto's concept of *critical making* [20], which focuses on how material production may support people in connecting embodied experiences with conceptual knowledge.

Ratto has highlighted the importance of "messing about" in Papert's vision constructionist learning [18], i.e. an experimental or playful approach to tools and materials. This closely aligns with Brown and Douglas' ideas of how tinkering and messing around can help people understand their relationship to their environment [6]. This seems crucial to imagining and shaping futures, as "messing" allows to prototype and experiment with different ideas. Hence, it seems that both playing and making may support this in conjunction. Kafai and Burke [14] add that through making games *for* others, people may create what Papert [19] has referred to as public entities: taking the output of the making process from personal knowledge objects to ones that can be shared with others.

Sullivan et al. note how critical making is often associated with critical game design practices [26]. Flanagan has used the idea of *critical play* to describe practices of playing and making games that raise or relate to questions about human life [10]. She proposes *unplaying* (playing in ways not intended by creators), *rewriting* (re-configuring the narrative) and *reskinning* (changing appearances) as ways of how criticality and subversion in play may appear. These activities could emerge as a result of messing about with existing games.

Drawing from these interconnected perspectives, we propose to focus on the intersection between playing and making for our purpose. We suggest thinking about this intersection in terms of *making as playing* and *playing as making*. Ratto [20] has suggested playful "messing about" as a pathway to making, whilst Brooks frames "designing as playing" [4] and encourages us to think of designing (which closely relates to making) as a process of playing with materials, allowing new ideas to emerge. She defines this as "*melded interactions, where* what if explorations *and* prototyping *by means of different kinds of material came together in experiential* making and breaking *endeavours*" [4, p. 9]. This view allows for interesting entry points to designing our workshop.

3 A Workshop for Co-designing Games About Futures

In the following, we outline how the concepts surveyed above were incorporated into each of the workshop stages (Table 1) and present results. We conducted the workshop with a group of 7 social/community workers aged 24–66 in a large German city who had an interest in exploring playful approaches for their work. The session was conducted at a local community centre and lasted for 4h, with some participants being familiar with each other through their work. None of participants had prior experience in game design. In addition to observation data, a 45min focus group discussion in which participants could reflect on and discuss their experiences was conducted immediately after the workshop. Data was analysed with thematic content analysis [11], using semantic coding and subsequently constructing key themes, to be presented in Sect. 3.5.

The general concept of the workshop was for participants to choose a topic relating to the future and design a prototype of a board game around this topic. We selected board games for this due to their rich material composition [22], consisting of many elements that represent space, roles, actions etc., that allow for many entry-points into embodied, analogue experimentation, and their relative accessibility.

Table 1. Workshop outline

Workshop stages	1. Explore & Disassemble	2. Invent & Conceptualise	3. Build & Make	4. Present & Play
Activities	game selection and analysis with template	select topic, experiment with materials, prototype	further prototyping, try to play game	present and play each others' games
Intention	*critically breaking the game* [5,10]	*making as playing, i.e. mess with materials* [4,18,20]	*playing as making, i.e. play to develop game* [4]	*deepen learning through sharing* [19]

3.1 Explore and Disassemble

After an introduction during which they collected ideas relating to the future that they would like to design a game about, participants were divided into two groups of 3–4 persons. Each group was asked to choose one board game to work with during the workshop out of a selection of 10 provided by the team. This selection was curated based on popularity and richness of material composition, e.g. *The Game of Life* [15] or*Labyrinth* [16], hoping that participants would grasp them quickly due to familiarity and find many entry-points into material experimentation.

Both teams were given a template for analysing their chosen game in regards to aspects such as theme, goals, materials or meaning (see Fig. 1 (a)). Including meaning in the analysis encouraged participants to critically examine the game's impact: one of the groups selected the *The Game of Life* and quickly noticed capitalistic values deeply embedded in it, whilst the other group chose a children's version of the *Labyrinth* and was able to draw out topics such as spatial thinking and accessibility from a seemingly simplistic game.

This exercise was intended for *critically breaking* the game (combining Brook's *breaking endeavours* [4] with the *critical play* concept [10]) and was reported by participants to be very effective in gaining an understanding of the connection between game mechanics and content. By reflecting on if the values in the games align with theirs, participants were able to not only learn more about each other's views but also consider what meanings they would like to put into their games and what kind of experiences they would like players to have.

3.2 Invent and Conceptualise

Then, each group selected one topic relating to the future for their game. Based on Flanagan's strategies for subversion [10], participants were encouraged to think about how appearance, content and ways of playing of their selected game might be changed to suit their vision for the future. After initial ideas had been articulated, participants were encouraged to explore and delve into prototyping materials (e.g. elements from existing board games covered with foil to be drawn on with whiteboard markers, blank cards, figurines, craft supplies etc.) to develop ideas - engaging in *making as playing*. In doing so, we hoped

(a) (b) (c)

Fig. 1. Workshop details: (a) participants analysing a game, (b) using prototyping materials and (c) discussing game board draft

to encourage "messing" and the emergence of imaginative *what if*-thinking (e.g. what if we include dice?) as Brooks suggested [4]. Participants were also given a concept template to help them keep in mind the most important elements of a game.

One group chose learning about one's own neighbourhood and improving it through incremental changes as their topic, building on the *Labyrinth*. Using its modular board to explore space, the group changed its appearance and made new tiles to represent their neighbourhood (see Fig. 1 (b)) and quickly got into a mode of playing with the board elements, exploring *what if*-questions arising from different moves (e.g. what if a figurine gets pushed off the board?).

The second group selected a more abstract topic: addressing structural inequalities in a re-imagining of *The Game of Life*. Troubled by the traditional ideas embedded in the original, they put aside the game board in favour of designing a new one (see Fig. 1 (c)). They came up with the concept of people moving through institutions and confronting inequalities. However, they struggled to translate their ideas into game mechanics, spending more time on conceptual discussion and making less use of prototyping materials.

3.3 Build and Make

After a break, participants continued building their games by incorporating additional elements. Both groups continued their discussions, trying to merge mechanics and meaning: for instance, the first group debated which features in a neighbourhood are framed as positive achievements and which as barriers (see Fig. 2 (a)). Participants were asked to consider how their games would be played step-by-step. Our intention here was to move from *making as playing* to *playing as making*. For the second group, attempting to *play* their game helped with making ideas more concrete: getting away from thinking through the lens of concept to the act of *playing* helped them prototype key steps and draft a game board much quicker (see Fig. 2 (b)).

(a) (b)

Fig. 2. Workshop progress: (a) participants attempting to play their game and (b) discussing players' steps

3.4 Present and Play

All groups were asked to briefly present their games to each other, following Papert's idea of public entities [19]. Whilst time did not permit to test the games, new ideas were being articulated and co-developed on the fly during the ensuing discussion. Participants expressed interest in enhancing their results by photographing and sharing them with others after the workshop, too, and potentially developing them further.

3.5 Reflection

In the subsequent focus group interview, most participants noted that they greatly enjoyed exchanging and co-developing ideas in a collaborative fashion, with one person summarising that they "*felt creative in the exchange with the group, collecting ideas or new impulses from what the others said*" [P4]. Many of the participants highlighted how they felt that the workshop's structure and materials were helpful in guiding their process and inspiring them.

There were mixed views on how the notion of "future" was addressed. The groups chose different approaches (combining a tangible topic with a simpler game or working a more abstract topic into a complex game) and thus felt they had different degrees of success in connecting their ideas to concrete and fun game mechanics. Hence, the second group reporting feelings at times more frustrated than playful. This led some participants to state that they thought some topics less suitable: "*the future topics were very, very big. And maybe a game needs a smaller approach.*" [P1]. This may indicate that guiding participants towards more concrete, tangible topics may help connect *making* to *futures.*

Participants did feel that their designs could be used to spark interesting conversations, e.g. about life in the neighbourhood: "*I found it exciting how much we can apply this to our work, in a playful way.*" [P5]). Generally, participants agreed that the experience was valuable to them, either because it allowed to deeply engage with their group and each other's ideas, or for deep reflection on games as medium and how they transport meaning.

4 Discussion and Conclusion

The workshop blueprint appears to have effectively supported people through a co-creative process. Melding of *breaking* and *making* [4] by having participants first analyse and then re-design a game helped guide them towards *critical making* [20] and inspire subversion, e.g. by changing appearance [10]. Including meaning in the analysis led participants to critically examine the values embedded in the games and learn about each other's positions. Both groups engaged in "messing" with game elements (materials, rules, goals etc.) as ways to think about the concepts they wished to convey (e.g. reducing inequality) as Ratto [20] suggested, connecting their experiential knowledge about games to their chosen topics in a process that they reported finding meaningful and constructive. Considering how participants were able to go from exchanging ideas to debating values and co-constructing goals indicates that a game co-design workshop can facilitate meaningful civic learning experiences [1,13]. It may also support people in engaging with emergent and complex anticipatory ideas [17].

While participants' reflections indicate that balancing playful, critical and focused thinking remains a challenge, the relative ease with which they moved through their process once they focused on the material and playful aspects of it suggests that these approaches were useful for a process of co-creation in which participants learned about each other's ideas. Providing a rich array of materials and extending the traditional properties of game elements, i.e. covering boards with foil to draw on, was useful to underscore the idea of breaking and re-making, hinting at how both games and futures can be unmade and remade.

Hence, we find that unmaking and re-making a game, and bringing the idea of play into the making, appears to be a productive concept for civic learning and engaging with futures. We hope that this will inspire other researchers in the field of games, learning and civic education to incorporate the ideas of making, breaking and "messing" into their work, considering how learners may engage with complex ideas and with each other by co-designing games.

5 Limitations and Future Work

This workshop was conducted with one small group, hence the results and analysis we can provide here are limited. Further testing and validation of the blueprint with more different groups is needed. Whilst conducting the workshop with a very broad focus allowed us to explore how constructionist approaches may be combined with criticality and playfulness in the context of civic learning and futures, we believe that focusing on a specific topic relating to the future may be helpful to analyse the learning effects achieved in more detail. Particular attention could also be paid to exploring more ways of incorporating playfulness. We encourage others to build on our linked workshop blueprint.

References

1. Ampatzidou, C.: Reinventing the rules: emergent gameplay for civic learning. In: de Lange, M., de Waal, M. (eds.) The Hackable City, pp. 187–203. Springer, Singapore (2019). https://doi.org/10.1007/978-981-13-2694-3_10
2. Brandt, E.: Introduction to (participatory) design games. Tijdschrift voor Hum. Factors **39**(4), 5 (2014)
3. Brandt, E., Binder, T., Sanders, E.B.N.: Tools and techniques: ways to engage telling, making and enacting. In: Simonsen, J., Robertson, T. (eds.) Routledge International Handbook of Participatory Design, pp. 145–181. Routledge, London and New York (2012)
4. Brooks, E.: Designing as play. In: Brooks, E., Dau, S., Selander, S. (eds.) Digital Learning and Collaborative Practices, pp. 4–11. Routledge, New York and London (2022)
5. Brooks, E., Sjöberg, J., Møller, A.K. (eds.): Design, Learning, and Innovation. LNICS, SITE. Springer, Cham (2022). https://doi.org/10.1007/978-3-031-06675-7
6. Brown, J.S., Douglas, T.: Learning for a world of constant change: homo sapiens, homo faber & homo ludens revisited. In: Weber, L., Duderstadt, J.J. (eds.) University Research for Innovation. Glion Colloquium series, pp. 321–336. Genève and Économica, London and Paris (2010)
7. Coulton, P., Burnett, D., Gradinar, A.: Games as speculative design: allowing players to consider alternate presents and plausible features. In: DRS2016: Future-Focused Thinking. Proceedings of DRS, Design Research Society (2016). https://doi.org/10.21606/drs.2016.15
8. De la Pena, D., Jones Allen, D., Hester, R.T., Jeff Hou, J., Lawson, L.J., McNally, M.J.: Design As Democracy: Techniques for Collective Creativity. Island Press, Washington, D. C. (2017). https://ebookcentral.proquest.com/lib/gbv/detail.action?docID=5602382
9. Findeli, A.: Searching for design research questions: Some conceptual clarifications. In: Chow, R.W.Y., Jonas, W., Joost, G. (eds.) Design Research Network, pp. 278–293. A DRNetwork publication, iUniverse Inc. (2010)
10. Flanagan, M.: Critical Play: Radical Game Design. MIT Press, Cambridge (2009)
11. Gareth, T., Hayfield, N., Clarke, V., Braun, V.: Thematic analysis. In: Willig, C., Stainton Rogers, W. (eds.) The SAGE Handbook of Qualitative Research in Psychology, pp. 17–37. Sage Publications, London and Thousand Oaks (2017)
12. Glăveanu, V.P.: Perspectival collective futures: creativity and imagination in society. In: de Saint-Laurent, C., Obradović, S., Carriere, K.R. (eds.) Imagining Collective Futures, pp. 83–105. Springer eBook Collection Behavioral Science and Psychology, Palgrave Macmillan, Cham (2018). https://doi.org/10.1007/978-3-319-76051-3_5
13. Hoggan, C., Hoggan-Kloubert, T., Owen, R.: Living democracy: social structures that promote civic learning. Adult Learn. **34**(3), 168–180 (2023). https://doi.org/10.1177/10451595221149765
14. Kafai, Y.B., Burke, Q.: Constructionist gaming: understanding the benefits of making games for learning. Educ. Psychol. **50**(4), 313–334 (2015). https://doi.org/10.1080/00461520.2015.1124022
15. Klamer, R., Markham, B.: The game of life. Boardgame (1977)
16. Kobbert, M.J.: Junior labyrinth. Boardgame (1995)

17. Miller, R.: Sensing and making-sense of futures literacy: towards a futures literacy framework (FLF). In: Miller, R. (ed.) Transforming the Future, pp. 15–50. Routledge Taylor & Francis Group and UNESCO, London and Paris (2018)
18. Papert, S., Franz, G.: Computer as material: messing about with time. Teach. Coll. Rec. **89**(3), 408–417 (1998)
19. Papert, S., Harel, I. (eds.): Constructionism: Research Reports and Essays, 1985–1990. Ablex Publ. Corp, Norwood, NJ (1991)
20. Ratto, M.: Critical making: conceptual and material studies in technology and social life. Inf. Soc. **27**(4), 252–260 (2011). https://doi.org/10.1080/01972243.2011.583819
21. Robertson, T., Simonsen, J.: Participatory design: an introduction. In: Simonsen, J., Robertson, T. (eds.) Routledge International Handbook of Participatory Design, pp. 1–18. Routledge, London and New York (2012)
22. Rogerson, M.J., Gibbs, M., Smith, W.: "i love all the bits": the materiality of boardgames. In: Proceedings of the 2016 CHI Conference on Human Factors in Computing Systems. CHI '16, pp. 3956–3969. Association for Computing Machinery, New York, NY, USA (2016). https://doi.org/10.1145/2858036.2858433
23. Sousa, C., Neves, P., Luz, F.: Barriers and hindrances to the effective use of games in education: systematic literature review and intervention strategies. In: European Conference on Games Based Learning, vol. 17, no. 1, pp. 611–620 (2023). https://doi.org/10.34190/ecgbl.17.1.1472
24. Srinivasa, K.G., Kurni, M., Saritha, K.: Embodied learning. In: Srinivasa, K.G., Kurni, M., Saritha, K. (eds.) Learning, Teaching, and Assessment Methods for Contemporary Learners, pp. 177–200. Springer Texts in Education, Springer, Singapore (2022). https://doi.org/10.1007/978-981-19-6734-4_8
25. Stoddard, J., et al.: Designing epistemic games for informed civic learning. Int. Soc. Learn. Sci. (2022). https://doi.org/10.22318/cscl2022.379, https://repository.isls.org/handle/1/8313
26. Sullivan, A., Salter, A., Smith, G.: Games crafters play. In: Dahlskog, S., et al. (eds.) Proceedings of the 13th International Conference on the Foundations of Digital Games, pp. 1–9. ACM Other conferences, ACM, New York, NY (2018). https://doi.org/10.1145/3235765.3235802
27. Thiel, S.K., Lyle, P.: Malleable games - a literature review on communities of game modders. In: Tellioglu, H., Teli, M., Nathan, L. (eds.) Proceedings of the 9th International Conference on Communities and Technologies - Transforming Communities, pp. 198–209. ACM, New York, NY, USA (2019). https://doi.org/10.1145/3328320.3328393

Envisioning Futures Through play – Embodiment Techniques for Futures Thinking in Business Contexts

Pelin Celik(✉) and Jana Picciani

Hochschule für Technik und Wirtschaft Berlin, Berlin, Germany
{pelin.celik,jana.picciani}@htw-berlin.de

Abstract. In the context of rapid technological and social changes futures thinking is essential for leadership and organizations to navigate uncertainties. Traditional methods might lack engagement and creativity in business contexts. This paper explores how play and embodiment techniques, such as Social Dreaming and the Polak Game, can enhance leadership skills in futures thinking. Utilizing Future Labs in collaboration with two Berlin based global industry partners, the research project demonstrates that integrating playful and embodied approaches fosters cognitive flexibility and emotional engagement with potential futures. The findings underscore the importance of these techniques in breaking traditional thought patterns, enhancing collaborative problem-solving and cultivating new perspectives for effective leadership in complex environments.

Keywords: Futures Thinking · Embodiment · Play · Futures Anticipation · Leadership Development

1 Introduction

In a world characterized by rapid technological progress and ever-evolving social dynamics, the ability to envision and prepare for diverse future scenarios is increasingly critical. Traditional methods in workshops for futures thinking such as backcasting, roadmaps or scenario planning might fail to engage participants and lack the creative embodiment needed to address complex and multifaceted challenges.

Embodiment, a concept grounded in cognitive science and philosophy, posits that cognitive processes are mainly influenced by physical interactions with the world. Thinkers like Dourish [1] have argued that our bodily experiences shape our understanding and perception of the world. In futures thinking, embodying potential scenarios through physical enactment and sensory engagement provides a more tangible and intuitive grasp of futures possibilities [2]. This approach goes beyond abstract theorizing, fostering empathy, emotional connection and a nuanced understanding of futures outcomes [3].

A. Schönbohm et al. (Eds.): GALA 2024, LNCS 15348, pp. 265–274, 2025.
https://doi.org/10.1007/978-3-031-78269-5_25

Play, on the other hand is deeply rooted in the human creativity and cultural development. The central role of play is fostering innovation and learning [4]. In the context of futures thinking, play facilitates a dynamic exploration of scenarios in a low-risk environment, encouraging creativity and adaptive thinking [5; 2]. Serious games, which are designed with specific educational or problem-solving objectives, harness the engaging and experimental nature of play. These games simulate real-world systems and challenges, allowing players to experiment with different strategies and observe the consequences of their actions in a tangible, interactive setting [6, 7].

The integration of embodiment and play in serious games offers an interesting way for enhancing futures thinking. By creating interactive environments where players can engage physically and emotionally with simulated future scenarios, serious games make abstract concepts tangible and relatable [8]. These embodied interactions foster a deeper, more intuitive understanding of complex future scenarios [9].

This paper seeks to explore the question how the integration of play and embodiment in serious games can transform futures thinking, making it more tangible in business contexts, allowing participants to engage with scenarios in a hands-on, experiential way. By grounding future scenarios in physical experience and playful exploration, a deeper understanding of potential outcomes can be developed, as well better preparation of management and organizations to navigate the uncertainties of the futures [7]. Therefore, the authors delved into the potentials of embodiment and play within the context of serious games in leadership development during the research project "Re:play", proposing that these innovative approaches might enhance futures thinking in business contexts. The research project took place at the University of Applied Sciences HTW Berlin and the University of Applied Sciences HWR Berlin in cooperation with two global industrial partners situated in Berlin.

2 Theoretical Framework

2.1 Future Labs for Futures Thinking

Future Labs are an innovative workshop framing designed to enhance participants' capacity to anticipate and navigate future challenges. These labs offer experimental environments where individuals and organizations can explore and co-create future scenarios with futures thinking [3].

Futures thinking emphasizes the open-ended exploration of a wide range of possible scenarios - the possible, probable and preferable futures [10]. This approach is less concerned with predicting specific outcomes and more focused on exploring uncertainties and imagining alternative futures [8]. By embracing the unknown and encouraging creative exploration, futures thinking helps businesses and organizations in Future Labs to be prepared for uncertainties and adapt to change by fostering a culture of innovation and flexibility [11].

2.2 Futures Thinking in the Concept of Play and Embodiment

A fundamental component of futures thinking is play, which allows individuals to explore ideas and scenarios in a risk-free environment. However, this exploration is closely tied to psychological safety, which enables innovation and creativity by fostering an environment where individuals feel safe to take risks [12]. In corporate settings, psychological safety has been shown to be essential not only for futures thinking, but also for successful strategy design and execution, organizational culture, employee engagement and overall well-being [12].

Play facilitates as well cognitive flexibility by enabling individuals to think divergently and consider multiple perspectives [13]. This cognitive flexibility is crucial for imagining a wide range of future possibilities and breaking away from existing cognitive biases. Play as such is one of the drivers of cultural development and creativity, as it allows individuals to experiment with new [4]. In the context of futures thinking, play provides a safe space for individuals to test different scenarios and explore the potential implications of their actions [11]. In a playful environment, individuals are more likely to share ideas, build on each other's contributions and create more robust and resilient scenarios to address complex challenges [14].

Building on the concept of play, another crucial aspect of futures thinking is embodiment, which involves physical and emotional engagement with future scenarios. Embodiment makes abstract concepts more tangible and enhances emotional connections to potential future outcomes [15]. In futures thinking, embodiment techniques such as role-playing allows participants to step into the shoes of different stakeholders and experience future scenarios from multiple perspectives. This tangible experience leads to a deeper understanding of the challenges and opportunities associated with different futures, as participants connect with the experiences and emotions of others [9].

3 Social Dreaming and Polak Game in Re:Play Future Labs

In order to assess the practical impact of playful embodiment techniques for futures thinking in leadership development, a full-day Future Lab with different games was arranged. This initiative included one Future Lab with company 1 from the healthcare sector and another with company 2 from the energy sector, as part of the research project "Re:Play – futures thinking games in leadership development," funded by the Berlin Institute for Applied Research (IFAF). Company 1 and company 2 were collaborative partners in this project.

The Future Labs served as workshops on futures thinking with interactive play as well as games, where potential futures were explored, and challenges were examined from diverse perspectives. The playful embodied methods and tools used in these labs are grounded in Systems Thinking and Futures Thinking using Inayatullah's Futures Triangle as an overarching methodology consisting of three variables: pull of the future, push of the present, weight of history [16]. The overall contextual framework revolved around envisioning potential futures for addressing internal challenges.

The authors used Social Dreaming, developed by Gordon Lawrence [17], as a technique to tap into the collective unconscious by sharing and interpreting "dreams" within a group setting. Social Dreaming shifts the focus from individual to collective meaning, uncovering hidden assumptions, emotions and insights that influence group dynamics and decision-making. Therefore, Social Dreaming addresses two components of the Futures Triangle: the influence of traditional experiences in the organization ("the weight of the past") and the aspirations for what is to come ("the pull of the future"). Studies have shown that Social Dreaming can enhance creativity, uncover hidden group dynamics and provide deep insights into organizational cultures and challenges [18]. In Futures Thinking and Speculative Design, Social Dreaming is utilized as a method for innovative exploration and discourse [19].

The authors utilized Social Dreaming in two Future Lab workshops with the companies, combining it with the Iceberg/Haptical Recording Model [20] to collectively envision a shared 'dream' for the actual entrepreneurial problem with the leaders. Methods like the Iceberg or Causal Layered Analysis enable a deeper understanding of underlying issues and the development of more comprehensive solutions in futures thinking [21].

Initially, each participant had to individually 'dream' a dream (Fig. 1). The participants sat in a circle of chairs with their backs turned to each other. First, they had to present their own dreams with their backs still turned to each other. Then, the participants could turn around, combine or group the individual dreams they had previously written down and presented and connect them to the dreams of others to eventually build a shared dream as a narrative of the organization's future.

Fig. 1. Participants engaging in Social Dreaming (l.) and the Polak Game (r.).

The arrangement of participants with their backs turned to each other created a physical experience that allowed the participants to dream undisturbed and focused on themselves. The physical arrangement was intentionally done to create a secluded, individual space for each participant while staying in the group. Presenting their dreams without looking at each other and only allowing discussion after they turned around provided a judgement-free environment. This was meant to help participants to freely engage in the activity.

At the beginning of the workshops, the Polak Game [22] invited leaders their futures thinking process. The game poses a meaningful and playful way to cast participants minds forward and focuses according to the Futures Triangle on the aspect of "the push of the present". They were first asked to imagine the next year and their own private future and position themselves accordingly. Next, they were asked to position themselves for the next 25 years and according to their company context. They started by standing in a line and could think and move through the space towards their stance. This two-step procedure was intended to gently transition the participants thought processes from their day-to-day work towards the futures thinking within the Future Labs. Another main aspect was for participants to experience the group constellation and mindsets present – and not present – within the room. Participants were encouraged to observe the room and explain and discuss their final position. The Polak Game invited participants to pay attention to themselves but also to the people around them. It was meant to visualize possible perspectives and help to embody playfully their image of their futures.

4 Observations and Findings Regarding Physical and Emotional Engagement Through Embodiment

4.1 Future Labs Play Group

Ten leaders from higher and middle management of Company 1 and twenty-one from Company 2 participated in the Future Labs following internal invitations and descriptions of the playful workshops. These leaders represented various professional backgrounds and departments within the companies, spanning from engineering, security, human resources, medical to accounting. The group from company 1 consisted of three female and six male leaders, while the company 2 workshop included four female and eighteen male leaders. 22 participants had been with their current company for more than 10 years.

Participant feedback was collected using both semi-structured interviews and questionnaires. The interviews were conducted to explore participants' detailed experiences within the Future Labs, while questionnaires provided quantitative data on their experience. Interviews were audio-recorded, transcribed verbatim and analyzed using qualitative content analysis as outlined by Mayring [23]. This method allowed for the identification of recurring themes and insights into how the serious games impacted participants' experience in futures thinking.

For the quantitative research, questionnaires including the User Experience Questionnaire (UEQ), the Adult Hope Scale and open ended questions were used. However, the data collected in this way is not statistically significant due to the small overall number of participants. Therefore, the main research focus lies within the action research observations and qualitative results from the additionally conducted interviews after each Future Lab.

4.2 Embodiment Aspects Within Social Dreaming

The Social Dreaming experience was set up to take advantage of the benefits that embodiment could evoke for futures thinking. From the questionnaire responses, statements within focus group interviews and projects action research approach, the following instances of embodiment could be observed. Leaders enjoyed the mix of solitary and group experience of Social Dreaming. They appreciated the way the play was executed and made them feel. One participant describes it this way:

"For example, I thought […] it was really good when we were sitting over there and now the 'future world', what was that, 2035, I think, right? That was also very well facilitated. We then somehow… everyone wrote down their own thing, which was also very, very well done. First sitting with your back and generate your own ideas. Then we discussed it together and then we said, well, we can really get there".

Being able to reflect on their own thoughts, sharing and comparing within the group to then come up with a shared dream was reflected to be a positive team experience. They liked the task of having to "come to an agreement within a relatively big group and then make it very specific." They stated that "it was challenging" and "it was very interesting what came out of it". It was a "positive" experience "that everything was going in one direction. [...] Everyone had a little bit of a different focus. But I think basically we all think the same way."

Three leaders appreciated the way the setup of the play promoted "relaxation", "dreaming" and being "allowed to think about their own ideal world" which would lead to a better understanding of their expectations of the future and how to get there:

"I liked the play, even if it was a bit tricky, because it forced us, every personality that was represented in the room, to just think big. And to move out of the small-small, so to speak, and simply paint an ideal picture of an ideal world. And [...] it was supposed to be a dream. And knowing that in the best-case scenario you'll probably end up here somewhere or something like that, that's totally fine. But if I do not put the North Star there, then I always start to act in the smallest possible way".

As described in this statement, coming from a very output-driven culture, one female participant from company 2 could engage with future scenarios and even draw parallels to known concepts like having a "North Star". The opportunity to "think big" and incorporating their personal perspective was mentioned as a major opportunity and a potential to actually take action towards change in their companies by another female participant in company 1:

"The fact that you really say, okay, I'm creating a positive vision, where could it go and just imagine that. I think it's a really great opportunity to do it in a playful way and for teams".

Within the Social Dreaming in company 1, the group thought about ways to innovate their ways of working. They proceeded to create a scenario imagining what they would want their children to experience if they ever worked for the company. In this instance, participants could mentally step away from their immediate problems and responsibilities and engage with personally meaningful scenarios:

"[...] And also the idea of... imagining to introduce my daughter into this scenario in my mind. What world do I want for her or what surroundings? It's definitely worth thinking about".

The emotional connection with a new perspective on their current situation then influenced the current next steps that were considered. Not only their own needs and wants in the now became relevant but also the way their own children or the next generations, would experience the future world. In that moment, they were aware of their responsibility but also their self-efficacy.

However, not only positive emotions were evoked with the play. At least three players in company 2 found it difficult to remove their thoughts from their current reality in that setting. It was also stated by one leader that thinking about a future that is far away (more than 2 years) was difficult and a hard concept to grasp. Another found the Social Dreaming approach "theoretical" in the sense that it conflicted with their belief that "there is no ideal world". What sense is there to imagine an ideal when this will never become true? This sentiment was prevalent especially within the group from company

2 whose working context was highly KPI driven and intricately outcome focused. One male participant from company 2 was describing that they were focusing almost solely on the required outcome of the play. Being asked to create a common dream within the group and having a time requirement in addition prevented them from freely engaging in the co-creative imagination. They stated feeling "stressed":

"The task was actually almost to find a consensus between ten different statements. So it was actually more: 'How do I find a consensus on any topic with communication'. It was almost just about that, about writing something down that every-one agreed on, detached from the topic [...] the actual stress that was triggered in my head was less about thinking about how the world would get better, but rather: 'How do we fill the card?'". So not only was it difficult to engage in the imagination because of it being "ideal" but also being used to a very outcome-driven approach proved a barrier to the effectiveness of the play to them.

Even though some participants had difficulties to engage with future scenarios within this play, it proved to be a segue for many to emotionally engage with futures thinking.

4.3 Instances of Embodiment Within the Polak Game

With the Polak Game, leaders were able to literally take a stance and position themselves in the now towards the future. The activity of positioning with the future in mind enabled at least three participants to "see, that [they] want to have influence", "opened up" and being able to "beam" themselves "into the future". Just taking a few steps within the room in regard to the future widely opened up thoughts and emotions along the realization what participants actually wanted for themselves.

Taking a stance, being in that room in relation to their coworkers was also a daunting experience to at least two participants in the group from company 2. They felt like they were in a "public viewing" and that the play was "judgmental" in its setup. Even though it was made especially clear that there were no right and wrong answers and the wording for the rules was deliberately chosen to convey that thinking "the world will be worse in the future", as well as "there is not much I can do" were not a negative personal trait, these participants were acutely aware of a mindset that would set them apart in a highly competitive and outcome-oriented culture.

Within the Polak Game, different perspectives, confidence and uneasiness alike could quickly surface, were acknowledged by the group and taken into account for their vision of the future.

5 Discussion

The Social Dreaming and Polak Game, designed to leverage embodiment techniques for futures thinking, provide valuable insights into how these methods can be employed to foster innovative and forward-thinking approaches in leadership. Analyzing the responses and feedback from leaders in the Future Labs reveals a spectrum of experiences and highlights both the strengths and limitations of these plays in various organizational contexts.

Leaders in the Social Dreaming play generally reported a positive experience, noting the benefits of blending solitary reflection with group discussion. This training allowed leaders to explore their own visions of the future in isolation before coming together to synthesize a shared dream. Comments highlighted the effectiveness of generating individual ideas and then discussing them within the group, which resonates with McGonigal's [2] arguments on the potential of games to enhance engagement and problem-solving. This approach was particularly appreciated by those from output-driven cultures, who found the play a refreshing departure from their usual focus on tangible outcomes.

However, not all leaders found the Social Dreaming play equally beneficial. Some struggled to detach from their current realities and engage with future scenarios, particularly when imagining a distant future proved challenging. This was especially apparent among leaders from company 2, whose highly KPI-driven and outcome-focused culture created friction with the idealistic nature of the play. The documented skepticism underscores Inayatullah's [20] emphasis on the need for multi-layered futures thinking to address pragmatic concerns. This highlights the importance of training cognitive flexibility and encouraging leaders to step outside their conventional cognitive frameworks, as suggested by Lawrence's [16] concept of Social Dreaming.

The Polak Game similarly leveraged embodiment techniques by allowing participants to physically position themselves in relation to future scenarios. This method aligns with Johnson's [14] theory of embodied cognition, emphasizing the role of physical experiences in shaping cognitive processes. The physical act of moving within the space prompted reflective thinking and emotional engagement, especially for leaders who felt more connected to the future by externalizing their thoughts and ideas. The Polak Game not only allowed for the exploration of diverse future perspectives but also fostered a shared language among leaders, supporting collaborative efforts [13].

Despite its strengths, the Polak Game also encountered challenges. Some leaders felt uncomfortable in their embodied experience with the public nature of the play and perceived it as judgmental. This discomfort was particularly pronounced among those from company 2, who were sensitive to appearing out of sync with their highly competitive and outcome-focused culture.

The investigation of the role of play and embodiment in futures thinking for leadership provided tangible insights into innovative methods for anticipating and responding to future developments. The results show that using Future Labs that integrate playful and embodied approaches not only promote cognitive flexibility and creativity among leaders but also foster a deeper emotional and physical connection to potential futures in organizations. This is particularly important in a context where traditional, analytical approaches may fall short in addressing the complexity and uncertainty of the future.

6 Conclusion

The experiences from both serious games, Social Dreaming and the Polak Game, in the Future Labs underscore the potential of embodiment techniques to enhance futures thinking in company settings by fostering emotional and cognitive engagement as the literature stated. However, they also highlight the importance of considering organizational cultures and individual perspectives when implementing such plays.

For future iterations, it may be beneficial to adapt the design and facilitation of future-oriented plays to fit the specific cultural and operational contexts of the leaders. This could involve adjusting the level of idealism, providing additional context to the experiences and providing clearer connections to practical outcomes. Facilitators of Future Labs using the Social Dreaming and Polak Game should also address the emotional and cognitive challenges leaders face when engaging with future scenarios, particularly in highly outcome-driven environments. It is important for facilitators to be aware of all emotions emerging within an embodiment instance. At the same time, playful experiences innately provide the required environment to safely address these emotions and guiding participants to understand underlying cognitive models, biases and inner resistances. Gaining these new perspectives will ultimately lead to participants creating new pathways towards a desirable future.

The strategic value of incorporating playful, embodied methodologies into business futures thinking practices is therefore twofold: One part is a deeper understanding of the prevalent cultural and organizational aspects that influence the futures thinking of the leaders within an organization. The second is the opportunity to foster a cultural shift towards innovation and adaption. Creating an environment where creative problem-solving and cognitive flexibility are valued and promoted should ultimately lead to a more effective preparation for any future challenges. In only two Future Labs, a tendentially open and trustful communication could be observed emerging from the playful activities and embodied engagement with the future. However, leaders will need to engage in these types of future thinking activities regularly by training sessions and workshops. Also, incentives and feedback loops can be motivators, while digital tools such as reminders or gamification elements may reinforce ongoing participation.

Future research should explore the scalability of these techniques across various organizational contexts and their long-term impact on leadership effectiveness and resilience, measuring productivity, innovation culture etc. Overall, this study highlights the transformative potential of play and embodiment in fostering a proactive and adaptive mindset among leaders, essential for thriving in the face of future challenges.

Acknowledgments. The Re:Play project was funded by IFAF – Institut für angewandte Forschung Berlin.

Disclosure of Interests. All authors declare that they have no conflicts of interest.

References

1. Dourish, P.: Where the Action is: The Foundations of Embodied Interaction. MIT Press, Cambridge (2001)
2. McGonigal, J.: Reality is Broken: Why Games Make Us Better and How They Can Change the World. Penguin Books, London (2011)
3. Kuzmanovic, M., Gaffney, N.: Enacting futures in postnormal times. Futures **86**, 107–117 (2017)
4. Stenros, J.: Behind games: playful mindsets and transformative practices. In: Walz, S.P., Deterding, S. (eds.) The Gameful World: Approaches, Issues, Applications, pp. 201–222. MIT Press, Cambridge (2014)

5. Dodgson, M., Gann, D.: The Playful Entrepreneur: How to Adapt and Thrive in Uncertain Times. Yale University Press, New Haven (2018)
6. Salen, K., Zimmerman, E.: Rules of Play: Game Design Fundamentals. MIT Press, Cambridge (2004)
7. McGonigal, J.: Imaginable: How to See the Future Coming and Feel Ready for Anything—Even Things That Seem Impossible Today. Penguin Life (2023)
8. McGonigal, J.: SuperBetter: A Revolutionary Approach to Getting Stronger, Happier, Braver and More Resilient. Penguin (2015)
9. Candy, S., Dunagan, J.: Designing an experiential scenario: the people who vanished. Futures **86**, 136–153 (2017)
10. Voros, J.: A generic foresight process framework. Foresight **5**(3), 10–21 (2003)
11. Miller, R.: Futures literacy: a hybrid strategic scenario method. Futures **39**(4), 341–362 (2007)
12. Edmondson, A.C.: The Fearless Organization: Creating Psychological Safety in the Workplace for Learning, Innovation, and Growth. Wiley, Hoboken (2018)
13. Ross, D.: Ambiguity and possibility: cognitive and educational grounds for play. Int. J. Play **2**, 22–31 (2013)
14. Byron, K., Keem, S., Darden, T., Shalley, C., Zhou, J.: Building blocks of idea generation and implementation in teams: a meta-analysis of team design and team creativity and innovation. Person. Psychol. **76** (2022)
15. Johnson, M.: Embodied Mind, Meaning, and Reason: How Our Bodies Give Rise to Understanding. The University of Chicago Press (2017)
16. Inayatullah, S.: The futures triangle: origins and iterations. World Futures Rev. **15**(2–4), 112–121 (2023)
17. Lawrence, W.G.: Introduction to Social Dreaming: Transforming Thinking, 1st edn. Routledge, London (2005)
18. Kets de Vries, M. F.R.: Dream journeys: new territory for executive coaching. IN: INSEAD Working Paper No. 2014/14/EFE (2014)
19. Dunne, A., Raby, F.: Speculative Everything: Design, Fiction, and Social Dreaming. The MIT Press, Cambridge (2013)
20. Celik, P.: Haptic recording experience: the iceberg model as a serious game for decision making in systemic design oriented leadership (SDOL). In: Dondio, P., et al. (eds.) GALA 2023. LNCS, vol. 14475, pp. 332–341. Springer, Heidelberg (2023). https://doi.org/10.1007/978-3-031-49065-1_32
21. Inayatullah, S.: Causal Layered Analysis A Four-Level Approach to Alternative Futures RELEVANCE AND USE IN FORESIGHT. Futuribles (2019)
22. Hayward, P., Candy, S.: The Polak game, or: where do you stand? J. Futures Stud. **22**(2), 5–14 (2017)
23. Mayring, P., Fenzl, T.: Qualitative Inhaltsanalyse. In: Baur, N., Blasius, J. (eds.) Handbuch Methoden der empirischen Sozialforschung. Springer, Wiesbaden (2019)

Learning Participatory Budgeting via Collaborative World-Building: A Case Study of *Empaville*

Richard Gomer(✉), Vanissa Wanick(✉), Lesia Tkacz, Kristina Risley(✉), Paolo Spada, Marco Meloni, and Matt Ryan

University of Southampton, Southampton, UK
{R.C.Gomer,vwv1n12,lesia.tkacz,k.risley,P.Spada,M.Meloni,M.G.Ryan}@soton.ac.uk

Abstract. Serious Games (SGs) can create a platform for democratic participation by allowing players to make decisions in scenarios that simulate real-world systems. Yet, little is known about what players get from such games and how learning takes place, particularly from a collective and structural point of view. This paper summarises and interprets the findings of 4 playtesting sessions of *Empaville*, a hybrid (digital and physical) Participatory Budgeting (PB) Role-Playing Game (RPG) in which players need to play a character, propose projects for a fictional city and vote for them. By utilising the Activity Theory Model of Serious Games (ATMSG) as a method of analysis, we identified that the core PB collaborative actions were empathy, ideation and decision-making, but these depended on each of the player's knowledge. We also identified that operationalising actions removes the learning opportunity (e.g., voting) and that sharing physical props was more engaging than sharing digital photos. World-building collaborative mechanisms that emerged were rooted in the structure of the city and access to services (via a shared map), social class and persuasion, and the players' knowledge of the real-world mechanisms. To conclude, we extend the ATMSG by proposing an analysis of collaboration and cooperation aspects in an SG as opportunities for learning by co-creating worlds.

Keywords: Democracy · Serious Games · Activity Theory · Participatory Budgeting · Civic Participation

1 Introduction

Games can offer scenarios for players to explore decision-making processes [20], such as dealing with futures of scarcity [14] or making policy decisions about food, water and energy [8]. Decisions in the realm of collective decision-making are systematically complex. These layers of complexity vary, from environmental challenges to social-economical values, but also posit new ways to demonstrate participatory democratic processes to citizens, policymakers, and practitioners.

A. Schönbohm et al. (Eds.): GALA 2024, LNCS 15348, pp. 275–284, 2025.
https://doi.org/10.1007/978-3-031-78269-5_26

Participatory democracy is viewed by many as a remedy to problems in democratic engagement and legitimacy, yet it remains a niche practice, with most citizens never being directly involved in decision-making processes, and decisions are typically taken in other ways at both local and national levels.

In this paper, we report on our experiences of designing a game, *Empaville*, that demonstrates one type of participatory democratic process: Participatory Budgeting (PB) via a 'hybrid' (blend of digital and physical game interactions) Role-Playing Game (RPG).

The core research question of this paper is *How might players collaborate and learn through democratic decision-making processes in games?* Using an exploratory approach, we expect to understand how decisions are made and how players navigate from the real world to the game world and learn through role-playing and collaborative world-building.

First, we decompose the game using [5] Activity Theory Model for Serious Games (ATMSG) to identify the actions that take place at different stages of the game. Second, based on observations gathered during play testing, we explore the importance and process of world-building within the game. Finally, we reflect on the activities, tools and actors from the gameplay experience and how the malleability of the gameworld shapes learning opportunities.

2 Related Work

2.1 Democratic Literacy and Civic Participation

Particularly important for legitimate community-based decision-making, participation is a process of iterative renegotiation that provides participants with an understanding of divergent opinions. [16] provides an example through a case study in Western Kenya (Kisumu Project), showing that providing opportunities for people to critically discuss a community project remains a challenge. Other challenges are the inclusion of underrepresented members of society, different actor roles, and ways people can engage and contest ideas in a safe environment.

Games can provide a sense of place, via connections with a location that allows a sense of transcendence from the 'real' location [3]. They provide an opportunity to develop player experiences that feel authentic due to affective connections, rather than being in an 'actual' physical place. Huizinga proposes the *Magic Circle* [11], the feeling of being part of a game world that players have 'entered into' [21]. [6] argues that the Magic Circle mixes rules from both the game world and the ordinary world, and that perhaps the best way to understand how players fluctuate from one another is through frames and keys instead of circles. For example, a fantasy world allows players to switch between common sense knowledge of the world, the rules of the world, and the fantasy world quite rapidly [6]. Keys are the transitional actions and interpretations of each frame. As such, we can argue that games can provide several frames for players to express and contest ideas, particularly around political contexts through multiple worldviews, in which they can use different 'keys'.

Yet, the participatory nature of games makes them an ideal medium for players to explore the process of democratic participation. Stipelman [20] posits that games function as metaphors for politics, in which stakeholders play 'resource management'. And hence we might use similar lenses to explore both games and democracy: game theory, activity theory, or political action. In this paper, we look at a specific case study in which a Serious Game (SG) was designed to raise awareness of Participatory Budgeting (PB) actions.

2.2 Collaborative World-Building

Imagination and world-building walk side-by-side. [12] argue that to be able to change the world, one needs to imagine the world and therefore consider narratives and counternarratives. In the democratic context, world-building can take the form of civic imagination: the possibility to imagine alternatives to current systems in which one is a civic agent [12]. Players and world builders (particularly analogue games, or tabletop RPGs) have different tools to navigate the worlds through safe spaces, active fiction engagement, embodiment, and performative agency [23]. Collaborative worldbuilding can also reflect radical democratic reflections, in which current systems are contested [22]. In games, collaborative world-building can have three aspects that enhance co-creation: player-driven decisions on what exists/does not exist in the game world, the adaptation of the world by the players and moderation by the community on what can be added to the game world [1]. In RPGs, the world provides a space for players to take on particular roles, including the creation of artefacts, timelines, drawing maps, and others [19]. Also in RPGs, it is possible to simulate other realities. Concepts in world-building fluctuate between fictional worlds (alternatives of our worlds and based on fictional storytelling), storyworld (can be fictional or non-fictional), possible worlds (usually grounded on cause-effect logic and social ideologies), virtual worlds (or simulated environments), transmedia storytelling (multiplatform storytelling) and transmedia world/universes (e.g., *Star Wars*) [19].

In RPGs, however, players are also worldbuilders, in which they provide interpretations of their stories (via the agreed characters' lens) and rules emerge from player interactions, not just from the Game/Dungeon Master. RPGs are also a space for performance as they require active participation and (re)interpretation of the character's worldviews. As such, the performative feature of RPGs brings critical perspectives on to which extent it reproduces and criticises the societal power relations that might emerge from the construction of these worlds [10]. This presents an opportunity for players to learn actively through co-creation of these worlds and creative experimentation [18]. This approach also resonates with the principles of social constructionists, which postulate that knowledge and realities are constructed through social interactions and that individuals learn through co-creation [4]. RPGs provide a space for players to explore and enact different roles, creating and interpreting their characters' identities, worldviews and relative power constraints. In this regard, these other realities often serve as psychologically safe [7] microcosms for larger real-world systems, allowing players to reflect, challenge, and reimagine societal norms and structures [9].

This approach resonates with social constructivism, in which learning is contextualised through social interaction [15]. Yet, although creative

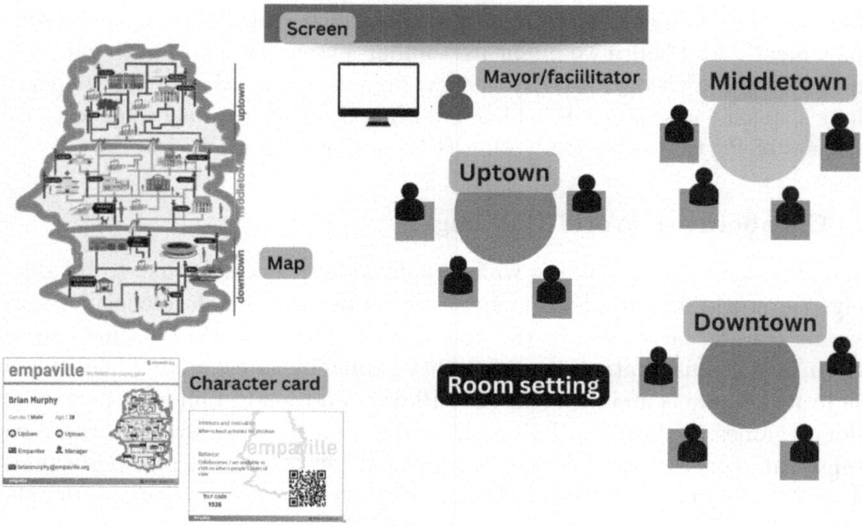

Fig. 1. Game setting, elements and tools

experimentation is facilitated in this context, other elements can be explored, particularly in the SG design setting, which includes reflection and debriefing [17].

3 Case Study: *Empaville* Gameplay

Empaville is a role-playing game (RPG) that simulates a game-like process of Participatory Budgeting (PB) that takes place in the fictional city of *Empaville*. The game is a hybrid form of RPG, that includes the use of printed and digital materials, with an in-person deliberation and digital voting component. The participants play as citizens of Empaville and are assigned to characters randomly. The game usually takes around 90 min and consists of eight steps: **1) Set-up and table division:** players are placed at different tables (each one is part of a city: Uppertown, Middletown, Downtown) in groups of four (see Fig 1); they are given character cards and asked to read these. Each character card has its motivation (which is kept in secret to entice role-playing) and demographic information, gender, name and where they work and live; **2) Presentation and entry:** the Game Master (GM) or instructor/facilitator roleplays as the 'Mayor' to convey game information to the players; **3) Ice-breaking:** players are asked to introduce each other based on their character cards. Here the character's motivation is an important element; **4) Ideation and town-level deliberation:** players are instructed to come up with 2 projects for their town as a 'team'; **5) Campaign and trading:** towns present their proposal to each table. They can use artefacts to convince others to vote for their proposal. Each proposal should be costed between low, medium and high. Players are invited to strike deals and negotiate with the others if they want; **6) Voting phase:** players vote individually using their mobile phones. They can give 2 positive votes and 1 negative vote; **7) Winning ceremony:** the winning team receives funding from the Mayor; **8) End:** exit of the game, analysis of the vote and critical reflections.

4 Research Design

Data collection took place in 2023 via four *Empaville* playtests (see Table 1 for details). During each session, participants (n = 12 per session) were assigned to tables (3 tables with 4 players) and provided with their character cards. They played the game, in the manner described in the gameplay section. Data collected took the form of observations, focus groups, interviews, and audio recordings.

4.1 Activity Theory and Serious Game Design

The Activity Theory-based Model of Serious Games (ATMSG) was developed to analyse the game component not as an isolated tool, but as part of a wider set of actors and motives [5]. By analysing the game as an 'actor' [13], it is possible to unlock networks, relationships, 'scripts' and understandings about what the game is and how it should be played [13].

Table 1. List of playtests, and methods deployed

Playtest Date and Location	Players	Data Collected
17 Feb 2023 (1) University of Southampton, UK	(1)Colleagues and students at our institution; members of the research team	(1) Observations, Surveys
17 July 2023 (2) University of Southampton, UK	(2) Students, members of the public, and elected councillors	(2) Observations, Surveys, Audio Recording, Focus Groups
12 September 2023 (3) Southampton, UK	(3) Attendees of the 4th International Conference on Evolving Cities and Towns; primarily academics	(3) Observations, Surveys, Interviews
30 November 2023 (4) Preston, UK	(4) Attendees at the This is the North Convention 2023	(4) Detailed Observations

5 Analysis and Findings

5.1 ATMSG Analysis

The ATMSG analysis decomposes the game into the goals that players pursue, the actions that they take, and the tools that help them. [5] suggest three primary activities: Gaming, Learning and Instructional. Figure 2 depicts the activity diagram of the stages of Empaville, overlayered by relevant SG components.

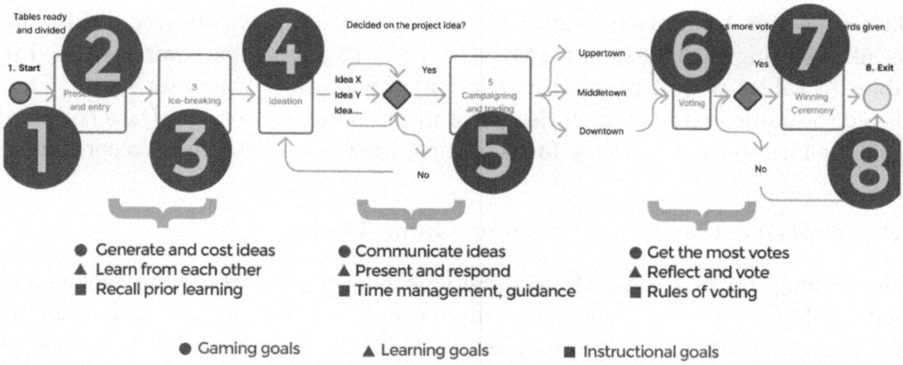

Fig. 2. Game sequence and SG components of Empaville based on ATMSG [5]

Activity: Gaming. The gameplay sessions took place in different contexts (conferences or invited events) and by different players, from academics to members of the community. Actions related to this activity were role-playing and performance, voting, providing ideas, brainstorming (ideation) and deliberation. Elements that supported such activities were the character card and the map. Some players would choose to take advantage of the opportunity to create leaflets or posters with pen and paper during the campaign stage to convince others about their ideas. The gaming tools were time (players had a specific time to finalise each stage), budget, and voting, which took the form of a leaderboard later in the process.

Activity: Learning. We have also observed that simple and actionable activities (e.g., pressing buttons to vote) removed the learning opportunity, as it was automated by the digital component. However, depending on the objective of the gameplay session, instructors could operationalise some elements of the ideation process, by giving pre-imagined ideas, for players to be able to focus on the campaign element, in which they discuss ideas. Elements that supported learning were the learner's previous experiences, as stated by one of the participants: *P1: "I did a climate degree, I like to think I know quite a lot about climate issues. I have also been a councillor, elected in real life, so I know quite a bit about the budget side of things, and what is actually feasible."*

Activity: Instructional. We observed that motivations for instructional activities were based on research outreach and PB advocacy. The subjects involved in this activity were political science researchers and PB advocates. As [5] state, the instructional activity relies on the person(s) 'teaching' via the game (i.e., the 'instructor'). We have observed that their activities were similar to those of a facilitator and Game Master (GM). At the start of each gameplay session, an instructor would roleplay a Mayor willing to get votes and be elected (at times this person would dress up as a Mayor and utilise props). The instructor was also a 'timekeeper' (making sure all tasks were completed by the groups so they could move on to the next stage of the game) and 'helper', in case players needed more clarification. Instructional tools observed were the use of a limited set of choices (voting 2 positives and 1 negative), deadlines, tips/assistance, storytelling and rewarding the winner at the end of the game. The voting mechanism slowed the pace of the game, as players had to go back to their mobile phones and vote individually for the projects they wanted/didn't want and it was not clear if they were voting for themselves or their character. Instructors had to remind players that they should vote according to their character's needs. During the debriefing stage, some players stayed in character, particularly if the ideas were contradictory. We did not observe intrinsic/extrinsic variations of the instructional activity in gameplay.

5.2 Collaborative World-Building

Blurring the Lines Between Real and Game Worlds. During our analysis, we observed that although the learning and the gaming activities are the same, they move between the real and game worlds. Players often relate to real-world experiences when dealing with complex decision-making whilst making proposals. For instance, players mentioned "*It is not it's central London*" or "*If you ever visited Tokyo... there is a lack of green spaces*". A particular group of players seemed to be very concerned about sticking to realistic budgets of what "1 million pounds" (instead of the fictional in-game currency) can buy: "We have to be realistic". Thus, by looking for knowledge references in the real world, players moved from character to their own needs, with the character's needs being forgotten along the game. The limitations of the ideas came across at times, but these were configured by the use of satire, as stated by the conversation:

- *P1: "How much is an average bridge?"*
- *P2: "An average bridge?"*
- *P1: "It also looks like this one doesn't have railings or anything."*
- *P3: "Yeah it doesn't look like a real...quite a risky bridge compared to the other ones."*
- *P4: "That's fine. *inaudible*."*
- *P3: "I mean like, think like how do the people at Downtown visit the hospital? It's a bit *inaudible* isn't it?"*
- *P2: "Oh right."*
- *P4: "We just die."*

- *P3: "Yeah. We just die on the bridge (P1: "I know") when the traffic's bad."*
- *P1: "Or there's like a massive traffic jam *inaudible*"*

Role Playing. Playing the character's motives was not consistent. While some players did not end up paying attention to their character card, other players did refer to their character information. For example, one player mentioned *"It's what Francis wants"*, meaning it was not what the player wanted, but what they imagined their character would want. At the same time, it was possible to see some players reflecting on the character's roles: *P1: "I don't care about trees in Downtown, I don't interact with Downtown *hand emphatically beats sounds against the table surface*, I won't pay my taxes for that."*

Idea Generation. One of the core activities in the game was proposing projects and having ideas. As [2] states, creativity in this setting is about framing the problem and not only trying to solve it. Therefore, most of the time during gameplay, and during the ideation stage, players had to define the problem for their character (and for themselves). For example, a player stated: *"We have one supermarket so we need to get home somehow."*. By looking at the character's needs, they posed a problem for the group to solve together. During this process, different tools were utilised: the character card to check the character's motives, the map and the mobile phone, where one player could submit the project with a corresponding image and text.

6 Discussion

The main ingredients of the collaborative world built around the game of Empaville were social class (embedded, implicitly, in the three areas), inequalities (access to services, structure of the city), and the public realm (parks, bridges, etc.). It was during the collaborative worldbuilding stage and idea generation that we observed the majority of the learning activities. Examples such as the 'bridge exchange', showed problems being defined at the same time as solutions. Thus, the malleability of the game world was well suited to crafting both at the same time; meaning that new problems can be invented to justify engaging solutions. By navigating between real and game worlds, players had to bring together their experiences and learn from each other. This concept aligns with social constructionism and expansive learning [4,5]. However, players made use of humour to discuss problems and build their world around the exaggeration of the problems. As a player mentioned *"I think it would be really cool to have some people who are just complete extremes, one of them who completely wouldn't believe in climate change, and like wants the world to like be polluted or something *laughs*"*. Thus, the exaggeration of the 'reality' and the game world (based on inequalities and social class) allowed players to reflect on their own experiences. The ATMSG allowed us to observe specific activities that relate to SG practices and design but also brought a new perspective that addresses its limitations

([5] mention that ATMSG does not account for social structures that mediate subject and objects). In this case, we propose that collaborative world-building, particularly via humour (as a tool) might enact social structures and allow players to generate ideas that are exaggerated but also allowed according to the budget given. We also noticed that in terms of PB, although the game may be created to simulate this type of decision-making, it does not teach "how much a real bridge will cost", but it provides a platform for participation, empathy (towards characters) and just to be able to 'play democracy'.

7 Conclusion and Future Work

In this paper, we analysed the activities of *Empaville*, a hybrid RPG designed to teach PB concepts. During the analysis, collaborative world-building emerged as a mechanism to facilitate learning, gaming, and instructional activities. We also observed the tools created to facilitate these, such as leaflets, posters, and props created by players. Humour also emerged as a tool utilised by players as a 'key' to move across different frames of the world (real/fictional). At times, the role-playing mechanic was blended between the real/fictional worlds. However, our findings show that the thin layers between the worlds (or frames) were spaces for learning opportunities through idea generation and learning from each other. This aspect opened up a new perspective whilst designing RPGs for serious contexts, as the 'game' of ideation proposed a blend of solution-problem dichotomies. As for learning 'democratic processes', the game provided diverse perspectives and supported agonistic views; however, these were dependant on the player's capability to role-play their character (e.g., some characters were deliberately conspiracy theorists). We also noticed a few limitations in our research, particularly due to the diverse nature of the player's background: 1) players who do not have RPG experience felt reluctant of performing, and 2) players that had previous PB knowledge dominated the discussions. In the future, we expect to explore with more depth character empathy and players' responses towards extremely different values, particularly as a way to unlock potential learning opportunities. We also expect to study more the role that previous knowledge plays in *Empaville* and how to manage power relations, so that all voices are heard and all have an equal opportunity to learn. In order to assess the long-term impact of the proposed learning activities, we also hope to conduct more studies with the same group at different times. We also expect to explore more possibilities for instructional activities, potentially via the use of Generative AI (GAI) and prompt engineering, by providing suggestions or predefined images, in order to concentrate the discussion around deliberation, campaigning, and world-building scenarios.

Acknowledgments. The game was supported by the EMPATIA H2020 and PHOENIX H2020 grants. The last iteration was funded by the DEMOPLAY grant (University of Southampton, 2023). OneSource, a Portuguese company from Coimbra, developed the digital platform.

References

1. Acharya, D., Wardrip-Fruin, N.: Building worlds together: understanding collaborative co-creation of game worlds. In: Proceedings of the 14th International Conference on the Foundations of Digital Games, pp. 1–5 (2019)
2. van Amstel, F.M., Silveira, G., Hartmann, T.: A problem-solving game for collective creativity. In: Annual INSCOPE-Conference, Enschede–Netherlands (2011)
3. Bowman, N.D., Banks, J., Rittenour, C.E.: Country roads through 1s and 0s: sense of place for and recollection of west virginia following long-term engagement with fallout 76 (2020)
4. Burr, V.: Social Constructionism. Routledge (2015)
5. Carvalho, M.B., et al.: An activity theory-based model for serious games analysis and conceptual design. Comput. Educ. **87**, 166–181 (2015)
6. Consalvo, M.: There is no magic circle. Games Culture **4**(4), 408–417 (2009)
7. Edmondson, A., Lei, Z.: Psychological safety: the history, renaissance, and future of an interpersonal construct. Annu. Rev. Organ. Psych. Organ. Behav. **1**, 23–43 (2014)
8. Ghodsvali, M., Dane, G., de Vries, B.: An online serious game for decision-making on food-water-energy nexus policy. Sustain. Urban Areas **87**, 104220 (2022)
9. Hoffman, S.: The practical use of other realities: taking berger and luckmann into the wild. Cult. Sociol. **10**, 109–124 (2016)
10. Hoover, S., Simkins, D.W., Deterding, S., Meldman, D., Brown, A.: Performance studies and role-playing games. In: Role-Playing Game Studies, pp. 213–226. Routledge (2018)
11. Huizinga, J.: Homo Ludens: A Study of the Play Element in Culture. Beacon Press, Boston (1955)
12. Jenkins, H., Peters-Lazaro, G., Shresthova, S.: Popular Culture and the Civic Imagination: Case Studies of Creative Social Change. NYU Press (2020)
13. Jessen, J.D., Jessen, C.: Games as actors. Int. J. Adv. Intell. Syst. **7**(3–4), 412–422 (2014)
14. Kelly, S., Nardi, B.: Playing with sustainability: using video games to simulate futures of scarcity. First Monday **19** (2014)
15. Kim, B.: Social constructivism. Emerg. Perspect. Learn. Teach. Technol. **1**(1), 16 (2001)
16. Kraff, H.: A critical exploration of agonistic participatory design. Des. J. **23**(1), 31–48 (2020)
17. Obikwelu, C., Read, J.C.: The serious game constructivist framework for children's learning. Procedia Comput. Sci. **15**, 32–37 (2012)
18. Rodriguez, H.: The playful and the serious: an approximation to huizinga's homo ludens. Game Stud. **6**(1), 1604–7982 (2006)
19. Schrier, K., Torner, E., Hammer, J.: Worldbuilding in Role-Playing Games. In: Role-Playing Game Studies, pp. 349–363. Routledge (2018)
20. Stipelman, B.: Making democracy fun: how game design can empower citizens and transform politics (2015)
21. Tekinbas, K.S., Zimmerman, E.: Rules of Play: Game Design Fundamentals. MIT press (2003)
22. Tomin, B.: Worlds in the making: world building, hope, and collaborative uncertainty. J. Am. Assoc. Adv. Curriculum Stud. (JAAACS) **14**(1) (2020)
23. Turner, J., Taboada, M.: Story-making: Re-imagining possible futures through collaborative world-building approaches (2021)

Horizon Makers: A Serious Game for Activating Futures Literacy Skills

Avo Schönbohm(✉)

Hochschule für Wirtschaft und Recht Berlin, Berlin, Germany
avo.schoenbohm@hwr-berlin.de

Abstract. Horizon Makers is a serious board game designed to nurture critical Futures Literacy skills such as creative imagination, storytelling, sense-making, critical thinking, and empathy. Drawing from narrative pedagogy and leveraging the Mechanics, Dynamics, Aesthetics (MDA) framework, the game immerses players in four distinct Sci-Fi-based future scenarios. The development followed an action-research methodology, incorporating iterative feedback from playtesting with academic and corporate participants. Results from the Game Experience Questionnaire (GEQ) and the User Experience Questionnaire (UEQ) indicate high levels of engagement, enjoyment, and meaningful learning, with minimal negative emotions. Future plans include expanding the Horizon Makers framework to new scenarios, such as urban development and nanotechnology applications, to enhance educational outcomes further and foster a forward-thinking mindset.

Keywords: Serious Game · Futures Literacy · Game Design · Action Research

1 Introduction

Futures literacy, future skills, and foresight competencies - often referred to as "21st-century skills" have emerged in recent years [1–3] as essential tools to address the future shocks [4] induced by the accelerated rate of change. These include digitalization, AI, job automation, bioengineering, and political instability, all of which challenge our ability to maintain agency [5] in a century marked by dramatic and dramatized changes [6]. In response, we have seen a wave of books and playful approaches to promote hope and hopeful futures [7], graduate programs have been established to teach future skills and tools, fostering the development of professional futurists, while reskilling initiatives have been launched to prepare for the new work of the future [8]. Theoretical considerations on using serious games for training these skills have led to the creation of various serious games and the first reviews on serious game design approaches for future skill training [9]. Horizon Makers is a serious board game designed to nurture essential futures literacy skills such as creative imagination, storytelling, sense-making, critical thinking, and empathy. Drawing from narrative pedagogy [10] and effective game design, the serious game enacts aspects of futures literacy through storytelling [11]. Players learn and actively discuss the interplay between technology and society in a competitive setting. They are encouraged to envision future solutions, highlighting the power of group dialogue in shaping societal viewpoints.

A. Schönbohm et al. (Eds.): GALA 2024, LNCS 15348, pp. 285–294, 2025.
https://doi.org/10.1007/978-3-031-78269-5_27

In 2023 and 2024, Horizon Makers was designed, play-tested, and further enhanced following an action-research methodology with more than 100 participants in academic and corporate settings. We gathered rich and encouraging data through surveys, focus-group interviews, and observations and used triangulation to reach conclusions.

The remainder of this paper is structured as follows: Section 2 discusses Horizon Makers' pedagogical objectives. Section 3 details the key elements of the game design. Section 4 explains the methodology followed, with a discussion of results in Sect. 5. Section 6 concludes critically and offers a research outlook.

2 Learning Objectives of Horizon Makers – Futures Agency!

Various frameworks have emerged to describe future skills, foresight competencies, or future literacy, including endeavors by UNESCO and OECD [12]. However, in a rather elaborate field, the researcher is still confronted with a conundrum of skills and competencies associated with future literacy. To define a limited future literacy skill set for the purpose of our paper, we identify and briefly discuss five "superpowers" that have consistently been part of future skills reviews [12]: Creative imagination, storytelling, collaborative sense-making, critical thinking, and empathy, as illustrated in Fig. 1.

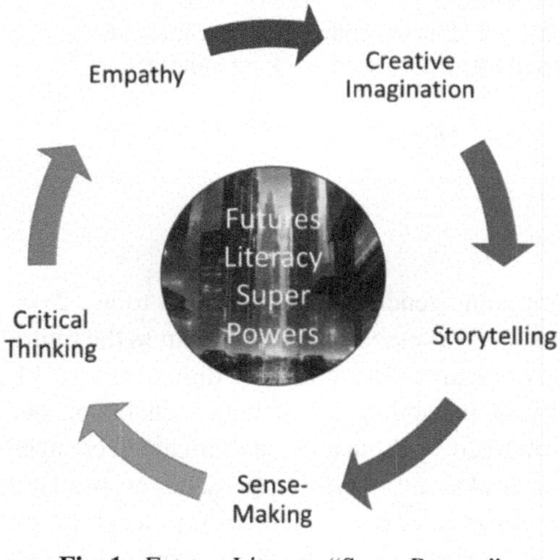

Fig. 1. Futures Literacy "Super Powers"

Future thinking starts with **creative imagination**. This involves going beyond the availability bias or the principle of "minimal departure" [13]. Here, the genre of Science Fiction might serve as a playing and training ground for imaginative thinking [14]. Other authors suggest that **storytelling** skills are a fundamental future skill since "worldmaking" [15] and narrative-based speculative practice have the power to change locked-in futures and related narratives [11]. Interactive and collaborative **sense-making** has also been identified as a crucial future skill. Based on Karl Weick's ideas, sense-making is the process of interpreting and constructing meaning from complex and ambiguous situations through social interaction and reflection [16]. In the context of futures literacy, it involves envisioning and making sense of potential future scenarios to guide present actions and decisions, fostering resilience and adaptability.

Critical thinking is essential for analyzing and evaluating future scenarios, allowing individuals and organizations to question assumptions, consider diverse perspectives, and make informed, strategic decisions [8].

In the context of futures literacy, **empathy** is a crucial skill that enables individuals to understand and anticipate the needs, perspectives, and emotions of others, fostering inclusive and innovative solutions for future challenges [17, 18].

These learning objectives formed the foundational motivation for designing Horizon Makers, ensuring that the game effectively fosters the critical futures literacy skills identified.

3 Horizon Makers – Shaping Futures!

Horizon Makers is a serious board game [19] designed to foster the above-described futures literacy skills, leveraging the MDA (Mechanics, Dynamics, Aesthetics) framework [20] to create an engaging and educational experience. Although it is fundamentally a new game, it borrows the key concept of technology-driven narratives from Future Blocks [21]. A graphic designer was contracted to design a professional look for the game. To evoke unconventional thinking, Horizon Makers is set in four distinct Sci-Fi-based future scenarios: Cyber Punk, Bio Punk, Solar Punk, and Politico Punk. For each scenario, there is a different design (see Fig. 2).

Fig. 2. Horizon Maker Board - Solar Punk

Mechanics: The game accommodates up to six players who navigate these scenarios through a series of challenges and strategic decisions. Each scenario features 30 unique challenge cards that present specific problems to be solved using 50 futuristic technology cards. Players assume various roles—narrators, jurors, and investors—each with 30 juror persona cards defining the judging criteria (see Fig. 3) to activate all their futures skills. An hourglass enforces a one-minute time limit for pitches, promoting quick thinking and creativity. Players rotate roles after each challenge, ensuring diverse experiences and perspectives.

Dynamics: Horizon Makers encourages interactive and collaborative play through narrative battles where narrators develop and pitch creative solutions. Jurors evaluate these pitches based on their persona cards, while investors strategically invest in technologies they believe will win favor with the jurors. These dynamics foster empathy, perspective-taking, and strategic thinking as players must anticipate jurors' preferences and make informed decisions.

Aesthetics: The game aims to create an engaging and thought-provoking experience through its immersive scenarios and creative problem-solving elements. Each Sci-Fi-based future scenario provides a rich thematic backdrop, and the role-playing aspect allows participants to embody different personas, fostering empathy and diverse perspectives. The elements of surprise with challenge and technology cards, combined with strategic investment and judgment, keep the gameplay dynamic and unpredictable. Although players compete to earn the most coins, the game also requires collaboration and mutual reflection, blending competitive and cooperative dynamics.

Fig. 3. Examples of Challenge, Technology and Persona Cards

The gameplay of Horizon Makers begins with the setup, where players choose a future scenario and set up the corresponding board. This involves arranging the challenge, technology, and juror persona cards specific to the selected scenario. Once the setup is complete, the game proceeds to the challenge phase. In this phase, a challenge card is drawn, and two narrators are selected to pitch their solutions to the presented problem. In the investing phase, investors place their bets on the technologies they believe will be favored by the jurors. This adds a strategic layer to the game, as investors must anticipate the jurors' preferences. During the pitching phase, narrators use technology cards to develop innovative solutions, which they pitch within one minute, monitored by an hourglass. This element of time pressure encourages quick thinking and creativity. Following the pitches, the judging phase ensues, where jurors evaluate the solutions based on their persona cards, which are made public to the narrators, ensuring that the evaluation criteria are clear. After each challenge, the game incorporates role rotation, where players rotate their roles clockwise, ensuring everyone experiences different perspectives and responsibilities.

The ultimate game objective of Horizon Makers is to earn gold coins, which are awarded for winning narrative battles, making correct investments, and aligning with the juror personas. The player who accumulates the most gold coins by the end of the game is declared the winner, highlighting the blend of creativity, strategy, and adaptability required to succeed in the game. Horizon Makers is a versatile and dynamic board game designed to nurture essential futures literacy skills such as creative imagination, storytelling, sense-making, critical thinking, and empathy. Through immersive scenarios, role-playing, and strategic thinking, players engage in a competitive yet collaborative environment, fostering critical reflections and innovative solutions for future challenges.

4 Methodology

The development and refinement of Horizon Makers followed a structured action-research methodology, allowing iterative improvement based on thematic feedback and real-world testing [22]. For data generation, we followed a mixed-method approach, including surveys, observations, focus-group interviews, and triangulation of results [23].

Initial Design and Prototyping: The initial prototype of Horizon Makers was created to foster key future literacy skills. Our experiences with the Game Future Blocks and its shortcomings informed this design. The original game design included four distinct future scenarios: Cyber Punk, Bio Punk, Solar Punk, and Politico Punk. Each scenario featured unique challenge cards, while the technology and juror persona cards were consistent across scenarios.

First Round of Testing: The prototype was first tested with four international student groups in 2023 (December 6 and 12) and 2024 (January 9) at the Berlin School of Economics and Law and the Hochschule für Technik und Wirtschaft Berlin. These sessions aimed to gather preliminary feedback. During this phase, multiple playtesting sessions were conducted with diverse student groups, ranging from first-semester Bachelor students to an applied MBA program with highly skilled participants, including two PhDs and professionally experienced students. Overall, approximately 60 students participated in the first round of testing.

Pre- and Post-Game Surveys, including the Game Experience Questionnaire (GEQ) [24] and the User Experience Questionnaire UEQ-S scales [25], were conducted. 48 participants fully completed the surveys. Observations were made to gather practical insights, such as the visibility of text on card fields, and dynamic aspects like balancing the gold coin feedback system and enhancing the roles of jurors and investors. Additionally, post-game interviews were conducted to collect thematic feedback on gameplay, roles, and overall experience. These interviews were recorded and analyzed thematically.

Feedback and Redesign: Based on the feedback from these initial sessions, several vital changes were made to the game. The boards were redesigned to improve thematic coherence and visual appeal, with each scenario having its dedicated board and the challenge card taking center stage (before all different scenarios could be played on one board). Minor changes included color-coding juror decisions in the investment area to facilitate the game flow. The roles of juror and investor were further strengthened to enhance gameplay dynamics and strategic depth. Additional juror persona cards were created to introduce more variety and complexity to the judging process.

Second Round of Testing: A second round was conducted with the redesigned game. This phase involved complete testing as in the first round, with two student groups from the Berlin School of Economics and Law (24 participants, split between MBA and IDB) and two Future Labs within corporate settings (25 participants in total, split between BA and SE groups). Minor changes to the game rules were made based on observations and player feedback during this phase. Feedback was collected on various scales, including engagement, educational value, and overall enjoyment.

Action-Research Approach: Throughout the development process, an action-research approach was employed [26]. Each design, testing, feedback, and redesign cycle allowed for continuous game improvement. Participants were actively involved in providing feedback and suggestions for improvement. The game was also applied in real-world settings (Future Labs) to validate its effectiveness and educational impact. This methodology ensured that Horizon Makers evolved into a robust and engaging tool for fostering Futures Literacy skills tailored to the needs and preferences of its target audience.

5 Results and Discussion

Due to space restraints, we will limit ourselves to presenting the survey results to the results of the second testing round with two corporate groups (BA and SE) and two academic groups (MBA and IDB) and then giving an overview of the observations and interviews. The Game Experience Questionnaire (GEQ) results for Horizon Makers provide a detailed view of players' engagement and overall experience across four distinct groups: Table 1 presents the average scores for various GEQ items, reflecting participants' perceptions of the game. The average enjoyment score ("I thought it was fun") is 3.07, indicating that players generally found the game enjoyable. BA participants reported the highest enjoyment (3.6), followed by MBA (3.4), SE (3.0), and IDB (2.7). The game induced minimal negative emotions, with low scores for "It gave me a bad mood" (0.89) and "I felt annoyed" (0.82). MBA and IDB participants reported slightly lower negative emotions than BA and SE groups. Participants rarely thought about other things during the game, with an average score of 1.07. The IDB group reported the highest distraction (1.4), while MBA participants were the least distracted (0.3). The game was well-received aesthetically, with a high average score of 3.35 for "It was aesthetically pleasing." IDB participants rated this aspect the highest (3.5), followed by BA (3.4), MBA (3.3), and SE (3.2). The game successfully maintained player engagement, with a low average score of 0.77 for "I felt bored." MBA participants reported no boredom (0.0), while IDB scored the highest (0.9). Players felt imaginative (2.78) and capable of exploring things (2.73) during the game. MBA participants felt the most imaginative (3.4) and exploratory (3.1), while SE participants felt the least in both categories (2.5 and 2.7, respectively). The game achieved good concentration levels, with an average score of 2.74 for "I was deeply concentrated in the game." BA and MBA participants reported the highest concentration (3.1), while IDB participants reported the lowest (2.3). Frustration levels were generally low, with an average score of 0.91. MBA participants reported the highest frustration (1.3), while IDB participants reported the lowest (0.5). The Social Presence Module, which measured psychological involvement – empathy, indicated that the game successfully activated empathy, with scores of 2.70 for MBA and 2.1 for IDB. Despite the empathy scores being available only for the academic groups for usability reasons, these results suggest that Horizon Makers effectively fosters empathy among participants.

The GEQ results indicate that Horizon Makers is an engaging and enjoyable game that effectively maintains player focus and minimizes negative emotions. Differences across groups suggest that while MBA participants experienced higher levels of imagination, exploration, and frustration, BA participants found the game most enjoyable and concentrated. Conversely, IDB participants, being the youngest group, experienced higher distraction and slightly more boredom but rated the game highly in terms of aesthetics. These findings highlight the game's ability to cater to diverse audiences, providing a balanced mix of fun, aesthetic appeal, and cognitive engagement. Future iterations could further tailor the experience to different groups' preferences and learning needs, enhancing its educational impact and enjoyment.

Table 1. Selected GEQ results [24] Key: 0 = not at all | 1 = slightly | 2 = moderately | 3 = fairly | 4 = extremely

GEQ #	Question	Horizon Makers				
		Total	BA	SE	MBA	IDB
		n=49	n=8	n=17	n=8	n=16
		Ø age	51	44	32	21
4	I thought it was fun	3.07	3.6	3.0	3.40	2.7
7	It gave me a bad mood	0.89	1.1	1.2	0.60	0.6
8	I thought about other things	1.07	1.1	1.1	0.30	1.4
12	It was aesthetically pleasing	3.35	3.4	3.2	3.30	3.5
16	I felt bored	0.77	0.8	1.0	0.00	0.9
18	I felt imaginative	2.78	2.5	2.7	3.40	2.7
19	I felt that I could explore things	2.73	2.9	2.7	3.10	2.5
22	I felt annoyed	0.82	1.0	0.9	0.50	0.8
28	I was deeply concentrated in the game	2.74	3.1	2.9	3.10	2.2
29	I felt frustrated	0.91	1.3	0.8	1.00	0.8
Social Presence Module						
Psychological Involvement – Empathy		n. a.	n. a.	n. a.	2.70	2.1

Overall, the game, even in its first prototype, received a warm welcome. The students were partly excited about it and impressed by the aesthetics and the gameplay. The user experience was overall very good. Nonetheless, we recognized a difference in reception based on age and academic experience: The young students were enthusiastic but had to "google" many terms and technologies, which enhanced the learning experience but by some means hampered the game flow. It also took the young students longer to get into the flow of the game since the rules were perceived as too complicated. They were also more fixated to their mobile phones. Very few of the younger students were obviously in a state of shame and perceived helplessness in the beginning. However, this became less troubling after a few rounds. Usually, after the second or third round and the change of roles, the game flow emerged. Some participants noted they would need help with the rules and suggested cards in their mother tongue. The participants from company SE especially said that English posed a barrier for many participants. But as one corporate participant noted: "*I liked about Horizon Makers assuming different roles and observing colleagues in these roles, and the creativity required to establish the connection between the problem and the given solution.*" (BA2) This feedback emphasizes the game's ability to foster dynamic role-play and creative problem-solving while activating empathy, which are critical components of futures literacy. We observed several groups that experienced spontaneous LARPing [27], where players fully embodied their personas, the narrators played out certain imagined personas, and even the investors took over the idea of making ethically based investments. Those groups had particular fun and a truly immersive experience. When asked for their favorite roles, the majority of participants stated the narrator role, but we identified players who enjoyed the jury role the most, and some even preferred the investor role, which allowed for a more contemplative part. All said that the role change and perspectives made the game particularly interesting.

Fig. 4. LARP Mode

Regarding the learning goals, participants demonstrated remarkable levels of creativity after a few rounds, and the pitches and storytelling were engaging and self-confident. We observed intense group discussions to collaborate in the sense-making of the scenario, challenge, and solution, especially in the groups that were immersed in full LARP mode (see Fig. 4). Critical thinking was required and trained not only by the jurors but also by the investors since they decided on the persona-integrity of the jurors. Here also, the empathy training was visible: Not only had the participants put themselves into the shoes of the others during one round, but they also changed their roles frequently and thus enhanced their interest in and empathy with the different roles with each additional round.

6 Critical Conclusion and Outlook

Horizon Makers has demonstrated its effectiveness in fostering critical futures literacy skills through an engaging and immersive gameplay experience. The positive feedback from both academic and corporate participants underscores its potential as a valuable educational tool. Players reported high levels of engagement, enjoyment, and meaningful learning, particularly in areas such as creative imagination, storytelling, sense-making, critical thinking, and empathy. The iterative design and action-research methodology allowed for continuous refinement, ensuring the game meets the needs and preferences of diverse player groups. The game experience was generally delightful, and reactions indicated both learning effects and enjoyment.

However, the game primarily serves as an activation tool for future skills rather than a comprehensive educational solution. While Horizon Makers has shown promising results in fostering futures literacy skills, one significant limitation is the lack of objective measures for the skills and learning these skills. We are aware of the criticism of the Game Experience Questionnaire [28] and the potential for deeper quantitative analysis of our results. Another limitation is the absence of a control group, which makes it difficult to isolate the effects of the game from other variables that might influence the outcomes. A more comprehensive experimental setting, including control groups, would provide a clearer understanding of the game's effectiveness in fostering futures literacy skills. A long-term study would be beneficial to determine if participants retain and apply the skills learned during gameplay over an extended period.

We plan to expand the Horizon Makers framework by developing cards in German, creating an ambiance and rules video, and elaborating on new scenarios and games based on the same game mechanics. Upcoming projects include "Berlin City Futures," a game focused on urban development, and "Nano Tech Dreams", which aims to apply and expand players' knowledge of nanotechnology. These new games will continue to leverage the proven mechanics of Horizon Makers, offering diverse and specialized learning experiences tailored to different thematic areas.

Acknowledgement. The development and research of the game were facilitated by the Re: Play Project, funded by the *Institut für angewandte Forschung Berlin (IfaF Berlin)*, reflecting Berlin's dedication to pioneering educational strategies. I thank Dr Maria Saridakis, Jana Picciani, and Jonny-Bix Bongers for their research assistance.

Reference

1. Miller, R.: Learning, the future, and complexity. an essay on the emergence of futures literacy. Eur. J. Educ. **50**(4), 513–523 (2015)
2. Rincón, G.B., Díaz-Domínguez, A.: Assessing futures literacy as an academic competence for the deployment of foresight competencies. Futures **135**, 102872 (2022)
3. Larson, L.C., Miller, T.N.: 21st century skills: prepare students for the future. Kappa Delta Pi Record **47**(3), 121–123 (2011)
4. Toffler, A.: Future Shock. Bantam, New York (1970)
5. Häggström, M., Schmidt, C.: Futures literacy–to belong, participate and act!: an educational perspective. Futures **132**, 102813 (2021)
6. Žižek, S.: Too Late to Awaken: What Lies Ahead when There is No Future? Random House, New York (2023)
7. McGonigal, J.: Imaginable: How to See the Future Coming and be Ready for Anything. Random House, New York (2022)
8. Thornhill-Miller, B., Camarda, A., Mercier, M., Burkhardt, J.M., Morisseau, T., Bourgeois-Bougrine, S., et al.: Creativity, critical thinking, communication, and collaboration: assessment, certification, and promotion of 21st century skills for the future of work and education. J. Intell. **11**, 54 (2023)
9. Gurbuz, S., Celik, M.: Serious games in future skills development. a systematic review of the design approaches. Comput. Appl. Eng. Educ. **30**(5), 1591–1612 (2022)
10. Armstrong, J.P., McCain, K.D.: Narrative pedagogy for leadership education: stories of leadership efficacy, self-identity, and leadership development. J. Leadersh. Stud. **14**(4), 60–70 (2021)
11. Liveley, G., Slocombe, W., Spiers, E.: Futures literacy through narrative. Futures **125**, 102663 (2021)
12. Kotsiou, A., Fajardo-Tovar, D., Cowhitt, T., Major, L., Wegerif, R.: A scoping review of future skills frameworks. Irish Educ. Stud. **41**(1), 171–186 (2022)
13. Ryan, M.: Fiction, non-factuals, and the principle of minimal departure. Poetics **9**(4), 403–422 (1980)
14. Milburn, C.: Modifiable futures: science fiction at the bench. Isis **101**(3), 560–569 (2010)
15. Goodman, N.: Ways of Worldmaking. Hackett Publishing, Indianapolis (1978)
16. Weick, K.: Organized sensemaking: a commentary on processes of interpretive work. Hum. Relat. **65**(1), 141–153 (2012)

17. Pouru-Mikkola, L., Wilenius, M.: Building individual futures capacity through transformative futures learning. Futures **132**, 102804 (2021)
18. Rifkin, J.: The Empathic Civilization: The Race to Global Consciousness in a World in Crisis. Penguin, London (2009)
19. Abt, C.: Serious Games. University Press of America, Lanham (1970)
20. Hunicke, R, LeBlanc, M., Zubek, R.: MDA: A formal approach to game design and game research. In: Proceedings of the AAAI Workshop on Challenges in Game AI, vol. **4**, no. 1, p. 1722 (2004)
21. Schönbohm, A., Walter, J.: Future blocks: sci-fi storytelling as a serious game for leadership development. In: Dondio, P., et al. (eds.) International Conference on Games and Learning Alliance, pp. 396– 401. Springer Nature Switzerland, Cham (2023). https://doi.org/10.1007/978-3-031-49065-1_39
22. Schönbohm, A., Zhang. T.: Evaluating the effectiveness of serious games in facilitating strategic decisions-making under COVID-19 crisis conditions. J. Work Appl. Manag. **14**(2), 257–271 (2022)
23. Ivankova, N., Wingo, N.: Applying mixed methods in action research: methodological potentials and advantages. Am. Behav. Sci. **62**(7), 978–997 (2018)
24. IJsselsteijn. W., de Kort, Y., Poels K.: The game experience questionnaire. eindhoven: technische universiteit eindhoven (2013)
25. Schrepp, M., Hinderks, A., Thomaschewski, J.: Design and evaluation of a short version of the user experience questionnaire (UEQ-S). Int. J. Interact. Multimedia Artif. Intell. **4**(6), 103–108 (2017)
26. Elliot, J.: Action Research for Educational Change. McGraw-Hill Education, London (1991)
27. Bowman, S.: Educational live action role-playing games: a secondary literature review. In: Bowman, S. (Ed.) The Wyrd Con Companion Book 3, pp. 112–131. Wyrd Con, Los Angeles (2014)
28. Law, E. Brühlmann, F., Mekler, E.: Systematic review and validation of the game experience questionnaire (GEQ) - implications for citation and reporting practice. In: Proceedings of the 2018 Annual Symposium on Computer-Human Interaction in Play, pp. 257–270 (2018)

Serious Games for Health and Immersive Learning: E-Health and Pharmacology

Games as a Non-pharmacology Therapy for Chronic Pain – A Mixed Method Pilot Study in Older People

Marlene Rosa[1](✉), Susana Lopes[1,2], Natália Martins[1], and Elena Lacomba-Arnau[3]

[1] ciTechCare - Center for Innovative Care and Health Technology School of Health Sciences (ESSLei), Leiria, Portugal
marlene.rosa@ipleiria.pt
[2] University of Salamanca, Salamanca, Spain
[3] Departament de Psicologia, Sociologia i Treball Social, Universitat de Lleida, Lleida, Spain

Abstract. This pilot study investigates the use of games as a non-pharmacological therapy for chronic pain in older adults. A group of institutionalized older adults experiencing persistent pain, without cognitive impairment, was recruited. Sociodemographic data were collected, and pain intensity was measured using the Visual Analogue Pain Scale (VAS) before and after a 20-min game-based intervention. Post-intervention, participants were interviewed about their personal experiences with the game. The "Tree Game," a giant floorboard game (Agilidades.pt), was selected for its unique properties conducive to this study (e.g., multi-stimuli approach). Significant differences in VAS scores before and after the Tree Game intervention were analyzed using the Wilcoxon test. Qualitative analysis of participants' feedback was also conducted. Results indicated that seventeen participants reported a reduction in pain following the game-based intervention (Group 1). The VAS scores demonstrated significant improvement in pain perception post-intervention (median = 4.50 vs. 3.00; P = 0.005). Six themes emerged from the qualitative analysis, describing the "Tree Game" as a playful and engaging experience that positively influenced pain perception.

Keywords: Non-pharmacological therapy · chronic pain · older adults

1 Introduction

Chronic pain is a common symptom among older adults, whether at home, in hospitalization, or institutionalization, with a substantial impact on their quality of life. It affects about 50% of older people living in the community and about 83% of those institutionalized in nursing homes [1]. Factors that influence pain improvement or worsening have been identified, and medication remains the preferred treatment [2]. More than 58% of institutionalized old people experience chronic pain, and 26.4% have a history of more than ten years. Interestingly, 33.3% of older people adopted medication treatment;

A. Schönbohm et al. (Eds.): GALA 2024, LNCS 15348, pp. 297–306, 2025.
https://doi.org/10.1007/978-3-031-78269-5_28

however, the pain did not improve in 41.7% or worsened in 34.7% of the cases [3]. Therefore, when comparing pain incidence and characteristics between community-dwelling and institutionalized older people, there is a significant trend for the worst scenario in institutionalized people [4].

Older adults are particularly vulnerable to chronic pain's consequences since the deterioration of functional capacity is one of the main symptoms of chronic pain [5]. Pain can limit body movement, contributing to both loss of overall physical and mental performance [5]. The experience of chronic pain can cause not only physical suffering but also emotional and psychosocial reactions. Moderate to severe or chronic pain was independently associated with a high incidence of disability [6, 7].

Non-pharmacological therapy should be an essential component of an overall treatment plan for older people, especially for those with chronic pain [8]. Common non-pharmacological strategies for treating chronic pain include exercise, local application of heat or cold, massage, ultrasound, immobilization, surgery, transcutaneous electrical nerve stimulation, pain management and education, cognitive strategies, and distraction [9, 10]. Many older adults with chronic pain use different non-pharmacological therapeutic strategies on their own before consulting a doctor [11].

According to Marcia et al. (2023), combined education and behavioral change, using coping strategies, are crucial interventions for managing chronic pain and its impact [12]. Behavioral and cognitive interventions help deconstruct negative thought patterns, beliefs, emotional states, and maladaptive behaviors. For the efficient stimulation of coping strategies, Vugts et al. (2020) concluded the positive effect of regular involvement in Serious Games (SGs) [13]. These authors investigated a group of patients with chronic pain or fatigue symptoms that received a short additional blended mindfulness-based serious gaming intervention (four 1-h sessions) during a rehabilitation program, concluding that a serious game can facilitate additional learning about coping, which ultimately reduces the burden of chronic pain. In a review paper on the challenge of virtual gaming technologies, the authors concluded about the successful effect on relief for acute pain and the increasing interest in the study of the effect on chronic pain. Interestingly, while distraction is a powerful tool in the case of both acute and chronic pain, interventions that rely exclusively on distraction are insufficient to address the needs of many individuals with chronic pain [14]. The gaming experience should provide mechanisms of graded-exposure therapy and other contemporary treatment modalities rather than seeking to escape the pain experience altogether. There is a consensus that immersive environments created by SGs decrease the pain experienced by upregulating non-painful neural signalling. This effect can inhibit the pathways that carry pain signals, making pain less noticeable and shifting our focus away from it [15]. This is increasingly important for chronic pain management (pain that persists beyond the time of expected healing), a medical field in which pharmacological approaches can be surprisingly ineffective [15]. Few studies have included non-digital games for pain education, and no studies are using these strategies for chronic pain management. Therefore, more research about the possible effects of analogue games for chronic pain and their impact on older people is necessary. Thus, due to the gap in the research, this article aims to explore the experience of pain in a ludic and interactive context provided by a giant floor analog game.

2 Methodology

One group pre-test and post-test design were used in the present study. Quantitative and qualitative data were collected between July and September of 2023.

2.1 Sample

A group of institutionalized older adults was recruited from the central region of Portugal, considering the following inclusion criteria: (i) 60 years old or older; (ii) no cognitive impairments, confirmed by the Mini-Mental Examination - a score of >24 points is an accepted cutoff value indicating preserved cognition [16]; (iii) no diagnosis of speech or comprehension disorders; and (iv) persistent pain complaints (more than three months); (v) doing/not pharmacological therapies; (vi) tolerant to light/moderate exercise. We excluded participants if they did not agree to participate in this study or were undergoing physiotherapy or other non-pharmacology treatments for pain. This study was approved in February of 2023 by the Polytechnic Institute of Leiria ethics committee with the reference CE-IPLEIRIA-40-2023.

2.2 Procedures

The evaluation was carried out by three investigators (MR, ES, AC) duly trained to implement the evaluation protocol, which took place on two consecutive days. The first day was dedicated to collecting participants' data on their sociodemographic and clinical characteristics. A specific questionnaire was used to evaluate the general properties of pain (4 open questions: history of pain; daily behaviour; attenuation factors; tolerance to exercise) and to decide on the criteria to participate. On the second day, the investigators implemented a game-based intervention, and they evaluated the pre- and post-pain intensity (Fig. 1). After that, a brief interview was conducted to explore the personal experience with the game, lasting about 5–7 min.

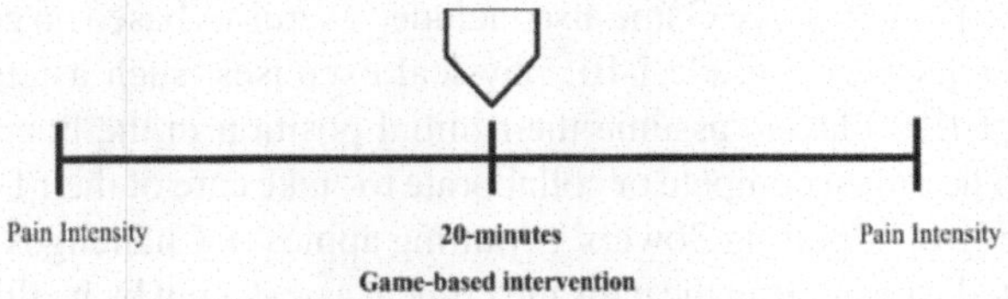

Fig. 1. Procedures for game-based intervention and pre- and post-pain assessment.

2.3 Sociodemographic and Pain Evaluation

The sociodemographic and clinical characterization of the sample was carried out using a questionnaire organized according to the following elements: (i) questions about gender, age, educational qualifications (can read/write, primary education, secondary education, others), retired (yes or no), institutionalized (yes or no), whether they live alone (yes or no); and (ii) open-ended questions related to the presence of comorbidities (disease, disorder, or injury), and if the answer to the previous question was positive, the onset of symptoms (number of days, weeks, months, or years). Pain intensity was assessed using the Visual Analog Pain Scale (VAS). This simple tool is validated for the Portuguese population and consists of a horizontal line (10 cm) with the endpoints "No pain" and "Worst imaginable pain". Participants were asked to make a mark that best represents the level of pain intensity they were experiencing (score 1–3, mild pain; 4–6, moderate pain) [17]. As explained before, the VAS was implemented before and after 20 min of the game-based intervention.

2.4 Evaluation of the Personal Experience with the Game

The interview used in this study was designed by the investigators involved, considering the importance of feeling immersed in the game to achieve results on pain perception. The interview was written and implemented in Portuguese language and translated to English for publication and data analysis. The investigators discussed the importance of asking about three different dimensions of immersive experiences: focus, thinking, and feeling. Consequently, they designed four open-ended questions: (i) "What was the focus of your attention in the last 20 minutes? What did you think about?"; (ii) "During the intervention, did you feel, perceive, or remember something that you want to highlight?"; (iii) "Explain what your main thought on this experience".

2.5 Game-Based Intervention

The game selected for this study was the Three Game (Agilidades, Inc.), a giant board game (250 cm x 250 cm) that transforms the floor into an enriched environment. It was specially designed thinking on major geriatric syndromes in Portugal, specifically for the initial stages of frailty. This game has a highly immersive context, as it allows the inclusion of different stimuli (e.g., physical, speech, and cognitive) into the same action. According to the recommendations of gaming properties for encouraging patients to positively manage pain, the Tree Game also included exercises based on graded-exposure therapy (motor sequences – grade I-III; physical exercises, such as strengthening, or balance – grade I-III). Players assume their initial position in the board game, in two different teams. They must compete or collaborate to "take care of their farm", playing to do the tree growing up ("putting flowers", "putting apples"). Challenges in the game are previously selected, considering the pain and clinical assessment by health professionals. Successful challenges (e.g., motor sequences, physical exercise, etc.) are necessary to complete the tree with a flower or an apple. The winner was the player with a more complete tree, in the available session time (https://agilidades.pt/agilmagazine-abril-junho-2023/). Table 1 explains the design elements of the Tree Game, including the simulation context, feedback elements, body and mind elements included in the game's dynamics, main challenges, and grading exposures principles. Participants were invited to participate in a 20-min game-based intervention using Tree Game.

Table 1. "Tree Game" (AGILIDADES, INC.) and their design elements.

Design elements				
Simulation context	Feedback elements	Body and mind functions	Challenges	Grading exposure
I have a farm to take care of. I need to move around to perform different actions: (1) the tree needs springer flowers (2) the tree needs winter apples 	**The tree must grow up** + number of flowers, + number of apples **Giant Dice** Game is going wrong: your tree will grow towards the opposing player **Game is going well:** If I complete the game-actions and take care of my farm, in this case, my tree **Game is going wrong:** If I don't complete the game-actions; my tree is losing the floors and the apples	Walk Move the trunk (rotate, flex, extend the trunk) Move the upper limbs (up, down, cross the midline) Spin the body Unilateral body support Global coordination Memory Speech Understanding Attention	**Motor sequences** e.g., You must return to the fruit basket taking 2 long steps in between with 3 steps toe to toe **Physical Exercise** e.g., to climb the tree, let's make sure our shoes are clean so we don't slip. To do this, drag one foot backwards on the floor **Cognitive exercises** e.g., repeat the following words alternating the order I am going to say with the opposite order: clock, days, tree! **Speech exercises** e.g., name as many objects as there are in the kitchen	**Grade I** Light exercises without dual task **Grade II** Moderate, easy dual tasks (e.g., speech exercises) **Grade III** Vigorous exercises, demanding dual task (e.g., cognitive exercises)

3 Statistical Analysis

Participants were divided into two main groups: (i) Group 1 - participants who perceived improvements in pain intensity after the intervention program, and (ii) Group 2 - participants who did not perceive any modification in pain perception after game-based intervention. Descriptive statistics (%, frequencies, and means) were applied for the analysis of sociodemographic data. For the analysis of possible differences in pain intensity (VAS scale) before and after game-based intervention, the normal distribution of variables was calculated using the Shapiro-Wilk test ($n < 50$). The normality of the sample was not confirmed ($p < 0.05$). Comparisons were made between the pre- and post-intervention moments using non-parametric statistics (Wilcoxon test, $p < 0.05$). The IBM SPSS statistics version 21.0 was used for this analysis. The brief interviews were fully transcribed and analyzed independently by two researchers (ES and AC) to identify the main topics and subtopics related to the participants' personal experience with the game. After the initial classification, these two researchers scheduled a consensus meeting with a third independent researcher. During this meeting, the main discrepancies were discussed and resolved.

4 Results

From the 39 participants, 7 were excluded from data analysis because they (i) presented an inconsistent pain pattern, which limits the classification of persistent pain ($n = 5$), or (ii) missed at least one evaluation moment ($n = 2$). Therefore, thirty-two elderly individuals participated in this study (2 males; 30 females). Participants had a mean age of 75.50 ± 9.88 years, and more than 50% were living alone. Thirty participants (93.75%) were retired. Twenty-eight (87.5%) participants had health comorbidities. The results regarding pain intensity in the pre-intervention period reveal that moderate pain was the most prevalent in the entire sample group, representing approximately 47.22% ($n = 15$) of the responses. Seventeen participants reported pain improvement after game-based intervention (Group 1). Group 1 has the highest percentage of individuals with moderate pain (52.9%), while Group 2 had the highest rate for the "mild" classification (53.3% of responses). The score on the VAS scale for the global sample ($N = 32$), demonstrates improvements in pain perception post-intervention (Fig. 2) (median pre-intervention = 4.50; IQR = 6 vs. median post-intervention = 3.00; IQR = 5; $P = 0.005$). There are non-significant differences in age (75.88 ± 11.14 vs 75.75 ± 9.37 yrs) and gender (2 male vs 1 male) distribution between groups.

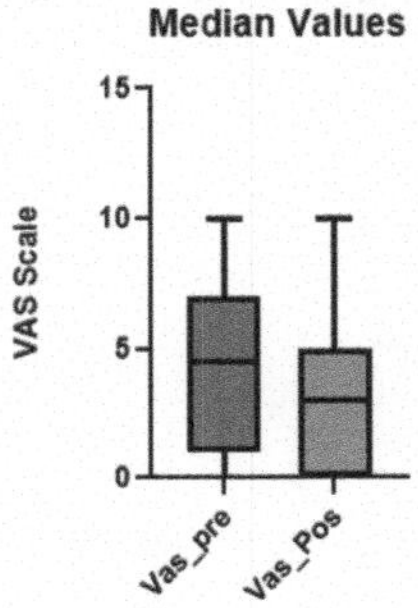

Fig. 2. Median values chart (boxplot comparing pain intensity between groups).

At the end of the study, 18 participants agreed to participate in a brief interview about their experience during the intervention. After the independent analysis of the short interview content, the level of consensus between the two evaluators was 0.728, indicating good reliability between raters. Table 2 presents the thematic analysis of participants' personal experiences.

The predominant topic, reported by 15 participants, was "focus and attention" during game-based intervention. This topic included a variety of experiences. A dichotomy between feeling distracted and simultaneously focused was reported. Some participants described an intense focus on the activity (Participant 1). Participant 4 highlighted the focus on the words he had to say, suggesting a cognitive-linguistic concentration on the activity. Participant 8 mentioned being focused on the cognitive part of the game, indicating active mental involvement. However, there were also reports of distraction and confusion, such as Participant 5, who expressed: "I couldn't think. I was so confused.". Only one participant addressed the perception of cognitive planning during the activity, offering a unique perspective. There were some perspectives suggesting that the activity requires focus, creative thinking, memory, and consolidation of thoughts. Participant 7 discusses the need to plan and think about what to do. The perception of difficulties was discussed by four participants. Participant 1 felt blocked initially, and Participant 5 also described feeling confused. Participant 2 specifically highlighted the difficulty in saying the names, suggesting a challenge in verbal recall. Participant 8 described the experience as an unusual challenge. Eleven participants discussed the activity in terms of "playfulness" and engagement. Their descriptions conveyed a sense of fun and enjoyment. For example, Participant 4 used words like "great," "I enjoyed it a lot," "a good initiative," and "very interesting", indicating a general appreciation for the activity. Three participants commented on perception and control of movement. Participant 2 noted that his actions were "very controlled". Participant 7 discussed the importance of training in lowering/raising the body, a fundamental game element. Participant 3 felt that with more training, he could play better. Eleven participants approached the topic of pain perception. Some of the experiences described suggest that activity may have had a role in pain management. Participant 4, for example, mentions that the movement was exciting and helped "manage the pain". Participant 5 reported that while playing, he felt no pain. However, not everyone has the same experience, as illustrated the Participant 9, who mentioned that the pain continued and limited the movement.

5 Discussion

This study explores the experience of pain in a ludic and interactive context provided by a game-based intervention using a giant floorboard game, Tree Game (Agilidades, Inc.). Seventeen participants (53.13% of individuals) reported pain improvement in intensity after game-based intervention (Group 1). These pilot data encourage further research in this area, including methodologies based on the implementation of analogue game strategies to manage chronic pain in elderly people, since most of the promising studies have used digital game strategies [14]. Implementing digital gaming might be challenging for older people with lower digital literacy [18], and therefore it is important to investigate analogue-game-based protocols, as a valid alternative.

In the present study, Group 2 had the highest rate for the "mild" classification (53.3% of responses), including older people with non-improvement in pain intensity after game-based intervention. In a previous study, Jensen et al. (2017) found that higher pain intensity is associated with greater pain catastrophizing and more significant interference in daily activities [19]. This is a very important conclusion to explain the more positive

Table 2. Analysis of participants' personal experiences playing the Tree Game.

Topic	Example of expression	N[a]
Focus and attention	*"I'm only focused on the game's challenges" (Participant 13)*	15
Cognitive planning	*"…in the words i need to say, things to plan and thinking in what to do …" (Participant 7)*	1
Perceiving difficulties	*"Give us the perception of how we are in special challenges, that we don't face in daily routines" (Participant 8)*	4
Playfulness and engaged experience	*"It's great! I like it very much! It is a good activity, very interesting to us!" (Participant 4)*	11
Perception and Movement control	*"I've performed very perfect movements. I'm very glad about my performance!" (Participant 2)*	3
Pain perception	*"Very good! As while I am playing, I don't feel any pain" (Participant 5)*	11

[a] Number of participants reported topic

interference of the Tree game in Group 1, which had 52.9% of participants with moderate pain and are susceptible to interferences and pain modelling.

The present study demonstrated improvement in pain perception post-intervention, considering the VAS scale results for all participants. Previous research has demonstrated similar results in studies using gaming mechanisms based on passive engagement [20]. Therefore, our results might be innovative because the mechanisms in Tree Game include multidimensional challenges, most of them involving active body movements, providing a new interesting topic for gaming research and pain relief related to physically active gaming mechanisms.

According to Rienzo & Cubillos (2020), collecting self-experience is a key determinant to obtain a real achievement in the game [21]. As already described, the Tree Game in this study was implemented to promote pain relief in older people. Therefore, it is important to analyze if self-experiences with this game reflect an immersive and satisfying experience. The analysis of the personal experiences during the game highlighted the following most representative topics: (i) focus and attention in the game; (ii) a playfulness and engagement experience; and (iii) the game's important role in pain management. Therefore, we can conclude that the self-experiences collected support pain-positive achievements in the game.

The methodology used in this study is appropriate for a pilot investigation, consisting of a quasi-experimental pre- and post-design. However, the positive and interesting results from this study should encourage future related research, and several recommendations should be considered, based on methodological limitations. First, there were pain characteristics that were not considered in this methodology (e.g., localization, exacerbator factors, etc.), which might be limiting the data analysis. In future research, different pain assessment instruments should be selected, including, e.g., catastrophizing measures, comprehensive pain questionnaires and biomarkers (e.g., salivary cortisol or heart rate). Otherwise, the study is focused on measuring the game's immediate effect on pain. Future studies on this topic should explore the long-term effects of game-based interventions in chronic pain, exploring the relationship with other relevant variables (e.g., functionality). The "Tree game" has an interesting design perspective for pain approaches, however, the methodology used was not sufficient to understand how each game element influences pain, for example: does the focus and attention connect to the grade III exposure? The adequate prescription of the Tree game might depend on testing different protocols (changing body and mind functions, challenges, grade of exposure) in future studies on this topic.

In conclusion, analogue game-based interventions potentially reduce pain intensity in older people, especially in those participants with moderate pain intensity. The intervention with the Tree Game demonstrated a very pleasant self-experience, and participants were conscious of the positive effect of pain distraction.

Acknowledgments. This work has been made possible through the financial support of two key scholarships - FI scholarship program of the Agència de Gestió d'Ajuts Universitaris i de Recerca de la Generalitat de Catalunya provided under the code "2023 FI-3 00107"; doctoral research scholarship program of the Foundation for Science and Technology of Portugal, with funding granted under the reference "2023. 02549.BDANA." Thank you Emanuel Silva and Ana Carolina, for their participation in the transcription of the interviews.

Disclosure of Interests. The company "Agilidades" and their consultants were not involved in the analysis or interpretation of the data collected.

References

1. Frondini, C., Lanfranchi, G., Minardi, M., Cucinotta, D.: Affective, behavior and cognitive disorders in the elderly with chronic musculoskeletal pain: the impact on an aging population. Arch. Gerontol. Geriatr. **44**, 167–171 (2007). https://doi.org/10.1016/j.archger.2007.01.024
2. Chan, H.K.I., Chan, C.P.I.: Managing chronic pain in older people. Clin. Med. **22**(4), 292–294 (2022). https://doi.org/10.7861/clinmed.2022-0274
3. Paz, M.G., et al.: Factors associated with quality of life of older adults with chronic pain. Rev. Bras. Enferm. **74**(suppl), 2 (2021). https://doi.org/10.1590/0034-7167-2020-0554
4. Ali, A., et al.: Managing chronic pain in the elderly: an overview of the recent therapeutic advancements. Cureus (2018). https://doi.org/10.7759/cureus.3293
5. Puto, G., Repka, I., Muszalik, M.: Factors correlating with functional capacity in older people with chronic pain. Int. J. Environ. Res. Public Health **20**(3), 2748 (2023). https://doi.org/10.3390/ijerph20032748
6. Makino, K., et al.: Pain characteristics and incidence of functional disability among community-dwelling older adults. PLoS ONE **14**(4), e0215467 (2019). https://doi.org/10.1371/journal.pone.0215467
7. Linton, S.J., Shaw, W.S.: Impact of psychological factors in the experience of pain. Phys. Ther. **91**(5), 700–711 (2011). https://doi.org/10.2522/ptj.20100330
8. Tang, S.K., Tse, M., Leung, F., Fotis, T.: The effectiveness, suitability, and sustainability of non-pharmacological methods of managing pain in community-dwelling older adults: a systematic review. BMC Public Health **19**(1), 1488 (2019). https://doi.org/10.1186/s12889-019-7831-9

9. Fox, L., et al.: Cognitive coping style and the effectiveness of distraction or sensation-focused instructions in chronic pain patients. PLoS ONE **11**(4), e0142285 (2016). https://doi.org/10.1371/journal.pone.0142285
10. Lehmann, J.F., Lateur, B.J.: Ultrasound, shortwave, microwave, laser, superficial heat and cold in the treatment of pain. In: Handbook of Pain Management, Elsevier (2003), pp. 473–483 (2003). https://doi.org/10.1016/B978-0-443-07201-7.50035-7
11. Dagnino, A.P.A., Campos, M.M.: Chronic pain in the elderly: mechanisms and perspectives. Front. Hum. Neurosci. **16** (2022). https://doi.org/10.3389/fnhum.2022.736688
12. Bruce, M., et al.: Understanding the chronic pain journey and coping strategies that patients use to manage their chronic pain: a qualitative, patient-led. Canadian Study. BMJ Open **13**(7), e072048 (2023). https://doi.org/10.1136/bmjopen-2023-072048
13. Vugts, M.A., Zedlitz, A.M., Joosen, M.C., Vrijhoef, H.J.: Serious gaming during multidisciplinary rehabilitation for patients with chronic pain or fatigue symptoms: mixed methods design of a realist process evaluation. J. Med. Internet Res. **22**(3), e14766 (2020). https://doi.org/10.2196/14766
14. Gava, V., Fialho, H.R.F., Calixtre, L.B., Barbosa, G.M., Kamonseki, D.H.: Effects of gaming on pain-related fear, pain catastrophizing, anxiety, and depression in patients with chronic musculoskeletal pain: a systematic review and meta-analysis. Games Health J. **11**(6), 369–384 (2022). https://doi.org/10.1089/g4h.2021.0232
15. Tao, G., Garrett, B., Taverner, T., Cordingley, E., Sun, C.: Immersive virtual reality health games: a narrative review of game design. J. Neuroeng. Rehabil. **18**(1), 31 (2021). https://doi.org/10.1186/s12984-020-00801-3
16. Santana, I., et al.: Mini-mental state examination: screening and diagnosis of cognitive decline, using new normative data. Acta Médica Portuguesa **29**(4), 240–248 (2016). https://doi.org/10.20344/amp.6889
17. Ferreira-Valente, M.A., Pais-Ribeiro, J.L., Jensen, M.P.: Validity of four pain intensity rating scales. Pain **152**(10), 2399–2404 (2011). https://doi.org/10.1016/j.pain.2011.07.005
18. Regalado, F., Ortet, C.P., Costa, L.V., Santos, C., Veloso, A.I.: Assessing older adults' perspectives on digital game-related strategies to foster active and healthy ageing. Media Commun. **11**(3), 88–100 (2023). https://doi.org/10.17645/mac.v11i3.6796
19. Jense, M.P., Tomé-Pires, C., Vega, R., Galán, S., Solé, E., Miró, J.: What determines whether a pain is rated as mild, moderate, or severe? The importance of pain beliefs and pain interference. Clin. J. Pain, **33**(5), 414–421 (2017). https://doi.org/10.1097/AJP.0000000000000429
20. Evans, E., Naugle, K.E., Ovispo, A., Kaleth, A.S., Arnold, B., Naugle, K.M.: Active virtual reality games reduce pain sensitivity in young, healthy adults. Front. Virtual Real. **2** (2021). https://doi.org/10.3389/frvir.2021.772293
21. Rienzo, A., Cubillos, C.: Playability and player experience in digital games for elderly: a systematic literature review. Sensors **20**(14), 3958 (2020). https://doi.org/10.3390/s20143958

Serious Games as Emerging E-Health Interventions: Design of an Exergame for the SMILER Project

Agnese Augello[1(✉)], Giuseppe Caggianese[2], Giuseppe Fulvio Gaglio[3], Luigi Gallo[2,4], Velia Malizia[5], Stefania La Grutta[5], Giancarlo Tancredi[6], Attilio Turchetta[7], Rosa Anna Vacca[8], and Iris Scala[9]

[1] Institute for High Performance Computing and Networking, CNR, Palermo, Italy
agnese.augello@icar.cnr.it
[2] Institute for High Performance Computing and Networking, CNR, Naples, Italy
[3] University of Palermo, Palermo, Italy
[4] Department of Information Science and Technology, Pegaso University, Naples, Italy
[5] Institute of Translational Pharmacology, CNR, Palermo, Italy
[6] Pediatric Department, Sapienza University of Rome, Rome, Italy
[7] Sport Medicine Unit, Bambino Gesù Children's Hospital, Roma, Italy
[8] Institute of Biomembranes Bioenergetics and Molecular Biotechnologies CNR, Bari, Italy
[9] Department of Maternal and Child Health, Federico II University, Napoli, Italy

Abstract. This paper outlines the design and implementation of an exergame developed under the strategic Italian CNR project SMILER (Serious gaMes in chILdren with nEurological or Respiratory disorders). The project aims at investigating how Serious Games (SG) can enhance the health conditions of young people with chronic diseases, specifically targeting two categories: individuals with Down Syndrome and those with Asthma. The SG employs a narrative strategy within an immersive, interactive setup. The child's movements are captured and translated into actions performed by an in-game avatar, who is central to the story. Additionally, a wristband continuously monitors the child's physiological data, ensuring they remain within the aerobic zone. In this document, the game's architectural modules and design decisions are described, along with introducing the experimental plan to explore the game's impact on transcriptome profiling (CTRA) gene patterns and neuropsychological outcomes through an upcoming pilot study.

Keywords: Serious Games · Digital Therapeutics · Running Game · Exergame · Health Intervention · Down syndrome · Asthma

1 Introduction

Serious Games represent an innovative tool for improving various health outcomes, by enhancing knowledge, changing behaviors, and reducing emotional

A. Schönbohm et al. (Eds.): GALA 2024, LNCS 15348, pp. 307–316, 2025.
https://doi.org/10.1007/978-3-031-78269-5_29

problems; their appeal across all ages relies on features such as interactivity, responsive feedback, user control, identity and immersion [15]. It is well known that individuals with chronic diseases, particularly children and adolescents, represent a vulnerable segment of the population. Neurodevelopmental disorders (NDDs) pose significant cognitive, motor, and behavioral challenges that negatively impact quality of life [18]. For instance, individuals with Down Syndrome (DS) often experience chronic immune dysregulation and inflammation, which lead to heightened behavioral and psychological issues such as anxiety and depression [5]. Similarly, Asthma (A) severely affects the quality of life due to its intensity and inadequate symptom control, with children suffering from persistent A being particularly susceptible to psychological problems, even in this case, anxiety and depression. Despite their different origins and manifestations, both DS and A share common features of chronic immune and neurobehavioral disturbances [4,7]. Moreover, children with DS or A may encounter limitations in engaging in physical activity, which is crucial for their growth, health, and well-being [16,17].

Recently, in a narrative review, [14], we discussed the potential of Serious Games as digital-health interventions for managing neurobehavior in NDDs, highlighting improvements in emotional recognition, cognitive abilities, and social skills for conditions such as Autism Spectrum Disorder (ASD), Attention-Deficit Hyperactivity Disorder (ADHD), Down Syndrome (DS), and Fragile X Syndrome (FXS). Among the various Serious Games (SG) developed in this field, have been proposed videogame-based therapeutic tools complementing traditional interventions for children [12], exergames promoting both physical activity and cognitive functioning [1] and improving visual-motor skills [13], and multiplayer games that enhance social interaction and provide positive reinforcement [2]. Additionally, SGs have been proposed as non-pharmacological training therapies for improving emotional awareness and emotion regulation, such as the parent-assisted SG Zirkus Empathico [8]. Systems that combine gamification and virtual reality (VR) have also been developed, such as the one presented in [9], which demonstrates effective support for self-regulation in mindful breathing practices. In chronic diseases such as A, poor access to medical prescriptions poses a significant barrier, particularly for children [10]. Engaging technologies like gamified interventions can play a crucial role in improving health outcomes. For instance, gamified approaches, including humanoid robots and innovative apps, are being used to enhance therapy adherence in children with A [3,6,10]. Social robots have been used in therapies for children with Down Syndrome to improve proprioception, postural balance, and gait, and have also been extensively employed in psychosocial therapies for children with ASD [11].

The SMILER project aims to design, develop, and evaluate an exergame as a digital therapeutic tool to address the common clinical challenges associated with DS and A. Recognizing that patient engagement and the effectiveness of SGs depend on various factors, the game integrates a narrative strategy within an immersive, interactive environment. The child's movements are mirrored by an in-game avatar who has a main role in the storyline, and a wristband continuously monitors physiological data to ensure the child stays within the aerobic zone. The game aims to engage these vulnerable groups in gamified physical activity, with the ultimate goal of examining its effects on both physical and neurobehavioral outcomes. In fact, the objectives of this study, beyond promoting physical activity, will be to investigate the impact of SGs on physical, neurobehavioral and biological patterns through two pilot randomized controlled trials involving adolescents with DS and A, respectively. More specifically, the impact of SG-derived experiences will be directly assessed by both the analysis of the transcriptome profiling of the enrolled children and by positive neurobehavioral changes. The hypothesis to be tested in the coming months is that the use of the SG may positively influence the Conserved Transcriptional Response to Adversity (CTRA) gene pattern, known for its association with increased inflammation related gene expression and decreased Type I interferon responses, which can impair immune function. By modulating CTRA profiles, SGs might positively affect the immune system, the children's health and their general behavior. In the remainder of the document, the game's design and architecture, and the experimental plan aimed at exploring its impact are discussed.

2 The SMILER SG

The game is designed to immerse children in a running adventure where they directly control an avatar with their physical movements. In the game, the child assumes the role of the avatar, navigating through a virtual forest and overcoming obstacles by performing physical movements. The correct execution of movements is demonstrated by a translucent avatar, which also explains how to collect rewards. As shown in Fig. 1, the SG is displayed on a large wall using a 4K ultra-short throw projector, and it is controlled by tracking the child's movements through the Microsoft Azure Kinect sensor, which allows it to operate without the need for physical markers, which could be invasive. The game includes an adaptive module that personalizes the experience by adjusting the game's intensity according to the child's physiological data, by continuously monitoring, through a wristband, the child's heart rate, ensuring that it remains within the aerobic zone, set at 60–80% of the maximum heart rate (to optimize physical exertion). This technological infrastructure will be deployed across two experimental sites-Naples, where the game will be tested with a group of children with DS, and Palermo, where it will be tested with a group of children with A. Each location will be equipped in the next months with a projector, a high-performance graphical workstation, and a Microsoft Azure Kinect sensor for markerless motion tracking.

2.1 Game Design

All project partners were involved throughout the entire game design process, since input and feedback from domain experts in DS and A were essential for developing a game with scenarios, mechanics, and exercises suitable for both

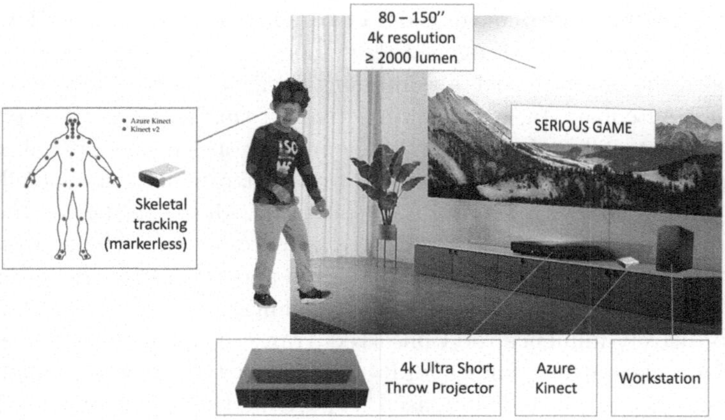

Fig. 1. The figure shows the hardware components and the gaming setup.

groups. A forest environment with clear elements, shapes, and colors was selected as the game setting. The avatar, representing the alter ego of the child, was designed as a teen superhero, allowing customization in gender, hair color and style, and wearable accessories have been defined as rewards during game-play.

Physical Exercises to Control the Avatar. The following four exercises have been defined: Marching in place (see Fig. 2); Squats (see Fig. 3); Lateral bends (see Fig. 4); Jumping in place (see Fig. 5). By setting the repetition and/or combination of the exercises, it will be guaranteed the child will stay in the optimal aerobic zone.

Fig. 2. Example of marching in place to try to reach the ogre.

The game's exercises, as shown in the previous images, were well contextualized into the chosen scenario, defining in this way the mechanics to interact with the game elements. The avatar runs through the forest and overcomes obstacles

Fig. 3. Example of squats to pass under obstacles.

Fig. 4. Example of side bends to open a portal and advance in the game.

according to the child's movements. An example of contextualization is summarized in Table 1.

Modeling of Avatar and Scenario and Game Development. The avatar, designed as a teenage superhero, was developed using Blender. The process included sculpting with detailed brushes for 3D modeling, Vertex Painting for skin and hair texturing, and UV Mapping for the costume. The sculpting mode was used for creating the avatar's complex shapes, with separate modeling of body parts like the head, arms, trunk, and legs to ensure proper animation without unrealistic deformations. Textures and materials were applied to enhance realism. Rigging involved creating an armature with Blender's rigify add-on for animation, while facial animations were achieved through Shape Keys, allowing different positions of the face's vertices to be memorized for varied expressions. Customization features allow players to personalize the avatar's appearance and accessories, such as gloves, boots, belts, hair color, hairstyle, and suit color, introduced as game rewards. Both male and female versions were created to allow users to customize their character according to their preferences. Figure 6 depicts two examples of avatar customization.

Fig. 5. Example of jumping in place to overcome barriers.

Table 1. Movements and scenarios description

Movement	Scenario	Description
Marching in place	Chasing the antagonist	The player marches in place, lifting their knees moderately (running avatar).
Squat	Overcoming a high frontal obstacle	The player performs squats to help the hero pass under obstacles (running avatar).
Lateral bends	Moving an obstacle to clear a passage	The run is interrupted by an obstacle. The player performs a series of lateral torso bends to enable the hero to remove the obstacle and clear the passage. The player's lateral bends allow the hero to lift the rock blocking the passage by pulling a rope (avatar not running).
Jumping in place	Overcoming a low frontal obstacle	When encountering a low frontal obstacle, the player jumps to help the hero overcome it, possibly collecting coins along the jump path (running avatar).

The virtual forest scenario was created in the Unity game engine using free assets. Developing the game in Unity allowed for rapid prototyping and seamless integration with the SMILER technology. The SG is customizable to meet user needs, with doctors who can configure a personalized exercise sequence for each participant. As previously mentioned, the avatar's speed is continuously adjusted by an adaptive module to ensure the user's physical activity remains within the aerobic range. A physical exercise tracking module utilizes the Microsoft Azure Kinect SDK to interpret movements and poses, collecting 36 joint positions to recognize exercise execution and adjust the avatar's behavior. Additionally, a heartbeat detection module employs a purpose-built smartwatch app for the Samsung Galaxy Watch 3 device and an HTTP server to transmit heart rate data to the game, providing real-time updates on the screen.

Fig. 6. Examples of avatar customization

Narrative Engagement and Rewards. To enrich the gaming experience and engage the players, the game incorporates a narrative component. Players are introduced to a forest that has lost its vitality. The avatar explains the situation and informs players that their mission is to restore the forest. The narrative reveals that a villain is responsible for draining the forest's energy, presenting a clear conflict that players must resolve. By performing the exercises, players work towards revitalizing the forest and overcoming the antagonist's impact.

Players earn rewards, represented by three accessories, belt, cloak and shield, which recognize their achievements and enhance their abilities for upcoming challenges. Initially, the character only has the basic accessories (basic belt, no cloak, no shield). Each skill can be acquired up to three times. Accessories can be adorned with symbols representing the acquired skills (for example, resistance, speed, and dexterity). The character can simultaneously wear multiple accessories, each fully or partially decorated.

Motivational messages further engage players, providing encouragement and reinforcing their connection to the story. Figure 7 illustrates the game's interface, featuring the translucent guide avatar, real-time heart rate display, collected rewards and the feedback on the player's movements.

Fig. 7. Game interface with the translucent guide avatar, heart rate, rewards, and movement feedback

2.2 SMILER Project Phases: Current Status and Study Design

At the current stage of the project, we have completed the preliminary design, procurement, and modeling and implementing phases. The implementation achievements include the successful completion and release of the first version of the SG, featuring the adaptive module that adjusts in real-time to the user's physiological data.

The ongoing phase involves a randomized controlled trial aimed at evaluating the impact of the SG. The study will conducted at two centers: CNR-Institute of Translational Pharmacology (IFT), in Palermo (A) and the University Federico II in Naples (DS). Participants are divided into groups to receive either the SG or standard care. Participants will be enrolled as follows:

- **Group A:** Receives the SG (10 participants with A and 10 with DS).
- **Group B:** Receives standard care (10 participants with A and 10 with DS).
- **Group C:** Age-matched peers without any condition (20 participants, 10 from each center).

The SG will be administered twice a week, two hours after lunch, with each session lasting 45 to 60 min. Participants' blood pressure, oxygen saturation and heart rate will be measured before and after each session. Participants will undergo assessments at various intervals, covering several key areas. Behavioral outcomes will be evaluated through measures of irritability, social withdrawal, stereotypic behavior, hyperactivity, and inappropriate speech. The Child Behavior Checklist will help identify problematic behaviors in children. Quality of life will be assessed using the PedsQL Questionnaire, which evaluates health-related quality of life across physical, emotional, social, and school domains. Physical activity levels among participants will be determined using the International Physical Activity Questionnaire. For biological analysis, blood samples will be collected and processed for RNA analysis. The analysis will focus on evaluating the CTRA transcriptome profile. The study protocol has been approved for the Palermo site. For the Naples site, the protocol has been submitted and is currently awaiting approval.

3 Conclusion and Future Works

The game described was developed and implemented as part of the strategic Italian CNR project, SMILER (Serious Games in Children with Neurological or Respiratory Disorders). The objective of this project was to create a SG designed to enhance physical activity and psychosocial well-being in children with DS or A. The SG was specifically designed as a running adventure, where an avatar, acting as the child's alter ego, navigates through a forest and overcomes obstacles through physical exercises. These exercises were carefully designed and contextualized with input from the project's medical partners. The game is projected onto a large wall, and the child interacts with it by mimicking the movements demonstrated by a translucent avatar. The SG has been completed and released. In the coming months, an experimental study will be conducted to assess how the SG might improve health outcomes for the children enrolled in the study.

Author Contributions. All authors contributed to the design of the game. The serious game (SG) was specifically designed by LG, GC, AA, and GFG. LG, who is the project lead for the ICAR-CNR unit, played a crucial role in the overall project definition alongside the other authors not listed in this subset, who are responsible for the health component of the project and defined the experimental scenario. GC contributed to all phases of the project, with a particular focus on design and engineering, game mechanics, implementation, and modeling in Unity. AA primarily contributed to game's design and engineering, focusing particularly on game mechanics, narrative and reward components. GFG contributed to the character modeling and the scenario development in Unity. AA and GC are co-first authors of the article, having contributed equally to its writing.

Acknowledgments. This work is funded by the projects @CNR SMILER: Serious gaMes in chILdren with nEurological or Respiratory disorders and FOE 2020 CLEVERNESS Tecnologie supporto delle fasce più deboli: giovani e anziani SOTTOPROGETTO: TECNOLOGIE EDUCATIVE BASATE SU SERIOUS GAMES.

References

1. Alba-Rueda, A., Moral-Munoz, J.A., De Miguel-Rubio, A., Lucena-Anton, D.: Exergaming for physical therapy in patients with down syndrome: a systematic review and meta-analysis of randomized-controlled trials. Games Health J. **11**(2), 67–78 (2022)
2. Berg, P., Becker, T., Martian, A., Danielle, P.K., Wingen, J.: Motor control outcomes following nintendo wii use by a child with down syndrome. Pediatr. Phys. Ther. **24**(1), 78–84 (2012)
3. Brage, A., Jean-Daubias, S., Loisel, E., Basset, T.: JOE: le robot-compagnon des enfants asthmatiques. In: APIA-Conférence Nationale sur les Applications pratiques de l'Intelligence Artificielle, pp. 115–118 (2018)
4. Hossny, E., Caraballo, L., Casale, T., El-Gamal, Y., Rosenwasser, L.: Severe asthma and quality of life. World Allergy Organ. J. **10**(1), 28 (2017). https://doi.org/10.1186/s40413-017-0159-y
5. Illouz, T., et al.: Immune dysregulation and the increased risk of complications and mortality following respiratory tract infections in adults with down syndrome. Front. Immunol. **12** (2021). https://doi.org/10.3389/fimmu.2021.621440
6. Ishiguro, K., Minamino, S., Kawahara, J., Majima, Y.: Development of a robot intervention program in medication instruction at a pharmacy. In: 2018 7th International Congress on Advanced Applied Informatics (IIAI-AAI), pp. 954–955. IEEE (2018)
7. Kharaba, Z., et al.: An assessment of quality of life in patients with asthma through physical, emotional, social, and occupational aspects. a cross-sectional study (2022). https://doi.org/10.3389/fpubh.2022.883784
8. Kirst, S., et al.: Fostering socio-emotional competencies in children on the autism spectrum using a parent-assisted serious game: a multicenter randomized controlled trial. Behav. Res. Ther. **152**, 104068 (2022)
9. Miner, N., et al.: Stairway to heaven: a gamified VR journey for breath awareness. In: Proceedings of the CHI Conference on Human Factors in Computing Systems, pp. 1–19 (2024)

10. Montalbano, L., Augello, A., Pilato, G., La Grutta, S.: A gamified interaction with a humanoid robot to explain therapeutic procedures in pediatric asthma. arXiv preprint arXiv:2306.04422 (2023)
11. Panceri, J.A.C., Freitas, E.V.S., Schreider, S.L., Caldeira, E., Bastos-Filho, T.F.: Proposal of a new socially assistive robot with embedded serious games for therapy with children with autistic spectrum disorder and down syndrome. In: Bastos-Filho, T.F., de Oliveira Caldeira, E.M., Frizera-Neto, A. (eds.) XXVII Brazilian Congress on Biomedical Engineering, pp. 1399–1405. Springer International Publishing, Cham (2022)
12. Peñuelas-Calvo, I., et al.: Video games for the assessment and treatment of attention-deficit/hyperactivity disorder: a systematic review. Eur. Child Adolesc. Psychiatry, 1–16 (2020). https://doi.org/10.1007/s00787-020-01557-w
13. Raygoza-Romero, J., Gonzalez-Hernandez, A., Bermudez, K., Martinez-Garcia, A.I., Caro, K.: Movelearn: an adaptive exergame to support visual-motor skills of children with neurodevelopmental disorders. In: Proceedings of the Conference on Information Technology for Social Good, p. 169–174. GoodIT 2021, Association for Computing Machinery, New York, NY, USA (2021). https://doi.org/10.1145/3462203.3475904
14. Vacca, R.A., et al.: Serious games in the new era of digital-health interventions: a narrative review of their therapeutic applications to manage neurobehavior in neurodevelopmental disorders. Neurosci. Biobehav. Rev. **149**, 105156 (2023)
15. Wang, Y., et al.: Application of serious games in health care: scoping review and bibliometric analysis. Front. Public Health **10**, 896974 (2022)
16. Wentz, E.E., Looper, J., Menear, K.S., Rohadia, D., Shields, N.: Promoting participation in physical activity in children and adolescents with down syndrome. Phys. Therapy **101**(5), pzab032 (2021). https://doi.org/10.1093/ptj/pzab032
17. Williams, B., Powell, A., Hoskins, G., Neville, R.: Exploring and explaining low participation in physical activity among children and young people with asthma: a review. BMC Fam. Pract. **9**(1), 40 (2008). https://doi.org/10.1186/1471-2296-9-40
18. Zavadenko, N.N.: Neurodevelopmental disorders in children: neuroplasticity and the possibilities of nootropic pharmacotherapy. Neurochem. J. **17**(2), 202–210 (2023). https://doi.org/10.1134/S1819712423020228

Escape from PharmaZ: A Game to Boost Pharmacophore Learning Through Immersive Augmented Reality

Iza Marfisi[1(✉)], Hubert Santuz[2], Camille Bisson[3], Marc Baaden[2], Nicolas Férey[4], Antoine Taly[2], and Olivier Delalande[5]

[1] Le Mans Université, LIUM, 72085 Le Mans, France
iza.marfisi@univ-lemans.fr
[2] Laboratoire de Biochimie Théorique, 75005 Paris, France
taly@ibpc.fr
[3] TeachingLab, Université de Rennes, Rennes, France
[4] Laboratoire Interdisciplinaire des Sciences du Numérique, Université Paris-Saclay, CNRS, 91400 Orsay, France
[5] IGDR, Université de Rennes, Rennes, France
olivier.delalande@univ-rennes.fr

Abstract. Pharmacophores are abstract descriptions of the properties of drug-like molecules that are necessary to understand how they interact with their biological target and hence, characterize their medical action. Mastering pharmacophores is essential for pharmaceutical science but this concept is very hard to grasp. This is mainly due to the difficulty of perceiving the three-dimensional aspect of pharmacophore models but also their combinatorial nature. We therefore designed *Escape from PharmaZ*, a hybrid serious game for undergraduate students. It is composed of a collaborative board game and a dedicated Augmented Reality (AR) smartphone application that allows the students to visualize and manipulate 3D molecular structures. The preliminary tests of this game, with 24 volunteers, show that it helps understand the pharmacophore concept, especially for novices in chemistry. The results also show that the game mechanics and the AR rendering help players better understand the nature of pharmacophore features and the importance of their spatial and combinatorial positioning.

Keywords: serious games · molecules · pharmacophores · *in silico* drug design · collaborative games · augmented reality

1 Introduction

According to the International Union of Pure and Applied Chemistry, "a **pharmacophore** is an ensemble of steric and electronic features that are necessary to ensure the optimal supramolecular interactions with a specific biological target to trigger or block its biological response". In other words, pharmacophores play a key role in the discovery of new active molecules for *in silico* drug design and is therefore taught in Pharmacy undergraduate curriculums. Yet, learning pharmacophores is very challenging for students. This is mainly due to two reasons.

A. Schönbohm et al. (Eds.): GALA 2024, LNCS 15348, pp. 317–327, 2025.
https://doi.org/10.1007/978-3-031-78269-5_30

The first is related to the difficulty to **identify the relevant combinations of pharmacophoric features** [1]. The main features are Aromatic, Hydrophobic, Negative Ionizable, Positive Ionizable, Hydrogen Bond Donor and Hydrogen Bond Acceptor, and are usually represented as colored spheres [2]. For example, in Fig. 1, the representation of the F molecule shows that it bears three Hydrophobic features (cyan spheres) and one Hydrogen Bond Acceptor (green sphere).

The second challenge, related to mastering pharmacophores, is to **perceive their spatial dimension** [1]. Molecules are usually represented with schematic formulas (A, B and C in Fig. 1). However, these formulas need to be mentally pictured as 3D models (D, E, F in Fig. 1) to fully understand their molecular structure. Indeed, it is the combination of pharmacophoric features and their 3D position on the molecule that characterize the way this molecule interacts with its biological target, and hence, its action as a drug. For example, G shares the same therapeutic properties as D, because they present the same 3D arrangement of pharmacophoric features, even though they do not have the same formula. On the other hand, the molecules F and E have the same pharmacophoric features (three Hydrophobic features and one Hydrogen Bond Acceptor) but their relative positioning is different and they therefore differ in terms of pharmaceutical action. Visualizing the spatial distribution of pharmacophoric features is therefore particularly important to understand therapeutic equivalences.

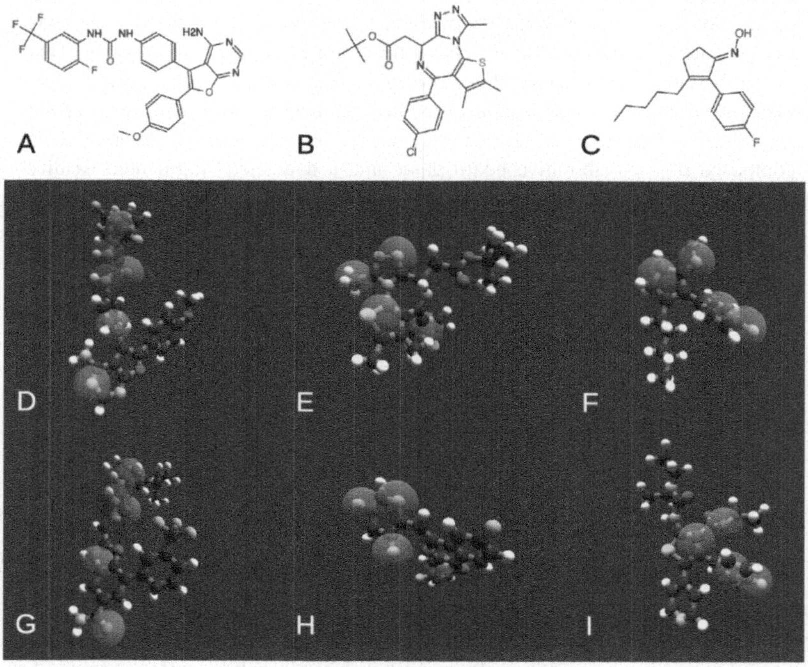

Fig. 1. Molecule formulas (A-C) with their 3D representation (D-F, respectively). Other molecules that share the same pharmacophore model but not the same formula (G-I). Equivalences are shown in columns (D is equivalent to G, E to H and F to I).

In order to make pharmacophores easier to master, we designed a serious game, called *Escape from PharmaZ*. Our objective is to help undergraduate students learn how to identify the pharmacophoric features and practice mentally visualizing them in 3D with the help of a dedicated Augmented Reality (AR) smartphone application. This study aims to address the following key research question:

- RQ1: Can the game help understand the main pharmacophoric features and the fact that they need to be combined in a specific way to build a pharmacophore model?
- RQ2: Does the use of AR help understand the three-dimensional nature of pharmacophores and hence, their possible variability through molecular structures and dynamics?

To this end, the next section begins with a brief review of the current serious games and AR applications to teach molecular concepts. Section 3 presents *Escape from PharmaZ*. Section 4 discusses the preliminary study, the data collection method, the initial results and limitations. Finally, Sect. 5 will conclude our research.

2 State of the Art

The use of **serious games** in education is becoming increasingly widespread, with applications in many fields. Their interest and added value have recently been the subject of a systematic literature review [3]. In the field of human health, many serious games are used for training, for informing the general public about common illnesses, motor rehabilitation, etc. [4]. Chemistry and pharmacology are no exception, and there are many serious games applied to these fields [5, 6]. However, chemistry games are usually focused on combining atoms to create molecules, and rarely on 3D molecular structures themselves. For instance, recent games such as *Molecular Builder Laboratory* [7] and *Elementium* [8] use 2D visualizations. Nevertheless, other recent games address biomolecular interactions with physical or virtual 3D molecular representations: *Pangu* [9], *DocMolecules* that aims at teaching antihistamine drug action [10] and a Virtual Reality simulation dealing with enzyme catalysis [11]. However, to our knowledge, no serious game proposing a three-dimensional approach of the pharmacophore concept has yet been developed, even if the software developed by Frey [12] could be seen as a 2D premise to pharmacophores.

The use of **AR** has proven its effectiveness for STEM learning, particularly in the fields that need 3D representations such as anatomy [13]. Concerning Molecular Science and Chemistry, several research projects have recently shown that the use of 3D digital models that students can explore in AR, is a good way to help them understand complicated concepts [14]. In particular, tools such as the web platform *MoleculARweb* [15] propose AR illustrations of a wide range of chemistry concepts. This platform uses letters or QRCodes as markers for displaying the 3D models.

3 Serious Game Escape from PharmaZ

Escape from PharmaZ is a **collaborative game** for three groups of two players (students). The game also needs a game master, played by the teacher or a student, with the help of an answer booklet. The game is intended to be used during a lab session, with approximately 16 students, followed by a debriefing session.

The game proposes a sci-fi setting in which the players are astronauts that have just crashed on an unknown planet (PharmaZ). Several of the crew members are gravely injured or sick because of the air breach. The players impersonate three healthy crew members (the astronaut pawns) that need to explore the planet to find local plants, animals or minerals that provide the right type of molecules for curing their fellow astronauts. The goal is to find molecules that are equivalent to terrestrial drugs (with an equivalent pharmacophore model). Players need to collaborate to find the appropriate molecules and bring them back to the spaceship, before the sun storms hit the planet in 40 min.

3.1 Game Material

Escape from PharmaZ is a **hybrid game,** composed of a **board game** (Fig. 2) and a dedicated **smartphone application called *Nanoscope*** (Fig. 3). The board game is shown in Fig. 2 (A). It has 12 tiles (B) that represent the land of the planet PharmaZ that needs to be explored. Each team has a pawn (C) that shows the position of their astronaut and a control panel (D), placed in front of them. This control panel helps them remember the right terms for the pharmacophoric features and holds the two goal molecule cards (E) they are looking for.

Fig. 2. Escape From PharmaZ game material

The *Nanoscope* smartphone application is used to show the 3D pharmacophores, in AR. As shown in Fig. 2, the tiles are initially placed with the landscape face up. During the game, the players can turn over the tile, on which their pawn is, to scan the resource face with *Nanoscope* and view the 3D pharmacophore (Fig. 3).

Fig. 3. Nanoscope: dedicated smartphone application that shows the 3D pharmacophore model

3.2 Game Rules

At the beginning of the game, each team (two players per astronaut pawn) gets two goal cards that are placed on the control panel. These cards show the 2D molecular formulas of a terrestrial drug. Their objective is to find the alien molecule that shares an equivalent pharmacophore model. Before the first turn, they are encouraged to identify possible pharmacophoric features and mark them, with translucent tokens, on the goal molecule formulas (Fig. 2, E).

During their turn, players first move their pawn one or two spaces to an adjacent tile. They then turn the tile over, on its resource face, and scan it with *Nanoscope*. The AR technology enables the players to view the 3D pharmacophore model from all angles by simply turning the tile or moving their smartphone like a virtual magnifying glass. As show in the state of the art, this interaction should be very useful to understand the spatial distribution of the pharmacophoric features.

Once they have analyzed the 3D model, the players need to decide if this alien pharmacophore corresponds to one of the terrestrial molecules they are looking for. Remember, these goal molecules are only shown as a 2D molecular formula and the players will therefore have to imagine them in 3D. During this step, verbal exchanges are crucial within the team (Fig. 4). If they decide that it does not correspond to one of their goal molecules, they place the tile back on the board. If they decide that it does correspond, they keep the tile and, during their next turn, must go back to the center of the board, where the spaceship crashed. Indeed, it is the central computer of the spaceship, personified by the game master, which will validate the correspondence with the help of the answer booklet. If the players are right, they validate their goal card. If the players are wrong, the game master can either reveal the exact pharmacophore model of the goal molecule or give them clues, like the number of a specific feature they should be looking for, depending on their level of expertise.

Note that if two or more astronauts are in the spaceship at the same time, they can argue if a proposed molecule is relevant or not and switch to another correspondence with their own goal molecules. The game ends after the 40 min limit or once the players have validated all their goal molecules.

Fig. 4. First test of Escape from PharmaZ

3.3 Important Game Mechanics

The game integrates several game mechanics to reach the target educational goals.

First of all, players are encouraged to **learn and use the appropriate vocabulary to designate pharmacophoric features**. The names of the main features are printed on the control panel (Fig. 2, D) that is in front of them during the entire game. In addition, each team needs to name the right features and represent them with translucent tokens they place on a goal card (Fig. 2, E) at the beginning of the game. Furthermore, each time they turn a tile and discover an alien molecule and its pharmacophore, team members should use the vocabulary again to decide whether the pharmacophore model could correspond to one of their goal molecules.

Secondly, the molecules used in the game were carefully selected to illustrate the fact that several 3D pharmacophore models could correspond to the same molecule. This should **encourage debate among the players and mobilize their knowledge about chemistry**. Furthermore, all the molecules in the game come from real scientific studies that are referenced in the answer booklet in the hopes that the players would want to learn more about them.

Thirdly, *Escape from PharmaZ* **encourages collaboration** between players. Indeed, in the game scenario, the radio system is broken and two teams can only communicate if their pawns are in the spaceship (center of the board) at the same tile. Since the objective of the game is for all the teams to find their goal molecules in less than 40 min, the players need to pay attention to the tiles turned by other teams and, if they believe the tile corresponds to one for their goal cards, they should meet up to discuss further similarities. These verbal exchanges should also help the teacher identify the difficulties students might still have to help them immediately or during the debriefing session. In an advanced version of the game, each crew member has specific skills (*e.g.* move faster, excavate faster) which encourages players to collaborate even more to take advantage of these skills.

Finally, the game is designed so that learners constantly need to compare 3D pharmacophore models to 2D molecular formulas. This should **train them to imagine molecules in 3D** and understand the three-dimensional specificity of pharmacophore models.

3.4 Game Design and Development

The game was designed by one pharmacy teacher and two chemistry experts with the help of one educational engineer, one graphic designer, one developer and two serious game experts who animated a professional training course [16]. The game design also relied on the expertise and experience of previous projects [9, 10].

The game materiel was made in the university fablab. The tiles were produced by laser etching on a cardboard-wood material and the pawns were made with the same technique on translucent plexiglass. Only the tokens were commercially purchased.

The *Nanoscope* application was developed with the *UnityMol* [10] software that displays molecules using *Unity 3D*. This solution allows high performance rendering. *Vuforia* was also used for the image recognition and AR rendering. It offers fast and efficient image recognition and allows to associate any mesh (in our case the 3D molecule computed by *UnityMol* from coordinates in the standard Protein Data Bank format) with any picture. This technology avoids using QRcodes that would have altered the games esthetics and immersion.

4 Preliminary Experiment

4.1 Experimental Protocol

This preliminary experiment aimed at measuring the effectiveness of the game with a selection of volunteers and improving it before use in class planned next year.

Before the players tested the game, they were asked to answer a **questionnaire to determine their profile** (age, degree of expertise in pharmacophores, experience with games and technological devices and ease with tridimensional visualization) and **eight course questions** to measure their knowledge of pharmacophore concepts. These course questions could be answered by "yes", "no" or "I don't know" (examples in Figs. 5 and 6) for a maximum score of 8. After the game session, participants were asked the exact same course questions to measure if they had progressed. The participants also provided **written feedback** after the game, related to the rules, the control panel and AR.

24 subjects participated, in 5 sessions. They were between 15 and 57 years old with 15 males and 9 females. Their profiles varied: 6 university professors and/or researchers, 3 engineers or technicians, 8 master's degree or PhD students and postdoctoral fellows and 7 high-school students. The players' ease with tridimensional visualization of molecules is well distributed and a large majority are novices with pharmacophore concepts. Half of them frequently play board games and more than half are familiar with advanced technologies such as AR.

4.2 Results

A majority of players considered the rules of *Escape from PharmaZ* easy (67%) or very easy (21%) to understand. The duration of a game (40 min) was perceived as just right (71%) or rather short (17%).

Furthermore, all the participants progressed on their knowledge score after the game with a final average score of 4.96/8 points with $p\text{-value} < 0.01$ for high-school students and $p\text{-value} < 0.001$ for the older profiles. More interestingly, while there is a significant difference in the score between novices versus non-novices in chemistry before the game ($p\text{-value} < 0.01$), no significant difference is measured between these populations after the game ($p\text{-value} > 0.05$). This could show that *Escape from PharmaZ* is effective for learning pharmacophore because novices have reached a similar score to experts. In addition, by distinguishing the questions related to concepts that were directly integrated in the game (vocabulary of pharmacophoric features, geometry) from the questions related to concepts less frequently mobilized in the game, the progression is only clear for the first type of questions ($p\text{-value} < 0.001$) while it seems less pronounced for the second type ($p\text{-value} > 0.03$).

This preliminary study also provides some answers for the two research questions. For instance, the study shows a significant improvement of the rate of correct responses for questions related to ***RQ1: Can the game help understand the main pharmacophoric features and the fact that they need to be combined in a specific way to build a pharmacophore model?*** (Fig. 5). In addition, players state that they used the vocabulary on the control panels always (25%) or frequently (54%). This points to the fact that the game helped them mobilize the right terms to describe pharmacophoric features during their verbal exchanges.

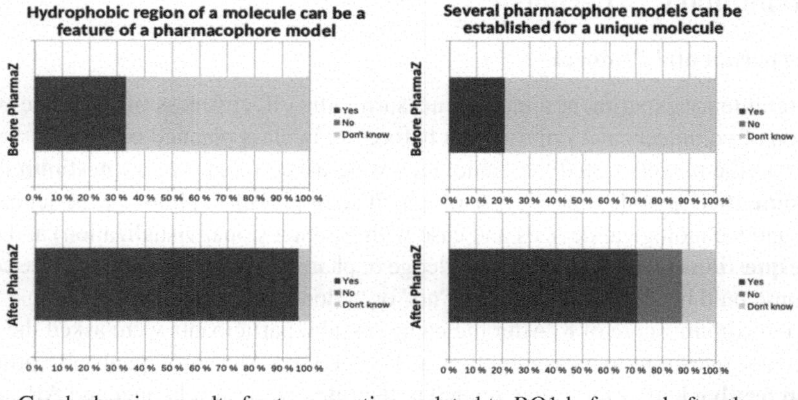

Fig. 5. Graph showing results for two questions related to RQ1 before and after the game. For both questions, the expected response was "yes" (in dark blue).

Concerning ***RQ2: Does the use of AR help understand the three-dimensional nature of pharmacophores and hence, its possible variability through molecular structures and dynamics?,*** this first study shows that 38% of players frequently described relative positions of features with geometric marks and also 38% did it a bit. In addition, the players clearly understood that a pharmacophoric feature can involve a group of atoms (Fig. 6, left). However, the game did not seem to help understand the effect of dynamic geometrical changes of a molecule (Fig. 6, right).

4.3 Limitations and Discussion

This preliminary experiment has several limitations. First of all, 24 participants are hardly enough to determine if the game is effective and to answer the research questions. In addition, classes had already finished at the time of the experiment so the game was tested with volunteers that are not representative of the undergraduate students and the class setting the game will be used in. Nevertheless, this first experiment provided valuable feedback to improve the game. For example, we changes the colors of the spheres representing the pharmacophore features because they were too hard to distinguish and we added a "flip" button to the *Nanoscope* application that allows players to better view the 3D molecule from all sides.

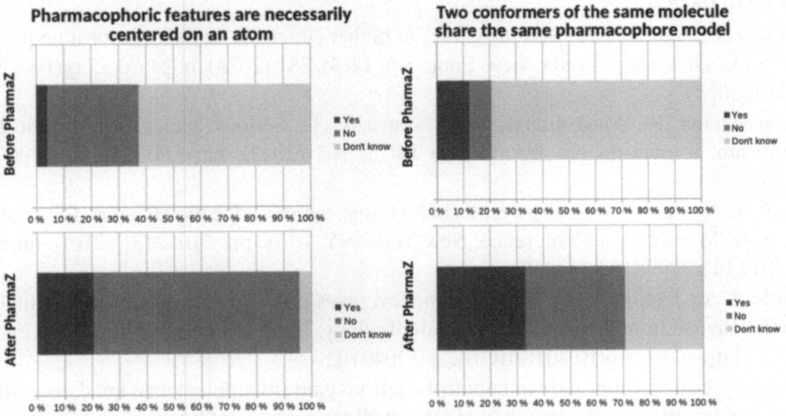

Fig. 6. Graph showing results for two questions related to RQ2 before and after the game. For both questions the expected response was "no" (in red). (Color figure online)

5 Conclusion

We designed *Escape from PharmaZ*, a hybrid serious game to familiarize undergraduate students with the concept of pharmacophores. The game exploits both the advantages of a classic multiplayer board game to provide a collaborative learning context, and the advantages of an Augmented Reality (AR) smartphone application to visualize and manipulate 3D molecules. The preliminary experiment, with 24 volunteers, shows that it helps them practice mentally visualizing 3D molecules to better understand the three-dimensional aspect of pharmacophores and helps them develop knowledge about pharmacophoric features. In particular, the comparison of answers to course questions shows that players, who were initially novice in pharmacophore concepts, could not be distinguished from experts after the game.

Acknowledgements. This project was financed by Université Rennes and the project AIR. It was also supported by the labex DYNAMO (11-LABX-0011) and ANR project PIRATE (ANR-21-CE45-0014). We thank the entire team: Louis Ernenwein (project manager), Ghislain Nouvel (IT development), David Baya (graphic design), Bastien Cravi (UX designer), Julien Lassimonne (educational engineer), Audrey Lachal (educational engineer & game design) and Bertrand Marne (serious game designer). We also thank Florent Barbault for his expertise in pharmacophores, all the early players of the game and Anthony Roussel for the video capture.

References

1. Qing, X., et al.: Pharmacophore modeling: advances, limitations, and current utility in drug discovery. J. Receptor Ligand Channel Res., 81–92 (2014). https://doi.org/10.2147/JRLCR.S46843
2. Kohlbacher, S.M., Langer, T., Seidel, T.: QPHAR: quantitative pharmacophore activity relationship: method and validation. J. Cheminform. **13**, 57 (2021). https://doi.org/10.1186/s13321-021-00537-9
3. Brandl L.C., Schrader A.: Serious games in higher education in the transforming process to education 4.0, systematized review. Educ. Sci. **14**(3), 281 (2024). https://doi.org/10.3390/educsci14030281
4. Damaševičius, R., Maskeliūnas, R., Blažauskas, T.: Serious games and gamification in healthcare: a meta-review. Information **14**(2), 105 (2023). https://doi.org/10.3390/info14020105
5. Mayfield, K., et al.: Designing a molecular biology serious educational game. In Proceedings of the ACM Southeast Conference, New York, NY, USA, pp. 210–213, (2019). https://doi.org/10.1145/3299815.3314462
6. Gauthier, A., Jenkinson, J.: Serious game leverages productive negativity to facilitate conceptual change in undergraduate molecular biology. Int. J. Game-Based Learn. **7**(2), 20–34 (2017). https://doi.org/10.4018/IJGBL.2017040102
7. Bjørner, T. et al.: Design and evaluation of a serious game to supplement pupils' understanding of molecular structures in chemistry. In Proceedings of the Joint International Conference on Serious Games, vol. 12945, pp. 263–275 (2021). https://doi.org/10.1007/978-3-030-88272-3_19
8. Filippas, A., Xinogalos, E.: Elementium: design and pilot evaluation of a serious game for familiarizing players with basic chemistry. Educ. Inf. Technol. **28**, 14721–14746 (2023). https://doi.org/10.1007/s10639-023-11791-9
9. Taly, A.: Is the boundary of fun redefined in a mixed-reality serious game? In Proceedings of the International Toy Research Association World Conference (ITRA), Paris, France (2018). https://sorbonne-paris-nord.hal.science/hal-02081028
10. Baaden, M., et al.: Ten simple rules to create a serious game, illustrated with examples from structural biology. PLoS Comput. Biol. **14**(3), e1005955 (2018). https://doi.org/10.1371/journal.pcbi.1005955
11. Bennie, S.J., et al.: Teaching enzyme catalysis using an open source framework for interactive molecular dynamics in virtual reality. J. Chem. Educ. **96**(11), 2488–2496 (2019). https://doi.org/10.26434/chemrxiv.7819982
12. Frey, K.M.: Structure activity relationship (SAR) maps: a student-friendly tool to teach medicinal chemistry in integrated pharmacotherapy courses. Curr. Pharm. Teach. Learn. **12**(3), 339–346 (2020). https://doi.org/10.1016/j.cptl.2019.12.014

13. Barat, G., et al.: Comparing learning retention in medical students using mixed-reality to supplement dissection: a preliminary study. Int. J. Med. Educ. **13**, 107–114 (2022). https://doi.org/10.5116/ijme.6250.0af8
14. Abdinejad, M., et al.: Student perceptions using augmented reality and 3D visualization technologies in chemistry education. J. Sci. Educ. Technol. **30**(2), 87–96 (2021). https://doi.org/10.1007/s10956-020-09880-2
15. Rodríguez, F. et al.: MoleculARweb: a web site for chemistry and structural biology education through interactive augmented reality out of the box in commodity devices. J. Chem. Educ. **98** (2021). https://doi.org/10.1021/acs.jchemed.1c00179
16. Marfisi-Schottman, I., et al.: 10 commandments of the serious game Padawan. In: Proceedings of the Games and Learning Alliance Conference, Tampere, Finland, pp. 63–73 (2022). https://doi.org/10.1007/978-3-031-22124-8_703885394

Short Papers

Online Learning Platform and Gamification Features Preferences: Gender-Based Analysis Among Estonian Students

Ayaz Karimov(✉) and Mirka Saarela

Faculty of Information Technology,University of Jyväskylä, P.O. Box 35, 40014 Jyväskylä, Finland
{akarimov,mirka.saarela}@jyu.fi

Abstract. With the increasing integration of technology in education, online platforms have become essential for learning, but understanding students' preferences is crucial for their effectiveness. This study explores how students' preferences for online educational platforms and gamification features vary across genders. We collected data from 406 students in Estonia, including 250 females, 142 males, and 14 others (such as non-binary, gender-neutral), and analyzed their usage patterns and preferences. The results show that platforms like Kahoot and Quizlet are widely favored among all genders. While females tend to prefer badge collection, males and others show a preference for competing with unknown players. However, there is little difference in preferences for point collection across gender groups.

Keywords: Educational Technology · Gamification · Gender · Online Educational Platforms

1 Introduction

In the implementation of gamification in educational settings, not all students benefit from it equally. In some cases, gamification even had a negative impact on students' motivation, learning outcome, and engagement [14]. Thus, there is no commonly accepted rule about designing and adopting gamified learning environments. One factor that affects the successful implementation of gamification is being able to personalize the experience based on learners' academic and social background, and gender is one of these important social factors. According to Denden et al. (2021), gender moderates the effect of personality on students' perception of the implemented game elements, and it should be considered in the application of gamification in educational settings [6].

A common research gap in studies examining the impact of gender on gaming is the limited scope of gender definitions. Existing research typically adopts binary gender classifications, overlooking the diverse spectrum of gender identities [9]. However, it is crucial to acknowledge and incorporate other gender groups

A. Schönbohm et al. (Eds.): GALA 2024, LNCS 15348, pp. 331–336, 2025.
https://doi.org/10.1007/978-3-031-78269-5_31

to foster fairness and inclusivity in learning environments since personality and identification are considered an important factor of individual differences [8]. Our study seeks to address this gap by expanding the sampling pool to encompass non-binary gender identifications among students. Estonia's significance as a research context for exploring students' preferences for online educational platforms and gamification features lies in its distinct socio-cultural landscapes. On the one hand, it stands out for its progressive stance on gender equality [1]. On the other hand, Estonia's educational system showcases intriguing patterns in gender-based academic performance, conforming with traditional global norms with boys excelling in mathematics and girls in reading [19].

2 Literature Review

Gender differences in response to gamification in educational contexts show significant variations in how individuals perceive and interact with gamified elements [7]. Research consistently shows that these differences are influenced by social, psychological, and cultural factors. People who identify as male, female, or non-binary often show distinct preferences for certain types of gamification features [6,11]. Males, for example, are frequently more motivated by competitive elements such as leaderboards, points, and direct competition. Hamari and Koivisto (2015) found that these elements align with the typical preference for achievement and status, which can be influenced by socialization processes that encourage competitiveness and assertiveness from a young age [12]. Many individuals thrive in environments where their accomplishments are publicly recognized and where they can compare their performance with that of their peers [13]. On the other hand, females and non-binary individuals may exhibit a preference for collaborative and narrative-based aspects of gamification [15]. Bopp et al. (2018) noted that these groups are more likely to engage with gamification features that offer social interaction, storytelling, and community building [10].

Several studies have explored the main reasons for these gender-specific preferences [11]. Chou (2019) suggested that individuals who prefer collaborative gamification elements might do so because they provide a safer and more supportive environment [2]. In competitive settings, some may experience higher levels of anxiety and lower levels of self-efficacy, which can negatively impact their engagement and performance. Others may report feeling more confident and motivated in competitive scenarios, where their skills and achievements are continually tested and validated. Moreover, the different responses to gamified learning elements are also evident in the types of games preferred by each gender [4]. Males are typically drawn to games that involve strategic planning, direct competition, and action-oriented tasks [20]. Females and non-binary individuals, however, often prefer games that incorporate elements of creativity, cooperation, and social interaction. Simulation games, role-playing games, and puzzles that require players to work together or follow a storyline are more popular among these groups [18].

The role of cultural context cannot be overlooked when discussing gender differences in gamification [3]. In cultures with rigid gender norms, the disparity in preferences and engagement with gamified elements is more pronounced. For example, in traditional societies where males are expected to be assertive and dominant, and females and non-binary individuals are expected to be nurturing and cooperative, these expectations shape their interactions with gamified learning environments. In contrast, in more progressive societies with greater gender equality, these differences tend to be less significant [5]. Despite these differences, it is important to note that there is considerable variability within each gender group [21]. Not all individuals who identify as male prefer competitive elements, and not all who identify as female or non-binary prefer collaborative elements. Individual differences, such as personality traits, previous experiences with games, and personal interests, also play a significant role in shaping preferences. This variability suggests that a one-size-fits-all approach to gamification is unlikely to be effective [17].

3 Methodology

We collected data through two main channels: (i) through the Ministry of Education and Research in Estonia and (ii) via direct communication with schools. We reached out to around 52 schools all over Estonia through their websites. The surveys were available in Estonian, Russian, and English to ensure that students understand and fulfill them clearly. In the development of the survey, we considered three main factors and agreed on survey questions based on these factors. These factors were the social background (i.e. age, gender, residence city), their attitudes toward the online educational platforms, and what types of gamification features they utilize. Furthermore, at the beginning of the survey, students were introduced to how the data would be used in this research, and by submitting the survey, they provided their consent. To analyze data, descriptive and inferential statistical analyses were employed.

Overall, 406 students fulfilled the survey, and their backgrounds differ. Approximately 61.6% of students identified themselves as "female", 25% identified as "male", and the remaining 3.4% preferred to identify themselves as "non-binary" or "gender neutral". The number of students in public and private schools studying in Estonia is based on gender. While the vast majority of students (94.09%) study in a public school, the average age of respondents was roughly 16 for all gender groups. The geographical location of students also varied with the majority of responses being from Tartu (13.3%), Tallinn (12.32%), and Võru (9.36%).

4 Results

The most commonly mentioned tools categorized by gender among the participants. Among females, Kahoot emerges as the most famous tool, with 215 mentions, followed closely by Quizlet with 199 mentions. Duolingo is also another famous tool preferred among females, with 120 mentions. In contrast, among male participants, Kahoot remains popular but with fewer mentions, totaling

116, followed by Quizlet with 108 mentions. Duolingo also receives mentions from males, though fewer in number compared to females, with 42 mentions. Moreover, 99math is mentioned by both genders, with a slightly higher count among females (14 mentions) than males (15 mentions). Interestingly, some tools, such as Quizizz, receive mentions exclusively from females, while others, like Khan Academy, receive mentions only from males.

The results indicate variations in the average values of preferred gamification features across gender groups (Fig. 1). In terms of badge collection, females exhibit a slightly higher average score (3.26) compared to males (3.07) and others (3.14). Males and others prefer competing with others whom they know compared to females. When it comes to competition with players whom they do not know, others have a higher preference (2.93) compared to males (2.67) and females (2.22). However, in terms of point collection, there is relatively little difference among gender groups, with females averaging 3.21, males averaging 3.15, and others averaging 3.21. The ANOVA test results indicate varying preferences for gamification features among gender groups ($F = 1.06$, $p = 0.35$). While badge collection preferences show no significant difference, distinct disparities emerge in preferences for competition. Significant differences are observed in both competing against known individuals ($F = 9.55$, $p < 0.001$) and unknown individuals ($F = 6.14$, $p = 0.002$). Preferences for point collection do not vary significantly between genders ($F = 0.11$, $p = 0.9$).

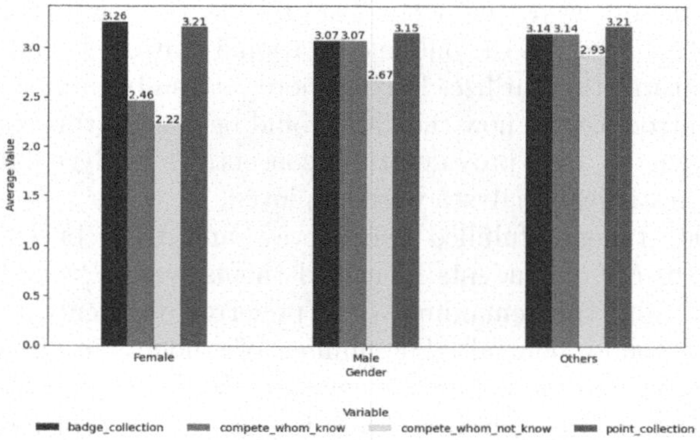

Fig. 1. Average Gamification Features by Gender Group

The analysis of geographical and demographic variations in preferences for online educational tools and gamification features among Estonian students demonstrated important differences based on city and school type. Students from urban areas like Tartu and Tallinn showed a higher preference for competitive elements such as point collection and competing with known individuals. In contrast, students from rural areas exhibited more varied preferences where they mentioned that they prefer collaborative and narrative-based features over competitive ones. Additionally, private school students generally showed higher preferences for competitive gamification elements compared to their public school counterparts.

5 Discussion and Conclusion

The findings of this study align with existing literature on gender differences in gamification preferences. Hamari and Koivisto (2015) found that competitive elements such as leaderboards and points appeal more to males, reflecting socialization processes that encourage competitiveness from a young age [12]. In our study, this trend is evident as males and some non-binary students preferred competition with unknown players. On the other hand, Bopp et al. observed that females and non-binary individuals tend to favor collaborative and narrative-based gamification elements, which align with their higher preference for badge collection in our findings [10]. Additionally, teachers' perceptions of data privacy and equitable access often shape their willingness to integrate gamified learning platforms into their classrooms [16]. For instance, educators who are more cautious about potential ethical concerns, such as the collection and use of student data or the reinforcement of competitive behaviors at the expense of collaboration, may be less likely to embrace these technologies. This variability in teacher adoption suggests that future research should explore how educators' ethical stances impact the successful implementation of EdTech platforms. The data collected were limited to a specific geographic region (Estonia), which may restrict the generalizability of the findings to broader populations.

Acknowledgements. This work was supported by the Academy of Finland (project no. 356314).

References

1. Alas, R., Kaarelson, T.: Gender equality in post-socialist country: case of estonia. Probl. Perspect. Manag. **6**(2), 13–20 (2008)
2. Chou, Y.: Actionable gamification: beyond points, badges, and leaderboards. Packt Publishing Ltd. (2019)
3. Cislaghi, B., Heise, L.: Gender norms and social norms: differences, similarities and why they matter in prevention science. Sociol. Health Illness **42**(2), 407–422 (2020)
4. Codish, D., Ravid, G.: Gender moderation in gamification: does one size fit all? (2017)
5. Connell, R., Pearse, B., et al. Gender norms and stereotypes: a survey of concepts, research and issues about change (2014)
6. Denden, M., Tlili, A., Essalmi, F., Jemni, M., Chen, N.-S., Burgos, D.: Effects of gender and personality differences on students' perception of game design elements in educational gamification. Int. J. Hum Comput Stud. **154**, 102674 (2021)
7. Eagly, A.H., Wood, W.: The nature-nurture debates: 25 years of challenges in understanding the psychology of gender. Perspect. Psychol. Sci. **8**(3), 340–357 (2013)

8. Essalmi, F., Tlili, A., Ayed, L.J.B., Jemni, M.: Toward modeling the learner's personality using educational games. Int. J. Distance Educ. Technol. (IJDET) **15**(4), 21–38 (2017)
9. Friman, U.: The concept and research of gendered game culture. In: DiGRA Conference (2015)
10. Education Games. International journal of game-based learning
11. González-González, C.S., Toledo-Delgado, P.A., Muñoz-Cruz, V. and Arnedo-Moreno, J.: Gender and age differences in preferences on game elements and platforms. Sensors **22**(9), 3567 (2022)
12. Hamari, J., Koivisto, J.: Why do people use gamification services? Int. J. Inf. Manage. **35**(4), 419–431 (2015)
13. Hanhela, T.: The achievement principle, education, and recognition. Distinktion: Scandinavian J. Soc. Theory **13**(1), 77–92 (2012)
14. Karimov, A., Saarela, M., Kärkkäinen, T.: Clustering to define interview participants for analyzing student feedback: a case of legends of learning. In: International Conference on Educational Data Mining (2023)
15. Karimov, A., Saarela, M., Kärkkäinen, T.: The impact of online educational platform on students' motivation and grades: the case of khan academy in the under-resourced communities. In: International Conference on Educational Data Mining, International Educational Data Mining Society (2023)
16. Karimov, A., Saarela, M., Kärkkäinen, T.: Understanding teachers' perspectives on ethical concerns and skills to use AI tools. In: International Conference on Learning Analytics and Knowledge. Society for Learning Analytics Research (SoLAR) (2024)
17. Lindqvist, A., Sendén, M.G., Renström, E.A.: What is gender, anyway: a review of the options for operationalising gender. Psychol. Sex. **12**(4), 332–344 (2021)
18. Lucas, K., Sherry, J.L.: Sex differences in video game play: a communication-based explanation. Commun. Res. **31**(5), 499–523 (2004)
19. OECD: PISA 2022 Results (Volume I) (2023). https://doi.org/10.1787/53f23881-en, https://www.oecd-ilibrary.org/content/publication/53f23881-en
20. Toda, A.M., Oliveira, W., Shi, L., Bittencourt, I.I., Isotani, S., Cristea, A.: Planning gamification strategies based on user characteristics and DM: a gender-based case study. arXiv preprint arXiv:1905.09146 (2019)
21. Veltri, N., Krasnova, H., Baumann, A., Kalayamthanam, N.: Gender differences in online gaming: a literature review (2014)

Motion Design for Emotion Design

Chris Hovey and Sara Jakubowicz(✉)

New York University, New York, NY 10012, USA
{chris.hovey,sarajakubowicz}@nyu.edu

Abstract. When designing learning experiences, there is evidence that affective features can improve learning. This paper explores the question of how spatial movements of NPCs impact a player's emotions in an executive function VR game. In two studies, NPC movement approaching players significantly increased arousal when compared to static distance movements. Though EF was not significantly improved following gameplay, a more challenging and adaptive level design may elicit the desired effect.

Keywords: Emotional Design · Animation · Virtual Reality · Game-Based Learning · Executive Function

1 Introduction

The emotions we experience are highly influenced by the world around us. Emotion can influence how we perceive the world, process information, and learn. When designing games for learning, intentionally creating game assets or environments that have certain emotion inductions can draw players' attention and enhance memory and learning.

The emotions experienced during learning can enhance attention, information processing, retention, and motivation [3]. Affective state, or "core affect" [11] can influence learning outcomes [9]. Heightened emotional states (arousal) enhance learning outcomes for both positive and negative valence [7]. Additionally, many features of multimedia environments have been identified as having an impact on affective states measured in a variety of ways, including active agent characteristics (non-player characters (NPCs)) [8].

Affective state is integral to learning skills such as executive functions (EFs). EFs are the intentional mental processes dedicated to problem solving and decision making that regulate other cognitive processes and actions [15]. Selecting design features to induce affective states has a relationship with cognitive training outcomes [5,12]. In a comparison of hot versus cool color designs in an executive function (EF) game, players in the 'hot' condition showed significantly greater improvements in EF of switching than players in a 'cool' condition [5].

1.1 Emotional Design

Emotional design for learning is the design of affective elements that are tied directly to the learning content without significantly increasing the learners'

A. Schönbohm et al. (Eds.): GALA 2024, LNCS 15348, pp. 337–342, 2025.
https://doi.org/10.1007/978-3-031-78269-5_32

cognitive load [8]. Affective features specific to the learning material lead to better educational outcomes [9]. Russell's circumplex model of affect which has two dimensions, arousal (activation) and pleasure (valence) allows fast capture of self-reported affective experience [10]. Bradley and Lang operationalized this construct for rapid capture by utilizing two semantic-differential scales in the Self-Assessment Manikin (SAM) [1], making it ideal to use in a repeated measure design because it minimizes participant fatigue.

Animations and Motion Design. In addition to character designs, the affective quality of character animations have influenced emotions. Even simple movement features can significantly impact the emotional experience of viewers when compared to still images, such as 2D user-approaching movements eliciting higher arousal [6]. The motion path of NPCs can also change the perceived affective quality of the animation. Increasing motion complexity on a traditional 2D display, from a near-line to wave-like or parabolic motion increases viewer arousal, with varied valence outcomes. Wave-like motions elicited more positive affective states while parabolic, character going down and back up, elicited more negative affective states [2]. Similarly, a "meandering" quadcopter flight path elicits significantly higher arousal and positive valence than simpler movements [13].

2 Studying Affective Animations in a Virtual Reality Executive Function Game

All You Can E.T.: A Virtual Reality Game. In this three-dimensional VR game, All You Can E.T., players feed hungry aliens a specific food based on what each is craving. All You Can E.T. (AYCET) was designed and validated as a two-dimensional game to enhance a player's executive functions of shifting, [4]. For Study 2, AYCET was recreated as a VR game, using two different animations to create two game versions based on the findings of Study 1.

2.1 2-Study Exploration of Character Motions, Emotions, and Learning

The purpose of this study was to explore and identify the affective quality of the movement path of fixed-feature NPCs in VR environments on stationary participants. Broadly, this research was guided by the question of 'How do character movements impact a user's emotions?'

For Study 1, characters animations were used to study the emotional responses to NPC movement out of the game's context. Study 1 was designed to establish the impact of character movement on players' affective state. Study 1 was conducted using a repeated measures, within-subject experimental design to account for individual differences. Study 2 investigated cognitive and affective outcomes using two versions of the VR game with either a high or low arousal animation.

The motion features for Study 1 included sinusoidal motion, a near-straight line [2], and a meandering path [13]; all three features were cross-modified toward the user versus toward the ground at a static distance [6] for a total of six animations. The 3×2 (path by trajectory) study design of motion features used in Study 1 are depicted in Fig. 1.

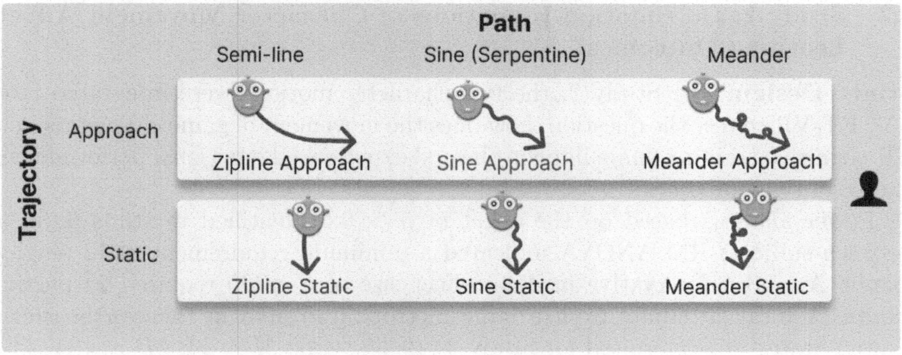

Fig. 1. Motion feature paths and trajectories used in Study 1. The movements integrated into the VR game for Study 2 are noted: the high arousal movement (zipline-static) is in blue while the low arousal movement (sine-approach) is in red. (Color figure online)

2.2 Study 1: Emotional Response on Motion Design Observations

Study Design. Power analysis of the main effects on arousal based on an anticipated effect of $\eta > .3$, alpha of .05, and power of .8 in a within-subjects ANOVA indicated a minimum of 8 participants. A more conservative medium effect of $\eta < .1$ required 12 participants. 15 participants were recruited from a medium Midwestern town in the United States (15–22 years; $M = 18$; $SD = 1.6$; 7F, 7M, 1 unspecified).

The Self-Assessment Manikin (SAM) [1] was used to measure affective responses to the six animations (Fig. 1). Demographic and gameplay history were administered to account for potential covariates.

Results. A Repeated Measures ANOVA was computed for mean emotion *valence* and *arousal* ratings on the six animations, it was found that trajectory had a medium sized main effect on arousal, $F(1, 13) = 17.43$, $p = .001$; $\eta = .3$. Path did not have a significant effect on arousal. Though, trajectory and path had a small interaction effect on arousal, $F(2, 26) = 3.41$, $p = .049$; $\eta = .02$.

Valence responses indicated a large main effect from path, $F(1.26, 16.37) = 3.95$, $p = .056$; $\eta = .12$, and a medium main effect for trajectory, $F(1, 13) = 7.6$, $p < .02$; $\eta = .08$. There was no significant interaction effect of path and trajectory on valence.

Statistically significant pairwise comparisons for arousal revealed that zipline-static vs. sine-approach had a large effect size and mean difference, $MD = -1.29$, $p < .001$, $d = 1.7$ and were selected for use in Study 2.

2.3 Study 2: Do Emotion Inductions of Character Movement Affect Learning Outcomes?

Study Design. For Study 2, the two character motions were integrated into AYCET-VR to test the question: how does the movement of game characters in a VR cognitive training game impact players' experienced emotions, performance, and cognitive outcomes?

Power analysis based on the effect of $\eta > 0.5$ identified in study 1, in a between-subjects RM ANOVA indicated a minimum requirement of 12 participants. A more conservative medium effect size of $\eta < .25$ required 24 participants. A total 29 adults from a large metropolitan area in the Northeastern United States were recruited for Study 2 (19–35 years; $M = 24$; $SD = 4.12$; 7F, 15M, 7 unspecified). Both groups played one of the two versions of AYCET-VR for ten minutes

The measures included the SAM, demographics, and gameplay - with the addition of accuracy and reaction time data as task performance measures. Gameplay data and scores on EF measures were the primary dependent variables of interest.

Executive function (EF) was measured in two forms, proximal and distal. The proximal measure included reaction times and accuracy scores during gameplay. The distal outcome was measured using a pre and post test of the Dimensional Change Card Sorting (DCCS) [14] task to assess improvements in EF of shifting between the two groups. For the VR session, participants were randomly assigned to play one of the two versions of AYCET-VR, rating their affective state on the SAM at the start and after playing each of the ten levels.

Results. A repeated measures ANOVA model was computed for each of participants' arousal and valence responses across the ten levels of *All You Can E.T-VR* played for each game type (approaching vs static animations).

Arousal was significantly different, $F(1, 19) = 6.7$, $p = .02$, $\eta = .14$, between the two game types. Participants playing AYCET-VR with approaching aliens experienced high levels of cognitive arousal, $M = 3.4$, $SD = .72$, while participants playing the game with static distance aliens experienced slightly negative levels, $M = 2.5$, $SD = .7$.

Valence was also significantly different, $F(1, 16) = 10.2$, $p = .006$, $\eta = .2$, between the two conditions. Participants playing AYCET-VR with approaching aliens experienced slightly negative levels of valence, $M = 2.7$, $SD = .7$, whereas those with static distance aliens experienced more positive levels of valence, $M = 3.7$, $SD = .6$.

An independent samples t-test for average reaction time and overall accuracy was not significant. Additionally, an ANCOVA for DCCS delta scores did not show significant improvements.

3 Discussion

Implications for Emotional Design. This research aimed to identify the affective quality of NPC animation features in path and trajectory, for a VR game for training EFs. Study 1 found that approaching animations elicited higher arousal than animations remaining at a distance. More complex movements approaching the user trended towards more positive valence in responses. Path results indicated more complex movements resulted in higher arousal for static distance animations, but not approaching.

Results from Study 2 confirmed the effect of approach vs static animations from Study 1. However, learners playing the high arousal version of the game did not improve EFs. More challenging level design, or longer play time may have resulted in a statistically significant finding for EFs.

Limitations. EF skills become more stable in adulthood, and the age range of participants for Study 2 was larger than anticipated. Overall, mild effects may be explained by the neutral designs of player surroundings and "plush" nature of NPCs rather than "living".

4 Conclusion

This research identified features in the affective quality of VR character animations for EF training. Approaching characters were found to elicit significantly stronger cognitive arousal than static characters in both age groups. While accuracy and EF skills were not significantly improved following gameplay, this does not mean that high arousal animations do not play a role in improving EF skills. The very large effect of reaction time hints that this player behavior and EFs training may be identified with better level design, limiting the upper age of participants, or increasing playtime.

The findings of this research may be applied to the affective design of VR games for learning. If players are intended to focus on specific features, then animations approaching users will elicit higher arousal and attention. If that is not an option, then increasing animation complexity of the target character may instead elicit the desired behavior. Future research in this area should include adaptive level design to properly challenge participants for improved EF outcomes.

Disclosure of Interests. The authors have no competing interests to declare that are relevant to the content of this article.

References

1. Bradley, M.M., Lang, P.J.: Measuring emotion: the self-assessment manikin and the semantic differential. J. Behav. Ther. Exp. Psychiatry **25**(1), 49–59 (1994). https://doi.org/10.1016/0005-7916(94)90063-9

2. Chafi, A., Schiaratura, L., Rusinek, S.: Three patterns of motion which change the perception of emotional faces. Psychology **3**(1), 82–89 (2012). https://doi.org/10.4236/psych.2012.31014
3. Heidig, S., Müller, J., Reichelt, M.: Emotional design in multimedia learning: Differentiation on relevant design features and their effects on emotions and learning. Comput. Hum. Behav. **44**, 81–95 (2015). https://doi.org/10.1016/j.chb.2014.11.009
4. Homer, B.D., Plass, J.L., Raffaele, C., Ober, T.M., Ali, A.: Improving high school students' executive functions through digital game play. Comput. Educ. **117**, 50–58 (2018). https://doi.org/10.1016/j.compedu.2017.09.011
5. Homer, B.D., Plass, J.L., Rose, M.C., MacNamara, A.P., Pawar, S., Ober, T.M.: Activating adolescents' "hot" executive functions in a digital game to train cognitive skills: the effects of age and prior abilities. Cogn. Dev. **49**, 20–32 (2019). https://doi.org/10.1016/j.cogdev.2018.11.005
6. Mühlberger, A., Neumann, R., Wieser, M.J., Pauli, P.: The impact of changes in spatial distance on emotional responses. Emotion **8**(2), 192–198 (2008). https://doi.org/10.1037/1528-3542.8.2.192
7. Pekrun, R.: The control-value theory of achievement emotions: assumptions, corollaries, and implications for educational research and practice. Educ. Psychol. Rev. **18**(4), 315–341 (2006). https://doi.org/10.1007/s10648-006-9029-9
8. Plass, J.L., et al.: Emotional design for digital games for learning: the effect of expression, color, shape, and dimensionality on the affective quality of game characters. Learn. Instr. **70**, 101194 (2020). https://doi.org/10.1016/j.learninstruc.2019.01.005
9. Plass, J.L., Kaplan, U.: Emotional design in digital media for learning. In: Tettegah, S.Y., Gartmeier, M. (eds.) Emotions, Technology, Design, and Learning, pp. 131–161. Academic Press, San Diego (Jan, Emotions and Technology (2016)
10. Russell, J.A.: A circumplex model of affect. J. Pers. Soc. Psychol. **39**(6), 1161–1178 (1980). https://doi.org/10.1037/h0077714
11. Russell, J.A.: Core affect and the psychological construction of emotion. Psychol. Rev. **110**(1), 145–172 (2003). https://doi.org/10.1037/0033-295x.110.1.145
12. Schweizer, S., Hampshire, A., Dalgleish, T.: Extending brain-training to the affective domain: increasing cognitive and affective executive control through emotional working memory training. PLoS ONE **6**(9), e24372 (2011). https://doi.org/10.1371/journal.pone.0024372
13. Sharma, M., Hildebrandt, D., Newman, G., Young, J.E., Eskicioglu, R.: Communicating affect via flight path exploring use of the Laban effort system for designing affective locomotion paths. In: 2013 8th ACM/IEEE International Conference on Human-Robot Interaction (HRI), pp. 293–300 (2013). https://doi.org/10.1109/HRI.2013.6483602
14. Zelazo, P.D., Anderson, J.E., Richler, J., Wallner-Allen, K., Beaumont, J.L., Weintraub, S.: II. NIH toolbox cognition battery (CB): measuring executive function and attention. Monogr. Soc. Res. Child Dev. **78**(4), 16–33 (2013). https://doi.org/10.1111/mono.12032
15. Zelazo, P.D., Blair, C.B., Willoughby, M.T.: Executive Function: Implications for Education. Tech. rep, National Center for Education Research (2016)

Comparing Interaction Modalities in VR Serious Games: A Study on Presence and Enjoyment

David Baberowski[1](✉), Thiemo Leonhardt[2], Josef Buchner[3], and Nadine Bergner[2]

[1] TU Dresden University of Technology, Dresden, Germany
david.baberowski@tu-dresden.de
[2] RWTH Aachen University, Aachen, Germany
[3] St.Gallen University of Teacher Education, St. Gallen, Switzerland

Abstract. This study investigates the impact of different interaction modalities on presence and enjoyment in VR serious games, focusing on two versions of a game designed to teach routing and network concepts. One version employs a catch and throw (CT) interaction, while the other uses a walk and place (WP) interaction. Conducted as a between-subject design field study with secondary school students, both versions achieved similar levels of presence and enjoyment among participants, with no significant differences. Nevertheless, a sensitivity analysis of the results indicates that the type of interaction has a minimal impact on the target variables of enjoyment and presence in the study, which are crucial for VR serious games.

Keywords: Virtual Reality · Serious Games · Interaction · Computer Science Education

1 Introduction

In disciplines characterised by a high degree of abstract content, such as computer science, there are frequently no real-life scenarios that can be effectively modelled and experienced in a virtual environment. Therefore, fictional environments must be constructed with the assistance of metaphors that accurately depict the learning content in a precise manner while simultaneously facilitating interactivity. In [2], a methodology for the development of an educational design that integrates learning content and metaphors as the foundation for game design is presented. Although this process supports the basic design of educational games, various aspects such as interaction modalities have not yet been sufficiently investigated for VR applications [6], especially for fictional worlds. For the purposes of this study, two versions of a VR serious game were developed, differing only in the type of interaction. The objective of this study is to examine the impact of the design aspect of interaction on the variables of presence and enjoyment, which are associated with learning success.

A. Schönbohm et al. (Eds.): GALA 2024, LNCS 15348, pp. 343–348, 2025.
https://doi.org/10.1007/978-3-031-78269-5_33

2 Theoretical Background

When developing serious games, it is important to consider psychological and emotional constructs, such as enjoyment and presence, as these factors contribute to the overall success of a learning setting. While there is no doubt that serious games are intended to have a serious purpose [7], it would be erroneous to assume that they are developed without an entertainment aspect as Laamarti et al. shows in their literature review [5]. In fact, the very notion of enjoyment is open to interpretation, particularly when we consider the potential of gamification elements and the positive impact they can have on intrinsic motivation [1,8].

The concept of presence is a widely discussed factor, particularly in the context of virtual reality applications. Presence is the feeling of actually being in a virtual place [10] and has established itself as an important metric for VR applications as there seems to be a positive correlation between presence, immersion and learning effect [6]. As postulated by Schubert [9], the concept of presence can be delineated by three sub-factors: involvement, spatial presence, and experienced realism. In environments that do not aspire to represent a real-world scenario, the experienced realism sub-factor is deemed unsuitable and thus merits a separate evaluation [3].

3 Game Versions

The objective of this study is to assess the impact of design choices pertaining to interaction in a VR serious game. To this end, two versions of the same game were developed, differing only in one aspect of the game design: the interaction. In this scenario, the learner assumes the role of a home router, responsible for forwarding data packets in a network based on their IP addresses.

The first version (see Fig. 1, left) is nearly identical to the version tested in a laboratory setting. It employs a catch-and-throw (CT) interaction, whereby the capsules come flying out of tubes placed approximately 10 m in front of the player. The player remains stationary throughout the duration of the game, as the capsules are directed towards a desk that delineates the player position. Subsequently, the player is required to grasp the capsule with a natural grip motion via the hand controllers and throw it back towards the designated target. This particular interaction was selected by the design team following an extensive process of evaluation and experimentation involving the consideration of multiple alternative options. During this process, the design team analyzed other VR games to identify motivating and enjoyable interactions. Existing VR games achieve engaging gaming experiences, even for repetitive tasks, with a considerable amount of dynamic motion, while players remain stationary. The interaction thus encourages the player to throw the packets with energy and even catch them earlier by jumping in the air. One potential drawback is that it may draw attention away from the origin of the packet. Given that every capsule is flying to the central player position, the origin tube may not matter to the players. However, the information which tube was ejecting, in theory, enables faster decision-making.

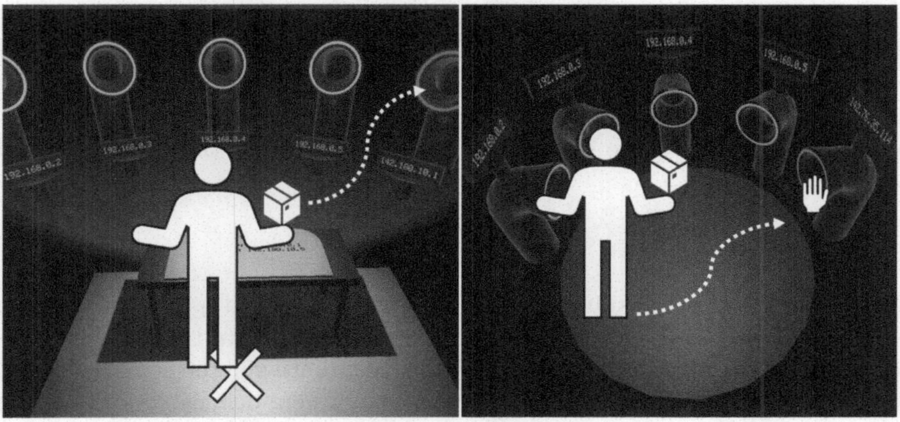

Fig. 1. Screenshots of the two game versions. On the left the Catch & Throw setup is shown, where the player stands in one place and throws the packet into a tube. On the right side the Walk & Place setup requires the player to walk up to a tube and then placing the packet into a tube.

The second version (see Fig. 1, right) employs a walk-and-place (WP) interaction to address this issue. The tubes are now positioned in a semicircle around the player, thereby delineating a circular play area with a diameter of 2 m. The capsules stay inside the opening of the tubes instead of being ejected like in the CT version, letting the player walk towards the tube and collect the capsule. Afterwards the player has to move towards the destination tube and place the package inside. This requires the player to cover a short distance to reach each tube, making it more pronounced where a capsule originated from, which is a beneficial information during the routing process. While the players engage in enacting activities and manipulation of objects, as in the CT version, a distinction can be made regarding their movements through the environment. In addition to manipulating the object (the capsule), the player is also required to change position and perspective within the environment. However, this presents a potential limitation, as the player is unable to observe all the tubes simultaneously. Consequently, there is a possibility that a capsule may emerge from a tube that is not immediately visible to the player. This issue is addressed through the use of supplementary cues such as spotlights, which illuminate a tube just before a capsule is about to exit.

During the design phase for the CT version a special focus was to create an enjoyable interaction, by using dynamic motions. In contrast, the WP version prioritized the integration of interaction, metaphor and learning content, which is anticipated to result in a more positive user experience for those engaging with the CT version. Therefore it is expected, that the interaction of the CT version is considered more enjoyable by the participants.

Second the versions do not differ in terms of immersion according to Slater [10], as identical hardware is used. In both versions, the player interacts with the same game objects through grasping movements. However, it is assumed that the more dynamic throwing motion (CT) requires more attention than the slower insertion of the packets (WP), which may have an effect on the presence subscale Involvement. At the same time, it is expected that looking around in the semi-circular arrangement of the WP version will have an effect on the subscale Spatial presence.

4 Results

The study is a between-subject design and was conducted as a field study in secondary schools in German-speaking Switzerland. Prior to the first questionnaire, the study leader introduced to the topic of "Routing in the home network". Following this, the subsequent stages of the study were delineated, after which the students commenced the preliminary survey. Once the initial questionnaire had been completed, the participants were instructed on how to use the VR glasses and controllers, after which they proceeded to the next phase of the study, which involved playing the game. The participants were not informed that two distinct versions of the educational game were available; instead, the headsets, which had only one version installed and operational, were randomly assigned to the groups. To ensure comparable levels of difficulty, the identical sequence of data packets had to be routed in both versions of the game. Additionally, the follow-up questionnaire was administered at this point, concluding the lesson and thus the study.

In total there where 158 completed questionnaires from students aged 13 to 15. 8 participants reported symptoms of motion sickness or nausea (3 or more on a scale from "0: no symptoms at all" to "4: strong symptoms") and were therefore excluded from the study. In a genuine classroom setting, external elements exert a considerable impact on students' ability to concentrate, thereby rendering experimental studies a challenging endeavor [4]. Since the goal of this article is not to evaluate the classroom setting but the influence of interactions on presence and enjoyment, students that did not engage with the learning application and learning content are excluded from the evaluation. For this purpose, learning tasks were used as an indicator and all students who showed a deterioration in the test score between pre and post test were excluded, leaving 118 questionnaires as basis for the evaluation.

Cronbach's α is used to confirm the reliability ($\alpha = 0.88$) of the included sub scale "enjoyment" from the intrinsic motivation inventory [11]. Enjoyment was assessed using a 5 point likert scale from 0 to 4 (see Table 1). Since an influence of prior knowledge on the enjoyment of the game cannot be ruled out, an ANCOVA with prior knowledge as a covariate is used here as well, according to which the game version did not have a significant effect on enjoyment ($p = 0.473$, $\eta_p^2 = 0.004$). Using G*Power in order to perform a sensitivity analysis ($p = 0.05$, $N = 118$, $df = 1$, 2 groups, 1 covariate) resulted in a limit of d = 0.396 (small effect), above which a significant effect would have been measured.

Presence was assessed using the Igroup Presence Questionnaire (IPQ) [9], which is composed from 3 subscales. The items where measured on a likert scale ranging from 0 to 6 (see Table 1). A comparison using a t-test showed no significant difference for presence or the subscales Spatial Presence and Involvement (see Table 1). A sensitivity-analysis using G*Power ($p = 0.05$, $N = 118$) showed, that for this setting, the detection of medium effects ($d > 0.5$) would have been expected with the necessary confidence level for presence and the two subscales considered.

Table 1. Differences in Presence and Enjoyment between game versions, different tests were used since not all scales satisfied all requirements (normality)

	CT		WP		CP versus WP		
	M	*SD*	*M*	*SD*	effect size	significance	power
Presence (t-test)	3.34	0.91	3.44	0.88	$d = .111$	$p = .550$	.77
Spatial Presence (u-test)	4.08	0.93	4.19	1.03	$d = .177$	$p = .410$	.58
Involvement (t-test)	3.25	1.02	3.04	1.13	$d = .191$	$p = .303$	.70
Enjoyment (ANCOVA)	3.23	0.80	3.32	0.75	$d = .126$	$p = .473$	.57

5 Discussion

The two versions of the VR game differed primarily in their interaction modalities, which were hypothesized to affect the enjoyment and presence experienced by the participants. The Catch and Throw version involved dynamic movements where players caught and threw capsules to target destinations. In contrast, the Walk and Place version required players to do a step to the source of the capsules, pick them up, and place them at the target destinations. Regarding enjoyment, the playful and dynamic interaction (throwing with high enjoyment) was suspected to perform better, than the deliberate and gradual interaction (picking and placing with lower enjoyment). However, no significant differences were measured. A sensitivity analysis showed, that medium and large effects (d > .396) would have been measured and can therefore be excluded for enjoyment according to Wilde. Interaction therefore appears to have had no or only a small influence on enjoyment in this study. A potential explanation is that the effect of the interaction on enjoyment may be overshadowed by the novelty of using VR headsets in the first place, which is likely to be similar for both versions. In this case, the scale may have reached saturation, making it difficult to detect smaller effects. The investigation of presence of the two interactions did not yield significant results, although medium effects (d > .5) would have been measurable. However, given that the interaction is only one of many factors influencing presence in virtual environments, this result is not unexpected. Nevertheless, there is evidence suggesting that other factors, such as visual and auditory stimuli, may be more influential than the type of interaction in the game with respect to the sense of presence.

The results are limited by the fact that the study was conducted as a field study in a school. While the associated problems of conducting the study (background noise, inclusion of the learning partner, room design) are present for all study participants, it is possible that there is a bias with regard to possible disturbances between the groups that cannot be ruled out. However, the findings indicate only a minimal impact of the interaction type on the target variables of enjoyment and presence, which are crucial for VR serious games.

Acknowledgments. This study was supported by the Society of Friends and Sponsors of TUD Dresden University of Technology.

References

1. Anolli, L., Mantovani, F., Confalonieri, L., Ascolese, A., Peveri, L.: Emotions in serious games: from experience to assessment. Int. J. Emerg. Technol. Learn. (iJET) **5**(SI3), 7 (2010). https://doi.org/10.3991/ijet.v5s3.1496
2. Baberowski, D., Leonhardt, T., Bergner, N.: Inside the system - designing VR serious games for computer science education. In: Dondio, P., Rocha, M., Brennan, A., Schönbohm, A., De Rosa, F., Koskinen, A., Bellotti, F. (eds.) Games and Learning Alliance, vol. 14475, pp. 311–320. Springer Nature Switzerland, Cham (2024). https://doi.org/10.1007/978-3-031-49065-1_30
3. Baberowski, D., Leonhardt, T., Lilienthal, L., Bergner, N.: Beyond realism: Rethinking presence in virtual environments for abstract concept learning. Proceedings of DELFI 2024 (2024). https://doi.org/10.18420/delfi2024_09
4. Dengel, A., Buchner, J., Mulders, M., Pirker, J.: Levels of immersive teaching and learning: influences of challenges in the everyday classroom. In: MacDowell, P., Lock, J. (eds.) Immersive Education: Designing for Learning, pp. 107–122. Springer International Publishing, Cham (2022). https://doi.org/10.1007/978-3-031-18138-2_7
5. Laamarti, F., Eid, M., El Saddik, A.: An Overview of Serious Games. Int. J. Comput. Games Technol. **2014**, 1–15 (2014). https://doi.org/10.1155/2014/358152
6. Makransky, G.: The immersion principle in multimedia learning. In: Mayer, R.E., Fiorella, L. (eds.) The Cambridge Handbook of Multimedia Learning, pp. 296–303. Cambridge University Press, 3 edn. (2021). https://doi.org/10.1017/9781108894333.031
7. Michael, D.: Serious Games: Games That Educate. Train and Inform. Thomson Course Technology, Boston, Mass (2006)
8. Rheinberg, F., Engeser, S.: Intrinsic motivation and flow. In: Heckhausen, J., Heckhausen, H. (eds.) Motivation and Action, pp. 579–622. Springer, Cham (2018). https://doi.org/10.1007/978-3-319-65094-4_14
9. Schubert, T.W.: The sense of presence in virtual environments: a three-component scale measuring spatial presence, involvement, and realness. Zeitschrift für Medienpsychologie **15**(2), 69–71 (2003). https://doi.org/10.1026/1617-6383.15.2.69
10. Slater, M.: A Note on Presence Terminology. Presence Connect **3** (2003)
11. Wilde, M., Bätz, K., Kovaleva, A., Urhahne, D.: Testing a short scale of intrinsic motivation. Zeitschrift für Didaktik der Naturwissenschaften **15**, 31–45 (2009)

Gamification and Artificial Intelligence in the Educational Context: Analysis of Scientific Literature

Angel Torres-Toukoumidis[1(✉)], María Mercedes Fernández Jiménez[2], Julio Merchán-Romero[3], and Javier Feliciano Arnaldo Vega-Ramírez[4]

[1] Universidad Politécnica Salesiana, 010105 Cuenca, Ecuador
atorrest@ups.edu.ec
[2] Universidad de Valladolid, 47002 Valladolid, Spain
[3] Universidad Santiago de Compostela, 15782 Santiago de Compostela, Spain
[4] Universidad Austral de Chile, 5110566 Valdivia, Chile

Abstract. Gamification and artificial intelligence have gained an important role in education, so much so that they have been considered to improve learning and skills development. Hence, the aim is to analyze the conceptual patterns between gamification and artificial intelligence in education, by reviewing 41 scientific articles from the databases Web of Science and Scopus that combine both terminologies to examine the level of education, role in the educational process, artificial intelligence technology used, elements of games and contributions to education. The results show their connection is mostly observed in higher education and in secondary education for the learning process of students, while the use of artificial intelligence is mostly used in the processing of computerized vision, natural language and use of algorithms through assisted digital platforms. In turn, the main elements incorporated in these experiences are points, levels and competence, giving added value in the teaching process. Finally, the significant contributions are directed towards the teaching of new skills and to the optimization of performance. While there are positive effects on the use of artificial intelligence and gamification as adaptive tools that allow optimizing feedback and help students achieve their objectives, there is still a need to explore this connection at other educational levels, in other roles and with other artificial intelligence and playful technologies, making it possible to expand the implementation in this context.

Keywords: Artificial intelligence · gamification · education · learning · natural language

1 Introduction

The new technological dynamics have been combined in the current educational ecosystem, establishing itself as a space of learning and development with multiple functionalities. The fusion of gamified strategies developed by Artificial Intelligence (AI) emerges as a promising approach aimed at creating more personalized and motivating

A. Schönbohm et al. (Eds.): GALA 2024, LNCS 15348, pp. 349–354, 2025.
https://doi.org/10.1007/978-3-031-78269-5_34

learning experiences. The deployment of cutting-edge technologies, including Artificial Intelligence (AI) and gamification, has gained remarkable importance in education over the past decade. As defined by Deterding et al. (2011) [1], gamification involves the incorporation of game-design elements in non-play environments. In turn, Hamari et al. (2014) [2] state the use of playful strategies as powerful tools to promote motivation and user engagement. In addition, various educational contexts have corroborated the integration of AI and gamification in teaching systems, exploring a wide range of applications yielding a variety of results related to performance, motivation and assessment of learning.

However, the use of AI and gamification in education comes with challenges. The technical barrier, resistance to change by professors and the real effectiveness of these technologies in different educational contexts are some of the problems identified in previous research [3]. There are also notable challenges that include technical aspects, accessibility, ethics and privacy. At the technical level, the implementation and maintenance of AI technologies and gamified platforms may require robust infrastructure and advanced technical knowledge [4]. Regarding accessibility, the aim is to ensure that AI and gamification-based solutions are inclusive and accessible to all students, including those with disabilities or special needs [2]. Finally, as for ethics and privacy, student data management and safeguarding privacy emerge as crucial issues [5].

Despite these challenges, this research underscores the transformative potential of AI-infused gamification in education. Navigating through these obstacles can pave the way for a more inclusive, engaging, and personalized educational landscape that fosters not just knowledge acquisition but also critical thinking, problem-solving, and creativity among learners. As educators and stakeholders grapple with these challenges, understanding and mitigating these issues are pivotal in harnessing the full potential of AI and gamification to revolutionize the educational experience.

2 Methodology

Considering these theoretical precepts and since gamification and artificial intelligence are emerging areas in education, reflected in their growth in the most prominent databases for the academic community as evidenced by Surendeleg et al. (2014) [6] in gamification and Xia et al. (2022) [7] in artificial intelligence, this research carries out a systematic review of the scientific literature with the aim of analyzing the conceptual patterns that arise between gamification and artificial intelligence in education. Based on the analysis criteria [8–11]. The following specific objectives were established: 1. Examine the artificial intelligence technologies incorporated in research on playfulness in education, 2. Review the elements of games used in experiences of artificial intelligence in the educational environment.

Regarding the criteria for selecting publications, two phases were applied. In the first phase a series of search characteristics were established: databases, search word, type of publication and range of years. For the database section, Web of Science and Scopus were the object of study [12]. Considering the language of the search words, only articles published in English were selected, although the search was also performed in Spanish in the three databases, without obtaining results. Therefore, the final words selected were: "gamification" with the Boolean operator "AND" together with "artificial intelligence". In the types of publication, it focused only on scientific articles, because they contain an average length for a thorough review and a structure that facilitates the understanding and review of the results, hence excluding books, reports and proceedings of conferences.

Regarding the range of years established, it was estimated from 2019 to August 2023*. The reason for selecting these years is that the scientific contributions in this area were doubled since 2019 until august 2023.

There were 256 baseline papers in the time range established between 2019–2023*, which after the configuration of the selection criteria regarding the language and exclusivity of scientific articles, a total of 160 scientific articles were obtained, in which a second phase was performed through the revision of Prisma-P flowchart [13] which consisted in reducing the sample through three screening: identification, which excludes duplicate documents (n = 35); projection, which excludes documents that are not in open access (n = 47); and eligibility, which excludes documents for particular justifications such as those outside the field of education (n = 37). In summary, the Prisma-P flowchart with its 3 screening yielded a total of 41 articles that will be reviewed in the analysis.

Regarding the analysis criteria, those from previous systematic reviews of scientific literature linked to gamification [8–10] and artificial intelligence [11] were selected and combined for developing systematized patterns in education. Each of the 41 selected articles were reviewed individually by each of the authors taking into account the 5 criteria mentioned from September 10th to October 25th, 2023, demonstrating the concurrency revealed and attending whether the potential intersection between gamification and artificial intelligence generate significant contributions to education or is simply a temporary and superficial complement to the educational process.

3 Results

3.1 Artificial Intelligence Technology in Gamification Experiences

Artificial intelligence is closely related to educational objectives and the type of content presented in the teaching-learning process. In the case of program-type tools, whose technology is based on natural language processing, environments designed from three-dimensional computer schemas are used [14]. This approach provides the user with a more immersive experience, establishing a more direct contact with the virtual environment. In this regard, virtual reality glasses are specifically designed, and the virtual worlds created help to turn education into an immersive subject. The use of this technology is considered particularly suitable for specific groups, taking into account factors such as the time of use and the number of students involved.

These perspectives are supported by fundamental arguments, Artificial Intelligence lies in promoting critical thinking in teaching [15]. In addition, it seeks to improve the skills and abilities of the students from the perspective of their professional career. It is also considered that gamification acts as a stimulus for students by increasing their motivation and commitment in practical activities, since this approach is based on challenges and scores with reward elements. AI-led tools tend to be more responsive and thus easier to use and familiarize compared to other types. The flexibility of AIs allows instructors to use infrastructure in various engineering domains for teaching, thereby facilitating teaching.

On the other hand, the computerized methodology in artificial intelligence is described as a personalized approach and gamification method valid for the teaching of certain activities that could theoretically be developed as a single gamification system that students could adapt as necessary through a system of motivation and incentives [16].

In the field of digital tools, such as artificial intelligence-assisted platforms, where interaction is exclusively through computers, teacher adaptation has proven to be remarkably agile, revealing results that students interpret positively during self-evaluations. In contrast to programs that depend on a specific physical support, AI-based assistance platforms become more accessible tools for platform management [17] generating results adapted to the needs of the student and the availability of the teacher.

Indeed, it express the need for teachers to acquire skills to integrate various educational technologies related to artificial intelligence. They propose a vision that involves merging the educational environment with several tools, first making them available and adapting them to professionals before implementing them in the teaching. In this context, it is necessary to plan the responsibilities between teachers and digital tools to support learning [18], ensuring an adaptive digital transformation and adequate interaction.

3.2 Game Elements in Artificial Intelligence

The presence of game elements in learning processes directly influences the tools available to educators. Students show more interest in a task when presented with recognition of achievements and the option to customize the associated character. This methodology allows students the freedom to adapt learning at their own pace, relating the educational process with autonomous motivation and generating a positive association with the social norm [19]. In this context, teaching with games shows that video games can be valuable tools for teaching social behaviors.

However, personalization is not the only way students can connect to video games and retain more information, but also the recognition and competition for scores, strengthening the sense of competition and adding a reward value that allows the student to develop problem-solving skills [20]. This approach, combined with the tiered structure, creates a stepped interpretation of learning, freeing the student from the pressure associated with traditional assignments [21].

4 Conclusions

This research explores the relationship between gamification and artificial intelligence (AI) in education, highlighting the positive outcomes and potential challenges. The use of gamification combined with AI has shown to enhance student performance, motivation, and communication skills, facilitating adaptation to educational content. This combination also supports critical thinking and provides a controlled environment that offers feedback, helping students meet curriculum and personal learning objectives while mitigating potential negative impacts of these technologies on education.

The majority of studies focus on higher education and secondary education, indicating significant advantages and hurdles in merging AI with gamification. Notably, there is a gap in research concerning elementary education, possibly due to bioethical considerations. In terms of perspectives on the use of AI and gamification, there is a dichotomy between a preventive approach, emphasizing the need for careful evaluation of digital tools before widespread implementation, and an experimental approach, which observes immediate improvements in learning quality and critical thinking.

AI technologies are praised for their user-friendliness and flexibility, making them more accessible than complex alternatives. Their adaptability to individual student needs is crucial for optimizing learning and enhancing educational outcomes. Environments crafted from the interplay of AI and gamification offer immersive experiences that support both accessibility and evaluation processes.

References

1. Deterding, S., Dixon, D., Khaled, R., Nacke, L.: From game design elements to gamefulness: defining "gamification". In: Proceedings of the 16th International Academic MindTrek Conference, pp. 9–15. ACM, Tampere, Finland (2011). https://doi.org/10.1145/2181037.2181040
2. Hamari, J., Koivisto, J., Sarsa, H.: Does gamification work? A literature review of empirical studies on gamification. In: Proceedings of the 47th Hawaii International Conference on System Sciences, pp. 3025–3034. IEEE, Waikoloa, HI (2014). https://doi.org/10.1109/HICSS.2014.377
3. Akgun, S., Greenhow, C.: Artificial intelligence in education: addressing ethical challenges in K-12 settings. AI Ethics **1**(1), 1 (2021). https://doi.org/10.1007/s43681-021-00096-7
4. Porayska-Pomsta, K., Mavrikis, M., Pain, H.: Technology-enhanced personalised learning: untangling the evidence. Study Health Technol. Inf. **258**, 125–129 (2018). https://pubmed.ncbi.nlm.nih.gov/30942728/
5. Zawacki-Richter, O., Marín, V., Bond, M., Gouverneur, F.: Systematic review of research on artificial intelligence applications in higher education – where are the educators? Eur. J. Open Distance E-Learn. **22**(1), 1–25 (2019). https://doi.org/10.2478/eurodl-2019-0001
6. Surendeleg, G., Murwa, V., Yun, H., Kim, Y.: The role of gamification in education – a literature review. Contemp. Eng. Sci. **7**(29), 1609–1616 (2014). https://doi.org/10.12988/ces.2014.411217
7. Xia, Q., Chiu, T., Zhou, X., Chai, C., Cheng, M.: Systematic literature review on opportunities, challenges, and future research recommendations of artificial intelligence in education. Comput. Educ. Artif. Intell. **3**, 100118 (2022). https://doi.org/10.1016/j.caeai.2022.100118
8. Torres-Toukoumidis, A., Romero Rodríguez, L., Pérez Rodríguez, A.: Ludificación y sus posibilidades en el entorno de blended learning: revisión documental. RIED: Revista Iberoamericana de Educación a Distancia **21**(1), 95–111 (2018). https://doi.org/10.5944/ried.21.1.18792
9. Klock, A., Gasparini, I., Pimenta, M., Hamari, J.: Tailored gamification: a review of literature. Int. J. Hum. Comput. Stud. **144**, 102495 (2020). https://doi.org/10.1016/j.ijhcs.2020.102495
10. Zeybek, N., Saygı, E.: Gamification in education: why, where, when, and how? Syst. Rev. Games Cult. (2023). https://doi.org/10.1177/15554120231158625
11. Zhang, C., Lu, Y.: Study on artificial intelligence: The state of the art and future prospects. J. Ind. Inf. Integr. **23**, 100224 (2021). https://doi.org/10.1016/j.jii.2021.100224

12. Aghaei Chadegani, A., et al.: A comparison between two main academic literature collections: web of science and Scopus databases. Asian Soc. Sci. **9**(5), 18–26 (2013). https://doi.org/10.5539/ass.v9n5p18
13. Shamseer, L., et al.: Preferred reporting items for systematic review and meta-analysis protocols (PRISMA-P) 2015: elaboration and explanation. BMJ **349**, g7647 (2015). https://doi.org/10.1136/bmj.g7647
14. de Back, T.T., Tinga, A.M., Nguyen, P., Louwerse, M.M.: Benefits of immersive collaborative learning in CAVE-based virtual reality. Int. J. Educ. Technol. High. Educ. **17**(1), 1–18 (2020). https://doi.org/10.1186/s41239-020-00228-9
15. Vinichenko, M., Ridho, T., Karácsony, P., Li, N., Narrainen, G., Chulanova, O.: The feasibility and expediency of gamification activities in higher education. Int. J. Educ. Pract. **7**(4), 459–468 (2019). https://doi.org/10.18488/journal.61.2019.74.459.468
16. Niu, S., Luo, J., Niemi, H., Li, X., Lu, Y.: Teachers' and students' views of using an AI-Aided educational platform for supporting teaching and learning at Chinese schools. Educ. Sci. **12**(12), 858–876 (2022). https://doi.org/10.3390/educsci12120858
17. Andriushchenko, K., Oleksandr, R., Tepliuk, M., Semenyshyna, I., Kartashov, E., Liezina, A.: Digital Literacy development trends in the professional environment. Int. J. Learn. Teach. Educ. Res. **19**(7), 55–79 (2020). https://doi.org/10.26803/ijlter.19.7.4
18. Cheng, K., Koo, A., Nasir, J., Wong, S.: An evaluation of online Edcraft Gamified Learning (EGL) to understand motivation and intention of recycling among youth. Sci. Rep. **12**(1), 14843 (2022). https://doi.org/10.1038/s41598-022-15709-2
19. Benhadj, Y., Messaoudi, M., Nfissi, A.: Artificial intelligence in education: integrating serious gaming into the language class ClassDojo technology for classroom behavioral management. IAES Int. J. Artif. Intell. **8**(4), 382–395 (2019). https://doi.org/10.11591/ijai.v8.i4.pp382-390
20. Durrani, U., Naymat, G., Ayoubi, R., Kamal, M., Hussain, H.: Gamified flipped classroom versus traditional classroom learning: which approach is more efficient in business education? Int. J. Manag. Educ. **20**(1), 100595 (2022). https://doi.org/10.1016/j.ijme.2021.100595
21. Ruiz, L., Moll-López, S., Nuñez-Pérez, A., Moraño, J., Vega-Fleitas, E.: ChatGPT challenges blended learning methodologies in engineering education: a case study in mathematics. Appl. Sci. **13**(10), 6039–6084 (2023). https://doi.org/10.3390/app13106039

uFood: Concept for a Serious Moral Game on Social-Media Marketing

Johannes Katsarov(✉), Tammo Rabener, Tim Wagenbach, Evgeniya Zakharova, Yolanda Blanco Hoppmann, Lisa Tran, Paul Drews, and Hannah Trittin-Ulbrich

Leuphana University Lüneburg, Universitätsallee 1, 21335 Lüneburg, Germany
Johannes.katsarov@leuphana.de

Abstract. Many ethical problems and risks are connected to the use of social media for purposes of marketing. Serious games have been shown to be particularly effective in promoting ethical sensitivity in other domains. In this paper, we outline the concept of uFood, a serious moral game to sensitize students of business and technology to issues related to social-media marketing. We present the game's educational strategy before the background of findings from moral psychology and studies of game-based learning.

Keywords: social media · serious game · game-based learning · ethical sensitivity · moral sensitivity · advertising ethics

1 Introduction

A wide range of ethical problems and risks are associated with social media, including the spreading of misinformation [14] and the promotion of self-destructive attitudes and behaviors – especially among vulnerable groups [13]. Since many ethical problems associated with social media are not regulated to an extent that could protect users from various risks [13], there is a growing awareness that citizens need to develop *social-media literacy*, including competences to protect themselves and others from mental risks, cyberbullying, the spreading of misinformation, etc. [9].

One avenue that has been used to promote social-media literacy, are serious games. In ethics education, serious games, and other forms of experiential learning have been found to be among the most effective teaching approaches [7]. Serious games have been developed to sensitize people to a wide range of ethical issues related to social media, including cybermobbing [4], data protection and cybersecurity [5, 10], misinformation and trolling [e.g., 1], and political radicalization [e.g., 8]. However, thus far, we have not been able to find any serious games on a responsible use of social media in marketing or advertisement, more specifically.

In this paper, we outline the concept of "uFood: The Social Media Marketing Game", a serious moral game to sensitize students of business and technology to issues related to social-media marketing. We present the game's educational strategy before the background of findings from moral psychology.

A. Schönbohm et al. (Eds.): GALA 2024, LNCS 15348, pp. 355–360, 2025.
https://doi.org/10.1007/978-3-031-78269-5_35

2 Educational Goals and Considerations

A key finding of research into moral psychology is that people who act unethically are often unaware that their behaviors are problematic (e.g., in being dishonest, harmful, or unfair). For example, Singhapakdi et al. [11] found that marketing professionals were unlikely to disagree with unethical marketing practices when they did not recognize that the described behaviors involved ethical issues or problems. People who were aware of the given risks, were much more likely to say that they would avoid the described behaviors. Other researchers found that marketing professionals frequently fail to recognize ethical problems [3, 12]. What these findings show, is that a sensitivity to ethical risks and problems of marketing is crucial for the prevention of business misconduct. We have therefore decided to make the promotion of ethical sensitivity in advertising the focus of our game. The main goal is to sensitize students and practitioners of marketing to a range of 16 ethically problematic practices advertising practices, as identified by Yildirim et al. [15]. Some of the more recent ethical issues in marketing revolve around the use of social media, including the promotion of products through social-media influencers, and targeted advertising that relies on triggering emotional responses in individuals based on sophisticated data on their desires and needs. For this reason, our game focuses on social-media advertising, although its lessons can be applied to any area of advertising ethics.

As Katsarov argues, it is crucial for learners to develop three forms of ethical sensitivity, which complement each other [6]:

1. *Recognitional ethical sensitivity* enables people to notice explicit ethical issues when they arise – even when they are facing time pressure, while they are pursuing challenging goals, and when they are exhausted. For this purpose, our game represents a large range of ethical problems in advertising and highlights how they can be perceived as problematic.
2. *Sympathetic ethical sensitivity*, on the other hand, implies that people need to learn to care for people unlike themselves (e.g., people of other ages, genders, ethnicities) and consider how they could be affected. To build this sensitivity, our game represents a wide range of identities positively and shows how diverse people can be affected negatively by problematic advertising strategies.
3. Finally, people require *critical ethical sensitivity*, an ability to notice when their own moral judgment and perception can be clouded. Our game is designed to sensitize learners for four central drivers of ethical blindness in the domain of business, namely (1) a mental preoccupation with business goals, (2) conflicts of interest, (2) a one-sided framing of issues in terms of business objectives, and (3) a gradual erosion of ethical standards (slippery-slope effect). These "blinders", in the language of Bazerman and Tenbrunsel usually affect people subliminally, i.e., without people's conscious awareness [2]. Critical ethical sensitivity enables people to recognize situations where they may fail to notice or evaluate ethical issues appropriately – akin to the knowledge that having a few alcoholic drinks reduces our driving competence and reaction time substantially.

3 Educational Strategy and Game Mechanisms

uFood has been designed for use in the classroom. Playing the game takes 45 min on average. No introduction to the game is required, but gameplay should be followed by a structured debriefing immediately.

3.1 Role and Challenge

uFood places players in the role of a social-media manager at a large company who is supposed to advertise a protein shake called "uFood" on social media for 10 weeks. Their boss expects them to attract 200.000 new customers for uFood within this short period of time, and to generate a revenue of more than 2 million Euros. Players always find their current statistics in the main menu of the game (Fig. 1).

Fig. 1. Main menu of uFood

Every week, players can choose from a range of advertising campaigns to reach their challenging business goals. To achieve their goals, players must decide among diverse possible actions each week. They can choose between advertisements that they can post on of six social-media outlets, and among influencers that they can hire for product promotion. Each week, they receive a limited amount of in-game currency (9 action points). Each choice costs a specific number of action points. For example, influencers with many followers are usually more expensive. Players can end a week without spending all their action points, saving the rest of their action points for the next week.

Social-media endorsements and product revenue are the two central metrics of the game. After each action, players see immediate effects in terms new followers. For instance, they will gain 1,440 new followers on one of the social-media platforms. At the end of the week, they learn what volume of sales they achieved, whereby their weekly sales figures depend on the number of current followers.

Most of the decisions that players can make in the game are relatively unproblematic from an ethical perspective. Some options are problematic, however, and they are not highlighted as such: players need to make up their own mind about the strategic and ethical appropriateness of each promotional activity that is presented to them (Fig. 2). This makes it difficult for learners to notice ethical issues, and likely that they will ignore some of them – especially since they are preoccupied with reaching business objectives and struggling to make sense of various business-related information. Some of the most problematic strategies are presented as "low-hanging fruit", promising high returns for little investment, and therefore creating egoistic temptations for players. The combination of these game mechanisms makes it very likely for players to make several problematic decisions throughout gameplay. In playtesting the game with more than 200 students, only very few students played the entire game without taking a single problematic choice.

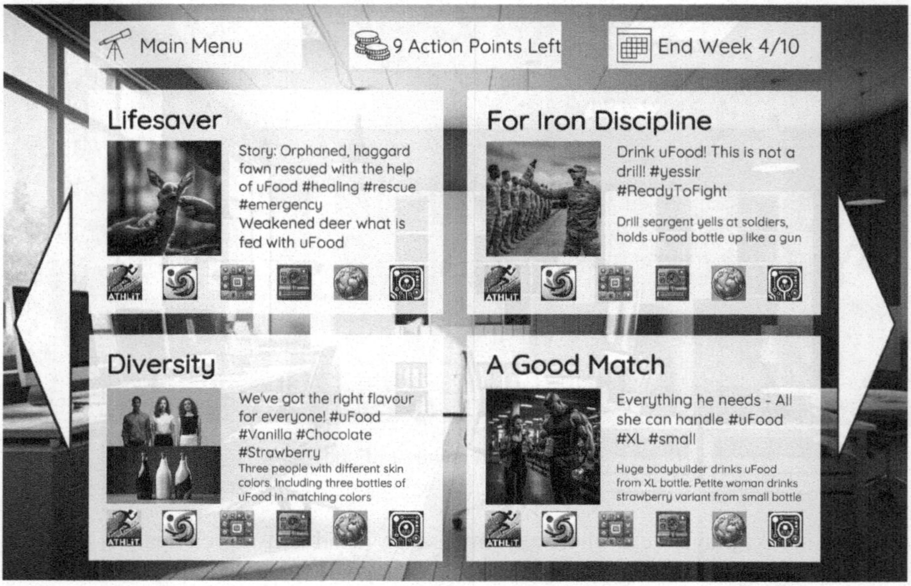

Fig. 2. Four random advertising concepts from uFood, including ethical issues.

3.2 Feedback System

uFood makes it likely for players to engage in problematic advertising behavior *unintentionally*. As a corrective, the game uses several feedback strategies to sensitize players for the problematic nature of the respective actions. First, they receive immediate evaluative feedback from their "critical friend" in the game, a self-selected mentor who expresses worries or concern when players make bad decisions. Second, delayed consequences are used to demonstrate what negative effects some forms of advertising can have for diverse people, and the company. For example, a baby who was fed with uFood for an entire week may end up in an intensive care unit, after players cooperated with a vegan food influencer who suggested that uFood was an appropriate substitute for breast milk. Third, the consequences are designed to integrate business-related and ethical considerations. In the long run, ethical misconduct also has a negative impact on business performance in the game: Negative events result in losses of followers and brand reputation. One of the bosses' expectations, which is explicitly mentioned in the beginning of the game, is for players to ensure that the uFood brand's reputation is protected. If the brand reputation dips below a rating of 3 stars, players will be fired.

At the end of week 8, the game culminates in a scandal, with one of four possible scandals arising. For instance, two parents may publicly accuse uFood of triggering an eating disorder in their teenage daughter. The likelihood and gravity of each scandal is influenced by previous decisions, e.g., by cooperating with an influencer who propagates a radical weight-loss regime. In the rare event that players took no problematic actions, a random scandal is displayed. Players can react to the scandals by ignoring them, apologizing publicly, trying to make amends, rejecting the accusations, or by attacking the accusers through social-media campaigns. Depending on the degree to which the accusations are justified, these choices lead to different results. For example, a public apology made in reaction to unjustified accusations erodes trust in uFood and has a negative effect on followers and brand reputation. The goal of the scandals is to sensitize learners for more systemic issues in social-media advertising, e.g., how the promotion of problematic beauty ideals can cause harm.

At the end of the game, the bosses either promote players, demote them to their previous role, or fire them, whereby all three business targets are considered. For example, players with a reputation below 3.5 will be demoted – irrespective of how high their revenues and follower numbers are. Additionally, players receive final feedback from their critical friend, who focuses on the ethical integrity they demonstrated in the game. In the worst case, players will lose this friendship. When the degree of players' ethical misconduct was moderate, the critical friend emphasizes the importance of learning and sensitivity and offers further support in the future.

4 Discussion and Outlook

In this paper, we have introduced the educational strategy and concept for the game uFood, which we have just finalized. Our aim is to publish the game as an open educational resource alongside exercises and teaching materials for the game's usage in education and training soon. At the Leuphana University in Lueneburg, we have tested uFood with more than 300 students meanwhile. We hope to publish results from our experimentation soon. Generally, our experience is that the game helps to facilitate a high degree of critical ethical sensitivity in students when the debriefing highlights common human fallacies in noticing ethical problems.

Acknowledgements. This work has been funded by the German Foundation for Innovation in Higher Education (Stiftung Innovation in der Hochschullehre) as part of the project Digital Transformation Lab for Teaching and Learning (DigiTaL). We would like to thank the members of our scientific committee, Jascha Brandes, Ina Cramer, Nicolas Dierks, Chiara Ludwig, Katharina Trostorff, and Markus Zimmer for their advice and recommendations on the development of uFood.

References

1. Basol, M., Roozenbeek, J., van der Linden, S.: Good news about bad news: gamified inoculation boosts confidence and cognitive immunity against fake news. J. Cogn. **3**(1), 2 (2020). https://doi.org/10.5334/joc.91
2. Bazerman, M.H., Tenbrunsel, A.E.: Blind Spots: Why We Fail to Do What's Right and What to Do About It. Princeton University Press (2011)
3. Beggs, J.M.: Seamless Integration of Ethics. Mark. Educ. Rev. **21**(1), 49–55 (2010). https://doi.org/10.2753/MER1052-8008210107
4. Calvo-Morata, A., Alonso-Fernández, C., Freire, M., Martínez-Ortiz, I., Fernández-Manjón, B.: Serious games to prevent and detect bullying and cyberbullying: a systematic serious games and literature review. Comput. Educ. **157**, 103958 (2020). https://doi.org/10.1016/j.compedu.2020.103958
5. Dewes, T., Gasiba, T., Schreck, T.: Understanding the usage of IT-security games in the industry and its mapping to job profiles. In: Paper presented at the Third International Computer Programming Education Conference (ICPEC 2022), vol. 3, pp. 1–12 (2022). https://doi.org/10.4230/OASIcs.ICPEC.2022.3
6. Katsarov, J.: Virtuous Play. Promoting Moral Sensitivity with Digital Games. Doctoral Dissertation. University of Zurich (2023)
7. Katsarov, J., Andorno, R., Krom, A., van den Hoven, M.: Effective strategies for research integrity training—a meta-analysis. Educ. Psychol. Rev. **34**(2), 935–955 (2022). https://doi.org/10.1007/s10648-021-09630-9
8. Playing History. Hidden Codes. Bildungsstätte Anne Frank (2022)
9. Polanco-Levicán, K., Salvo-Garrido, S.: Understanding social media literacy: a systematic review of the concept and its competences. Int. J. Environ. Res. Public Health **19**(14), 8807 (2022). https://doi.org/10.3390/ijerph19148807
10. Ryan, M., McEwan, M., Sansare, V., Formosa, P., Richards, D., Hitchens, M.: Design of a Serious Game for Cybersecurity Ethics Training. In: Proceedings of DiGRA 2022. Paper 156, 1–18 (2022). http://www.digra.org/wp-content/uploads/digital-library/DiGRA_2022_paper_156.pdf
11. Singhapakdi, A., Rao, C.P., Vitell, S.J.: Ethical decision making: an investigation of services marketing professionals. J. Bus. Ethics **15**(6), 635–644 (1996). https://www.jstor.org/stable/25072789
12. Sparks, J.R., Hunt, S.D.: Marketing researcher ethical sensitivity: conceptualization, measurement, and exploratory investigation. J. Market. **62**(2), 92–109 (1998). http://www.jstor.org/stable/1252163
13. Strycharz, J., Duivenvoorde, B.: The exploitation of vulnerability through personalised marketing communication: are consumers protected?. Internet Policy Rev. **10**(4) (2021). https://doi.org/10.14763/2021.4.1585
14. Trittin-Ulbrich, H., Scherer, A.G., Munro, I., Whelan, G.: Exploring the dark and unexpected sides of digitalization: toward a critical agenda. Organization **28**(1), 8–25 (2021). https://doi.org/10.1177/1350508420968184
15. Yildirim, E., Mert, K. Cebeci, H.: Comprehensive review of the marketing ethics literature: a bibliometric approach. Turk. J. Bus. Ethics **14**, 242–269 (2021). https://doi.org/10.12711/tjbe.2021.14.2.2176

Historical Tabletop Role-Playing Games: Integrating Historical and Cultural Content into the Character Creation Process

Sofia Despoina Kyrgiafini(✉), Ioanna Afroditi Mazi, Varvara Garneli, and Ioannis Deliyannis

Department of Audio and Visual Arts, Ionian University, Tsirigoti Sq. 7, 49100 Corfu, Greece
sofiakyrgiafini@gmail.com

Abstract. Historical Role-Playing Games (RPGs) allow players to immerse themselves in past worlds, experiencing firsthand various social, political, and economic realities. Given this potential, further research is necessary to explore practical and innovative methods for integrating historical information into gameplay mechanics. We developed the Player's Guide (PG) for a TableTop RPG (TTRPG), systematically incorporating social and political elements from a specific historical era. This study contributes to the growing body of knowledge on the educational potential of TTRPGs, offering valuable insights into the role of the PG in enhancing historical understanding.

Keywords: Tabletop RPGs · Character Creation Process · Historical Education

1 Introduction

Historical games like Call of Duty: World War II and Assassin's Creed Origins often reference past events and historical figures or incorporate history as a functional element of the user experience, enhancing authenticity [1]. While some historical games link their content to the past without providing relevant historical information, the interactive nature of commercial game titles can promote innovative and deep communication of historical data, arguments, and debates [2]. In particular, historical RPGs can transcend the limitations of the present and immerse players in the worlds of the past, allowing them to experience firsthand the social, political, and economic realities that shaped previous eras [3], often with satisfactory historical accuracy. More research is needed to investigate practical and innovative ways of historical content integration, engaging players with a variety of historical experiences.

In this study, we will employ TableTop Role-Playing Games (TTRPGs), a form of interactive storytelling where players take the roles of characters in a fictional setting, guided by a set of rules and the Game Master (GM) who runs the game. These games combine narrative and mechanics, allowing players to influence the story through their decisions and actions [4]. The integration of historical elements in these games can be achieved through carefully selected narratives and appropriate system design.

A. Schönbohm et al. (Eds.): GALA 2024, LNCS 15348, pp. 361–367, 2025.
https://doi.org/10.1007/978-3-031-78269-5_36

Narratively, the games could be based on historically accurate stories, characters, and settings, immersing players in the relevant time period. Mechanically, game systems could incorporate rules that reflect historical realities, such as social hierarchies and economic and political systems [5]. In this viewpoint, a crucial component of incorporating historical elements in TTRPGs could be the Character Creation Process (CCP). This process requires players to design their Player Characters (PCs) by assigning names, backgrounds, and personalities and selecting traits that reflect the historical setting [6]. For example, Ars Magica features a detailed medieval European setting where players create characters deeply rooted in the historical and mythical context of Europe, with abilities that mirror professions and skills from that time.

Inspired by games like Ars Magica[1], our approach will engage players with a historical period, challenging them to understand its key features in order to create characters that align with both the era and their imagination, following the guidelines provided in the Player Guide (PG). By encouraging players to deeply explore their characters' backgrounds and motivations, we aim to foster a strong connection between the player and the character, sparking greater interest in their journey. We believe our work will resonate with Game Designers, History Teachers, GMs, and Researchers, inspiring further exploration and research in this field.

2 Methodology

The CCP involves several key decisions as players design their PCs according to the instructions outlined in the PG. These decisions typically include choosing their PC's class and origin. The class represents the PC's primary role or specialization within the game, ranging from traditional archetypes like fighters, mages, and rogues to more unique ones based on the game's design needs. In addition, players select their PC's origin or background, another crucial element that defines their identity and place within the game world. Origin encompasses factors such as place of birth, family history, social status, and formative experiences, all of which influence the PC's personality, skills, and motivations [7]. By carefully designing the PG, we utilized the CCP as a means to integrate historical content into the game.

2.1 Game Setting

We set the game in 1716 Corfu during the Ottoman siege. At that time, the island was under Venetian control, which shaped its social, cultural, and political dynamics. Corfu's strategic location made it a key Mediterranean trading hub, contributing to its economic prosperity under Venetian rule. Trade brought wealth to the island and facilitated the exchange of goods, culture, and ideas [8]. Corfu became a center where artistic, intellectual, and scientific ideas were exchanged and disseminated [9]. Meanwhile, the military organization of Venetian possessions followed Venice's overarching defensive strategy, aimed at maintaining its territories against Turkish threats and protecting against frequent pirate raids [10].

[1] https://www.atlas-games.com/arsmagica/.

2.2 Design Process

The first step of creating our PG involved brainstorming and researching to ensure the accuracy of the game's content. We focused on various aspects of Corfu in the early 18th century, including its history, mythology, and social and political settings. Additionally, we delved into details of daily life, such as architecture, habits, clothing, items, names, and even the island's flowers. Key sources included historical texts, records, and literature recommended by historians and local scholars. We then aimed to provide flexible and dynamic gameplay by following an iterative design process, allowing continuous refinement.

2.3 Content Integration

We linked the CCP to the social dynamics of Corfu, influenced by Venetian rule. In doing so, we aligned historical roles relevant to the period with traditional TTRPG archetypes, assigning corresponding responsibilities. Players' choices in this context influence their PCs' statistics, abilities, and health, as well as determine the items they possess. Additionally, we introduced social status to reflect the social hierarchy of the Ionian Islands [11], where society was divided into nobles, townspeople, and commoners [12]. Social class was linked to factors, such as access to wealth and education, relationships and alliances, commanded respect, lifestyle, resources, responsibilities, and societal expectations. Finally, we designed character origins to capture the migratory waves and socio-political dynamics of the time [13], with each origin granting unique attributes that mirrored the historical backgrounds of Corfu's inhabitants.

3 Player's Guide

We developed the PG[2], including instructions about the character creation process, which consists of the following: Classes, Social Status, and Origin.

3.1 Classes

We designed six classes tailored to the historical and social context of Corfu and inspired by popular RPG classes, each with its own unique abilities and role. The Soldier and Rifleman are combat specialists [10], while the Musician [8] and Cleric [12] focus on support and enhancement. The Scholar [8] and Rogue [11] are versatile classes, balancing offense and support. These classes incorporate traditional RPG mechanics while reflecting the island's rich cultural and military history. We also integrated historical elements like items, clothing, and visual representations into the game's art for a more immersive experience (See Table 1).

---

[2] https://heyzine.com/flip-book/2957dd0682.html.

Table 1. Character Classes

Name	Items	Description
Soldier	Schiavona[3]	Close-range assaults, significant physical strength, limited mental prowess
Rifleman	Muskets[4]	Precision, firepower. They integrate land and naval elements, tactical versatility in historical skirmishes
Scholar	Encyclopedia	Balanced class excelling in detection and intellectual endeavors; strong intelligence attribute; reflects scholarly traditions and educational institutions of the island
Cleric	Healing scrolls	Supportive roles with healing and defensive abilities. Inspired by the Jewish Community's role against the Ottomans
Musician	Musical Instrument	Enchants allies through music; supports with storytelling; reflects Corfu's vibrant cultural and musical heritage
Rogue	Venetian Daggers	Thrives on espionage and swift maneuvers; excels in reconnaissance and critical strikes; navigates Corfu's underworld and intricate social-political landscapes

3.2 Social Status

Another critical decision is the PC's social class, which reflects the social hierarchy of the Ionian Islands under Venetian rule from the mid-14th to late 18th century. At the top were the nobles, who held hereditary titles and occupied key positions in administration and the military. The middle class, the *Asti*, consisted of professionals, merchants, and craftsmen who drove economic growth. The *Popolari*, or working class, had fewer privileges and performed essential labor [12] (See Table 2).

3.3 Origin

In 1537, the Turks under Barbarossa attacked Corfu but failed to capture the city. They devastated the countryside, enslaving 20,000 people and leaving rural areas deserted [11]. To mitigate further destruction, the Venetians offered land and privileges to settlers. This prompted significant migration from Epirus, Peloponnese, Crete, Venice, and Malta. Many modern Corfiots trace their ancestry to this period, with entire neighborhoods and some villages populated by their descendants [13]. We included the origins from Venice, Peloponnese, Crete, and Hepirus and enriched them with phantasy and cultural elements (See Table 3).

---

[3] Venetian sword.

[4] Rifles of the historical era.

Table 2. Character Status

Social Classes	Advantages	Disadvantages
Nobles	Start with ten coins, enabling the purchase of expensive items. High connections and access to exclusive areas due to their names' inclusion in the "Libro d'Oro"	High expenses to maintain a lavish lifestyle. Increased public scrutiny, making illegal activities harder. Lack of practical skills. Difficulty connecting with ordinary citizens
Asti	Start with six coins, providing financial stability. Can navigate both high society and common environments. Bonuses in trade negotiations. Extra item slot	Moderate advantages and privileges. There are no exceptional bonuses. Compromises needed for a balanced approach
Popolari	Strong community ties offering support and local insights. Practical skills in craftsmanship and repair. Bonus in navigation actions and improvised items	Start with minimal resources (2 coins). Financial vulnerability. Social barriers to accessing exclusive areas. Challenges in interactions with nobles and the wealthy

Table 3. Character's Origins

Origin	Attribute's Name	Attribute
Venetian	"The Spider's Bite"	Grants agility, allowing a reroll of failed dodge attempts once per game
Peloponnesian	"The Wrath of Morea"	Offers +2 dice for physical actions at the cost of health once per game
Corfiot	"Botanical Revival"	Enhances healing, granting +2 on healing rolls once per game
Cretan	"Unshakable Morale"	Provides immunity to intimidation and +2 morale points once per game
Epirote	"Endurance of Epirus"	Grants 2 extra energy points at the cost of mental health once per game

4 Conclusions

We designed the PG for a historical TTRPG set in Corfu during the 18th-century Ottoman siege, systematically integrating social and political historical elements into the CCP. Players select Class, Social Status, and Origins to create their PCs, a process that encourages research while tables and images aid their decisions. Our goal was to spark players' historical curiosity, prompting deeper investigation into the past through their engagement with the game. The CCP is designed to involve players actively, motivating them to explore their characters' backgrounds and motivations, thereby fostering a strong connection to their PCs. However, this feature may appeal primarily to players drawn to this aspect of TTRPGs. Future work will involve systematic testing of the PG and the overall game experience by specialized testers and end users.

This study contributes to the growing body of knowledge on the educational potential of TTRPGs, offering insights into the impact of the PG on player engagement with historical content. Our aim was to engage players deeply with the historical material, promoting a deeper exploration of the past and fostering attachment to their characters. However, factors such as player familiarity with TTRPG gameplay and individual preferences should be carefully considered.

Acknowledgments. We would like to thank the Dr Charalambos Kourgiantakis and Assistant Professor Fotios Baroutsos for their help and access to historical references.

Disclosure of Interests. The authors have no competing interests to declare that are relevant to the content of this article.

References

1. Wainwright, M.: Virtual Historians: How Video Games Portray the Past. Routledge, NY (2019)
2. Houghton, R.: World, structure and play: A framework for games as historical research outputs, tools, and processes. Práticas da História. Journal on Theory, Historiography and Uses of the Past vol. (7), pp. 11–43 (2018)
3. McCall, J.: Teaching history with digital historical games: an introduction to the field and best practices. Simul. Gaming **47**(4), 517–542 (2016). https://doi.org/10.1177/1046878116664669
4. Hitchens, M., Drachen, A.: The many faces of role-playing games. Int. J. Role-Playing (1), 3–21 (2008). https://doi.org/10.33063/ijrp.vi1.185
5. Kuran, M.Ş., Tozoğlu, A.E., Tavernari, C.: History-themed games in history education: experiences on a blended world history course. In: 17th International Conference on Information Technology Based Higher Education and Training (ITHET) 2018. LNCS, pp. 1–8. IEEE (2018). https://doi.org/10.1109/ITHET.2018.8424767
6. White, W.J., Arjoranta, J., Hitchens, M., Peterson, J., Torner, E., Walton, J.: Tabletop role-playing games. In: Role-Playing Game Studies: Transmedia Foundations, pp. 63–86. Taylor and Francis, Routledge (2018). https://doi.org/10.4324/9781315637532-4
7. Iantorno, M., Consalvo, M.: Background checks: disentangling class, race, and gender in CRPG character creators. Games Cult. **18**(8), 979–1003 (2023). https://doi.org/10.1177/15554120221150342
8. Fusaro, M.: Political Economies of Empire in the Early Modern Mediterranean: The Decline of Venice and the Rise of England, 1450–1700. Cambridge University Press, Cambridge (2015). https://doi.org/10.1017/CBO9781107447158
9. Gekas, A.: Migrants, Merchants and Philanthropists: Hierarchies in Nineteenth-Century Greek Ports. In: Jarvis, A., Lee, R. (eds.) Trade, Migration and Urban Networks in Port Cities, pp. 1640–1940. Liverpool (2008). https://doi.org/10.5949/liverpool/9780973893489.003.0007
10. Gasparinatos, G.S.: Venetian rule on the Ionian Islands. Η Βενετοκρατία στα νησιά του Ιονίου Πελάγους. Private Edition (2009)
11. Pappas, T.G.: Corfu: Manual of Local History. Κέρκυρα:Εγχειρίδιο Τοπικής Ιστορίας. Pedagogical Institute, Athens (2000)

12. Klemis, O.K.: Sociology of the Corfiot People. Κοινωνιολογία του Κερκυραϊκού Λαού. Papazisis, Athens (1998)
13. Kollas, Ch.B.: Region and Population of Corfu in the 17th Century: Toponyms - Settlements – Demographics. Χώρος και Πληθυσμός της Κέρκυρας του 17ου Αιώνα: Τοπωνύμια –Οικισμοί – Δημογραφικά στοιχεία. Corfu (1988)

Modelling and Verification with Petri Nets of Asymmetric Role-Playing Learning Scenarios

Gaëlle Guigon[1,2(✉)], Mathieu Muratet[1,3], Mathieu Vermeulen[2], and Thibault Carron[1]

[1] Sorbonne Université, CNRS, LIP6, 75005 Paris, France
[2] IMT Nord Europe, Institut Mines-Télécom, University Lille, Centre for Digital Systems, 59000 Lille, France
gaelle.guigon@imt-nord-europe.fr
[3] Sorbonne Université, CNRS, INS HEA, LIP6, 75005 Paris, France

Abstract. Students need realistic practice in their future professions, including teamwork. Our goal is to enhance student cooperation and simulate real-life scenarios through educational activities. We support teachers in designing asymmetric role-playing games using a specific model and tools. These games are relevant across various disciplines and educational levels, focusing on fostering cooperation. Our verification system helps ensure optimal cooperative opportunities in these scenarios. This article presents a method using Petri nets for modelling and verifying these role-playing scenarios, ensuring they promote collaboration. The method translates game tasks into reusable Petri net patterns, adaptable to various combinations. The system's effectiveness has been tested in games with two to three players, providing valuable metrics for teachers on synchronisation risks but it needs adjustments for scenarios with repeated tasks and random resources.

Keywords: Petri net · serious game · co-design · automated check

1 Introduction

An increasing number of teachers are adopting innovative methods to enhance student engagement [5]. Serious games (SGs) have proven effective [2], and many are designed for specific purposes [1]. Our focus is on aligning these games with students' future careers. Known as learning games (LGs), most are single-player with uniform roles. However, multiplayer, multi-role games offer greater realism and promote collaboration [3]. We want to prepare students for teamwork and diverse career roles through games asymmetric scenarios that we call "Role Learning Games" (RLGs).

RLG design is complex [6], particularly in synchronising tasks for collaboration. We developed a model and two tools to aid teachers in designing RLG

A. Schönbohm et al. (Eds.): GALA 2024, LNCS 15348, pp. 368–374, 2025.
https://doi.org/10.1007/978-3-031-78269-5_37

scenarios [4]. This paper introduces a method using Petri nets for scenario modelling and automated verification, focusing on ensuring collaboration synchronicity. Our research question is: How can we automatically ensure that players will be able to collaborate at the intended times? The following sections discuss the Petri net modelling, verification system, and its evaluation, preceding a discussion.

2 Scenario Modelling with Petri Nets

Our contribution is inspired by the work of Muratet [8] that helps designers to model LGs with Petri nets. A Petri net is a mathematical representation that models systems based on discrete events and states [9]. It is recognised as a powerful tool for analysis, validation, and verification.

2.1 Petri Nets and Pattern Propositions

A Petri net is a graphical and mathematical tool used to simulate complex systems. It is a bipartite graph with two sets of vertices: Places (P) and Transitions (T). As a graphical model, it's readable by humans and computable to generate all reachable states from the initial state by firing transitions, forming the reachability graph. This graph is our core model for scenario analysis.

In this context, a "quest" is a set of tasks for a role, and a "scenario" is a set of quests making up a game, with roles possibly played by multiple players. Places represent quest states, and transitions depict tasks roles perform to progress. Game tasks are simulated in the Petri net by firing the associated transitions, keeping it synchronised with the quest state.

In summary, we use Petri nets to model asymmetric role-playing game scenarios and the reachability graph to analyse role behaviours. Thus, for example, we can answer questions like: which are the triggerable transitions for each role in the quest at a given time? What is the shortest path to common tasks that necessitate simultaneous actions by at least two roles?

We have modelled six fundamental Petri net patterns in Fig. 1 to build various scenario elements based on Sun's work [10]. These patterns (Fig. 1) reflect the variety of tasks and scenarios in RLGs. Pattern 1 models a basic task, where completing the task moves a token from "ready 1" to "TU 1"[1] via the "do 1" transition, indicating time spent. After validation, the token moves to "ready after 1". Pattern 2 requires to complete several mandatory tasks before advancing, while pattern 3 unlocks multiple tasks after one is finished. Pattern 4 represents a situation where a role chooses one or more tasks, and pattern 5 models a situation where the role needs to decide on a path. In our current context, each RLG quest is constructed using combinations of these six patterns. The next subsection explains how they are combined to model a quest.

[1] TU: Time Unit.

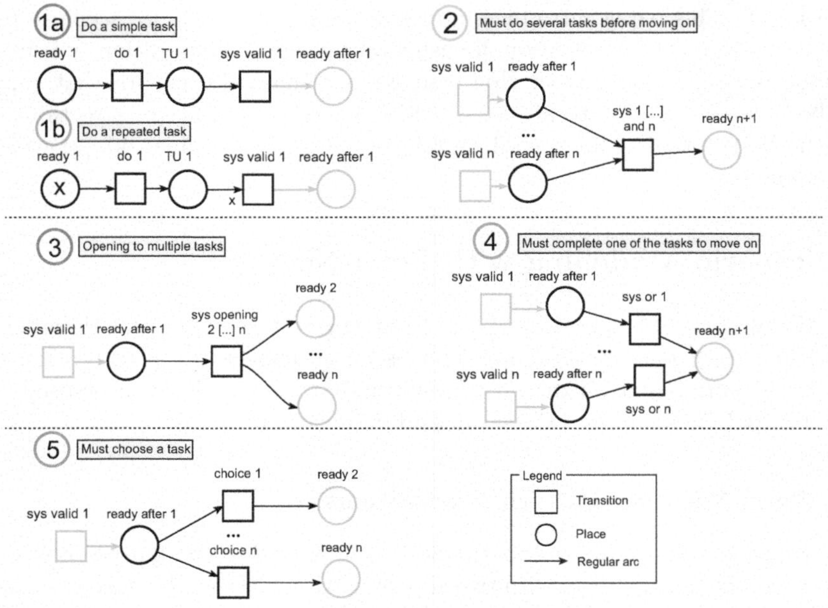

Fig. 1. Petri net patterns representing various RLG situations

2.2 Combining Petri Net Patterns

Firstly, we use one Petri net per role, so a scenario has at least two Petri nets for multiplayer games. In cooperative games, roles need to perform some tasks together, called "common tasks" (CT). Figure 2 illustrates a two-role scenario with three CTs, corresponding to pattern 1a in Fig. 1. Switching between tasks C and D, E & F corresponds to pattern 3, and switching between tasks D, E & F and H corresponds to pattern 2. System actions (grey transitions) fire automatically and do not cost time units, while player actions (white transitions) cost 1 TU. Designers must ensure that both roles perform the CTs in the correct order and simultaneously.

Tasks marked as optional, such as tasks S, Y, O, Q, N and R for Role 2 in Fig. 2, adjust timing, keeping players occupied while waiting for common tasks. To account for side tasks, the first Petri net of each role is derived to obtain a constrained version that calculates the shortest path, including side tasks, to the CT. For Role 2, the constrained net connects the optional tasks to the common task transition with read arcs, thus, it does not affect mandatory task progress. If there are no side tasks, the constrained and unconstrained nets are identical, as shown for Role 1.

3 Automatic Verification System

The core objective of our system is to automatically verify whether CT in the quests can be performed concurrently. This consists in computing the overlap

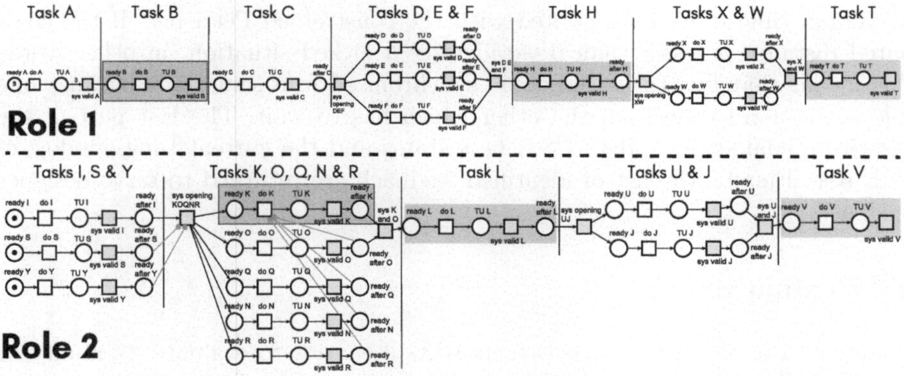

Fig. 2. Example of a scenario composed of two quests represented with Petri nets

window for each role involved in a common task to perform it. To achieve this, we use Laalys [7]. We choose to use this tool for two reasons: it enables to process the extended Petri nets that includes another type of arc: inhibitor arcs (this type of arc is used in specific conditions: the weight of the arc blocks the activation of the transition if there are too many tokens in the Place; and it provides an API to query Petri nets); in our case we used it to block a player's action when too many resources (tokens) were available in a reserve (Place).

3.1 Requirements

As mentioned, each quest is represented by two Petri nets: an unconstrained version (to compute the shortest path to a specific task) and a constrained version (where side tasks are connected to ensure Laalys calculates the shortest path including side tasks). For each transition, we define whether it is a system transition (automatically executed) or player-activated. The last requirement for our algorithm is to define the list of CT to check. Each common task includes the roles involved, and each role references the two Petri nets (unconstrained and constrained) modelling its quest.

3.2 Algorithm Overview

Our main algorithm, named "RLGchecker"[2] computes, for a given order of common tasks, the overlap time windows to perform these tasks by roles involved. The algorithm parses all given CT and calculates the minimum distance, in TU, between the minimum TU of each role to reach a common task and the minimum of the maxima TU of the other roles involved in this common task. The minimum time units is computed with the unconstrained Petri net while the

[2] Sources of the algorithm: https://github.com/GuigonGaelle/RLGchecker/releases/tag/v1.0.

maximum time units is computed with the constrained Petri net. If the computed distance is lesser than 0 we identify a locked situation, in other words this means that two roles cannot be synchronised in a same task because one role needs more time than the other which has to wait. The last part of the algorithm enables to update Petri nets states and the current time window of each role. Finally, the list of identified feedback are returned to serve designer feedback.

4 Evaluation

We tested the algorithm with various RLG scenarios to evaluate its ability to detect synchronisation issues and suggest improvements. The first test involved a real RLG for a French class with two roles (R1 and R2) seen in part 3. In this scenario, each common task (CT) had a narrow cooperation window of only 1 TU. When we tested it with students, one role completed tasks faster than the other, leading to uneven pacing and waiting periods. Here, we were expecting warnings from the algorithm to prevent this type of problem so that the designer can occupy the other role instead of waiting. For each common task (for example, 'do H' and 'do L', in blue in Fig. 2), a message was displayed, as this one:

> R1 'do H ' is accessible after 8 TU. // R2 'do L ' is accessible after 4 to 8 TU. // Concerning 'R1': 'do H', 'R2': 'do L': Overlap WARNING. The common tasks (CTs) will be accessible on only one TU: There is no margin of time to complete this CT. If the estimated duration does not correspond to reality, a role may be waiting for another one. We suggest you to add some side tasks to compensate for differences in speed between players.

The algorithm flagged potential issues with such narrow windows, recommending the inclusion of side tasks to keep players occupied. This feedback would have been valuable in preventing these timing mismatches. The teacher expressed interest in using side tasks to avoid downtime, showing the algorithm's practical utility in refining scenarios to accommodate different player speeds.

We tested our system on other scenarios including one with random exchanges of resources between players and tasks repeated an indefinite number of times. The algorithm's results showed a major synchronicity problem, expected due to the game's mechanics. Overall, initial tests of our algorithm show encouraging results regarding its effectiveness in identifying synchronisation issues and providing actionable feedback. The results are very positive for linear scenarios but the system can be refined to better analyse more complex scenarios.

5 Discussion

A concise set of Petri net patterns enables designers to build multiplayer, multi-role scenarios, with our algorithm automatically checking if roles can interact at the right times. Initial results are promising, as the algorithm effectively identifies synchronisation issues and provides guidance for adjustments, making scenario testing efficient. However, complexities arise in scenarios involving resource management and multiple game turns, as demonstrated in a second test. The system currently struggles to reflect how one role's tasks impact another, particularly with inter-role resource management, since each role operates within its own Petri net. We are investigating solutions, such as dynamic arc weighting, to address this limitation. RLGs are uncommon, with little research available to guide designers. This paper provides a method to ensure that CTs can be executed concurrently, accounting for differences in player task completion speeds. The algorithm's feedback helps designers identify and resolve potential waiting times, allowing for smoother game flow.

6 Conclusion

To address our research question, we developed an algorithm that analyses each role's quest using Petri nets. This algorithm evaluates the time needed to reach common tasks and compares the timings across roles, offering feedback for improvement when synchronisation is not optimal. It performed well in linear scenarios but encounters challenges in non-linear ones with resource exchanges, indicating the need for refinement.

Future developments include automating Petri net generation through an online tool. This automation would simplify the design process for teachers and instructional designers, allowing them to export Petri nets easily without requiring prior expertise.

References

1. Alvarez, J., et al.: A formal approach to distinguish games, toys, serious games and toys, serious repurposing and modding, and simulators. IEEE Trans. Games **15**(3), 399–410 (2023)
2. Cahier, J.P., El Mawas, N.: Co-designing a serious game to train emergency medical services. In: CTS, pp. 588–593. San Diego, United States (2013)
3. Di Loreto, I., Divitini, M.: Games for Learning Cooperation at Work: the case of crisis preparedness. In: ECTEL meets ECSCW 2013. Paphos, Cyprus (2013)
4. Guigon, G., Vermeulen, M., Muratet, M., Carron, T.: Tangible or digital? A comparison between two tools for designing asymmetric role-playing games for learning. In: CSEDU. Angers, Fr (2024)
5. Jaffray, A., Finn, C., Nurse, J.: SherLOCKED: a detective-themed serious game for cyber security education. In: Furnell, S., Clarke, N. (eds.) HAISA. vol. AICT-613, pp. 35–45. Springer Intl Publishing, Virtual, UK (2021)
6. Marfisi-Schottman, I.: Designing Serious Games, Mobile Learning and Extended Reality Applications for and with teachers. thesis, Le mans Université (2023)
7. Muratet, M., Yessad, A., Carron, T.: Understanding Learners' Behaviors in Serious Games. In: ICWL. LNCS, vol. 10013, pp. 195–205. Springer, Rome, Italy (2016)
8. Muratet, M., Yessad, A., Carron, T.: How to assist designers model learning games with Petri nets? In: Foundations of Digital Games 2022. Athènes, Greece (2022)

9. Peterson, J.L.: Petri Net Theory and Modeling of Systems. Prentice Hall, Reading, Mass (1981)
10. Sun, W., Li, T., Peng, W., Sun, T.: Incremental workflow mining with optional patterns and its application to production printing process. Int. J. Intell. Control Syst. **12**, 45–55 (2007)

Combining 360° Spaces and Social VR

Suryaprakash Reddy Kalvakolu[1], Heinrich Söbke[1,2(✉)], Jannicke Baalsrud Hauge[3,4], and Eckhard Kraft[1]

[1] Bauhaus-Universität Weimar, Goetheplatz 7/8, 99423 Weimar, Germany
{suryaprakash.reddy.kalvakolu,heinrich.sobke, eckhard.kraft}@uni-weimar.de, soebke@hsw-hameln.de
[2] Hochschule Weserbergland, Am Stockhof 2, 31785 Hameln, Germany
[3] Bremer Institut für Produktion und Logistik (BIBA), Hochschulring 20, 28359 Bremen, Germany
baa@biba.uni-bremen.de, jmbh@kth.se
[4] Royal Institute of Technology, Kvarnbergagatan 12, Södertälje, Sweden

Abstract. 360° spaces are representations of real locations created using 360° images, enabling viewers to walk through by changing position. As basis for virtual field trips, they have proven to be valuable learning tools. In technological terms, 360° spaces are to be characterized as single-user applications. In contrast, Social VR applications are characterized by multi-user capability and user-specific avatars. From a learning perspective, the concepts of collaborative learning and embodiment have long been proposed as conducive to learning. Both concepts might be supported using Social VR. However, there is hardly any knowledge about the use of 360° spaces and Social VR. Accordingly, the research question arises how Social VR-based 360° spaces are perceived by learners. This article presents a mixed-method evaluation study (N = 16) – using a questionnaire and focus group discussions – of a 360° space based on the Social VR platform Mozilla Hubs used on PCs. The study highlighted the opportunities offered by Social VR-based 360° spaces but also revealed several challenges that need to be addressed to embrace the potential of Social VR-based 360° spaces to be utilized regularly in education. Accordingly, the study represents relevant preparatory work for the use of multi-user 360° spaces in playful learning environments, such as educational escape rooms.

Keywords: social presence · collaborative learning · avatar · embodiment · playful digital environment · escape room game · desktop VR

1 Introduction

360° technology allows projection of spherical images to render the surroundings, where a camera view is positioned at the center of the image plane to realize human-eye behavior. Spherical images are generated either from machine-aided applications (e.g., building information modelling) or from photographic imagery. **360°-based virtual environments** offer low-cost, easy-to-capture, non-computer-generated simulations that

A. Schönbohm et al. (Eds.): GALA 2024, LNCS 15348, pp. 375–380, 2025.
https://doi.org/10.1007/978-3-031-78269-5_38

can provide a true-to-reality representation of the location [1]. The application of 360° imagery evokes a unique sense of presence and immersion that has potential in teaching and learning [2]. Accordingly, 360° virtual environments, also called **360° spaces**, support virtual field trips (VFTs), which have proven to be powerful learning activities that promote exploratory learning through the visualization of real (physical) locations [3–5]. In the context of this article, the term VFT is defined as a 360° space that is visualized highly realistic [6, 7]. Even though VFTs do not fully achieve the authenticity and information content of field trips [8, 9], despite the evidence of the comparability of photos and reality [10], there are advantages such as location and time independence, avoiding weather issues, overcoming physical inaccessibility, or avoiding dangerous places [11]. Furthermore, they are less time and cost-consuming to use [3, 12, 13]. 360° virtual environments are mostly single-user applications, which limits many learning processes, like situated learning that requires the collaborative solving of tasks [14]. Consequently, collaborative learning is also not inherently promoted [15]. One example in which collaborative work is achieved via organizational measures outside the virtual environment rather than via technological means is the implementation of the VFT as a serious game: an educational escape room game [16]. Furthermore, a few prototypes are using multi-user environments for VFTs (e.g., [17]). A type of virtual environment, which on the one hand uses the spatial metaphor, and on the other hand is multi-user capable by definition is **Social Virtual Reality**, i.e., a multi-user virtual reality platform lets learners interact and communicate in virtual environments using avatars [18, 19]. Social VR allows learners to meet in virtual environments, participate in activities, and communicate. Further, Social VR is considered essential for remote collaboration in virtual environments [20–23]. Combining the advantages of Social VR with the advantages of 360° spaces may therefore be seems therefore to be a promising approach for fostering collaborative learning. The purpose of this study is therefore to evaluate the learners' attitudes towards a Social VR-based 360° space as learning tool?

Theoretical Background. To our knowledge, **Social VR** has not been used based on 360° spaces. One of the important characteristics of Social VR is that it supports collaborative learning [24, 25]. Collaborative learning takes place in a situation in which two or more learners learn or attempt to learn something together to build a shared body of knowledge. In contrast to individual learning, learners participate in a collaborative learning process to benefit from each other's resources and competencies [26]. In other words, collaborative learning refers to methods and specific environments in which learners participate in a shared task and in which learners are interdependent and responsible for each other [27]. Social VR platforms allow learners to interact with each other and possibly also with teachers in virtual environments using avatars. This promotes a sense of social presence and facilitates communication, interaction and collaboration, and therefore collaborative learning takes place [28–30]. **Social presence** is seen as being with real people in a virtual environment [31, 32]. Social presence enables multiple learners to communicate with each other, usually through visual and auditory cues [33, 34] and enables communicative behavior during virtual field trips. It is hypothesized that the stronger the feeling of being physically present in the 360° space is, the more it encourages learners to be more confident and intrinsically motivated to learn [35]. In addition, social presence contributes significantly to learner engagement in the virtual environment [36]. Accordingly, Social VR-based learning experiences enable learners to observe other learners and subsequently emulate models for successful learning [37]. Since social presence is considered a prerequisite for learning [38], we consider the increase in social presence through Social VR to be an important argument in favor of Social VR-based 360° spaces. A striking feature of social VR is the representation of participants through three-dimensional representations, so-called **avatars**. Participants can customize such avatars and control these avatars through the social VR environment. The use of avatars is one of the factors that increase social presence [39], especially in Social VR environments [40]. Furthermore, the concept of Sense of Embodiment (SoE) to a body B is described by Kilteni et al. [41] concerning virtual reality as 'the sense that emerges when B's properties are processed as if they were the properties of one's own biological body'. Accordingly, we hypothesize possible effects of avatar embodiment, i.e., the conceptual extension of embodied cognition [42] beyond the learner's own body to its digital representation, the avatar. Although in this study both concepts, collaborative learning and avatar embodiment, are not investigated in detail, we believe that this study provides preliminary work by investigating a potential virtual environment, which is a prerequisite for a more detailed investigation of both concepts.

2 Methodology

The prototype – representing a 360° space of a composting plant – was developed in line with the design guidelines in [43], starting with collecting requirements, then generating mock-ups (in our case scenarios), assessing these and then starting the validation, which is described in more detail below. The prototype was finally validated in a study comprising 16 researchers and assistants (4 female, 12 male) recruited by convenience sampling from the chair of waste management of the university three of the authors belong to. The participants had an average age of 33.9 years (SD = 9.65, range 21–56). The validation was carried out in the following way: 1. The participants were invited to an online meeting. 2. In the online meeting, the participants got an introduction to the virtual environment, further they watched an onboarding video on how to create their avatar and how to use the virtual environment. 3. The participant joined the virtual environment desktop-wise, i.e. using their PC, received an introduction to the navigation dashboard and moved to the area of the virtual lecture hall. 4. The facilitator – the first author – took the role of guiding the participants through the lecture hall and the navigation dashboard. 5. Within a time-frame of 15 min the participants explored the virtual environment and the participants were guided through the first four panoramas discussing the content of the panoramas. 6. The participants completed the questionnaire, which also asked about their prior knowledge of the subject and media technology. In addition, the demographic data already reported was requested. The questionnaire also consisted of three self-designed item sets with a total of 17 items on handling, participants' impressions and appropriateness for learning. 6. Finally, a focus group discussion was held for approximately 25 min involving lively contributions from the participants. The results are presented in detail in [44].

3 Discussion and Conclusions

In this study, aiming at educational virtual field trips (VFTs), we combined 360° spaces with the concept of Social VR: a virtual environment was created using the Social VR software Mozilla Hubs. The established spatial metaphor of Social VR needed to be adapted for the 360 spaces: Each 360° panorama becomes its room within a room, in which learners can be teleported via buttons. In each 360° panorama itself, it is possible to teleport to the dashboard and to previous and subsequent panoramas in the context of the VFT. In general, we received a positive assessment of the potential of the proposed virtual environment in learning contexts. However, several challenges had to be overcome during the development of the virtual environment like the limited support for 360° panoramas, which resulted in a spherical, round floor area as well as that the answers showed clearly that social presence is not optimally promoted. Further, it should also be investigated to what extent lifelike avatars lead to an increase in social presence. A specialized authoring software for 360° spaces that supports inherently the concept of Social VR may reduce the challenge. On the positive side, the study has confirmed the potential of a combination of 360° spaces and Social VR to host learning environments as powerful learning tools, especially also as a foundation for spatial playful environments, such as educational escape rooms.

Acknowledgements. This work has been partly funded by VR VET (No. 01132959 - ERASMUS-EDU-2023-PI-FORWARD-LOT2) co-funded by the European Commission through the Erasmus+ program and the work also acknowledges the support by Förderfond "Lehr-Innovationen" (IN_WiSe23_02) by Bauhaus-Universität Weimar. The presented work represents the authors' view.

References

1. Eiris, R., et al.: Desktop-based safety training using 360-degree panorama and static virtual reality techniques: a comparative experimental study. Autom. Constr. **109**, 102969 (2020). https://doi.org/10.1016/j.autcon.2019.102969
2. Reyna, J.: The potential of 360-degree videos for teaching, learning and research. In: 12th International Technology, Education and Development Conference, Valencia, Spain, March 2018. https://doi.org/10.21125/inted.2018.0247
3. Norris, E., et al.: Teacher and pupil perspectives on the use of Virtual Field Trips as physically active lessons. BMC. Res. Notes **8**, 719 (2015). https://doi.org/10.1186/s13104-015-1698-3
4. Seifan, M., et al.: The effect of virtual field trip as an introductory tool for an engineering real field trip. Educ. Chem. Eng. **27**, 6–11 (2019)
5. Wolf, M., et al.: Virtualised virtual field trips in environmental engineering higher education. Eur. J. Eng. Educ. **48**, 1312–1334 (2023)
6. Pham, H.C., et al.: Virtual field trip for mobile construction safety education using 360-degree panoramic virtual reality. Int. J. Eng. Educ. **34**, 1174–1191 (2018)
7. Ritter, K.A., Chambers, T.L.: Three-dimensional modeled environments versus 360 degree panoramas for mobile virtual reality training. Virtual Real. **26**, 571–581 (2022)
8. Springer, C., et al.: Virtualization of virtual field trips. In: Proceedings of DELbA 2020. CEUR-WS, Online (2020)

9. Wolf, M., et al.: 360°-based virtual field trips to waterworks in higher education. Computers **10**, 118 (2021). https://doi.org/10.3390/computers10090118
10. Rossetti, T., Hurtubia, R.: An assessment of the ecological validity of immersive videos in stated preference surveys. J. Choice Model. **34**, 100198 (2020)
11. Klippel, A., et al.: Transforming earth science education through immersive experiences: delivering on a long held promise. J. Educ. Comput. Res. **57**, 1745–1771 (2019). https://doi.org/10.1177/0735633119854025
12. McCaffrey, et al.: Virtual fieldtrips for petroleum geoscientists. PGC **7**, 19–26 (2010). https://doi.org/10.1144/0070019
13. Schulze, D.G., et al.: Virtualizing soil science field trips. Nat. Sci. Educ. **50**, e20046 (2021). https://doi.org/10.1002/nse2.20046
14. Lave, J., Wenger, E.: Situated Learning: Legitimate Peripheral Participation. Cambridge University Press, Cambridge (1991)
15. Dillenbourg, P.: Collaborative learning: Cognitive and computational approaches. In: Advances in Learning and Instruction Series. ERIC (1999)
16. Wolf, M., et al.: Low-threshold digital educational escape rooms based on 360VR and web-based forms. Electron. J. e-Learn. **22**, 01–18 (2024)
17. Eiris, R., Gheisari, M.: iVisit-collaborate: online multiuser virtual site visits using 360-degree panoramas and virtual humans. In: Linner, T., et al (eds.) Proceedings of the 39th International Symposium on Automation and Robotics in Construction, Bogota, Colombia, pp. 276–282. IAARC (2022). https://doi.org/10.22260/ISARC2022/0039
18. Li, J. et al.: Social VR: a new medium for remote communication and collaboration. In: Extended Abstracts of the 2020 CHI Conference on Human Factors in Computing Systems, Honolulu, HI, USA, pp. 1–8. ACM (2020). https://doi.org/10.1145/3334480.3375160
19. Wang, M.: Social VR : a new form of social communication in the future or a beautiful illusion? J. Phys. Conf. Ser. **1518**, 012032 (2020)
20. Ahlers, T. et al.: Foreign language tandem learning in social VR: conception, implementation and evaluation of the game-based application Hololingo! i-com **21**, 203–215 (2022). https://doi.org/10.1515/icom-2021-0039.
21. Barreda-Ángeles, M., et al.: Easily applicable social virtual reality and social presence in online higher education during the covid-19 pandemic: a qualitative study. Comput. Educ. X Real. **2**, 100024 (2023). https://doi.org/10.1016/j.cexr.2023.100024
22. De Simone, F.: Measuring user quality of experience in social VR systems. In: Proceedings of the 3rd International Workshop on Multimedia Alternate Realities, Seoul Republic of Korea, pp. 25–26. ACM (2018). https://doi.org/10.1145/3268998.3277702
23. Gunkel, S.N.B., et al.: Social VR platform: building 360-degree shared VR spaces. In: Adjunct Publication of the 2017 ACM International Conference on Interactive Experiences for TV and Online Video, Hilversum, The Netherlands, pp. 83–84. ACM (2017)
24. Mystakidis, S., et al.: Deep and meaningful e-learning with social virtual reality environments in higher education: a systematic literature review. Appl. Sci. **11**, 2412 (2021). https://doi.org/10.3390/app11052412
25. Rante, H., et al.: Development of social virtual reality (SVR) as collaborative learning media to support Merdeka Belajar. IJIET **13**, 1014–1020 (2023)
26. Collis, B., Moonen, J.: Collaborative learning in a contribution-oriented pedagogy: In: Howard, C., et al. (eds.) Encyclopedia of Distance Learning, pp. 277–283. IGI Global (2005)
27. González-Ruiz, V., et al.: Collaborative project-based learning: an experience. Presented at the EDULEARN19 Proceedings (2019)
28. Dunmoye, I.D.: An exploratory study of social presence and cognitive engagement association in a collaborative virtual reality learning environment. Comput. Educ. X Real. **4**, 100054 (2024). https://doi.org/10.1016/j.cexr.2024.100054

29. Montagud, M., et al.: Towards SocialVR: evaluating a novel technology for watching videos together. http://arxiv.org/abs/2104.05060 (2021)
30. Van Brakel, V., et al.: Feelings of presence and perceived social support in social virtual reality platforms. Comput. Hum. Behav. **139**, 107523 (2023). https://doi.org/10.1016/j.chb.2022.107523
31. Biocca, F., et al.: Toward a more robust theory and measure of social presence: review and suggested criteria. Presence Teleoper. Virtual Environ. **12**, 456–480 (2003). https://doi.org/10.1162/105474603322761270
32. Oh, C.S., et al.: A systematic review of social presence: definition, antecedents, and implications. Front. Robot. AI **5**, 114 (2018). https://doi.org/10.3389/frobt.2018.00114
33. Churchill, E.F., Snowdon, D.: Collaborative virtual environments: an introductory review of issues and systems. Virtual Real. **3**, 3–15 (1998). https://doi.org/10.1007/BF01409793
34. Snowdon, D., Churchill, E.F., Munro, A.J.: Collaborative virtual environments: digital spaces and places for CSCW: an introduction. In: Churchill, E.F., Snowdon, D.N., Munro, A.J. (eds.) Collaborative Virtual Environments. CSCW, pp. 3–17. Springer, London (2001). https://doi.org/10.1007/978-1-4471-0685-2_1
35. Cheng, K.-H., Tsai, C.-C.: A case study of immersive virtual field trips in an elementary classroom: students' learning experience and teacher-student interaction behaviors. Comput. Educ. **140**, 103600 (2019). https://doi.org/10.1016/j.compedu.2019.103600
36. Lee, K.M., et al.: Are physically embodied social agents better than disembodied social agents? Int. J. Hum. Comput. Stud. **64**, 962–973 (2006). https://doi.org/10.1016/j.ijhcs.2006.05.002
37. Morrison, L., et al.: Social presence in virtual professional learning. JDLL **1**, 93–110 (2021). https://doi.org/10.51357/jdll.v1i1.160
38. Richardson, J.C., et al.: Social presence in relation to students' satisfaction and learning in the online environment: a meta-analysis. Comput. Hum. Behav. **71**, 402–417 (2017). https://doi.org/10.1016/j.chb.2017.02.001
39. Yoon, B., et al.: The effect of avatar appearance on social presence in an augmented reality remote collaboration. Presented at the 2019 IEEE Conference on Virtual Reality and 3D User Interfaces (VR) (2019)
40. Heidicker et al.: Influence of avatar appearance on presence in social VR. In: 2017 IEEE Symposium on 3D User Interfaces (3DUI), Los Angeles, CA, USA, pp. 233–234. IEEE (2017). https://doi.org/10.1109/3DUI.2017.7893357
41. Kilteni, K. et al.: The sense of embodiment in virtual reality. Presence Teleoper. Virtual Environ. **21**, 373–387 (2012). https://doi.org/10.1162/PRES_a_00124
42. Foglia, L., Wilson, R.A.: Embodied cognition. WIREs. Cogn. Sci. **4**, 319–325 (2013)
43. Camburn, B., et al.: Design prototyping methods: state of the art in strategies, techniques, and guidelines. Des. Sci. **3**, e13 (2017). https://doi.org/10.1017/dsj.2017.10
44. Kalvakolu, S., Söbke, H., Baalsrud Hauge, J., Kraft, E.: Educational virtual field trips based on social VR and 360° spaces (2024). https://arxiv.org/abs/2409.05496

Puzzle Playground – Teaching VR Interactions Through a Puzzle Game

Vincent Albertsson, Patrick Hibbs, Csanád Farkas, Qinxin Ren, Amir Zaidi, Ricardo Marroquim, Elmar Eisemann, and Rafael Bidarra(✉)

Delft University of Technology, Delft, The Netherlands
R.Bidarra@tudelft.nl

Abstract. In recent years, it has become clear that modern education is not currently equipped with the proper tools to fully support remote teaching. Virtual reality (VR) has the potential to make remote education viable in the future. Nevertheless, many teachers and students lack experience and familiarity with this technology, which poses a challenge to its adoption in education. In this paper, we introduce Puzzle Playground, a game that builds familiarity with VR by teaching object interactions through puzzles in an interactive experience tailored for educators. Players gradually learn VR interactions by completing various puzzle levels. A preliminary user study indicated that people who learned with Puzzle Playground grasped VR interactions faster than those who learned with printed or visual methods.

Keywords: Virtual reality · Interaction techniques · Educational technology

1 Introduction

Recent efforts to modernize educational tools in classrooms with novel technologies have brought a resurgence in interest in virtual reality (VR) for education. Although VR is a promising technology, educators have remained inexperienced with it, which is a major roadblock to its adoption in this context.

Many VR applications employ similar interaction and control schemes, making it easier to switch between them. Nevertheless, the initial hurdle remains: people with no VR experience struggle to understand these mechanisms during their first tries. By overcoming this difficulty, they can acquire a solid foundation that prepares them for using a wide variety of VR applications in the future.

The contribution of this paper is twofold: (i) we identify the common basic interactions and controls in most VR applications, and (ii) propose *Puzzle Playground*, a very accessible game designed to introduce inexperienced VR users to

This work was partially funded by the HORIZON-CL2-2021-TRANSFORMATIONS-01 Project E-Diploma (project number 101061424).

A. Schönbohm et al. (Eds.): GALA 2024, LNCS 15348, pp. 381–387, 2025.
https://doi.org/10.1007/978-3-031-78269-5_39

interaction mechanisms. Preliminary evaluation of the game suggests that the learning retention and performance of its players is higher than that of other participants, who learned with either a written explanation or a recorded video.

2 Related Work

VR continues to develop, extending its applicability in many domains. Medical applications, for one, can significantly benefit from VR [7,13]. Moreover, many other application domains show promising enhancements with such technologies, including simulating military battlefields [11], learning physics [3], assisting surgery [11], and conducting medical simulations [10].

Specific to VR in education, there are several surveys available analysing recent research [1,9,12]. Elston et al. [4] try to address this issue by giving general guidelines to teachers adopting VR for medical education. Holly et al. [5] discuss how to design VR experiences for teaching.

Apart from general guidelines, Carpenter et al. [2] discuss the readiness of such technologies in education. Furthermore, they point out, from their survey, that a limiting factor is teachers' familiarity with the technology and the lack of training material.

Specifically for interactions in VR, a few attempts have been made to facilitate the user experience and their learning curve. Yang Li et al. [8] provide an analysis of gesture interaction in VR, covering the classification of gestures and input devices to enhance the user experience in VR environments. Users may be helped in understanding these gesture interactions with smart visualizations. For example, Xin-Yu Huang et al. [6] used fingertip tracking and a first-person perspective to facilitate interaction between users and game objects. Still, no evaluation was performed to assess if fingertip tracking could assist users in becoming familiar with VR.

In conclusion, while the potential of using VR in education is enormous, user familiarity remains a problem and hinders the practical inclusion of VR in educational settings. This paper addresses this gap specifically for VR interaction.

3 Game Design

We designed and developed Puzzle Playground, a first-person puzzle game in a sandbox playground centered around common VR interactions. It consists of several levels, each with a single objective to complete. For each level, players learn one VR interaction type and must subsequently apply it to solve the task at hand. The levels' setup allows the players to make mistakes and easily recover from them, encouraging them to explore the interactions until they have fully mastered them.

As the game is aimed at beginners, the number of interaction mechanisms is kept small. Based on the most popular VR games and applications, we identified the following interaction categories as the most important to learn:

- *grabbing and displacing* objects
- *rotating* objects
- *scaling* objects
- *bringing distant objects into your hand* (informally known as 'tele-grab')

The introductory levels present one of the four basic interactions above, and are expected to be easy to complete. Since the players are introduced to the mechanics one by one, they can fully focus on each learning objective. The challenging levels test players' skills by requiring them to combine multiple interactions to complete the level. These levels reinforce and deepen players' skills through repetition and recall in different contexts.

Every level contains instructions in the form of floating UI elements, with helpful explanations on accomplishing the interaction(s) needed for the level. Therefore, players of Puzzle Playground also get familiar with how to interact with basic UI elements.

3.1 Game Environment

The game scenario is a stylized kindergarten environment. This environment is beneficial for the learning objectives due to two reasons. First, a kindergarten creates an analogy to the inherent learning experiences associated with early education. A kindergarten is typically the first educational institute. The goal of Puzzle Playground is to educate inexperienced players on interactions in VR. A concrete example is stacking blocks to practice grabbing and moving objects. Stacking blocks is a typical activity in a kindergarten, thus players who understand the analogy could intuitively start stacking blocks. Second, a kindergarten has the benefit of being a fairly simple environment. This reduces distractions for the player, as opposed to being indulged in a more thrilling environment, which might then drive attention away from the puzzles and the learning goals.

To focus on interactions, there are no navigation mechanisms, meaning that the player can not move around the environment.

3.2 Level Design

The game consists of six levels, with one elementary puzzle per level. This section will explore and justify each level's design in depth.

Out of the six levels, two are dedicated to picking up and placing objects: one to introduce the player to the interaction and another to complement with a more precise placement of objects. These two are followed by one level dedicated to grabbing distant objects ('tele-grabbing'), as it is similar to regularly grabbing objects.

Grabbing and tele-grabbing are the interactions that are most likely to be included in a VR game or application. Therefore, the first three levels at the start of the game are dedicated to teaching these mechanisms.

The following three levels focus on less popular interactions, that may occur less often in games and applications, but are nevertheless very helpful in a interactive classroom setting, e.g. to better visualize or appreciate an object or phenomenon. The fourth level introduces object rotation. Two options are available to the player. They can either use the orientation of their hand to rotate an object they are holding or use a stick on a VR controller to rotate it.

Finally, the last two levels introduce object scaling. The player learns how to enlarge and shrink objects via gestures. All levels are further detailed below.

Table Cleanup. This level introduces grabbing, moving and dropping objects. The player sees several blocks on a table. The goal is to tidy up the table and put them in a bin next to the table. The start of the level is depicted in Fig. 1a.

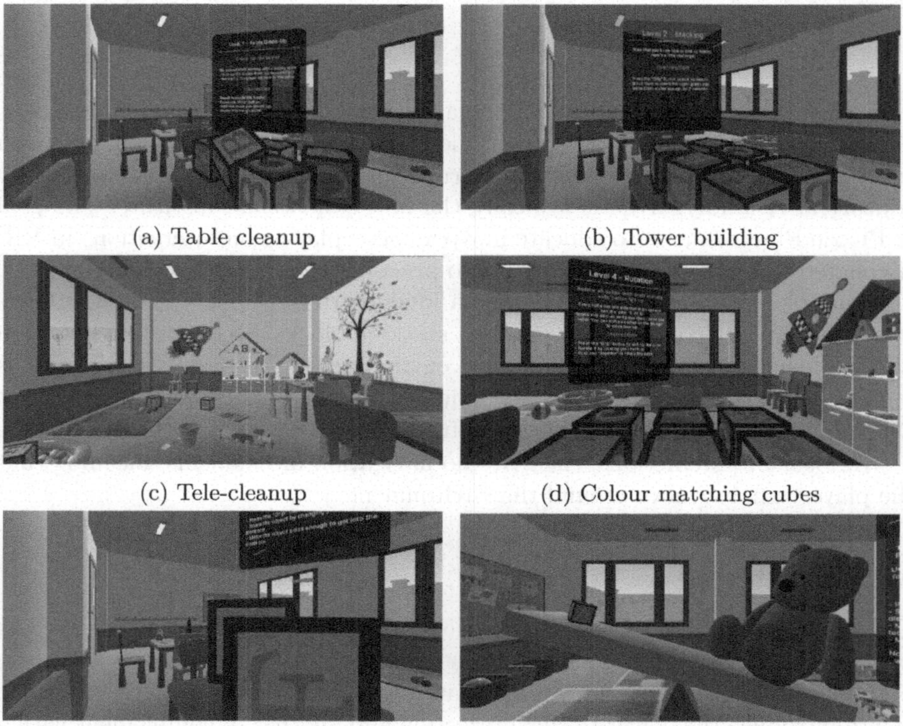

(a) Table cleanup (b) Tower building

(c) Tele-cleanup (d) Colour matching cubes

(e) Scale down (f) Scale up with mass

Fig. 1. Current game levels of Puzzle Playground.

Tower Building. This level helps players master the basic grabbing interaction of the previous level by requiring more precision to complete the objective.

The player starts in front of the same table with blocks, as before. The task is to build a tower taller than a given threshold, indicated with a green-tinted transparent plane. The final tower must stay stable for a few seconds after the player releases the controller grab button. The start of the level is depicted in Fig. 1b.

Tele-Cleanup. This level introduces the 'tele-grab' mechanic, which players can use to pick up objects too far away to be reached with their hands. Teaching this interaction early makes it easier for players to recover from mistakes at later levels, e.g. pick up an object without crouching, if they dropped it. Similar to the first level, the objective is to put a set of cubes into the bin to the right of the player. However, this time the cubes are scattered on the floor, out of the player's reach. The start of the level is depicted in Fig. 1c.

Colour Matching Cubes. This level introduces rotation, a new interaction for grabbed objects. The cubes on the table have six differently coloured sides; initially, they show a random side facing upwards. The objective of the level is to rotate all cubes so that they all show the same color facing upwards. Asking the player to rotate multiple cubes, should help remember how to use the rotation. Additionally, since the rotation is randomized, the player should not get bored with this repetition. A possible start of the level is depicted in Fig. 1d.

Scale Down. This level introduces the scaling interaction. Comparable to the first level, the task is again to place all blocks into the bin, but the objects are now oversized. So, to fit a block into the bin, the player must first scale the block down, by simultaneously grabbing it with both hands and then moving their hands closer together. Using a setup similar to the first level helps the player focus on the interaction. The start of the level is depicted in Fig. 1e.

Scale Up with Mass. This level focuses on scaling objects up rather than down. The player is challenged to solve a simple physics puzzle: flipping a balance scale with a heavy object on one side and a lighter one on the other. To flip the balance to the other side, the player has to scale up the smaller object, and place it back on the balance scale. The start of the level is depicted in Fig. 1f.

4 Game Implementation

Puzzle Playground was implemented in Unity Engine[1], using OpenXR[2] and the XR Interaction Toolkit[3], which includes the grab and tele-grab interactions

[1] https://unity.com.
[2] https://www.khronos.org/openxr.
[3] https://docs.unity3d.com/Packages/com.unity.xr.interaction.toolkit@2.5/manual/index.html.

by default. The rotation and scaling mechanics were manually implemented. Teleportation and other locomotion methods were entirely disabled to restrict the game to only interaction. The game environment uses the Kindergarten Interior Unity package[4] as a base, to which several other assets were added. For deployment and testing, the HP Reverb G2 Omnicept HMD[5] was used on various systems. All systems achieved a stable 90 FPS during testing. A short trailer[6] of Puzzle Playground illustrates its game mechanics and environment.

5 Conclusion

There is a significant lack of VR experience among educators, and solving this technological hiccup can drastically improve education in the near future. We presented Puzzle Playground, a VR game expressly designed and developed to teach players how to interact with objects in VR. The game approaches this in a structured, step-by-step manner, guiding players through basic VR interactions and letting them play through various puzzle levels. A preliminary evaluation of Puzzle Playground indicates that learning VR interactions with the game is more time-efficient than other methods, such as oral or written explanations.

References

1. AlGerafi, M.A.M., Zhou, Y., Oubibi, M., Wijaya, T.T.: Unlocking the potential: a comprehensive evaluation of augmented reality and virtual reality in education. Electronics **12**(18) (2023). https://doi.org/10.3390/electronics12183953
2. Carpenter, R., McWhorter, R., Stone, K., Coyne, L.: Adopting virtual reality for education: Exploring teachers' perspectives on readiness, opportunities, and challenges. Int. J. Integr. Technol. Educ. **12**, 27–36 (2023). https://doi.org/10.5121/ijite.2023.12303
3. Dorland, B., et al.: Quantum physics vs. classical physics: introducing the basics with a virtual reality game. In: Games and Learning Alliance, 8th International Conference GALA 2019. LNCS, vol. 11899, pp. 383–393. Springer (2019)
4. Elston, P., Canale, G.P., Ail, G., Fisher, N., Mahendran, M.: Twelve tips for teaching in virtual reality. Med. Teach. **46**(4), 495–499 (2024). https://doi.org/10.1080/0142159X.2023.2285396
5. Holly, M.S., Pirker, J., Resch, S., Brettschuh, S., Gütl, C.: Designing VR experiences - expectations for teaching and learning in VR. In: Educational Technology and Society, vol. 24, pp. 107–119 (2021). https://api.semanticscholar.org/CorpusID:236166326
6. Huang, X.Y., Tsai, M.S., Huang, C.C.: 3D virtual-reality interaction system. In: 2019 IEEE International Conference on Consumer Electronics - Taiwan (ICCE-TW), pp. 1–2 (2019). https://doi.org/10.1109/ICCE-TW46550.2019.8991800

[4] https://assetstore.unity.com/packages/3d/props/interior/kindergarten-interior-111197.

[5] https://support.hp.com/us-en/document/c06994662.

[6] https://surfdrive.surf.nl/files/index.php/s/o6P8IVttg84PwVs.

7. Javvaji, C.K., Reddy, H., Vagha, J., Taksande, A., Kommareddy, A., Reddy, N.: Immersive innovations: exploring the diverse applications of virtual reality (VR) in healthcare. Cureus **16** (2024). https://doi.org/10.7759/cureus.56137
8. Li, Y., Huang, J., Tian, F., Wang, H.A., Dai, G.Z.: Gesture interaction in virtual reality. Virtual Reality Intell. Hardw. **1**(1), 84–112 (2019). https://doi.org/10.3724/SP.J.2096-5796.2018.0006
9. Marougkas, A., Troussas, C., Krouska, A., Sgouropoulou, C.: Virtual reality in education: a review of learning theories, approaches and methodologies for the last decade. Electronics **12**(13) (2023). https://doi.org/10.3390/electronics12132832
10. Philippe, S., et al.: Multimodal teaching, learning and training in virtual reality: a review and case study. Virtual Reality Intell. Hardw. **2**(5), 421–442 (2020)
11. Singh, R.P., Javaid, M., Haleem, A., Suman, R.: Internet of things (IoT) applications to fight against COVID-19 pandemic. Diab. Metabol. Syndr. Clin. Res. Rev. **14**(4), 521–524 (2020). https://doi.org/10.1016/j.dsx.2020.04.041
12. Zhao, X., Ren, Y., Cheah, K.S.L.: Leading Virtual Reality (VR) and Augmented Reality (AR) in education: bibliometric and content analysis from the web of science (2018–2022). SAGE Open **13**(3), 21582440231190820 (2023). https://doi.org/10.1177/21582440231190821
13. Zhou, Y., Mac Gillavry, M., Yang, P., Xu, Z., Zhang, B., Bidarra, R.: Astral body: a virtual reality game for body ownership investigation. In: Games and Learning Alliance, 12th International Conference GALA 2023. LNCS, Springer (2023)

Experiencing Forced Migration: A Participatory Approach to Developing a Serious Video Game

Kseniia Harshina(✉), Imke Alenka Harbig, Mathias Lux, and Tom Tucek

Alpen-Adria-Universität Klagenfurt, Klagenfurt, Austria
{kseniia.harshina,imke.harbig,mathias.lux,tom.tucek}@aau.at

Abstract. Forced migration affects millions worldwide due to conflict, disasters, and persecution. This paper presents a participatory approach to serious game development, engaging individuals with lived migration experiences to create authentic and impactful narratives. Based on qualitative research, we propose a game design methodology to enhance empathy and raise awareness of forced migration. Our study demonstrates the potential of participatory games to bridge the gap between forced migrants and the broader public, fostering empathy, social change, and empowerment for marginalized communities.

Keywords: Forced Migration · Serious Video Games · Empathy · Participatory Design · Qualitative Study · VR Video Game Design

1 Introduction

Forced migration is an increasingly pressing issue in the current global landscape, encompassing a broader range of experiences beyond the legal definition of 'refugee' and including people displaced by conflict, persecution, or climate change. As millions are continuously forced to leave their homes, the relevance of understanding and addressing these experiences becomes increasingly critical [1]. This shows the importance of developing effective means to accurately portray and raise awareness of the lives and stories of those affected. Our research project aims to develop a serious VR video game that fosters empathy and awareness of forced migration experiences by offering players a deeper, more interactive engagement with the topic. The game will reveal how players' actions affect others, highlighting the hidden pain many individuals with experiences of forced migration carry, while also providing empowerment and validation for those with such experiences. Recognizing the importance of authenticity and dialogue, we have adopted a participatory approach by involving individuals with forced migration backgrounds in the development process. This paper presents the initial findings of our ongoing qualitative study, which gathers diverse perspectives to inform the game design methodology. These insights can help shape guidelines for developing serious games that not only educate but also empower those whose stories are being told.

A. Schönbohm et al. (Eds.): GALA 2024, LNCS 15348, pp. 388–393, 2025.
https://doi.org/10.1007/978-3-031-78269-5_40

2 Related Work

Recent advances in extended reality (XR) technologies enable increasingly realistic empathy tools and experiences [2]. A recent example that stands out is the work of Herrera et al. [3], who conducted an experiment comparing traditional perspective-taking tasks with VR perspective-taking tasks to evaluate their effectiveness in promoting long-term empathy for homeless people. Participants with the VR tasks showed more significant and lasting positive attitudes toward the homeless population, as well as a high likelihood of engaging in supportive behaviors. Similarly, Bujić et al. [4] found that immersive experiences through VR had a significantly more positive impact on attitudes towards human rights than traditional 2D formats or articles. However, the use of VR as an empathy tool is not without its ethical challenges, such as deceptive and unintended outcomes [5]. Similarly, Sora-Domenjó stresses the need for rigorous research and caution regarding long-term effects [6]. These considerations led us to adopt a participatory approach, allowing those affected by forced migration to shape the game's development.

Several existing video games explore forced migration. *Path Out*, an autobiographical adventure about a Syrian artist fleeing war [9]. *Bury Me, My Love* portrays text messages exchanged between a Syrian refugee and her husband, highlighting the difficult decisions faced by refugees [10]. Our work builds on these foundations by combining serious gaming, VR, and participatory design to create a tool for empathy and awareness regarding forced migration. Unlike existing games, our project aims to create a multifaceted experience that educates those without forced migration experiences and empowers those who have undergone such experiences.

3 Method

This study aims to explore the wishes and desires of individuals affected by forced migration in the development of a video game centered on their experiences. We conducted an online study in English, German, and Ukrainian. Potential participants were invited through non-profit organizations and messenger group chats for individuals affected by forced migration. All survey questions were optional. The survey first collected demographic data, the country participants had fled, their destination, and asked to what extent they identify with the term refugee. Open-ended questions explore (1) what a video game on forced migration should depict, (2) what people with no experience of forced migration, and (3) what people with such experiences should gain through it. Participants were also asked to share personal stories they wished to (4) see depicted or (5) "replay" in the game. Participants are asked for their consent to utilize their stories in the development of our video game and whether they have any final comments.

We conducted qualitative content analysis following Mayring's (2010) [7] systematic approach. The analysis involved coding participant responses, grouping codes into broader categories, and identifying overarching themes that captured the core findings. In particular, we were interested in their wishes regarding (1) the content, (2) the takeaways for individuals not affected by forced migration, and (3) the takeaways for individuals affected by forced migration. Furthermore, we (4) collected stories about personal experiences with forced migration for the purpose of an accurate depiction of said video game.

Fourteen participants completed our survey. Two participants had to be excluded due to self-identifying as not having experienced forced migration or leaving hateful comments. This resulted in a total sample size of 12 participants (7 female, 5 male) aged 16 to 85 years ($M = 32.42$, $SD = 20.31$). Most of our participants (91.7%) fled from Ukraine, and only one reported having fled Iran. Participants migrated to various countries, including Austria (50%), Germany (16.7%), Slovenia, France, the UK, and the USA (each 8.3%). The main reason for the experienced forced migration was war (91.7%). Other reasons named by participants included political reasons, power outages, unstable economic situation, living conditions, anxiety, and not feeling safe. Interestingly, only two-thirds of our participants (66.7%) identified with the term refugee. Participants preferred the terms "forcedly relocated" and "guest".

4 Results of the Qualitative Study

Participants' responses to the open-ended questions varied in length and depth. Responses to the first three questions were categorized using qualitative content analysis [7], while responses to the fourth and fifth were summarized for this paper.

Our analysis of participants' video game content suggestions resulted in three categories: overarching message, narrative style, and game content. Table 1 summarizes these. One participant highlighted the significance of everyday tasks, sharing: "When you're in a store and can't figure out if you're buying a sweet bun or a meat bun because you don't know the language. That minor inconvenience makes you question your whole situation." Another expressed feelings of homesickness tied to leaving family memorabilia behind: "The hardest thought is that my childhood photos and family albums were left behind. I may never reconnect with those memories."

Qualitative analysis of responses about non-migrants' learning outcomes revealed three stages:

1. Specific knowledge: Participants wanted players to understand forced migration processes, challenges, and opportunities to help. For some, migration may offer opportunity; for others, it's a struggle.
2. Understanding: Participants emphasized a desire for empathy and self-reflection, noting that outward appearances can mask inner pain: "Migrants may seem cheerful but are often deeply depressed."
3. Behavior change: Participants hoped players would engage more compassionately with migrants and actively help them.

Table 1. Categorized Participant Suggestions for Game Content

Category	Content
Overarching Message	Need for support, finding a home, differences between voluntary and forced migration, complexity and variety of forced migration experiences
Narrative Style	Personal stories, symbolic migration journey, diverse age perspectives, exploration of various environments (war zones, refugee camps, urban areas), and identity search/integration challenges
Specific Content	1. Struggles: language barriers, financial issues, discrimination, leaving memorabilia, starting over, identity search 2. Emotions: loneliness, homesickness, nostalgia, mixed feelings (necessity vs. reluctance), emotional burden (existential questions)

Table 2. Participant-Identified Outcomes for Individuals with Forced Migration Experiences

Category	Content
Sense of Belonging	Feeling understood, validated, and supported
New Perspectives	Feeling empowered, seeing positive aspects of the journey, and appreciating diversity
Practical Information	Tools for integration, info on the host country (e.g., education system)

For participants with migration experience, the game should foster a sense of belonging and hope, offering practical tools for integration and positive messages like, "People always have a way out and shouldn't give up" (Table 2).

The final two questions gathered stories that participants wanted to see or replay in the game. Seven themes emerged:

- Cultural challenges: Language barriers, ignorance, and intrusive questions.
- Exploitation and discrimination: Unfair labor practices and housing discrimination.
- Concealing pain: Struggling to hide emotional distress from others.
- Relocation challenges: The emotional and physical strain of moving, especially for older individuals.
- Unity and support: Early support and unity during the crisis.
- New discoveries: Positive experiences with new cultures and places.
- Empowerment: Replaying significant interactions, like conversations with border officials, to choose different outcomes.

Based on our qualitative analysis, we have developed a game design framework that will be used to create a prototype for the serious game. In this prototype, players will navigate scenarios either with agency – allowing people with experiences of forced migration to replay situations and express their frustrations – or without agency, helping those without such experiences to better understand the daily challenges faced by forced migrants. Environmental storytelling will guide players through discovering diaries and voice messages, while empowerment scenarios will offer emotional expression. A story-sharing feature will foster community engagement by enabling people with experiences of forced migration to share their narratives. The game will utilize VR to create immersive environments, deepening players' emotional connection and empathy by placing them directly into the experiences of forced migration.

5 Discussion

This study offers valuable insights into the desires of individuals affected by forced migration for a video game based on their experiences. It is noteworthy that all participants who shared their personal stories consented to incorporating their stories. This highlights the great potential of participatory game development as a platform that encourages individuals to share their experiences. Two key themes emerged from participants' overall responses: the importance of authenticity and representing the diversity within the forced migration community. These further highlight the value of our participatory approach, involving individuals with lived experiences to ensure authentic narratives. By continuing to collect stories from individuals with different backgrounds, we furthermore aim to create a game that reflects the diversity of such experiences.

The desired takeaways for individuals with and without forced migration experiences differed significantly. Participants wanted those without experience to gain knowledge, understanding, and motivation for change, while those with such experiences should be offered a sense of belonging, new perspectives, and practical information. Incorporating a variety of desired takeaways into one game may seem like a big challenge in development. It could be tempting to make separate games for each group. However, this risks further separating them. Instead, we urge video game designers to incorporate both perspectives into one game. Our framework includes two game modes aimed at different audiences, offering a more inclusive and comprehensive experience.

As the game involves VR, before any formal evaluation studies are conducted, rigorous playtesting will be necessary to ensure the physical, emotional, and mental safety of the players. VR can be a highly immersive tool, and it is critical to address any potential risks, especially for individuals with past traumatic experiences. Ensuring the safety of the prototype will be a priority to create an experience that fosters empathy while protecting the well-being of all players.

As the study is ongoing, we have not yet reached theoretical saturation, where no new insights emerge. Another key limitation is the small sample size, which does not capture the full diversity of forced migration experiences yet. Additionally, the focus on those affected by the Ukraine invasion limits the representation of other regions. Our current efforts aim to reach a more diverse participant pool to ensure well-rounded representation. Despite these limitations, our initial results demonstrate the potential of participatory video game development.

6 Conclusion

The study highlights the potential of participatory approaches in developing serious games that authentically represent forced migration experiences. By involving individuals with lived experiences in the development process, the project ensures the game will educate and foster empathy among those without such experiences and provide therapeutic benefits to those who have been affected. The data revealed a need for the game to offer specific information, foster understanding, and promote behavioral change to people without forced migration experiences while offering a sense of belonging, empowerment, and practical information to individuals with such experiences. Future development will focus on integrating these diverse insights into a cohesive gaming experience that bridges the gap between these groups.

References

1. UNHCR: Refugee statistics (2024). https://www.unhcr.org/refugee-statistics/
2. Paananen, V., Kiarostami, M.S., Lee, L.-H., Braud, T., Hosio, S.: From digital media to empathic spaces: a systematic review of empathy research in extended reality environments. Comput. Surv. **56**(5), 114:1–114:40 (2023)
3. Herrera, F., Bailenson, J., Weisz, E., Ogle, E., Zaki, J.: Building long-term empathy: a large-scale comparison of traditional and virtual reality perspective-taking. PLoS ONE **13**(10), e0204494 (2018)
4. Bujić, M., et al.: Empathy machine: how VR affects human rights attitudes. J. Media Psychol. **32**(1), 25–38 (2020)
5. Ramirez, E., et al.: What it's like to be a ...: why it's (often) unethical to use VR as an empathy nudging tool. J. Virtual Reality Ethics **7**(2), 45–60 (2021)
6. Sora-Domenjó, C.: Disrupting the empathy machine: the power and perils of virtual reality in addressing social issues. Front. Psychol. **13**, 814565 (2022). https://doi.org/10.3389/fpsyg.2022.814565
7. Mayring, P.: Qualitative Inhaltsanalyse. In: Mey, G., Mruck, K. (eds.) Handbuch Qualitative Forschung in der Psychologie, pp. 601–613. VS Verlag für Sozialwissenschaften, Wiesbaden (2010). https://doi.org/10.1007/978-3-531-92052-8_42
8. Oktay, J.S.: Grounded Theory. Oxford University Press (2012)
9. Causa Creations: Path Out (2017). https://path-out.net
10. The Pixel Hunt: The Pixel Hunt, Figs, and ARTE France, Bury Me, My Love (2017). https://burymemylove.arte.tv

Learning Through Designing: A Visual Inquiry Tool for Digital Educational Escape Games

Michael Louis Eulenstein[1(✉)], Stephanie Stiegel[2], Sarah Cortes Czech[1], Rana Zeynep Erkan[1], and Thorsten Schoormann[3]

[1] Betriebswirtschaft und Wirtschaftsinformatik, Informationssysteme und Unternehmensmodellierung, Universität Hildesheim, Universitätsplatz 1, 31141 Hildesheim, Germany

{eulensteinm,cortes,erkan}@uni-hildesheim.de

[2] Universität Flensburg, Auf dem Campus 1, 24943 Flensburg, Germany

stephanie.stiegel@uni-flensburg.de

[3] Business Information Systems, Data-Driven Enterprise, TU Braunschweig, Universitätsplatz 2, 38106 Braunschweig, Germany

thorsten.schoormann@tu-braunschweig.de

Abstract. Digital escape games are getting attention for educational purposes, typically by letting students play a certain game to engage with a new topic and gain knowledge. But what about letting students design escape games instead of just playing them? By following a design-oriented learning approach, this paper explores the educational potential of students creating their own escape games as part of their coursework. We introduce the *Escape This! Canvas*, a visual inquiry tool that supports the process of designing educational escape games from creating a first idea and theme, over specifying a game structure, to reflecting and measuring the actual learning objectives. Our canvas aids in exploring, structuring, and communicating key design elements important for building new digital escape rooms. This paper contributes to understanding the components necessary for crafting educational escape games, offering a practical tool for iterative planning and project communication, and sheds light on the value of the design of escape rooms for educational purposes.

Keywords: Design Canvas · Digital Escape Room · Serious Games

1 Introduction

Playful concepts entered the education sector in recent years. Educational escape games are a prime example for this trend. Usually played in teams, it is the goal to evade a room by solving tasks within a time limit. Originally part of entertainment, they are now popular in education and training, promoting skills like collaboration, problem-solving, and resilience [1]. Typically, students play these games, and teachers assess knowledge gains [2]. In contrast to that, we asked how the process of designing an escape room through students affects the learning. Designing a game has the potential to offer deeper

A. Schönbohm et al. (Eds.): GALA 2024, LNCS 15348, pp. 394–400, 2025.
https://doi.org/10.1007/978-3-031-78269-5_41

engagement with a certain topic, requiring students to plan, solve problems, and make several decisions. We propose that creating a digital educational escape game helps students familiarize themselves with new field or phenomenon by working through key components like defining learning goals and crafting puzzles.

To support this design process, we developed and evaluated a visual inquiry tool, the *Escape This!–Design Canvas*. This canvas provides a structured framework for designing educational escape games, promoting creativity and collaboration. Canvases help manage cognitive load, support joint ideation, and have seen success in various fields, including education [3, 4]. In this paper, we discuss the use of Escape This!–Canvas, developed as part of a research project at the University of Hildesheim, exploring the potential of serious games in higher education. Emphasizing lifelong learning skills, we argue that educational tools like these escape games can effectively integrate into existing structures while promoting sustainability education.

2 Research Design

Our research design is informed by design science research and the principles for visual inquiry tools [5, 6]. Design science is a problem-solving paradigm that allows us to rigorously create purposeful artifacts, here in the form of visual inquiry tools, and has already been used to craft results from this class of tools (e.g., [4, 7]). We created checklists and visual guides, including the Design Canvas, to help students design and test escape rooms, focusing on learning gains. Our approach to developing the final version of the Design Canvas was systematic and iterative. Initially, we grounded our work in the existing literature on escape rooms, which informed the first version of the canvas crafted by our team of authors. This initial version was applied in introductory courses to gather feedback. Further refinement was achieved through discussions in workshops and presentations with experts in the field. We then evaluated the canvas through focus groups and interviews. Over 1.5 years, the canvas underwent multiple revisions based on its application in various seminar courses. This paper reports on the final version of the canvas, presenting an in-depth account of the development process, evaluation, and the lessons learned from its implementation.

3 Artifact Description: Escape This!–Canvas

Through several activities for building and evaluating the artifact, we culminated in the current iteration of the Escape This!–Canvas. Capturing eight building blocks to re resent main design decisions (see Fig. 1) and guiding questions to prompt users to reflect on important aspects of each building block (see Table 1). In the following, we describe the building blocks in more detail to provide references to the underpinning literature and building activities of the canvas.

The first block *players* seek to get an understanding of the target user, the students who are learning. Numerous factors can have an impact on the escape game's design, including age, prior knowledge, etc. In alignment with the student's background, appropriate *learning goals* need to be formulated. The designers can draw on existing templates, such as SMART [8], to describe these goals. Additionally, they should consider supplemental skills that can be trained through escape games, such as social or problem-solving skills. Closely intertwined with the objectives, *evaluation* techniques are demanded. This enables distinguishing and assessing the two key dimensions of the functionality of the escape game (i.e., does it work? Is it playable?) and the actual increase in knowledge and skills (i.e., what has been learned?) can be distinguished and investigated by the designers.

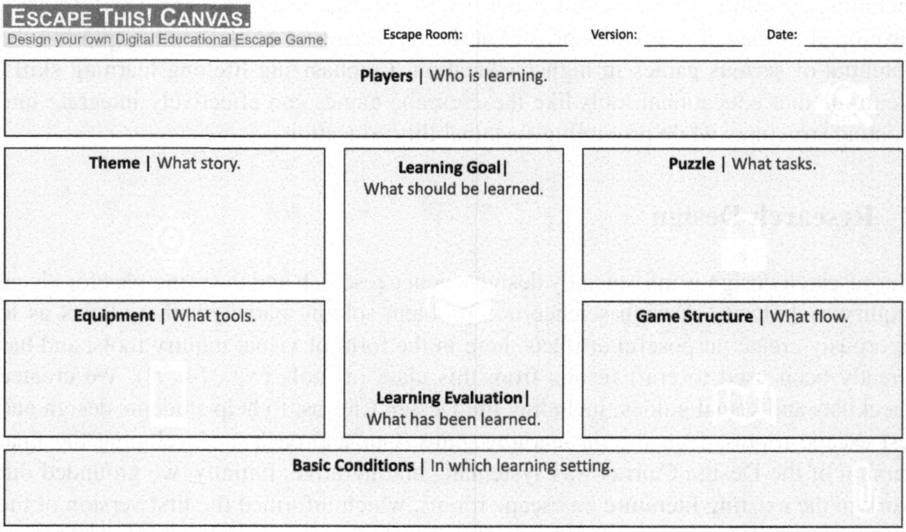

Fig. 1. A canvas for designing educational escape rooms.

Similar to physical escape games, designers in digital environments can use a series of *equipment*. The options span from text-based tools (e.g., created in Google Forms), through basic graphical games (e.g., created with PowerPoint, Genially, or Whiteboards) to 3D environments in which users can perform activities (e.g., DeckToys, Gathertown, Articulate 360, virtual reality applications). Depending on the setting, various types of *puzzles* can be implemented, such as quizzes to query knowledge or locks, passwords, and combinations to challenge problem-solving abilities. Those elements are interwoven through the underpinning *game structure* and the overall narrative to follow. Escape games can be linear formats (e.g., specific order of tasks), non-linear approaches (e.g., puzzles in any order), or iterative models [9]; some employ gated designs in which a set of tasks needs to be completed to continue the game. It is important to ensure a balance between inputs (e.g., knowledge nuggets), tasks, and rewards to create a seamless game experience. The *basic conditions* describe the setting in which the game is played. For example, games can be designed for home settings where students participate individually or with family members, or in school environments where they work in groups under teacher supervision. The evaluation was only conducted by students in the master seminar and included sometimes multiple rounds of testing, questionnaires, and interviews with the participants.

Among the key ingredients for a good escape game is the *theme*. In our case the topics surrounded the sustainability development goals (SDGs) which resulted in environmental settings like a boat or a botanical garden. Designers might ask themselves which story, narrative, genre (e.g., mystery, fantasy, future), and characters (e.g., protagonist vs. antagonist) best align with the learning goal. For instance, in terms of sustainability one might want to draw on future scenarios depicting how the world will be in 50 years if nothing (e.g., world systems) is changed. The remaining game elements must be harmonized with this theme to create an immersive environment.

Table 1. Example key questions to guide the canvas's usage.

Building block	Key questions	Example outcome
Players	Personal, cultural, or educational background? What prior knowledge can be built on?	Age, education, needs, prior knowledge, …
Learning goals	What learning needs should be fulfilled? What learning goals should be achieved? What competencies and skills should be trained?	Goals, skills, abilities, …
Learning evaluation	How to measure learning success? How to ensure the game's applicability	Proof of concept, success, …
Theme	Which story fits the learning goal? Which characters (e.g., protagonist) are helpful?	Story, genre, character, …
Equipment	Which are supporting digital tools? Which digital material should be embedded	Design software, resources, …
Puzzle	What types of quizzes are suitable? What types of locks, passwords, combinations?	Quizzes, locks, tasks,…
Game structure	Linear, non-linear, iterative game flow? How to balance tasks and rewards?	Flow, sequence, balance, …
Basic conditions	How much time (e.g., restricted by lectures)? Any budget, equipment, or content constraints?	Constraints, context, …

4 Demonstration and Evaluation

4.1 Course Context and Educational Goal

The course where the design canvas was tested aimed to teach serious game design and sustainable development through the creation of digital educational escape rooms. The main goal was to enhance student's ability to apply theoretical knowledge in a practical setting, specifically focusing on the design of engaging learning experiences through games. This process was part of the seminar's examination, allowing students to build games aligned with specific educational goals, such as promoting sustainability or fostering problem-solving skills.

4.2 Illustrating the Applicability of the Design Canvas

Feedback collected from students during the summer and winter terms of 2023 emphasized the canvas's ability to reduce design complexity and support structured project organization. Students noted that the canvas helped break down the design of escape rooms into manageable steps, making it easier to focus on specific tasks. This structure facilitated better self-organization and more effective time management. By guiding students through a step-by-step process, the canvas provided a clear orientation in managing the complexity of creating an escape game. Additionally, the students appreciated the supporting resources, such as PDFs and tool links, which fostered clear instructional guidance and topic familiarization.

4.3 Exploring the Usefulness of the Design Canvas

Students successfully designed and implemented educational escape rooms during the seminar. A digital escape room with a "time travel" theme showcased the practical application of the canvas. In post-course evaluations, we gathered qualitative feedback from focus groups comprising 13 students across four groups. The feedback sessions aimed to understand student experiences and their perception of the course content.

Key highlights from the course included the opportunity to work in teams, which fostered communication, cooperation, and collaborative problem-solving skills. The visual nature of the canvas greatly facilitated communication and collaboration, ensuring everyone was aligned. As one Master student noted: "*The canvas was really helpful in making sure we all understood what needed to be done and how to go about it.*"

Our approach allowed students to apply their theoretical knowledge in a practical context, helping them grasp complex concepts more effectively. For example: "*What I enjoyed about it was definitely when you do it with friends, it can end up chaotic. I don't think the focus was on learning success there, but it was more about getting to know people and doing something together to strengthen the bond as a team.*"

Students appreciated the balance between creative freedom and structured guidance provided by the course. The flexibility to design their escape rooms from scratch, while having access to resources and support, was particularly valued. For instance: "*We could create it ourselves, and the challenge of designing was both rewarding and educational.*" Overall, the canvas helped to reduce the complexity of the design process by providing a structured approach (e.g., *[…] break down the complexity of designing an escape room into manageable components.*" This was crucial in helping students focus on specific tasks and elements of their escape rooms without feeling overwhelmed.

5 Conclusion

Initial feedback indicated a high level of engagement and enjoyment among participants. The use of the Escape This!–Canvas significantly contributed to making the complex process of designing educational escape rooms more manageable and engaging. Participants showed a marked improvement in their understanding of sustainability. The canvas facilitated the creative and interactive aspects of the course. Students appreciated the opportunity to apply their knowledge practically while being guided through a structured design process. In the words of a participant: "*The highlight was that we could create it ourselves. Taking on the other perspective of designing was challenging and rewarding.*" The initial results indicate that the canvas was effective. Our findings suggest that serious games, under certain conditions, can enhance learning outcomes and student engagement in higher education. This study has several limitations. The small, homogeneous sample puts in question whether the findings can be transferred. A control group for comparison is needed. Lastly, long-term effects on learning and skill development were not assessed, necessitating longitudinal studies. As we concluded our seminar, we were able to show the effectiveness of design thinking tools as a pedagogical tool. The data gathered from the seminar can help education, where serious games and or escape games can become cornerstones of effective learning strategies. In conclusion, we hope to complement the stream of research on gamification, serious games, and educational escape games as well as shed light on the design and communication of escape game projects (e.g., through students).

Acknowledgments. "Escape This!" is funded by Freiraum, Stiftung Innovation in der Hochschullehre (Innovation in Higher Education). We like to thank them for their support.

References

1. Ouariachi, T., Wim, E.: Escape rooms as tools for climate change education: an exploration of initiatives. Environ. Educ. Res. **26**(8), 1193–1206 (2020). https://doi.org/10.1080/13504622.2020.1753659
2. Liapis, G., Zacharia, K., Rrasa, K., Vlahavas, I.: Serious escape room game for personality assessment. In: Dondio, P., et al. (eds.) GALA 2023. LNCS, vol. 14475, pp. 420–425. Springer, Cham (2024). https://doi.org/10.1007/978-3-031-49065-1_43
3. Täuscher, K., Abdelkafi, N.: Visual tools for business model innovation: recommendations from a cognitive perspective. Creat. Innov. Manag. **26**(2), 160–174 (2017). https://doi.org/10.1111/caim.12208
4. Schoormann, T., Behrens, D., Fellmann, M., Knackstedt, R.: On your mark, ready, search: a framework for structuring literature search strategies in information systems. In: Ahlemann, F., Schütte, R., Stieglitz, S. (eds.) WI 2021. LNISO, vol. 46, pp. 558–575. Springer, Cham (2021). https://doi.org/10.1007/978-3-030-86790-4_38
5. Avdiji, H., Elikan, D., Missionier, S., Pigneur, Y.: A design theory for visual inquiry tools. J. Assoc. Inf. Syst. **21**(3), 695–734 (2020). https://doi.org/10.17705/1jais.00617
6. Schoormann, T., Möller, F., Chandra Kruse, L., Otto, B.: BAUSTEIN—a design tool for configuring and representing design research. Inf. Syst. J. (2024)
7. Morana, S., Scheid, M., Gau, M., et al.: Research prototype: the design canvas in MyDesignProcess.com. In: DESRIST 2018 Conference Proceedings (2018)

8. Költzsch, T.: Google bringt zahlreiche neue Funktionen für Workspace Golem (2021). https://www.golem.de/news/smart-canvas-google-bringt-zahlreiche-neue-funktionen-fuer-workspace-2105-156601.html,%202021. Accessed 14 Mar 2024
9. Ali, F., Aslam, W., Ali, K., et al.: New family of iterative methods for solving nonlinear models. Discrete Dyn. Nat. Soc. (2018). https://doi.org/10.1155/2018/9619680

Evaluation of Escapade: An Engaging, Collaborative Multi-role Learning Game on History

Alf Inge Wang(✉), Jakob Endrestad Kielland, and Wictor Zhao

Norwegian University of Science and Technology, N7491 Trondheim, Norway
alfw@idi.ntnu.no

Abstract. Game-based learning positively impacts learning performance, classroom dynamics, and attitudes of both students and teachers. While digital learning games have existed since the 1960s, most remain single-player. Although social learning games have gained popularity, they are often competitive, like student response systems. There is a growing need for collaborative learning games, especially those with distinct student roles. Escapade is a multi-role collaborative game for teaching history, inspired by GeoGuessr. This paper examines its effects on motivation, collaboration, learning, engagement, and enjoyment, analyzing factors such as collaboration mode, gaming interest, history class interest, and player roles.

Keywords: Game-based Learning · Collaboration · Student Perceptions

1 Introduction

Engagement is crucial for effective learning, with student engagement shown to impact outcomes [1]. Educational games have been found effective [2, 3], though most game-based learning (GBL) remains single-player. Social gameplay is becoming more common in GBL, especially with game-based student response systems, which enhance learning, classroom dynamics, attitudes, and reduce anxiety [4, 5]. While collaborative gameplay in GBL has been beneficial [6], few studies explore games where players assume different roles to solve challenges [7, 8].

This paper presents findings from an experiment evaluating Escapade, a collaborative, multi-role history game inspired by GeoGuessr. The game includes three roles: the *explorer* (questions/answers), the *geography expert* (maps/flags), and the *history expert* (historical events/technology). The study examines how the game influenced motivation, collaboration, learning, engagement, and enjoyment, considering collaboration modes, gaming interest, history interest, and player roles. Further details on the game and experiment are in [9].

A. Schönbohm et al. (Eds.): GALA 2024, LNCS 15348, pp. 401–406, 2025.
https://doi.org/10.1007/978-3-031-78269-5_42

2 Research Questions and Experiment

This study examined the impact of a collaborative multi-role learning game in a history course on students' motivation, collaboration, learning, engagement, and enjoyment (RQ1). It also explored how the collaboration mode (RQ2), students' gaming interests (RQ3), interest in the subject (RQ4), and the roles they played (RQ5) influenced their overall gaming and learning experience.

The experiment took place at a local high school with 36 participants selected via cluster sampling. Students, grouped in threes or fours, played different roles on their own computers. After a tutorial, they played the main game on the Cold War, while being observed. Following gameplay, participants completed a questionnaire on their experience. One class (16 students) followed a jigsaw approach, restricting (separate) screen views, while the other class (20 students) was encouraged to share screens.

The questionnaire included 15 statements and 11 questions related to the research questions and demographics. Statements were based on [10], using a five-point Likert scale from "fully disagree" to "fully agree," but results are presented using a simplified three-point scale (disagree, neutral, agree). Statistical analysis was done using the Mann-Whitney U test [11].

3 The Game: Escapade

The Escapade concept was inspired by the browser game GeoGuessr, where players guess locations from random Google Street View images [12]. It also draws on several theoretical models, including the jigsaw method [13], Malone's taxonomy of intrinsic motivation [14], the GameFlow model [15], game reward systems [16], and the LEAGUE framework [17].

Escapade is a collaborative puzzle game where players work together to determine the situation, time, and place of a historical image. Each player has a distinct role: the *Explorer* views the image and submits the final answers, while the other players act as experts with specialized information. The *Explorer* answers three questions: "What is the picture of?" (multiple choice), "When did it happen?" (entering a date), and "Where did it happen?" (placing a pin on a map). The *geography expert* accesses a wiki of maps and flags, while the *history expert* consults a database of historical events and technology, sorted by year. Figure 1 shows screenshots of the Explorer, and geography roles.

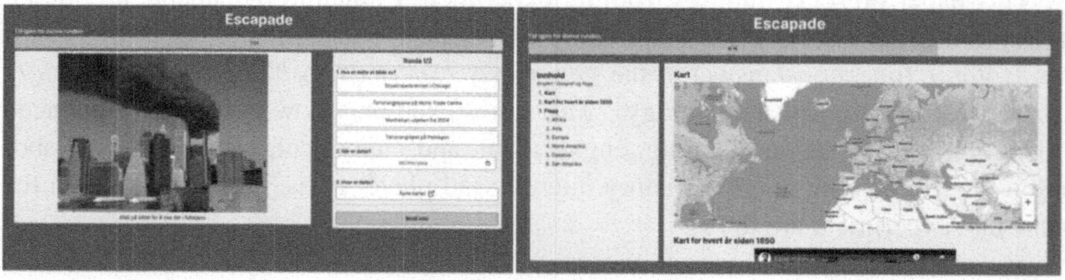

Fig. 1. Screenshots of Escapade: Explorer (left), Geography (right)

4 Results

Table 1 presents the Likert scale responses (disagree to agree) for the 15 statements in the questionnaire, comparing the jigsaw and non-jigsaw classes, along with overall agreement percentages. The results indicate a generally positive impact of the game on motivation, collaboration, learning, engagement, enjoyment, and session duration.

Table 1. Results on Motivation, Collaboration, Learning, Engagement and Enjoyment

		Jigsaw (%)			Non-jigsaw (%)			All (%)
ID	**Statement**	**D**	**N**	**A**	**D**	**N**	**A**	**A**
S1	Important to do well in Escapade	0	13	88	5	30	65	75
S2	Did not try hard to do well in Escapade	69	31	0	80	10	10	6
S3	Playing Escapade is valuable to me	0	13	88	25	15	60	72
S4	Playing Escapade made me less motivated for the class	94	0	6	90	5	5	6
S5	I wanted to learn more about the situations in the game	19	25	56	10	35	55	56
S6	I felt it was easy to cooperate with my team	0	25	75	5	5	90	83
S7	I felt that cooperation made the game harder	56	31	13	55	30	15	14
S8	I felt that I learned something from playing Escapade	0	13	88	10	10	80	83
S9	I felt that I was focused while playing	0	19	81	5	10	85	83
S10	I felt that I had to concentrate to do well in the game	0	19	81	0	30	70	75
S11	I thought it was boring to play Escapade	100	0	0	90	10	0	0
S12	I felt an increased pulse while playing	50	19	31	40	25	35	33
S13	Playing Escapade was fun	0	19	81	0	20	80	81
S14	I wish the game was a part of the history class at school	6	0	94	0	25	75	83
S15	I thought there was too little time for each round	75	25	0	80	10	10	6

D = Disagree, N = Neutral, A = Agree

The statistical analysis comparing collaboration modes, gaming interest, interest in history and roles in the game revealed the following: *Students in the jigsaw mode* (strict role separation) found Escapade more valuable and expressed a stronger desire for the game to be part of their history class compared to those in the *non-jigsaw mode*. Jigsaw players also felt they learned more from the game, although this was a borderline finding. *Gamers* were more motivated, found the game more valuable, wanted to learn more about the historical events, and felt it was easier to collaborate. Gamers also reported a greater increase in pulse while playing. This trend aligns with research indicating that gamers are more favorable towards GBL. *Students with a high interest in history* exhibited higher motivation, learning motivation, cooperation, focus, engagement, and enjoyment. They were also more likely to disagree that the game was boring, although this was a borderline result. The *role played in the game* influenced student experiences. *History experts* were more motivated, *geography experts* were less focused and engaged, while *explorers* experienced higher engagement and a greater increase in pulse. Overall, Escapade demonstrated positive effects on motivation, learning, and engagement, with variations based on collaboration mode, gaming interest, and role played.

The *survey* also asked about participants' contributions to their team. *Explorers* reported leading their teams by directing experts and analyzing details in the image. *Geography experts* focused on identifying flags, which they felt was crucial for success, particularly in jigsaw groups. *History experts* filtered information based on the explorer's needs and found their role challenging. Further, the survey invited to additional feedback. Responses were generally positive, with participants finding the game enjoyable and wishing it were part of the history class. Suggestions included improvements to the historical map, adjusting difficulty, reducing round time, adding background music, and increasing the workload for geography experts.

Observations confirmed most survey results. Participants were generally engaged and talkative, with jigsaw groups interacting more than non-jigsaw groups. Teams overheard others, which increased engagement and competitiveness. However, real-time play meant faster teams had to wait for others to finish, reducing their enjoyment. Meanwhile, teams still playing experienced increased stress to complete the game.

5 Discussion

The experimental results indicated that Escapade positively affected motivation, with only three students reporting decreased motivation (S4). This was supported by open-ended responses and informal feedback, consistent with findings from other cooperative learning games in high schools [6]. Additionally, over half of the students were motivated to learn more about the historical events featured in the game (S5).

The game's strengths lie in its collaborative and competitive elements. The per-round time limits, intergroup collaboration, and intra-group competition drove immediate goal-setting and enthusiastic engagement, as students frequently compared scores between rounds. Perceived learning was notably positive, with 83% of students reporting learning from the game, and jigsaw mode players (88%) felt they learned more compared to non-jigsaw players (80%).

Engagement and enjoyment were also high, with students reporting increased focus and fun, essential for experiencing gameflow [15]. One-third experienced an increased pulse while playing, and 83% wished the game were part of the history class, indicating high immersion.

Comparing jigsaw and non-jigsaw modes, the jigsaw mode was found more valuable by 88% of students versus 60% in non-jigsaw mode (S3). This difference may be due to dominant students overshadowing others in non-jigsaw mode, a behavior observed during the experiment. Additionally, more jigsaw students wanted the game included in the history class (94% vs. 75%).

Gaming interest had a significant impact. Gamers showed higher motivation, found the game more valuable, wanted to learn more, and felt easier collaboration. They also reported a greater increase in pulse. Previous studies have noted that gamers are more favorable toward GBL, though differences in motivation effects compared to non-gamers were not always found [18]. Other research supports that interest in game-based environments relates to better performance and engagement [19].

Students' interest in history also influenced their experience. Those with higher interest exhibited greater motivation, focus, engagement, and enjoyment, and expressed a stronger desire to learn more about the game's historical scenarios. This aligns with findings that greater subject interest enhances educational game experiences [20]. GBL has been shown to boost domain-specific motivation, such as math games improving attitudes towards math [21]. Our data indicated increased interest in history for over half of the students (S5).

Finally, the role students played in Escapade affected their experience. History experts were more motivated, explorers experienced a greater pulse, while geography experts reported less concentration and engagement. Studies of MMORPGs suggest that role impact can significantly influence learning outcomes [22]. Overall, the roles in Escapade were well-balanced, providing an enjoyable experience for all participants.

6 Conclusion

This study aimed to assess the impact of a collaborative multi-role learning game, Escapade, on teaching history. The evaluation indicated that the *game positively influenced* motivation, collaboration, perceived learning, engagement, and enjoyment (RQ1). Notably, students in the *jigsaw mode*, where they could not view each other's screens, found the game more valuable and were more inclined to integrate it into the history class compared to those in the non-jigsaw mode (RQ2). Jigsaw students also tended to report greater learning.

The study revealed that students' gaming interest had a more significant impact on their experience than the collaborative play mode. *Gamers* were more motivated, valued the game more, found collaboration easier, and showed greater immersion (RQ3). Additionally, students with a *higher interest in history* experienced more substantial benefits, including increased motivation, learning motivation, collaboration, focus, engagement, and enjoyment (RQ4). *Role* differences also affected student experiences (RQ5). *Explorers* were more engaged, *history experts* were more motivated, and *geography experts* experienced less concentration and engagement.

Overall, the use of Escapade in history classes showed promising results. Further exploration into collaborative multi-role learning games could help maximize their educational potential.

Acknowledgments. Thanks to teachers Ove Sollazzo Syrstad and Arnt Selnes and their students at Kristen Videregående skole Trøndelag for participation in the experiment.

References

1. Guthrie, J.T., Wigfield, A.: Reading Engagement: Motivating Readers Through Integrated Instruction. ERIC (1997)
2. Kebritchi, M., Hirumi, A., Bai, H.: The effects of modern mathematics computer games on mathematics achievement and class motivation. Comput. Educ. **55**, 427–443 (2010)
3. Suh, S., Kim, S.W., Kim, N.J.: Effectiveness of MMORPG-based instruction in elementary English education in Korea. J. Comput. Assist. Learn. **26**, 370–378 (2010)
4. Wang, A.I.: The wear out effect of a game-based student response system. Comput. Educ. **82**, 217–227 (2015)
5. Wang, A.I., Tahir, R.: The effect of using Kahoot! for learning–a literature review. Comput. Educ. **149**, 103818 (2020)
6. Jong, B.-S., Lai, C.-H., Hsia, Y.-T., Lin, T.-W., Lu, C.-Y.: Using game-based cooperative learning to improve learning motivation: a study of online game use in an operating systems course. IEEE Trans. Educ. **56**, 183–190 (2012)

7. Raybourn, E.M., Fabian, N.D., Tucker, E.M., Willis, M.: Beyond game effectiveness. Part II, a qualitative study of multi-role experiential learning. Sandia National Laboratories (SNL), Albuquerque, NM, and Livermore, CA (2010)
8. Guigon, G., Vermeulen, M., Muratet, M., Carron, T.: Towards an integration of the multi-role dimension in the design of learning games: a review of the literature. In: de Rosa, F., Marfisi Schottman, I., Baalsrud Hauge, J., Bellotti, F., Dondio, P., Romero, M. (eds.) GALA 2021. LNCS, vol. 13134, pp. 258–264. Springer, Cham (2021). https://doi.org/10.1007/978-3-030-92182-8_26
9. Kielland, J.E., Zhao, W.: Utilising Collaboration in Escapade: An Engaging Learning Game. NTNU (2022)
10. Wang, A.I., Lieberoth, A.: The effect of points and audio on concentration, engagement, enjoyment, learning, motivation, and classroom dynamics using Kahoot! In: Proceedings from the 10th European Conference of Games Based Learning. Academic Conferences and Publishing International Limited (2016)
11. Mann, H.B., Whitney, D.R.: On a test of whether one of two random variables is stochastically larger than the other. Ann. Math. Stat., 50–60 (1947)
12. Girgin, M.: Use of games in education: GeoGuessr in geography course. Int. Technol. Educ. J. **1**, 1–6 (2017)
13. Aronson, E.: The Jigsaw Classroom. Sage (1978)
14. Malone, T.W.: What makes things fun to learn? Heuristics for designing instructional computer games. In: The 3rd ACM SIGSMALL Symposium and the first SIGPC Symposium on Small Systems, Palo Alto, California, United States. ACM Press (1980)
15. Sweetser, P., Wyeth, P.: GameFlow: a model for evaluating player enjoyment in games. ACM Comput. Entertain. **3** (2005)
16. Wang, H., Sun, C.-T.: Game reward systems: gaming experiences and social meanings. In: DiGRA Conference. Citeseer (2011)
17. Tahir, R., Wang, A.I.: Codifying game-based learning: development and application of LEAGUÊ framework for learning games. In: European Conference of Games-Based Learning. Academic Conferences and Publishing International (2018)
18. Recabarren, M., Corvalán, B., Villegas, M.: Exploring the differences between gamer and non-gamer students in the effects of gamification on their motivation and learning. Interact. Learn. Environ. **31**, 3529–3542 (2023)
19. Vargianniti, I., Karpouzis, K.: Effects of game-based learning on academic performance and student interest. In: Liapis, A., Yannakakis, G., Gentile, M., Ninaus, M. (eds.) GALA 2019. LNCS, vol. 11899, pp. 332–341. Springer, Cham (2019). https://doi.org/10.1007/978-3-030-34350-7_32
20. Li, Y., Chen, D., Deng, X.: The impact of digital educational games on student's motivation for learning: the mediating effect of learning engagement and the moderating effect of the digital environment. PLoS ONE **19**, e0294350 (2024)
21. Vankúš, P.: Influence of game-based learning in mathematics education on students' affective domain: a systematic review. Mathematics **9**, 986 (2021)
22. Williams, J.P., Kirschner, D., Suhaimi-Broder, Z.: Structural roles in massively multiplayer online games: a case study of guild and raid leaders in World of Warcraft. In: Symbolic Interaction and New Social Media, vol. 43, pp. 121–142. Emerald Group Publishing Limited (2014)

Promoting Cognitive and Psychosocial Rehabilitation with a Co-Designed Multiplayer Serious Game

Carolina Figueira[1(✉)], Simão Reis[1], Luis Paulo Reis[1], Marta Parreira[2], Ana Ramos[2], and Eliana Silva[1]

[1] LIACC/FEUP, Faculty of Engineering, University of Porto, Porto, Portugal
carolinacintraff@gmail.com
[2] NeuroGime - Clinica de Neurorreabilitação, Braga, Portugal
https://liacc.fe.up.pt/, https://www.neurogime.pt/,
https://www.neurogime.pt/

Abstract. Rehabilitation consists of interventions aimed at restoring, maintaining, or enhancing the skills required for daily living. Cognitive rehabilitation includes diverse techniques and strategies intended to improve deficits in memory, concentration, attention, learning, and other higher cognitive functions like language, logic, and reasoning. This study addresses the challenges of community reintegration faced by individuals with Acquired Brain Injuries (ABI) by developing a multiplayer serious games platform. Traditional cognitive rehabilitation methods are often repetitive and lack social interaction opportunities, which often causes abandonment. Through an innovative co-design approach involving eleven participants including patients, caregivers, and professionals, four mini-games were conceptualized and developed for the cognitive training of capacities such as visual and positional memory, mathematical reasoning, linguistics, and executive functions.

Keywords: Co-Design · Cognitive Rehabilitation · Serious Games · Multiplayer Games · Human-Computer Interaction

1 Introduction

Acquired Brain Injuries Disorders of cognitive functions are common following Acquired Brain Injuries (ABIs) and significantly impact independence, social relationships, and quality of life [1]. Cognitive deficits affect over 70% of stroke survivors [2]. Despite being a significant health challenge, studies show a gap in long-term outcome assessments and access to rehabilitation services, with only 30% receiving in-patient and 15% outpatient rehabilitation [5]. Non-TBIs, primarily caused by cerebral vascular accidents (CVA), or strokes, pose a growing concern due to their high global burden. In Portugal, strokes are the main cause of death and long-term disability [3], contributing to rising healthcare costs.

A. Schönbohm et al. (Eds.): GALA 2024, LNCS 15348, pp. 407–413, 2025.
https://doi.org/10.1007/978-3-031-78269-5_43

ABIs can significantly impair normal brain function, making community integration challenging for patients. Classical techniques often rely on therapist-led interventions in clinical settings, posing logistical and motivational challenges for patients.

Cognitive and Psychosocial Rehabilitation Rehabilitation encompasses a range of interventions aimed at restoring, maintaining, or enhancing essential daily life skills. Cognitive rehabilitation specifically targets deficits in memory, concentration, attention, and learning, among other higher cognitive functions such as language, logic, and reasoning, employing various methods and approaches [4]. However, conventional cognitive rehabilitation methods often face challenges related to patient motivation due to their repetitive and monotonous nature. Hence, there is a growing recognition of the importance of innovative approaches, such as serious games, which facilitate interaction and complement traditional treatments. Individuals with ABIs often face challenges fulfilling their fundamental need for social connection and belonging, with social isolation being a primary concern for many [6]. Social isolation, characterized by inadequate social relations at various levels, is exacerbated by motor, cognitive, and socio-emotional impairments typical in ABI patients, making them vulnerable to social exclusion [7]. Such changes, often enduring, lead to reduced participation in society and increased social isolation over time.

Serious Games Serious games (SGs), games designed for purposes beyond mere entertainment [8], find applications across diverse sectors including such as primary and secondary school education, adult and higher education, healthcare, or the workplace to promote desired motivational, behavioral, and learning outcomes [9]. Incorporating SGs into cognitive rehabilitation has shown promising results with various known platforms that assist the rehabilitation of many patients, such as RehaCom and CogniPlus. For the case of rehabilitation, SGs offer a promising avenue, providing a playful and social perspective to engage patients in their recovery without replacing traditional rehabilitation methods.

Co-Design The project places a strong emphasis on user experience and usability, recognizing the importance of collaboration between developers and individuals with diverse perspectives, including those with lived experience, service providers, and other stakeholders [10]. The co-design is the most important aspect of this project since it is particularly innovative and aims to acknowledge the potential challenges faced by patients of ABIs, including motor and cognitive disabilities, as well as potential age-related difficulties with technology.

2 Methodology

This project, developed by a multidisciplinary team of psychologists, neuropsychologists, and computer engineers, aims to innovate cognitive rehabilitation by incorporating multiplayer serious games (SGs) to enhance both cognitive and social aspects of therapy. The multiplayer games will foster social skills through cooperative gameplay and include mechanisms to ensure fair and challenging experiences for all patients. It seeks to fill a gap in traditional rehabilitation, which often relies on single-player games and lacks innovative, socially interactive approaches. Co-design methodology was used to tailor the platform to patients' preferences. The inclusion criteria for this study were patients over the age of 18 who have already started a cognitive rehabilitation process and who have preserved general intellectual abilities and comprehensive language skills to understand informed consent and perform the tasks required for participation, family members or caretakers of such patients, therapists or professionals in the field (e.g. neuropsychologists, neurologists, occupational therapists).

The co-design process comprises three phases: structured interviews tailored for each group to understand their needs and preferences, a consultation with professionals to gather opinions on general aspects of the game and their themes and visuals, and finally a usability study to validate the final prototype. The training programs were thought out having in mind the literature and the results of the first phase of co-design.

First Phase of Co-Design Due to patient availability, it was impossible to interview patients of ABI. Since the cognitive issues and training techniques are similar to the rehabilitation of patients with dementia, we conducted interviews with individuals with dementia undergoing cognitive training, their family members, and health professionals involved in the training. The interviews with the patients and family members were conducted at the clinic, and the ones with the professionals were conducted online due to lack of availability in their schedules. They were all around 15 min long, were audiotapes, and transcribed verbatim in an anonymous manner.

The semi-scrtuctured interviews targeted different objectives for each group. For patients, the focus was on their comfort with technology, design preferences, and daily challenges. Family members were asked about how to engage them in treatment and their design preferences. Health professionals discussed the games they currently use in therapy, their limitations, and features that could enhance the app's enjoyment and relevance. After the interviews, the team chose the cognitive areas that the mini-games focused on and changed specifics about the theme, the mechanics of the mini-games, and the aesthetics to meet the requirements of the participants. Participants were not compensated for their involvement. The study received approval from the Ethics Committee of the Faculty of Engineering at the University of Porto, and all procedures were conducted following the Declaration of Helsinki.

Our sample of professionals included 5 individuals (1 male, 20%), aged 26 to 40 years old (M= 32.8; SD= 5.76), the sample of patients was of 3 individuals (1 female, 33.3%), aged 65 to 72 years old (M= 69; SD= 3.06), and finally for family members, 3 individuals (1 male, 33.3%), aged 42 to 55 years old (M= 47.66; SD= 6.66). All of the professionals specialized in either Clinical Psychology (n= 3; 60%) or Neuropsychology (n= 2; 40%), and all of the participants were Portuguese.

Training Programs The game is called "CogniSpace" and each mini-game will approach a different cognitive function. After studying the literature and consulting with professionals, patients, and family members in the first phase it was possible to choose the best functions to tackle and design the mini-games. The mini-games, designed for Portuguese adults with Acquired Brain Injuries, will feature both written and audio content in Portuguese. To maintain player motivation, visual and audio feedback will be provided throughout the games, as recommended by a neuropsychologist. The games include both single-player and multiplayer modes, each lasting 10 min so to not cause cognitive fatigue. Players receive text-based instructions at the start, with an option for text-to-speech narration. A progress bar tracks progress without showing the exact time to reduce anxiety. Performance ratings are given as 'Good', 'Very Good', or 'Excellent'. The mini-games focus on daily tasks to enhance real-life applicability. Figure 1 shows examples of scenes in each mini-game.

Memory Tornado. This is a cooperative multiplayer game for the exercise of visuospatial memory. Working memory is essential for managing daily tasks that require retaining and processing information to achieve goals [11]. Training this cognitive function involves responding to visual stimuli within a set timeframe, helping to improve the patient's ability to store, update, and recall information efficiently. In this mini-game, players memorize the layout of items in different settings, such as a kitchen or garden, before a hurricane disrupts everything. They then work together to restore the scene by correctly placing the items back in their original positions. Each player is responsible for one half of the scene, and points are awarded for accuracy. If mistakes are made, players can retry. Hints are available if needed, and difficulty increases when players complete 3 out of 5 scenes correctly without using hints, with more items displaced in harder levels.

Perfect Pair. This is a single-player game for the exercise of linguistics. This game is designed for patients with alexia, a condition where they can write and spell but struggle to understand written text, even their own, which typically occurs after an ABI [12]. Based on feedback from professionals, it focuses on helping patients identify correct prepositions of location (e.g., "on," "under," and "next to") to describe scenes. As players progress, the game increases difficulty by adding more objects to the scenes. Difficulty is adjusted based on performance, with faster progression for high scores and hints available when needed. Players must correctly answer 3 out of 5 questions to advance to the next level.

Counting Change. This is a single-player game for the exercise of mathematical reasoning. The game targets rehabilitation for individuals with acalculia and dyscalculia, conditions affecting numerical skills, often linked to post-stroke cognitive deficits [13]. In this single-player game, players tackle money-related tasks that range from counting coins in simple scenarios to calculating larger sums involving coins and bills in more complex ones. The goal is to enhance arithmetic skills, particularly addition and multiplication, to prepare for real-life situations. Difficulty adjusts dynamically based on player performance, advancing to harder levels if the player excels, or remaining at the current level if more practice is needed, with clues available to assist players.

Everything Ready?. This is a cooperative multiplayer game for the exercise of planning and management (executive function). This game focuses on improving executive functions like planning, organizing, and decision-making, which can be impaired by brain injuries, particularly in the frontal lobe [14]. Players collaborate to complete tasks such as cleaning, cooking, or shopping by correctly pairing objects from two sets of images in the proper sequence. The game adjusts difficulty by increasing the number of steps in tasks and it provides hints when needed. Players advance to more challenging levels after correctly completing 3 out of 5 scenes without using hints.

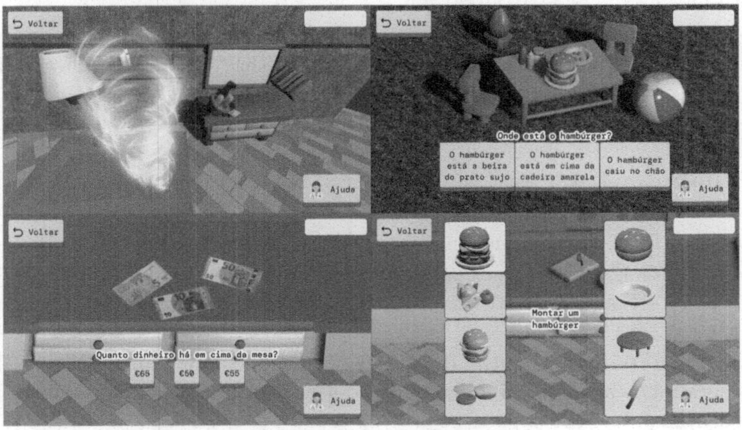

Fig. 1. On the top left, the animation of the tornado in "Memory Tornado" passing through the scene and reorganizing the objects. On the top right, an example of a scene in "Perfect Pair" with the scene above the questions regarding the position of the hamburger in regards to the empty plate. On the bottom left, an example of a scene in "Counting Change" with the money on the table and the question and options at the bottom of the screen. On the bottom right, an example of a scene of "Everything Ready?" with the task in the middle (Cooking a stew) and the steps on each side

3 Conclusion

The second phase of the co-design is being conducted, meaning the team has to wait for feedback about the first version of the game from neuropsychologists and psychologists working on a clinic focused on neurorehabilitation in order to improve it. Their feedback is crucial to better understand details in usability and the levels of difficulty the patients could face. The mini-games will be adapted to their ideas and suggestions before the usability tests.

Some limitations of this study include the reduced number of mini-games, which don't encompass all of the possible cognitive impairments that patients could experience. Other limitations include the small sample size for data collection and the limited number of phases per level of each mini-game.

The platform developed in this study aims to offer engaging and socially interactive mini-games to complement cognitive rehabilitation through cognitive training. By fostering social connections and increasing ecological validity, the goal of this project is to enhance the rehabilitation process, improve the lives of ABI patients, and facilitate their resocialization.

Acknowledgments. This work was financially supported by: Base Funding -UIDB/00027/2020 of the Artificial Intelligence Laboratory - LIACC -funded by national funds through the FCT/MCTES (PIDDAC).

Disclosure of Interests. The authors declare that they have no competing interests that are relevant to the content of this article.

References

1. Mantovani, E. et al.: Telemedicine and virtual reality for cognitive rehabilitation: a roadmap for the COVID-19 pandemic. Frontiers Neurol. **11** (2020)
2. S. Rost, N. et al.: Post-stroke cognitive impairment and dementia. Circ. Res. **130**(8), 1252–1271 (2022)
3. O AVC é a principal causa de morte e incapacidade em Portugal. https://www.spmi.pt/o-avc-e-a-principal-causa-de-morte-e-incapacidade-em-portugal/. Accessed 22 July 2024
4. Bahar-Fuchs, A., et al.: Cognitive training for people with mild to moderate dementia: a Cochrane Review. BJPsych Adv. **26**(2), 66 (2020)
5. Andelic, N., et al.: Unmet rehabilitation needs after traumatic brain injury across Europe: results from the CENTER-TBI study. J. Clin. Med. **10**(5), 1552–1555 (2021)
6. Lowe, N., et al.: 'Lonely in my head': the experiences of loneliness in individuals with brain injury. Br. J. Health. Psychol. **26**(2), 444–463 (2021)
7. Salas, C., et al.: Social isolation after acquired brain injury: exploring the relationship between network size, functional support, loneliness and mental health. Neuropsychol. Rehabil. **32**(9), 2294–2318 (2022)
8. Larson, K.: Serious games and gamification in the corporate training environment: a literature review. TechTrends **64**(2), 319–328 (2020)

9. Krath, J., et al.: Revealing the theoretical basis of gamification: a systematic review and analysis of theory in research on gamification, serious games and game-based learning. Comput. Hum. Behav. **125**, 106963 (2021)
10. Mulvale, G. et al.: Co-designing services for youth with mental health issues: novel elicitation approaches. Int. J. Qual. Methods **18**(10258) (2019)
11. Jung, H.T., et al.: Effectiveness of a serious game for cognitive training in chronic stroke survivors with mild-to-moderate cognitive impairment: a pilot randomized controlled trial. Appl. Sci. **10**(19), 6703 (2020)
12. D Barbosa AC., Asuncion RMD., Emmady PD.: Alexia. StatPearls Publishing, Treasure Island (FL) (2024)
13. Grimaldi, M., Jeanmonod, R.: Acute stroke presenting with isolated acalculia. Am. J. Emerg. Med. **36**(10), 1923.e1–1923.e3 (2018)
14. High WM. et al.: Early versus later admission to postacute rehabilitation: impact on functional outcome after traumatic brain injury. Arch. Phys. Med. Rehabil. **87**(3), 334–342 (2006)

Playful Adult Learning: LEGO® as a Playful and Pedagogical Approach

Dimitra Chasanidou[1,2](✉) and Natassa Raikou[2,3]

[1] Norwegian University of Science and Technology, 7491 Trondheim, Norway
[2] Hellenic Open University, 26335 Patras, Greece
dimitra.chasanidou@ntnu.no, std146411@ac.eap.gr, raikou.anastasia@ac.eap.gr, araikou@uth.gr
[3] University of Thessaly, 38221 Volos, Greece

Abstract. This paper explores the role of playfulness in adult learning and examines the case of LEGO seminars. This study interviewed trainees and educators in LEGO Education seminars and findings show that playful process in seminars could benefit adults in multiple ways. Playful elements in adult learning and psycho-pedagogical dimensions of the learning process reveal opportunities in this field. Limitations and future work are discussed at the end.

Keywords: LEGO® · Adult learning · Playful learning · Reflective Thinking · Pedagogical approach

1 Introduction

An increased emphasis on diverse skills over the last 5–10 years aims to fulfill the needs of a continuously changing work environment. Experts point out that personal, social, methodological skills are closely connected with employability, particularly for young graduates [17]. This is inline with lifelong learning which is adequately incorporated as an important part of the Sustainable Development Goals (SDG) that calls for "adult up-skilling and reskilling in fast changing labor markets" [13]. In order to address these challenges, new skills and learning approaches are necessary [5].

LEGO®, as a playful learning approach, could fill this gap. Research has consistently shown that play and playful approaches are crucial for learning and human development at all stages, from childhood to adulthood [8,14]. Play has been a fundamental part of our lives, creating an impact on cognitive, social, emotional development, while stimulating curiosity, creativity, and imagination [8]. Adult learning could embrace playful approaches in learning activities considering contextual factors, teaching practices, and instructional objectives. LEGO® applications have been applied in various educational settings and fields, demonstrating promising results in adult learning (e.g., [11,20]). LEGO® could be applied in adult learning with constructivist activities, where

A. Schönbohm et al. (Eds.): GALA 2024, LNCS 15348, pp. 414–420, 2025.
https://doi.org/10.1007/978-3-031-78269-5_44

learners try to associate meanings to learning from active inquiry of their life experiences [12]. Rooted to the essence of experiential learning and constructivism, learning with LEGO® can be achieved through own experiences and reflective practices [7,12]. However, an exploration of the literature shows that fun and enjoyment have been more discussed in relation to the learning of children and less in relation with adults [2,4]. Therefore, this study explores the topic of playfulness in LEGO® Education adult learning seminars and the associated playful elements. The remainder of this paper is organized as follows. Section 2 reviews theoretical foundations and empirical evidence of playful learning in adult learning. Section 3 describes the methodology and Sect. 4 presents findings in two sections. Finally, Sect. 5 discusses limitations and future research directions.

2 Playfulness and LEGO® in Adult Learning

Playful approaches and elements in adult learning encompass specific strategies and tools designed to make learning more engaging, enjoyable, and effective. These approaches are rooted in the understanding that play is not only beneficial for children but also for adults, enhancing motivation, creativity, and cognitive development [8,16]. Theoretical foundations of playful approaches are mainly rooted in constructivist and experiential learning theories. Constructivist Learning Theories, such as those proposed by Piaget in 1952 [15] and Vygotsky in 1978 [10], argue that knowledge is constructed through active engagement with the environment. This theory supports the use of playful elements in learning, as they provide a hands-on, interactive approach that encourages exploration and experimentation. Similarly, Experiential Learning Theory (ELT), proposed by David Kolb in 1984 [7], emphasizes learning through experience, particularly through a cycle of concrete experience, reflective observation, abstract conceptualization, and active experimentation. This theory aligns closely with playful learning approaches, where learners engage in hands-on activities that require them to reflect on their experiences, conceptualize their observations, and apply their knowledge in new contexts. According to ELT, playful elements such as simulations, role-playing, and hands-on building activities provide concrete experiences crucial for learning. Empirical evidence support the use of playful learning approaches in increasing engagement, motivation, social interaction, and collaboration among others (e.g., [19]). One example of playful application in adult learning refers to storytelling and narrative techniques that could leverage the power of stories to make learning more relatable and memorable.

As an innovative and effective educational tool, LEGO® applications in adult learning gained traction [1,3]. Traditionally associated with children's play, LEGO® has been recontextualised for adult education through LEGO® Serious Play and LEGO® Education. These approaches leverage the tactile, constructive, and playful nature of LEGO® bricks to foster engagement, creativity, and deeper learning. Specifically for LEGO® Education, this is an initiative by LEGO® Group aiming to promote hands-on, playful learning experiences

Fig. 1. Examples of LEGO® Education kits. Left: STEAM Park aims to build early STEAM skills in kindergarten. Right: SPIKE Essential aims to build programming skills in elementary.

for learners of all ages. By integrating LEGO® bricks into educational contexts, LEGO® Education seeks to foster creativity, critical thinking, problem-solving, and collaboration skills. This approach is grounded in constructivist and constructionist theories of learning, which emphasize on the importance of active, experiential learning. In addition, LEGO® Education focuses on developing essential 21st-century skills, such as collaboration, communication, creativity, and critical thinking. These skills are increasingly important in a rapidly changing, interconnected world [5]. LEGO® Education offers a wide range of sets and kits (e.g., Fig. 1) designed for educational purposes, where traditional LEGO® bricks, as well as specialized components such as motors, sensors, and programmable bricks are combined in model building. The company offers facilitated professional learning courses for educators to actively engage in experiential professional learning programs. Courses are designed to produce transferable instructional skills for educators that trigger student engagement through play. Successful participation lead to certification by LEGO® Education Academy.

3 Methodology

The paper follows a qualitative research methodology, with semi-structured, in-depth interviews which were completed in early spring 2024 with key informants [6,18]. Informed consent was obtained from all participants before interviews. Following an interview guide, participants were asked several open-ended questions. Interviews lasted for up to 60 min and they were recorded and transcribed verbatim.

In total, 11 trainees and 3 educators of LEGO® Education from Greece participated in interviews. All trainees were certified participants in LEGO® Education seminars and they were all teachers in preschool, elementary, high school or higher education. Regarding their professional profile, eight are engaged in their current work with education, while the remaining three are engaged in educational activities in private schools. All trainees completed LEGO® Education seminars, while most of them attended several other seminars in the past to advance their professional skills. Additionally, 3 educators participated in interviews, with long experience from 8–15 years, as certified educators by LEGO® Education Academy. Their educational background was in computer science and engineering, while they are engaged in LEGO® Education training of school teachers who teach robotics.

4 Results and Discussion

Interviews with trainees and educators provided rich results on two dimensions: the playful elements of the seminars, and its psycho-pedagogical aspects. First, we describe the structure of LEGO® Education seminars to gain an holistic perspective. Seminar's target group is mainly school teachers. One physical seminar lasts from 6–8 hours and typically, consists of 80% experiential training, 20% theoretical approaches. Seminars are categorized according to the LEGO® kit, and apply experiential learning to engage participants in "hands-on" learning through a playful process. Overall, seminars include both individual and group building activities. The educational objectives of the seminars include teaching of lesson plans, experimentation with LEGO® kits, integration of robotics into the understanding of subjects and concepts, improvement of skills such as empathy, problem solving, socialization, team spirit and cooperation. The most common educational techniques applied in such seminars involve problem solving, trial and error, and case study that allows learners to analyze and discuss real or hypothetical scenarios related to the use of LEGO®.

4.1 Playful Elements in Adult Learning

Study participants discussed as playful elements in LEGO® seminars those associated with (a) hands-on, creative learning, and (b) role-playing and simulations.
Hands-on, Creative Learning: According to Kolb's Experiential Learning Theory [7], engaging in concrete experiences is a crucial step in the learning cycle. Both educators and trainees discussed the characteristics of LEGO® seminars in relation with playfulness. For educators, practical application of hands-on learning enhance trainees' active engagement. They believe such hands-on activities created a dynamic and interactive learning environment, making seminars more engaging for both educators and trainees. Also, enthusiasm and engagement of trainees during hands-on activities motivated educators to a more vibrant and effective teaching experience. On the other hand, trainees believe that they benefit from the tangible, hands-on experience with LEGO® bricks, which helps to communicate abstract concepts and theories. Also, trainees seem to retain information better when they actively participate with hands-on activities where they could recall information more effectively. Trainees explored multiple ways to solve problems and build models, while working with LEGO® encourages creativity and innovation.
Role-Playing and Simulations: Educators and trainees believe they were significantly benefit from role-playing and simulations during LEGO® Education seminars. These approaches involved trainees taking on various roles and be

engaged in real-world scenarios, mimicking classroom situations, and providing immersive and practical learning experiences. Typical roles involve participants in pairs to become either a modeller who builds models by bricks or the supervisor who instructs modeller how to build something. One simulation example is the simulation of physics in an activity where trainees learn the impact of the weight of a car made by LEGO® bricks on its final distance from point A to point B. Role-playing allowed educators to understand different perspectives of a problem by participating in scenarios or by observing trainees. This created greater empathy and improved their teaching strategies to accommodate diverse viewpoints. Other playful approaches mentioned in the seminars involve point systems and small rewards in friendly competitions. Finally, the most common playful element is timed challenges where time-bound tasks add a layer of excitement and urgency to the learning activities.

4.2 Psycho-Pedagogical Dimension in LEGO® Education

The psycho-pedagogical dimension of LEGO® Education seminars involve various principles, both psychological and pedagogical, that aim to enhance the learning experience and outcomes for adult learners. Constructivism and reflective thinking describe the meaning of psycho-pedagogical dimension.

Constructivism: Constructivism constitutes the theoretical background of experiential learning activities [9]. Trainees reflected on the constructivist activities during seminars when they constructed their own understanding and knowledge through hands-on activities and building LEGO® models. Furthermore, social constructivism was experienced through collaborative learning, emphasizing in teamwork and peer interactions. Trainees perceived that they constructed knowledge together, benefiting from diverse perspectives, backgrounds and collective problem-solving.

Reflective Thinking: Reflective thinking elevates the building activity from an internal process to an external activity. Educators encouraged trainees to reflect on their learning processes and models, promoting deeper understanding and self-awareness. Educators reflected on the seminar's process and commented that through critical thinking and spatial reasoning try to enhance higher-order thinking skills by completing building tasks, problem-solving activities, and physical manipulation of LEGO® bricks. Apart from cognitive and social development, educators and trainees believe that seminars contribute to emotional development. Specifically, skills such as empathy, self-regulation, and interpersonal communication were connected with emotional intelligence developed in seminars. Furthermore, inclusion was mentioned as a particularly useful characteristic in classrooms.

5 Limitations and Future Work

This study is not without challenges, and although the benefits outweigh the limitations, they need to be disclosed. One limitation refers to the suitability of participants. Trainees were all school teachers, while future studies could take into consideration participants' background and explore more cross-disciplinary groups of trainees and educators. Another limitation is the time of the study. Since participants were trainees in such seminars one or more years ago, they might forget part of their experience with LEGO®. Longitudinal studies could deal with such issues and involve participants before, during and after their experience with seminars. Lastly, comparative studies of LEGO® Education seminars with other types of adult learning seminars could bring more light into this area.

References

1. Benesova, N.: Lego® serious play® in management education. Cogent Edu. **10**(2), 2262284 (2023)
2. Boghian, I., Cojocariu, V.M., Popescu, C.V., Mâţ, L.: Game-based learning. using board games in adult education. J. Edu. Sci. Psychol. **9**(1) (2019)
3. Cavaliero, T.: 'creative blocs': action research study on the implementation of Lego as a tool for reflective practice with social care practitioners. J. Furth. High. Educ. **41**(2), 133–142 (2017)
4. Charlier, N., Ott, M., Remmele, B., Whitton, N.: Not just for children: game-based learning for older adults. In: 6th European Conference on Games Based Learning, Cork, Ireland, pp. 102–108 (2012)
5. Chasanidou, D., Raikou, N.: Lego® for professional development: a systematic literature review. In: International Conference on Human-Computer Interaction, pp. 3–21. Springer (2024)
6. Hennink, M., Hutter, I., Bailey, A.: Qualitative research methods. Sage (2020)
7. Kolb, D.A.: Experiential learning: Experience as the source of learning and development. FT press (2014)
8. Leather, M., Harper, N., Obee, P.: A pedagogy of play: reasons to be playful in postsecondary education. J. Experiential Edu. **44**(3), 208–226 (2021)
9. Lewis, L.H., Williams, C.J.: Experiential learning: past and present. New Dir. Adult Continuing Edu. **1994**(62), 5–16 (1994)
10. Liu, C.H., Matthews, R.: Vygotsky's philosophy: constructivism and its criticisms examined. Int. Electron. J. **6**(3), 386–399 (2005)
11. McCusker, S.: Lego®, serious play tm: thinking about teaching and learning. Int. J. Knowl. Innov. Entrepreneurship **2**(1), 27–37 (2014)
12. Merriam, S.B., Baumgartner, L.M.: Learning in adulthood: A comprehensive guide. Wiley (2020)
13. Orlović Lovren, V., Popović, K.: Lifelong learning for sustainable development-is adult education left behind? Handb. Lifelong Learn. Sustain. Dev. 1–17 (2018)
14. Peabody, M.A., Noyes, S.: Reflective boot camp: adapting lego® serious play® in higher education. Reflective Pract. **18**(2), 232–243 (2017)
15. Piaget, J., Cook, M., et al.: The Origins of Intelligence in Children, vol. 8. International Universities Press, New York (1952)
16. Rice, L.: Playful learning. J. Edu. Built Environ. **4**(2), 94–108 (2009)
17. Succi, C., Canovi, M.: Soft skills to enhance graduate employability: comparing students and employers' perceptions. Stud. High. Educ. **45**(9), 1834–1847 (2020)
18. Turner, D.W., III.: Qualitative interview design: a practical guide for novice investigators. Qualitative Rep. **15**(3), 754 (2010)

19. Whitton, N.: Playful learning: tools, techniques, and tactics. Res. Learn. Technol. **26**, 1–12 (2018)
20. Zenk, L., Hynek, N., Schreder, G., Zenk, A., Pausits, A., Steiner, G.: Designing innovation courses in higher education using lego® serious play®. Int. J. Manage. Appl. Res. **5**(4), 245–263 (2018)

AI-Awareness: Fostering Teachers' Awareness of Artificial Intelligence Through a Board Game

Anna Re[1], Giuseppe Città[1], Manuel Gentile[1], Fabrizio Lo Presti[1,2], Vanessa Pitrella[1,2,3], Crispino Tosto[1(✉)], and Salvatore Perna[1]

[1] Institute for Educational Technology, National Research Council, via Ugo La Malfa 153, 90146 Palermo, Italy
crispino.tosto@itd.cnr.it

[2] Dipartimento Chirurgico, Medico, Odontoiatrico e di Scienze Morfologiche con Interesse Trapiantologico, Oncologico e di Medicina Rigenerativa, Università di Modena e Reggio Emilia, Modena, Italy

[3] Dipartimento di Scienze Psicologiche, Pedagogiche, dell'Esercizio Fisico e della Formazione, Università degli Studi di Palermo, Palermo, Italy

Abstract. The integration of Artificial Intelligence (AI) into educational practices offers numerous opportunities to improve teaching, learning, and assessment. However, for these tools to be used effectively, it is critical to address the role of teachers, their professional development, and the misconceptions that may hinder the adoption of AI technologies. On these premises, the idea of creating a board game designed specifically for teachers emerged. *AI-awareness,* in fact, was designed not only to introduce various AI tools and discuss their potential applications in the classroom but also to help teachers overcome biases and challenges they may face in their educational practice. By improving their awareness of AI tools, teachers can better understand the transformative possibilities of Artificial Intelligence in education, ultimately promoting a more informed and innovative teaching approach.

Keywords: Artificial Intelligence · teachers · training · board game · engagement · teacher feedback

1 Introduction

The integration of Artificial Intelligence (AI) tools and their application in the core domains of education (teaching, learning, and assessment practices) offers particularly promising prospects [1]. These opportunities - along with the related challenges - are connected to the need to ensure adequate training on the effective use of emerging AI technologies to teachers. Such training should promote a learning environment that contributes to the achievement of educational goals [e.g., 2, 3] and support the changes that these technologies impose on the teacher's role [4]. In fact, although the introduction of AI technologies offers significant opportunities, teachers are not fully aware of their potential and how these technologies can concretely support learning processes. On the

A. Schönbohm et al. (Eds.): GALA 2024, LNCS 15348, pp. 421–426, 2025.
https://doi.org/10.1007/978-3-031-78269-5_45

other hand, teachers' limited knowledge of AI may explain biases and fears that often emerge regarding its potential application in education. One these misconceptions is that AI will replace teachers [5], a fear that may limit the understanding of the role of that AI in education and that may be exacerbated by the lack of practical experiences. In this direction, the opportunities and challenges arising from the integration of AI in teaching should be accompanied by the need to ensure adequate training of teachers on the conscious and effective use of these technologies [6]. In fact, whether the application of AI tools occurs with awareness of their potential use, it can improve the effectiveness of the teaching and learning process, allowing teachers to promote personalized learning and innovative methods to engage students [7, 8].

In this direction, the use of board games may represent a particularly effective strategy for teachers' training as it can provide teachers with a fertile ground to explore a creative usage of AI for educational purposes in a collaborative context. Literature has indeed widely confirmed that board games are effective tool in promoting knowledge and skills acquisition across different subjects while involving players in social interactions, collaboration, and cooperation [9]. Moreover, empirical research has begun to provide evidence about the potential of board games in stimulating individuals' creativity [e.g., 10]. Based on these theoretical premises, within the framework of the AI4T project – an Erasmus+ K3 project (https://www.ai4t.eu/ - Project N° 626154-EPP-1-2020-2-FR-EPPKA3-PI-POLICY) developed by five European countries - the idea of designing a board game emerged.

2 Design Principles

AI-awareness is an educational game designed for teachers who already have a basic understanding of AI technologies focused on enhancing their awareness of the potential role that these technologies can play in education. The aim of the game is not to engage in abstract discussions but, on the contrary, to stimulate critical reflection on the potential offered by new technologies through the design of concrete learning interventions. Participants are given the task of collaboratively designing educational interventions that aim to resolve problematic situations typical of classroom teaching with the aid of technological tools based on artificial intelligence. The game has a duration of 1 h, and teachers are required to participate in groups. Through the collaborative design of practical solutions to different educational scenarios, teachers can familiarize themselves with AI technologies and understand how they can be effectively integrated into the school context. Moreover, they can start to critically reflect on the implications of such technologies while interacting with their peers, fostering the creation and discussion of new ideas.

2.1 Game Goals and Objectives

In accordance with the premises discussed in the previous section, the training objectives of the designed game can be summarized as follows:

- **Promote awareness on the use of AI technologies in education:** the fundamental objective of the game is to create an interactive experience that helps teachers to a) understand and define more accurately the dimensions of teacher-student interaction, and b) explore the potential of AI-based technologies through reflection on how these can be effectively integrated into the educational relationship to address common challenges and problems.

- **Involvement and collaborative interaction**: the game encourages the active involvement of teachers who must collaborate to address the challenges presented by the game. This can lead to the sharing and exchange of different ideas and points of view, which together encourage collaborative learning.
- **Experimentation and practical learning:** through the shared design of practical solutions to various educational scenarios, teachers can familiarize themselves with AI technologies and understand how they can be effectively integrated into the school context (simultaneous promotion of *knowledge* and suggestions for *educational use*).

3 The Game Dynamics

Fig. 1. Example of Scenario and Technology cards.

The game involves participating in small groups (usually between 4 and 5 teachers per group), so that all participants can express themselves and collaborate actively to develop solutions using a set of Scenario cards (which present challenging classroom problematic scenarios) and Technology cards (which describe AI tools, see Fig. 1 for examples of cards typology). The gameplay session is led by a facilitator whose role consists in enforcing rules, in promoting and guiding the interaction and collaboration. And in facilitating the gameplay by assigning each group a token/object which represents the group, and by drawing the *Scenario* card used in each turn. Each group discusses and proposes a solution, choosing the most appropriate Technology cards. The solutions are then presented to the other groups and peer-evaluated by voting. The group with the most voted solution advances a number of steps equal to the number of votes received, while the groups that voted for the winning solution advance one step. This scoring system is designed to promote voting sincerely for what each group think is the best solution rather than voting for their own solution: voting for the best solution (and striving to produce quality solutions) increases the likelihood of scoring higher. A group wins the game when it reaches the end of the game board. In the case a time limit is implemented, if the time is up before a group can reach the end, the closest to the finish line wins.

3.1 The Scenario and Technology Cards

Each Scenario card describes a typical problem situation that concerns classroom teaching, ranging from the impact of the diversity of learning styles on the outcome of an activity, to the emotional and learning challenges that students must face. The identification and description of the scenarios are based on the theoretical perspective of Pianta [11, 12] which identifies the interactions between teacher and students as the cornerstone of teaching and learning dynamics in the classroom. Furthermore, these interactions, and consequently the teaching dynamics of the class, can be described in terms of three fundamental dimensions: teaching domain, emotional domain and class organization [11]. In accordance with the theoretical proposal, we have therefore identified and described 13 possible class scenarios where one of these dimensions of class dynamics is salient. Table 1 describes three examples of problematic teaching scenarios, as they appear in the corresponding cards, together with the interaction dimension they respectively intercept.

Table 1. Example of cards for each interaction dimension.

Dimension	Scenario Description
Emotional domain	Your class consists of very different students. While some are outgoing and ready to ask for help, others are struggling to communicate their needs or doubts, while others are completely unmotivated. During a lesson, some of his students are having difficulty with a new concept. However, instead of asking for help, these pupils seem confused and silent
Organizational domain	During a class discussion, you notice that some students can express their ideas clearly and comprehensibly, while others seem to have difficulty communicating effectively, using confusing and unclear sentences
Instructional domain	During the exercise on a new topic, fractions, some students show difficulty in performing precise calculations and correctly applying the rules related to fractions; as a result, they struggle to keep up with the pace of the class

The Technology cards offer players the opportunity to explore the many applications of artificial intelligence (AI) in education. Each of the 14 cards offers a concise description of a category of technology solutions: from the most popular search engines to the most innovative image and text generators. Table 2 provides examples of the type of content included in the cards. The Technology deck also contains a bonus card (*Other Technology* to integrate a technology not available in the deck cards into solutions to the problem situations.

Table 2. Description of two technology cards content.

Technology	Description
Image Generators	AI-based image generation tools leverage advanced machine learning techniques to create different kinds of images from a textual description. Users often have the option to control specific parameters, such as colour schemes, styles, artists to use as inspiration, and compositions, providing a high degree of customization and flexibility. OpenAI DALL-E and Microsoft Bing Image Creator are examples of this technology
Translation Tools	A translation tool is software facilitating language conversion. Examples include Google Translate, DeepL, and Trados. These tools enhance cross-cultural communication by converting text between different languages

4 Future Directions

The integration of AI tools into everyday teaching practice is a fundamental issue that is not sufficiently addressed in terms of actions aimed at teachers training. In this regard, AI-awareness was conceived as a concrete response to make teachers aware of the various AI tools and to help them overcome the misconceptions often associated with the use of these technologies. The game aims to provide a space for teachers to explore the implications of AI in a practical and collaborative way, encouraging critical reflection on the tools and promoting greater awareness.

The game was tested during the final conference of the AI4T project in late January 2024 and involved 20 teachers. Participants particularly appreciated the peer-to-peer nature of the proposed solutions and insights created within the game rounds, which were thus perceived as emerging from the experience of their colleagues rather than from top-down directions formulated by experts far removed from the problems of everyday classroom practice. Moreover, teachers immediately demonstrated a high level of commitment and involvement, actively participating in the discussions both in relation to the creation of solutions to the proposed 'problem situations', within the group, and in relation to the feedback provided to the other groups' solutions and the acknowledgement of that provided to their own. The version of the game described in this article is a useful training tool for teachers, although further modifications are desirable. Firstly, future variations of the *'Technology'* cards will be necessary according to the technological development of the AI solutions themselves. In addition, further modifications to the gameplay might require the introduction of additional gamification elements to make the game more challenging and engaging. Finally, the systematic collection of data on game dynamics and the quality of proposed responses could be useful for an empirical evaluation of the use of the game in training.

References

1. Chiu, T.K., Xia, Q., Zhou, X., Chai, C.S., Cheng, M.: Systematic literature review on opportunities, challenges, and future research recommendations of artificial intelligence in education. Comput. Educ. Artif. Intell. **4**, 100118 (2023)
2. Celik, I.: Towards Intelligent-TPACK: an empirical study on teachers' professional knowledge to ethically integrate artificial intelligence (AI)-based tools into education. Comput. Hum. Behav. **138**, 107468 (2023)
3. Su, J., Yang, W.: Artificial intelligence in early childhood education: a scoping review. Comput. Educ. Artif. Intell. **3**, 100049 (2022)
4. Gentile, M., Città, G., Perna, S., Allegra, M.: Do we still need teachers? Navigating the paradigm shift of the teacher's role in the AI era. Front. Educ. **8**, 1161777 (2023)
5. Altinay, Z., et al.: Capacity building for student teachers in learning, teaching artificial intelligence for quality of education. Societies **14**(8), 148 (2024)
6. Pitrella, V., Gentile, M., Città, G., Re, A., Tosto, C., Perna, S.: La percezione dell'utilizzo dell'intelligenza artificiale nello svolgimento dei compiti a casa in un campione di insegnanti italiani. Annali online della Didattica e della Formazione Docente **15**(26), 300–318 (2023)
7. Choi, B.: A collaborative board game as an assessment environment to evaluate teacher's pedagogical design thinking for technology integration. J. Form. Des. Learn. **7**, 1–16 (2023)
8. Pitrella, V., et al.: Artificial intelligence for personalized learning in K-12 education. a scoping review. In: Casalino, G., et al. (eds.) HELMeTO 2023. CCIS, vol. 2076, pp. 372–382. Springer, Cham (2024). https://doi.org/10.1007/978-3-031-67351-1_25
9. Bayeck, R.Y.: Examining board gameplay and learning: a multidisciplinary review of recent research. Simul. Gaming **51**(4), 411–431 (2020)
10. Mercier, M., Lubart, T.: The effects of board games on creative potential. J. Creat. Behav. **55**(3), 875–885 (2021)
11. Pianta, R.C., Hamre, B.K., Allen, J.P.: Teacher-student relationships and engagement: conceptualizing, measuring, and improving the capacity of classroom interactions. In: Christenson, S., Reschly, A., Wylie, C. (eds.) Handbook of Research on Student Engagement, pp. 365–386. Springer, Boston (2012). https://doi.org/10.1007/978-1-4614-2018-7_17
12. Pianta, R.C.: Teacher-student interactions: measurement, impacts, improvement, and policy. Policy Insights Behav. Brain Sci. **3**(1), 98–105 (2016)

Author Index

A. Schönbohm et al. (Eds.): GALA 2024, LNCS 15348, pp. 427–429, 2025.
https://doi.org/10.1007/978-3-031-78269-5

SPRINGER NATURE

GPSR Compliance

The European Union's (EU) General Product Safety Regulation (GPSR) is a set of rules that requires consumer products to be safe and our obligations to ensure this.

If you have any concerns about our products, you can contact us on ProductSafety@springernature.com

In case Publisher is established outside the EU, the EU authorized representative is:

Springer Nature Customer Service Center GmbH
Europaplatz 3
69115 Heidelberg, Germany

The manufacturer's authorised representative in the EU is Springer Nature Customer Service Centre GmbH, Europaplatz 3, 69115 Heidelberg, Germany. If you have any concerns regarding our products, please contact ProductSafety@springernature.com

Printed and bound by CPI Group (UK) Ltd, Croydon, CR0 4YY
30/09/2026
02225585-0008